Ellee Thalheimer

D1352076

Cycling
ITALY

COASTAL RIDES

1 GARGANO

It's hard to get to, this lush promontory in the South of Italy. Without a car, it's pretty inconvenient. Maybe that's why its coastline is some of the most untrafficked on mainland Italy. Enter bicycle. A cyclist savours exploring these cliff-cut, shimmery-watered environs with the freedom of two wheels (p231).

2 SARDINIA

Step off the ferry, mount your bike and get ready for some of Italy's best coastal cycling. Soar along lightly trafficked, sometimes desolate, coastline with glittering emerald waters on one side and forested mountainsides pushing in from the other (p252).

3 CINQUE TERRE

Parco Nazionale delle Cinque Terre protects a slice of coast that will leave you awestruck and drop-jawed. It's a tour through splendour: cliffs, peaceful forests and steep, terraced slopes of vineyards falling to the churning sea. The dramatic landscape presents dramatic climbs that reward with scintillating descents (p94).

4 ALGHERO

The handsome and upbeat port town of Alghero on La Riviera de Corallo (the Coral Riviera) offers the very best of *il mare* (the sea) and *il monte* (the mountain) and has enduring panoramas across the entire northern and eastern expanses of the island (p270).

BIKE PATHS

1 ALTA ADIGE & DOLOMITI DI BRENTA

For those who like to wander, picnic and enjoy mesmerising mountain scenery – but could skip out on actually climbing the mountains – the highly maintained bike paths of the Dolomite valleys (p160) are a dream. Hulking Dolomite cliffs, gushing rivers and sparkling vineyards flank your route as you pedal happily along.

2 MILAN'S BIKE PATH

Is it a coincidence that you can cycle the pretty canalside bike paths around Milan in a dress? It's something to think about as you quickly leave Milan on the easy-access, ultra-flat paths. The quiet trails take you past swimming locals, verdant riverside nature and rural Lombardian countryside (p138).

3 PESCHIERA TO MANTUA

The 40km of magnificent riverside bike path is an incredible blessing to locals who use it extensively for recreation and exercise. The trail dabbles into forests and open fields, past fishermen and small towns. In the distance, the occasional castle graces the horizon (p148).

HIDDEN TUSCANY

1 MASSA MARTTIMA

Massa what? Exactly. This area of Maremma experiences an intermittent trickle of tourists on the good days. However, a cyclist will count their blessings finding such a sweet spot where the silent back roads visit sleeping, ancient hill towns that nestle in the rolling, thickly wooded heart of Tuscany (p59).

2 ROAD LESS TAKEN

Why are people not here? That's what we asked ourselves when cycling through the pin-drop quietude in the hills north of Arezzo. The scenery vacillates from dense forests to rocky moonscape outcrops to river valleys to fields. Bonuses include side trips to Michelangelo's birthplace and San Francesco di Assisi's monastery in the woods (p63).

3 SEASCAPES & CLIFF VILLAGES

From Orbetello in southernmost Tuscany, it's an Alice-in-Wonderland ramble through Feniglia Nature Reserve. Monstrous pines shroud a sun-dappled isthmus where nature gluttons tiptoe around for peeks of the prolific wildlife. Then the route steers calmly inland through farmland and vineyards to the gorge-flanked Pitigliano and Montalcino, the Brunello capital (p73).

MOUNTAIN PASSES

1 COLLE FAUNARIA/DEI MORTI (2481M)

After muscling up an unforgiving mountain road in the company of scurrying marmots, you summit this desolate, windswept pass. The energy from the alpine expanse unfolding in every direction and the feeling of soul-growing accomplishment makes you leave the mountains a slightly different person than when you arrived (p97).

2 RADICI PASS (1529M)

You definitely won't be able to get by on the typical croissant-and-cappuccino Italian breakfast today. The 14.5km climb through ruggedly gargantuan, utterly gorgeous, mountain country entails over a kilometre of what is signed as 18% grade near the top. It takes no prisoners. It completely rocks (p72).

3 DOLOMITI MOUNTAIN PASSES

The Dolomites heave imposingly from the rocky earth and stretch their chunky, looming spirals towards the heavens. A cyclist peers up at them, assesses their sheer height and brawn as a provocation and starts pedalling. This sublime, pass-laden mountainscape of extremes requires a cyclist's love and determination – and a bit of masochism (p170).

CITYSCAPES

1 ROME

The chaotic, make-up-your-own-rules traffic of Rome might deter a cyclist from exploring by bike. This is a shame because cycling Rome is not only an exhilarating proposition to ride a raucous, frenzied wave, it also provides a profound tool for unpeeling the rich layers of this famed and ancient metropolis (p39).

2 FLORENCE

Enticing vineyards and quiet forests surround Florence, but cyclists might be surprised at how satisfying it is to hop onto a bike, dodge the pedestrian crowds and discover Florence, the cradle of the Renaissance, by weaving through its alleyways and pedalling past its architecture: monumental shrines to the potential of human creativity (p80).

GLAM ITALY

1 AMALFI COAST

Though the Amalfi Coast is a finely-cut-sundress, expensive-linen-pants kind of place, the scenery and nature are so stunning to cycle that there's no keeping the lycra away. Undeniably, this coastline is one of the most awe-inspiring with its narrow road unbelievably clinging to sheer cliffs that plunge to the sea (p220).

2 LAKE COMO

Famous people have homes here and tourists arrive in droves. Thank goodness the route approaches this legendary lake from the backdoor to the north. Touching down in the small town of Lecco, a cyclist gets to relish the glorious, mountain-studded lake scenery while on the fringe of the crowds (p132).

WINE COUNTRY

1 LANGHE & ROERO

The fame of Piedmont's wine, food and truffles shadows the fact that this region is a spectacular cycling destination with its castle-topped hills and rolling expanse of vineyard-covered landscape. In fact, it might be one of the best ways to roll up to Barolo or Barbaresco and taste their world-famous wares (p102).

2 ALTA ADIGE & DOLOMITI DI BRENTA

Though sheltering some of the most dramatically gorgeous wine country in Italy, the valleys of the Dolomites aren't usually associated with Italian wine country. Who knows why? Bike paths snake through vineyards flanked by limestone cliffs and lorded over by monstrous mountain ranges. None too important, the wine is impressively sumptuous (p163).

3 TUSCANY

Steeped in age-old tradition, history and world renown, the luscious Tuscan wine country inspires many a cyclist to point their wheels in its direction. The Chianti (p48) region boasts its refined air and manicured hills. The wilder Brunello (p56) country produces a wine fit for the gods.

4 FRIULI-VENEZIA GIULIA

Not just a master of the reds, Italy also produces world-class white wine. Way over in the northeast corner of Italy, snuggled up next to the Slovenian border, are the Colle (hills) of Friuli that modestly produce award-winning white wine and provide tranquil countryside cycling through rural vineyards and farmland (p185).

HISTORICAL TOURS

3

1 ETRUSCAN LAZIO

Some of the most intriguing relics of the ancient Etruscan culture dot the Lazio countryside. A cyclist has the fantastic opportunity to enjoy a tour of the lazy, golden countryside while delving chest-deep into the fascinating history of the mighty Etruscans (p41).

2 ROME OLD & NEW

Known to the ancient Romans as the *regina viarum* (queen of roads), the Appia Antica (p39) was considered revolutionary for being almost perfectly straight and wonderfully drainable. Today, it's still there for your cycling pleasure and is dotted with churches and catacombs that take you back the days of the Romans.

3 TRULLI & SASSI

Whereas Rome and Florence flaunt *gargantuan* (iconic architecture), Puglia shelters a humbler building tradition that holds its own appealing intrigue. The *trulli*, cone-domed huts, and the *sassi*, Matera's cave dwellings, open a window into ancient countryside culture. A genuine introduction to these structures is cycling through the landscapes that inspired them (p224).

2

CICLISMO ITALIANO

1 ITALIAN CICLISTI

Italy has an incredibly rich and well respected history of cycling that is very much alive today. While you pedal along fully loaded, in any region, you're bound to be passed by Italian *ciclisti* in slickly matching lycra. They are everywhere, in love with their sport, upholding their proud tradition at full throttle (p33).

2 CYCLING MONUMENTS

Statues and shrines revering the cyclist are scattered throughout Italy: the Madonna dei Ciclisti on Colle Gallo, the Patron Saint of Cycling at Lake Como and Marco Pantani's statue on Colle Faunaria/dei Morti (p97). Reaching these statues – usually at the top of some excruciating climb – makes a cyclist proud to participate in such a rich and honoured tradition.

CYCLING IN ITALY

Dear cyclist, let Italy be your muse. To a bike tourist, she is one of the fairest in the world.

With her gastronomic superiority, long and venerated history of cycling, immensely diverse landscapes and vivacious culture, Italy entices the cyclist to rear up on one wheel and plunge into the unforgettable adventures to be had within her borders.

On a bike, you can access far-flung areas like Friuli-Venezia Giulia, where you soar through sun-soaked vineyards. All day you smell the freshly tilled earth, feel the wind cooling the sweat off your face and are lulled by the quiet rustling of the land. Then, that evening, on a sunset-rosy piazza, you sip wine created by the land you courted intimately all day...a juicy, dripping-from-your-mouth experience. Later, someone might ask, 'Do you know Friuli wines?' And you smile, as when you remember an old lover, and you say, 'Yes, I know them'.

With a bike, you can get stuck in a tiny train station in rural Umbria and decide to take a spin around town while waiting for a connection. You might run into a crowd of socialising strollers embarking on the ritual *passigata* (an evening amble on the main strip). When you ask a young couple for directions, you end up laughing, joking and eating pizza with them while yelling about politics over a bottle of wine until the wee hours. This small village now holds more charm for you than that of even the great city of Florence.

By bike, you can slug it out with a 15km ascent of an alpine pass. You reach the summit, legs thrashed and endorphins pumping, and peer out over a desolate alpine range that teaches you a little more about the depths of inspiration.

So, go ahead, perk your ears and open your senses to the call of your honey-voiced muse, who lures you to pack your bike and get ready for the best of the best.

Contents

THE MAPS

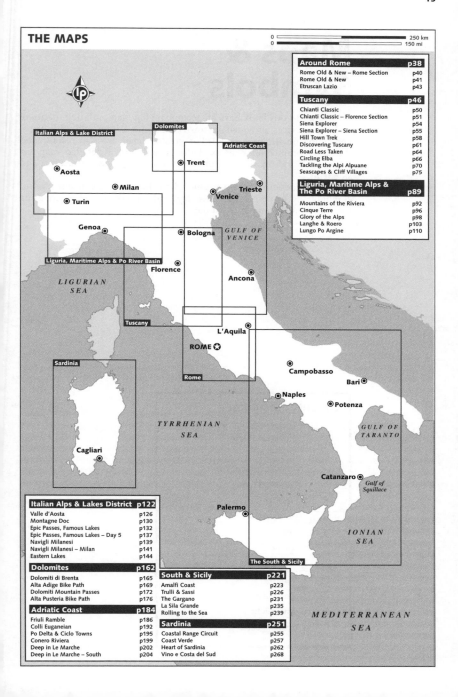

0 — 250 km
0 — 150 mi

Italian Alps & Lake District

Dolomites

Adriatic Coast

Aosta

Milan

Trent

Trieste

Venice

Turin

Genoa

Bologna

GULF OF VENICE

Liguria, Maritime Alps & Po River Basin

Florence

LIGURIAN SEA

Ancona

Tuscany

L'Aquila

ROME

Rome

Campobasso

Bari

Naples

Potenza

Sardinia

TYRRHENIAN SEA

Cagliari

Catanzaro

Gulf of Squillace

GULF OF TARANTO

Palermo

IONIAN SEA

The South & Sicily

MEDITERRANEAN SEA

Maps & Symbols

Most rides in this book have an accompanying map outlining the route and the services provided in towns en route (along with side trips, depending on the map scale). For greater detail, we also recommend the best commercial map available. You'll find a detailed map for every day of riding, showing the route, towns, services, attractions and side trips.

We provide an elevation profile when there is a significant level of climbing and/or descending on a day's ride. These are found alongside the cues near the map for that day.

CUE SHEET SYMBOLS

⌐►	right-hand turn
↗	veer right
↑	continue straight on
◄⌐	left-hand turn
↘	veer left
Rome	town/city
▲	hill
⚠	caution
●●	side trip
↺	return
★	point of interest
⊟	traffic light
◉	roundabout

Cue Sheets

Route directions are given in a series of brief 'cues', which tell you at what kilometre point to change direction and point out features en route. The cues and elevation profiles are found alongside the maps throughout the book. These pages could be photocopied or cut out for on-the-road reference and used with a recommended map. The only other thing you need is a cycle computer.

To make the cue sheets as brief and simple to understand as possible, we've developed a series of symbols (see the Map Legend on the inside front cover) and the following rule:

Once your route is following a particular road, continue on that road until the cue sheet tells you otherwise.

Follow the road first mentioned in the cues even though it may cross a highway, shrink to a lane, change name (we generally only include the first name, and sometimes the last), wind, duck and climb its way across the country. Rely on us to tell you when to turn off it.

Because the cue sheets rely on an accurate odometer reading we suggest you disconnect your cycle computer (pop it out of the housing or turn the magnet away from the fork-mounted sensor) whenever you deviate from the main route.

SEASCAPES & CLIFF VILLAGES – DAY 3

HOW TO READ A CUE SHEET	CUES			GPS COORDINATES
where possible rides start and/or finish at a visitor centre ▶	start		Castel del Piano tourist office	42°53'36"N 11°32'11"E
	0km	⌐	Via Marconi	
	0.3	⌐	to 'tutte le direzioni,' Via della Stazione	
	0.6	↰	SS323 to 'SS2 Cassia'	
towns or cities along the ride are highlighted in blue ▶	6.6		Seggiano	42°55'43"N 11°33'38"E
		↗	to 'San Quirco d'Orcia'	
			(or ↘ to 'centro' to enter town)	
climbs are graded as gradual, moderate, hard or steep ▶	6.8	▲	3.3km climb	
potential hazards are detailed ▶	10.1	⚠	6.2km steep descent	
	12.7	↘	SP22 to 'Montalcino'	
	16.5	▲	2.9km moderate climb	
read: at 20.6km turn left for the side trip to Abbazia di Sant'Antimo ▶	20.6	●●↰	Abbazia di Sant'Antimo 1.6km ↺	
	21.7	↗▲	to 'Montalcino' 7.8km moderate climb	
	26.1	★	Museo di Brunello	
Montalcino has a place of interest mentioned in the text ▶	29.5	↑★	Montalcino	43°03'28"N 11°29'25"E
		⌐	to 'Siena'	
		⚠	6km steep twisting descent	
read: at 31.3km turn left and take the second exit on the roundabout to Buonconvento (where roundabouts have more/less than four exits, the correct exit is given; not all roundabouts and traffic lights are included on the cue sheet, just those where a change of direction is needed)	31.3	◎↰	2nd Exit to 'Buonconvento' SP45	
	40.8	◎↰	SS2 to 'Siena'	
	42.8		Buonconvento station (RHS) on right	43°08'17"N 11°29'00"E

Table of Rides

ROME	DURATION	DISTANCE	DIFFICULTY
ROME OLD & NEW	3–7 HOURS	55KM	MODERATE
ETRUSCAN LAZIO	1 DAY	59.6KM	EASY–MODERATE

TUSCANY	DURATION	DISTANCE	DIFFICULTY
CHIANTI CLASSIC	2 DAYS	101.7KM	MODERATE–DEMANDING
SIENA EXPLORER	4–7 HOURS	75.8KM	MODERATE–DEMANDING
HILL TOWN TREK	3 DAYS	150KM	MODERATE–DEMANDING
DISCOVERING TUSCANY	3 DAYS	202.5KM	MODERATE
ROAD LESS TAKEN	1–2 DAYS	115.6KM	MODERATE–DEMANDING
CIRCLING ELBA	5–9 HOURS	92KM	MODERATE–DEMANDING
TACKLING THE ALPI ALPUANE	3 DAYS	155.3KM	MODERATE–DEMANDING
SEASCAPES & CLIFF VILLAGES	3 DAYS	179.8KM	MODERATE

LIGURIA, MARITIME ALPS & THE PO RIVER BASIN	DURATION	DISTANCE	DIFFICULTY
MOUNTAINS OF THE RIVIERA	2 DAYS	173.1KM	DEMANDING
CINQUE TERRE	5–8 HOURS	75.1KM	MODERATE–DEMANDING
GLORY OF THE ALPS	2 DAYS	164.8KM	DEMANDING
LANGHE & ROERO	3 DAYS	198.5KM	MODERATE
LUNGO PO ARGINE	3 DAYS	218.1KM	EASY

ITALIAN ALPS & LAKES DISTRICT	DURATION	DISTANCE	DIFFICULTY
VALLE D'AOSTA	2 DAYS	126.6KM	MODERATE
MONTAGNE DOC	3 DAYS	223.8KM	MODERATE–DEMANDING
EPIC PASSES, FAMOUS LAKES	5 DAYS	366.6KM	DEMANDING
NAVIGLI MILANESI	3 DAYS	253.4KM	EASY
EASTERN LAKES	3 DAYS	203.4KM	MODERATE

DOLOMITES	DURATION	DISTANCE	DIFFICULTY
DOLOMITI DI BRENTA	3 DAYS	173.6KM	MODERATE–DEMANDING
ALTA ADIGE BIKE PATH	3–6 HOURS	66.9KM	EASY
DOLOMITI MOUNTAIN PASSES	6 DAYS	319.5KM	DEMANDING–VERY DEMANDING
ALTA PUSTERIA BIKE PATH	2½–4 HOURS	40KM	EASY–MODERATE

ADRIATIC COAST	DURATION	DISTANCE	DIFFICULTY
FRIULI RAMBLE	3 DAYS	213.5KM	EASY–MODERATE
COLLI EUGANEIAN	5–7 HOURS	78.8KM	MODERATE–DEMANDING
PO DELTA & CICLO TOWNS	4 DAYS	242.7KM	EASY
CONERO RIVIERA	3–6 HOURS	54.6KM	MODERATE
DEEP IN LE MARCHE	6 DAYS	428.3KM	MODERATE–DEMANDING

THE SOUTH & SICILY	DURATION	DISTANCE	DIFFICULTY
AMALFI COAST	2 DAYS	81.5KM	EASY–MODERATE
TRULLI & SASSI	3 DAYS	237.5KM	EASY–MODERATE
THE GARGANO	2 DAYS	166.5KM	MODERATE–DEMANDING
LA SILA GRANDE	2 DAYS	138.6KM	MODERATE
ROLLING TO THE SEA	2 DAYS	138.3KM	MODERATE–DEMANDING

SARDINIA	DURATION	DISTANCE	DIFFICULTY
COASTAL RANGE CIRCUIT	2 DAYS	107.9KM	MODERATE
COSTA VERDE	3 DAYS	147.4KM	MODERATE
HEART OF SARDINIA	4 DAYS	293.4KM	DEMANDING
VINO E COSTA DEL SUD	2 DAYS	93.6KM	MODERATE

The Author

ELLEE THALHEIMER is a freelance writer, yoga instructor, bike tour guide and former wilderness guide living in Portland, Orgon (USA). Having toured extensively by bike in Argentina, Cuba, Trinidad and Tobago and across the US a number of times, Ellee has only grown more addicted to cycling. She loves long, beautiful ascents the most and appreciates all the lessons her bike, Sojo, has taught her. Whether she's commuting, teaching yoga for cyclists or mountain biking, this two-wheeled contraption provides boundless inspiration. After researching and writing this book, she is also now officially in love with cycling in Italy.

MY FAVOURITE RIDE

Climbing 16km to Colle di Sampeyre fully loaded with a non-functioning granny gear (that's another story), I vacillated between wondering about my career choice and believing I was the luckiest person in the world. The way one's mind unfolds on such a desolate, consistent climb is perhaps better than therapy. I was alone but for incredibly un-shy marmots most of the time and completely awestruck by the scenery. On the second day, it was at the top of the 18km ascent to Colle Faunaria/dei Morti where I decided for certain that these wild, boulder-strewn valleys and crowds of foreboding, jagged, cloud-grazing mountains were the most awesomely beautiful places I had ever been in the world over the entire course of my life.

CONTRIBUTING RESEARCHERS

Several people who helped verify cue-sheet accuracy include:

Jesse Sibley – Jesse's passion for cycling and everything Italian inspired him to start Broken Compass Tours. When he's not riding, he's giving private cooking lessons and organising tours throughout central Italy.

Gino Pirelli – Gino is an international bike tourist and Critical Mass advocate who loves getting to know different cultures and slow riding with good people.

ExperiencePlus! – Monica Price and folks at this bike tour company work the bike season in Italy and spend their winters travelling by bike or otherwise.

THANKS

I encountered an incredible number of angels during research. I send a huge shout out to my close friends and windows into the soul of Italy: Jesse and Dory Sibley (woo pig sooie), Leslie Baxter and GL Casetta, and Gino Pirelli. Furthermore, Monica and her family in Rome, the Braccicorti clan, L and A in Milano, and Giovanna from Ghilarza were inspiring, generous people to meet on the road. My father Bruce Thalheimer and Debra Rolfe were amazing cycling companions who put up with my late-night writing. Bridget Blair and Janine Eberle provided support and guidance, and Quentin Frayne and Ethan Gelber were generous with time and advice. Thanks goes to the wordsmiths of previous Italy guidebooks. Lello Sforza, Pietro Boselli and Lorenzo Giorgio are hard-working bike advocates who gave me inspiration. Trenitalia rocks my world. I love you, Italy. From home, as always, Mary Beth Wynne is my peer and saviour. Sandra Bao, Ben Greensfelder, Ryan Ver Berkmoes and Erin Corrigan are P-town lifelines. Gratitude to my friends and family who love me even though I disappear for long periods of time. Thanks to Diane Wilson and the studio for giving me the most important tools.

Route Descriptions, Maps & Charts

CYCLING ROUTES

This guide covers the best areas for on-road cycle touring that Italy has to offer. The rides do not traverse the country from north to south or east to west, but have been selected because they are scenic, they pass through interesting towns or historic areas, and they are lightly used by cars and easy to reach by public transport. Rides vary from one to six days and link easily with one another, offering continuity for extended trips. Various transport options for getting to and from the rides are suggested. Rides accommodate both the novice and the experienced cyclist.

In most cases, the rides have been designed to make carrying camping gear and food optional. Each ride is broken into a set number of days, with accommodation and food options available at each day's destination. In some cases alternative destinations are offered.

Cyclists can use this book as an introduction and planning tool, as well as in real-time on the road. We hope that once cyclists become familiar with local circumstances they start planning their own routes, too.

Times & Distances

Each ride is divided into stages, and we suggest a day be spent on each stage. In some cases the distance for a particular stage is relatively short, but attractions en route, or nearby, warrant spending extra time; distance junkies may decide to condense two stages into one day.

The directions for each day's ride are given in terms of distance (in kilometres) from the starting point (specified on the cue sheets).

A suggested riding time has been given for each day's riding. Because individual riding speed varies widely, these should be used as a guide only. They only take into account actual riding time – not time taken for rest stops, taking photographs, eating or visiting a museum – and are generally based on an average riding speed of between 10km/h and 20km/h.

Ride Difficulty

Each ride is graded according to its difficulty in terms of distance, terrain, road surface and navigation. The grade appears in the Table of Rides at the beginning of the book and at the start of each ride.

Grading is unavoidably subjective and is intended as a guide only; the degree of difficulty of a particular ride may vary according to the weather, the weight in your panniers, whether children are cycling, degree of pre-trip training, or how tired and hungry you are.

Easy These rides involve no more than a few hours' riding each day, over mostly flat terrain with good, sealed surfaces. They are navigationally straightforward.

Moderate These rides present a moderate challenge to someone of average fitness; they are likely to include some hills, three to five hours of riding, and may involve some unsealed roads and/or complex navigation.

Demanding These are for fit riders who want a challenge, and involve long daily distances and/or challenging climbs, may negotiate rough and remote roads and present navigational challenges.

MAPS & PROFILES

Most rides in this book have an accompanying map that shows the route, services provided in towns en route, attractions and possible alternative routes and side trips, depending on the map scale. The maps are based on the best available references, sometimes combined with GPS data collected in the field. They are intended to show the general routes only of the rides we describe and are not detailed enough in themselves for route finding or navigation. For greater detail, we also recommend the most suitable commercial map available in the 'Maps' section of each ride.

Most chapters also have a regional map showing the gateway towns or cities, principal transport routes and other major features. Map symbols are interpreted in the legend on the inside front cover of this book.

CUE SHEETS

Route directions are given in a series of brief 'cues', which point out features en route and tell you at what kilometre point to change direction.

These pages could be photocopied or cut out for on-the-road reference and used with a recommended map. The only other thing you need is a cycle computer.

To make the cue sheets as brief and simple to understand as possible, we've developed a series of symbols (see the Map Legend on the inside front cover) and the following rule:

Once your route is following a particular road, continue on that road until the cue sheet tells you otherwise.

Follow the road first mentioned in the cues even though it may cross a highway, shrink to a lane, change name (we generally only include the first name and sometimes the last), wind, duck and climb its way across the country. Rely on us to tell you when to turn off it.

Because the cue sheets rely on an accurate odometer reading we suggest you disconnect your cycle computer (pop it out of the housing or turn the magnet away from the fork-mounted sensor) whenever you deviate from the main route. Remember that most odometers have a range of accuracy that can vary up to 0.5km, so the cue sheets might not align exactly.

Planning

Some people like to plan, and some people like to fly by the seat of their pants (not advisable in August) and Italy accommodates both types of bike tourist. Italy is not particularly cheap, so it doesn't cater especially well to a poor tourist, although travellers adept at penny pinching can get by. Italy has the hardest and easiest of landscapes and arguably the best food and some of the most interesting architecture in the world. As a cycling destination in general it's world-class, accommodating all types of cyclists lavishly.

As this guide focuses on cycling and not general information about Italy as a travel destination, we suggest you also have one of Lonely Planet's regional or country guides to Italy.

WHEN TO CYCLE

Italy, although thrust deep into the tempering Mediterranean arena, has many climate zones. For the most part, the best biking times throughout the country are spring (April to early July) and autumn (September to October), when a fair and stable barometer is most likely and days can last until 9pm.

If you are trying to learn Italian before your trip, know that it will be helpful to learn the almost-as-important Italian language of hand gestures.

In northern mountain zones, the ideal pedalling window is slightly shorter (beginning in mid- to late-May and ending in early to mid-October) to allow for the melting of late-spring, high-pass snows and avoid the sharpened winter bite of late autumn's teeth. (Note that light, lingering snow can fall over the highest ground at any time of year.) Balmy autumn afternoons, when crop bounty is most plentiful, bring a fascinating assortment of local religious and harvest *fiere* (festivals).

In the south – a land of mild winters, early-spring high temperatures and long balmy autumns – winter trips are not impossible, especially in Sicily and Sardinia. Inland especially, unexpected frosts, heavy rains and even snow may still occur. Also be prepared to adjust to short hours of daylight – the sun sets as early as 5pm.

See Climate (p281) for more information.

The hottest months, July and August, are best left to the throngs of car-bound tourists and vacationers. Not only is it sweltering everywhere (particularly on the islands, throughout the south, and all coastal and lowland areas), competition for accommodation is fierce and even quiet roads are busy and service-industry patience is at a low ebb.

WHAT TO BRING

The well paved *vie* (roads) of Italy are perfectly suited to road bikes or stocky touring/hybrid frames with slick tyres. (If you put slicks on your wheels, you may also wish to bring foldable knobbies for the eventual off-road ride.) After that, as a general rule, keep gear to a minimum. If you can't decide if you need it, don't bring it. Every gram is noticeable on hills and if you do end up needing something, you can certainly buy it in Italy. It is, however, important to carry adequate protection from the elements. If you're camping or hostelling, you will, of course, need more equipment than if you stay in hotels. See the Your Bicycle chapter (p303) for handy tips about how to prepare your bike and pack your panniers. The Health & Safety chapter includes a First-Aid Kit checklist (see boxed text p324).

Clothing

Ideally, pack lightweight clothes that dry quickly. Clothes that you can wear on or off the bike, such as a plain black thermal top, help keep your load to a minimum. The more stylish among you might consider one going-out outfit of the lightest variety.

Go with the padded bike shorts designed to be worn without underwear to prevent chafing. If you don't like lycra, get some 'shy shorts' – ordinary shorts with padded, lightweight chamois inside. In colder weather, wear lycra tights over your bike shorts or padded thermal pants. Another option is a pair of lycra, individual leg warmers, easily removed when the temperature rises.

Cycling clothing should be light and breathable. Some shirts made of synthetic fabrics are designed to keep cyclists from overheating, but natural fabrics like wool and silk are preferable to many. Cotton is cool and it dries slowly. Many cyclists like to wear light, long-sleeved cotton shirts in hot weather. It makes for a fantastic cooling fabric on hot days, but it's dangerous to wear during cold, wet weather. Choose bright or light-coloured clothing, which is cooler and maximises visibility.

Sunglasses are essential, not only to minimise exposure to UV radiation, but also to shield your eyes from dust and insects. A helmet with a visor also affords some protection. A bandanna is great for soaking up sweat so it doesn't run into your eyes.

Be aware of the danger of exposure, especially during cooler months and at higher elevations where weather conditions can change rapidly. Layering (wearing several thin layers of clothing) is the most practical way to dress. Start with a lightweight cycling or polypropylene top, followed by a warmer insulating layer, such as a thin fleece vest (light and quick-drying) and then a rainproof, windproof jacket. Fine-wool thermal underwear is an excellent alternative to synthetic fibres.

Some great waterproof, yet 'breathable' cycling jackets are available, made of Gore-Tex and its many offshoots.

Fingerless cycling gloves reduce the impact of jarring and the likelihood of numb hands. They also protect against grazes in the event of a fall.

In cold weather you may want full-finger gloves (either thin gloves worn over bike gloves, or more wind- and rain-resistant ones). Thermal socks and neoprene booties that go over your shoes help keep blood in your toes on frigid mornings and during bad weather. A close-fitting beanie (winter hat) worn under your helmet is an essential part of your warmth artillery.

Helmets are not compulsory by law, but you shouldn't ride without one. If your helmet has been in a crash, replace it.

Cycling shoes are the ideal footwear (or, next best, stiff-soled ordinary shoes) because they transfer the power from your pedal stroke directly to the pedal. Spongy-soled running shoes are inefficient and may leave your feet sore. More and more people swear by cycling sandals – stiff-soled sandals with room for a pedal cleat. They're cool in summer and they dry quickly.

Bicycle

There are many different bikes people tour on these days, from recumbents to folding bikes to tandems with baby-seat additions. You can opt to carry panniers or haul a one-wheel or two-wheel trailer. Talk with your bike-shop personnel to explore and try out your options. See Your Bicycle (p303).

> 'You may have the universe if I may have Italy.' GIUSEPPE VERDI

EQUIPMENT CHECKLIST

This list is a general guide to the things that might be useful on a bike tour. Don't forget to take on board enough water and food to see you safely between towns.

BIKE CLOTHING

- cycling gloves
- cycling shoes and socks
- helmet and visor
- long-sleeved shirt or cycling top
- fleece or wool beanie
- fleece or thicker wool layer (for mountains and shoulder seasons)
- down or synthetic down vest (for mountains and shoulder seasons)
- neoprene booties (for mountains and shoulder seasons)
- full-finger gloves (for mountains and shoulder seasons)
- padded cycling shorts (two pair)
- sunglasses
- bandanna
- T-shirt or short-sleeved cycling top
- visibility vest
- waterproof, breathable jacket and pants

OFF-BIKE CLOTHING

- sandals
- something loose-fitting, made of natural fibres
- something slinky and black
- sunhat
- swimming gear

EQUIPMENT

- bike lights (rear and front) with spare batteries
- camera
- cycle computer
- day-pack (or bike luggage that can act like one)
- headlamp
- medical kit* and toiletries
- mosquito repellent
- panniers (waterproof liners if needed)
- pocket knife (with corkscrew)
- sarong (acts as towel, changing room, beach towel, clothing, sun protection, knapsack, sheet and yoga mat)
- sewing kit
- sleeping sheet
- small handlebar bag and/or map case
- sunscreen
- tool kit, pump and spares**
- two bungee cords
- U-lock (think about a cable as well)
- water containers (water bottles and/or camelback and an extra litre for your pannier)
- water purification tablets, iodine or filter*
- whistle for dogs and emergencies

*see the First-Aid Kit boxed text (p324) in the Health & Safety chapter
**see the Spares & Tool Kit boxed text (p324) in the Your Bicycle chapter

Buying & Hiring Locally

Almost all of the thousands of bike shops in Italy are small, independent businesses focusing on a single market. In fact, many bike stores are so specialised that they sell only certain brands based on retail arrangements with one or more of Italy's famous bicycle manufacturers or distributors. Any shop will carry the components or accessories you need, but not necessarily the specific brand you desire. Even the gear will probably be branded to match the retailer(s) featured by the store. Some of the larger boutiques do, however, have eclectic collections worth checking out.

Prices vary to wild extremes – shoddy, stopgap materials are very cheap, but the top-end models of high-profile brands can be extraordinarily expensive.

High-quality rental bikes and equipment are becoming more available. **ExperiencePlus!** (www.experienceplus.com) provides cyclists with rentals, touring equipment and other bike services in Italy, so you can leave your bike at home. Other rental options are mentioned within the regional chapters.

COSTS & MONEY

Italy isn't cheap, although compared with the UK and northern Europe the situation is not so bad. What you spend on accommodation (your single greatest expense) will depend on various factors, such as location (Turin is pricier than Taranto), season (August is crazy on the coast), the degree of comfort and luck. At the bottom end you will pay €14 to €20 at youth hostels where meals generally cost €9.50. The cheapest *pensione* (small hotel) is unlikely to cost less than €25 for a basic single or €40 for a double anywhere from Pisa to Palermo. You can stumble across comfortable rooms with their own bathroom from €50 to €80. Midrange hotels in the more expensive places such as Rome, Florence and Venice can easily cost from €80 to €150 for singles or €120 to €200 for doubles. In this guide, we provide (where appropriate) an approximate range of prices you can expect to pay for rooms at the upper price range in low and high seasons.

Eating out is just as variable. In Venice and Milan you tend to pay a lot (and sometimes get little in return), while tourist magnets such as Florence and Rome offer surprisingly affordable options. On average you should reckon on at least €20 to €50 for a meal (two courses, dessert and house wine), although you can still find basic set lunch menus for €10 to €15.

A backpacker sticking religiously to youth hostels, snacking at midday, and travelling slowly could scrape by on €40 to €50 per day. Your average midrange daily budget, including a sandwich for lunch and a simple dinner, as well as budgeting for a couple of sights and travel, might come to anything from €100 to €150 a day.

Public transport is reasonably priced, but car hire (p298) is expensive (as is petrol) and is probably best arranged before leaving home. On trains (p299) you can save money by travelling on the slower *regionale* (local) trains.

HOW MUCH?

Camping ground (tent and person)	€12–25
An espresso	€0.90
Supplementary Trenitalia bike ticket	€3.50
Make-it-yourself sandwich lunch	€3–6
Gelato	€1–3

BACKGROUND READING

The *Big Blue Book of Bicycle Repair* (Calvin Jones) is a bicycle repair and maintenance manual provides comprehensive instruction in clear, uncomplicated language and includes helpful accompanying pictures.

The *Metal Cowboy* (Joe Kurmaskie) is a cycle touring classic. He takes the reader on his quirky, outlandish adventures as he cycle tours around the world.

The *Heel to Toe: Encounter the South of Italy* (Charles Lister) explores the glory and sadness of the south in his trip aboard a clapped-out moped.

The *Treasures of the Italian Table* (Burton Anderson) is an older, yet fabulous and ageless book exploring the history and tradition of Italian food in a grabbing narrative style.

The *Italian Way* (Mario Constantino, Lawrence R Gambella) is a book provides provocative, insightful, truthful and pointed views about broad and quirky aspects of Italian culture.

The *Dark Heart of Italy* (Tobias Jones) criss-crosses the country and attempts to come to grips with everything from football corruption to Berlusconi. Still, Jones cannot help but admire Italy's complexity and its people's passion.

INTERNET RESOURCES

There are more region-specific websites embedded in the regional chapters.

Associazione Mountain Bike Italia (www.amibike.it) An informative website about mountain biking mostly in Northern Italy.

Bici Italia (www.bicitalia.org) A website affiliated with FIAB (see p29) that gives information about Italy's bike paths and routes.

Cycling (www.cycling.it) Online Italian cycling magazine.

Delicious Italy (www.deliciousitaly.com) This site takes you closer to immersing yourself in Italy's fabulous food and wine, from general information to cooking-school suggestions.

Ente Nazionale Italiano per il Turismo (www.enit.it) The Italian national tourist body's website has everything from local tourist office addresses to gallery and museum details.

GUIDED & GROUP RIDES

Local bike tour resources are mentioned in the regional chapters.

THE US

Andiamo Adventours (☎ 800 549 2363; www.andiamoadventours.com) Operates week-long cycling and hiking tours, including family-friendly itineraries.

Backroads (☎ 800 462 2848, 510 527 1555; www.backroads.com) Has week-long cycling and walking tours, including trips for families and solo travellers.

DuVine Adventures (☎ 888 396 5383; www.duvine.com) Offers deluxe cycling vacations in Italy.

ExperiencePlus! (☎ 800 685 4565, 970 484 8489; www.experienceplus.com) Leads one- to two-week cycling and walking tours, including trips for singles and families.

Womantours (☎ 800 247 1444; www.womantours.com) Facilitates yearly all-women's cycling trips to Italy.

THE UK

Cycle Rides (☎ 01225 428 452, 0800 389 3384) Formerly known as Bike Tours, this company operates a couple of tours.

RIDES QUICK REFERENCE

Beginner Ride Suggestions Trulli & Sassi (p224), Navigali Milanesi (p138), Alta Adige (p168), Friuli Ramble (p185)

Intermediate Ride Suggestions Valle d'Aosta (p123), Langhe & Roero (p102), Seascapes & Cliff Villages (p73)

Difficult Ride Suggestions Glory of the Alps (p97), Mountain of the Riviera (p90), The Gargano (231), Epic Passes, Famous Lakes (p132)

Historical Ride Suggestions Trulli & Sassi (p224), Appia Antica (p39), Etruscan Lazio (p41)

Coastal Ride Suggestions Anything in Sardinia (p249), Gargano (p231), Circling Elba (p66), Cinque Terra (p94)

Mountains Ride Suggestions Glory of the Alps (p97), Heart of Sardinia (p260), Epic Passes, Famous Lakes (p132), Tackling the Alpi Apuane (p69)

Wine Region Ride Suggestions Chianti Classic (p48), Hill Towns (p56), Friuli Ramble (p185), Vino e Coasta del Sud (p267), Dolomiti di Brenta (p163)

Federazione Italiana Amici della Bicicletta (www.fiab-onlus.it) Informative website of a countrywide organisation that supports, promotes and defends the use of bicycles in Italy.

Federazione Italiana Città Ciclabili (www.cittaciclabili.it) Organisation news, affiliate lists and links.

Italia Mia (www.italiamia.com) The best thing about this site is its mass of links. Click on art and, as well as a list of artists' biographies, you get links to museums and galleries. Elsewhere you can explore everything from Italian cinema to genealogy.

Lonely Planet (www.lonelyplanet.com) An up-to-date, cutting-edge website including comprehensive information on travel and adventure.

On Your Bike (www.lonelyplanet.com/thorntree) Online forum discussing travel by bike.

TurismoInBicicletta.it (www.turismoinbicicletta.it) An online bicycle travel agency of sorts that serves Lombardia, Trentino and the eastern lakes district.

Uffici Biciclette (www.ufficiobiciclette.it) Website of an Italian organisation that promotes cycling tourism and transport.

Environment

RESPONSIBLE CYCLING

Most cyclists know this, but there's nothing like a healthy reminder: as we are so blessed to experience the beautiful wildernesses of Italy, it is really important to respect and take care of the nature so enjoyed.

On the grand scale of things, a single trip might not seem particularly environmentally significant, but consider tourism's worldwide context: each year there are some 700 million holidays, a figure that is expected to grow to one billion by 2010. Most Mediterranean countries suffer from the over-development of tourism to some degree, especially in coastal areas, and Italy is no exception.

So what can you do to limit your environmental footprint even though you are already embarking on an ecofriendly bike tour?

Transport

For a start you might consider a low-emission form of transport. Train travel in Italy, especially between the major city centres, is easy and affordable. There are also numerous InterRail and Eurail passes available, and InterRail has now introduced a single-country ticket, which is worth considering if you're planning a big itinerary.

Most forms of transport emit carbon dioxide and carbon-offset schemes enable you to calculate your emissions so that you can invest in renewable energy schemes and reforestation projects. Some schemes focus just on emissions caused by flights, while others help you work out emissions from specific train, car and ferry journeys to enable you to offset your journeys whatever mode of transport used.

Accommodation

On the ground look out for ecofriendly places to stay; Italy has a good network of *agriturismo* (farm-stay accommodation). Locally run tours, markets and courses are another good way to engage with the country.

An increasing number of tourism businesses are now looking to cash in on the buoyant green euro. Look out for some of the telltale signs of a genuine commitment to the environment. The eco-labelling scheme **Legambiente Turismo** (www.legambienteturismo.it) has certified nearly 200 hotels, judging them on their use of water and energy resources and their reduction in waste production, as well as whether they offer good local cuisine and organic breakfasts. There's also an increasing number of family-run B&Bs and *agriturismo* (p278).

Slow Food

Try Paul Sterry's *Complete Mediterranean Wildlife* for a general guide to the flora and fauna of the region.

One of the best ways to help local economies is to shop locally. In Italy this isn't difficult, given that it is the home of the **Slow Food Movement** (www.slowfood.com) and the abundant markets, farm restaurants and seasonal, organic food available throughout the country. The guidebook *Osterie d'Italia* is an excellent source of information. In 2007 Slow Food opened its very first supermarket, **Eataly** (www.eatalytorino.it; p159), in Turin, which gives local producers direct access to consumers for the first time.

Rubbish

Always keep your wrappers and trash while on the road and throw it away in a rubbish bin later. For camping, cyclists can refer to the **Leave No Trace** (www.lnt.org) website that elaborates on responsible camping procedure.

THE LAND

Italy is one of the world's most easily recognised countries. Its high-heeled, knee-length boot shape embraces an area of just over 300,000 sq km and is caressed by four Mediterranean sub-seas: the Adriatic to the east; the Ionian in the south; the Tyrrhenian, between Sardinia and France's Corsica; and the Ligurian, lapping the northwestern Riviera.

Italy's terrain is 75% mountainous, divided between two major ranges: the Alps and the Apennines. The Alps dominate the north, rising from the Gulf of Genoa on the French–Italian border and arcing east to the Adriatic Sea. The Alps consist of three groups of peaks: the Maritime and Western Alps between Genoa and Valle d'Aosta; the Central Alps reaching east to Alto Adige; and the Eastern Alps of the Dolomites and Julian and Carnic Alps. The highest all-Italian summit is Gran Paradiso (4061m) in Valle d'Aosta; nearby Mont Blanc (4807m) and Monte Rosa (4634m) straddle Italy's borders with France and Switzerland respectively. Both Sardinia and Sicily also have significant mountain groups, and Sicily hosts Europe's highest active volcano, Mt Etna (3261m).

The 1220km-long Apennines are like a craggy, boot-length zipper from Liguria to Calabria and even into Sicily. Corno Grande (2914m) in Abruzzo's Gran Sasso d'Italia group is its zenith. Smaller Apennine spur ranges include the marble Apuan Alps in northwest Tuscany, the volcanoes in the south, and the limestone uplands on the Amalfi Coast–Sorrento Peninsula.

The densely settled Po plain (Pianura Padana) is Italy's vast and peerless lowland. Water from scores of rivers and some of Italy's 1500 lakes drains into the Po River, Italy's longest, which in turn empties into the Adriatic through a broad delta south of Venice. The largest inland bodies of water are the northern glacier-carved lakes of Garda, Maggiore and Como.

The coastline is varied, though notably short on sandy beaches. This is similar to Italy's Tyrrhenian Sea islands: Sicily and, off its north coast, the scattered Aeolian Islands, including Capri; Sardinia; and the handful between Corsica and the coast, notably Elba.

WILDLIFE
Animals

As with the flora, many animals that now inhabit the Alpine region migrated there after the ice ages. Some came from Arctic regions, while others were originally inhabitants of central Asia. Italy is home to remarkably few dangerous animals. It has only two poisonous snake species, the adder and the viper.

Many animals found in the Alps are also common in the Mediterranean zone. Not that many wild animals remain in Italy's most populous areas but you might spot a deer, a marmot, a wild boar, a fox or other smaller mammals from the road in remote areas.

Plants

Italy's two most distinctive floral zones are the alpine and the Mediterranean.

Alpine flora has been affected most by the ice ages, so today's alpine flora consist of relatively recent arrivals. In the mountains the growing

Wild Flowers of the Mediterranean by Marjoir Blamey and Christopher Grey-Wilson is a field guide to 2500 species of flowers, fruit trees, grasses and ferns of the Mediterranean.

Travel Foundation (www.thetravelfoun dation.org.uk) The UK-based sustainable tourism charity provides tips on how to travel more responsibly.

In the 20th century 14 species became extinct in Italy, including the alpine lynx, sea eagle, black vulture and osprey.

The Italian Ministry of Environment website (www.minambiente.it, in Italian) provides details on the country's biodiversity and protected areas, and links to agencies that work in conservation.

season (essentially the snow-free period) becomes shorter with increasing altitude, and therefore alpine plants take longer to recover from any setback in their growth cycle. Mountain bikers and hiking cyclists should keep this in mind and take particular care to avoid damaging the fragile flora of the Alps.

In the Mediterranean region, the long presence of humans on the Italian peninsula has resulted in widespread destruction of original forests and vegetation, and their replacement with crops, orchards, flower farms and *macchia*, a scrub that blankets the once-forested foothills in the south. There are, however, still isolated and protected pockets of naturally occurring early vegetation.

NATIONAL PARKS

Italy has 21 national parks and well over 400 smaller nature reserves, natural parks and wetlands, plus 33 Unesco World Heritage sites. The national parks cover just over 1.5 million hectares (5% of the country), and Italy's environmentalists are continually campaigning to increase the amount of land that is protected. The parks, reserves and wetlands all play a crucial part in the protection of the country's flora and fauna and there are regular conservation events to promote them.

To learn about biodynamic and organic living in return for a few hours' work, check out World-Wide Opportunities on Organic Farms (www.wwoof.it)

For more information go to the website of the **Federazione Italiana Parchi e Riserve Naturali** (Italian Federation of Parks and Reserves; www.park.it).

ENVIRONMENTAL ISSUES

Environmental awareness in Italy has improved in recent years, mainly in response to the effects of climate change, increasing urban smog and pollution of the country's extensive coastline. The Ministry for the Environment is taking an increasingly tougher line on environmental issues by gradually strengthening environmental laws in response to public opinion and as a result of EU directives.

Urban areas, the industrialised north of Italy and most of the country's main cities suffer from high levels of air pollution. Poor air quality can be attributed to the fact that Italy has one of the highest per-capita levels of car ownership in the world. The increase in the use of motor scooters emitting noxious fumes has also contributed to this pollution. Visible evidence of the damage this causes can be seen on buildings where the stone has become blackened due to constant exposure.

Inadequate treatment and disposal of industrial and domestic waste has affected areas including the Ligurian coast, the northern Adriatic, and areas near major cities such as Rome and Naples. However, it is possible to find clean beaches, particularly in southern Puglia, Calabria, Sardinia and Sicily. In particular, Sardinia still boasts some beautiful stretches of coastline, but a rash of development plans a few years ago set alarm bells ringing there, too.

Look for the Green Swan eco-label that flags up genuinely ecofriendly places to stay Legambiente Turismo (www.legambienteturismo.it) .

On the world stage, Italy is committed to many international agreements dealing with desertification, hazardous wastes, air pollution and marine dumping. Italy is a signatory to the Kyoto Protocol, under which it agreed to reduce greenhouse gas emissions by 6.5% below 1990 levels in the period from 2008 to 2012. A climate-change action plan was published in 2003, which included an increased reliance on natural gas and electricity (including renewable forms of energy). Since early 2005, Italy, along with France, Germany and the UK, has been participating in the European Union Emissions Trading Scheme.

History of Cycling

HISTORY OF CYCLING
Not a Da Vinci

Italians celebrated the late-1960s discovery of a distinctly bike-like sketch connected to Leonardo da Vinci's *Codex Atlanticus*. It was hailed as proof that an Italian was the first to conceive of the bicycle. Unfortunately, later studies and analyses of the Codex image concluded rather convincingly that the rough rendering was a forgery, and so Italy withdrew from the debate with France, Germany and Scotland over who really invented the bicycle. What is clear is that although the first great creative strides were made elsewhere, Italian genius was fundamental to the steady development of *la bicicletta* (the bicycle).

Anche Lo (Me Too)

The first Italian bicycle manufacturer, Raimondo Vellani of Modena, sent his models to market in 1867–68; the first Michaux-style *vélocipèdes* (known as a boneshaker because of the rough ride on cobbled streets) came from Carlo Michel of Alessandria at about the same time. In the 10 years that followed, more than 20 workshops set wheels in motion in Milan, Monza, Padua, Novara, Bologna, Turin and Verona.

Fausto Coppi (1919–60) was known as the soul of cycling in Italy. He won 151 races and was the first rider ever to win the Giro and Tour in the same year.

It wasn't until 1885 that the world got its first glimpse of the Italian genius for bicycle innovation. Following on an 1884 idea, Milan-based Eduardo Bianchi built a bicycle with two equal-sized, tension-spoked wheels (to avoid the perils of the ever-larger front wheel of the brakeless 'two-wheel' or 'bi-cycle' machine) and began a long career as Italy's – and eventually Europe's – foremost bicycle trendsetter and manufacturer. Shortly after, he used iron instead of hard wood for the frame and fork and, by 1888, had substituted pneumatic tyres for the solid rubber predecessors. The resulting 'pneumatic-tyred safety bike', manufactured throughout the north of the country with heroic brand names like Olympia, Frera, Lygie, Taurus, Legnano, Atala, Ganna and Gloria, spread like wildfire. Bianchi's notoriety and place in manufacturing were further assured when, in 1889, Italian cyclist Tomaselli raced a Bianchi to victory in the Grand Prix de la Ville (in Paris), the most important race of the times.

In 1895, the first international Bicycle Exposition was held in Milan and the vastly expanded state of the market, including Italy's newfound manufacturing stature on equal footing with others, was established.

In the history of cycling invention, three more great Italian accomplishments deserve mention, although they came decades later. In 1915, Bianchi committed his company to building bicycles for the WWI *bersaglieri*, a special Italian bicycle army corps. Today Bianchi boasts that the sturdy model produced was the first mountain bike, complete with dual suspension and large pneumatic tyres. In 1927, another Italian great, Tullio Campagnolo, made his mark by inventing the quick-release for bicycle wheels and, in 1930, the *cambio a bacchetta* (rod gear), which inspired the modern front and rear derailleur. These patents were the start of serious technical advancement in the sport and the dominance of Campagnolo components. Finally, Francesco Moser, the great Italian champion, designed the first disc wheels, with which in 1984 he broke Eddy Merckx's 12-year-old, one-hour world record and the 50km/h mark. Today's Italian bicycle manufacturers have continued the legacy and are considered some of the best and most innovative in the world.

Not Exactly a Love Affair

Unlike in other European countries where cycling flourished from its earliest days, the history of cycling in Italy was decidedly turbulent. In fact, *il ciclismo* (the cycle) has faced so much of an uphill battle that some historians can't speak of Italian cycling without mentioning *duelli* (duels); cyclists were always up against something.

The first challenge came from the Italian people themselves. Except during the cycling glory years of the fascist 1930s and after WWII in the 1940s to 1950s, cyclists faced rampant *ciclofobia*, a widespread fear of and hostility towards bicycles and all of the ideas they espoused: modernisation, emancipation, liberalisation etc. City folk considered the bicycle a dangerous and meddlesome nuisance, and country dwellers feared the invasion it made possible from the city. One famous writer-reporter named Lombroso even wrote a defamatory treatise supporting a popular theory linking the bicycle with delinquency (since the bicycle could be used to flee the scene of a crime). Even legislators erected obstacles: highly restrictive laws (the earliest from 1818) governed the handling of a bicycle, imposed taxes on its use and required its registration with authorities (including licence plates).

Despite this, two-wheel *appassionati* (an Italian term for people with a specific passion) gave in to their zeal, and two organisations formed at the end of the 19th century. Although fundamental to the advancement of cycling, they also fed directly into the duel paradigm since few good words passed between them. In 1884, hardened speedsters and racers – those practicing *ciclismo agonistico* (agonistical or athletic cycling) – rallied around the Unione Velocipedistica Italiana (UVI; Italian Velocipedallers Union). Around 10 years later, frustrated, leisure-minded enthusiasts of *ciclismo turistico* (cycling tourism) heeded the call of the Touring Club Ciclistico Italiano (TCI; Italian Cycle Touring Club), whose monthly newsletter *Rivista Mensile* carried news and inspiration to stalwart tourers. For years, the rivalry between UVI and TCI set cycling against itself, a battle that subsided only when new and powerful external duelling partners – first soccer and then the automobile – forced the cycling world to form a somewhat united front.

Social Revolution

Despite the setbacks, *la bicicletta* is an undeniable part of Italian history. As the first affordable means of individual transport, it revolutionised Italian life. Women, who took to cycling in respectably large numbers, were liberated by it. Workers traditionally confined to local markets could search further afield. The first of the *bersaglieri* (Italian army) units were formed to accelerate the speed of message delivery during army manoeuvres. Even the moneyed gentry, with time on their hands, turned

GIRO D'ITALIA

The Giro d'Italia is Italy's answer to the Tour de France. First run in 1909 (four years after the Tour got its start), the Giro, sometimes called the 'Feast of May', is cycling's second-greatest multistage race and Italy's biggest annual sporting event, attracting hundreds of thousands of spectators to the roadside and watched on television by more than 100 million people worldwide.

to the opportunities the bicycle opened. The greatest early example of this is the nearly 750km Milan–Rome *gita turistica* (tourist excursion) organised in 1895 by TCI and attended by Queen Margherita herself. She travelled in a private carriage, but was preceded by a parade of 70 elegant, saddle-mounted gentlemen in dress coats and bowler hats. The 1901 TCI tour in Sardinia made an equivalent splash, welcomed in every town by banners, bands and cheering locals throwing flowers.

In 1904, TCI celebrated its tenth anniversary with a *festa turistica della nazione* (national tourist feast), a pageant of 10,000 cyclists in Milan followed by a massive banquet for 3400 people. TCI, in addition to demonstrating the harmless and practical value of the bicycle, had been producing the world's first cycle-tourism maps with elevation charts and cue sheets not unlike those in this book. TCI was also the first group to lobby for improving roads that had been left to deteriorate after the railroad proved effective, and even bike paths.

In 1905 there were 242,000 bicycles (plus 5000 motorcycles and 4000 automobiles) on the roads of Italy. By 1913 more than 1.5 million bicycles were in use. For thousands of Italians, owning a bicycle was a quality-of-life improvement.

Of perhaps greater importance than the great bike races are the famous Italian personalities and grand cycling champions who dominated the sport. True to the tradition of duelling in *ciclismo*, the masters in the saddle always emerged in pairs and battled heroically for victory in ways that sometimes polarised and always electrified the nation. In one of the latest wheel-to-wheel battles, Marco Pantani, *il pirata* (the pirate), lost the 1999 Giro d'Italia to Ivan Gotti, when, at the end of the penultimate stage, he was removed from the race after testing positive for performance-enhancing drugs.

And Today?

The bicycle continues to duel for its survival. Whereas it was seen as a fascist vehicle in the 1930s, its nonpolitical utilitarian value came to the fore in an economically and materially depressed Italy. Once feared for its symbolic power, the bicycle was later adopted by neo-realist cinematographers and futurist artists to represent hope, renewal, opportunity and advancement. As a curious sign of the times, today the bicycle is sometimes thought of as a steed from which to fight the speed of modernisation.

Still, the bicycle rolls on with millions of Italian users. Mountain bikes hit the hills in the 1990s (see the boxed text p97). Races grow in stature, led by the Federazione Ciclistica Italiana. And cycle-tourism lobbies continue to demand quality, protected bike paths and recognition from the same stubborn automobile-minded lawmakers, urban planners and fellow citizens who have stumped them since the 1880s.

ROME

HIGHLIGHTS

- **Night riding** in the city centre (p39)
- Travelling through time on the **Appica Antica** (p39)
- Exploring the ancient **Etruscan sites**, tombs and museums (p41)

SPECIAL EVENTS
- Festa de Noantri street theatre, music and food (the last two weeks in July), Trastevere
- Holy Week procession through the city (main events on Good Friday and Easter Sunday)

CYCLING EVENTS
- Giro del Lazio (September), Lazio region

FOOD & DRINK SPECIALITIES
- *saltimbocca alla Romana* (veal fillet with prosciutto, wine and sage)
- *carciofi alla Romana* (artichokes stuffed with mint or parsley and garlic)
- *granita* (crushed ice with lemon or other fruit juices)

TERRAIN
Hilly, both in the city centre and surrounding countryside. Many city roads are cobbled and slippery. Suspension would be a blessing, especially on the Appia Antica.

| Telephone Code – 06 | www.enjoyrome.com |

Skip over Rome? Perish the thought. Her gigantic architectural and historical richness is hedonistic in its excess. While walking (or riding) her streets, you travel in the footsteps of insane tyrants, philosophers, hell-bent warriors and the slaves who made this sparkling and arrogant city a symbol of human potential.

Is Rome a city that nurtures cyclists? Undeniably, no. Cyclists have to fight their way through the traffic and chaos. Still, a small and dedicated group of urban cyclists grit their teeth and persist, but progress towards improved cycling conditions is slow. City riding is suggested only for the savvy cyclist who likes tackling mayhem.

While we'll leave you to find your own adventures in the city, the two rides in this chapter provide respite from the cityscape and let you burrow into the history not only of ancient Rome, but also of the ancient Etruscan culture. The Rome Old & New ride leaves the city via the famous Roman road, the Appica Antica, tours the suburbs and then ends up in Frascati, a town where weekenders flock to relax and drink wine. The Etruscan Lazio ride begins north of Rome in Tarquinia, not in the city centre. Once on your way, you immerse yourself in Etruscan history and sites while cycling through picturesque farmland.

HISTORY

Rome showcases evidence of two of the great empires of the Western world: the Roman Empire and the Christian Church. From the Roman Forum and the Colosseum to the Basilica di San Pietro and the Vatican – and in almost every piazza – lie so many levels of history that the saying 'Rome, a lifetime is not enough' must certainly be true.

It is generally agreed that Rome had its origins in a group of Etruscan, Latin and Sabine settlements on the Palatine, Esquiline and Quirinale Hills. These and surrounding hills constitute the now-famous seven hills of the city. Ancient Romans put the date of their city's foundation as 21 April 753 BC and, indeed, archaeological discoveries have confirmed the existence of a settlement on the Palatino in that period.

However, it is the legend of Romulus and Remus that prevails. According to legend, the twin sons of Rhea Silvia and the war god Mars were raised by a she-wolf. Romulus killed his brother during a battle over who should govern and then established the city of Rome on the Palatino, making himself the first king. Out of the legend grew an empire, which eventually controlled almost the entire world known to Europeans at the time.

ENVIRONMENT

The Comune di Rome covers roughly 150,000 hectares, of which 37% is urban development, 15% is parkland and 48% is farmland. Rome's most notable geographic features are its seven hills: the Palatine, Campidoglio, Aventine, Celian, Esquiline, Viminale and Quirinale. Two other hills, the Gianicolo, which rises above Trastevere, and the Pincio, above Piazza del Popolo, were never part of the ancient city. The Tiber (Tevere) winds through town, flowing from the Apennines.

Due to the number of private gardens once owned and maintained by Rome's elite, the city is decorated with exotic flora, not to mention 1300 native species.

CLIMATE

In July and August, Rome's average temperature is 25 to 30°C, although the impact of the sirocco, a hot, humid wind from Africa, can produce stiflingly hot weather in August, with temperatures in the high thirties for days on end. Winters are moderate and snow is rare. October, November and December are the wettest months.

PLANNING
Maps

Lonely Planet's *Rome City Map* is waterproof, lightweight and handy. It indicates all principal landmarks, as well as museums, shops and information points, and includes a street index. The most comprehensive road map of the city is the Michelin (1:10,000) map *Roma*, although it is unwieldy. The best map for the rides into the outskirts of the city is Touring Club Italiano's 1:200,000 map *Lazio*.

The Rome Tourist Board publishes an excellent pocket-sized city map, *Roma*, which is freely available at the tourist office in Via Parigi. Tourist information kiosks around the city also hand out *Charta Roma*, an A3-sized stylised map with the major sights and their opening hours. Plenty of maps are also available at newsstands and bookshops.

For maps of ancient Rome try the *Lozzi Archaeo Map* (€4), which has a plan of the Roman Forum, the Palatine and the Colosseum.

Cycling Events

If you happen to be in Rome with your bike on the last weekend of May, be prepared to participate in the largest two-wheeled protest of the year, **Ciemmona** (www.ciemmona.org). During the monthly **Critical Mass** (www.critical-mass.info), cyclists traditionally take over the streets, through sheer mass, in protest of car-culture. It first began in San Francisco in September of 1992, but now it's a worldwide event, with each city approaching the festivities a little differently.

For Ciemmona, cyclists of many creeds and agendas flood into Rome from across the country, Europe and even the world to participate. Highly colourful and tremendously decorated, a huge fleet of all sorts of bikes invades the usually car-dominated streets of Rome. A raucous crowd of bike advocates, bike lovers and bike geeks have their day in the sun as they Tarzan through parts of the city they usually don't dare ride. It is a good time – a fantastic time – that gives you the opportunity to understand

ROME

more fully the cycling issues of Rome and the cyclists who advocate for improvement. Beware that the people, though they're generally lighthearted, can get amped up.

GETTING THERE & AWAY

See Getting There & Away in Travel Facts for advice about getting to/from Rome.

AIR

The airport at Fiumicino (see p291) is easy to get to by train. The efficient Leonardo Express leaves from platform 24 at Stazione Termini and travels direct to the airport every 30 minutes from 5.52am until 10.52pm. It costs €11. From 11.30pm to 6am (when the train isn't running), there's a night bus service from Stazione Termini to Tiburtina station (40N from Piazza Cinquecento), where you can catch a Cotral bus to Fiumicino.

Getting to and from Ciampino (see p291) is more time-consuming by public transport despite its being only 15km southeast of the centre. From Ciampino airport, buses service the Anagnina Metro station (30 minutes, about every 1–1½ hours), where trains run to Stazione Termini (combined bus and train ticket is about €4).

Late or very early arrivals have little option other than to bike or take a taxi. Taxis have limited space for bikes, unless they are minivans, which have just enough room for a bike bag. Expect to pay around

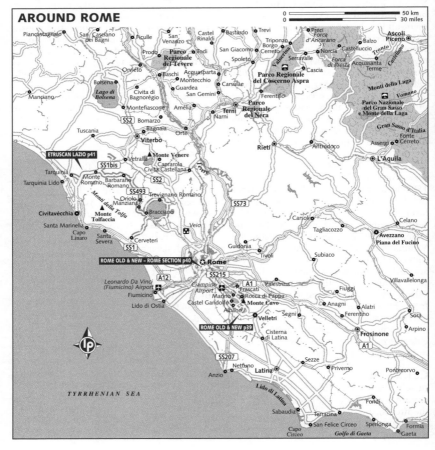

AROUND ROME

€30–40 from Ciampano/Fiumicino. Note that taxis registered in Fiumicino charge a set fare of €60 to travel to the centre – make sure you catch a Comune di Roma taxi instead.

You can ride to/from either airport (leave about 1½ hours for either ride). From Fiumicino, the least trafficked route is along the SS201 (the ancient Via Portunense), which deposits you near Trastevere. From Ciampino, head northwest on Via Appia Nuova until the first roundabout, then head southwest briefly on Grande Raccordo Anulare before turning right onto Via Appia Antica (see p40), which leads to the heart of Rome's city centre. Note, the latter ride should only be attempted with a hardy road bike or a mountain bike.

GETTING AROUND
Getting Started

A great way to get down the lay of the land and see one of the planet's most fascinating cities is to scour it on two wheels. Within minutes, you'll be smack in the middle of the ancient city centre, marvelling at how old and new worlds collide and intertwine to form the chaotic, mind-blowing wonder that is present-day Rome. Grab a map from the **tourist office** (p44) and plan your attack.

Deterrents to riding in Rome include unpredictable traffic tendencies, heavy traffic and pollution, colossal roundabouts, slippery cobbled streets, crowds of pedestrians, high incidents of petty crime and a dearth of good bike racks. On that note, always lock your bike securely and strip it of valuables.

That being said, if you are armed with a good map and you take your time to calmly and carefully manoeuvre, the city quickly becomes less daunting and can become a blast to ride. Beginners, try riding on a Sunday, when much of central Rome is closed to motorised traffic.

For more information on cycling Rome try **Bici Roma** (www.biciroma.it). Also, you can purchase *Roma in Bici* by Puglisi Romano, which gives cycling itineraries for the city – you can get it online or in Rome. **Bici e Bike** (☎ 06 704 76 491; www.biciebike.org; Via la Spezia 79) is an Italian community organisation that schedules walks and bike rides (for both mountain and road bikes).

Night Riding

To make your tour of Rome unforgettable in a way only possible on two wheels, take to the streets late on a weeknight – Sunday nights are great. Shadows and lamps quietly reveal the drama of edifices and other structures, winding cobblestone streets, and sculptures under the tranquillity of night. In the early hours, it's quiet enough to feel the pulse of this ancient city – you may even hear the echoes and whispers of buried treacheries and old alliances. Maybe you'll understand a bit more about the inspiration that struck the great artists who mucked about Rome over the centuries. This might be the moment when Rome becomes '*your*' Rome.

ROME OLD & NEW

Duration 3–7 hours

Distance 55km

Difficulty moderate

Start Stazione Termini

Finish Frascati

Summary See the many faces of Rome, from ancient vestiges to suburban, wine-happy enclaves in the surrounding hills.

It blows your mind to start in the heart of modern Rome and, after just 4km, to be warped into the Ancient Roman times, travelling on a road that has been trod for millennia. Along this famous road, the Appia Antica, Rome's robust and astounding history is crystallised in the ruins, temples and tombs that line the way as you make your way bumpily along.

Further down the road, you also get to experience the Rome that is alive and kicking. You'll pass through outlying Rome, through fancy suburbs and little towns, and you'll get a taste of the manner in which the city has chosen to expand. The traffic is unappealing in places, but the route tries to keep you away from them as much as possible.

Frascati, the final destination, is a popular place for Romans to enjoy the famous cheese, ham and wine of the area. It's customary for the youth of Rome to venture to Frascati (where the wine is famously cheap and infamously harsh the next day) to buy vino at the cantina and picnic supplies at the market, and to have themselves a wonderful time. Note there are a lot of cantinas that let you eat your food on site.

For certain, you'll enjoy really pretty stretches besides the Appia Antica and some fantastic views of the city valley. However, the ride doesn't stand out for scenery or lack of traffic. It stands out because it's an exceptional way to experience the complex layers that constitute the city of Rome.

HISTORY

Known to ancient Romans as the *regina viarum* (queen of roads), Via Appia Antica runs from Porta di San Sebastiano, near the Baths of Caracalla, to Brindisi, on the coast of Puglia. It was started around 312 BC by the censor Appius Claudius Caecus, but it did not connect with Brindisi until around 190 BC. The first section of the road, which extended 90km to Terracina, was considered revolutionary in its day because it was almost perfectly straight, yet slightly curved for drainage purposes. Sections of the original ancient roadway were excavated in the mid-19th century and remain in place.

PLANNING
When to Cycle

Sunday is the best day to cycle this route, as part of the Appia Antica is closed to motorised vehicles. However, some attractions (such as Catacombe di San Sebastiano p41) are closed on Sunday. The private road to the catacombs opens between 8.30am and noon and 2.30pm and 5pm daily, except Wednesday.

What to Bring

Bring a secure bike lock and lights for riding through the occasional tunnel.

Maps

Lonely Planet's *Rome City Map* will get you started along the Appia Antica, and Touring Club Italiano's 1:200,000 map *Lazio* provides enough detail otherwise.

GETTING TO/FROM THE RIDE
Rome (start)

See p44.

Frascati (finish)
TRAINS

From Frascati, trains run regularly to Rome's Stazione Termini (€1.90, 30 minutes, hourly). You should pre-buy your supplemental bike ticket (€3.50) in Rome.

THE RIDE

If you haven't visited the Colosseum or the Baths of Caracalla, this route swings by both. Ride towards Via Appia Antica through Rome's twisted streets to **Porta San Sebastiano** (4.6km), the largest and best preserved gateway to the city. Some sections of the original Appia Antica are in place, with colossal chunks of stone paving the way. Though the original cobble is an impressive testament to the road's durable construction, it makes for a somewhat bouncy ride, so tough tyres and a sturdy bike are recommended. The dirt paths that line the road can be a smoother option, but they are not contiguous. On a completely different note, the ruined tombs and scrubby forests that line the outskirts

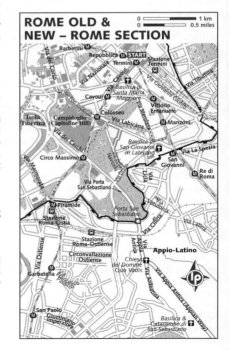

ROME OLD & NEW – ROME SECTION

ROME OLD & NEW

of the Appia Antica become seedy in the evening, so watch the time.

Near the beginning of the Appia Antica is a bike rental shop that hands out maps and historical information about the ride; minor repairs might be done here. At the fork between Appia Antica and Appia Ardeantina, you'll find the **Chiesa del Domine Quo Vadis** (5.5km), a church built at the point where St Peter is said to have met Jesus. Proceed onto the scenic private road that leads to the **Catacombs of San Callisto** (6.5km; ☎ 06 513 01 580; www .catacombe.roma.it), the largest and most famous of the catacombs, and the **Basilica and Catacombs of San Sebastiano** (7.1km; ☎ 06 785 03 50). Outgoing car traffic must exit left at 6.9km, as the road becomes one-way, but cyclists can proceed carefully, watching for the few oncoming cars. Further along are the well preserved **Circo di Massenzio** (7.5km) and picturesque **Tomb of Cecilia Matella** (7.6km), plus a section of original Appia Antica cobble. After you depart the Appia Antica, there's a 1km section of highway (Via Appia Nuovo, 16.2km), so stay to the shoulder.

The little towns like Castel Gandolfo (29.1km), Nemi (39.8km) and Rocca di Papa (47.5km; often referred to as 'daddy rock'), are interesting, teetering on beautiful. Choose to linger a bit – it's enjoyable, but save your appetite for the food and wine of Frascati (55km). **Pane e Tuttipani** (☎ 06 941 66 37; Via Mentana 1) is

a charming *enoteca* (wine shop) that serves plates of excellent and well-priced food. You can sample local cheeses and salamis (€7.50–12) with local wine or opt for a more substantial dish. Best of all is the fact that after sampling the local tipples, you can buy a few bottles here to take away with you.

There are some highlight descents: after you leave Nemi there's a fantastic 5km descent, and there's another long descent after Roca di Papa.

ETRUSCAN LAZIO

Duration 1 day
Distance 6.6km
Difficulty easy–moderate
Start/Finish Rome
Summary You can choose to immerse yourself in Etruscan history or you can just enjoy peaceful back roads through rolling farmland. Or make a cocktail of both.

Just over an hour's train ride north of Rome, in the gently rolling farmlands of Lazio, you can get your fill of Etruscan history. Some of the most fascinating and best preserved Etruscan sights in the country are en route.

Until the Etruscan's nautical trade routes were seized by the Greeks (5th century BC) and their culture absorbed by the more powerful Romans (1st century BC), they were known as skilled navigators, traders and artists. This route visits what is left of their culture: the mysterious tombs and ruins of Tarquinia and, if you like, Cerveteri, two of the main city-states in the Etruscan League (which peaked from 7th to 6th century BC).

It's fairly easy cycling as the route passes small towns, wheat fields and ruined Roman aqueducts; traffic tends to be on the sparse side. The ride starts in Tarquinia and ends in Bracciano, making it a do-able day ride from Rome with the help of our good friends at Trenitalia.

PLANNING

Tarquinia to Bracciano can be an easy day ride from Rome if you use the train system at the beginning and end of the route. If you want to fatten the ride into two days, you could spend the night in Bracciano and the next day ride the loop around the

ROME

lake (35.4km) before heading to Cerveteri (another 18km), on the alternative route, to see the Etruscan ruins and museum. Trains will take you back to Rome from there.

When to Cycle
This is a year-round ride, though weather will be more unpleasant in the winter. Summer weekends, especially Friday and Sunday afternoons, can have lots of traffic due to beach goers.

What to Bring
A torch (flashlight) is useful for the eerie Etruscan tombs.

Maps
Touring Club Italiano's 1:200,000 map *Lazio* covers the ride.

GETTING TO/FROM THE RIDE
Tarquinia (start)
TRAIN
Regular services run between Tarquinia's station and Rome's Stazione Termini (€6.20, 1 hour 20 minutes, about every 2 hours). The supplementary bike ticket is €3.50.

BICYCLE
The ride starts in Tarquinia because there is so much pollution and traffic leaving Rome.

Bracciano (finish)
TRAIN
Trains from Bracciano's station to Rome's Stazione Termini run every half hour (€2.70, 1 hour). The supplementary bike ticket is €3.50.

For cyclists continuing to Tuscany, taking the train north is suggested because the Aurelia highway up the coast is a traffic nightmare. Orbetello, the beginning of Seascapes & Cliff Villages ride (p73), is a short train ride away.

THE RIDE
It's surprising that a quick ride on a train from Rome can deliver you to an area that meanders through peaceful Lazio back roads. The terrain is rolling enough to make you sweat, but there are not outstandingly significant climbs, and the ride is short enough to allow for a leisurely tour of the Etruscan sites. Once you leave bustling Tarquinia, the route hops from one quaint

little town to another. The area is not frequented by tourists and you can get a taste of Lazio's small-village culture. Riding through the countryside, weaving through fields and smelling the earth, you can almost imagine what it was like when the area was dominated by the Etruscan culture.

The ride begins from the Tarquinia train station. For a warm-up on your Etruscan journey, visit the beautiful 15th-century Palazzo Vitelleschi in Tarquinia. It houses the **Museo Nazionale Tarquiniese** (☎ 07 668 56 036; Piazza Cavour; adult/child €4/2, incl necropolis €6.50/3.25), which contains a wealth of Etruscan artefacts. Just 4.7km into the ride, you'll come to the fascinating **Etruscan Necropolis** (☎ 07 668 56 308; adult/child €4/2, incl museum adult/child €6.50/3.25; 8.30am–6pm), boasting famous painted tombs. Almost 6000 tombs have been excavated, of which 60 are painted, but only

ETRUSCAN LAZIO

CUES			GPS COORDINATES
00		Train Station Tarquinia	42°14'27"N 11°43'37"E
	🚻	outside of Train station	
0.2	↰	to Tarquinia	
0.4	↱	at stop sign to 'Tarquinia'	
2.5	↑⊙	to 'Museo Nationale'	
3.2	↑⊙	to 'Museo'	
(50m)	↱	to 'Necropoli Etrusca'	
3.6	↰⊙	to 'Necropoli Etrusca'	
4.7	★	Necropoli Etrusca	
6.6	↰	to 'Viterbo'	
18.4	↱	to 'Blera'	
(■■↑)		Continue .1 km, signs to left for 'Norchia' Necropoli Etrusca, 12.2km ↱	
30.3	↱	to 'Barbarano Romano'	
33.8		Barbarano Romano	42°14'59"N 12°04'00"E
36.7	↙	to 'Vejano'	
39.9		Vejano	42°13'01"N 12°05'42"E
	↑	SS493	
48.7		Oriolo	42°09'32"N 12°08'20"E
51.9		Manziana	42°08'00"N 12°07'35"E
52.8	↙	to 'Bracciano,' Via Braccianese Claudia	
54.1	↘	SS493, to 'Bracciano'	
57.6	↱	to 'Bracciano', SS493	
58.4	↰	Via Principe di Napoli	
58.8	↱	Via Aurelio Saffi	
59.1	↰	Via Garibaldi	
59.2	↱	Via Armellini	
(70m)	↰	Via Salvatore Negretti	
59.5	↰	Via Principe Napoli	
(50m)	↱	Piazza IV Novembre,	
6.6		Bracciano Tourist Office	42°06'12"N 12°10'33"E

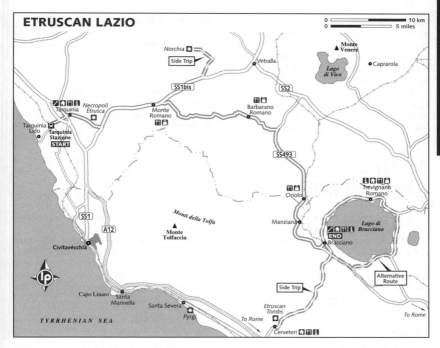

ETRUSCAN LAZIO

a handful are open to the public. The writer, DH Lawrence, who studied the tombs before measures were taken to protect them, wrote extensive descriptions, and it is well worth reading his *Etruscan Places* before seeing the tombs. Excavation of the tombs started in the 15th century and continues today.

Leaving the Etruscan Necropolis, you settle into a pleasant and easy ramble over gently rolling farmland. Look out for the ruined **Roman aqueduct** along the way. On Friday and Sunday evenings in the summer, when everyone is going to or coming back from the beach, traffic can be more intense between Tarquinia and the turn-off to **Blera** (18.4 km), but afterwards, it's very quiet.

If your appetite for Etruscan history has yet to be satiated, consider a 12km side trip (18.4km) to **Norchia**, another ancient necropolis perched dramatically on a rocky outcrop. **Barbarano Romano** (33.8km) is an endearing town and a good place grab a bite, as is **Oriolo** (48.7km). Continue to the lakeside village of **Bracciano** (52.8km), where you can hop on a train back to Rome and stay the night, or continue the Etruscan

tour de force by taking the alternative route to **Ceveterri**.

ALTERNATIVE ROUTE: BRACCIANO TO CERVETERI
18.1km one-way, with lake loop 53.5km

From Bracciano, you have the choice to continue cruising around Lazio and/or pursuing the Etruscans. The alternative route entails an optional scenic loop around Lago di Bracciano before it heads down to visit Cerveteri, one of the most important commercial centres in the Mediterranean from the 7th to the 5th century BC. As Roman power grew, however, so Cerveteri's fortunes faded, and in 358 BC the city was annexed by Rome. The first half of the 19th century saw the first tentative archaeological explorations in the area, and in 1911 systematic excavations began in earnest.

The tombs at the **Necropoli di Banditac-cia** (☎ 06 994 00 01; Via del Necropoli, 2km outside of Cerveteri; €4, incl museum €6.50; closed Mon) are built into *tumoli* (mounds of earth with carved stone bases), laid out in the form of a town, with streets, squares and terraces of houses. The result is a strange and haunting landscape. Treasures taken from the tombs can be seen in Cerveteri's medieval town centre at the **Museo Nazionale di Cerveteri** (☎ 06 994 13 54; Piazza Santa Maria; admission €4, incl necropolis €6.50; 8.30am–6.30pm Tue–Sun).

Trains from Cerveteri's station (which is 6.5km west of the centre) to Rome's Stazione Termini are very frequent (€3.20, 50 mins).

MOUNTAIN BIKE RIDES

If you are a mountain biker stuck in Rome, check out the **Biciurbana** (www.biciurbana.org) for the heads-up on the most nearby rides in the Lazio region.

CITY & FACILITIES

ROME
☎ 06 / pop 2.6 million

Information

There are **APT offices** all over town, such as on Via Parigi (☎ 06 488 99 212; www.romaturismo.it; Via Parigi), in Stazione Termini (☎ 06 487 12 70) and at Fiumicino airport (☎ 06 659 54 471). A good alternative is **Enjoy Rome** (☎ 06 445 18 43, www.enjoyrome.com; Via Marghera 8a), an excellent, private tourist office that publishes the free and useful *Enjoy Rome* city guide. Both APT and Enjoy Rome offer free hotel reservation services.

Supplies & Equipment

Good bike shops in Rome include **Cicli Collalti** (☎ 06 688 01 084; Via del Pellegrino 80a; closed Mon), a friendly place for quick, competent repairs. **Bikeaway** (☎ 06 454 95 816; www.bikeaway.it; Via Monte delGallo 25a) also rents bikes, and **Lazzaretti** (☎ 06 855 38 28; www.ciclilazzaretti.it; Via Bergamo 3a/b) has been in business since 1916. For more information on supplies and equipment in the city, go to www.slowbike .info/assistenza%20bici.htm.

Sleeping & Eating

Finding accommodation in Rome can be tiring, especially during the summer season.

Bed and breakfasts are becoming increasingly popular in Rome, and the **Rome Tourist Board** publishes a full list. **Albergabici** (www.albergabici.it) provides cyclist-friendly accommodation listings. The **Bed & Breakfast Association of Rome** (☎ 06 553 02 248; www.b-b.rm.it; Via A Pacinotti 73) offers online booking.

All of Rome's camping grounds are a fair distance from the city centre. **Village Camping Flaminio** (☎ 06 333 26 04; Via Flaminia 821; per person/tent €7.50–9.50/€7) is close-ish to the city centre. Tents and bungalows are available for hire.

The **Associazione Italiana Alberghi per la Gioventù** (Italian Youth Hostels Association; ☎ 06 487 11 52; www.ostellionline.org; Via Cavour 44) has information about all youth hostels in Italy. The two accommodations listed are around Stazione Termini. **Funny Palace** (☎ 06 447 03 523; www.funnyhostel.com; 5th Fl, Via Varese 31; dm €15–29, d €70–75) has had a stellar reputation since it opened in 2005. There are doubles, triples and quads, all with a comfortable, homey feel. Thoughtful touches such as clean towels, a bottle of wine on arrival and vouchers for coffee and cornetto breakfasts in a nearby café make it a truly excellent choice. **Beehive** (☎ 06 447 04 553; www .the-beehive.com; Via Marghera 8; dm €20–22, d €70–75) is the leading 'hip hostel' in Rome. Run by an American couple, it's brightly painted and features stylish furniture and fittings. Best of all are the on-site internet lounge, book exchange, vegetarian café, garden courtyard and yoga studio. Book well ahead.

A 24-hour **Conad** supermarket is on the lower level of Stazione Termini and at the Tiburtina train station. A large, cheap fruit and **vegetable market** is on the north side of Piazza Vittorio Emanuele. **Casa del Pane** (☎ 06 495 83 37; Via Goito 9), a posh bakery in the Termini area, rustles up a tasty slice of pizza, as well as some mighty fine bread. At Stazione Termini try **Trimani Wine Bar** (☎ 06 446 96 30; Via Cernaia 37b; meals €32) for a top-quality lunch.

TUSCANY

HIGHLIGHTS

- Savouring **Florence** (p48) and **Siena** (p53), then leaving them for the countryside
- Climbs into rewarding hill towns: **Pienza** (p56), **Montepulciano** (p57) and **Pitigliano** (p74)
- Sipping Brunello in **Montalcino** (p57) and Chianti Classico in **Greve** (p51)
- The traffic-free mountainscapes of the **Alpi Apuane** (p69)
- Rolling through the tranquil fairyland of **Feniglia Park** near Orbetello (p73)

SPECIAL EVENTS

- Il Palio horse race (July & August), Siena
- Explosion of the cart fireworks display (Easter), Florence
- Feast of St John festivities for Florence's patron saint (June), Florence

CYCLING EVENTS

- Giro di Toscana, Tuscany region
- Gran Fondo della Versilia, Viareggio
- Gran Fondo del Brunello mountain-bike race, Montalcino
- 24 Ore del Vivo (24-hr mountain-bike race), Val d'Orcia
- Sbiciclettata community event, Grosseto (mid-June)
- Gran Fondo Elba Ovest, Elba
- Fondo del Citta Tufo, Pitigliano

FOOD & DRINK SPECIALITIES

- *crostini* (grilled bread covered with chicken-liver pâté)
- *cinghale* (wild boar, often served in pasta dishes or as a sausage)
- *panaforte* (dense dried-fruit-and-nut tart)
- Chianti Classico (a blended red-and-white wine)

TERRAIN

Rolling hills in the Chianti and Crete regions; flatter in the south near Orbetello and along the coast by Viareggio; steep climbs and descents in the mountainous Alpi Apuane.

Telephone Code – 05	www.discovertuscany.com

The blessing of this chapter is two-fold, dear cyclist. First of all, it outlines routes that explore hidden parts of Tuscany, which are every bit as soul-shaking as the dense tourist areas of Florence, Siena and the Chianti region. Second of all, it allows you to explore those very same astounding, tourist haunts from the unbeatable seat of the saddle. You have an unparalleled opportunity to experience the many faces of Tuscany that many think are the 'best of the best' – architecture, art, countryside, gastronomy, wine, hill towns, seascapes and mountain regions.

HISTORY

The Etruscans founded Florence in about 200 BC. It later became the Roman Florentia, a strategic garrison built to control the Via Flaminia. The city suffered during the barbarian invasions of the Dark Ages.

In the late 14th century, Florence was ruled by the Guelfi under the Albizzi family. Among the families opposing them was the Medici, whose influence grew, as they became the papal bankers.

In the 15th century, Cosimo de' Medici became Florence's ruler. Artists Alberti, Brunelleschi and Donatello flourished under his patronage. Cosimo was followed by his grandson, Lorenzo il Magnifico, whose rule (1469–92) ushered in the Italian Renaissance. In 1492, the Medici bank failed and the family was driven out of Florence.

After Florence's defeat by the Spanish in 1512, the Medici returned to the city but were expelled in 1527, this time by Emperor Charles V. Charles later allowed the Medici to return to Florence, where they ruled for another 200 years.

In 1737, the Grand Duchy of Tuscany passed to the House of Lorraine, which retained control for the most part until it was incorporated into the Kingdom of Italy in 1860.

Florence was badly damaged during WWII by the retreating Germans. Floods ravaged the city in 1966.

ENVIRONMENT

If you regard Tuscany's coast as the base, the region forms a rough triangle covering 22,992 sq km. Crammed within that triangle are various land forms: from mountains in the north and east to relatively flat plains in the south – from islands off the coast to rolling hills in the interior.

Much of the coast is flat, with the exception of a stretch south of Livorno and the Monte Argentario peninsula. The northern flank of the region is closed off by the Apennines and the Alpi Apuane.

In all, two-thirds of Tuscany is mountainous or hilly. Lower hill ranges rise in the south and are separated by a series of low river valleys, the most important being the Arno. The Arno rises in the Apennines, flows south to Arezzo and then meanders northwest. Although the river was once an important trade artery, traffic is virtually nonexistent on it today.

Of the islands scattered off Tuscany's coast, the central and eastern parts of Elba, along with Giannutri and parts of Giglio, are reminders of an Apennine wall that collapsed into the sea millions of years ago. Western Elba and parts of Giglio are the creation of volcanic activity.

CLIMATE

Tuscan summers are hot and oppressive. From late June to September, highs of 35°C are common. The Chianti region is the hottest. Temperatures along the coast are marginally lower. Mountainous areas, such as the Alpi Apuane, are cooler and wetter.

Spring and autumn are the nicest times of year, but rainfall in November can be heavy. Specifically, April to early June and September to October are the most pleasant months. Average daytime highs around 20°C to 25°C are ideal for cycling.

Winter is chilly across the region. Snowfalls and temperatures around zero are possible in inland hilly areas (such as Siena and Cortona).

PLANNING
Maps

The best general reference map of the region is Touring Club Italiano's (TCI) 1:200,000 *Toscana*. For individual rides,

---

BROKEN COMPASS TOURS

Broken Compass Tours (☎ 34 060 39 913; www.brokencompasstours.com; Arezzo) is a grassroots guiding service that is passionate about cycling and Tuscany. Even better, it makes sure you point your wheel off the beaten path. The company specialises in week-long tours but is available to guide single day tours as well. It's a blessing that the bilingual owner Jesse Sibley is a total foodie. Doubling as a chef, he enjoys sharing his intimate knowledge of regional cuisine and wine and can prioritise well-selected visits to wineries and local olive farms for tastings. With Broken Compass Tours, you will eat well and learn much while pedalling the quiet back roads of Tuscany.

Edizioni Multigraphic's 1:100,000 individual province maps, *Carta Stradale Provinciale*, provide additional detail. For more information on Tuscany and Florence, see Lonely Planet's *Florence* and *Tuscany*.

To purchase maps and books in Florence, try **Feltrinelli International** (☎ 05 52 921 96; Via Cavour 12r), opposite the APT office, and **Internazionale Seeber** (☎ 05 52 873 39; Via de' Cerratani 16). An informal website about cycling in Tuscany is www .tuscanybike.org.

Cycling Events

For information on International Cycling Union rides, such as the Giro di Toscana, visit www.uci.ch/english/index.htm. To learn more about the Gran Fondo della Versilia, check out the race's website (www .versiliabike.it). For information on the Gran Fondo del Brunello and mountain biking in the Val d'Orcia, contact **Club Orso on Bike** (☎ 34 705 35 638; www .bikemontalcino.it).

The **Sbiciclettata** (www.gol.grosseto.it /asso/asbici/indexe.html) is a bike ride/ ecological walk/party from Grosseto to Istia d'Ombrone and back. The **Gran Fondo Elba Ovest** (www.granfondoelbaovest.com) is a low-to-high mountain bike race. The **Fondo del Cittá Tufo** (www.gcpitigliano. it) is an annual road race in Pitigliano.

EVERYONE'S BELLA TOSCANA

Tuscany's popularity as a tourist destination makes for a steady stream of traffic between the major regional attractions, specifically from late June to August. Take an overabundance of foreigners unfamiliar with the roads and mix in hordes of Italians fleeing the cities on vacation (especially in August), and you have a recipe for traffic-induced disaster. Be particularly alert when entering and leaving Florence and Siena, as they tend to clog in summer.

GETTING THERE & AWAY

As it is such a popular tourist attraction, Florence can easily be reached by land or air.

Air

Aeroporto di Firenze (Florence Airport; ☎ 05 530 61 300; www.aeroporto.firenze.it), 5km northwest of the city centre – caters for domestic and a handful of European flights. Pisa international airport **Galileo Galilei** (☎ 05 08 49 300; www.pisa-airport.com), one of northern Italy's main international and domestic airports. It is closer to Pisa but well linked with Florence by public transport.

Train

Florence is on the Rome–Milan train line, which means that most of the trains for Rome, Bologna and Milan are **Intercity** or **Eurostar Italia,** which do not carry bikes unless they are disassembled and bagged (see box p297). Diretto and regionale trains, however, both take bicycles and run between Florence and Rome (€15.80, 3¾ hours, every 2 hours). It is possible to catch a train from the Galileo Galilei airport to Florence.

Bus

Lazzi (☎ 05 52 15 155; www.lazzi.it, in Italian; Piazza Stazione) forms part of the **Eurolines** network of international bus services and sells tickets for buses to various European cities, as well as regionale tickets.

From the **SITA bus station** (☎ 80 037 37 60; www.sitabus.it, in Italian; Via Santa Caterina da Siena 17r; information office 8.30am–12.30pm & 3–6pm Mon–Fri, 8.30am–12.30pm Sat–Sun), just west of Piazza della Stazione; there's service to/from Siena (€6.50, 1¼hours, at least hourly). Direct buses also serve Arezzo.

GATEWAY

See Florence (p80).

CHIANTI CLASSIC

Duration 2 days

Distance 101.7km

Difficulty moderate

Start Florence

Finish Siena

Summary You get to pedal through two of Italy's most gorgeous cities and explore the intoxicating vineyards, forests and wine of the Chianti region along the way.

This ride touches down in two spectacular Tuscan cities, **Florence** (p80) and **Siena** (p85). They are both major points on the tourist track, for good reason, and you get to experience them uniquely from two wheels.

The true glory of this ride lies in the fact that you navigate between the cities not in a train, bus or car, but rather seeing, feeling and smelling the luscious **Chianti wine region** in the middle. What a treat it is to pedal out of Florence's beautiful mayhem into a landscape unfolding into gorgeous fields of perfectly rowed vines, olive groves and forests. Tranquillity emanates from these rolling hills where its inhabitants have for centuries nurtured and honed the sacred art of wine making. The verdant hillsides perfume the air and stoke your anticipation for the evening, when you will savour sumptuous wine or simply eat fantastic, Tuscan-style handmade pasta after a day of pedalling.

You also have the opportunity check out the castle of **Montefioralle** and the impressive abbey **Badia di Passignano** on a side trip from Greve. On Day 2, you meander through the lovely hamlets of **Radda** and **Castellina** in Chianti before descending into Florence's Gothic rival, **Siena**. Some will find the ride challenging, some won't: there's a hearty share of climbing, but the distances aren't brutal.

PLANNING
When to Cycle
See the Climate section (p47) for information on the best weather conditions. Florence and Siena are swamped with tourists in July and August, making accommodation very difficult to secure. April to early June and September to October are the most pleasant times to cycle.

What to Bring
Don't underestimate the power of the scorching Tuscan sun in July and August. If you're embarking on this ride in summer, bring sunscreen and plenty of water. A corkscrew is also very handy for uncorking wine.

Maps
The ride crosses two provinces (Florence and Siena). TCI's *Toscana* does the job. Another good map is Selca's hard to find 1:70,000 *Il Chianti*. Ask for it at APT tourist offices or contact the Provincia di Firenze office (☎ 05 52 76 01; Via Cavour 37) in Florence.

Information Sources
Florence by Bike (www.florencebikepages .com) is a site dedicated to cycling around Florence and Tuscany. **Firenze in Bici** (www.firenzeinbici.net) is associated with FIAB and has the latest and greatest on bike activism in town, in case you want to get involved. For itineraries and events in Florence, check out www.firenze turismo.it. Go Tuscany's website (www.firenze.net) has an events calendar and tips on places to stay. See Siena Information sources (p85).

FLORENCE FROM THE SADDLE

What better way to distinguish your experience of Florence than by seeing this magnificent city by bike? Here are some bike companies that can hook you up with a cyclo-city tour amongst other things.

Tour Bike Florence (☎ 05 523 43 048, 34 063 51 800; www.tourbikeflorence.it; Via Fiesolana 14r) Bike rental (per 1/3/5/7 days including self-guiding itineraries €13/32/50/65), three-hour city tours (€35) and day trips to Fiesole and Il Chianti (both €65 incl lunch).

Florence by Bike (☎ 05 54 88 992; www.florencebybike.it; Via San Zanobi 120–122r) Straight bike rental (per 1 or 5 hours €2.70/7.50, 1 or 3 days €14/34.50 include self-guided city itineraries) and a 32km-long day tour of Chianti (incl lunch €75).

GETTING TO/FROM THE RIDE
Florence (start)
See Getting There & Away (p48).

Siena (finish)
BUS
The hub for buses is at Piazza Gramsci. TRA-IN and SITA express buses race up to Florence (€6.50, 1¼ hours, up to 30 daily). SENA buses run to/from Rome (€18, 3 hours, 8 daily) and Milan (€25.50, 4¼ hours, 3 daily) and there are seven buses daily to Arezzo (€5, 1½ hours).

TRAIN
Unfortunately, Siena isn't on a major train line, so buses are generally a better alterna-

---

Days 1 & 2: Chianti Classic

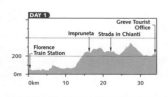

DAY 1

Florence Train Station

Impruneta Strada in Chianti

Greve Tourist Office

200

0m

0km 10 20 30

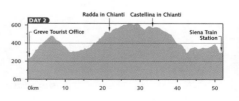

DAY 2

Radda in Chianti Castellina in Chianti

Greve Tourist Office

Siena Train Station

600

400

200

0m

0km 10 20 30 40 50

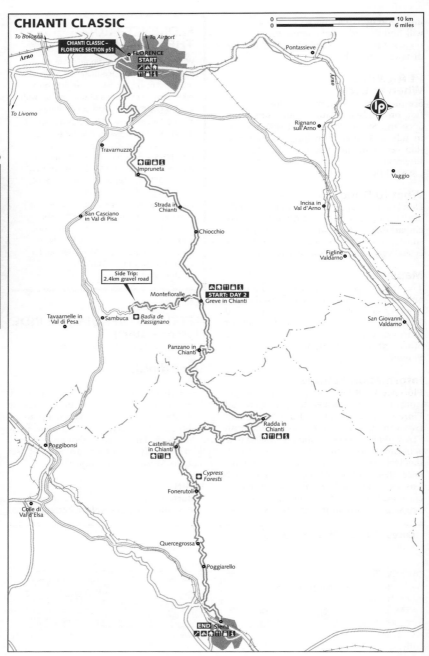

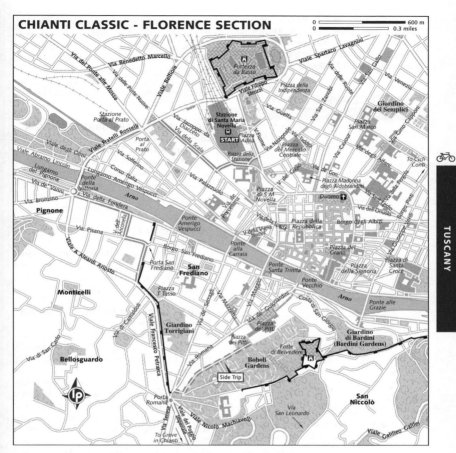

CHIANTI CLASSIC - FLORENCE SECTION

tive. That said, the ease of travelling with a bike on a train and frequency of train departures make an argument for taking the train anyway. By train, change at Chiusi for Rome and at Empoli for Florence. Trains arrive at Piazza F Rosselli, north of the city centre. Supplementary bike tickets are €3.50.

BICYCLE

Siena is the starting town for three other rides, Hill Town Trek (p56); Siena Explorer (p53); and Discovering Tuscany (p59). It's possible to bike on secondary roads to Arezzo. It will be pretty, but it will be hilly.

THE RIDE
Day 1: Florence to Greve in Chianti
2½–5 hours, 32.2–47.1km

Leaving the splendour of Florence's Renaissance art, cathedrals and gardens, you'll ride across the Arno into the heart of the Chianti region, which is adorned with undulating hills and acclaimed vineyards.

At the beginning of the ride, there is the option to detour at the **Porta Romana** (4.3km), an imposing city gate that once marked the outer limits of Florence, so that you can explore the touted **Boboli Gardens**. The route then sets you to the task of climbing out of the city and rewards you with splendid views of Florence's skyline. After about 7 to 10km, the bustle of Florence fades as the route winds steadily upwards past airy olive groves towards **Impruneta** (16.2km). Terraced vineyards line both sides of the hilly route from Impruneta to Strada in Chianti (21.8km).

CHIANTI CLASSIC – DAY 1

CUES			GPS COORDINATES
0km		Florence train station	43°46'40"N 11°14'54"E
90m	⊙⌐↱	at Piazza della Stazione	
0.3km	↗	Via Della Scalla, 'to Sienna'	
0.9km	⊙↱↱	'to Siena'	
1.7km	⊙⌐↱	'to Siena'	
2.1km	↱↱	to 'Porta Romana'	
2.3km	↖	Via Giovanni Della Casa	
2.6km	↗	to Porta Romana	
2.7km	⌐↱	to Porta Romana	
4.3km	⊙↟	onto Poggio Imperiale	
	●●↱↱	Under arch to Boboli Gardens	
5.2km	⌐↱	Due Strada, Via del Gelsomin	
6km	↱↱	at T, unsigned Via Seneze	
7.9km	↗	to 'Scandicci'	
8.3km	↱↱	to 'Firenze, Sienna'	
8.6km	⌐↱	to Sienna SR 2	
10km	⊙↱↱	to Impruneta	
11km	↱↱	to Impruneta	
11.3km	▲	2.6km moderate climb	
16.2km		Impruneta	43°41'05"N 11°15'10"E
18.2km	↱↱	to Greve	
20.9km	⌐↱	to 'Greve' SS222	
21.8km		Strada in Chianti	43°39'43"N 11°17'40"E
	↗	to continue on SS429	
22km	⊙↖	to 'Greve'	
29.5km	★	Castello di Veranzzano	
31.6	●●★	Montefioralle and Badia di Passignano ⌐↱ 14.9km	
	⌐↱	to 'Montefioralle', Viale Lino Falsetattacchi, Via del Buondelmonti RT	
32.2		Greve Tourist Office	43°35'18"N 11°18'53"E

For a sample of the famed **Chianti Classico**, stop when you see a sign with a 'black cockerel', at one of the dozens of wineries littering the route, especially in the last 3km. If you're lucky enough to be riding through on the last Sunday of the month in summer, the wineries are all open with free tastings.

SIDE TRIP: MONTEFIORALLE & BADIA DI PASSIGNANO
1–2 hours, at 31.6km, 14.9km RT

Drop your panniers where you're staying in Greve before doing this side trip – if it suits you. After unloading, backtrack on your route then turn west (31.6km) at the point just before you entered Greve and grunt up the steep hill to the ancient castle-village of **Montefioralle** (1.4km). If your equipment is sturdy enough for a short stretch of gravel, pay a visit to **Badia di Passignano**, 14.4km up the road, to an abbey founded in 1049 by Benedictine monks, and then retrace the route back to Greve.

Day 2: Greve in Chianti to Siena
3–6 hours, 53.5km

Climbing the 7km out of Greve, you'll be absorbed into the rolling landscape of carefully preened vineyards and olive groves. Along the way, *agriturismi* (farm-stay accommodation) and wineries dot the route. Eventually, the sparkling vineyard landscape becomes tempered with forest as the winding and well-paved road heads to **Radda di Chianti**. Quiet, lightly trafficked SS429 offers stretches of easy riding. However, you will climb into the delightful Radda in Chianti (21.9km), where you can take a quick stroll

---

L'EROICA

While you're two-wheeling around Tuscany, you may see signs in an old-fashioned style that say L'Eroica with an arrow. That is a sign for one of the most endearing, and incredibly enough, elegiac bike races ever to be put on. Hundreds of mostly Italian cyclists get together for this cyclotouristic rally, dress up in vintage cycling clothing, use antique cycling apparatus and in one bombastic lament for times gone by, ride their hearts out in the Tuscan hills. Their mission statement proclaims that they re-enact 'heroic times of cycling: dust or mud, no organised service, vintage refreshment, wonderful and demanding roads, great ability to adapt and suffer'.

We know that their inertia is stoked by veneration of the past as well as the desire to reclaim a former standard of hardiness and simplicity, if not masculinity. But when they all dress up together in their precious wool jerseys and cycling goggles, it's actually really cute. Seriously.

For more information check out: www.eroica.it.

CHIANTI CLASSIC - DAY 2

CUES		GPS COORDINATES
start	Greve tourist office	43°35'18"N 11°18'53"E
0km	S on Viale G. Verrazzano	
0.2	▲ moderate 7km climb	
10.4	◥⌐ SS429 to `Radda in Chianti'	
20.7	◥⌐ to `Radda in Chianti'	
21.8	★ Radda in Chianti	43°29'14"N 11°22'32"E
22.8	↘ to `Castellina in Chianti'	
31.4	◥⌐ SS222 to `Castellina. in Chianti'	
33.4	★ Castellina in Chianti	43°28'17"N 11°17'08"E
36.8	★ Cypress Forests	
51.7	↘ to `Stazione F.S.'	
52.6	◎ (3rd exit) to `Stazione F.S.'	
53.2	◢◎ (1st exit) train symbol	
53.4	◢◎ (1st exit) train symbol	
53.5	↰ into Siena station	43°19'55"N 11°19'22"E

on the quaint main road. Radda's tourist office (☎ 05 777 38 494; Piazza Castello 6) has information on winery tours and local walks. Radda's speciality meat and cheese shops, near the base of Via Roma, make a nice place to grab a quick bite. **Castellina in Chianti** (33.5km) also boasts plenty of medieval charm as well as adorable cafés to grab lunch. Both of these little towns have venues that advertise wine and olive oil tastings.

It's a rip-roaring descent approaching Siena past **cypress forests** (37km) towards the distant marble domes and red-brick towers on the horizon. The traffic of Siena doesn't pick up until the last 3–4km, and there are two short, steep hills coming into town. Once in the city (55km), you and your bike can collapse in the middle of Piazza del Campo, the exquisite main plaza, which whets your palate for the marvels of Siena.

SIENA EXPLORER

Duration 4–7 hours
Distance 77.5km
Difficulty moderate–hard
Start Siena
Finish Buonconvento
Summary In the matter of a day, you can go from the architectural masterpiece, Piazza del Campo, to the enormous ruins of a countryside abbey, to secluded hills deep in the Tuscan forest.

If you have a spare day in Siena, consider doing this day ride. It will satiate your urge to hightail it from the city in search of the countryside and wilder surroundings of Siena. The route is jaw-droppingly beautiful in places and is strewn with intriguing stops. You can meander through the ruined Gothic abbey of San Galgano and taste olive oil and wine at the conservation-oriented organic farm of Tenuta di Sannocchia. This route is not for the weak of thigh – there are some major ascents, especially in the second half of the day. But the payback descents scintillate you with a luxurious natural high. Plus, you'll get to wind your way through a truly gorgeous area of the forested Tuscan hills seldom snapshot by visitors.

The ride ends in Buonconvento where you can hop a quick train into Siena. If you want an easier ride, you can make it an 'out-and-back' from the San Galgano.

FARM WITH A MISSION

The Sienese day trip passes an ambitious working organic farm, **Tenuta di Spannocchia** (☎ 05 77 75 21; www .spannocchia.org). Situated on 1200 acres of vineyards, olive groves, fields and forests, Spannocchia is also a wildlife sanctuary, a centre for educational programmes and conservation projects.

Those interested in a cooking class, historical tour of the grounds, or farm tour should call in advance for accommodation, rates and reservation information. To stay you must be a member of the Spannocchia Foundation (student/adult €30/45). The membership, good for one year, helps support the farm. Those wishing to purchase any of the farm's organic products (wine, olive oil, honey etc) may simply drop by.

PLANNING
Maps

The free *Siena* APT map handed out at the main APT office in Siena is adequate for this ride, as is TCI's *Toscana* map and Litografia Artistica Cartografica's 1:150,000 *Siena: Carta della Provincia*, which can be purchased at most tourist offices and bookstores.

Information Sources

Terre di Siena in Bici (www.terresienainbici .it) is an internet resource and free guide book found at the tourist office that describes cycling itineraries and resources in the region. Siena has a very active local cycling club, **Amici della Bicicletta F Bacconi** (☎ 05 774 51 59; www.adbsiena .it; Via Mazzini 55), which is affiliated with the FIAB and organises rides to nearby attractions.

GETTING TO/FROM THE RIDE
Siena (start)
See p85.

Buonconvento (finish)
TRAIN

From the Buonconvento station, trains leave regularly to Siena (€2.30, 20 to 30 minutes, six daily), the last leaving around 9pm. Note that you can't buy supplementary bike tickets at this station. You can go south, catching connecting trains to Orbetello, the beginning of Seascapes & Cliff Villages (p73).

BICYCLE

Buonconvento is on the Hill Town Trek (p56) and Seascapes & Cliff Villages (p73) routes.

THE RIDE

Leaving Siena can be a bit hectic, but after turning on Via Ricasoli (3.2km) the busy medieval streets of Siena begin to give way to seemingly endless stretches of wheat and sunflower fields. The first 20km on the way to San Galgano are rolling while the last 15km gets steeper.

The 13th-century Ponte della Pia (20.5km), once an important point on the Massetana Road, linked Siena with Massa Marittima in the Middle Ages. The bridge can be crossed by foot, and adventurers may want to tromp around in search of the nearby ruins of the Santa Lucia monastery. Further down the road is Tenuta di Spannocchia (21.8km; see side trip below and boxed text p53). **Ristorante Montebello** (23.2km; ☎ 05 777 99 086) is run by

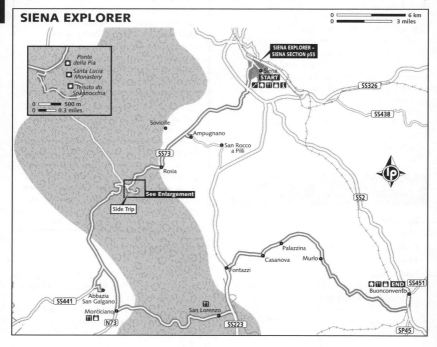

SIENA EXPLORER

CUES			GPS COORDINATES
start		Siena train station	43°19′54″N 11°19′23″E
0km		Turn right at station exit, heading under overpass	
0.5	◎	First exit	
1.3	↘	To Porto Camollia, Viale Minzoni	
1.4	↟🚉	Continuing on Garibaldi	
1.7	⬑	Via di Camollia	
1.8	⬏	Via dei Gazzini	
1.9	⬏	Via R Franci (becomes Viale Cadorna), to 'Fortezza'	
2.2	↗	Via Armando Diaz (past fort)	
2.5	↘	to 'tutte le direzione,' Viale Sauro	
2.7	⬑	Via Ricasoli ('tutte le direzione')	
5.5	↑	Tutte le Direzione	
6.2	↑	to 'Roma'	
7.7	⬏	to 'Sovicille'	
17.6		Rosia	43°15′00″N 11°13′24″E

CUES CONTINUED			GPS COORDINATES
20.5	★	Ponte della Pia bridge (LHS)	
	★	Santa Lucia monastery	
{21.8	●●⬑	Tenuta di Spannocchia 4km ↻}	
{33.7	●●⬏	to 'Abbazia San Galgano' follow signs 5.8km ↻}	
36.3	★	Sculpture Garden	
37.3	⬑	to 'San Lorenzo,' SP32A	
49.4	★	San Lorenzo, Pieve di San Serenzo	
50.9	⬑	to Siena, SS223	
52.9	⬏	to 'Fontazzi'	
56.8	↘	to 'Sienna'	
58.1	↗	to Vescovado di Murlo	
64.7	↗	to 'Buonconvento'	
66	↘	to 'Buonconvento'	
73.9	↘	to 'Buonconvento'	
77.4	⬏	at unsigned T intersection	
77.5	★	Buonconvento train station on left	43°08 05 N 11°29 04 E

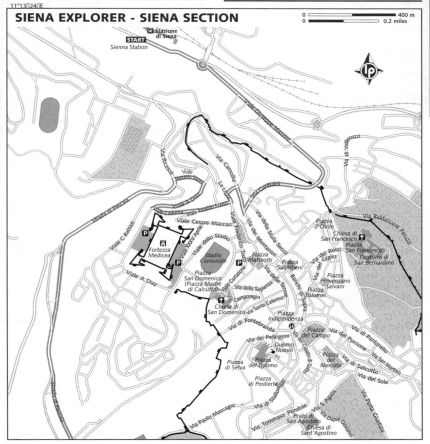

SIENA EXPLORER - SIENA SECTION

Sicilians (on the verge of changing its name) and makes a great lunch choice.

The ride then entails some switch-backed inclines and descents, though it's not long before the turn-off for the **Abbazia San Galgano** (33.7km). From the *abbazia* (abbey), you head east to San Lorenzo (49.9km), backtracking to a tiny Tuscan village whose epicentre is narrow, winding, steep, flowered, cobbled and seemingly untouched by modernity. You can grab a coffee and check out the **Pieve de San Serenzo**, a church whose first recorded mentioning was in 1108. You'll have to take the highway (51.4km) for 2km, after which you plunge into the Tuscan forest and tuck into some major climbs before soaring finally through golden, undulating farmland into Buonconvento.

SIDE TRIP: SIENESE DAY TRIP
1 hour, at 22.3km , 4km RT

See boxed text Farm With a Mission p53.

SIDE TRIP: ABBAZIA SAN GALGANO
1–2 hours, at 34.2km, 5.8km RT

The monks of this former Cistercian abbey were among Tuscany's most powerful. By the 16th century, the monks' wealth and importance had declined and the church deteriorated. On a hill overlooking the abbey is the **Romanesque Cappella di Monte Siepi**, where the original Cistercian settlement lived. Inside the chapel are badly preserved frescoes by Ambrogio Lorenzetti, depicting the life of St Galgano. A real-life 'sword in the stone' is under glass in the floor of the chapel, put there, legend has it, by San Galgano.

HILL TOWN TREK

Duration 3 days
Distance 150km
Difficulty moderate–demanding
Start Siena
Finish Cortona

Summary Delve deeper into Tuscan wine country that is jewelled by small, walled medieval towns that watch you sternly as you fight to pedal to their hilltops.

Touring from hill town to hill town, you'll test your climbing muscles and truly know why the towns' placements prevented invasion. But it's worth it. While travelling across the strikingly dramatic landscape, you'll see medieval walled towns burst into the horizon, and your sense of history becomes a live thing, not merely conceptual.

The towns themselves are laid-back, accustomed to tourists, and casual about their own beauty. Furthermore, if you patronise restaurants in the region, it'll be hard to figure which is more intoxicating, the wine or food.

The three days of riding include mostly rolling hills, with steep climbs into the towns. Though the climbing is significant, the daily distances aren't overwhelming. The route wanders through the undulating, cypress-lined wheat fields of the stark Crete region before you settle in for a night in Montalcino. Then terrain changes from fields to vineyards – the source of the region's famed Brunello wine – and passes by the sulphurous baths of Bagno Vignoni, the Renaissance hill town, Pienza, before arriving in Montepulciano. The final leg is short and rolling to Cortona (p58), the growingly popular town and point of departure.

PLANNING
Maps

TCI's *Toscana* covers the ride. Otherwise, a good, cheap map is the 1:150,000 *Siena: Carta della Provincia* by Litografia Artistica Cartografica, which can be found at tourist offices.

GETTING TO/FROM THE RIDE
Siena (start)

See p85.

Cortona (finish)
BUS

From the bus station at Piazza Garibaldi, LFI buses connect the town with Arezzo (€2.60, 1 hour, at least 10 daily), via Castiglion Fiorentino.

TRAIN

Because Cortona is on the Rome–Florence train line, it is quite easy to get to/from either location. It's a bit tougher to get back to Siena. Cortona/Camucia is the closest train station to Cortona (about 4km downhill from town,

FOR THE CITY-PHOBES AND NATURE-LOVERS

If you don't want to stay in Siena at the start of the Hill Town Trek, there are *agriturismi* in the first 20km of Day 1.

Agriturismo Santa Lucia (☎ 05 773 65 892; www.agriturismosantalucia.com; at 10.8km, which is 2km down a signed road; rents apartments, price depends on season)

Casa Vacanza Santa Caterina B&B (☎ 05 777 17 320; www.casavacanzes caterina.com; SS438, at 16.6km; per person €40, plus €5 for breakfast)

signed off the road to Montepulciano). Note that there is no way to buy supplementary bike tickets at this station, so plan ahead.

Destinations include Arezzo (€2.20, 20 minutes, hourly), Florence (€6.70, 1½ hours, hourly), Rome (€9.40, 2¼ hours, every 2 hours) and Perugia (€2.80, 40 minutes, at least 12 daily).

To return to Siena, first take the Florence–Rome train to Chiusi, then change for Siena (€7.70 plus €3.50 bike supplement, 2½–3½ hours, every 2 hours).

BICYCLE

There are hilly, beautiful possibilities to ride secondary roads from Cortona to Arezzo and to ride to the Le Marche ride. Ask the tourist office or local cyclists.

THE RIDE
Day 1: Siena to Montalcino
3½–7 hours, 56.7km

The scenery along this stretch varies from exposed, undulating landscapes to green and succulent, but it's dramatic throughout and makes for some stellar cycling. The ride is hilly, especially before you reach Asciano. Then there a couple more climbs, including the final steep 6km. At the end, the wine gods shall smile upon you because you have arrived in the Brunello capital, **Montalcino**.

Departing from Siena, proceed straight through a series of roundabouts, following signs for Arezzo. You'll think you've accidentally merged onto the highway, but hold tight for the Taverna D'Arbia Nord exit (7.3km). About 8km from Siena, busy arterial roads give way to the spacious wheat fields and olive groves of Le Crete.

The landscape in the region radiates violet or golden hues depending on the season. On the way, you might see signs for fresh pecorino and ricotta; worth a stop if you want a delectable snack. Cypress-lined roads meander to the Abbazia di Monte Oliveto Maggiore (34.8km), where things look considerably less parched. The Abbazia, a 14th-century monastery, is famous for its Signorelli and Sodoma frescoes. The monastery is open from 9.15am to noon and 3.15pm to 6pm daily.

After a 2.6km climb, enjoy a rip-roaring descent into Buonconvento and then the stunning grunt up to Montalcino, a town prized by wine aficionados and lovers of age-old Tuscan charm alike.

SIDE TRIP: ASCIANO
30 min–2 hours, at 19.1km; 0.6km RT

Not on the tourist track, Asciano is a great place to refuel after hard rides. **L'Angolo dello Sfizio** (☎ 05 777 17 128; Corso Matteotti €35/37) is where Tuscan folk enjoy Tuscan food like bruschetta clobbered by fresh tomatoes dripping in olive oil and pasta that melts in your mouth.

SIDE TRIP: FATTORIA DEI BARBI AND THE MUSEO DI BRUNELLO
2 hours, about 5km RT

South of Montalcino on SP14 (you'll see signs to turn, at 3.9km on Day 2), you'll find the **Fattoria dei Barbi** (☎ 05 778 41 111; www.fattoriadeibarbi.it; Località Podernuovi), a winery that has been in the Colombini family since 1790. You can try Brunello, olive oil, salami and pecorino all made on site and stay in the *agriturismo* (farm stay accommodation). There are tours of the cellars and on-site is the **Brunello Museum** (www.museodelbrunello.it), which has displays on the winemaking tradition over the centuries. Even though it's right on Day 2's route, it might be nice to drop your stuff in Montalcino after Day 1 and wander over at leisure.

Day 2: Montalcino to Montepulciano
3½–7 hours, 58km

It's a day of thrilling, switch-backed descents and arduous climbs, with typically

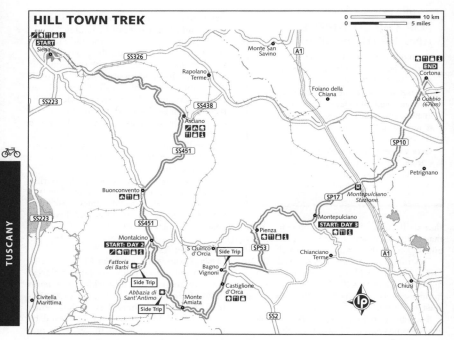

HILL TOWN TREK

charming scenery. You'll pass the famous Sant'Antimo church (where you might hear some Gregorian chanting), the Roman baths of Bagno Vignoni and the pinch-yourself-pretty town of Pienza.

As you leave Montalcino, the sweeping vistas foretell a hefty descent. The pavement is chunky, so beware. At 9.3km, visit the 12th-century **Romanesque Abbazia di Sant'Antimo,** built on the site of a monastery founded by Charlemagne in AD 781. The climb to Castiglione d'Orcia is hard work, but the view on the descent to Bagno Vignoni (29.8km) is generous compensation. You can visit this hot-spring pool built by the Medici before pedalling to Pienza (43.5km), a superb example of Renaissance architecture and town planning. In Pienza, **Baccus Osteria** (☎ 05 787 49 080; Corso Rosellino 70; baccus.osteria@libero.it; closed Tue) serves wonderful Tuscan food, both carnivore- and vege-friendly.

Enjoy a relatively flat, vineyard-lined ramble en route to Montepulciano (58km), until the final 500m – a brutally steep incline.

Day 3: Montepulciano to Cortona

2–4 hours, 35.2km

This rolling ride is easier than previous days and the scenery, though pleasant, doesn't 'grab a fistful of your jersey and shake you' to such a degree. After a quick, thrilling descent out of Montepulciano,

JOIN THE VINO NOBILE DI MONTEPULCIANO FAN CLUB

Paul III gushed about *Vino Nobile di Montepulciano* in his late 16th-century poem 'Bacchus in Tuscany'. Subsequently, this red wine – which dates back to 1350 – was granted the description of 'noble' in the second half of the 18th century, about the same time that Voltaire was dropping the name in his 1759 novel *Candide*. Slightly more recent admirers have included the ex-American presidents Martin Van Buren and Thomas Jefferson.

it's a roly-poly downhill ride until a butt-kicker ascent into Cortona. The landscape is mainly wheat fields, vineyards, olive groves and sunflowers. After about 20km, Cortona looms grandly above you on an intimidating ridge – a pretty though more crowded hill town. When you're ready to jump off to the next adventure, the train station is back the way you came at the bottom of the final climb (follow signs).

It's not a bad choice to overnight in picturesque, romantic (less crowded) Pienza. This is also a good option if you are tuckered out and/or not interesting in climbing into Cortona.

DISCOVERING TUSCANY

Duration 3 days
Distance 202.5km
Difficulty moderate
Start Siena
Finish Massa Marittima
Summary Rich both in panoramas and back roads canopied by dense forest, this route takes you deep into Tuscany where many visitors never venture.

As the honking, exhaust and traffic of Siena fade behind you with each pedal stroke, you make your way through the golden-green hills of Tuscany towards the worthy tourist destinations of **San Gimignano** and **Volterra**, before delving into some fantastic, less explored countryside near verdant Massa Marittima. Terrain-wise, expect rolling hills, some longer climbs and some short, steep hauls into the towns. The low daily mileage is the moderate aspect of this ride; the amount of climbing earns it difficult points.

Day 1 ends in Volterra, a walled, Tuscan town snuggled into the splendour of an expansive panorama. Day 2 leads you pleasantly further away from the crowds to the sleepy 8th-century mining town of **Massa Marittima**. The last day is a loop that explores some of the most picturesque, undiscovered hill towns in Tuscany: Montemassi, Sassofortino and Roccatederighi. The route takes you through sleepy hamlets, thick forests and along deserted roads.

This ride provides you with an excellent option to take an alternative route to Piombino and the start of the Elba ride (see Circling Elba ride p66). Logistically speaking, the route works well if you're planning a visit to Elba or continuing on to Rome. Consider your pre-/post-ride itinerary before embarking because getting from Massa Marittima to Florence or Siena is more complicated.

PLANNING
When to Cycle
Visiting San Gimignano in July or August can be a permanently scarring travel experience, as tourist hordes clog the narrow streets and entrance lines to attractions wind endlessly about. Any other time is preferable.

Maps
TCI's *Toscana* covers the route as does 1:150,000 *Siena: Carta della Provincia*. Touring Club Italiano's *La Via Francigena in Provincia di Siena* is also good and it's free at the Siena tourist office. The Volterra Tourist Office provides a free bike guide and map, *I Centri Commerciali Matural della Valdicecina in Bicicletta*. Though rudimentary and decorated with a cyclist in a bikini, it does give some good ideas for further exploring the area.

GETTING TO/FROM THE RIDE
Siena (start)
See p85.

Massa Marittima (finish)
BUS
To get back to Siena, consider catching a bus. There are two daily buses to Siena (€4.40), at 7.05am and 4.40pm, and around four buses to Volterra (changing at Monterotondo). All buses stop on Piazza XXIV Maggio.

TRAIN
To get to Florence or Rome, the train is a better option. The nearest train station is Follonica on the coastal Rome–Turin line. Cycling to Follonica is a 20km breeze – downhill or flat all the way. Diretto trains run to Rome (€12.25, 2½–3 hours, every 2–4 hours). To get to Florence, take the Rome–Turin train north to Pisa, then

VERNACCIA: A PROVOCATIVE WHITE

'It kisses, licks, bites, thrusts and stings.' That's how Michelangelo, clearly drawing upon the purple end of his palate, described San Gimignano's **Vernaccia** white wine. Smooth and aromatic with a slightly bitter aftertaste and pale golden yellow in colour, it was Italy's first DOC (Denominazione di Origine Controllata) wine. Boccaccio fantasised about flowing streams of cool Vernaccia, Pope Paul III reputedly bathed in it and the ever demure St Catherine of Siena used it as medicine. When you ride through San Gimignano, be a little less ambitious and just manage to ride in a straight line out of town.

SWISS FAMILY BIKE HAVEN: FAT TYRE POSSIBILITIES IN MASSA

Just 5km away from Massa off SR439 (there are signs), is a mountain biking enclave at the *agriturismo* **Massa Vecchia** (☎ 05 669 03 885; www.massavecchia. it; *Località* Massa Vecchia; per person €30–44) where they offer MTB tours in the area and also on Elba. In the community-oriented, relaxed atmosphere, clients sit pretty with very nice Scott rental bikes on hand.

Cyclist-friendly touches include in-room bike nooks to park your steed, drying racks and a properly gigantic breakfast. Half-board is a yummy and economical deal; make sure to try the house wine from their vineyards. Even if you aren't up for mountain biking, you'll have access to internet and a pool, and it's just a nice bike friendly place to stay in beautiful surroundings.

change for Florence (€10.30, 2½–3 hours, every 2 hours). The supplementary bike ticket is €3.50.

BICYCLE
There is an alternate route (see p62) that goes to Piombino part way through the second day. Otherwise, Abbazia San Galgano on the Siena Explorer ride (see p53) is rugged and scenic - it's 32km away from Massa Maritima and you could use it to loop back to Siena.

THE RIDE
Day 1: Siena to Volterra
3½–7 hours, 65.4km

As you leave Siena, the atmosphere becomes more serene as you meander through rolling farmland with mountains in the distance. The flat stints are peppered with some rolling hills and a few significant climbs: after Colle Val d'Elsa and San Gimignano, and then into Volterra.

At 12.3km reigns the 13th century, medieval stronghold of **Monteriggioni**, whose walls and towers constitute one of the most complete examples of a fortified bastion in Tuscany. At the turn to Colle Val d'Elsa (13.3km) there's a good restaurant/bar/bakery for grabbing tasty snacks and water. Continue by ambling along through sunflower fields towards the famed, towered skyline of **San Gimignano**, a worthwhile side trip (35.6km). To get the low-down on the area, walk your bike to the **Pro Loco tourist office** (☎ 05 779 40 008; www.sangimignano.com; Piazza del Duomo 1). Leaving San Gimignano, the route twists and turns through lush olive groves and farmland before reaching the ancient Etruscan town of Volterra, which offers plenty sites of its own.

Day 2: Volterra to Massa Marittima

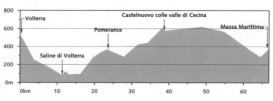

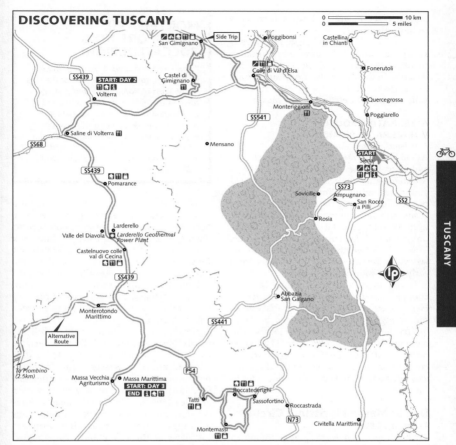

DISCOVERING TUSCANY

If you are low on time or want to skip the crowds, you can forgo San Gimignano and enjoy a quiet, lovely lunch at **Tre Archi** (☎ 05 779 53 099; Via Castel Gimignano 35/b, Castel Gimignano; closed Tue), where the route reconnects with SS68. This jovial local haunt makes delectable Tuscan pasta and meat dishes accompanied by good house wine.

Day 2: Volterra to Massa Marittima
4–7 hours, 66.3km

Unlike the vineyard-filled, terraced hills in the Chianti region, the Maremma's hills are adorned with grand chestnut, beech and evergreen oak forests. As the day progresses, the greenery will thicken around you and the air will become slightly more invigorating and fresh. The terrain is rolling, with a couple of steeper climbs thrown into the mix. You fly down from Volterra into **Saline** then settle into a significant climb. Traffic will be deliciously minimal for most of the day.

Pass through **Pomarance** (22.9km), a largely industrial town, before encountering a climb past the colossal boric acid plant near **Larderello** (34.5km). Located in the Valle del Diavolo (Valley of the Devil), Larderello has geothermal vents that once terrified passing travellers. Today, it is Italy's largest boric acid producer. What it lacks in appeal it makes up for in bizarreness. A steep 2km climb leads you into **Castelnuovo** (38.5km), a good place to grab a bite. A pizzeria is right on the route.

From Castelnuovo to Massa, the ride has sweeping views of the forested mountains to the south and east, which are particularly dazzling in the dying afternoon sun. You'll break from the lush forest into an open valley right before climbing to Massa.

ALTERNATIVE ROUTE: VOLTERRA TO PIOMBINO
7–10 hours, 112km

At 48.9km of Day 2, you can duck out and head for the coast. Turn off SS439 to Monterotondo on SS398, which will lead you to Piombino. You'll cruise down a picturesque descent via beautiful mountain roads with views of the sea and countryside until you hit flat coastal lands. The 15.5km of uninterrupted descent will make you giddy. The route is free of traffic until around the last 9km. Ferries leave daily to Elba from early in the morning until 8pm to 10pm.

If you miss your ferry, **Piombino** is a cool place to hang your hat for the evening (see box on p66). When the tourists drain out at night, this harbour town becomes 'pretty and twinkly' for the locals who hang out on Piazzetta del Mare. The tourist office hands out the *Costa degli Etrucshi cicloturimso* maps (☎ 05 862 04 611; www .costadeglietruschi.it) detailing day rides in the area.

Day 3: Massa Marittima Circuit
4–7 hours, 70.8km

There's top-notch scenery and cycling in store for you in this seldom trod corner of Tuscany. It's unlikely that you'll encounter any tourists after leaving Massa Marittima, even in summer. With the sublime tranquillity comes challenge: it's probably the toughest day of the tour.

MONTEMASSI, SASSOFORTINO & ROCCATEDERIGHI

Known as 'Roccastrada's Villages', these picturesque towns dot the tops of the hills to the west of Roccastrada, the primary town in the district. If you're interested in spending a night in a medieval hill town, or in trekking along the district's eight trails, visit the following website for information: www.comune.roccastrada .gr.it. Alternatively, call tourist information (☎ 05 645 63 376).

Your descent out of Massa Marittima boasts spectacular valley views. The route becomes especially quiet after you turn to **Tatti** (14.2km) into narrow, winding back roads canopied by lush forest. Watch out for sections of switch-backed road that have steep drop-offs and no rails (21km). Tatti (22.7km) is a nice town for a café stop, and **Montemassi** (34.4km) is an imposing medieval village with several pleasant cafés and restaurants.

Heading north again, grunt uphill towards Sassofortino and Roccatederighi. Consider a quick side trip to castle-adorned hill town **Sassofortino** (42.6km) before continuing on to **Roccatederighi** (45.2km). One of the most well preserved and least visited medieval villages, Roccatederighi seems to emerge straight from a craggy outcrop, providing wonderful views of the valley and towns below. Plus, there's a wine museum in its Piazza dell'Orologio.

Meander back towards Massa on a different, but equally appealing, wooded road before retracing your steps along the main roads back into Massa Marittima.

Day 3: Massa Marittima Circuit

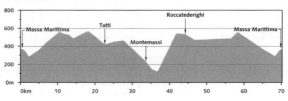

ROAD LESS TAKEN

Duration 1–2 days
Distance 115.6km
Difficulty moderate–demanding
Start/Finish Arezzo, Florence
Summary Both St Francis of Assisi and Michelangelo spent a deal of time in this forgotten corner of Tuscany, laced with incredibly scenic and deserted roads.

Could this be real? A magnificent corner of Tuscany without the crowds or the hype or many people knowing about it at all, even cyclists? Yes, we testify. And the roads and scenery are straight from cyclist heaven. The route, for the most part, is seldom trafficked and weaves through diverse landscapes of forest, rivers, valleys, and even moonlike rocky outcrops.

Sages and artists fancied this area – there is little reason why you won't. There's an intriguing and scenic side trip to Santuario di San Francesco, supposedly where St Francis of Assisi received stigmata. It doubles as a destination for modern-day pilgrims. Plus, you can follow the footsteps of Michelangelo as you visit his birthplace and the rock on which he posed his model for Creation of Adam.

PLANNING
When to Cycle

See Climate section (see p47). You will rarely have the issue of traffic on this route. Around August you might start seeing truffle vendors by the **Abbazia di San Francesco Assisi.**

What to Bring

If you plan to visit the *abbazia*, both men and women should bring something to

---

CARAPAX

European Centre for Conservation of Turtles; (☎ 05 669 40 083; Località Venelle CP 34) is a wildlife (primarily turtles) refuge and restoration site where you can also check out the white stork, now extinct in Italy, and cute, fuzzy donkeys.

ROAD LESS TAKEN

CUES			GPS COORDINATES
00		Arezzo Tourist Office, Stazione	
			43°27'36"N 11°52'40"E
	↰	Viale Michelangelo	
0.8	↗	to 'centro storico'	
1.2	↱	Via B. Dovizi	
1.5	↱ ⊙	to 'Municipio,' Via F. Mochi	
2.1	↰	to 'Canile Comunale'	
9.4	↰	to 'Anghiari,' SP43	
(50m)	↱	to Anghiari	
14	▲	3.3km moderate to hard	
25.5	▲	1.4km moderate to hard	
26.9	●● ↱	after little park with fountain to	
		Anghieri Centro	
28.2	↘	to 'Caprese'	
39.6	↘	to 'Caprese'	
41.9	▲	1km moderate to hard climb	
43.6	●●↑	to 'Casa Natale,' Caprese 'centro'	
	↰	to 'Lama'	
46.1	▲	5.4km moderate to hard climb	
55	▲	2.1km moderate to hard climb	
55.9	↗	to 'Chiusi della Verna'	
56.8	↰	to 'Arezzo'	
57.1	★	Centro Visite Chiusi (on right)	
	▲	1km moderate-hard	
58.1	⚠	11.2km descent	
64.1		Dama	43°41'55"N 11°53'52"E
77.9	↱	to 'Arezzo'	
		Bibiana	43°41'51"N 11°48'52"E
78.2	↘	to 'Arezzo'	
79.3	↰	to 'Arezzo'	
85.5	↱	to 'Salutio'	
86.2	●● ↱	to Etruscan Ruins	
88.2	↰	to 'Montanina'	
96.8	↰	Viale di Subbiano	
		Capolona	43°34'20"N 11°52'10"E
97.1	↱	to 'Aretina'	
97.4	↑	over busy road, not Right to Arezzo	
103.4	↰	to 'Sansalpolcro'	
106.3	↱	to 'Chiassa Superiore,' across bridge	
113.6	↱	to 'Centro'	
114.1	↰ ⊙	to 'Stazione'	
114.3	↱	to 'Stazione'	
115.1	↱	Via Guido Monaco	
115.2	↱ ⊙	at Piazza Guido Monaco	
115.3	↱	to 'Stazione'	
115.6	↰	Arezzo Tourist Office, Stazione	
			43°27'36"N 11°52'40"E

cover exposed shoulders. They have loaner shawls available for those who forget.

Maps

TCI's *Toscana* covers this region.

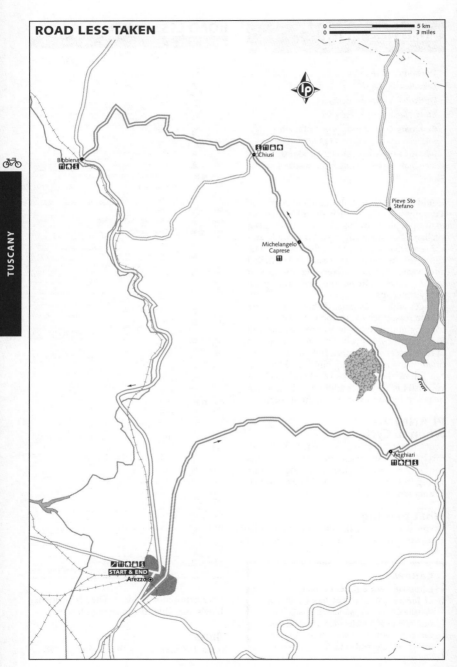

GETTING TO/FROM THE RIDE
Arezzo, Florence (start/finish)
TRAIN

Arezzo is on the Florence–Rome train line, with frequent service to and from Florence (€5.60, 1½ hours, frequently). Add €3.50 for a supplementary bike ticket.

To get to the start of the rides beginning in Siena, as well as to transfer to the beginning of other southern Tuscany rides, it might be better to catch a bus at the station at Piazza della Repubblica (€5, 1½ hours, 7 daily) because you'll have to transfer by train in Florence, and that takes much longer.

BICYCLE

There is a network of secondary roads that go to Florence from Arezzo, all doable in a day's time.

THE RIDE

After an hour and 15 minutes on the train from Florence, you'll be at the start of the ride in Arezzo. In the shadow of Florence, Arezzo harbours a wealth of architecture, culture and atmosphere that is largely under the tourist radar – just like this ride. Think about staying in **Arezzo** instead of Florence to delve deeper into the experience of Tuscany.

En route, you soon leave the city trappings of Arezzo in exchange for the fresh countryside. After completing two significant climbs, you'll hit **Anghiari** (26.9km), a picturesque medieval town that's worth a café break. At 43.6km, you come to the birthplace of Michelanglo, **Caprese Michelangelo**, where there's a small museum.

Before you arrive at **Chiusi della Verna** (57km), there's 8km more of climbing. Just as you enter the village, you'll see signs for the **Santuario di San Francesco** (56.5km).

If you want to make this long cycling day into two shorter days, stay in **Chiusi,** a village snuggled up to the Castentino nature reserve, where hiking opportunities abound. The **tourist office** (☎ 05 755 99 611; www.comune.chiusi-della-verna.ar.it) is a good source of information about accommodation, trekking and attractions. In Chuisi, you can take a short, signed detour to the site where *Creation of Adam* was modelled for Michelangelo. On the way back to Arezzo, which is definitely the easier portion of the ride, you'll cash in on all the climbing with an amazing 11km descent through equally gorgeous scenery into a river valley and past Tuscan hamlets.

SIDE TRIP: SANTUARIO DI SAN FRANCESCO
At 56.5km, 7km RT

In this impressive Franciscan monastic complex you can check out some of the saint's clothing stained with blood from stigmatic wounds and the whip with which he used to impose a little self-discipline …you know, like you do to fortify your uphill determination. Right?

It's quite inspiring to see the see San Francesco's meditation spot in nature and the cave in which he slept. There are also frescoes in a corridor in one of the buildings that recount the saint's life. On a more hedonistic thought, leaving the abbazia you might run into vendors selling wild truffles.

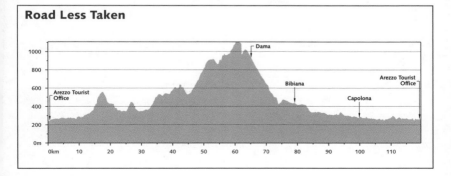

Road Less Taken

TUSCANY

CIRCLING ELBA

Duration 5–9 hours
Distance 92km
Difficulty moderate–demanding
Start/Finish Portoferraio
Summary Her woodsy slopes, unrelenting cliffs and soft-sand beaches all make Elba a coy resort island that motions to tourists, including cycle tourists, with the curling of her finger.

Elba rises out of the Tyrrhenian Sea like the sharpened top of a volcano. Indeed, the central and eastern parts of the island are remnants of an Apennine wall that collapsed into the sea, and the western part of the island was created by volcanic activity. For cyclists, the geological origins of the

STUCK IN PIOMBINO?

No problem. Family run and owned, **Albergo Italia** (☎ 05 652 20 922; Via XX Settembre 39; albergo-itlaia@libero.it; s/d €60/90) is a nice place to crash and it has a bike garage. It's just a stone's throw from restaurants and the circuit of Piombino's *passeggiata* (traditional evening stroll) on Corso Vittorio Emauele.

island translate into steep climbs, thrilling descents and views upon vistas upon views. Little Elba, 28km long and 19km across at its widest, still manages to entice cyclists, trekkers and sun-seekers alike.

Some high points of the ride include touring Portoferraio's walled old town, the tranquil beaches near Marciana Marina, the snaking, cobbled alleys of Poggio and cycling the roller-coaster ride of the wild

CIRCLING ELBA

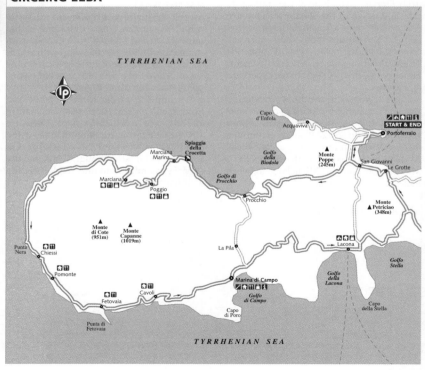

and windblown west coast section. Elba will have more tourists and crowds than the coastal riding in Sardinia or the rural vistas of Tuscany, but is easy to reach and spectacular all the same.

Though this ride is routed for one day, lingering is a nice option. Marina di Campo has a fair share of accommodation, the west coast has some lodging options, and in Lacona, camp grounds are many. However, riding this island fully loaded will definitely up the ante.

HISTORY
Elba has been inhabited since the Iron Age. Ligurian tribespeople were the island's first inhabitants, followed by Etruscans, Greeks from Magna Graecia and Romans, the richer of whom began building holiday villas. Centuries of peace under the Pax Romana were compromised during the barbarian invasions. By the 11th century, Pisa was in control and it built fortresses to help ward off attacks by Muslim raiders operating out of North Africa. In the 16th century, Cosimo I de' Medici founded the port town of Cosmopolis (today Portoferraio). Napoleon was exiled to Elba, arriving in 1814 and staying only a year before attempting another shot at imperial greatness. By the beginning of the 1980s, tourism had arrived to take the place of mining and smelting.

PLANNING
Maps
Beside the standard TCI's *Toscana* map, you can purchase detailed, cycling specific maps at many bike shops and *tabacchi* (small shops selling tobacco and sundries).

GETTING TO/FROM THE RIDE
Portoferraio (start/finish)
BOAT
Unless you're flying directly into Elba, the only way to get there is by ferry from Piombino. Several companies (Moby Lines, Toremar and Elba Ferries) operate ferries and have offices in Piombino and Portoferraio. Unless it is the middle of August, you shouldn't have any trouble buying a ticket on departure. Prices for the one-hour trip are around €14 per person one-way, plus an additional €5 per bike. All lines offer a special deal on certain runs (indicated in timetables).

BUS
From Via Leonard da Vinci 12 in the centre of Piombino, buses depart to many destinations including Motorotondo and Massa Marittima, where you can hook up with the Discovering Tuscany ride (see p59).

TRAIN
Piombino's train station is to the north on the Rome–Genoa line. It can shoot you down to Orbetello, the beginning of the Seascapes & Cliff Villages (see p73) ride.

BICYCLE
If you go back up to the Discovering Tuscany ride via the alternative route (see p59) (which is in reverse from Piombino), you have our respect.

THE RIDE
After knocking around Portoferraio's old town, begin the circuit at the APT tourist

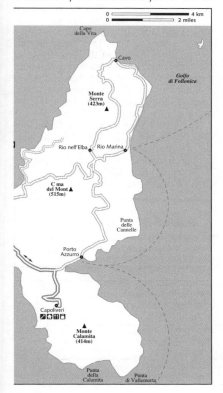

TUSCANY

office near the ferry terminal. Not more than 3km out of town, en route towards Procchio, the chaotic, traffic-jammed arteries of Portoferraio give way to twisting, steep roads. After a brief climb, the road plunges in healthy descent.

From Procchio to Marciana Marina, the road hugs the dramatic cliffs, and tiny, picturesque villages cling to the thickly forested mountainside above. Keep an eye out for signs indicating beaches, as some of the prettiest (and smallest) coves lie along this stretch. Visit **Spiaggia della Paolina** (11.9km) by locking your bike and scrambling down the steep steps. **Marciana Marina** (16.7km) is a lovely revitalising point before the hefty climb up to Marciana. The cliff town of **Poggio** (21.9km) would be easy to pass, but if you choose to poke around its maze of cobbled alleys and tiny plazas, it might prove a treat. If you want to climb higher (not by your own volition), stop in the car park on the left about 500m before Marciana (24.7km) for a cable car ride to the top of **Monte Capanne.**

From Marciana to **Marina di Campo** (50.8km), the Tyrrhenian Sea crashes at your right, and to your left, mountains crowd to the coastline. This stretch of rolling coastline is some of the best riding on the island, and the least trafficked. At 44km, **Fetovaia** has a broad, sandy beach, if you're looking to cool off. The waterfront cafés, promenade and beach in Marina di Campo are worth a side trip.

The route then climbs to Capoliveri (76km). To explore the town, take the middle of three roads to the right, Via Calamita, at the roundabout (76km). From Capoliveri it's a simple cruise to Portoferraio.

To the tourist herds, this region is just ground

CIRCLING ELBA

CUES		GPS COORDINATES
start	Portoferraio Ferry	42°48'58"N 10°19'13"E
0km	at Western Ferry Exit, to 'tutte le direzione'	
0.2	Via Teseo Tesei (at Coop)	
0.9	to 'Procchio'	
1.8	to 'Procchio'	
3.3	2.3km hard climb	
9.9	to 'Marciana'	
10.5	to 'Marciana'	
11.9	Spiaggia della Paolina	
	{16.7 ●● Marciana Marina 2km}	
	to 'Poggio'	
	5.4km hard climb	
21.9	Poggio	42°47'12"N 10°10'59"E
24	Monte Capanne (LHS)	
24.7	Marciana	42°47'35"N 10°10'08"E
38.2	Chiessi	42°45'35"N 10°06'45"E
40.4	Pomonte	42°44'55"N 10°07'16"E
44.0	Fetovaia	42°44'06"N 10°09'07"E
47.7	Cavoli	42°44'17"N 10°11'08"E
50.8	to 'Marina di Campo'	
53.6	Marina di Campo	42°44'56"N 10°14'06"E
	to Portoferraio	
	{53.8 ●● beach/promenade 1km}	
	to 'tutti le direzione,' Via Roma	
55	to 'Capoliveri,' first exit	
56.3	3.2km hard climb	
64.4	Lancona	42°45'43"N 10°18'07"E
68.9	to 'Capoliveri'	
72.1	to 'Capoliveri'	
72.3	to 'Capoliveri'	
75.1	to 'Centro'	
76.3	Capoliveri	42°44'37"N 10°22'51"E
	{retrace route to cue 72.1}	
83.7	Continue to Portoferraio	
90.2	first exit to 'Porto'	
90.9	second exit to 'Porto'	
91.4	to 'Porto'	
91.9	to 'Porto'	
92.0	Portoferraio Ferry Terminal	42°48'58"N 10°19'13"E

ELBA'S BEACHES

Italy's third largest island indulges beach-loving tourists with 10km of sandy beaches.

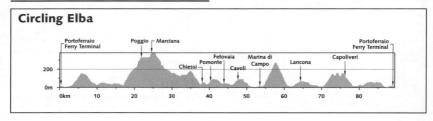

Circling Elba

TACKLING THE ALPI APUANE

Duration 3 days
Distance 155.3km
Difficulty moderate–demanding
Start Castelnuovo di Garfagnana
Finish Viareggio
Summary It's astounding that alpine mountains thrusting ostentatiously over the radiant blue horizon would be easily missed. Yet, many visitors do miss them. If you come with your bike, the only word is 'epic'.

TRADE YOUR SKINNIES FOR SOME FAT KNOBBIES IN THE ALPI APUANE

It's breathtaking enough to cycle through the mountain roads of the Alpi Apuane. Just wait till you dig further into the heart of it on a mountain bike. **Garfagnana Adventures** (☎ 05 836 49 195; www .garfagnanaadventures.com; *agriturismo* room €60–80; guided touraround €130 per day for up to eight people, bike rental per day €25) is 6km out of Castelnuovo di Garfagnana on SP16. They also operate a cozy *agriturismo* nestled against the forest 6km outside of Castelnuovo di Garfagnana.

to cover on their way to Cinque Terra. This is a blessing to you. Tucked into the northwest of Tuscany, this magnificent mountain range hosts a treasure trove of excellent cycling opportunities, especially if you're a climber. You're bound to share the road with ripped local cyclists clad in bright lycra as you tour the craggy forests that dwarf the age-old villages nestled in their skirts. You'll soar down descents and muscle up hills on deserted roads veiled in foliage. Not so bad.

The route's base town is Castelnuovo di Garfagnana, a tiny village with a half-cocked tourist infrastructure. The first two days are circuit rides that begin and end in the town's centre. Day 1 goes through the 10th-century town of Barga and climbs up to hilltop hamlet, Sillico. Day 2 is the Radici Pass: an epic climb peppered with 18% grade and an epic 31km descent…'epic' being the theme. On Day 3, you heave on the panniers and twist through the valleys and tunnels of the Parco Naturale delle Alpi Apuane en route to the coastal party town of Viareggio.

PLANNING
When to Cycle

Unlike other regions in Tuscany, Garfagnana can be downright unpleasant in the winter months. Despite its proximity to the coast, the Alpi Apuane does get snow. Garfagnana also gets more rain, on a year-round basis, than the rest of Tuscany.

What to Bring

If you're cycling in the late spring, summer, or early autumn, a waterproof shell and lightweight fleece should suffice. If you are

hard core enough to ride in winter, bring appropriate cold-weather gear. Remember lights for the tunnels along the route.

Maps

The best map of the region, which can be used for all three days, is the 1:50,000 *Parco delle Alpi Apuane* by Edizioni Multigraphic. TCI's *Toscana* map covers everything as well.

GETTING TO/FROM THE RIDE
Castelnuovo di Garfagnana (start)
BUS

If coming from Lucca, catching an unfortunately acronymed CLAP bus is a viable option (€3.60, about 1 hour, every 2 hours). You'll be charged for two tickets – one for you, one for your bike.

TRAIN

From Florence, catch a train on the Florence–Viareggio line to Lucca then change to the Lucca–Aulla line, on which Castelnuovo is a stop (€7.70, 1 hour, hourly). Rome to Castelnuovo (€43.80; 4½–5hours, every 2 hours) is more difficult, involving three stops.

BICYCLE

Though the distance is manageable, cycling from Lucca to Castelnuovo is not recommended. The road is narrow and heavily travelled by overloaded, marble-hauling tractor-trailers. You can cycle to the Cinque

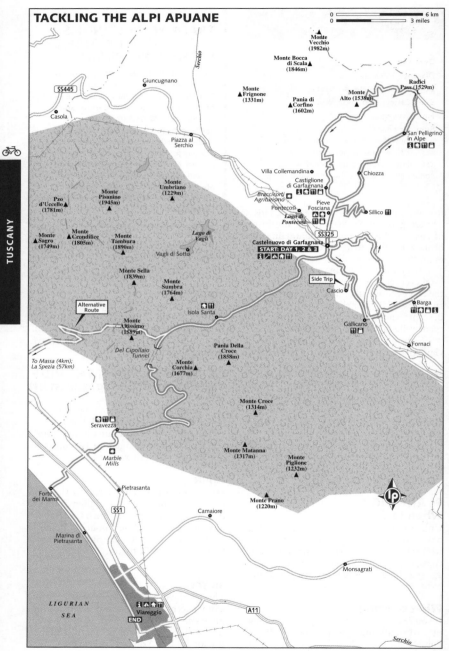

TACKLING THE ALPI APUANE

0 — 6 km
0 — 3 miles

SS445

Giuncugnano

Casola

Monte Vecchio (1982m)

Monte Bocca di Scala (1846m)

Monte Frignone (1331m)

Pania di Corfino (1602m)

Monte Alto (1538m)

Radici Pass (1529m)

San Pelligrino in Alpe

Piazza al Serchio

Serchio

Villa Collemandina

Chiozza

Castiglione di Garfagnana

Monte Umbriano (1229m)

Braccicorti Agriturismo

Pieve Fosciana

Sillico

Pontecosi

Pzo d'Uccello (1781m)

Monte Pisanino (1945m)

Lago di Vagli

Lago di Pontecosi

SS325

Monte Sagro (1749m)

Monte Crondilice (1805m)

Monte Tambura (1890m)

Vagli di Sotto

Castelnuovo di Garfagnana
START: DAY 1, 2 & 3

Monte Sella (1839m)

Side Trip

Cascio

Barga

Monte Sumbra (1764m)

Alternative Route

Isola Santa

Gallicano

Monte Altissimo (1589m)

Del Cipollaio Tunnel

Fornaci

To Massa (4km);
La Spezia (57km)

Pania Della Croce (1858m)

Monte Corchia (1677m)

Monte Croce (1314m)

Seravezza

Marble Mills

Monte Matanna (1317m)

Monte Piglione (1232m)

Pietrasanta

Monte Prano (1220m)

SS1

Forte dei Marmi

Camaiore

Marina di Pietrasanta

Monsagrati

LIGURIAN SEA

Viareggio
END

A11

Serchio

Day 1: Tackling the Alpi Apuane

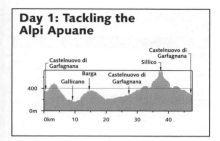

Terra ride from Castelnuovo by way of Massa to Fosdinovo to La Spezia.

Viareggio (finish)
BOAT
June to September, **Consorzio Marittimo Turistico** (☎01 877 32 987; Via Minzoni 13, La Spezia) runs passenger boats connecting Viareggio with the Cinque Terre villages and Portofino.

BUS
Lazzi (☎05 844 62 34) and **CLAP** (☎05 843 09 96) buses run from Piazza d'Azeglio in Viareggio, where both have offices, to destinations around Tuscany. Long-distance buses run to such destinations as Milan (€23.50).

TRAIN
Florence and Rome can both be reached by train from Viareggio. To get to Rome, catch a train to Pisa (€2.40, 20 minutes, hourly), then the slow train to Rome (€17, 3½ hours, hourly). If Florence is your destination, take the Viareggio–Florence line (€5.90, about 2 hours, hourly). You can catch a train to La Spezia (€4, 1 hour, regularly), the beginning of the Cinque Terre ride. Also, you can take the coastal line south to both Piombino and Orbetello, the beginnings of the Circling Elba (see p66) and Seascapes & Cliff Villages (see p73) rides respectively. The supplementary bike ticket is €3.50.

THE RIDE
Day 1: Garfagnana Circuit
2½–5½ hours, 48km
This day involves a loop that begins in Castelnuovo and circles back through the town on the way to the out-and-back to Sillico, at the end of the ride. Therefore,

TACKLING THE ALPI APUANE – DAY 1

CUES		GPS COORDINATES
start	Castelnuovo di Garfagnana tourist office	
		44°06'37"N 10°24'46"E
0km	NE from Piazza delle Erbe	
	⌐► (50m) Via Olinto Dini	
	⌐ (30m) exit through town wall	
0.1	⌐► Via Roma	
0.2	⌐► to `Monteperpoli' (after bridge)	
	↖ (50m) to `Monteperpoli'	
	▲ 2.8km steep climb	
3	↑ to Cascio	
{3.7	●●⌐► Cascio 2km ↻	
7.7	↗ towards black and white sign for Gallicano	
8.8	⌐► to `Molazzana'	
9.1	Gallicano	44°03'44"N 10°26'20"E
	⌐ to `Barga' (hard left)	
10.7	▲ 3.8km moderate climb	
10.9	↑ to `Barga'	
13.1	↑ on Pietro Funai	
{14.5	Barga	44°04'32"N 10°28'56"E
	⌐ to 'Castelnuovo di Garfagnana,	
	Via Largo Roma (stay right)	
20.3	↗ SS445 (cross bridge)	
20.5	⌐► SS445 to `Castelnuovo di Garfagnana'	
	⚠ narrow shoulder, busy road	
	★ Osteria Paseliana	
28	Castelnuovo di Garfagnana	44°06'37"N 10°24'46"E
	↗ to 'ospedale,' Via Roma/SS324 (across bridge)	
31.1	⌐► to `Sillico'	
32.3	↗ staying on main road	
34	▲ 4km hard climb	
38.0	★ Sillico	44°07'59"N 10°26'40"E
	{!retrace route to Castelnuovo di Garfagnana}	
48.0	Castelnuovo di Garfagnana tourist office	
		44°06'37"N 10°24'46"E

this could make for two smaller day rides if you want to split the tough climbs, thrilling descents, and mind-blowing views of the Alpi Apuane. You'll pass through the interesting villages of Barga and Sillico, which are worth a gander. The toughest climb, the switch-backed ascent to Sillico, comes late in the day and will send you home tired.

After leaving Castelnuovo, the route climbs steeply, providing picturesque glimpses of the town. After 3km, consider a side trip to **Cascio**. An important military fortification in the 17th century, Cascio today is a quaint village town with a fine view. The ascent into Barga follows a shady, tree-lined roadway with its fair share of steep switchbacks. In **Barga** (14.5km), you can visit the medieval town centre and pay a visit to the crenellated duomo and its exquisitely carved pulpit. Make sure to notice the view across the valley of the **Parco Naturale delle Alpi Apuane** before heading back towards Castelnuovo. The small-shoulder, much-traffic combo on SS445 (20.5km) gets tedious.

Pass through Castelnuovo on your way towards Pieve Fosciana before turning onto a quiet back road and climbing up to **Sillico** (38km), a winsome, sleepy hamlet perched on the side of a mountain. You can lock your bike in the car park and wander through the town's twisting cobbled alleys before sipping a coffee at the café. Retrace your steps back to Castelnuovo, carefully navigating the steep descent's hairpin curves.

Day 2: The Radici Pass
3–5 hours, 50.2km

Oh, Radici! How you cook and stuff little cyclist egos and serve them on a platter. But somehow we love you and value the reward of unparalleled mountain vistas and endorphin surges. In 18km, this route rises 1300m. In the last relentless 5km, there's well over 1km of what is signed as 18% grade. Once you've triumphed, however, more than 30km of amusement-ride downhill awaits your wheels.

After the first 4km of the ride, the tough climbing begins. Settle in for 14km of relentless, switch-backed climbing. **Chiozza** (10km) is a good place to enjoy the view and refill water bottles. In summer, raspberries line the next segment of road, not to mention the meadows of waving grass, wildflowers and patches of

TACKLING THE ALPI APUANE – DAY 2

CUES		GPS COORDINATES
start	Castelnuovo di Garfagnana tourist office	44°06′37″N 10°24′46″E
0km	NE out of Piazza delle Erbe	
	⌐ (50m) Via Olinto Dini	
	⌐ (30m) exit through town wall	
0.1	↑ Via Roma/SS324 (crossing bridge)	
3.9	↗ to `Chiozza'	
	▲ 14.5km steep hard climb	
10.1	Chiozza	44°09′20″N 10°26′16″E
16.8	★ San Pellegrino	44°11′31″N 10°28′56″E
18.4	★ Top of climb	
	⚠ 31km descent	
19.4	↘ SS324, Radici Pass	
42.3	↘ to `Castelnuovo di Garfagnana'	
43.2	★ Castiglione di Garfagnana	44°08′57″N 10°24′40″E
46.3	↗ staying on SS324	
	{!retrace route to Castelnuovo di Garfagnana}	
50.3	↑ through old town wall	
50.1	⌐ (30m) Via Olinto Dini	
	⌐ (50m) into Piazza delle Erbe	
50.2	Castelnuovo di Garfagnana tourist office	44°06′37″N 10°24′46″E

woods. After you pass a cluster of sturdy, weather-worn homes on the left, the ascent becomes savage. **San Pellegrino** (16.8km), known as the 'balcony of Garfagnana' for its dramatic location, provides a worthy break point. If you're a wimp. To the west, take in the peaks in the Parco Naturale delle Alpi Apuane, which muscle their way radically into the sky. Occasionally, the notorious 'sea of fog' blankets the valley below.

The top of the climb and the beginning of the 31km descent (18.4km) comes before actual **Radici Pass** (19.4km), through which you jubilantly bomb (unless you want to

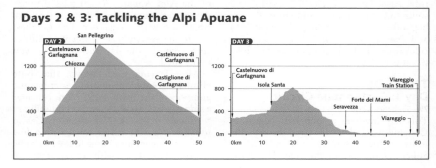

Days 2 & 3: Tackling the Alpi Apuane

stop at the restaurant). If you want to cool your brakes, medieval, walled **Castiglione di Garfagnana** (43.2km) has a 12th-century fortress to check out before sailing into Castelnuovo di Garfagnana.

Day 3: Castelnuovo di Garfagnana to Viareggio
3–5½ hours, 57.7km

Though less than 60km away, rowdy Viareggio is laid-back Castelnuovo's antithesis. The riding is moderate, with a steady climb for the first 20km, followed by a long, slow descent to sea level.

Just a few kilometres out of Castelnuovo, past marble mines (about 2km), you'll start to see mesh retaining wire securing the valley walls. Chunks of rock do slip by, so be aware.

Meander through the ferny woods of the **Parco Naturale delle Alpi Apuane** to **Isola Santa** (13.1km), a picturesque town on the edge of a man-made lake. You'll weave into an amazing landscape flanking a ravine on winding roads with steep mountains crowding you on either side. When you reach the spooky, 1125m-long **Del Cipollaio tunnel** at 19.1km, lights are essential. We were freaked but local cyclists don't seem to be bothered.

TACKLING THE ALPI APUANE – DAY 3

CUES		GPS COORDINATES
start	Castelnuovo di Garfagnana tourist office	44°06'37"N 10°24'46"E
0km NE	out of Piazza delle Erbe	
⬏	(50m) Via Olinto Dini	
⬑	(70m) exit through town wall	
0.1 ⬏	Via Roma	
0.2 ⬏	to 'Monteperpoli' (after bridge)	
⬈	where road forks	
13.1 ★	Isola Santa	44°03'59"N 10°18'40"E
19.1 ⚠	1125m Del Cipollaio tunnel	
⚠	20.3 km descent	
37.6	Seravezza	43°59'40"N 10°13'39"E
37.7 ⬏	at T intersection, to 'Pietra Santa'	
43.2 ⬆◎	Via Michelangelo Buonarroti	
43.7 ⬑🚻	Via dell' Acqua	
44.1 ⬏🚻	at T intersection, Duca D'Aosta	
45.3 ⬑🚻	when you hit the esplanade. Bike lane right of road	
	Forte dei Marni	43°58'04"N 10°10'37"E
55.7	Viareggio	43°52'02"N 10°15'24"E
56.8 ⬑	to 'Satzione,' Via Giuseppi Mazzini	
57.7	Viareggio train station	43°52'25"N 10°15'11"E

Enjoy the euphoria of the final descent while it lasts, because upon dead-ending at the sea, the flat haul to Viareggio passes the dizzying profusion of bars, beach clubs, discos and two- to four-star hotels that line the strip. The route ends at the train station, where you can promptly leave if a raucous beach party isn't your style.

ALTERNATIVE ROUTE: CASTELNUOVO TO MASSA
3–5 hours, 40.7km

If you want to avoid the hustle and bustle of the Viareggio strip trip, local cyclists have recommended an alternative route to Massa that involves some climbing but gets major votes for scenery. Pedal 4.4km after Isola Santa (13.1km) and take the right turn-off to Massa, which sits on the Rome–Genoa train line.

SEASCAPES & CLIFF VILLAGES

Duration 3 days
Distance 179.8km
Difficulty moderate
Start Orbetello
Finish Montalcino/Buonconvento
Summary This ride is for those easily distracted. The scenery keeps on changing, with a little of everything: sea, wine country and medieval villages.

This three-day route is fantastically diverse: from the magical fairyland of Orbetello's Feniglia isthmus – with gigantic looming pines and sun-dappled paths covering its strip of ocean bound earth – to Pitigliano's ogle-worthy splendour to Montalcino's voluptuous wine and vineyard views. The remote, dramatic landscape, historical quality and minimal traffic of this ride make it spectacular.

Depart from the bike-friendly, oft-ignored coastal town of **Orbetello**, heading inland over **Feniglia** isthmus, through farmland and poppy fields, towards the perching spectacle of **Pitigliano**. Day 2 entails **Etruscan tombs** and forested hilly stretches west of **Monte Amiata** (Tuscany's highest peak at 1736m). On Day 3, the air thickens with aromatics of the famous Brunello vineyards as you weave towards Montalcino. You can either spend the night in **Montalcino** (possibly linking up with the Hill Towns ride the next day) or zip into Buonconvento to catch the next train to Siena.

PLANNING
Maps

The most helpful map is probably Touring Club Italiano's 1:200,000 *Toscana*. Once you make it to Castel di Piano, the *tabacchi* around the corner from the unhelpful tourist office sell a detailed *Kompass* map 1:50,000 (€7), which shows cycling routes in the Monte Amiata area and has an accompanying written guide (in German and Italian).

Information Sources

Vivi La Maremma (☎ 05 644 13 499; www .vivilamaremma.it; Corso Carducci 90) is based in Grosseto and offers cycle tours in the area. Pitigliano doesn't have a bike shop, but you can go to **Caffè del Teatro** (☎ 34 939 09 811; Piazza Garibaldi 55), where the coffee is amazing and the owner, Cesari, an avid motorcyclist (ex-cyclist), will dry you off, hand you a bike pump and tell you about the stellar cycling routes in the area.

GETTING TO/FROM THE RIDE
Orbetello (start)
TRAIN

The Orbetello/Monte Argentario train station is easily reached from Rome on the Rome–Turin diretto line (€7.55, 2 hours, every 2 hours). From Florence, go through Pisa first, then hop on the Turin–Rome line (€13.80, 3½hours, every 2 hours); add €3.50 for a supplementary bike ticket.

Buonconvento (finish)

See p54.

BICYCLE

Follow the Siena Explorer (see p53) in reverse and then make a day ride to Siena. Buonconvento is also on the route of the Hill Town (p56) ride.

THE RIDE
Day 1: Orbetello to Pitigliano
4½–9 hours, 81.8km

Riding through the Duna Fengalia Park, you'll join other entranced pedestrians and

SEASCAPES & CLIFF VILLAGES – DAY 1

CUES			GPS COORDINATES
start		Orbetello tourist office	42°26'22"N 11°12'37"E
0km		Head through parking lot to Via Mura di Ponente (towards water)	
	↰	(20m) Via Mura di Ponente	
0.5	↱	to `Porto Ercole' (bike lane on this road)	
1.8	↰	to `Porto Ercole' (bike lane to the left of this road)	
3.3	↰	to `Feniglia' (bike lane ends)	
3.9		sign for `Duna Feniglia'	
4.2	↑★	past gate; Duna Feniglia	
	⚠	6km dirt road	
4.5	✗	On main road, not straight onto lesser road	
4.8	↰	at unsigned road junction	
10.3	↘	onto path that goes around gate (30 meters before the gate)	
10.4	↰	on paved road crossing river	
	★	Ristorante La Campara	
10.5	↱	Via delle Mimose (stop sign)	
13.5	↑	to `Capalbio Scalo'	
18.3	↑	to `Charione Scalo'	
27.2	↰	to `Charione Scalo'	
27.4	↰	to `Aurelia SS1'	
28.6	✗	to `Aurelia SS1'	
32.8	★	Giardino del Tarocchi	
34.5	↰	SP75 to `Capalbio'	
37.5	↑	SP101 to `Manciano'	
48.5	↑	SP101 to `Manciano'	
54.5	↱	to `Manciano'	
	▲	8km moderate climb	
62.5	↘	to Pitigliano	
or	✗	to Manciano Centro	
81.7	↰	Via Cavour to `Centro Storico'	
81.8		Pitigliano tourist office in Piazza Garibaldi	42°38'07"N 11°40'12"E

cyclists wondering over this miraculous sea-bound landscape canopied by giant pines. It's renowned for birdwatching and has some nice beaches. The road through the park is gravel, but the verdict is that it's easily done with a hefty road bike. We did it on a fully-loaded bike with slick 28 tyres. Take your time on the gravel; enjoy the park. At 10.4km over a river, after the park, Ristorante La Campara sells fresh granita to fortify you for the fields of wildflowers and protected coastal flood plains to come as the route begins to flank the Tyrrhenian Sea. If you're lucky, poppies will alight the fields with explosions of red.

As you veer towards the heart of Tuscany, the landscape turns to vineyards and rolling picturesque farmland. The last part

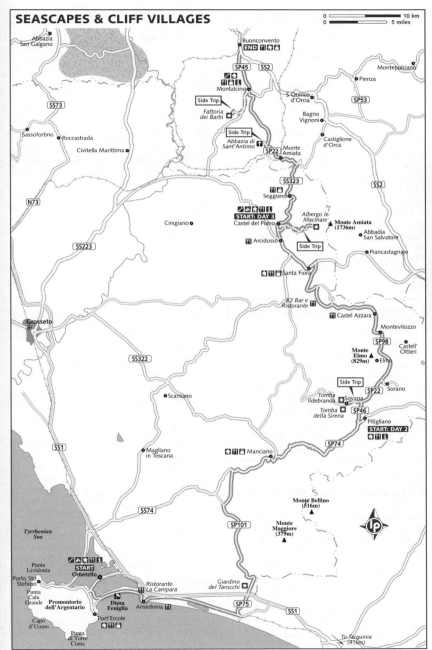

Day 1: Seascapes & Cliff Villages

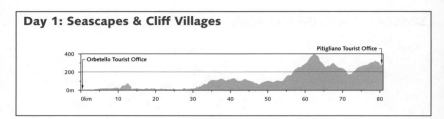

of the ride is hillier, including the 0.8km hard climb into the fortress of Pitigliano, but the majority of the ride is flat. As you approach Pitigliano, there are a number of agriturismi if you want to stay in the countryside. Also, the Conara Winery (79.2km) offers tastings.

Pitigliano sits tranquilly in its fortress-like splendour. The lush gorges flanking three of its sides make the cliff-hanging medieval town even more dramatic. The gorgeous main piazza with its *tufo* structures provides expansive vistas of the valley.

ORBETELLO GOES BY BIKE

Who would have known that this little town squeezed onto an isthmus would be so 'cyclofied'? The locals travel all over on bikes with baskets, racks, panniers and baby holders. And why not? It's flat as a pancake and the weather is lovely for much of the year. Plus, cycling is pleasant in this little town (which is relatively off the tourist radar) boasting a gorgeous historic centre and a number of green public spaces, including a lovely boardwalk.

Day 2:
Pitigliano to Castel del Piano
3–6 hours, 55.2km

This classic Tuscan ride climbs and descends through picturesque patchwork landscape that is manicured by an agriculture of distinct Italian aesthetic. Traffic is wonderfully light. Etruscan tombs (5.4km) just past Sovana are well worth the detour. The Tomba della Sirena is on the left, and the Tomba Ildebranda is about 200m down the road on the right. After leaving **Castel Azzara** (23km), which is a good lunch stop, full-horizon views of the valley and rolling hills inundate your scope until you enter

SEASCAPES & CLIFF VILLAGES – DAY 2

CUES			GPS COORDINATES
start		Pitigliano tourist office	42°38'07"N 11°40'12"E
0km		go back under the arch the way you entered	
0.1	↱	at stop sign (retracing previous day)	
0.7	↑	SP46 to 'Sovana'	
1.7	▲	1.8km moderate-hard climb	
{5.4	●●↰	to 'Sovana' Etruscan tombs 8.3km ↺	
	↱	SP22 to 'Sorano'	
9.4	↑	to 'Sorano'	
9.7	↖	to 'S. Valentino'	
12.3	▲	.9km hard climb	
14.6	↙	to 'Montevitozzo, Castel Azzara'	
14.8	▲	2.9km hard climb	
18.7	↖	to 'Castel Azzara, Montevitozzo'	
19.1		Montevitozzo	42°44'28"N 11°42'22"E
	↘	to 'Castel Azzara	
19.6	▲	2.9km moderate climb	
23	↖	to 'Castel Azzara	
24.7	↱	at T intersection on Via Marconi	
		(↖ to go into town)	
	↘	at fork! (10m)	
30.2	↘	to 'S Fiora'	
38	↗	to 'S Fiora'	
41.6	▲	2.5km moderate to hard climb	
43.8	↙	to 'Castel del Piano'	
or	↘	to S Fiora Centro	
44.1	↖	to 'Castel del Piano'	
44.9	↙	to 'Castel del Piano'	
48.9	↙	to 'Castel del Piano'	
	⚠	twisting, steep descent into Arcidosso	
51.8	↙	to 'Castel del Piano'	
		Arcidosso	42°52'21"N 11°32'19"E
54.7	↑ ⊙	Via Vittorio Veneto	
55.2	↱	at Piazza Garibaldi	
	↱	(20m) Via Marconi	
		(10m) Castel di Piano Tourist Office on the right	
			42°53'36"N 11°32'11"E

denser forest scenery. The descent into **Arcidosso** (51.8km) is steep with hairpin curves, and traffic starts to increase. **Castel del Piano** is a lovely small town whose main square has decadent views of the valley.

K2 **Bar e Ristorante** (34.8km) and the cafés, markets and restaurants in **Santa Fiora** (43.8km) are some of the only places to grab a bite and water up on this remote stretch of road.

Day 3: Castel del Piano to Montalcino/Buonconvento
2½–5 hours, 42.8km

Today, the stellar cycling continues, but the shorter distance allows enough time to explore the famed hill town of Montalcino or catch a train to Siena before nightfall.

You'll consistently ascend and descend through the wine country – the toughest portion of rollers begins at 16.5km and continues to 29.5km). The 12th-century Romanesque church, **Abbazia di Sant'Antimo** (20.6km), built on the site of a monastery founded by Charlemagne in AD 781, is the first significant point of interest along the way. You pass the turn-off for the **Fattoria dei Barbi** and **Museo di Brunello** (26.1km, p57), which might be appealing. After Montalcino, it's virtually all downhill to Buonconvento.

Montalcino warrants a visit or a night's stay. The notorious, luxurious, delicious Brunello wine is produced here. See the

SEASCAPES & CLIFF VILLAGES – DAY 3

CUES			GPS COORDINATES
start		Castel del Piano tourist office	42°53'36"N 11°32'11"E
0km	↱	Via Marconi	
0.3	↱	to 'tutte le direzioni,' Via della Stazione	
0.6	↰	SS323 to 'SS2 Cassia'	
6.6		Seggiano	42°55'43"N 11°33'38"E
	↗	to 'San Quirco d'Orcia'	
		(or ↘ to 'centro' to enter town)	
6.8	▲	3.3km climb	
10.1	⚠	6.2km steep descent	
12.7	↘	SP22 to 'Montalcino'	
16.5	▲	2.9km moderate climb	
20.6	●●↰	Abbazia di Sant'Antimo 1.6km ↺	
21.7	↗▲	to 'Montalcino' 7.8km moderate climb	
26.1	★	Museo di Brunello	
29.5	↟★	Montalcino	43°03'28"N 11°29'25"E
	↱	to 'Siena'	
	⚠	6km steep twisting descent	
31.3	◎↰	2nd Exit to 'Buonconvento' SP45	
40.8	◎↰	SS2 to 'Siena'	
42.8		Buonconvento station (RHS) on right	43°08'17"N 11°29'00"E

Hill Town Trek (p56) for more information on Montalcino.

Otherwise, it's easy to catch a train to Siena at Buonconvento's dusty brick train station (42.8km).

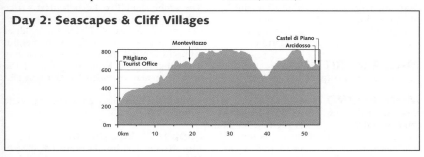

Day 2: Seascapes & Cliff Villages

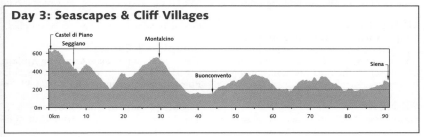

Day 3: Seascapes & Cliff Villages

MOUNTAIN BIKE RIDES

ALPI APUANE
See **Garfagnana Adventures** (p69).

AREZZO
Valtibike (www.valtibike.it) is an online source about mountain biking in the area with itineraries replete with maps and elevation charts.

CASTEL DEL PIANO
Albergo Le Macinaie (☎ 05 649 55 983; www.lemacinaie.com; Via Pozzo Stella 57) is an agriturismo outside of Castel del Piano that specialises in adventure and cycle vacations. They will rent you a bike and put you up for the night if you want to explore the Monte Amiata's mountain biking possibilities, such as the famous **Anello di Monte Amiata**, which circumnavigates the mountain. You'll tour through beechwood and chestnut forests and catch some stellar views.

ELBA
Maremma in Bici (www.maremmainbici.it) is based inland but does mountain bike rentals and tours on Elba, as does Massa Vecchia (see p60), out of Massa Maritima.

MASSA MARITTIMA
See Massa Vecchia (p60).

MONTALCINO
Orso on Bike (☎ 34 705 35 638; www.bikemontalcino.it) in Val d'Orcia in the Montalcino region conducts mountain-bike tours, from easy rides of touring and wine tasting to difficult climbing rides.

ORBETELLO
Gruppo Ciclistico Monte Argentario (www.argentaribike.it) is a good online information source about MTB (mountain biking, of course) in the area, including mapped itineraries.

PIENZA
Ciclo Posse (☎ 05 787 16 392; Via Matteotii 45; www.cicloposse.com) offers guided and self-guided tours as well as quality road-bike rentals.

SIENA
Centro Bici (☎ 05 772 82 550; Via Toselli 110) rents mountain bikes and runs tours from Siena. **Gruppo Ciclistico Val di Merse** (www.rosiabike.it) is a cycling group that is a good resource for MTB in the Siena province.

TOWNS & FACILITIES

CASTEL DEL PIANO
☎ 05 / pop 4330
Castel del Piano, nestled near the base of Tuscany's highest mountain, the volcanic Monte Amiata (1736m), serves as a base for Italians (not many tourists) who've come to enjoy the area's hiking and mountain bike trails. It is a quiet, pleasant town with a vista-rich main square, Piazza Garibaldi, and a winding, maze-like old city with five historic cathedrals.

Information
The ambivalent **Pro Loco tourist office** (☎ 0564 97 35 34), which claims to be open year-round, is just off Piazza Garibaldi at Via G. Marconi 9. At the more helpful tabbachi around the corner you can buy a cycling specific Kompass guide of the area, with map included (in German and Italian).

Several ATMs and banks line the Viale Vittorio Veneto.

Supplies & Equipment
Motofficina Giallini Loriano (☎ 05 649 55 611; Pizza RG Carducci 9), which is half a motorcycle/scooter shop, will perform bicycle repairs and sell basic bike supplies.

Sleeping & Eating
The nearest camping is at **Camping Amiata** (☎ 05 649 55 107; www.amiata.org; Via Roma 15; per person/tent €5–6.50/5–9), on your left as you enter town.

Albergo Impero (☎ 05 649 55 337; Via Roma 7; s/d €30/45, with bathroom €43/60) is the best and most spacious accommodation in town, with a large lawn, a decent restaurant and a shed in the back to put the bikes.

The centre is dotted with fresh produce, meat and cheese shops stocked with fresh and local goodies. **Antico Frantoio** (Corso Nasini 31; pizzas and pastas about €5; closed Tue) is an excellent brick-oven pizzeria with a quiet backyard garden.

CASTELNUOVO DI GARFAGNANA
☎ 05 / pop 6060

Left generally unnoticed because of its relative lack of historical sites, Castelnuovo deserves recognition as the delightful town it is. Once referred to by a former governor as a 'land of wolves and bandits' because of its popularity with robbers and adventurers, Garfagnana today is refreshingly modest and uncongested. Unlike other parts of Tuscany, Castelnuovo has cheap accommodation and summer days that stay cool and pleasant.

Information

There are two excellent information centres in town, both of them on the small, main square, Piazza delle Erbe. The helpful **Pro Loco tourist office** (☎ 05 836 41 007; www. garfagnanaturistica.info) has maps and information on accommodation and outdoor activities. Across the street, the **Centro Visitatori Parco Alpi Apuane** (☎ 05 836 44 242; www.parcapuane.it) has an extensive selection of maps of the park and its vicinities and guides. You might be lucky to find *Garfagnana by Bicycle*, a collection of 22 mountain-bike rides and five touring routes. During the time of writing, the new edition of the book was in the making.

ATMs are found on the Piazza Umberto.

Supplies & Equipment

For bicycle repairs, head to **Cicli Maggi 2** (☎ 05 836 39 166; Via N Fabrizi 40) run by ex-cyclocross champion Alessandro Iori. They do rentals as well.

Sleeping & Eating

The nearest camping is at **Parco La Piella** (☎ 05 836 29 16), about 4km away in Pieve Fosciana.

Da Carlino (☎ 05 836 44 270; www .dacarlino.it, in Italian; Via Garibaldi 15;

s/d/tr/q incl breakfast €50/70/85/90, per person €60–70) is a flower-bedecked hotel-restaurant; some rooms have mountain views. Lock bikes to the iron fence beneath the hotel's entrance or store them in the basement. **Trattoria Marchetti** (☎ 05 836 39 157; Via Testi 10; mains from €6) is an earthy, inexpensive lunch spot dishing up massive plates of delicious local dishes.

Small *alimentari* (fruit and vegetable stands) and bakeries selling fresh local food dot the centre.

CORTONA
☎ 05 / pop 22,000

Set into the side of a hill covered with olive groves, Cortona, which has changed little since the Middle Ages, offers sensational views across the Tuscan and Umbrian countryside. It was a small settlement when the Etruscans moved in during the 8th century BC, and it later became a Roman town.

Information

The **APT tourist office** (☎ 05 756 30 352; Via Nazionale 42) can assist with a hotel list and the useful Cortona brochure – a complete guide to tourist essentials. There are several ATMs on Via Nazionale, including one on Piazza Garibaldi just as you enter the town. There are no bicycle shops in Cortona.

Sleeping & Eating

Getting a room in Cortona around the **Mostra Antiquaria**, one of Italy's main antique furniture fairs, late August to early September, is virtually impossible without a reservation. Otherwise, the city has several cheap hotels and a hostel, and finding a room doesn't normally pose a problem.

Ostello San Marco (☎ 05 756 01 392; ostellocortona@libero.it; Via Maffei 57; dm/d €13/34, incl breakfast) is an HI-affiliated youth hostel, which is a short, steep ride east of Piazza Garibaldi. Though it's undeniably budget-friendly, its premises are not cared for.

Stanta Margherita (☎ 05 756 30 336; comunita cortona@smr.it; Via Cesare Battisti 15; s/d/tr/q €32/46/56/76) is run by sweet, obliging nuns, and the cloister-quality rooms are clean. This is a popular place,

CASTELLO DI VERRAZZANO

Castello Di Verrazzano (☎ 05 585 42 43; www.verrazzano.com; guided tours 10am & 11am Mon–Fri), is a castle on an estate where the best of Tuscany – Chianti Classico, *Vin Santo*, grappa, honey, olive oil and balsamic vinegar – has been crafted for centuries. Tour its historic wine cellar and gardens, then taste four different Verrazzano wines (1 hour, €18), or go the whole hog and lunch on five estate-produced courses in the company of five different wines (3 hours, €42). It also has an affiliated *agriturismo* (p278).

so call ahead (with an Italian phrasebook at the ready).

Hotel Italia (☎ 05 756 30 254; www .planhotel.com/hitalia; Via Ghibellina 5/7; s/d/tr €79/105/135) is in a 17th-century palazzo just off Piazza della Repubblica. A roof-level breakfast room, massages, wi-fi and mountain bike hire are available.

Piazza della Repubblica hosts a produce market each Saturday and several grocery shops dot the area. **Trattoria Dardano** (☎ 05 756 01 944; Via Dardano 24; meals €24; closed Wed) is just one of a half-dozen reliable, no-nonsense trattorias that line Via Dardano. **Pane e Vino** (☎ 05 756 31 010; Piazza Signorelli 27; snacks €6) is a hugely popular dining hall in the centre of town serving regional specialities. There are more than 500 wines to choose from and most of the pasta is homemade.

FLORENCE

☎ 05 / pop 352,200

In a valley on the banks of the Arno River and set among low hills covered with olive groves and vineyards, Florence (Firenze) is immediately captivating. Cradle of the Renaissance and home of Machiavelli, Michelangelo and the Medici, the city seems incomparably laden with art, culture and history. The French writer Stendhal was so dazzled by the magnificence of the Basilica di Santa Croce that he was barely able to walk for 'faintness'. He is apparently not the only one to have felt overwhelmed by the beauty of Florence – Florentine doctors supposedly treat a dozen cases of 'Stendhalismo' a year.

Information

The main **APT office** (☎ 05 529 08 32; www .provincia.firenze.it; Via Cavour 1) is just north of the duomo. The Comune di Firenze (city council) operates a **tourist office** (☎ 05 521 22 45; www.comune. fi.it; Piazza della Satzione) just outside the southeastern exit of the train station, Stazione di Santa Maria Novella. The Comune di Firenze has another **office** (☎ 05 523 40 444; at Borgo Santa Croce 29r).

Two useful websites devoted to the Chianti region are www.chianti.it and www .chiantinet.it.

Banks and ATMs are scattered everywhere throughout the city centre, including several inside the train station.

Supplies & Equipment

Some bike shops in town include **Giuseppe Bianchi** (☎ /fax 05 521 69 91) on Via Nazionale 130r; and the family-run **Cicli Conti** (☎ 05 557 92 08; www.cicliconti.it; Via Marconi 120) in the northeastern part of the city. On the first day of the Chianti Classic (see p48), at 16.9km, you will pass **Piaggio Centre Folli**, which is a moto-shop that could possibly help you with your bike. To rent a road or mountain bike, contact **Florence by Bike** (☎ 05 548 89 92, www .florencebybike.it; Via San Zanobi 120). It can supply you with panniers and extra gear if necessary. (See boxed text p49 for tour company recommendations.)

Sleeping & Eating

Establishments close to the train station are most convenient if you intend to cycle the Chianti Classic (see p48). For this reason, the majority of the accommodation is listed in this area. Many of the budget hotels around the train station are clean and safe, but there are also a fair number of seedy establishments. However, it's a short trip to the ride's start no matter where you end up. Book ahead in the summer and for the Easter and Christmas–New Year holiday periods.

The **Consorzio ITA office** in the train station can check the availability of rooms and make bookings (reservation fee €3). The APT office has a list of B&Bs. **Albergabici** (www.albergabici.it) is a great resource for cyclist-friendly accommodation.

Campeggio Michelangelo (☎ 05 568 11 977; www.ecvacanze.it; Viale Michelangelo 80; per person/tent €9–11/€11–12), just off Piazzale Michelangelo, south of the Arno, is the closest camp site to the city centre.

The HI **Ostello Villa Camerata** (☎ 05 560 14 51; Viale Augusto Righi 2–4; dm/d/tr with breakfast €18/60/69) is one of the most beautiful hostels in Europe. It accepts HI members only. About 4.5km from the Stazione di Santa Maria Novella, ride east along the Arno then northeast on Via Campfiore.

Hotel Pensione Ferretti (☎ 05 523 81 328; www.pensioneferretti.it; Via delle Belle Donne 17; s €40–75, with bathroom €50–85, d €50–85, with bathroom €60–105, extra bed €30, all incl breakfast) is run by Roberto and Sandra, who will make you feel right at home in their no-frills, unpretentious hotel with 16 rooms.

Hotel Consiglia (☎ 05 521 41 72; www.hotelconsigli.com; Lungarno Amerigo Vespucci 50; d €100–150, tr €120–170, all incl breakfast) is a short walk from town. This riverside Renaissance palace is perfect for peace-seeking guests happy to cycle to dinner. It is next door to the road-blocked US embassy, meaning motorised vehicles are kept well away.

Note that dining is more expensive here than elsewhere in Tuscany. If time permits, be adventurous and seek out the little eating places in the **Oltrarno** (roughly the downtown area from the duomo to Ponte Vecchio) and near Piazza del Mercato Centrale in the San Lorenzo area, where you'll eat authentic Italian food.

Locals flock to **La Canova di Gustavino** (☎ 05 523 99 806; Via della Condotta 29r; meals €25), a laid-back *osteria* (restaurant focussing on wine) where the bread comes in a bucket and the oil and vinegar in a wooden box. **Trattoria Bordino** (☎ 05 521 30 48; Via Stracciatella 9r; meals €20) requires you to arrive promptly to score a table at this astonishingly simple bistro, hidden on a dead-end street, seconds from the Ponte Vecchio crowds. Fare is wholly traditional Tuscan and the €6 lunch deal is a steal.

Getting There & Away
TRAIN
Florence's central train station is Stazione di Santa Maria Novella (Piazza della Stazi-

one). Florence is on the Rome–Milan line. There are regular trains to/from Rome (€30, 1½–2 hours), Bologna (€14.20, 1 hour), Milan (€29.20, 2¾–3¼ hours) and Venice (€26.60, 3 hours). To get to Genoa (€18), change in Pisa; for Turin (€35), in Milan.

BUS
From the **SITA bus station** (☎ 80 037 37 60; www.sitabus.it, in Italian; Via Santa Caterina da Siena 17r), just west of Piazza della Stazione, there are *corse rapide* (express services) to/from Siena (€6.50, 1¼ hours, at least hourly).

GREVE IN CHIANTI
☎ 05 / pop 22,700
Approximately halfway between Florence and Siena, Greve in Chianti, sprung into existence in the 13th and 14th centuries. Originally accommodating the overflow population from castle communities, Greve quickly grew into an important trade centre and marketplace. The recent discovery of ancient grape seeds in a local archaeological excavation suggests that cultivated vineyards have been in existence here for nearly 23 centuries. Today, Greve serves as the centre for tourist excursions focused on wine and olive oil tasting in the Chianti region.

Information
The **tourist office** (☎ 05 585 46 287, www.chiantiechianti.it; Piazza Matteotti 11) is just outside the city centre on the main road from Florence. Staff will book accommodation, recommend local vineyards for wine and olive oil tasting, and provide maps. A good website with tourist information is www.greve-in chianti.com.

There is a bank and ATM on Viale Vittorio on the way into town. There are no local bike shops.

Sleeping & Eating
Budget accommodation is not the area's strong point. Booking well ahead is a good idea – and be prepared to loosen purse strings since it's a popular area for tourists year-round. **Castello di Verrazzano** (☎ 05 585 42 43; www.verrazzano.com; rooms from €100) runs a lovely *agriturismo* (see box p81). The breakfast is plentiful, but

you will have to climb, on foot or bike, a pretty 2km to get to the main estate from the rooms below. Greve has a couple of good hotels on its central square, like **Albergo Giovanni da Verrazzano** (☎ 05 85 31 89; www.albergoverrazzano.it; Piazza Matteotti 28; s/d/tr/q incl breakfast €93/118/155/190; Mar–Jan), which has been run by the same family for three generations. It also runs a restaurant and cooking school.

Greve's Coop supermarket is located on Viale Vittorio, the main street through town. **Antica Macelleria Falorni** (☎ 05 85 30 29; www.falorni.it; Piazza Matteotti 7) is a centuries-old *macelleria* (butcher shop) that is renowned throughout Tuscany for its prime-quality meat. **Caffe S Anna** (☎ 05 585 30 95; Via Italo Stecchi 1) has scrumptious pastas and salads, plus free wi-fi – and you can rent a laptop.

MASSA MARITTIMA
☎ 05 / pop 8800

This is, perhaps, the most interesting town in the Maremma region of Tuscany, dating back to the 8th century. The walled nucleus of the old town was in place by the 12th century. The medieval town thrived on the local metal mining industry until the plague hit in 1348 and mining ended 50 years later. Only in the 18th century, with the draining of marshes and re-establishment of mining, did Massa Marittima come back to life.

Information
The **Ufficio Turistico** (☎ 05 669 02 756; www.altamaremmaturismo.it; Via Todini 3/5) is beneath Museo Archeologico. The Banca Toscana at Piazza Garibaldi 17 has an ATM.

Supplies & Equipment
In a pinch, **Massa Vecchia** (☎ 05 669 01 838; www.massavecchia.it; Localitá Massa Vecchia) is an *agriturismo* that has a repair station and sells some bike supplies. There are no bicycle repair shops in the town centre.

Sleeping & Eating
Overnight options in town are thin. If you find them all full, the tourist office has a detailed list of the fantastic *agriturismi* in surrounding area and can make you a reservation.

Ostello Santa Anna (☎ 05 669 02 665/33 927 86 272; Via Gramsci 3; per person €15; reception 9–12pm & 5–7.30pm) is a quiet, budget option a 1km uphill ride from the centre, with six-bed dorms each with bathrooms.

Hotel Il Girifalco (☎ /fax 05 669 02 177; Via Massetana Nord 25) is a good bet. It is about 500m from the town centre, back towards Volterra, and has a pool, nice rooms, a good breakfast and a garage for bikes.

You won't be disappointed by hanging out for a night at the mountain bike *agriturismo*, **Massa Vecchia** (see box text p60), which can also assuage your knob-by needs.

There are plenty of above-average restaurants. **Osteria da Tronca** (☎ 05 669 01 991; Vicolo Porte 5; meals €23–28) is an intimate stone-walled restaurant squeezed into a side street. **L'Antica Osteria** (☎ 05 669 02 644; Via Norma Parenti 19; meals €25) is an osteria offering good value, several lip-smacking vegetarian options and inexpensive pizza.

MONTALCINO
☎ 05 / pop 5100

A pretty town perched high above the Orcia valley, Montalcino is best known for its wine, the **Brunello** (p57). Produced only in the vineyards surrounding the town, it is said to be one of Italy's best reds.

Information
The **Pro Loco tourist office** (☎ 05 778 49 331, www.prolocomontalcino.it; Via Costa del Municipio 1) is just off Piazza del Po-polo, near the towered Palazzo Comunale. The office sells Orso on Bike's *Biking in Val d' Orcia*, a guide to mountain biking in the region. There's an ATM in Piazza del Popolo and several others sprinkled throughout town.

Supplies & Equipment
LM Bike (☎ 05 778 48 282; Viale Piero Strozzi 31) operates out of the town's only petrol station IP. The store has a modest supply of gear and performs minor repairs. It also rents mountain bikes.

Sleeping & Eating

The hotel possibilities in Montalcino are limited but the surrounding countryside is dotted with agriturismi. The tourist office has complete lists.

Casa Degli Orsi (☎ 05 772 22 140; caaorsi@hotmail.com; Via Spagni 20; r €90–120) has been in the Orsi family for generations and is now part B&B. Highlights include a gorgeous garden that's home to a family of turtles, a lovely patio, views of the medieval buildings and the countryside, and a glass floor in the bottom room that displays the old cellar. It's a fabulous find, complete with a garage for bikes, but bring something to augment the inclusive breakfast.

Il Giardino (☎ /fax 05 778 48 257; Piazza Cavour 4) is excellent value with a small courtyard for bikes.

Albergo Il Giglio (☎ /fax 05 778 48 167; www.gigliohotel.com; Via Soccorso Saloni 5; s/d €70/100) has comfortable rooms and is an excellent choice. Doubles have panoramic views.

There's a Coop supermarket on the corner of Via Sant'Agostino and Viale della Liberta.

Al Baccanale (☎ 05 778 47 263; Via G. Matteotii, 19; meals €30, cheapest bottle of Brunello €27; closed Wed) is right on a gorgeous piazza and serves food that makes your eyes roll back in your head – like gnocchi with truffle sauce. **Taverna Il Grappolo Blu** (☎ 05 778 47 150; Scale di Via Moglio 1; meals €28) does ingenious things with local ingredients – try the juicy *coniglio al Brunello* (rabbit cooked in Brunello wine). **Enoteca La Fortezza di Montalcino** (☎ 05 778 49 211; Piazzale Fortezza; wine by the glass from €4) is within the fort itself and is perfect for trying out one of countless varieties of Brunello, buying a bottle and/or climbing up onto the ramparts. **Alle Logge di Piazza** (☎ 05 778 46 189; Piazza del Popolo 1; winebarlelogge@email.it) serves a mean cappuccino and has free wireless.

MONTEPULCIANO

☎ 05 / pop 13,900

Set atop a narrow ridge of volcanic rock, Montepulciano, like Montalcino, is set in Tuscany's superb countryside, where some of Italy's finest wines are produced.

Information

The **Pro Loco tourist office** (☎ 05 787 57 341; www.prolocomontepulciano.it; Piazza Don Minzoni) will make free hotel reservation. There are a few banks with ATMs scattered about the town, including a Banca Toscano across from the tourist office.

Supplies & Equipment

Ciclo Posse (☎ 05 787 16 392; www.cicloposse.com; Via Matteotii 45) is the closest shop. It's in Pienza.

Sleeping & Eating

Accommodation in Montepulciano is limited, so plan ahead. The tourist office has a list of B&Bs.

Bellavista (☎ 34 782 32 314; bellavista@bccmp.com; Via Ricci 25; d €56–70) is at the budget end and an excellent choice; nearly all of its rooms have fantastic views.

Albergo Il Marzocco (☎ 05 787 57 262; www.albergo ilmarzocco.it; Piazza Savonarola 18; s/d incl breakfast €60/95) has been run as a hotel by the same family for over a century. The rooms are large and comfortable, some with balconies and views.

Osteria dell'Acquacheta (☎ 05 787 58 443; Via del Teatro 22; meals €15–20) is a small eatery with the look and feel of a country trattoria. The food is excellent, but mainly meat orientated. **Trattoria Diva e Maceo** (☎ 05 787 16 951; Via di Gracciano nel Corso 90; meals €24–28) is uncomplicated and popular with the locals – it carries a good selection of local wines.

ORBETELLO

☎ 05 / pop 14, 600

Once an island, the Monte Argentário promontory came to be linked to the mainland by an accumulation of sand that is now the isthmus of Orbetello. The tiny, oval town of Orbetello is located in the middle of this narrow strip. Further sandy bulwarks form the Tombolo della Giannella and the Tombolo di Feniglia to the north and south. They enclose a lagoon that is now a protected nature reserve.

Information

The **Pro Loco tourist office** (☎ /fax 05 648 60 447; Piazza della Republica 1) across from the cathedral provides accommodation and dining information, as well as a free map of the city.

ATMs line the Corso Italia.

Supplies & Equipment

There are a couple of bike shops in bike-infested Orbetello. **Girobike** (www.giro bike.net; Viale Carravaggio; Mon to Fri 9–12pm & 1.30–7pm, Sat 5–7pm, closed Sun) is right outside of centre has a nice supply of gear and parts, provides repairs and rents bikes. In Castel di Piano, there is a bike shop in the centre, **Giallini Loriano** (☎ 05 649 55 611; Piazza Guarnieri; closed Sun).

Sleeping & Eating

On the southwest fringe of Duna Feniglia beach, **Camping Feniglia** (☎ 05 648 31 090; www.campingfeniglia.it; near Porto Ercole; per person/tent €5–10/€5–13) is the closest and best camping ground. It also rents four- and six-person bungalows by the week.

Ask the tourist office for B&B and budget options. Most of the hotels are bike-friendly. **La Perla** (☎ 05 648 65 227; www .albergolaperla.it; Via Volontari di Sangue 10; s/d €50/70, s/d with bathroom €40/80), as one of the cheaper hotel options in town, is adequate. It's right outside the old city walls.

Park Hotel and Residence (☎ 05 648 63 318; www.parkhotelresidence.com; Viale Marconi and Via Tintoretto) is outside of the old city walls, with a picturesque patio on top that's perfect for a bit of yoga or splitting a bottle of wine.

Hotel Sole (☎ 05 648 60 410; www. hotelsoleorbetello.com; Corso Italia & Via Colombo) is an 18-room boutique-style hotel smack dab in the middle of the centre.

Osteria il Nocchino (☎ 05 648 60 329; Via Furio Lenzi 64; meals €30) is an excellent choice with limited seating capacity where they serve food like mama used to make.

PITIGLIANO

☎ 05 / pop 4100

The visual impact of this town is unforgettable. It seems to grow organically out of a high, volcanic outcrop that towers over the outlying valley. The gorges that surround the town on three sides constitute a natural bastion, completed to the east by the manmade fort.

Information

The **tourist information office** (☎ 05 646 14 433; Piazza Girabaldi) is supposedly open from 10am to 1pm, and 3pm to 7pm Tue to Sun, and has limited hours, sometimes no hours in winter.

A Banca di Credito Coopertivo ATM stands next to the tourist office. There are no bicycle repair shops in the tiny town.

Sleeping & Eating

One of the coolest and best deals in town is **Rosanna Camilli's B&B** (☎ 05 641 720 359; Via Unitá d'Italia 92; s/d €30/50). Rosanna has a garage for bikes, and the rooms have panoramic views of the city and come equipped with kitchens. It's throwing distance from the centre – and Rosanna is fabulous.

Albergo Guastini (☎ 05 646 16 065; Piazza Petruccioli 4; s/d €37/62), and they make you pay to put your bike in their unceremonious garage. Not cool.

Hotel Valle Orientina (☎ 05 646 16 611; www.valleorientina.it; Località Valle Ori-entina), a self-proclaimed bike hotel, has fine rooms and its very own 7th-century thermal baths it's 3km outside town on the road to Orvieto.

On Piazza Petruccioli there is a little *alimentari* with lovely fresh, local food. **Osteria Il Tufo Allegro** (☎ 05 646 16 192; Vico della Costituzone 2, just off Via Zuccarelli; full meal with wine €27) is definitely the place to eat. **Panificio Celata** (☎ 01 050 780 533; Via Unita d'Italia 3) is an absolutely amazing bakery to stop into for your road fuel, selling delectable focaccia, pizza and brioche. **Caffé del Teatro** (☎ 34 939 09 811; Piazza Garibaldi 55) is where the locals hang, to laugh and tease each other. **Jerry Lee Bar** (Via Roma 28) has internet access (per hour €3) and lures many young locals in to grab a drink.

PORTOFERRAIO

☎ 05 / pop 10,200

Known to the Romans as Fabricia and later Ferraia, this small port was acquired by Cosimo I de' Medici in the mid-16th century. It was from this time that the fortifications and the town that exists today took shape.

Information

The main **APT tourist office** (☎ 05 659 14 671; www.aptelba.it; Calata Italia 26) can assist with accommodation and provides a list of shops that rent and repair bikes. Pick up the free map of Portoferraio as well. There are banks and ATMs on Calata Italia and Via Giosue Carducci in the new part of town, and in the Piazza Cavour in the old town. Laundry can be done at Laundrette (Viale Elba 51).

Supplies & Equipment

A bike shop in Portoferriao is **Cicli Brandi** (☎ 05 659 14 128; Via Carducci 33), which rents mountain bikes. You'll probably find what you need at **Ciclo Sport** (☎ 05 659 14 346; Via Carducci 146; closed Sun) as well. Also, you'll be able to find shops inland in Piombino, like **2G Moto Sport** (☎ 05 653 32 42; Via C Pisacane 84), which has the basics.

Il Libraio (☎ 05 659 17 135; www .elbalink.it; Calata Mazzino 10), on the waterfront beside the old town, stocks a variety of walking and biking maps for the island.

Sleeping & Eating

Note that at the height of summer many hotels operate a compulsory half-board policy. The **Associazione Albergatori Isola d'Elba** (☎ 05 659 15 555; www .albergatorielbani.it; Calata Italia 20) can help you reserve a room.

The closest camping grounds are about 4km west of Portoferraio, in Acquaviva. **Acquaviva** (☎ 05 65919 103; www .campingacquaviva.it; per person/tent €7–14/10–20) is near the beach and easily found. The Lacona area has many camping options.

Hotel Acquamarina (☎ 05 659 14 057; www.hotelacquamarina.it; Localitá` Paduella; s €52–104, d €78–180) is close to the centre, and rooms are sunny with large balconies overlooking the naturally wild gardens.

Cafescondido (☎ 340 340 08 81; Via del Carmine 65; meals €25; closed Sun) is a raucous café up the hill serving delicious food with Elba-centric culinary permutations. **La Libertaria** (☎ 05 659 14 978; Calata Matteotti 12; meals €30; Apr–Oct) has divine food.

SIENA
☎ 05 / pop 48,000
Siena is an iconic Italian city that lures the masses with a medieval centre bristling with Gothic buildings, such as the **Palazzo Pubblico** on Il Campo (Siena's main square). A wealth of artwork is contained in its numerous churches and small museums. Like Florence, Siena offers an incredible concentration of attractions.

Siena also makes a good base for exploring central Tuscany. Note, however, that it can be difficult to find budget accommodation in Siena unless you book ahead. In August and during the city's famous twice-yearly festival, **Il Palio**, it's nearly impossible to find accommodation without a reservation.

Information

The **APT office** (☎ 05 772 80 551; www .terresiena.it; Piazza del Campo 56) has information booklets, maps and other resources for cyclists wanting to explore the region. ATMs are scattered throughout Siena, the highest concentration being on Banchi di Sopra. Don't pass by **Internet Train** (Via di Cittá 121; per hr €4; 8am–8pm; Sun–Fri), a popular café with cables for laptop hook-ups. There's another branch at Via di Pantaneto 57. **Wash & Dry** (Via di Pantaneto 38; 8am–10pm) is a laundry in town.

Supplies & Equipment

Bike shops include **Rossi Bike** (☎ 05 774 83 06; Via Camollia 204–206), just near the Porta Camollia, and **Centro Bici** (☎ 05 772 82 550; Via Toselli 110), which also rents mountain bikes and runs tours.

Sleeping & Eating

Siena's accommodations are not of the most bike-friendly variety. Make sure when you make your reservation you tell them you have a bike. Check the **Albergabici** website (www.albergabici.it) for recommendations. Otherwise, for help finding a room, contact the APT or **Siena Hotels Promotion** (☎ 05 772 88 084; www.hotelsiena.com; 2 Piazza San Domenico).

Colleverde (☎ 05 772 80 044; Strada di Scacciapensieri 47; per person/site €7.75/7.75; open late Mar–early Nov) is a camping ground north of the centre.

TUSCANY

TUSCANY

Guidoriccio (☎ 05 775 22 12; Via Fiorentina 89, Località Stellino; B&B per person €14.30) is a non-HI youth hostel about 2km northwest of the city centre. Leave the city by Via Vittorio Emanuele II, which is an extension of Via di Camollia.

Piccolo Hotel il Palio (☎ 05 772 81 131; www.piccolohotelilpalio; Piazza del Sale 19; s €55-80, d €70-110) has bland, somewhat tired rooms, but they have a locked garage for bikes.

Hotel Minerva (☎ 05 772 84 474; www.albergomir nerva.it; Via Giuseppe Garibaldi r €72–80/90–110) is a more upmarket affair, with small, clean rooms with spectacular views. They have a storage place for bikes and a 10% discount for FIAB members.

At **Conad Market** (Galleria Metropolitan, Piazza Matteotti) self-caterers can stock up on piazza-picnic nosh. **L'Osteria** (☎ 05 772 87 592; Via dei Rossi 79-81; meals €25) is no-nonsense but has savoury dishes at prices locals will pay. Pop over to Kopa Kabana for something *dolce* (sweet) afterward. **Osteria da Cice** (☎ 05 772 80 26; Via San Pietro 32; meals €25, tourist menus €12) is in the hands of a friendly team, reflecting its mainly youthful clientele. It's the place for an informal, relaxed meal, and it has plenty of vegetarian options among its *primi piatti* (first courses).

VIAREGGIO
☎ 05 / pop 58,200
Italy's second Carnevale capital after Venice, Viareggio is the leading resort town on the northern Tuscan coast. To some, Viareggio epitomises the ultimate party, but others find the town a nightmare. If beach clubs aren't your thing, proceed directly to the train station and escape to greener pastures. Both Lucca and Pisa are but a 'hop, skip and jump' away.

Information
APT tourist office (☎ 05 849 62 233; www.viareggioturismo.it; Viale Carducci 10) In summer, a smaller office also operates at the train station.

There are ATMs at both the tourist office and the train station.

Sleeping & Eating
There are about a half-dozen camping grounds spread out between Viareggio and Torre del Lago in the Pineta di Levante woods, most open from April to September. **Campeggio dei Tigli** (☎/fax 05 843 41 278; www.campingdeitigli.com; Viale dei Tigli; per person/tent €5–10/10–15) is the biggest and best.

Viareggio boasts more than 120 hotels of all classes. They mostly jostle for space near the waterfront. There are plenty of restaurant options, although the waterfront places tend to be expensive and uninspiring.

Peralta (☎ 05 849 51 230; www.peraltatuscany.com; d from €90, apt per week from €700; May–Oct), although it's a 10km ride up a side valley from Viareggio, is a relaxing hamlet resuscitated by an Anglo-Italian sculptor. There are courses in painting and cooking, plus hearty hill walking. Find it signposted from the village of Camaiore.

Da Giorgio (☎ 05 8 44 44 93; Via G Zanardelli 71; meals around €35) is the place for fish – and exclusively fish – of the freshest kind, succulently cooked. Advance reservations are essential.

VOLTERRA
☎ 05 / pop 11,300
Mounted high on a rocky plateau, Volterra's medieval ramparts give the windswept town a proud and forbidding air. Volterra, originally an Etruscan settlement, was absorbed into the Roman confederation around 260 BC.

Information
The **tourist office** (☎ 05 888 72 57; www.comune.volterra.pi.it; Piazza dei Priori) is in the centre of town. ATMs can be found in the Piazza dei Priori, and along the Via Gramsci as you enter town.

Supplies & Equipment
There are no bicycle repair shops in Volterra. However, between Siena and Volterra, the route passes right by bike/moto shop **Antichi Officina** (☎ 05 779 233 666; Via Livini 1/3) in Colle di Val D'Elsa.

Sleeping & Eating
Camping Le Balze (☎ 05 888 78 80; Via di Mandringa 15; per car/tent/person €3/7/8; Easter–Oct) is the closest camp site to town with a pool, new bathrooms and a position right on Le Balze.

Seminario di Sant'Andrea (☎ 05 888 60 28; semvescovile@diocesivolterra.it; Viale Vittorio Veneto 2; d €28, d with bathroom €36) is a mere 600m or so from Piazza dei Priori and makes an excellent budget choice.

Albergo Nazionale (☎ 05 888 62 84; www.hotelnazionale-volterra.com; Via dei Marchesi 11; s/d €65/85, tr €100, all incl buffet breakfast), a late-19th century hotel claiming to have once hosted writer DH Lawrence, sits smack in the middle of Volterra's centre. Rooms vary in size and style and some have balconies.

Agriturismo San Lorenzo (☎ 05 883 90 80; www.agriturismosanlorenzo.it; B&B d €85, apt without breakfast €90–110) is a giddying fusion of sustainable tourism, countryside vistas, mod cons and wonderful food. It's 3km outside Volterra en route from Siena.

Pizzeria da Nanni (☎ 05 888 40 47; Via delle Pregioni 40; pizzas €5.80–7.50) is a hole-in-the-wall where Nanni spatulas from his oven while sustaining a vivid line of backchat, notably with his long-suffering wife. **Ristorante Don Beta** (☎ 05 888 67 30; Via Giacomo Matteotti 39; meals €30–35, menus €13–18), with its slew of truffle-based dishes, is the place to sample the prized fungus, which abounds – insofar as it abounds anywhere – in the woods around Volterra.

TUSCANY

LIGURIA, MARITIME ALPS & THE PO RIVER BASIN

HIGHLIGHTS

- Seldom-trod **Ligurian back roads** through thick forest (p90)
- Adventurous routes through the unprecedented beauty of the **Maritime Alps** (p96)
- Vineyard-covered and castle-crowned **Langhe hills** (p102)
- Surprisingly bike-centric **Pavia** and **Cremona** and the peaceful countryside in between (p108)

SPECIAL EVENTS

- Sagra del Pesce (2nd Sunday in May), Camogli
- Regatta of Ancient Maritime Republics, Genoa – every four years (May 2010)
- Food/wine festivals: cheese (Bra), wine (Barolo), white truffles (Alba), chestnuts (Cuneo) – September to November
- Palio d'Asti horserace (3rd Sunday in September)

CYCLING EVENTS

- Tours of Riviera Ligure delle Palme and Riviera Ligure Ponente (February/March)
- Milan–San Remo Classic (late March)
- Bicincittà (late May), in 150-plus cities

FOOD & DRINK SPECIALITIES

- *taggiasca* olives and olive oil
- *pesto genovese*
- *trifula bianca* (white truffle)
- Langhe wines
- *bollito* (boiled meat in sauce)
- *focaccia* and *farinata* (breads)

TERRAIN

Pancake-flat plains in the Po River basin – the wine region's rippling hills get higher and harder in the south – surprisingly steep, coastal Ligurian Alps plunge dramatically to the Riviera – long, arduous climbs and high passes in the Maritime Alps.

Telephone Codes – 01 / 03   www.italiantourism.com/liguria

This chapter covers a lot of ground, some of it rolling coastal, some mountainous, and some as flat as can be. But that, in many ways, is why Italy is so enticing. Over a 150km span, you can rise from a flood plain's swelter to the nip of an exposed mountain pass, and still finish the day smoothing out any muscular wrinkles in the warm welcome of the Mediterranean's waters.

GATEWAY
Turin (see p158).

LIGURIA

Seaside Liguria is best known for its Riviera, which simply means 'coast' or 'shore'. However, if properly inflected and crowned with a capital 'R', the words 'the Riviera' call much more to mind. But don't be misled into thinking that coastal charm makes for easy, flatland pedalling. Rising dramatically to impressive heights a few kilometres inland, the **Maritime Alps** (Alpi Marittime, p96) and the **Apennines** (Apennini, p96) give the Riviera its climate and its agricultural richness. It's into these thigh-sacrificing mountains a cyclist must venture to substantiate a true veneration of Liguria.

HISTORY
Liguria has been blessed and cursed as a transit land caught between Rome and all points north and west. Since prehistory,

Ligurians have seen Neanderthals, Cro-Magnon man, the Carthaginians, Romans, Goths, Vandals, Byzantines, Lombards, Franks, Saracens, Germans, French, Spanish and Austrians climb through their mountains and move along their shores. Despite this tumult, Liguria grew into its own. With Genoa in the lead as one of Italy's four great maritime powers, Liguria used the Crusades, the discovery of the New World (Columbus was Ligurian) and the wars of succession to forge an identity. It wasn't until the 19th century when two more local lads, Mazzini and Garibaldi, began the Risorgimento, leading to the unification of Italy, that Liguria joined the rest of the peninsula.

ENVIRONMENT
One of Liguria's most enduring qualities is its natural diversity. The 'eternal spring' of the riviera and the proximate classic mountain climate have allowed for a marvellous mix of flora. From the profusion of coastal flowers to the higher terraced gardens, and further into the hills where

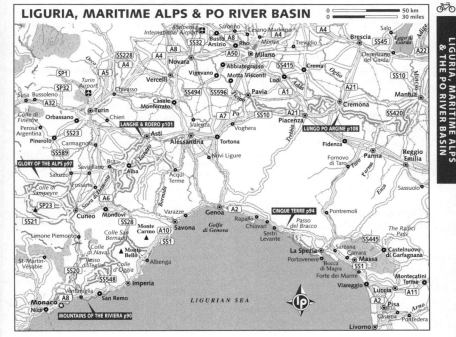

LIGURIA, MARITIME ALPS & PO RIVER BASIN

trees proliferate and give way to upper-elevation fields, you can see it all in just a few hours of cycling. The steep-walled valleys and coastal precipices are also perfect for the cultivation of olives, grapes, citrus and a variety of vegetables. Foods and their by-products (olive oil, wine, pesto) make the area is justly famous.

MOUNTAINS OF THE RIVIERA

Duration 2 days
Distance 173.1km
Difficulty demanding–very demanding
Start Ventimiglia
Finish Albenga
Summary The towering slopes of the Riviera make you earn the experience of their staggering beauty with your sweat, and muscle-twinging thighs.

To the west of Genoa stretches the **Riviera di Ponente**, the Alp-squished 'coast of the setting sun' that boasts about 3000 botanical species, the papal palms, delicious light wines and arguably the best olive oils in Italy. Here you will find magnificent beach meccas for sun worshippers – evidence of the **Roman 'Salt Roads'** (see p96) – picture-perfect fortified towns – splendid mountain panoramas – and acres of planted, terraced valley slopes.

PLANNING
When to Cycle
Spring and autumn are best for biking, with days light and mild enough for outdoor enjoyment, free from summer hordes and full of festivals. Summer, too, is good, although very hot and crowded.

Maps & Booklets
The Touring Club Italiano 1:200,000 *Liguria* map is best, although the free *Regione Liguria* 1:250,000 provincial map available at tourist offices is a good alternative. Ask for other free Regione Liguria maps that detail cycling routes.

Olive fans should pick up the free *La Strada del Vino e dell'Olio dale Alpi al mare* information packet.

GETTING TO/FROM THE RIDE
Ventimiglia (start)
TRAIN
Ventimiglia is on the main coastal train line that runs through Genoa (3 hours) and Nice (45 minutes), with hourly services to/from both cities. Ventimiglia is also the terminus of a nearly hourly train service from Turin (3½ hours) via Cuneo (1¾ hours).

BICYCLE
Ventimiglia is an enjoyable, rolling 41km ride from Nice along the *basse corniche* (coastal road) via downtown Monte Carlo and Menton.

Albenga (finish)
TRAIN
Albenga is on the principal coastal railway, midway between Ventimiglia (1½ hours) and Genoa (1½ hours). It takes about 4½ hours to reach La Spezia (€9.30).

THE RIDE
Day 1: Ventimiglia to Pieve di Teco
6 ½–11 hours, 88.3km
Be prepared to go to your special place today because you are about to climb, climb, climb, and then you'll climb some more. But the route is as unforgiving in its splendour as it is in its challenge. You'll weave through desolate mountainscapes laden with sublime panoramas that you'll appreciate in profound ways because you will have earned them with each burning pedal stroke.

The elevation can be softened by taking the alternative route that is more trafficked. An early start is advisable either way. At the end of the day, you can look forward to a fabulous pitch headlong into the heart of nature-rich alpine Liguria.

For the stout of lung and thigh, the main route drives over a dramatic, wooded panoramic road to the 1504m pass near **Monte Ceppo** and the 1387m **Passo di Teglia.** In the route's lower reaches, it's blanketed by a patchwork of mute olive, sun-bright grape greens and peppered lightly with stone-clad medieval villages. At its heights, there is the beauty of remote open-field vistas to the **Maritime Alps** (see p96). Plan ahead for lunch – there is not much available for the last 36.5km – and be realistic about time, as this is a tough route that will take longer than you may think.

From the eastern edge of Ventimiglia, head north into the **Nervia Valley**, considered the most beautiful in the western Riviera, and home to the medieval, castle-crowned villages of **Dolceacqua** (8.7km) and **Isolabona** (12.6km). Soon you'll also pass the spectacular hilltop-villages **Apricale** (244m, 15.4km) and **Baiardo** (851m, 26.4km). They are striking enough to distract you from the magnificence of the densely forested hills and valley views.

From Apricale, you'll tackle the first major climb (15.4km), which keeps the heat on for 13.3km until you cross over **Passo Chimbegna** (898m) and hit Baiardo. But don't think you're off the hook yet. Soon after, at 33.7km, you'll embark on another 4.3km hard climb, after which you'll plummet for 15.5km at 38km. The narrow road impossibly clings to the mountainside. On an overcast day, the clouds that settle into the mountain skirts below inspire a sense of other-worldly flight.

Not messing around with anything flat, the route begins to climb again at 54.1km. The 11.6km, 950m climb to **Passo di Teglia** very well might hand your butt to you. Before you start the climb, **Molini di Triora** is a good point to refuel with lunch – you could also take a load off 3km into the climb at **Andagna** (57.2km). Even as you climb, it's hard to not feel ultimately blessed to be cycling on this tranquil, dramatic mountainside.

After you've triumphed, a descent into the **Rezzo Valley** awaits, through western Liguria's largest forest, an area used for animal grazing since the earliest days of written history.

MOUNTAINS OF THE RIVIERA – DAY 1

CUES		GPS COORDINATES
start	Ventimiglia Tourist office	43°47'28"N 7°36'29"E
0.0	↰ Via Cavour/SS1	
1.5	◎ ↰ to 'Dolceacqua'	
{1.5	◎ ↑ alt route: 56.5km}	
8.7	★ Dolceacqua	
12.6	Isolabona	43°52'52"N 7°38'22"E
12.8	↱ to 'Apricale'	
	▲ Hard climb 13.3km	
15.4	Apricale	43°52'49"N 7°39'41"E
	{ ↱ to 'Centro'}	
15.5	↘ to 'Baiardo'	
26.4	Baiardo	43°54'13"N 7°43'12"E
	↱ to 'San Remo'	
	{ ↰ to 'Centro'}	
26.2	↘ to 'Monte Ceppo'	
31.3	↘ to 'Carmo Langan'	
33.7	▲ 4.3km hard climb	
38	⚠ 15.9 descent of varying grades	
44.9	↱ unsigned, not to 'Pigna'	
54.1	↱ to 'Pieve di Teco at stop sign	
	▲ 11.6km hard climb	
57.2	↱ to 'Rezzo'	
	{ ↰ to Andagna centro}	
65.7	★ Passo di Teglia (1387m)	
70	↰ not to San Bernardo	
79.6	{alt route rejoins}	
80.7	Rezzo	44°01'20"N 7°52'30"E
86.9	↰ to 'Imperia' (at 'Stop' sign)	
87.4	↱ SS28 `to Pieve di Teco'	
88.3	↱ `to Armo'	
	(30m) Pieve di Teco, Piazza Cavour	
		44°02'44"N 7°55'03"E

ALTERNATIVE ROUTE: GOING COASTAL
5–8 hours, 56.5km
This route is shorter with fewer climbs (and more traffic), but it's not a walk in the park. Liguria's most famous road, the

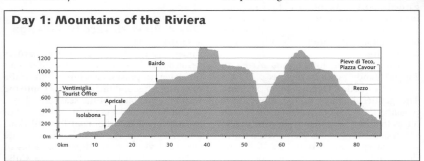

Day 1: Mountains of the Riviera

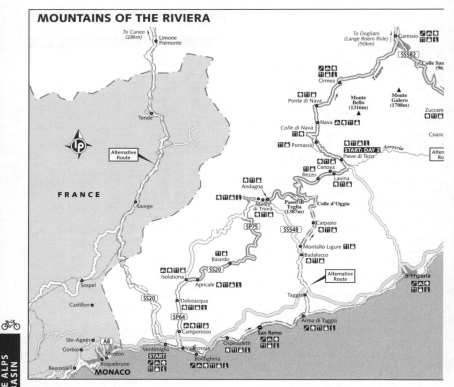

MOUNTAINS OF THE RIVIERA

Via Aurelia, glides along part of one of Italy's most famous stretches of coast, the Riviera dei Fiori. Ventimiglia and beach-abundant, villa-rich Bordighera are at the start of a gentle, coastal pedal along a busy road past the **Exotic Plant Garden** to San Remo (17km). The latter's medieval centre, art and architecture, villas and gardens, port and century-old casino were instrumental in attracting bygone British holidaymakers and making the Riviera a hot vacation destination. It's still a hectic tourist target.

Now come the hills. From Arma di Taggia's sandy beaches, there is a 27.5km crank up to **Colle d'Oggia** (1167m, 52.8km). The gentler inclines of the lower Valle Argentina – fields of small, black taggiasca olives that have lent detour-worthy **Taggia** (28km) and its olive oils such acclaim – give way to steeper, wooded and less-forgiving slopes. But the views are tremendous.

Think ahead about lunch: **Badalucco** (36.5km), **Montalto Ligure** (41km) and **Carpasio** (46.5km) are the last chances for prepared food until **Rezzo** (68.8km).

From the top of Colle d'Oggia, Pieve di Teco is 24km away, all downhill. The quiet low-traffic road descends into the prime valley named after the slate-roofed town of Rezzo.

Day 2: Pieve di Teco to Albenga
5–9 hours, 84.8km

Today's ride is longer but not as hard as yesterday's. The route climbs three medium-length passes, all within sight of the towering Alps, and then eases back into the warmth and colour of the seashore.

You barely feel the 400m getting out of town before the start of your first (10.1km) uphill. Pause in **Pornassio** to take in the westward view of the 'little Dolomites of Liguria'. The busy, touristy crest of **Colle**

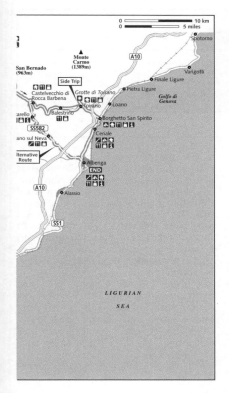

MOUNTAINS OF THE RIVIERA – DAY 2

CUES			GPS COORDINATES
start		Pieve di Teco, Piazza Cavour	44°02′44″N 7°55′03″E
0km		(30m) down to main road SS28	
0.4	▲	10.1km hard climb	
5.8		Pornassio	44°04′12″N 7°52′13″E
{10.5		Colle di Nava (941m)}	
14.2		Ponte di Nava	44°07′05″N 7°52′08″E
19.8	⌐→	to 'Turin'	
		{↑Via Roma through Ormea Centro}	
			44°08′54″N 7°54′38″E
31.6	↑	ignore signs 'to Albenga'	
32.5	↗	at stop sign and fork, SP582	
33.1	↑🏠★	Garessio	44°12′12″N 8°00′53″E
34.1	▲	6.1km hard climb	
40.2		Colle San Bernardo (963m)	
	⚠	14.2km twisting steep descent	
54.2	▲	8.5km hard climb	
54.8	↰	'to Castelvecchio'	
		{■■↑ alt route: Zuccarello 16.6km}	
57.2	★	Castelvecchio di Rocca Barbena	
			44°07′51″N 8°07′04″E
58.2	⌐→	'to Balestrino'	
62.7	⚠	11.3km twisting steep descent	
68.4	★	Balestrino	44°07′29″N 8°10′20″E
		{72.8 ●●↰ Grotte di Toirano 6km ↺}	
75.1	⌐→◎	'to Borghetto S.S.'	
76.3	↰	'to Ceriale'	
76.4	⌐→	'to Ceriale'	
	◎↗	(50m) to 'Ceriale'	
78.3		Ceriale	44°05′33″N 8°13′48″E
80.1	↰1🏠	Via Muragne 'to mare'	
80.5	⌐→	Via Pineo @ T intersection (along tracks)	
83.8	↗	unmarked road at fork	
83.9	↰	(50m) Via Patrioti	
84.4	⌐→	Viale dei Mille	
84.7	↰	Via Genova	
		{alt route rejoins (turn right)}	
84.8	★	Piazza di Popolo	
		Albenga tourist office (middle of piazza)	
			44°03′05″N 8°12′54″E

di Nava (941m, 10.5km) and its two 18th-century forts lie ahead, followed by a rewarding, gentle downhill through lavender-filled fields and Piedmont's **Val Tanaro**.

Lunch in medieval **Ormea** (19.8km) or **Garessio** (33.1km) is a pleasure. Ormea is the first place since Ventimiglia with a bike shop, while elongated Garessio is known as 'the pearl of the Maritime Alps' for its mineral spas, historical vestiges and rich natural surroundings.

Garessio is at the foot of the easiest climb of the day, 6.1km up to **Colle San Bernardo** (963m, 40.2km). The twisting descent on the ocean side of the pass is an excellent breather before the 8.5km haul up past **Castelvecchio di Rocca Barbena's castle** and typical Ligurian fortified village (57.2km). The palazzo at **Balestrino** (68.4km), on the down side of the same ridge, is also striking.

Back in the seaside flats, a small road hugs the coast to Albenga's doorstep. The ancient towers of this monument-rich city appear long before the square near a modern suspension bridge at the heart of town.

As an alternative to the third climb, the road from Colle San Bernardo continues all the way down to the coast at Albenga. It's the more traffic-rich option as well. On the way, brake for the perfect medieval village

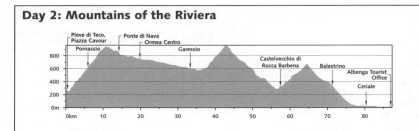

Day 2: Mountains of the Riviera

of **Zuccarello**, once the most important town in the Neva Valley.

SIDE TRIP: GROTTE DI TOIRANO
72.8km, 1–2 hours 6km RT

More than 200 million years ago, underground rivers carved the Varatella system of 70 caverns into an other-worldly tangle of calciferous wonders in the karstic dolomite complex outside the village of Toirano. Who knows what hibernating bears, Paleolithic Neanderthals and their later Cro-Magnon cousins (who left footprints behind!) thought of these formations? There are 1280m of galleries open to the public. It's open from 9am to noon and 2pm to 5pm daily.

CINQUE TERRE

Duration 5–8 hours
Distance 75.1km
Difficulty moderate–demanding
Start La Spezia
Finish Sestri Levante
Summary You'll understand why everyone loves Cinque Terre, with her precipitous cliffs falling to the sea, vineyards etched into the steep mountainside, and quiet wooded roads.

To get there, just before the right turn towards Borghetto San Spirito on the outskirts of Toirano, turn left onto Via Carretto, signed for 'Grotte di Toirano'. Turn left again after 30m and then follow signs 3km to the cave entrance.

If you have a strong set of legs, cycling is the ultimate way to experience the prized, World Heritage-listed Cinque Terre. Known to be frequented by dirt-bag backpackers as well as your classic sunhat-and-zinc-oxide tourist, Cinque Terre's steep, vineyard-covered slopes and wooded landscapes perched above the deep-blue sea have boundless appeal. Needless to say, the cycle-tourist will pedal away with a matchless experience. At the end of the ride, in the beach town Sestri Levante, you can stretch out on the silky sand in preparation of eating mouth-watering seafood.

You can choose to keep on cycling north after a night in Sestri. The trafficky coastal road to Genoa is dotted with some amazingly picturesque beach towns. Otherwise, let Sestri Levante be your final destination. Stay the night or easily catch a train back to La Spezia, making it a day ride, if climbing hills with panniers doesn't do it for you.

PLANNING
When to Cycle

Spring and autumn are climatically ideal for outdoor adventuring; days are still long, the light is bright and the temperature is no longer beastly. That said, crowds flock to this area even well outside the peak summer months.

Maps

The Touring Club Italiano 1:200,000 *Liguria* map (6.20) is best, although the free *Regione Liguria* 1:250,000 provincial map available at tourist offices is a good alternative. Ask for other free Regione Liguria maps that detail cycling routes.

GETTING TO/FROM THE RIDE
La Spezia (start)
TRAIN

La Spezia is on the coastal Genoa–Rome train line, which is connected to Milan and

Turin via Genoa (1–2 hours), and to Pisa (1–1½ hours). The slowest of the frequent services from Genoa makes local stops the length of the Paradiso Gulf, the Gulf of Tigullio and the Cinque Terre. ATC buses cover the short distances to Lerici and Portovenere.

Sestri Levante (finish)
BOAT
Consorzio Maritimo Turistico Cinque Terre Golfo dei Poeti (☎ 01 879 67 676; www.navigazionegolfodeipoeti.it; Passeggiata Constantino Morin) runs boat services to Genoa and Lerici, as well as to coastal towns including all Cinque Terre towns except Camogli.

TRAIN
Also on the Genoa–Rome line, Sestri Levante connects directly to La Spezia (€6.90, 1 hour, frequently) and Genoa (€3.30, 1–1½ hours, frequently).

BICYCLE
Pisa is approximately a 75km ride from La Spezia along the busy SS1 or the touristy, seaside SS432. Parma is a more difficult 125km ride on the SS62 over the 1039m Passo della Cisa. It's possible to bike to Castel di Gandolfo as well.

THE RIDE
La Spezia to Sestri Levante
4½–8 hours, 77.3km

The route tours **Parco Nazionale di Porto Venere**, a protected spread of precipitously steep terraced vineyards, olive groves, cluster pines and forests of chestnut trees. The only road climbs to a perch high above the coast and the five ravine-lining fishing villages

RIDING THE COAST TO GENOA
3–6 hours, 53.4km

This is a short and moderate ride, albeit with incredible traffic in summer. If it's the off-season or you don't care about traffic you might want to cycle the shoreline road running the length of the Gulf of Tigullio, which gains some altitude as it summits the ridge behind Monte di Portofino and then drops back to roll along the Paradiso Gulf's edge all the way to downtown Genoa.

The beaches at **Lavagna** and **Chiavari** are wide and welcoming, and Portofino is a worthy side trip. On the way down, detour through **Camogli** for its decorated buildings gleaming along the port like a homing beacon for wayward sailors. On lots of buildings you'll see painted 3-D features, which one might think to be tacky, but it's just so Italian that it ends up being aesthetically pleasing.

Before hitting Genoa, the route rolls the length of the Paradiso Gulf through beach front communities of great renown, like **Recco**, the 'gastronomic capital of Liguria', which boasts Italy's best focaccia.

of **Riomaggiore, Manarola, Corniglia, Vernazza** and **Monterosso al Mare** (the Cinque Terre or 'Five Lands') before dropping to lunch and the lapping of waves at Levanto. A swim is *de rigueur* before the grind up 615m to Passo del Bracco and a screaming plunge back to sea level at Sestri Levante.

From **La Spezia**, head out of the traffic and into the hills. And hills there are: 300m up from the city limits to a lookout

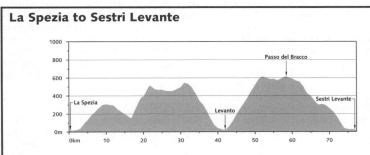

La Spezia to Sestri Levante

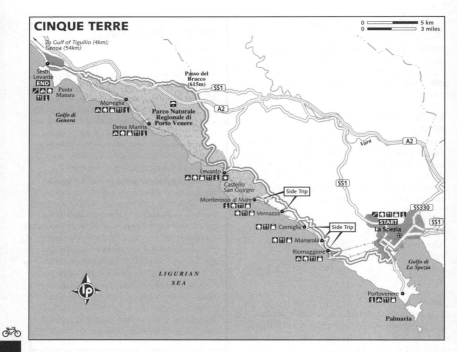

CINQUE TERRE

over the whole of the Cinque Terre, and then 25km of (sometimes steeply) 'rolling' terraced terrain through some of Italy's most extraordinary countryside. The turns for the villages fly by. Visit each seaside settlement at your own peril – every metre down is a metre met again coming up. As for the tunnels at 8.3km and 11.7km, there is a walkable, if unpleasant, sidewalk if you're squeamish about 'subterranean' travel.

Take lunch in **Levanto** (40.1km), the only seaside town to which all roads necessarily lead. If there is time after a beach break, check out the medieval **Castello San Giorgio**, **Chiesa della Costa** and **Loggia Medievale**, off Piazza del Popolo in the eastern part of town.

Then it's back to work. A long, stiff climb leads away from the coast to **Passo del Bracco** (615m, 58.5km). The start of the climb is particularly brutal and almost shadeless, but the sweet views and quiet coastal forests are worth it. From the Passo del Bracco, almost 20km of windy descent finishes in the heart of civilisation at Sestri

Levante. As you approach the town, the traffic becomes increasingly tighter.

MARITIME ALPS

The Maritime Alps (Alpi Marittime) are a spur of snow-capped giants that reach down from Colle della Maddalena, the length of the southern French–Italian border, and splash into the Mediterranean Sea, rippling the landscape for hundreds of kilometres. The sierra also sweeps southeast as the Ligurian Alps (see p89) before giving way to the Ligurian Apennines behind Genoa. Veiled in a quiet and wild obscurity but easily accessible, the Alpi Marittime are rich in culture, lush forests, rugged ridges and glacial valleys sheltering high meadows.

HISTORY

The valleys on either side of the Maritime Alps have been populated since the Bronze Age, when pastoral peoples (ie the 'ancient Ligurians', whose rock engravings from about 1800 BC to 1500 BC have been uncovered) first cherished their value. Best known during Roman times for the **Sentiero del Sale** (Salt Road), a sea-to-scree trade route that passed through the Maritime Alps. The area was also recognised for its Gallic cultural unity, which found full voice in the Middle Ages through a single language – *langue d'Oc* – and a palpable Occitan identity. It wasn't until the **1713 Treaty of Utrecht** that the region's lands (then part of the Savoy state) were divided. In recent years, especially since borders have dissolved in the European Union, interest has surged in long-forgotten, cross-border **Occitan culture.**

ENVIRONMENT

Despite the cultural unity in the Maritime Alps, its position at a geographical and geological crossroads is characterised by a large variety of landscapes, plants and animals. In contrast to the solid and squat white-granite massifs in Parco Naturale delle Alpi Marittime to the west, to the east are wind-carved and mottled limestone giants rooted over extensive networks of karstic caves in Parco Naturale dell'Alta Valle Pesio e Tanaro. To the south, the middle slopes rich in a Mediterranean abundance unusual at such elevations (warmed by the tempering effect of the sea) give way in less than 10km to sparse, northern alpine pastures and plants. Even animals rarely seen in lower climes – chamois, ibex, alpine marmot – are a mere bray away from their woodland neighbours – deer, boar, fox, badger, marten and hare.

GLORY OF THE ALPS

Duration 2 days
Distance 164.8km
Difficulty demanding
Start/Finish Cuneo
Summary It might make you cry. How beautiful the enormous jagged mountains and rugged valleys are. Or the watering eyes just might be from the pain in your leg muscles.

This route navigates some of the most overwhelming and ravishing landscapes of

MOUNTAIN BIKE VALLE MAIRA

Pensione Ceaglio (see p112) in tiny Marmora happens to be an epicentre of mountain biking. Specifically catering to the Northern European cyclist community, Ceaglio is impressively prepared with maps, directions, routes, tools and an amazing restaurant that prepares guests for the hundreds of kilometres of single track and abandoned military roads. Don't miss out on a shot of their homemade genepy, a *digestivo* (after-dinner drink) made from high alpine plants.

Ceaglio doesn't rent bikes, but specialised rentals can be arranged through a shop in Piasco, **Mattio** (☎ 07 527 00 58; Via Dante 21). Ex-professional Lukas Stöckli runs mountain bike camps and guided trips (www.mtb-piemonte.it) based from Ceaglio. The riding here is extremely diverse, both in landscape and challenge level, and is recommended.

Italy, but for the casual pedaller, this is not an easy ride. Grinding up the remote, awesome passes of Colle di Sampeyre, Colle d'Esischie and Colle Faunaria/dei Morti, you start to forget any other reality besides climbing, one pedal stroke after the other. You fight and you stagger – and the mountain doesn't care – but eventually you conquer the pass and welcome an unparalleled satisfaction.

Is it worth it? Yes, and yes. Besides the fact that the gruelling climbs feed your soul, you experience the sublime, craggy mountain ranges and valleys in a way that makes the place a part of you. With each summit, you are birthed afresh. Dramatic? Riding the passes fully loaded will inspire drama in you as well.

This ride is for the adventurous. Marmots (rodents) casually cross your path as you climb and descend through raw wilderness and rural herding land. The very occasional motorcycle rider and daring motorist (and even you yourself) think you're crazy. It's only the passing Italian *ciclisti*, in their matching lycra on bikes nicer than your car, who don't think you're crazy. They understand your fervour and share the passion.

PLANNING
When to Cycle

Relative to the northern Alps, the weather slap in the Maritime Alps is softened by the proximate Mediterranean climate. But we're still talking about mountains: chilly and rainy springs, brisk autumns and cold and snowy winters. The best time for two-wheeling is from May to October, although even at the height of summer, in the higher elevations, nights (and many days) can be chilly, rainy, foggy and even snowy.

What to Bring

Brings lots of food and water, as the riding is strenuous and services are few and far between. Also, bring insect repellent, as there is nothing more annoying than climbing a pass while being harassed by tiny flies. Have lights on hand for riding through small tunnels and carry extra layers because the alpine climate is a fickle thing.

Maps

The Touring Club Italiano 1:200,000 *Liguria* or *Piemonte* maps are best. The free *Regione*

Liguria 1:250,000 and *Cuneo* 1:200,000 provincial maps available at tourist offices are also good.

GETTING TO/FROM THE RIDE
Cuneo (start/finish)
TRAIN

Regular trains run from Cuneo's central train station, at Piazzale Libertà, to Saluzzo (€2.45, 35 minutes, up to 6 daily), Turin (€4.70, 1¼ hours, up to 8 daily), San Remo (€6, 2¼ hours, 3 daily) and Ventimiglia (€4.80, 2 hours, around 4 daily), as well as Nice (2¾ hours, at least 6 daily) in France. A second train station for the Cuneo–Gesso line serves the small town of Mondovì, where there are connections to Savona and Genoa.

THE RIDE
Day 1: Cuneo to Marmora–Vernetti
5–9 hours, 89.5km

This day is a killer, but getting out of Cuneo is civilised and painless. The flatlands slowly start a gentle, almost imper-

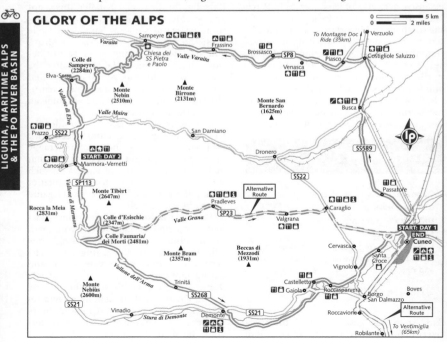

GLORY OF THE ALPS

LIGURIA, MARITIME ALPS & THE PO RIVER BASIN

Day 1: Cuneo to Marmora

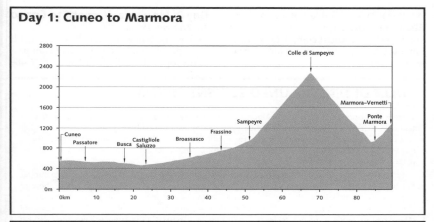

Day 2: Marmora to Cuneo

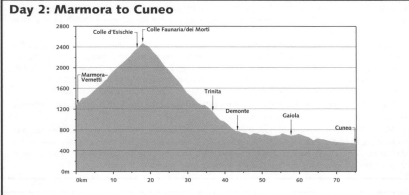

ceptible climb. It's the calm before the storm. There are castles, baroque churches and medieval towers at **Busca** (17.5km) and **Costigliole Saluzzo** (23.3km), and you can take the short snack detour into the market centre of **Venasca** (31.8km) for its famous bread and salami. Self-caterers and snack fiends should stock up in **Sampeyre**. Other than a small store in Canosio, there are no good markets until tomorrow afternoon at Demonte. At 74.7km, after the pass, you can revitalise at the restaurant in **Elva-Serre**.

After you cycle 51.4km to the bottom of the pass, you might notice that the mild, then eventually not so mild, climb has worn your freshness before you take on the big daddy of a pass, **Colle di Sampeyre** (63.7km, 2284m). As you tuck into

the climb though, you distance yourself from the trappings of civilisation. As you head into the heart of the unrelentingly gorgeous Alps, the route ascends through dense alpine forests and a panorama of monstrous mountains. The euphoria of sailing down the other side is tempered by the steepness and narrowness of the road that is chipped into the bare rock of a sheer ravine wall.

After the descent comes yet more climbing: you have the final testament-to-faith 5km climb to **Marmora**.

This day is long and it requires you to be self-sufficient in terms of water (bring a tonne), food and repair equipment. There's an option of splitting up the mileage of this day by staying in the economical and pleasant lodging in **Sampeyre**

(51.4km). One adorable hotel is **Albergo Ristorante Alte Alpi** (☎ 01 759 77 100; hotelaltealpi@hotmail.com; Via Vittorio Emanule 98; s/d €35/50), which serves wonderful food.

Day 2: Marmora–Vernetti to Cuneo
4½–7½ hours, 75.3km

Today, the route doesn't dink around. It immediately sends you up the 17.9km pass to the top of the Vallone di Marmora, Colle

---

COLLE DI TENDA: CUNEO TO VENTIMIGLIA
7–11 hours, 107.3km

There is an option of cycling to the Mountains of the Riviera ride via the Colle di Tenda, a mountain pass that Italian cyclists will raise their eyebrows at, as if remembering the pain. On the other side of the pass, you ride through France for a stint (buy some cheese) then return to Italy. This has several significantly hairy and tenuous sections, but it's legendary – so you, Lonely Planet reader, will get the lowdown.

From downtown Cuneo, the road leads through commercial sprawl to Borgo San Dalmazzo, at the bottom of the Vermenagna valley. At Limone Piemonte, if the legs won't go where the ego urges, a little train barrels through the mountain you would otherwise go over (erasing 32km, almost 900m of climbing and a difficult 550m descent). The one-stop rail trip (10 trains a day; all take bikes) to Tende in France takes about 20 minutes. The station in Limone Piemonte is above town on its northern edge. As you enter town, take the first left towards the centre, then turn left again just before the first roundabout. In Tende, after leaving the station, turn left on the main road to rejoin the main route.

True mountain gluttons must be prepared with food, drink and determination. Ahead lies a stout 14.7km hike up 890m, the last 8.2km on 17 windswept switchbacks – very tough. Near the top, the paved road turns gravel over a penultimate ridge and then finally to **Colle di Tenda** (1871m, 42.5km) at the unmarked French border. Unfortunately, the downhill is almost as brutal as the climb: 7.6km of loose gravel through tight hairpins – take care because it's steep, slippery and sans guardrails!

Pavement reappears at the start of the **Roia valley**. Take in the precipitous valley walls, dramatic gorges and pastel-coloured cliff side villages.

Almost 5km after crossing back into Italy, the second tunnel is off-limits to bikes! The left turn to Airole is an odd wandering road that disappears once (forge through the mountain bike-worthy dirt section). After that, back on the main road you'll approach the flat lower valley to the coast at Ventimiglia. We hope you won't be permanently scarred, mentally or physically.

Day 3: Cuneo to Ventimiglia

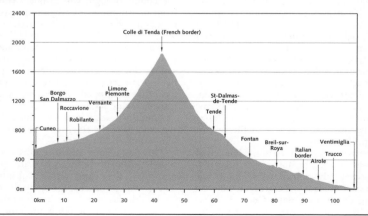

Faunaria/dei Morti. It is not easy. Your compensation is the diversity, immensity and simply overtaking beauty of the mountains and valleys. The desolation can make you think you're the only person left on earth. Marmots frantically scamper and dart around in the sidelines, and sometimes right across your path, as if there was a sounding of a marmot alarm. You are obviously the most drama they've had in a while.

On the far side of the intermediate pass – **Colle d'Esischie** (2374m, 16.4km) – there is a choice between a left to the alternative route **Valle Grana** (one of Italy's steepest) or a right to the final pass **Colle Faunaria/ dei Morti** (2481m, 17.9km), visible 1.4km away up to the right. The Valle Grana alternative route drops 1535km in 20km to **Pradleves** and then continues down 250m and 13.2km to **Caraglio**, before a right on SS22 across the edge of the flatlands to Cuneo.

Following the Colle Faunaria/dei Morti the 25.1km tear-jerking descent flies through the Stura valley's sea of green, which is distantly flanked by sharp-peaked mountains. Then it's a 32.3km roll back to Cuneo.

After **Demonte** (43km), the converted military road on the far side of the valley is a nicer, lightly trafficked alternative to the main thoroughfare. Above **Gaiola**, the route shifts back to the north side of the river for a quiet spin through the villages of **Castelletto** and **Roccasparvera**. The high plateau on the far side of the river is the mesa on which Cuneo is the northern tip, just 15km away.

WINE COUNTRY

Looking longingly into a bottle of Italy's best northern red wine evokes visions of undulating, vineyard-covered hills, ancient stone villages, the smell of busy agriculture and the feel of juicy grapes mashing between toes. There's no better way to experience the real thing – Langhe, Roero and Monferrato – than on two wheels. Cycle through namesake **Barolo**, **Barbaresco**, **Moscato**, **Asti** and **Dolcetto**, whose names alone ring like the crystal into which they are decanted. Furthermore, the route cruises you through the unforgettable,

food-famous cities of **Acqui Terme**, **Alba**, **Bra** and **Asti**, making the ride not only a lavishing exploration of the landscape but also of the senses.

Unlike Tuscany, an iconic Italian cycling destination, the **Langhe** and **Roero region** rests on its food and wine laurels and doesn't emphasise itself as a cycling destination. You'll find out that it is very much worthy, due to its many untrafficked roads through voluptuous hills preened with vineyards, and post-cycling meals that will blow you over to the next ride.

HISTORY

Traces of the region's first inhabitants date back to the Neolithic times. The Romans also frequented this fertile area, and plentiful evidence remains of life in the centuries that followed, from ancient hilltop surveillance towers to medieval castles, churches and buildings, baroque and Gothic palaces and so much more. This is a land that has been fiercely fought over, divided between and passed through the hands of the area's wealthiest and most powerful people, as well as the Savoys, Spanish, Austrians, Napoleonic French and Russians, before landing back in Italian territory. Curiously, although wine production dates back to before the Roman arrival, written mention isn't made until the 14th century.

ENVIRONMENT

The soil of this unique area is the result of millions of years of layered underwater deposits. Alternating drifts of clay and sand settled at the bottom of the Padano Gulf, an arm of the then-larger and deeper early Mediterranean Sea. Later, an uplifting of the land thrust this ground above water and bent the hardened strata into today's hills. Wind and water erosion have continued to shape the terrain. Rivers, in particular, having coursed eastwardly, gave the hills a characteristic shape: steep but stable, dry and exposed to the southeast versus gently inclined, higher in water content and less stable to the northwest. These contrasting slopes of nutrient-rich soils and differing degrees of exposure to the elements are ideal for the growing of grapes, as well as forests and pastures whose rich earth gives birth to highly prized truffles, hazelnuts, cheese and flowers.

LIGURIA, MARITIME ALPS & THE PO RIVER BASIN

LANGHE & ROERO

Duration 3 days
Distance 198.5km
Difficulty moderate
Start Acqui Terme
Finish Asti
Summary This ride is an odyssey for the senses: a truffle-sprinkled, odouriferously decanted, vineyard-cruising, bike-loving good time.

Be prepared to fall in love with the vineyard-dotted landscape of Langhe and Roero. There is a wistful, almost romantic sensation that fills you as you soar downhill through the sun-soaked countryside, wind blasting past your face, scented by tilled earth and fresh vines. Those descents, as sensuous as they are, conversely signify that you'll be ascending. The climbs will make you sweat but are moderate enough to allow you to sip Barolo in Barolo and savour truffle-infused homemade pasta at lunch.

PLANNING
When to Cycle
The full impact of the Po plain weather patterns, especially the hot summers, is felt here. Thus, the best pedalling times are spring and autumn. Keep in mind that hotels fill quickly during the autumn festival and harvest season, especially in September during **Asti's madcap** and **medieval Palio** (p114).

Maps & Booklets
For overall coverage, Touring Club Italiano's 1:200,000 *Liguria* or *Piemonte* maps are best, although the provincial maps of Asti, Alessandria and Cuneo, available at information offices, are free and fine, especially the *Terre e Vini d'Asti* 1:160,000 map.

Keep an eye out for the free brochures and maps, particularly those dealing with wine trails. The Alba tourist office hands out brochures with cycling itineraries (€1.50) themed on Barolo (see p107), cheese, hazelnuts, stone, Moscato (see p107) (a sweet, golden wine) and religion.

LANGHE & ROERO – DAY 1

CUES			GPS COORDINATES
start		Acqui Terme tourist office	44°40'39"N 8°28'07"E
0km	↖	Corso Roma	
0.2	↱	Via Cavour, to 'Castel Rocchero'	
0.6	⚠	cross tracks	
	▲	4.4km hard climb	
4.9		Moirano	44°42'05"N 8°26'26"E
6.5	▲	1.9km moderate hill	
8.3	↱	Castel Rocchero, `to Nizza'	44°43'12"N 8°24'55"E
9.3	↖	to 'Nizza'	
16.3	↙◎	(2nd exit) to 'Nizza centro'	
16.7	⚠	ignore signs to 'Cannelli'	
17.1	↖	after Traffic Light on Via Corsi	
		Nizza Monferrato	44°46'26"N 8°21'16"E
17.3	↱	Via Girabaldi, following ◎ around Piazza Garibaldi	
17.5	↱	Via Valle San Giovanni	
24.8	↑◎	onto Viale Italia	
31.2		to 'Alba'	
	★	S Stefano Belbo	44°42'31"N 8°13'49"E
31.5	↖	after bridge `to Mango'	
	▲	5.5km tough climb	
37.7	↖	Valdivilla, `to Mango'	44°42'34"N 8°10'56"E
39.6		Busa	44°42'33"N 8°10'07"E
		{42.7 ●● ↱ Mango 1km ↻}	
43.6	↙◎	(1st exit) `to Alba'	
	⚠	5.9km descent	
48.5	↙◎	(1st exit) `to Neive'	
		{49 ●● ↱ Neive 1 km ↻}	
49.5	◎	2nd exit to 'Barbaresco'	
51.5	▲	1.6km hard climb	
		{52.9 ●● ↱ Barbaresco 4km ↻}	
	★	Enoteca	
59.5	▲	`to Alba' 1.6km steep climb	
60.5	↙◎	(2nd exit) Via Acqui to center	
60.7	↖	Via Giraudi	
	↱	(40m) Piazza Risorgimento/Duomo, Alba tourist office	44°42'03"N 8°02'10"E

GETTING TO/FROM THE RIDE
Acqui Terme (start)
TRAIN
The rails through Acqui Terme are infrequently used: the Savona–Alessandria service passes fewer than 10 times a day in each direction (30 minutes from Alessandria, 1½ hours from Savona) and the Asti–Genoa service about a dozen (1 hour from Asti, 1¼ hours from Genoa). Supplementary bike tickets cost €3.50.

BICYCLE
Acqui Terme is an easy 35km pedal from Alessandria on the SS30, a hilly 50km from

LIGURIA, MARITIME ALPS & THE PO RIVER BASIN

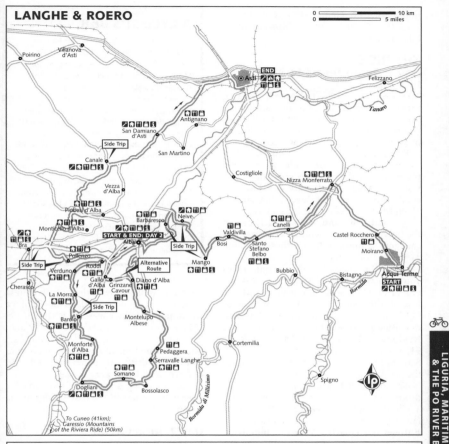

LANGHE & ROERO

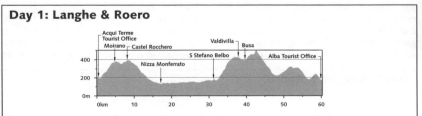

Day 1: Langhe & Roero

LIGURIA, MARITIME ALPS & THE PO RIVER BASIN

Asti via the SS456, a difficult 60km from Savona on the SS334 and a no-nonsense 25km from Ovada.

From Dolgliani, at the southernmost part of the loop, you can bike 50km south to hit the Italian Riviera ride at Garessio.

Asti (finish)
TRAIN

Asti is on the Turin–Genoa railway line and is served by hourly trains in both directions. Journey time is 30 to 55 minutes to/from Turin (€3.50); and 1¾ hours to/from Genoa (€6), stopping at Alba (€2.45, 40 minutes). Supplementary bike tickets cost 3.50.

THE RIDE
Day 1: Acqui Terme to Alba
3½–6½ hours, 60.7km

Today's route climbs two ridges dividing three rivers and weaves through the land of Moscato and Barbaresco, which will leave you throughout the day in varying degrees of awe – and possibly debauchery.

From Acqui, the route immediately ascends from the Bormida valley then plunges into the vineyards of the Belbo valley. At **Nizza Monferrato** (17.1km), the route continues for a lovely, flat stretch along the river before the hills ahead.

At **Santo Stefano Belbo** (31.1km), at the heart of Moscato wine production, you can grab a meal and visit the crumbling medieval tower above the city.

Then the second 5.5km climb takes you on a twisty road of terraced Moscato vineyards with outstanding views. At the top of the ridge, the village of **Mango** (44.1km) has the 16th-century **Castello dei Busca**, which houses the **Enoteca Regionale del Moscato** (☎ 01 418 92 91; www.enotecamoscato.com; Piazza XX Settembre 19), a visitors centre featuring the acclaimed Moscato wines.

The 280m, 5.9km descent from Mango drops into the lower Langhe region. There's a side-trip option to **Neive** (49km) for its famous *centro storico* (historic centre) and **Bottega dei Quattro Vini** (an important wine centre). Also, if you're a lover of the noble rot, it would be a shame to skip **Barbaresco** (55.4km), the village that gave its name to the wine. It's the site of an impressive 13th-century church and

A CYCLIST'S B&B

Near the town of Canale, about halfway into Day 3 of the route, **B&B Le Cicale** (☎ 01 736 50 70; www.lecicale.com; Via Montaldo Roero 46; per week/day with half-board €300/45) is situated in the hamlet of Vezza d'Alba. You can't get much closer to having a casual visit in an Italian home than staying with the Servetti family. Maria will gladly teach you how to cook local dishes, and Domenico is an avid cyclist who offers his 'homemade cycling maps' to guests.

Catering specifically to cyclists, the Servettis serve large breakfasts and provide post-ride snacks. Domenico also has tools on hand should you need them. Bonuses are the pool and organic garden. At Le Cicale, the folks are stellar and the place is a proper base for cycling adventures.

tower, as well as the 18th-century Chiesa di San Donato, now used as the **Enoteca Regionale del Barbaresco** (☎ 01 736 35 251; www.enotecadelbarbaresco.it; Piazza del Municipio 7). The *enoteca* (wine bar) offers information and tastings, and bottles from 113 different wineries, and 130 different area labels are for sale.

The final ridges and hills into Alba are especially radiant in the rosy shades of the afternoon sun.

Day 2: Alba Circuit
4–7 hours, 71.7km

Today's route sweeps through lower Langhe, over hills in the region's alto area, and then back down a long and intensively scenic ridgeline to Alba. Fortunately, panniers can

Day 2: Langhe & Roero

be left at the hotel or carried empty for wine purchases.

From Alba, speed west through an uninspiring strip. Flashes of distant hilltop castles are a harbinger of brilliant things to come. There's a possible detour through **Roddi** (7.3km), the first of the 11 Barolo-producing *comuni* (municipalities), for a peek at its 13th-century bell tower and medieval castle.

After a steep 0.6km climb at 8.6km, you'll come to **Verduno** (11.5km), whose **Piazza Don Borgna** makes for an interesting stop. Leaving Verduno, you'll run into some *enoteche* (wineries offering tastings, 11.9km and 12.4km). Continuing on this rural road, you will feel genuinely nestled into the heart of wine country. **La Morra** (14.8km) also has an elegant bell tower, the Castello della Volta, a 17th-century church, and a Cantina Comunale for the tasting and purchase of local wines. The view from La Morra's Piazza Castello at the ridge summit looks to a ridiculously beautiful panorama of the Langhe hills.

To the lowlands south of La Morra is **Barolo** (19.9km), the village that gave its name to the wine now known as 'the king of wines, the wine of kings'. The 10th-century Castello di Barolo houses the **Enoteca Regionale del Barolo** (☎ 01 735 62 77; www.baroloworld.it; Castello Falletti), which has a lavish tasting area and an ethnographic museum. You feel refined just by walking in – and that's a hard feat when you're wearing cycling gloves. Around the corner, **Barolando** (☎ 01 73 56 28; Piazza Municipio 2) is an excellent *osteria* (wine bar serving some food) for a lunch of fresh pasta and a fat glass of Barolo.

You climb to **Monforte d'Alba** (25.7km) whose horizons are filled with picture-perfect vistas. It's located at the southern edge of the Barolo hills and is the site of another medieval castle and 13th-century tower. On the descent, the scenery changes dramatically. You will tour through groves of trees and pastures fundamental to the production of the region's cheeses and hazelnuts. **Dogliani** (33.4km), at the bottom of the hill, has a fine medieval centre, complete with a castle and tower.

The last 9.7km climb of the day is a tough-ie – it pushes to the crest of a long ridge. The route stays high for a few kilometres

LANGHE & ROERO – DAY 2

CUES		GPS COORDINATES
start	Alba tourist office	44°42'03"N 8°02'10"E
0km	S on Via Vittorio Emanuele	
0.2	⌐► Via Belli	
0.7	◥ Corso Bandiera	
1	⌐►◉ Via L Enaudi bridge, become Corso Europa	
5.1	⌐►◉ `to Roddi'	
6.1	◥◉ `to Roddi'	
6.7	◥ Via Prati Riva `to municipio'	
{7.3	●● ◥ Roddi 1km ↺}	
7.3	⌐► Via Cavour	
7.9	◥ downhill	
8.2	⌐► Strada Roddi Verduno `to Verduno'	
8.6	▲ 0.6km steep climb	
11.5	★ Verduno	44°39'57"N 7°55'57"E
	⤢◉ (3rd exit) `to La Morra'	
11.6	▲ 3.2km moderate climb	
11.9	★ enoteca	
12.4	★ enoteca	
13.2	◥ unsigned road, not to 'Rivalta'	
13.8	◥ to 'La Morra'	
14.8	↑ La Morra	44°38'23"N 7°56'03"E
14.8	⌐► Via Roma `to Barolo'	
17.9	◉ 2nd exit `to Barolo'	
19	◥ Via XXV Aprile `to Barolo'	
	▲ 1.3km descent	
20.2	⌐► `to Barolo, centro'	
{20.8	●● ◥ Barolo 1km ↺}	
20.8	↑ `to Monforte'	
	▲ 5.9km moderate climb	
24.5	◥ `to Monforte'	
26.6	★ Monforte d'Alba	44°35'00"N 7°58'05"E
	⤢ (20m)Via Garibaldi `to Dogliani'	
33.4	★ Dogliani	44°31'57"N 7°57'15"E
	◥ Via Codevilla `to Bossolasco'	
34.4	▲ 9.7km moderate-hard climb	
36	★ enoteca	
39.2	★ Somano	44°32'09"N 8°00'33"E
44.1	⤢◉ `to Alba'	
48.1	Serravalle Langhe	44°33'37"N 8°03'35"E
50.8	Pedaggera	44°34'41"N 8°04'23"E
57.3	◉ `to Diano'	
63.7	Diano d'Alba	44°39'04"N 8°01'43"E
	{64.5 ■■ ◥ alt route: Grinzane Cavour 12km}	
70.3	◥ Corso Langhe	
71.2	↑◉ Piazza Savona, to information icon	
	(road becomes Via Vittorio Emanuele after RA)	
71.7	Piazza Risorgimento, Alba tourist office	44°42'03"N 8°02'10"E

and envelops you in vistas of the dazzling Langhe to the west (the same surveyed from the east this morning) before the final 18km, luscious descent back to Alba.

LIGURIA, MARITIME ALPS & THE PO RIVER BASIN

An alternate route from **Diano d'Alba** (63.7km) leads to the medieval castle and **Enoteca Regionale Piemontese di Grinzane Cavour** (☎01 732 62 159; www.castellogrinzane.com; Via Castello 5) in Grinzane Cavour, which showcases a wide variety of regional libations. An ethnographic museum, a restaurant and guided tastings are available.

The route then drops to the valley floor at **Gallo d'Alba**, from where Alba is an easy ride.

Day 3: Alba to Asti
3½–6 hours, 66.1km

Where the wine hills of Langhe cover the southern sweeps of the Tanaro River, **Roero** rules the north. Though not as well known or frequented as Langhe, Roero holds much appeal. The route is essentially a rollicking ride on quiet back roads through rolling hills of vineyards, forested former estates and fields.

From Alba, take the same Roddi road as yesterday. The leg towards Bra is the most trafficked of the day. Think about a worthwhile side trip to **Pollenzo** (13.5km), the site of the rich Roman community of Pollentia, which preceded the founding of nearby Bra, and the Palazzo Traversa Museum. The city of **Bra**, visible at the top of a hill to the west, is the third (after Asti and Alba) of the area's great wine centres. The side trip to Bra's many medieval and Renaissance churches and palaces and its museums is recommended. Plus, Bra is the birthplace of the **Slow Food Movement** (www.slowfood.com), so you're bound to find a righteous meal.

Stretching for miles from Bra to the northeast is the **Rocche of Roero,** the rocky outcropping bisecting the region. The route tinkers around it and its most famous vineyards and castle-topped towns. While cruising over gentle rollers, you'll be able to see **Monticello d'Alba**'s medieval **Castello dei Conti Roero. Canale** (37.3km), the main town of Roero's 24 *comuni* (municipalities) contains the 14th-century Castello dei Malabaila and the **Enoteca del Roero** (☎01 739 78 228; www.enotecadelroero.it; Via Roma 57), which is directly on the route at 37.6km. They have a restaurant and feature some wine varieties a bit removed from the limelight, like Roero

Arneis, Cisterna d'Asti, Barbera 'Alba and Nebbiolo d'Alba.

Although it officially leaves the Roero region and dips into the province of Asti and its Monferrato wine estates, the route climbs into hills whose draping vineyards

LANGHE & ROERO – DAY 3

CUES			GPS COORDINATES
start		Alba tourist office	44°42'03"N 8°02'10"E
0km		S on Via Vittorio Emanuele	
0.2	⌐►	Via Belli	
0.7	⌐◄	Corso Bandiera	
1	⌐► ⊙	Via L Enaudi bridge, become Corso Europa	
5.1	⌐► ⊙	`to Roddi'	
6.1	↑⊙	`to Pollenzo'	
		{13.5●● ⌐► Pollenzo1km ↻}	
		{15.1●● ⌐◄ Bra 7.8km ↻}	
16.8	⌐►	at stop sign to 'Pocapaglia'	
		{18.1 ●● Pocapaglia, 2km RT (hotel, food, info)	44°42'59"N 7°53'02"E
20.4	⌐►	to 'Monticello'	
22.6	⌐◄⊙	to 'S. Guiseppe'	
25.4	⌐►	to 'Corneliano'	
27.3	⌐◄⊙	to 'Canale'	
33.1	⌐►	to 'Canale'	
37.3	⌐◄	T intersection, Piazza San Bernardino	
	⌐►	(50m) Via Roma	
		Canale	44°47'52"N 7°59'58"E
37.6	★	Enoteca del Roero	
38	★	Pedalata Sport bike shop	
38.1	⊙	Second Exit to 'Asti'	
38.8	⌐►⊙	`to S Damiano'	
43.4	⌐◄⊙	`to S Damiano'	
45.2	★	enoteca	
44.5	↗	`to centro'	
45.5		San Damiano d'Asti	44°50'05"N 8°03'54"E
	⌐►	with traffic, Via G Peano	
46.5	⌐►	`to Govone'	
49.2	⌐◄	`to S Martino'	
50.7	⌐◄	Via Asti `to Antignano'	
55		Antignano	44°50'43"N 8°08'08"E
64.2	↑⊙	(2nd exit) SS458 `to Turin'	
64.2	↑	`to Acqui T'	
64.8	↘	Corso Venezia,to 'Acqui T'	
65.2	⌐◄⊙	Corso Savona `to centro'	
65.7	⌐►	to 'ospedale'	
65.9	↘	`to ospedale' around Campo del Palio	
66	↑	following information icon	
66.1	↙	Piazza Vittorio Alfieri	
		(50m) Asti tourist office	44°54'03"N 8°12'24"E

LIGURIA, MARITIME ALPS & THE PO RIVER BASIN

WINES OF LANGHE & ROERO: MAKE YOUR TOUR

Barolo wine, a product of the Nebbiolo grape, is the Langhe region's premium wine. This and other wines in the area have been awarded one of Italy's precious quality seals: DOC (Denominazione di Origine Controllata). Barolo's prominence as the 'the king of wines, the wine of kings' began in the early 19th century when the last marquess of Barolo, Giulia Colbert, asked the Count of Cavour to help enhance her cellar. With the aid of a French specialist, they developed a robust, complex, full-flavoured and fragrant red like those in vogue in Bordeaux. A true Barolo is still unlike most of its lighter Italian kin.

Other worthy wines in Langhe include **Barbaresco**, another vigorous and delicious red, the poor cousin of which is believed to have been produced during Roman times; **Barbera**, a lately improved red reputed for its complexity – **Dolcetto**, the local, long-standing red table wine and favourite of many; and **Moscato d'Asti,** a sweet, white dessert wine whose bubbly spumante is legendary.

En route, you have an amazing opportunity to savour these fine wines:

DAY ONE
Moscato Enoteca Regionale del Moscato (☎ 01 418 92 91; www.enotecamoscato.com; Piazza XX Settembre 19, Mango), a free presentation centre for the region's wines and other products.
Barbaresco Enoteca Regionale del Barbaresco (☎ 01 736 35 251; www.enotecadelbarbaresco .it; Piazza del Municipio 7) offers information and tastings, and sells bottles from 113 different wineries and 130 different labels from the area.

DAY TWO
Barolo Enoteca Regionale del Barolo (☎ 01 735 62 77; www.baroloworld.it; Castello Falletti) has a lavish tasting area and an ethnographic museum.
Various regional wines Enoteca Regionale Piemontese di Grinzane Cavour (☎ 01 732 62 159; www.castellogrinzane.com; Via Castello 5) in Grinzane Cavour showcases a wide variety of regional libations.

DAY THREE
Barbera d'Alba Enoteca del Roero (☎ 01 739 78 228; www.enotecadelroero.it; Via Roma 57) features some more unusual wine varieties, such as Roero Arneis, Cisterna d'Asti, Barbera 'Alba and Nebbiolo d'Alba.

still feed the Roero wine cycle. This is one of the most picturesque parts of the ride.

The day's final leg is a descent from **Antignano** (55km) back to the banks of the Tanaro River, and then an easygoing spin into downtown Asti.

PO RIVER BASIN

HISTORY

Milan, one of the biggest cities along the Po, has been the heart of Lombardy since as far back as the time of Romanised Cisalpine Gaul and the Germanic Langobards. While Piedmont enjoyed relative stability, the Lombards, when under attack by the Franks, formed the Lombard League, whose collapse resulted in centuries of wrangling between powerful families and their political and religious allies. Over the last two centuries before Italian unification, Piedmont joined Lombardy in watching successions of conquering foreign powers pass through. Today, Turin and Milan are Italy's industrial poles.

ENVIRONMENT

The source of the Po River is in the Piano del Re on the slopes of Monviso, 40km west of Saluzzo. From its high-elevation peat bogs through the steep-cut valley of the pre-Alps, the river emerges onto a vast plain and begins its meandering flow to the Adriatic, collecting the contents of scores of waterways. The whole plain used to be the floor of the Tethys Ocean, the larger precursor to what is now the Mediterranean Sea. Sediment accumulated over millennia and, after the water level dropped, was shaped by glaciers, wind and water. Rice and other

LUNGO PO ARGINE

Duration 3 days
Distance 218.1km
Difficulty easy
Start Pavia
Finish Mantua
Summary Hail, hail, to the gods of flatness. Thank you for these tranquil country roads and riverside meandering.

grains, sugar beets and fruit are now the most important crops emerging from the nutrient-rich soil. Industry, too, has benefited from the advantages of the river and its plain.

This three-day pedal, easily completed in two by the ambitious, runs along some of the best of the Po's flow. The route *lungo* (along) the Po takes advantage of the tranquil *argine* (dike) paths, dense riparian nature and rich accompanying history.

The Po River took many millennia to shape the wide, fertile plain through which it meanders. Humankind has been swifter in making its mark on the land. As it is prone to flooding, the Po has over the years been lined by a series of argine and a considerable riverside lowland zone called a *golena*, both used for water-level control and agricultural purposes. The river serves as the primary artery of the country's most important industrial and agricultural region.

In general, this area is not high on the tourist checklist, but the medieval cities are quite intriguing and the inhabitants take advantage of the flat landscape by commuting industriously about on bicycles. Furthermore, the regional food is outstanding and a perfect complement to a day of cycling.

PLANNING
When to Cycle
The lower elevations in Italy, particularly in the flats of the Po River basin, get uncomfortably muggy during summer, particularly in July and August. If you go during a hot spell, leave early in the day. The best pedalling seasons are the spring and autumn.

PO CITIES LOVE THE BICI

Cremona and Pavia are infiltrated by pedestrians and cyclists. Motorists think they run the show, but you'll constantly see them frustrated and waiting in their cars as they navigate the maddening one-ways and tangle of signs of vague indication. All the while, cyclists jive on by. Within the city centres, there are no-car zones and bike lanes, and motorists are polite to cyclists. These intriguing medieval cities are great places to explore by bike while bunches of local cyclists, from grandmother with grandchild in tow to the lycra-fied roadie, swirl around you.

Maps & Booklets
For getting out of the mazelike towns, the tourist office or your hotel will have free city maps.

For overall coverage, the Touring Club Italiano 1:200,000 *Lombardia* map (6.20) is best. The free *Regione Lombardia* 1:400,000 Lombardia map and *Lombardia – Tourist* map of rivers can also be used with the free provincial maps of Pavia, Piacenza, Cremona and Mantua, available at tourist offices.

The Mantua tourist office stocks an excellent booklet in English detailing cycling itineraries along the Po River, in the **Parco del Mincio** (☎ 03 763 62 657; Via Marangoni 36), and around the lakes. One route takes cyclists around Lago Superiore to the Santuario di Santa Maria delle Grazie. The Cremona APT has cycling guides (in Italian only) for the areas around Cremona, Casalmaggiore and Crema.

Information Sources
Check with the FIAB affiliate, **Amici della Bicicletta** (www.fiab-mantova.it) about local group rides in Mantua.

GETTING TO/FROM THE RIDE
Pavia (start)
TRAIN
Direct trains link Pavia train station with Milan (€2.95, 30 minutes, up to 8 daily), Genoa (€6, 1½ hours) and beyond.

BICYCLE
See the Navigli Milanesi ride (see p138) for the route to Milan. Otherwise, Pavia

LUNGO PO ARGINE – DAY 1

CUES		GPS COORDINATES
0.0	Pavia leaving tourist office and Piazza Petrarca	
		45°11'07"N 9°09'13"E
	(70mts) Viale Matteotti	
0.2	unsigned Corso Strada Nuova (one-way for cars, bikes permitted)	
0.9	unsigned Corso Girabaldi, to 'San Michelle'	
1.9	to 'Lodi'	
5.2	SS617 to 'Stradella'	
6.6	to 'Stradella'	
9.4	Ponte della Becca	
14.3	argine to San Cipriano Po'	
18.6	San Cipriano Po	45°06'25"N 9°16'56"E
	argine to Portalbera	
20.4	to Portalbero	
22.4	Portalbero	45°06'03"N 9°19'14"E
	to 'Arena Po'	
25.8	Arena Po	45°05'37"N 9°21'40"E
28.9	to 'Parpanese'	
32	at stop sign to 'Parpanese'	
32.5	Parpanese	45°05'26"N 9°25'30"E
38.1	gravel road 3.5km	
38.6	at T intersection	
42.1	unsigned road	
	Sarmato	45°03'35"N 9°29'29"E
42.6	to 'Piacenza'	
57.6	3rd Exit	
	Piacenza	45°03'15"N 9°40'38"E

CUES CONTINUED		GPS COORDINATES
58	to 'Milano' exit	
59.9	to 'Milano' exit	
62.1	hard turn onto unsigned road (after gas station, before sign to Casalpustelengo)	
63.3	to Caselle Landi	
67.2	to 'Caselle Landi'	
68.3	to 'Caselle Landi'	
72.4	Caselle Landi	45°06'08"N 9°47'27"E
74.6	to Meleti	
78.9	to Meleti	
80	to Meleti	
80.5	Meleti	45°07'09"N 9°50'13"E
	to 'Maccastorna'	
80.8	to 'Maccastorna'	
83.9	to Crotta D'A (not to 'Maccastorna')	
	{●● to 'Maccastorna' 2km }	
85.8	to Aqua Negra	
88.4	at T intersection on unsigned SS234	
	{■■ (90m) unsigned road to Spinadesco}	
92.7	to 'Cremona,' 'Centro'	
98.6	to 'Centro'	
99.1	at fork (not under arch)	
99.4	Corso Campi	
99.7	Corso Cavour	
99.8	Via Gramsci	
99.9	Giovani Baldesio	
	(60m) Piazza del Duomo	
100	Cremona Tourist Office	45°07'59"N 10°01'26"E

is 35km from Milan on the busy SS35 or SS412. Supplementary bike tickets are €3.50.

Mantua (finish)

TRAIN

The Mantua train station (Piazza Don Leoni) has direct trains to/from San Benedetto Po, Cremona, Milan and Verona. Trips to every major hub usually require at least one change of train. Supplementary bike tickets are €3.50.

BICYCLE

Mantua is the end of the Eastern Lakes ride, which can be ridden in reverse to Bergamo. A direct, albeit trafficky, route to Verona is approximately 40km north on SS62. Parma is about 60km to the southwest via SS420.

THE RIDE
Day 1: Pavia to Cremona
5½–10 hours, 100km

One important feature of the Po plain is that it's flat, very flat. In fact, the steepest roads on today's ride are mere ramps, linking 'low' roads through extensively cultivated fields to the elevated argine paths along which part of the route runs. It's easy touring made marvellous by the natural beauty and serenity of the surroundings.

Head east out of Pavia and then south across the Po-spanning, century-old, 1km-long **Ponte della Becca** (9.9km). At **Albaredo Arnaboldi**, turn left onto the first of many argine. This raised embankment goes all the way to **Arena Po** (25.8km) and then, after the road dips inland and over a highway, picks up again after **Parpanese** (32.5km). Unfortunately, after **Sarmato** (42.1km) and its vast fortifications, there is no choice but to fight traffic on the busy SS10 for 15km to **Piacenza** (57.6km).

Piacenza is a prosperous town often overlooked by tourists. Its central Piazza dei Cavalli is fabulous, dominated by **Il Gotico**, the 13th-century town hall. Nearby, the 12th-century duomo (cathedral) is a sober building at the end of Via XX Settembre, although Basilica di **Sant'Antonio** is even older (11th century).

LUNGO PO ARGINE

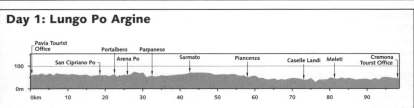

Day 1: Lungo Po Argine

Don't miss the **Palazzo Farnese** on Pi-azza Cittadella, home to three museums, including the Museo Civico. A 2km side trip to **Maccastorna** (83.9km) leads to a teeny-tiny, 14th-century walled town that's worth a visit.

Cycling again, head north out of Piacenza, back to the far side of the Po. Return to the argine for a meandering ride through rich agricultural country between the Po and Adda Rivers.

ALTERNATIVE ROUTE: ACQUANEGRA CREMONESE TO CREMONA
1–2 hours, at 88.4km, 17.7km

Yes, there is a way to enter Cremona without getting on the busy SS234 for 11.6km. Will you get lost in the maze of unmarked back roads? Most likely, but it could beat SS234. It might be worth a shot if you hate traffic, are prepared for gravel roads, have a good chunk of time and carrying plenty of water. At least you know that you won't cross the

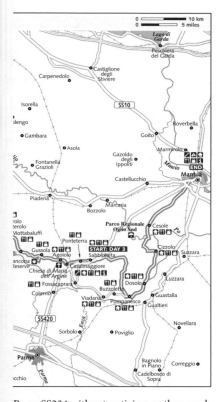

LUNGO PO ARGINE – DAY 2

CUES		GPS COORDINATES
Start	Cremona tourist office	45°07'59"N 10°01'26"E
0km	W on Via Baldesio	
0.7	↰⊙ via del Giordano, 4th exit	
0.9	↱ via del Sale	
1.6	via del Sale, not via Portinari del Po	
2	↰ to "Ciclabile Golena del Po", bikepath	
6.1	↑ not ↱ to "Ciclabile Golena del Po", through gates	
10.7	↑ Follow "Po" bike path sign	
12.2	↑ to "Ciclabile Golena del Po"	
13.5	↗ follow "Po" bike path sign	
14.5	↑ follow "Po" bike path sign	
	★ Bodrio delle Gerre natural monument	
15.2	↑ follow "Po" bike path sign	
16.7	↱ to "Golena del Po"	
17.3	↰ to "Ciclabile Golena del Po"	
18.8	↱ unsigned road, not "to Cremona"	
21.8	↱ to "via Po"	
22.1	↰ not to "via Po"	
23	↱ to "Ciclabile Golena del Po"	
23.4	↱ to "Ciclabile Golena del Po"	
25.4	↱ via Argine Capoluogo, to "Trattoria del Cacciatore"	
25.7	↖ via A. Faverzani	
26.4	San Daniele Po, via G. Marconi 45°03'53"N 10°10'49"E	
30.2	↱ Via Argina Cremona "to Solarolo M"	
38.4	↗ to "Ciclabile Golena Po"	
39.7	↑ not "to Ciclabile Golena Po"	
49.7	★ Santuario della Madonna dell'Argine	
50.2	↑ on levee, pass gate	
50.7	↑ bike lane on levee	
50.9	↑ into town	
51	↰ hard turn on via del Lino,	
51.	↱ (50m) via Angelo Brofferio	
	↱ (30m) P.zza Garibaldi, Casalmaggiore 44°59'10"N 10°24'54"E	
51.2	↰ P.zza Garibaldi/via Cavour	
55.4	↰ via C. Monteverdi, Ponteterra	
57.6	↑⊟ via Giulia Gonzaga	
57.9	Sabbioneta Tourist Office	44°59'55"N 10°29'22"E

Po or SS234 without noticing, as they sandwich the area you'll be navigating.

You take a left into **Spindesco**, continue east (right) on Via Marconi and hook onto Via Acquaviva, which dumps you across SS234 towards Pincenengo, after which you take a right on Via Sesto that takes you into the city. Got it? Good luck.

Day 2: Cremona to Sabbioneta
3–6 hours, 57.9km

Like yesterday, there is little today to challenge the thighs. In fact, the route is even easier since there is no stretch on a main road and the distance is less, leaving time for exploration in Cremona. This will be some relaxed riding.

From central Cremona, head back to the banks of the Po to join a vast network of bike paths along *argines* through picturesque countryside. Though it's oh-

so-close, you'll rarely see the river itself. These new bike paths are fantastic and some of the levee roads are open to bikes but closed to most motor traffic. Mostly the route follows the **Ciclabile Golena del Po** – otherwise, you'll be meandering along country roads.

On land many *cascine* (large farms) have settled between colourful fields of crops and wildflowers, *bodri* (ponds) and canals, and protected nature reserves.

LUNGO PO ARGINE – DAY 3

CUES		GPS COORDINATES
start		Sabbioneta Tourist Office(Piazza delle Armi 44°59'55'N 10°29'22''E
0km		N on via Giulia Gonzaga
0.1	⌐	via Vespasiano Gonzaga
0.3	⌐	via Colonna
	↰	(50 m) via Porta Imperiale
0.5	↑	through city gate
	⊟	(50m) cross highway
2.8	⌐	unsigned road at large warehouse on ⌐, T-intersection
	↰	(50m) via Viazzola, into town
3.1	⌐	via Motta
8.3	↰	unsigned, not to "Valle"
8.9	↑	via Ottoponti Bragagnina/via Ottoponti Salina
13.2	⌐	to "Viadana"
13.8		Salina
	⌐	to "Viadana," "Pomponesco" 44°57'06'N 10°34'28''E
14.2	↘	not on via Volta, on via Maranghino Orlandelli
15	↰	via San Giulio/via Sant'Antonio
16.3	↑	cross SP57
16.7	↗	to "Garzaia di Pomponesco"
17.1	↰	to "Garzaia di Pomponesco" on levee road, bike path
17.8	★	Pomponesco 44°55'42'N 10°35'32''E
24	★	Dosolo 44°57'14'N 10°38'32''E
29.5	↰	descend from levee, before gravel road
29.7		Cavallaro 44°59'53'N 10°39'25''E
29.9	↑	on via Montesauro
31.1	↰	via C. Poma

CUES CONTINUED		GPS COORDINATES
31.8	↰	Via Argine Po
32.9	⌐	unsigned road, SP57
34.2	⌐	`to Cesole'
37	★	Oglio River pontoon bridge
37.3		on levee road to "Agriturismo La Motta", not to "Cesole"
41.7	↰⚠	on gravel road for 250 m, unsigned
41.9	↑	via Chiarella, cross SP57
43	↘	to "Buscoldo"
47.5		Buscoldo (place to sleep—B&B Ninna Nanna) 45°05'32'N 10°41'55''E
	⌐	via Marconi
48	↰	strada argine Fossaviva
48.1	⌐	(50 m) strada S. Salmaso
49.1	⌐	Strada Zaitina, not on main road
50.3	↰	unsigned road
53.2	↑	to "S. Silvestro", via Punte
54.7	⌐	via Pisacane
55.1	↑⊙	unsigned bike path (near cemetery)
56.5	↰⊙	strada Spolverina
56.8	↑⊟	cycle underpass on left
56.9	⌐	unmarked bike path (before gas station).
57.2	↰	along bike path on Strada Lago Paiolo
57.9	↰	on via Albertoni (bikepath)
58.1	⌐	via Avis/viale Oslavia/Viale Gorizia
58.8	↘⊙	2nd exit "to centro" via Bugoni/Via Chiasso
59.8	↑	via Roma
60.2		Piazza Mantegna, Mantua Tourist Office 45°09'37'N 10°47'52''E

Follow the cues steadfastly while using a detailed map between **Stagno Lombardo** (15.3km) and **Mottabaluffi** (32.8km). Many of the turns are unsigned. After Mottabaluffi, the route is clearer. You'll pass by more small agricultural towns, many with fine 18th-century villas and churches, and the riverbank nature setting is more splendid. You might want to check out the baroque **Chiesa di Maria dell'Argine** on the right, 1km before Casalmaggiore.

The last few kilometres pass quickly once **Casalmaggiore**'s unmistakable skyline comes into view. There you'll leave the levees for the final sweet leg east into Sabbioneta.

Day 3: Sabbioneta to Mantua
3½–6 hours, 60.2km

Like the two previous days' routes, this ride is flatter than flat, and for 24.6km it hugs the banks of the Po River to its confluence with the **Oglio River**. From there, Mantua is only 18.5km away.

Pay attention between 2.1km and 17.1km because the route follows several unsigned roads until it meets the levee roads at **Pomponesco** (17.8km), which boasts a 16th-century porticoed square. When the route hits the river, it meanders riverside past poplar plantations grown in its flood plain.

Past **Cavallaro** (29.7km), after rejoining car traffic, the route swings through a lovely poplar grove. At **Torre d'Oglio** (37km) on the mouth of the Oglio River, it crosses a curious **pontoon bridge**. You enter Mantua along bike paths and lanes. At 56.8km, if you decide to take the bike underpass, follow that path across the street at the gas station and rejoin the bike path at 56.9km.

MOUNTAIN BIKE RIDES

MARMOLI
Pensione Ceaglio (☎ 01 719 98 117; Frazione Vernetti 5; per person €34–49, half-pension €44–59) is one of the only

options in this one-horse town. It's specifically geared to Northern European mountain bike tourism (see p97).

TOWNS & FACILITIES

ACQUI TERME
☎ 01 / pop 19,000

This town's strategic position at a sulphurous thermal water source on a trade route (later the Roman Via Emiliana) between the Po plain and the Mediterranean brought it attention long before Romans bathed. Acqui Terme was, however, a famous spa town during Roman times, and it was eventually controlled by the Monferrato family after the tumultuous medieval period. In 1708 the city went to the House of Savoy and then followed the standard bumpy road to Italian unification. Acqui is deep in Alto Monferrato, the higher elevations of a hilly zone of woods alternating with fields of the Moscato d'Asti white grape.

Information
The **IAT office** (☎ 01 443 22 142, www .acquiterme.it; Piazza Levi 12) can help with accommodation and provide details for the thermal centres.

There are a few banks near the IAT office, and more in Corsos Vigan and Dante.

Supplies & Equipment
La Bicicletteria di Pernigotti Fabio (☎ 01 443 20 826; Via Nizza 36) is a bicycle shop in town.

Sleeping & Eating
Relais dell'Osso (☎ 01 445 68 77; www.osso .it, in Italian; Via dei Dottore 5; s/d €42/73) is a charming place right in the heart of the tranquil old town. Rooms are sunny and bright; breakfast is an additional €5.

Grand Hotel Nuove Terme (☎ 01 445 85 55; www.grandhotelnuoveterme.it; Piazza Italia 1; s/d €100/130) dominates Piazza Italia. This glamorous Art Nouveau hotel has been in business for more than a century offering stylish and comfortable rooms.

Almost all hotels have good attached restaurants. Elsewhere in town, for cheap eats head to the pizzerias in Piazza Addolorata and Via Mazzini. **Antica Hosteria da Bigāt** (☎ 01 443 24 283; Via Mazzini 30/32; 1st/2nd courses from €6/5.50; Thu–Tue), with its wooden beams and brick walls, is a welcoming option. This trattoria in the historic centre is known for its *farinata* (a type of thin focaccia).

ALBA
☎ 01 / pop 29,900

Solid red-brick towers rise above the heart of Alba, a wine town with good evidence of its medieval past. Alba's modern claims to fame, in addition to wine, include its late-autumn white truffle crop and festival, and a *palio* (race) on donkeys. Towards the end of WWII, the town's citizens proclaimed Alba an independent republic for 23 days after partisans liberated it from the Germans.

Information
The main **IAT** (☎ 01 733 58 33; www .langheroero.it; Piazza Medford 3) is in the northwest of the city in Palazzo delle Mostre. There is another **office** (☎ 01 733 62 562; Via Vittorio Emanuele 19).

A cluster of banks are on Piazza Savona.

Supplies & Equipment
Cicli Gagliardini (☎ /fax 01 734 40 726; Via Ospedale 7 just off Piazza Garibaldi), is an excellent bike shop.

Bikes are available for hire at **Motocicli DeStefanis** (☎ 01 734 40 462; Via S Margherita 2; per day €13).

Sleeping & Eating
You shouldn't have any problems finding a room unless you're coming in October, when an advance booking is essential. A popular alternative to staying in town is to lodge in one of the many *agriturismi* in the surrounding countryside. The tourist office stocks extensive lists of local *agriturismi* as well as B&B's.

Albergo San Lorenzo (☎ 01 733 62 406; fax 01 733 66 995; Piazza Rossetti 6; s €60–70, d €80–90) is a superb all-around choice. It may be the poshest two-star in Piedmont. The affiliated gourmet café below provides your (included) breakfast that is very tasty and hearty with dairy-free, gluten-free and vegetarian choices.

Albergo Leon d'Oro (☎/fax 01 734 41 901; Piazza Marconi 2; s €28–42, d €45–60) has white wooden shutters that hide a flower-filled terrace and spotlessly clean, if old-fashioned, rooms.

Vincafé (☎ 01 733 64 603; Via Vittorio Emanuele II 12; cheese and meat platters €8–16) is a clever mix of old and new. This contemporary wine bar, popular with locals and tourists, serves up a splendid feast of platters in a vaulted stone cellar or al fresco in the pedestrian quarter. Diners can choose from the 350-label wine list.

L'Osteria del Teatro (☎ 01 733 64 603; Via Generale Govone 7; mains about €12), in the heart of the *centro storico*, is a classical Piedmontese restaurant. The menu is traditional and the wine list satisfying.

ALBENGA
☎ 01 / pop 23,000
Historically, Albenga is one of the most important cities of coastal Liguria – its physical history – remnants from Roman, Byzantine, medieval, Renaissance and Baroque times – is, in many ways, the story of Liguria. The silting up of the Cento River has today left a fertile cultivated plain and an extensive beach. Now, it's a relatively touristed Italian Riviera town with an intact medieval centre.

Information
The **IAT office** (☎ 01 825 58 444; www .inforiviera.it; Viale Martiri della Libertà 1) is just off Piazza del Popolo.

Many banks are on Piazza del Popolo and adjacent Piazza Petrarca.

Supplies & Equipment
The best bike shop is **Bike Race** (☎ 01 825 07 72; Via Genova 71).

Sleeping & Eating
There are more than 15 camping grounds spread along the seashore.

Piccolo Paradiso (☎ 01 825 17 34; www .piccoloparadiso.com; Via Che Guevara 19; per person/site €7–9/€15–20) is 1.5km away from Piazza di Popolo near the beach.

Albenga's **Hotel Torino** (☎/fax 01 825 08 44; Viale Italia 25, s €30–40, d €50–70, with bathroom s €40–60, d €60–80) is on

the main street to the beaches. Just west of the train station, try

Hotel Concordia (☎ 01 825 0 263; Viale Patrioti 46; s €40–€50, d €50–€80). Charming **Hotel Ancora d'Oro** (☎ 01 825 18 56; Via Sauro 90; s/d €35/55) is right on the water.

Most hotels have restaurants and cafés. **Da Puppo** (☎ 01 825 18 53; www .dapuppo.it Via Torlaro 20; closed Mon) has Albenga's best pizzas and *farinata* (flat bread). Elsewhere in the old town, **La Linguaccia** (☎ 01 825 08 11; Via Cavour 40) is a hip place to eat traditional food. **La Pazzazucca** (☎ 01 825 08 00; Via Torlaro 34) caters to vegetarians and organic food aficionados. For a splurge, reserve ahead at **Antica Osteria dei Leoni** (☎ 01 825 19 37; Via Lengueglia 49; meal €40–50).

ASTI
☎ 01 / pop 72,000
Settled long before it was made a Roman colony in 89 BC, Asti has a rocky history. An independent city-state in the 13th and 14th centuries, it was subsequently passed around among Spain, Austria, Napoleon's France and finally the Savoys, prior to Italy's unification. Today, Asti attracts a food-and wine-focused kind of tourist, and this ancient city's largely pedestrianised centre makes it a fine place to kick around.

Information
The **Asti information office** (☎ 01 415 30 357; www.terredasti.it; Piazza Alfieri 34) is under the southern arches. Banks can also be found on this piazza.

Supplies & Equipment
Asti's bike gurus work at **Piemontesina** (☎ 01 412 18 809; Corso Torino 9), east of the centre.

Sleeping & Eating
Booking ahead is always a good idea in Asti; around Palio time (September) it's essential.

Campeggio Umberto Cagni (☎ 01 412 71 238; Via Valmanera 152; per person/site €6.50/8) is the nearest camp-site, off Corso Volta.

Hotel Cavour (☎/fax 01 415 30 222; Piazza G Maconi; s €39–44, d €58–64), opposite the train station, is family-run, welcoming and comfortable.

Hotel Reale (☎ 01 415 30 240; fax 01 413 43 57; www.hotel-reale.com; Piazza Alfieri 6; s €75–85, d €110–140) languishes in a majestic 18th-century mansion on Asti's central square. The hallmark is Old World style with 21st-century comfort.

Asti is a culinary centre of more than 60 restaurants that suit most budgets. Explore the blocks under the arcades around Piazza Alfieri and the streets around Piazzas San Secondo, Statuto and Marconi, as well as the connecting Via Cavour. Many *supermercati* (supermarkets) and *alimentari* (delis) are located here too.

Enoteca Audisio (☎ 01 414 36 326; Via Cavour 83) is a simple brick and wooden wine-bar-cum-café that is a laid-back place to sip and taste locally produced wines. **Da Aldo di Castiglione** (☎ 01 413 54 905; Via Giovanni Gioberti 8; mains around €13) serves local meat dishes that are succulent and tasty.

CREMONA
☎ 01 / pop 70,000

Home of the violin, Cremona jealously maintains its centuries-old status as premier exponent of the delicate art of making stringed instruments. All of the great violin-making dynasties started here – **Amati, Guarneri** and **Stradivari**. An independent city-state until the 14th century, Cremona today boasts a compact but impressive medieval city centre. It's a first-class example of a 12th- to 13th-century urban centre surrounded on all sides by significant structures: the main cathedral; its adjoining 111m **Torrazzo** (belfry), touted as Italy's tallest; the Bertazzola, a Renaissance loggia; the octagonal baptistry; Palazzo Comunale or town hall; and a small porticoed Loggia dei Militi. Elsewhere throughout the city are churches and palaces from many eras.

Information

The **APT office** (☎ 03 722 32 33; www .aptcremona.it; Piazza del Comune 5) is opposite the cathedral.

Banks are also located here and on Corso Vittorio Emanuele II and Corso Palestro, both off Piazza Stradivari.

Supplies & Equipment

A good bike shop is **Cicli Priori** (☎ 03 722 27 00; www.clipriori.it; Via Milano 2).

Sleeping & Eating

Accommodation in central Cremona is surprisingly limited (but well-priced), so think about booking ahead if you plan to stop here.

Just southwest of the city centre along the Po is **Camping Parco Al Po** (☎ 03 722 12 68; www.campingcremonapo.it; Lungo Po Europa 12a; tent sites from €15).

Albergo Duomo (☎ 03 723 52 42; fax 037 245 83 92; Via Gonfalonieri 13; s/d €45/65) is just a few steps from Cremona's cathedral and ablaze with wrought-iron flower boxes in spring, Albergo Duomo also runs its own rather eccentric **pizzeria** (mains €7–18).

Hotel Astoria (☎ 03 724 61 616; www. astoriahotel-cremona.it; Via Bordigallo 19; s €45–50, d €70–80) is a charming spot, with French-washed corridors and immaculate rooms.

Dellearti Design Hotel (☎ 03 722 31 31; www.dellearti.com; Via Bonomelli 8; s €70–138, d €99–186) is a hi-tech vision of glass, concrete and steel equipped with a Turkish bath, a gym and suitably chic rooms. You should fit in perfectly.

Open-air market stalls on Piazza della Pace sell fresh fruit and vegetables every morning.

On summer nights the piazza spills over with alfresco bars and live music. **La Sosta** (☎ 03 724 56 656; Via Sicardo 9; mains €10–15) is surrounded by violin makers' workshops. It's a beautiful place to feast on regional delicacies such as *gnocchi vecchia Cremona* (old-fashioned Cremona gnocchi; filled with Lombard cheese), the house speciality. **Il 21 w.a.y.** (☎ 03 723 49 88; Piazza Stradivari 20–21; mains €9–16), Cremona's hippest new hangout, is a restaurant/wine bar whose pared-down menu features generous salads.

CUNEO
☎ 01 / pop 50,000

The largest city in the province of the same name, Cuneo is the self-proclaimed 'green capital' of Piedmont (Piemonte). The compact old town lies in the northern *cuneo* (wedge), perched atop an impressive butte overlooking the Stura di Demonte and Gesso rivers, and the western edge of the Po plain. Cuneo's foundations were laid in the 12th century. Known as the 'city of the seven sieges', Cuneo has a history replete with conflict from the medieval period to the modern era. Visiting low-key Cuneo is a treat. The grand-scale architecture and the friendly folks make this a great gateway city to the mountains.

Information

The **IAT office** (☎ 01 716 93 258; www .cuneoholiday.com; Via Roma 28) is in the old town.

Banks line Corso Nizza, the main street south of Piazza Galimberti.

Cuneo Bike Hotels (www.cuneobike hotels.it) is an interesting organisation whose free booklets (available in tourist offices) include information about cycling in the area, plus maps and a list of bike-friendly hotels in the region. They also distribute free packets describing both road and mountain biking itineraries (maps included).

Supplies & Equipment

The well established bike shop here is **Ciclo Pepino e Chiapale** (☎ 01 716 90 985; Corso Kennedy 13).

Sleeping & Eating

About 1km south of the centre is **Campeggio Bisalta** (☎ 01 714 91 334; www.cuneo camp.it; Fraz Castagnaretta, Via S. Maurizio 33; per person/site €5.50–6.50/€5.50–6.50).

Ostello OASI (☎ 01 716 73 90, after hours ☎ 33 820 97 893; Via Mons. Peano 8; s without bathroom €20) is the nearest thing Cuneo has to a youth hostel. This religious institute situated within a stone's throw of the *centro storico* (historic centre) has 11 simple, clean rooms.

A true accommodation gem is **B&B Angeli** (☎ 01 746 30 344; Viale degli Angeli 6; s/d €35/56); it's excellent value, especially taking into account the wonderfully furnished, high-ceilinged rooms that take you back in time, and the scrumptious breakfasts (one of the best we had) for hungry cyclists – they even take requests.

Hotel Royal Superga (☎ 01 716 93 223; Via Pascal 3; s €52–57, d €68–82) is just off Piazza Galimberti. This 19th-century hotel is a welcoming place with charming and spacious three-star rooms.

Supermarkets can be found near Piazza Galimberti (Via Ponza di San Martino) and

an easy walk from the train station (cnr Corso IV Novembre & Via Felice Cavallotti).

Pizzeria & Ristorante Piedgrotta (☎ 01 716 02 093; Corso Giovanni XXIII 28) is a locals' haven a handful of blocks away from the high profile central piazza. You will eat and drink well here. **Osteria della Chiocciola** (☎ 01 716 62 77; Via Fossano; mains €12) is half-enoteca, half-restaurant and a wine lovers' kind of place. Browse the comprehensive wine collection downstairs before heading upstairs to tuck into the regional cuisine.

LA SPEZIA
☎ 01 / pop 90,000

La Spezia's facade is an uninspiring hodge-podge of 19th- and 20th-century architecture and industrial ports. But there is something appealing about this bypassed naval centre – perhaps it's the fact that the masses have skipped it. It's also a perfect base from which to launch walks and pedals into the thrilling surrounding countryside.

Information

The main **APT/IAT** (☎ 01 872 54 311; www.aptcinqueterre.sp.it; Viale Mazzini 45) is near the waterfront, and there's also a branch in the train station. The **Cinque Terre Park Office** (☎ 01 877 43 500) is in the train station as well; the staff there can give you all the info you need about the park.

Numerous banks have branches on Via Chiodo.

Supplies & Equipment

One of the best bike shops in town is **Bellotto** (☎ 01 872 03 54; Viale Italia 109), 500m east of the tourist office.

Sleeping & Eating

There are no camping grounds at La Spezia. There's camping in neighbouring Arcola and Lerici; check out www.camping.it for listings. Also ask at IAT offices about agriturismo and B&B options.

One of the nearest hostels is **Ostello Cinque Terre** (☎ 01 879 20 215; www. hostel5terre.com; Via Riccobaldi 21; dm/d €20–23/€55–65), in Manarola.

There are a number of cheap hotels around the train station, but many tend to be scruffy.

Albergo Teatro (☎ 01 877 31 374; www.albergoteatro.it; Via Carpenino 31; s €25–30, d €38–50, d with bathroom €45–65) is adjacent to the theatre. It's a spartan but perfectly adequate place in a handy location in the historic centre, a couple of blocks' stroll from the port.

Hotel Firenze e Continentale (☎ 01 877 13 200; www.hotelfirenzecontinentale. it; Via Paleocapa 7; s €50–94, d €68–134) retains some of its early-1900s atmosphere and is one of the best options near the train station.

For homemade meal makings, shop at the daily market on Piazza Cavour. There are a number of excellent bakeries on Via Prione.

The waterfront has plenty of relaxed places to wine and dine, including **Vicolo Intherno** (☎ 01 872 39 98; Via della Canonica 22; mains around €10). Take a seat around chunky wooden tables beneath beamed ceilings at this Slow Food–affiliated restaurant and wash down the *torte di verdure* (Ligurian vegetable pie) or stockfish (cured without salt) with local vintages. **Nettare e Ambrosia** (☎ 01 877 37 252; Via Fazio 85 and 86; mains €10–15) is simple and authentic, yet it more than lives up to its goddess-pleasing name. 'Nectar & Ambrosia' is *the* place to sample great wines with seafood-based specialities such as *zuppa di calamari* (calamari soup).

MANTUA
☎ 03 / pop 47,000

On the shores of lakes Superiore, Mezzo and Inferiore (a widening of the Mincio River) is serene and beautiful Mantua (Mantova), a town settled by the Etruscans in the 10th century BC. Mantua's greatest years (known as 'La Gloriosa') came under the House of Gonzaga during the Renaissance and ended with the arrival of the Austrians in 1708. Mantua joined the rest of Italy in 1866. The old city is on a small peninsula at the heart of which is a string of five piazzas capped at the northern end by the Palazzo Ducale complex. The centre of the old city is medieval **Piazza Sordello**, site of the duomo and the incomparable **Palazzo Ducale**, also known as the Reggia dei Gonzaga. Behind the palazzo's facade is a city within the city, an extensive complex of open piazzas and structures.

Information
The **APT office** (☎ 03 764 32 432; www .turismo.mantova.it; Piazza Mantegna 6) is on the corner touching the market-laden Piazza delle Erbe.

A good cluster of banks can be found in Via Umberto I.

Supplies & Equipment
Check out **Mantua Bike di Giovanni** (☎ 03 492 20 909; Viale Piave 22/b) for parts and repairs. Renting city bikes is possible from **La Rigola** (☎ 03 763 66 677; Via Trieste; per day from €8).

Sleeping & Eating
Hotel ABC (☎ 03 763 23 347; www .hotelabcmantova.it; Piazza Don Leoni 25; s/d €33/44, s with bathroom €66–88, d with bathroom €77–121) is right opposite the train station; it's a reasonable and very convenient option with clean, comfortable rooms.

Libenter B&B (☎ 03 762 22 414; www. libenter.org; Via Pomponazzo 15; apt incl breakfast €70–120) has two one-room apartments and a two-room apartment, offering independence in a central location. Breakfast is served at **Libenter Moderna Osteria**.

Hotel Broletto (☎ 03 762 2 3678; www. hotelbroletto.com; Via dell'Accademia 1; s/ d €70/120), just off Piazza Broletto, is less than a five-minute stroll to the lake. You won't find a friendlier family than the one who runs this place. Rooms are somewhat old-fashioned, but with contemporary comforts.

Open-air cafés abound on Piazzas Sordello, Broletto and Erbe. **Fragoletta Antica** (☎ 03 763 23 300; Piazza Arche 5; mains €7–10) is a rustic eatery just back from the waterfront serving tasty dishes, such as gnocchi with ricotta, burnt butter and parmesan, in a cosy dining room. **Hosteria dei Canossa** (☎ 03 762 21 750; Vicolo Albergo 3; mains €8–13.50) is a local gem dishing up regional risotto, pasta and meat dishes teamed with hard-to-find Lombard wines.

MARMORA–VERNETTI
☎ 01 / pop 100

Marmora–Vernetti is a tiny, remote and beautiful mountain hamlet overlooking the confluence of two small rivers and their valleys. Facing Marmora, across a deep, open dip and towered over by the Monte

Cassorso massif, is the slightly larger village of Canosio.

Information

For local information, check the bulletin board outside Pensione Ceaglio.

Sleeping & Eating

Lucky for you, **Pensione Ceaglio** (☎ 01 719 98 117; Frazione Vernetti 5; per person €34–49, half-pension €44–59) is one of the two options in this one-horse town. It's specifically geared to Northern European mountain bike tourism (p97) and has your basic tools and supplies on hand. The rooms are comfortable, and dinners are copious and excellent.

The other option is **La Marmu** (☎ 01 079 98 307; Via Roma 18; s/d €25/50), which has some acceptable rooms for rent and is owned by the same family that runs the adjacent hangout bar, **Osteria delle Croce Bianca**, where you can get a simple meal.

PAVIA

☎ 03 / pop 71,200

Originally Roman Ticinum, Pavia is on the Ticino River just north of its confluence with the Po. Now just a satellite of Milan, Pavia was once its rival as the capital of the Lombard kings until the 11th century. During the Renaissance, however, the city became a pawn of power politics; it was occupied by Spain in the 16th century, then Austria in the 18th century, and finally France from 1796 to 1859. Today it's a thriving industrial, agricultural and educational centre. The sprawl and traffic of Pavia surround a cobbled, old-city nucleus, which is quite pleasant. Plus, many people, from students to older folks, buzz about on *biciclettes*.

Information

Pavia's **IAT/APT** (☎ 03 822 21 56; www .provincia.pv.it/provinciapv/brick/turismo; Piazza Petrarca) is right by the daily open-air market. Banks are on Corso Cavour between the station and Piazza della Vittoria.

Supplies & Equipment

A good bike shop, one of several in town, is **Cicli Zamai** (☎ 03 825 78 242; Viale Tasso Torquato 57).

Sleeping & Eating

Just west of town, **Campeggio Ticino** (☎ 03 825 27 094; www.campingticino.it; Via Mascherpa 10; per person/site €5.70– 6.40/€4–4.50) can be rather noisy.

Hotel Rosengarten (☎ 03 825 26 312; www.rosengarten.pv.it; Via Cesare Lombroso 21/23; s/d €70/100) has a bike storage space equipped with a pump. Facilities are nice and the staff helpful.

Hotel Excelsior (☎ 03 822 85 96; www. excelsiorpavia.com; Piazzale Stazione 25; s/d €58/84) is first-rate for the value-for-money ratio. The location, outside the station's main exit (the higher of the two staircases when you get off the train), is handy if you're catching an early train. Breakfast costs an extra €6.

Self-caterers have to check out the fantastic daily open-air market in Piazza Petrarca by the tourist office for fresh produce, meat, cheese, bakery items etc.

Broadway Café (☎ 03 822 47 33; Via XX Settembre 35; dishes €5.50–6) is a funky spot that specialises in bruschetta served on wooden plates. It also has salads and daily special choices for a starter (€5.80) and a main (€6.50). **Bardelli Ristorante** (☎ 03 822 74 41; Viale Lungo Ticino Visconti 2; mains €14–18) is Pavia's grandest restaurant, set in a beautiful old house down by the riverside. Regional wines by the bottle, such as a Di Frara, start around €18.

PIEVE DI TECO

☎ 01 / pop 1340

This quiet mountain town doesn't look important, but since it's at a key economic and geographical crossroads in the Valle Arroscia, Pieve di Teco has always controlled the flow of people and produce between the Mediterranean and the mountains. Pieve di Teco continues to be the leading *comune* (municipality) in the valley and retains its Old World charm, despite the destruction of its medieval walls and gates.

Information

The **information office** (☎ 01 833 64 53; www.prolocopievediteco.it; Via S Giovanni 1) is next to the post office.

Banks are clustered towards the southern end of Via Eula.

Sleeping & Eating

At the north end of town is the friendly **Albergo Dell'Angelo** (☎ 01 833 62 40; Piazza Carenzi 11; s/d €30/50, s/d with bathroom €40/65), which is actually going to be your only hotel choice in town, so you should check availability before you arrive. Otherwise, **Da Guisteppi** (☎ 01 833 66 565; Via Umberto I 75) and **Palazzo Manfredi** (☎ 33 877 67 824; Via Umberto 21; s/d without bathroom €35/50) advertise as B&Bs with one and three rooms respectively.

Markets and speciality food shops are in Corso Ponzoni. On Piazza Cavour, bars and a quick-serve pizza place have cheap eats for the hasty. Other places for meals are **Pizzeria 'Da Rita'** (closed Thu) on Corso Ponzoni and Pizzeria dal Maniscalco (Via Roberto Manfredi).

SABBIONETA

☎ 03 / pop 4300

Coming up on Sabbioneta, the 16th-century 'little Athens' of the Gonzaga clan, you'll see bizarre, star-shaped walls accessed by a narrow driveway. Inside lies the surreal settlement of Sabbioneta. The town was created in the 16th century by Vespasiano Gonzaga Colonna in an attempt to build a Utopian city. Though it's a shadow of what it used to be, there's still a strong local community, thanks in part to its size and Roman layout on the surrounding plains.

Information

Sabbioneta tourist office (☎ 03 755 20 39; www.sabbioneta.org; Piazza d'Armi).

Sleeping & Eating

There are a handful of options in this small town. Check out the tourist office or their websites for detailed information. You can try **Albergo Al Duca** (☎ 03 752 20 021; www.italiaabc.it/az/alduca; Via della Stamperia), which also has a restaurant, or **Albergo Guila Gonzaga** (☎ 03 755 28 169; Via Vespasiano Gonzaga).

A handful of simple café/restaurants are scattered along Sabbioneta's streets.

SESTRI LEVANTE

☎ 01 / pop 19,100

Sestri Levante shares the shores of the Gulf of Tigullio with famous neighbours **Chiavari**, **Rapallo** and **Portofino**. The bay's beauty, climate and bounty have held attention of the nobility for centuries and today draw more than one million visitors a year. Rich in artistic and religious significance, Sestri Levante's past is particularly well evoked by the yesteryear Genovese gentry's grandiose villas, now also symbolic of the region's present-day splendour. For a change of pace, this town is a good base for excellent one-day hikes in **Parco Nazionale delle Cinque Terre** and along the promontory at Portofino.

Information

The **IAT office** (☎ 01 854 57 011; www .sestri-levante.net; Piazza San Antonio 10) is closed Sundays. Banks are on the central roundabout.

Sleeping & Eating

Sestri Levante has more than 30 hotels.

Camping Fondeghino (☎ 01 854 09 209; Loc. Villa La Rocca 59; tent sites €20–30) is not the closest camping ground, but in contrast to those nearer, it's clean and peaceful.

Albergo La Neigra (☎ 01 854 17 56; Viale Roma 49; s/d without bathroom €35/50) is near the train station and has a good-value restaurant but no private toilets. In the centre, **Villa Jolanda** (☎ /fax 01 854 13 54; www.villaiolanda.com; Via Pozzetto 15; s €35–55, d €60–85) is right on the peninsula.

Grand Hotel dei Castelli (☎ 01 854 85 780; www.hoteldeicastelli.com; Via Penisola 26; s €110–130, d €205–265) represents the height of luxury.

A wide variety of food options is clustered on the isthmus on Via Rimembranza and the main alleyway (Via XXV Aprile). Try the *stoccafisso* (salted cod in a crispy batter or tasty sauce) and other sea fare at **La Cantina del Polpo** (☎ 01 854 85 296; www .cantinadelpolpo.it; Piazza Cavour 2). For dessert, slurp a glass of the Cinque Terre's unique dessert wine, Sciacchetrà.

VENTIMIGLIA

☎ 01 / pop 24,700

The last Italian city before the French border, Ventimiglia was founded in the 2nd century. It has three distinct parts: the hilltop medieval town, the commercial centre and a new apartment-building spread. People pressing towards more noteworthy beaches and towns usually skip Ventimiglia; for this reason alone, it should be given its due.

Information
The **IAT office** (☎/fax 01 843 51 183; www.turismoinliguria.it; Via Cavour 61) is on the main drag. Most banks are in Via Roma and Corso Repubblica.

Supplies & Equipment
A good bike shop, **Cicli Action** (☎01 842 32 007; www.cicliaction.it; Corso Genova 18a), is 500m east of the central traffic light.

Sleeping & Eating
Along the Fiume Roia just north of downtown is **Camping Roma** (☎01 842 39 007; www.campingroma.it; Via Freccero 121; per person €7–10, site €8–12).

A 10-minute stroll along the seafront from Ventimiglia's town centre, the family-run **Hotel Seagull** (☎01 843 51 726; www.seagullhotel.it; Passeggiata Marconi 24; s/d €60/75) has simple but appealing sky-blue-and-white rooms, a fragrant garden and a breezy terrace.

Pretty near to the train station, you'll find **Hotel Calypso** (☎01 843 51 588; www.calypsohotel.it; Via Matteotti 8; s €50–64, d €64–82).

For self-caterers, a **supermercato** (cnr Via Roma & Via Ruffini), the central covered market (Corso Repubblica) and other speciality stores adorn the centre. The Friday market extravaganza runs along the Roia.

Otherwise, Ventimiglia is awash in passable places to eat. Cheap sandwich places line Via Stazione and spill over into Via Hanbury. Choose among the seafood menus posted along the seaside Passeggiate Oberdan, Cavallotti and Marconi. Another concentration of trattorias includes the western stretch of Via Roma and parallel Via Aprosio.

ITALIAN ALPS & LAKES DISTRICT

This chapter is for the 'wobbly', beginning cyclist who just likes to pedal around in the sun and smell the flowers. They will go to the bike paths of Milan and the Lakes District. This chapter is also for the 'pass-happy masher' who won't be satiated until they've wrung the very last ounce of energy from the quivering fibres of their muscles. They will head to the Alta Rezia and Montagne Doc. There's also a bit for the layperson who likes to dabble in the happy medium. For them, the Valle d' Aosta will showcase high-class mountain scenery that is scandalously enjoyed with only a moderate level of challenge. Also, sections of the Lakes District will have their serene bikeways tempered with some up-and-overs.

The common thread: all these diverse routes are fantastically cycle-worthy, and furthermore, you will have to try very hard to find a bad meal, because the gastronomic standards of this region rival the heights of Monte Blanc.

THE ALPS

The alpine spine stretched across southern-central Europe always draws the eye. Because these mountains seem impassable, people have tried to conquer them. Similarly, cyclists look to the mountains and seek to triumph. Is it out of masochism, hell-bent determination, endorphin chasing, the love the dramatic faces of nature …or a little of each? Who knows, but the fact is we flock to the mountains with bicycle in hand ready to feel the burn, capture the exhilaration and earn the deep satisfaction of accomplishment.

The Valle d'Aosta (see p123), Montagne Doc (see p128) and Epic Passes, Famous Lakes (see p132) rides each offer a different experience of the Alps. Cycling the Valle d'Aosta offers extravagant scenery reigned over by Mont Blanc, but the riding is only moderately difficult, so it's accessible to

many levels of rider. On the Montagne Doc ride, you get to climb through deep forest to mountain passes, cycle through summer-slumbering ski towns and meander in the splendid Susa Valley. On the Alta Rezia, you pool all your determination, love and neuroses into one focused effort to navigate up and over mountains of such exquisite beauty you'll have to reconceptualise your frame of reference.

HISTORY

Italian alpine mountain peoples, despite their distinguishing regional particularities and unique customs, have a lot in common. Descended from ancient tribes, they lived for centuries coupled to a harsh environment in unfrequented regions. Singular identities developed relatively unencumbered by the squabbling and bickering of the plains' residents. However, there was contact with the outside world. Mountain

ITALIAN ALPS & LAKES DISTRICT

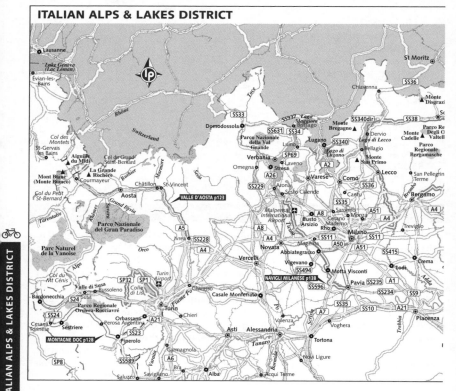

valleys were valuable crossroads controlling access to the laborious passes over which pilgrims, merchants and princes had to travel. These important trade and communications choke points were first waylaid by the Romans and have been hotly contested in the centuries since. Over time the strategic locations of these mountain communities led to their development as important commercial, administrative and religious centres. In the 21st century, rekindled curiosity over cross-border identities has revived interest in high-valley culture – agricultural still, but increasingly bankrolled through controlled exploitation of outdoor adventure opportunities (particularly skiing) in the vast, protected alpine parklands.

ENVIRONMENT

The Italian Alps are the broad mountainous arc stretching north and east from Cuneo along the French and Swiss borders to the high passes north of Sondrio. Millions of years ago, they were formed by the collision and overlapping of the African and European tectonic plates. During the Pleistocene age, five great glacial waves gouged coarse valleys into the uplifted rock, whose features have since been somewhat softened by torrents and wind. The valley floors have also been left by the retreating ice behemoths with a thick alluvial layer of fertile soil.

Despite differences in rock content, the superficial natural flavours remain constant. The frequently tilled low-valley land is usually thick with vegetation. Higher forests shade productive undergrowth and woodland animals. Further up, scented pine forests open onto gardens of alpine fauna and foliage, which, in turn, stretch into shrub-spotted alpine fields. Stern, weather-beaten rock and the barren white tracts of everlasting ice tower over it all.

GATEWAYS

See Milan (p153) and Turin (p158).

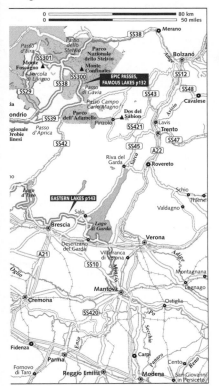

VALLE D'AOSTA

Duration 2 days
Distance 126.6km
Difficulty moderate
Start Aosta
Finish Ivrea
Summary A captivating alpine mountain ride in the skirts of Mont Blanc that won't break the energy bank.

The glacially incised **Valle d'Aosta** (Aosta Valley) offers a castle-spangled approach to the soul of the Alps at their highest and grandest. It has long attracted oglers and merchants seeking solace in, passage through, and control over its 13 side valleys and soaring passes. Today's Italian governments have reaffirmed Aosta's special autonomous status, recognising rights originally bestowed in 1191. Close ties with French-speaking Europe since AD 757 often make it feel both French and Italian. In fact, the French language (introduced into the valley in 1861) is afforded equality alongside the Italian language.

ITALIAN ALPS & LAKES DISTRICT

PLANNING
When to Cycle
With sudden Alp-prompted cold snaps and frequent rainfall aside, muggy summers still grip the Valle d'Aosta, especially in the lower elevations. Since this ride tackles no high passes, the best ride times are from mid-May to mid-September, with the standard caveat about August overcrowding. Prevailing daytime winds blow up the valley, but usually not fiercely enough to hinder the cyclist.

What to Bring
There are some longish tunnels en route, so be prepared with lights. Some tunnels have haggard sidewalks that you can limp along (if you don't like riding through tunnels).

Maps
Touring Club Italiano's 1:200,000 *Piemonte e Valle d'Aosta* map covers everything, as does the free 1:115,000 *Valle d'Aosta* map produced by the province. Tourist offices give a detailed, totally adequate and free road map of the region. Furthermore, the tourist office has an amazing (and incredibly pretty) free cycling booklet with rides all over the valley mapped in full detail.

GETTING TO/FROM THE RIDE
Aosta (start)
BUS
Buses operated by Savda (www.savda .it) run to Milan (1½–3½ hours, 2 daily), Turin (2 hours, up to 10 daily) and Courmayeur (1 hour, up to 8 daily), as well as French destinations including Chamonix. Services leave from Aosta's **bus station** (☎ 01 652 62 027; Via Giorgio Carrel), virtually opposite the train station.

TRAIN
Aosta's train station, on Piazza Manzetti, is served by trains from most parts of Italy via Turin (€7.10, 2–2½ hours, more than 10 daily). Travellers from Milan must change trains at Chivasso. Local service continues to Pré-St Didier (50 minutes), 5km short of Courmayeur.

BICYCLE
Of the few ways to bicycle into Aosta, two are part of the route described here, from Ivrea and Courmayeur. The magnificent, but brutal, road over the 2473m **Colle di Grand San Bernardo** gets you to Aosta from Martigny (Switzerland).

Ivrea (finish)
TRAIN
The train line between Turin (1 hour) and Aosta (1–1½ hours) runs through Ivrea's station, south of the centre on Via Nigra.

BICYCLE
To cycle to the ride, you would logically bike to Ivrea and do the second day in reverse. It's possible to ride to Ivrea from Turin. Ask local shops for their route recommendations.

THE RIDE
Day 1: Aosta Circuit
3–5 hours, 51.6km
The first thing today is a train ride up the hill. And a roar comes from the crowd!

But grumbles also come from the corner…something about not earning the downhill. Since today's route is an out-and-back, going up by train is a good option if you don't want to overlap the route or ride on the busy SS26. Of course, one can always ride. Also, don't fret – there's some climbing in store up to **Val Ferret**. Trains to **Pré-Saint Didier** leave Aosta almost every hour and take 50 minutes. This is the same train line that you can jump on at many points on the ride if you want to hightail it back to Aosta. That's why this route can accommodate many levels of rider.

From the second you step off the train, you'll be immersed in the scenery of the **Valle d'Aosta**, quietly thick with trees before a horizon chock-full of mountains – the hulking front liner being **Mont Blanc**. From Pré-Saint Didier, where you can buy a snack or gelato, you'll work your way up a gentle to moderate incline. The peaceful back roads weave you up the valley through lush-smelling forest and mountain-flanked pastoral fields – so picturesque you think a rosy-cheeked Heidi swinging a basket of wildflowers might jump out from behind a tree at any moment.

You'll pass appealing alpine mountain towns, which fully embrace the flower-decorated, varnished-wood aesthetic expectations of an alpine mountain experience.

VALLE D'AOSTA – DAY 1

CUES			GPS COORDINATES
start		Aosta tourist office, Piazza Chanoux	45°44'14"N 7°19'30"E
0km		S on Viale Conseil des Commis	
0.3	↑◎	Aosta train station {!take train to Pré-Staint Didier}	
	⤴	out of train station	
0.5	↑	at stop sign into Pré-Staint Didier	
		Pré-Staint Didier	45°45'50"N 6°59'30"E
1.1	⌐→	to 'Champex'	
1.5	⤴	at stop sign	
	▲	8.7km	
3.2	↘	at stop sign, to 'Verrand'	
5.4		Courmayeur	45°47'34"N 6°58'19"E
6.5	⤴	to 'Entréves'	
6.8	↗	to 'Entréves'	
9.2		'Entréves'	45°48'58"N 6°57'52"E
9.8	★	Funevie Monte Bianco	
10.2	●●↑	Val Ferret, 10km RT	
		Retrace route to Pré-Staint Didier Train Station	
20.3	↑	keep going past train station	
23.6	⌐→	to 'Aosta'	
24.9	↘	to 'La Ruina'	
25.3	●●⌐→	La Cave Enoteca and Restaurant (.6km RT)	
	↑	to 'La Salle'	
27.5	⌐→	at stop sign to SS26	
27.8	⤴	to 'Villair' (ignore signs to Aosta)	
28.7	↗	to SS26	
29.8	↘	at fork	
30.3	↘	to 'Aosta'	
30.5	⤴	to 'Aosta'	
34.2	⚠	Tunnel .4km	

CUES CONTINUED			GPS COORDINATES
35.7	⚠	Tunnel	
36.5	⚠	Tunnel	
31.7	↙◎	to 'Les Combes, Introd'	
32		Arvier	45°42'12"N 7°09'55"E
	▲	1.8km moderate climb	
34.5	↑	to 'Introd'	
34.9	↘	to 'Aosta'	
	▲	3.3km descent	
36.9	↗	to 'Villeneuve'	
38.2	⌐→	at stop sign by Church	
		Villeneuve	45°42'09"N 7°12'28"E
41.4	⌐→	at stop sign	
	▲	1km steep climb	
42.4	⤴	to 'Urbains'	
		Aymavilles (info sign about Castello)	45°42'05"N 7°14'57"E
42.5	★	Castello de Aymavilles	
42.9	↘	to 'Aosta'	
43	⤴	to 'Aosta	
44	⌐→	at stop sign	
44.9	⌐→	at T intersection	
46	↑◎	unsigned road	
49.5	◎	3rd exit to 'Aosta'	
49.9	◎	2nd exit to 'Centre Ville'	
50.1	◎⤴	to 'Centre Ville'	
50.7	⌐→	under arches	
51	⌐→	to Caribineri	
51.2	↑	Via Edouard Aubert	
51.4	↑	Via Tillier	
51.6		Piazza Chanoux, Aosta Tourist Office	45°44'14"N 7°19'30"E

Subsequently, they are fat and sleek from their healthy tourist industries. You'll first pass through **Courmayeur** (5.4km), where people embrace trekking and trekking apparel, and then **Entreves** (9.2km).

At 9.8km, the **Funivie Mont Blanc** (☎ 658 99 25; www.montebianco.com) in **La Palud** (1369m) runs cable cars into (and even over) the Alps – beside Europe's highest peak, **Mont Blanc**, that imposing, megalithic apex that has begin inspiring your awe the entire ride. Cars depart every 20 minutes to a number of destinations (€17–36 RT, depending on destination). An outing to the highest point, **Aiguille du Midi** (3842m), and back will take around four hours. Plant lovers should pause at the Pavillon du Mont Fréty station for the **Alpine Garden Saussurea**.

We suggest you continue up through Val Ferret (see Side Trip: Val Ferret, p126). The ride back down to Aosta is just as glorious: a good bit of downhill, flanked by high mountains, blessed with outstanding panoramic views and peppered by quaint ancient villages and castles. You'll weave down the valley as if it were a half-pipe, avoiding SS26 for the most part, and exploring the rural outreaches of the region. **Morgex** (23.5km), capital of Valdigne, is worth a short detour for its 10th-century castle, 15th-century church, Romanesque belfry and a number of towers – as well as its lovely cantina.

After a short stint on SS26, you head into rolling land rich in vineyards and orchards – this valley is as famous for apples as it is for grapes. The silent, narrow country roads touch down in tiny hamlets, each boasting a castle or ancient architecture. Particularly mentionable is the Gothic **Castello di Aymavilles** (www.comune.aymavilles.ao.it), which was built in 1278. While most visitors are riding in a cable

ITALIAN ALPS & LAKES DISTRICT

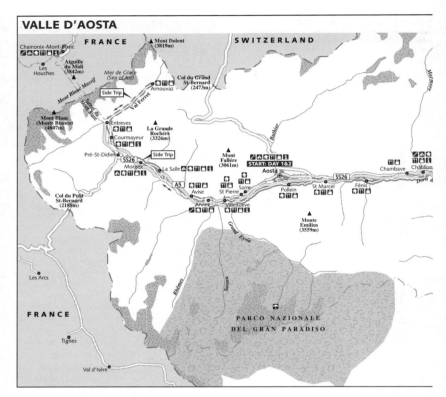

VALLE D'AOSTA

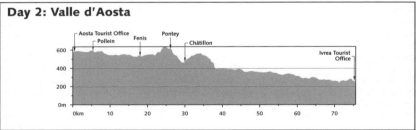

Day 2: Valle d'Aosta

car to the heights of the mountain, you'll be cycling in a spectacularly handsome area that really opens a window for you into the rural, modest and vivacious culture of the Aosta Valley.

SIDE TRIP: VAL FERRET
1–2 hours, at 10.2km, 20km RT

Before heading back down the valley, ponder the gorgeous, highly recommended side trip in Val Ferret – on a road skirting a pristine, galloping river at the base of the Monte Bianco monolith. It's 426m in and 10km up to **Arnouvaz**, where the paved road runs out. This is where mountain bikers embark on an 'epic' seven-day ride around the massif (see the text Mountain Bike Rides on p149).

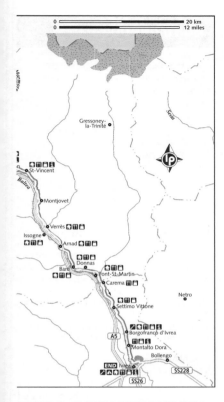

SIDE TRIP: TASTING FAMOUS WHITES OF THE VALLEY

30 minutes–2 hours, at 25.3km, 1.2km RT

The Valle d'Aosta is home to vineyards producing sought-after wines that are rarely available outside the region – including those from Europe's highest vineyard, **Morgex et La Salle** (☎ 01 658 00 331; www.caveduvinblanc.com; Chemin des Iles 31, La Ruine), named for the two villages strung together by its vines. You can stop in to taste the best of the valley and also have lunch at the highly acclaimed restaurant that shares the building.

Day 2: Aosta to Ivrea

4–7½ hours, 74.8km

Serene secondary roads creep through sedate Old World villages over the first 31.1km, and reach to the upper slopes along the edge of the vale. A plethora of Romanesque and Gothic castles dot the

VALLE D'AOSTA – DAY 2
DAY 2: AOSTA TO IVREA

CUES			GPS COORDINATES
start		Aosta tourist office, Piazza Chanoux	
			45°44'14"N 7°19'30"E
0km	⬏	Via Tillier	
0.3	↑	Via Edouard Aubert	
0.5	↑	Continue wrong way on one-way using bike path	
0.7	↑	Via Battiglione Aosta	
0.8	↑	Via Lys	
0.9	⬑	tutte le Direzione	
1.1	⬏	to 'La Pila'	
1.3	⬑	after arches, to 'La Pila'	
1.8	⬏	with traffic, to 'La Pila'	
2.1	◎	2nd exit to 'Gressan'	
2.4	◎	3rd exit to Pollein	
5.3		Pollein	45°43'43"N 7°21'13"E
2.4	⬑	first after bridge `to Pollein'	
5.3	⤴	to 'Brissagne' SR15	
11	⤴	`to Neyran,' red road	
11.2	⚠	Rough road .4km	
11.6	⬏	Under overpass	
	⬑	(30m) at T insection	
13.3	↑	to 'Fénis'	
17	⬏	to 'Fénis'at stop sign	
17.8		Fenis	45°44'17"N 7°29'07"E
	▲	1km moderate, steepish climb	
21.2	⤴	to 'Pontey'	
22.4	⤴	at fork to 'Pontey'	
	▲	steep climb (1.5km?)	
26.	⬂	to 'Blanchet Centro'	
		Pontey	45°44'21"N 7°35'07"E
28.7	↑	Cross bridge	
29.1	★	S. Vincente train station	
29.6	◎↑	under overpass	
30	⬏	unsigned T intersection	
		Châtillon	45°44'59"N 7°37'06"E
30.2		1km climb	
31.1	⤴	SS26 to 'Torino'	
56.4	◎⬏	to Turin	
72.8	⤴	Corso Garibaldi `to Biella'	
74.4	⬂	Corso Cavour (GPS track goes to Stazione)	
74.6	⬂	Corso Cavour unsigned.	
74.8	⬑	Piazza Ferruccio Nazionale	
	⬏	(70m) Via Palestro	
75	⬑	Piazza Ottinetti	
		Ivrea tourist office	45°28'00"N 7°52'33"E

route, each within view of the next. Even though jumping onto SS26 is essential some of the time, you can take a free map from any tourist office and divert as you see fit. If you have time, that's a pretty way to go.

ITALIAN ALPS & LAKES DISTRICT

From Aosta, head south across the Dora Baltea River and turn east towards the magnificently restored 13th- to 14th-century **Castello de Fénis** (17.8km), considered the classic medieval Aosta castle, featuring rich frescoes and period graffiti.

Just to the east, in **Châtillon** (30km), three castles grace the hillside. The 14th-century Castello di Ussel (across the river), Castello Passerin d'Entrèves, surrounded by gardens and visible above the centre of town, and Castello Baron Gamba, circumscribed by the route, are all worth a visit as is the Roman bridge (to the right of the Chanoux bridge just before town). Châtillon is the jumping-off point for trips (by bus and/or bike) up Valtournenche to Breuil-Cervinia and the back of the Matterhorn.

The section of the route on SS26, though more trafficked, is still scenic. If you don't want to explore back roads, there are many historical and architectural points of interest on the way to Ivrea. They are as follows:

Past **St-Vincent**, the sober 14th-century Castello di Verrès looks like an archetypal stronghold, doing sentinel duty atop its rocky perch. Across the river, the restored 15th-century Castello d'Issogne, built over the ruins of a Roman city, was later converted into the sumptuous Renaissance residence it now resembles. You can visit here on a side trip or while taking an alternative route on the rolling lanes west of the river.

There are also Roman remains along this path of the ancient route to Gaul, known to pilgrims as the Via Francigena. **Donnas** is the site of one of the best-preserved bits of this Roman road and, 3km later, the river crossing at **Pont-Saint-Martin** is just downstream of the original 1st-century BC Roman bridge that was used until 1831.

Further along is **Borgofranco d'Ivrea**. Little is left of its Roman origins, but the prosperity of its 13th-century *ricetto* (tax-free zone centre) survives, as does the elegant Palazzo Marini.

Montalto Dora harbours the remains of a Roman aqueduct and the 18th-century Villa dei Baroni Casana, now a Benedictine monastery. The defensive *castello* (castle) atop Monte Crovero has protected the road to **Ivrea**, today's next and last stop, for more than 600 years.

MONTAGNE DOC

Duration 3 days
Distance 223.8km
Difficulty moderate–demanding
Start Turin
Finish Pinerolo
Summary From the desolate climb to the Colle del Lys, to the flat, mountain-hugged Susa Valley; this is a party pleaser.

Turin is the hub of radiating spokes of notoriously high-elevation valleys. The best rides are those that slide a few lengths into the valleys and then vault the dividing ridges, giving a cyclist a little bit of everything. This three-day pedal hits three of the valleys (and the two passes dividing them), including those elected to host the 2006 Winter Olympics: Alta Val Chisone and the Valle di Susa. This ride, though it has its challenges, infuses enough easy pedalling that it is accessible to the intermediate rider who has the gumption to make it over a couple of passes.

PLANNING
When to Cycle
This ride goes to some high elevations, thereby escaping the heat of the plains and running the risk of hitting periodic high-elevation weather mess. The best time for pedalling is from mid-June to mid-September, although holidaying crowds in August can be a pain.

Maps
The *Piemonte e Valle d'Aosta* 1:200,000 map by Touring Club Italiano includes the area west of Turin. Instead, try the free Instituto Geografico DeAgostini 1:180,000 *Province of Turin* map distributed at tourist offices. For the ride from Avigliana to Susa, ask in Turin for the *Ciclostrada Valle di Susa* map.

Information Sources
Bici & Dintorni (☎/fax 01 188 89 81; www .biciedintorni.org) is the FIAB affiliate of urban cyclists promoting two-wheeling in Turin. It has a busy calendar of organised activities open to anyone (sometimes for a small fee).

Contact Provincia di Torino's Servizio **Turismo e Sport** (☎ 011 861 26 39; www .provincia.torino.it, Via Maria Vittoria 12) for the free bicycling maps.

GETTING TO/FROM THE RIDE
Turin (start)
See p158.

Pinerolo (finish)
TRAIN
The Pinerolo train station is the last stop on a spur line from Turin (40 minutes, 15 trains daily).

BICYCLE
You can take bike paths from Pinerolo into Turin, but make sure that you aren't in a hurry because they are a confusing maze. It's a 44km ride to Costigliole Saluzzo, and from there you drop onto SR589. Alternatively, you can bike 37km east to Carmagnola, on the main Cuneo–Turin train line, to arrive at Cuneo, the starting point of the ride.

THE RIDE
Day 1: Turin to Avigliana
4½–8 hours, 87.5km
Today's ride gambols north into the Valli di Lazio, a scramble over the Colle del Lys before soaring into the heart of the Valle di Susa.

Getting out of large cities can be a pain – getting out of Turin, although it's well supplied with bike paths, is moderately so. However, it's a nice way to get a scope of the city and her riverside paths. About 10km will pass before there is real air and the traffic begins to relax. After you pass **Druento**, you'll breathe a sigh of relief and exhilaration as you enter a quieter valley, clearly heading away from the city, towards a mountain-clad horizon.

As you continue towards the pass, the landscape becomes more rugged and picturesque. Adorable and curious little **Viù** (39km) is a halfway point of the climb. It's a tiny town equipped with a gigantic church and an immense wood sculpture of **Pinocchio**. You can fill up with water at Viù's public fountain and grab a bite to eat.

A mountain lane under the cool shroud of thick forest leads to the top of the **Colle del Lys** (67.7km, 1311m).

Spend a minute taking in the enveloping panorama, and you may want to join the sunbathers languishing about, soaking up the mountain rays on the grassy alpine knoll. The descent will eloquently and decadently remind you why we go to so much trouble climbing.

From **Almese** (82km), on the edge of the Susa Valley floor, the village of **Villar Dora** and its **storybook castle** are 1km away. Also keep an eye out for the castle and towers of Avigliana, today's terminus.

SIDE TRIP: LANZO TORINESE
30 minutes–1 hour, at 36.5, 2km RT
Beyond the ring of suburbs, medieval Lanzo Torinese is a short side trip from the main route. You can wander the *chintane* (medieval alleys) and appreciate the Gothic Chiesa di Santa Croce, medieval Torre Civica and the Ponte del Diavolo.

Day 2: Avigliana to Oulx
4–7 hours, 59.1km
The Valle di Susa provokes one to leisurely explore the little villages nestled into its expansive valley walled by particularly magnificent mountains. The lower-valley Valle di Susa Ciclostrada from Avigliana to Susa, seen during the first part of the day, contrasts with the climb-intensive portion from Susa to Oulx.

If you are tuckered out, you can stay in anti-climactic Oulx. Alternatively, if it's

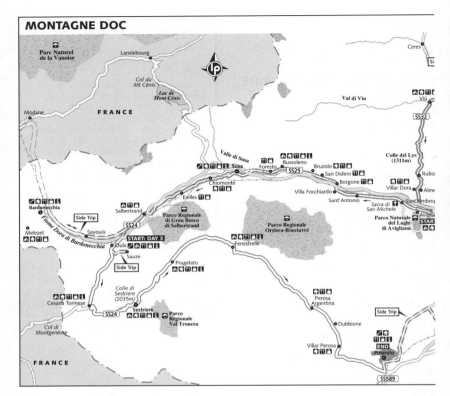

MONTAGNE DOC

also about the destination for you, and not just the ride, choose to go left to the beautifully set, cosy mountain ski town of **Sauze** or up the valley to **Bardonecchia** for a single-track interlude. This is the beating heart of mountain bike adventures in Piedmont, and both Sauze and Bardonecchia have extensive mountain biking parks (although rentals are more easily available in the latter). For all the info you need to ride Bardonecchia check out www.bardonecchiabike.com.

Either way, you'll have to return to Oulx to rejoin the next day's route. If you want to stay in one of these towns, from the Oulx train station you can opt to take a bus up the steep, gorgeous 6km slug to Sauze or a train straight to Bardonecchia, a gradual and more traffic-heavy climb 13km away.

The **Valle di Susa** shelters a profusion of religious buildings – in fact, it's nicknamed Valle delle Abbazie. The **Path of the Franks** once linked its five core religious centres – Sacra di San Michele, Monte Benedetto, Certosa di Banda, Madonna della Losa and the Abbey of Oulx – all but Losa being on today's route.

From **Avigliana**, a signed bike path wobbles up the shallow valley through the medieval burgs of **Sant'Ambrogio** and **Sant'Antonio** to **Villar Focchiardo**. It's a lovely route for enjoying magnificent scenery and ancient, lazy hamlets at a meandering pace.

From Villar Focchiardo, the bike path crosses the Fiume Dora Riparia and touches several villages on the north bank: **Borgone** and its 11th- to 12th-century chapel – San Didero – and **Bruzolo** and **Bussoleno**

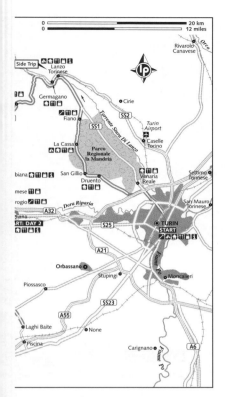

origins and marked the border with Dauphiné country until the 1713 Treaty of Utrecht.

Day 3: Oulx to Pinerolo
5–8 hours, 77.2km

At the beginning of the day, wherever you start from, there is a singular and determined focus: 920m to the top of **Colle di Sestriere**. It's highly suggested that you break from the grind and enjoy the mesmerising alpine environs before you plummet an unbelievable 55.8km into the flatlands.

From Oulx, the climb starts gradually then intensifies after about 2.2km for 2.5km. The next fateful uphill mash will lead you to the glory of Colle di Sestriere (21.4km 2035m) and its characterless namesake resort conceived by Mussolini and built by the Agnelli clan (of Fiat fame).

Jump on the gravity party train and fly fast to the villages of **Pragelato** (and its Folk Museum), **Fenestrelle**, **Perosa Argentina** and **Villar Perosa**, which make good pit stops. As you're soaring through the plains at the bottom of the Valle del Chisone, Pinerolo will soon appear.

SIDE TRIP: LAGHI BAITE
2 hours, 14km

So, you're hot and sweaty and not amused over being torn from your world-class mountain scenery and thrown into the sweltering, trafficked flatlands around Pinerolo. We know what will cheer you up: swimming with penguins.

Take a side trip to **Laghi Baite** (☎ 00 190 70 419; www.laghibaite.it; Strada Piscina 38, Cumania; per person €7) and you can do just that in their glass-partitioned swimming pool, which is half for humans and half for penguins.

This family favourite, part conservation project and part animal park, showcases a menagerie of rescued beasts and fowl, even a couple of tigers. From Pinerolo, it's a slight downhill slant on inoffensive SP895 to **Madonna della Neve**, where you turn right towards Piscina and follow signs to Laghi Baite. When you leave the park, it's a 2km pedal to the Piscina train station, which has regular departures to Turin.

(26.2km). Before you make your way into **Susa** (34.1km), a prime place for lunch, you'll pedal past a gorge that feels like it was a sacred place back in the day.

Susa started life as a Celtic town and boasts a host of charms, from its Roman Arch of Augustus, amphitheatre and Acquedotto delle Termi Graziane, to the 3rd-century Porta Savoia (Savoy Gate) and attached 11th-century Cattedrale San Giusto, as well as the medieval Castello di Marchesa Adelaide, Borgo dei Nobili and Chiesa del Ponte.

The road out of Susa immediately begins to climb through steep forested mountains, with jagged, snow-dolloped ones in the distance. With the exception of one brief dip, it never stops. Along the way is a short alternate route to the forbidding **Exilles fort** (46.1km). It has obscure medieval

EPIC PASSES, FAMOUS LAKES

Duration 5 days
Distance 366.6km
Difficulty demanding (last day moderate)
Start Prato allo Stelvio (Prad am Stilfserjoch)
Finish Lecco
Summary Infamous Stelvio Pass initiates you into a ride of colossal alpine landscapes, rigorous climbing and sizzling descents. The mellower last day ends in the sweet shore-side town on renowned Lake Como.

The passes in this ride are the stuff of Italian cycling lore. The **Stelvio**, **Gavia**, **Bernina**, **Livigno**, **Foscagno** and **Mortirolo**. They cluster tightly together, at once daring you like a gang of bullies and inspiring you like a gathering of wise elders. Between them sprawl elegant valleys, like **Valfurva**, the **Viola**, the **Poschiavo**, the **Corteno**, the **Malenco** and many more, all spry tributaries of the great **Valtellina**. It's an odyssey of a ride really, both testing the determination of your own heart and exploring the incomprehensible landscape around you. The cherry on top is ending up at the relaxing Lake Como village Lecco.

PLANNING
When to Cycle
Snow can fall in the high passes in any month – the best time to tackle this ride is between mid-June and mid-September. Mid-August is best avoided due to the usual crowds.

What to Bring
Make sure you've got plenty of liquid and solid sustenance for the marathon high-altitude passes – there are often no services over long stretches. Also be prepared for tough weather conditions. Bring a bike light for fog or snow, and for brief tunnels.

Maps & Booklets
Touring Club Italiano's 1:200,000 *Trentino Alto Adige* map shows this ride as far as Tirano (17km short of the end at Sondrio) and the *Lombardia* map begins in Trafoi (10.9km from the start). The free *Provincia di Sondrio* 1:115,000 map covers everything. Another good free map for the rides along

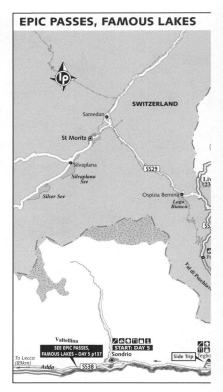

EPIC PASSES, FAMOUS LAKES

the Adda River is the *Regione Lombardia–Tourist* map of rivers.

Two comprehensive and free information booklets available in English are: the *Alta Rezia Pocket Guide* (complete with a trekking/mountain-biking map) and the *Vademecum Alta Valtellina*.

Information Sources
For organised cycling activities in Bormio, check with the **Unione Sportiva Bormiese** (☎ 03 429 01 482; www.bormiese.org; Via Nesini 6).

The local FIAB affiliate, with a fistful of organised cycling activities and information, is **Amici della Bicicletta Sondrio** (☎ /fax 03 479 226 682; Vicolo degli Orti 3).

GETTING THERE & AWAY
Prato allo Stelvio (start)
Spondigna, a flat 3km ride north of Prato at the junction of SS38 and SS40, is where the

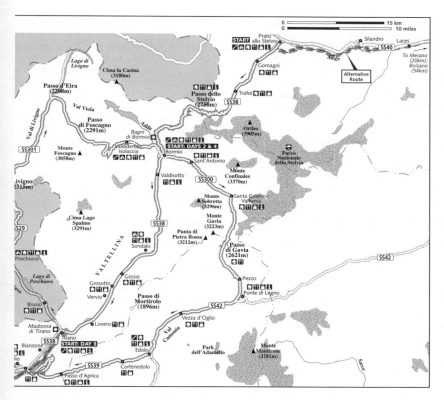

lines of public transportation will mostly drop you when you arrive in Prato.

BUS
The most convenient local bus stop is at Spondigna. *SAD* operates bus No 401 hourly from Bolzano to Merano (40 minutes); in Merano, catch the connecting bus to Spondigna (1½ hours, every 30 minutes). There's an extra fee for bikes.

TRAIN
Hourly trains from Bolzano to Merano (40 minutes) can transfer to the private uber bike-friendly **Val Venosta line** (www .ferroviavalvenosta.it) that takes you to Spondigna.

BICYCLE
Cycling is a very nice way to arrive, thanks to the bike paths. The Val Venosta bike route connects Prato allo Stelvio with Bolzano

(87km), Merano (53km) and Nauders, in Austria (36km). The paths are well-signed and you can get maps from tourist offices. Between Prato and Merano, there are a couple of sections that are unpaved.

Lecco (finish)
See p152.

THE RIDE
Day 1: Prato allo Stelvio to Bormio
3–6 hours, 46.6km
The eerie, mesmerizing 48 switchbacks climbed in the course of a 25km ascent are part of what is now an iconic Italian cycling route. In the summer, you might see more cycling traffic – recumbents, tandems, mountain bikes, whatever – than cars. Check with the tourist office because there is a day in the summer when all traffic is barred from the pass and hordes of

ITALIAN ALPS & LAKES DISTRICT

pass-hungry cyclists take over. This is Italy's highest pass (and the Alps' third-highest) on the 'highest road in Europe', and it rewards its faithful climbers with a 22km plummet to **Valtellina's Bormio**. Just don't forget to look up folks. The entire ride is within the limits of **Parco Nazionale dello Stelvio**, Italy's biggest national park and the largest protected area in Europe.

The ascent starts out of Prato and gets steeper beyond **Gomagoi** (6.3km), where the Solda valley turns southeast while the route continues southwest up the Rio Trafoi. The first of the Stelvio's 48 numbered curves appears 2.2km later, signalling the beginning of the long haul ahead. **Trafoi** (10.4km) is the last chance for food and drink before the pass. **Hotel Bellavista** (11km; ☎ 04 736 11 716; www.gustav-thoeni.com), run by Olympic skiing champion Gustav Thoni, is a great place to grab calories and shelter (ask about discounts for cyclists).

From Trafoi, the almost surreal succession of switchbacks heads for the pass, quickly climbing above the tree line and affording remarkable views over the surrounding mountains and glaciers and even the road itself. At Passo dello Stelvio (2758m, 25.1km), actually the largest summer ski area in the Alps – hotels, restaurants and cafés allow for a celebratory drink/snack with throngs of other exhilarated tourists. To mark the occasion further, the **tourist office** (☎ /fax 03 429 03 030; www .passostelvio.com) will issue a laser-printed colour certificate with the date, your name and address, and the time it took you to climb the pass (be honest!). There are even memorials to **Fausto Coppi**, Italy's most famous cyclist. **Carlo Donegani Museo Storico**, recounting the hows and whys of the Stelvio road (and the role it played in WWI), is an interesting museum.

What took hours to climb can take less than an hour to descend. Other than the snowscapes, extraordinary natural sights, some short, dark, wet, one-way tunnels and tough road twists, there is nothing to stop a determined decliner from reaching record speeds. It goes without saying that brakes should be in good working order.

Day 2: Bormio to Tirano via Gavia

5½–10 hours, 97.9km

After yesterday's heroic hike followed by a full afternoon's rest, today's labours may seem like out-and-out masochism. The climb to 2621m **Passo di Gavia** covers approximately the same distance, but the day's distance tally is 50km longer and includes a second (much easier) afternoon ascent. It's not as hellish as it sounds. The net change of elevation is 763m down and the surrounding natural grandeur is incomparable.

From Bormio, head straight for the Valfurva, whose lead town, **Santa Caterina Valfurva** (12.4km), is a winter ski resort and summer alpine centre for the neighbouring Forni, Cedec and Zebrù Valleys. Food and drink purchased here will be the last until the top of the pass, for the right turn in town marks the start of an arduous climb. No fewer than 10 switchbacks force you to sweat through pine forests to the tree line, above which the Val di Gavia arena of cold, rocky, alpine desolation dominates. Never fear, there will be snow! The welcome **Rifugio Bonetta** (☎ 03 649 18 06) at the top of Passo di Gavia (2621m, 25.8km) has hot and cold water, warm drinks, postcards stamped with proof of location, Giro d'Italia pictures of snow-covered cyclists at the pass, and, if necessary, lodging.

Now begins an approximately 37km descent. The steepest part covers 1363m in 18.3km down the Val delle Messi to **Ponte di Legno** (43.8km). The remaining 559m and 19.4km are in the verdant Val Camonica via **Vezza d'Oglio** to **Edolo** (65km).

POST PASSO DI STELVIO INDULGENCE

A restorative soak in healing hot springs sounds pretty good after pedalling many kilometres of steep switchbacks. Mud therapy? Many swear by it. Join the many other people who come to Bormio today for its nine thermal-mineral springs – famous for curative qualities since Roman times. **Bormio Terme** (☎ 03 429 01 325; www.bormioterme.it; Via Stelvio 10; admission 1hr €8–11; 9am–10pm Mon & Wed, 9am–10.30pm, all other days 9am–9pm, closed May) offers scads of spa treatments (inhalations, mud therapies and so on). The prices given include access to the indoor and outdoor pools.

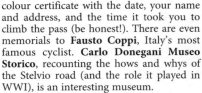

From Edolo, the route turns back uphill the length of the Valle di Corteno to the **Passo d'Aprica** (1176m, 81.4km) in the same-name resort town surrounded by protected natural areas like the peat bogs of Pian di Gembro at Trivigno (13km north) and the **Parco Regionale Orobie Valtellinesi**. From Aprica the route drops back to the Valtellina floor a few kilometres from Tirano.

Day 3: Tirano to Bormio via Livigno
3½–6 hours, 57.6km

Thanks to Swiss engineering genius, the ride begins at 2265m. Three passes later (none of which requires more than 400m of climbing) and following a visit to the duty-free city of Livigno, Bormio is back in view. Passports are mandatory for the brief incursion into **Switzerland**. Of, course, if there's a voice in your head saying 'cheater cheater pumpkin eater', or if you just want to go get it, then go get it! Ride up the darn thing. The alternative route from Tirano points 31.8km up the valley on SS38A/Swiss route 29 via Poschiavo.

From Tirano's Ferrovia Retica station, the building next door to the main station on Piazzale Stazione, the Swiss-run **trenino rosso** (☎ 03 427 01 353; www.rhb.ch), Europe's highest non-cogwheel train, chugs up 1824m to the **Ospizia Bernina station** (1¾ hours, extra bicycle fee). The trip up the Alta Valposchiavo into the Engadin region is possible in chilly open cars with unobstructed views of the curious circular viaduct in **Brusio**, blue-green **Lago di Poschiavo**, and then the Bernina mountain range glaciers.

From the Ospizia Bernina station (2265m), a short climb crests at the top of the **Passo del Bernina** (2328m). The sublime beauty of this bit of the Alps is absolutely mind-boggling – it's almost hard to concentrate on riding. The road heads down from the pass to a left turn (4.1km) back through the border and a climb to the Forcola di Livigno (2315m, 8km), from which it's 14.7km down to lunch in the centre of Livigno.

Livigno (turn-off at 19.8km) is a sunny holiday resort spread for kilometres along the single road through its valley. Most people come here for the outdoor experience, but shopping is also a draw for some. Livigno has been a duty-free zone since the 16th century.

Passes two and three lie above Livigno to the east. **Passo d'Eira** (2208m, 26.4km) is the lowest of the day, but the longest given the depth of the Livigno valley. The dip into La Vallaccia makes the 263m climb to **Passo di Foscagno** (2291m, 33.2km) a breeze.

The remainder of the ride drops the lengths of Valdidentro to Bormio. Along the way, take in the 12th-century **Chiesa San Gallo** (in Valdidentro Isolaccia, 49.4km).

Day 4: Bormio to Sondrio
4–7 hours, 75.7km

Today's ride heads downhill the length of the Alta Valtellina to Tirano and then into the lower river area to the provincial capital at Sondrio. Sounds easy, right? Guess again. Starting in the early afternoon, a brutal not-to-be-underestimated wind blows east up the valley. Get a jump on things, friend.

In **Valdisotto** (8km), the inexplicable increase in elevation is the result of a massive landslide that on 28 July 1987 buried three *borghetti* (small villages) but just missed the 13th-century Chiesa de S. Bartolomeo di Castelaz.

The city of massive high-rises clinging to the northern hillside is **Sondalo**, famous in the 1930s and 1940s as a curative spa for pulmonary diseases and today is the region's hospital.

Grosio (24.5km) has lots to see, most important of which is the Parco delle Incisioni Rupestri, conserving the Bronze-Age carvings of the ancient Ráter people. Nearby are ruins of the 11th- to 14th-century **Castello Visconti Venosta** and 12th-century Chiesa di Santo Giorgio. The people of Grosio are some of the last in the valley to wear traditional clothes in everyday life. Before automotive vehicles became prevalent, they used to hike the road south of Grosio to Edolo over the **Passo del Mortirolo** (1896m), one of the steepest of the Giro d'Italia.

Grosotto (27.2km) has the lovely 17th-century Santuario B.V. delle Grazie, and **Mazzo** (29.7km) the 12th-century Torre e Contrada Pedenale.

One word of warning just in case: starting south of Bormio, and until just north of Tirano, bicycles are not allowed on SS38. Tirano (38.9km) is at the dividing point between the Alta Valtellina (and an alpine climate) and the lower valley's more Mediterranean look and feel.

From Tirano, hop onto the newly improved bike path that goes all the way to Sondrio. There are a couple of hairier places, and the path goes on SS38 for a blip, so just follow the bike path signs. You can duck off the path a bit early in Piano if you wish. Via Stelvio takes you straight into Sondrio.

Day 5: Sondrio to Lecco
5–9 hours, 88.8km
Although it involves no major changes in elevation, today's ride is fairly long with lots of rolling hills along the lower 44km of Valtellina to the top of Lago di Como. The next 44km follows the steep contours of the encircling mountains that plunge dramatically into the waters of Europe's deepest lake.

From Sondrio, a half-dirt, half-paved, former carriage road called the Sentiero Valtellina charts the south bank of the Adda River (with one deviation up to the main road in Gherbiscione, 11km) as far as Fusine. When it disappears into a maze of cornfields (12.4km), common sense and determination lead you to small country lanes on the far side.

Shortly after **Sirta** (21.1km) and its Chiesa di San Giuseppe (with the largest dome in the region), the main road crosses the bike route. Jog over the bridge here to the north side of the Adda and then make an immediate left. A short but steep hill on a lovely, gravel back road climbs to **Desco** (24.7km) before finally and definitively returning to pavement.

The beautiful, triple-arched, stone bridge 4.2km further is the 15th-century **Ponte di Ganda**. It marks the turn for the side trip to **Morbegno**, the last large village in Valtellina and a pleasant medieval centre. Morbegno is also the start of the Antica Via Privia that climbs the 1985m Passo di San Marco through the heart of the Alpi Orobie to Bergamo.

Back at the base of the Costiera dei Cèch, the last few kilometres of Valtellina unwind.

Colico (46.3km) is the first of the magical Lago di Como villages packed with history and attractions. Ruins here of the early 17th-century Spanish fort fit the bill. About 25km later, the side trip at **Olgiasca** to the 11th-century **Abbazia di Piona** takes in one of the lake's most important Romanesque structures. Crenelated Castello Recinto

and an impressive church devoted to Saint Thomas of Canterbury crown the rocky spur of **Corenno Plinio** (55.6km). Don't speed past the fabulous Orrido (gorge) at Bellano formed by the Torrente Pioverna.

Varenna (66.3km) is the pearl of Lario. Gaze up at the ruins of its medieval Castello di Vezio (from which the lake panorama is unrivalled) and the length of the multitiered gardens of 17th-century Villa Cipressi or the 1km-long botanical spread of the 13th-century former Cistercian Villa Monastero. Take in the 10th- to 11th-century Chiesa di San Giovanni Battista, one of the area's oldest churches. Nature lovers can visit the ornithological museum or the banks of the Fiumelatte, Italy's shortest river (only 250m long).

Further down the lakeshore, once-fortified **Mandello del Lario** (78.3km) is an important stop for motorcycle lovers. Museo Moto Guzzi is set in the former factory.

Just past **Abbadia Lariana**, the major vehicular road that has stuck to the upper slopes merges with the *lungolago* (lakeshore drive). It's an unpleasant 3.6km stretch, but the only road to the next and final stop at Lecco.

SIDE TRIP: PAYING HOMAGE TO THE PATRON SAINT OF CYCLISTS AND THE CYCLING MUSEUM
4–6 hours, 57.4km RT
It is only right that one has to pilgrimage up a 8.9km climb to reach the **Madonna del Ghisallo**, patron saint of (Italian) cyclists, a bestowment made by Pope Pious XII in 1949. Today, her sanctuary/chapel in the hamlet of Magreglio (above Bellagio) is a shrine to cycling's past and present greats. Right next door is the must-see, inspiring and well-done **Museo del Ciclismo** (www. museociclismo.it). The chapel grounds also have an evocative Pope-blessed **Monumento al Ciclista** that holds claim to a panoramic lookout over the lake and mountains.

In the half-light of the small Madonna del Ghisallo sanctuary (built in 1623), you can immediately tell that it is no ordinary chapel. Cloaking the walls between votive plaques are glass-framed bike jerseys, and packing the rafters is a curious collection of bicycles. On the left, amid others, is the *steed il campionnissimo* cycle that **Fausto Coppi** rode to victory in the 1949 Giro

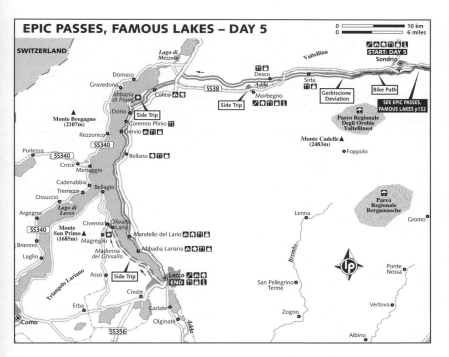

EPIC PASSES, FAMOUS LAKES – DAY 5

d'Italia. There too is the tortured frame from **Fabio Casartelli**'s fatal crash in 1995. On the right, the aerodynamic machine is from **Francesco Moser's** 1984 record-breaking, one-hour ride. And how about **Gino Bartali**'s 1948 Tour de France coup wheels? Or, yes, that's **Gianni Motta**'s pink jersey from his 1966 Giro triumph. The other names represented are a who's-who of cycling giants: **Bottechia**, **Moser**, **Merckx**, **Hinault**, **LeMond**, **Magni** and **Felice**. Any cycling devotee gets the shivers.

Then, get your lycra-clad hiney over to the Museo del Ciclismo, where elaborate displays focus on everything from the history of cycling and the greats of racing to the latest carbon technology to an 'entirely' wooden bike. It is such a thrill to learn more about our passion and to see the vast amounts of time, resources and energy dedicated to it.

To get there head up SS583 and take the left right before the Bellavista hotel and restaurant (at 19.8km). There is only one fork before you arrive – take the unsigned left.

THE LAKES DISTRICT

The 'land of the lakes' stretches from Lago Maggiore in the west, on the border between Piedmont and Lombardy, to Lago di Garda in the east, on the border with Veneto and Trento. It includes the lakes of Como, Endine, Iseo and Idro and a variety of smaller *meres* and *tarns* (lakes and pools) pooled between the pre-alpine crags at the edge of the Lombard Po plain. It's a vast land rich in art and history that has caught the fancy of artists and poets since Roman times. Characterised by a mild climate, fresh air, a varied environment and plentiful distractions, it remains a major destination for travellers seeking a small piece of paradise. Cycle around these lakes, over the mountains dividing them, and along the canals connecting them and you will come to a profound appreciation for what this region brings to the table.

ITALIAN ALPS & LAKES DISTRICT

HISTORY

Humans seem to have been drawn to the shores of Italy's northern lakes since Neolithic times (3rd millennium BC). Despite the vast territory, subsequent historical trends were shared: the flourishing of independent city-states – their domination by wealthy dynasties (notably those from Milan) – and the fluctuating fortunes of the local economic mainstays, which are small industries based on local natural resources. Despite the upheavals caused by the mid-19th century campaign for independence, WWI and WWII, the Lakes have remained retreats for European nobility and transalpine travellers.

ENVIRONMENT

The three major lakes – Maggiore, Como and Garda – and their smaller satellites share their origins in the southward thrust of glaciers during the Quaternary era about three million years ago. Yet they differ strikingly in the configurations of mountain ranges, ridges and valleys. Each individual lake is itself surrounded by an array of contrasting landscapes. In geological make-up, too, there are differences, as the predominant limestone of Garda gives way to the crystalline rocks around Maggiore. Everywhere there is an abundance and diversity of wildflowers, especially in limestone country, and magnificent chestnut, beech and oak woodlands. The dearth of readily observed fauna is perhaps due in part to the long history of intensive settlement.

NAVIGLI MILANESI

Duration 3 days
Distance 253.4km
Difficulty easy
Start Sesto Calende
Finish Lecco
Summary Milan, Italy's world-famous business and fashion centre is surprisingly situated in the middle of a tranquil network of canalside bike paths.

Milan wasn't built on a river, but through an astonishing web of canals it has benefited from the power and utility of flowing water. Its Naviglio Grande, begun in the 12th century, and was the first navigable manmade canal of the modern world. Like other area canals, it has been used for irrigation and transport (building blocks for Milan's cathedral mined near Lago Maggiore were floated down this canal), once facilitating trade between foreign destinations and interior ports.

Today, the Milanese canals' connections to nearby rivers – like the Ticino, Adda and Po – are protected nature zones used primarily for recreational use. Though Milan is more a business powerhouse than a tourist magnet, these canal side paths – in total three times longer than their more famous Venetian cousins – have great appeal for the cyclist. Within a couple of kilometres, the intrepid cyslist can be out of the traffic on tranquil paths headed for the countryside, an aspect of cycling infrastructure that many smaller cities cannot boast.

Please note that during the time of research there were several instances of construction that warranted extensive detours. Don't take the cue sheets as gospel.

PLANNING
When to Cycle

Smouldering summers in the Po Plain are tempered by the lakes and rivers in the foothills of the Alps. Industry-rich Milan and its suburban sprawl intensify the heat, making spring and autumn the best times of year for pedalling.

Maps & Books

Touring Club Italiano's 1:200,000 *Lombardia* map is ideal for this ride. The free *Regione Lombardia* tourist map detailing rivers sections is helpful when spinning along the Ticino and Adda Rivers.

Interested in organised cycling activities? Check with Milan's very active FIAB affiliate, **Ciclobby** (☎ /fax 02 693 11 624; www .ciclobby.it; Via Borsieri 4e). Its offices are due north of the Garibaldi train station. Otherwise, the Provincia di Milano produces Italian-language cycling brochures that have detailed information on cycling itineraries in the region.

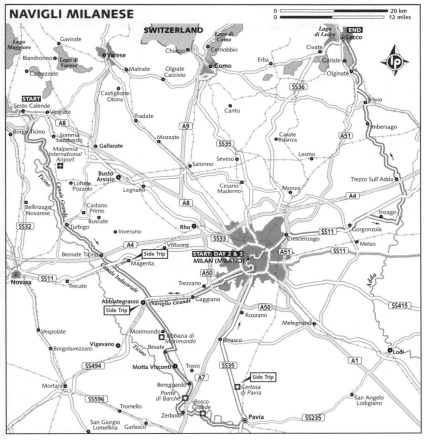

NAVIGLI MILANESE

Day 1: Navigli Milanesi

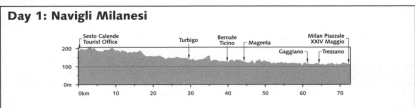

GETTING TO/FROM THE RIDE
Sesto Calende (start)
TRAIN
Sesto's train station is on the main Milan–Domodossola line that skirts Lago Maggiore's southwest shore (1 hour to/from Milan, 12 trains daily).

Lecco (finish)
TRAIN
From Lecco, it's an easy train ride (€2.65, 45 minutes) to Bergamo, the start of the Eastern Lakes ride and south to Milan (€2.60, 1 hour). Both have regular services and require a €3.50 supplementary bike ticket.

NAVIGLI MILANESI – DAY 1

CUES			GPS COORDINATES
start		Sesto Calende tourist office	45°43'24"N 8°37'49"E
0km	↰	E on Viale Italia	
0.4	↑	Alzaia Mattea (at Piazza Guarano)	
1.4	⚠	1km gravel path	
2.5	↱	unsigned main road	
3	↱	bike path to 'Milano' (just before hill)	
8.6	↱	to 'Milano'	
9.2	↰	at T intersection by Porto della Torre	
10.4	↱	E/1 Alleanza Assicurazioni path to 'Milano'	
10.8	⚠	0.5km cobblestones	
11.7	↑	cross canal	
11.8	↰	hard turn, bike path by canal	
12.6	↑	Canale Industriale bikepath	
17.2	⚠	cross to other side of canal	
27.2	↑	end of bike path	
27.6	↑	Via Alzaia 'to Turbigo'	
28.1	↑	Via E. Fermi	
29.3	↱	Via Milano (main road)	
29.3	↱	(10m) hard turn, Via A. Boromi	
29.3	↰	(50m) along Canale Grande	
29.5	★	Turbigo	45°31'36"N 8°44'01"E
37.8	↑	leave E/1 bike path	
39.7	★	Bernate Ticino	45°28'42"N 8°49'08"E
44.4	★	Magenta	45°26'24"N 8°53'10"E
49.4	↙	via Case Nuove (main road)	
49.6	↑	do NOT cross canal	
50.6	↑	Via per Castelleto	
53.5	↑	cross bridge over Naviglio Grande	
53.6	↰	Via Alzaia Naviglio Grande	
61.4	↰★	cross canal in Gaggiano	45°24'22"N 9°02'00"E
61.4	↱	(20m) along canal	
64.4	★	Trezzano	
73.1	↱	Viale Gorizia	
73.3		Milan Piazzale XXIV Maggio	45°27'09"N 9°10'44"E

BICYCLE

Lecco is the last day of the Epic Passes, Famous Lakes ride (p132). You can take the somewhat trafficked SS583 to Como (52km).

THE RIDE
Day 1: Sesto Calende to Milan
4–7½ hours, 73.3km

Today's ride is never far from gently flowing water and is as flat as the terrain that keeps the flow so slow. The route has four parts: the meandering lane along the Ticino River in the **Parco Regionale Valle del Ticino** – the tranquil, car-free bike path along the Canale Industriale – the small roads along the Canale Grande through the **Parco Lombardo della Valle**

NAVIGLI MILANESI – DAY 2

CUES			GPS COORDINATES
start		Milan Piazzale XXIV Maggio	45°27'09"N 9°10'44"E
0km		W on Viale Gorizia	
0.2	↘	Naviglio Grande	
8.9	★	Trezzano	45°25'08"N 9°04'18"E
12.7	↰★	Gaggiano, cross canal	45°24'22"N 9°02'00"E
	↱	(20m) along canal	
20.5	↑	to R is bridge from Lecco route	
21.9	↑	Parco Ticino bike path	
		{21.9 ●● ↱ Abbiategrasso 3km ↻}	
		{26 ●● ↱ Abbazia di Morimondo 3km ↻}	
43.5	↱	bike path ends	
44	★↱	Bereguardo, 'to Garlasco'	45°15'30"N 9°01'39"E
49.8	◉↰	'to Garlasco,'2n exit	
50.5	↰	'to Zerbolo'	
66.8	↰	Viale Giulietti/Viale della Liberta	
67.8	↙	Viale Battisti	
68.4	↰	Via Filzi, to 'Centro'	
68.7	↱	Piazza Petrarca	
	★	(50m)Pavia tourist office	45°11'19"N 9°09'14"E
68.8	↱	out of Piazza Petrarca, Viale Matteotti	
68.9	↰	Via XI Febbraio	
69.3	◉↑	(2nd exit) continue	
69.9	↱	cross bridge over Naviglio Pavese	
	↰	(20m) V. Alz. Continue following BP	
		{76.7 ●● ↱ Certosa di Pavia 5km ↻}	
92.2	↰	to 'Milano'	
99.8	↰	following route over bridge to turn on Via Della Chiesa Rosa	
102.3	▤↰	Via San Gottardo	
102.4		Milan Piazzale XXIV Maggio	45°27'09"N 9°10'44"E

del Ticino – and the eastern dash along the much-storied Naviglio Grande through the Parco Agricolo Milano Sud straight into Milan's trendy Navigli area.

The first 13km passes effortlessly along the eastern bank of the Ticino. This uninterrupted bike-only corridor doesn't get much shade, but the kilometres just whiz by. Signs pointing the path across to the east side of the canal at the Castelnovate lock complex (17.2km) are a little confusing.

Nosate, 2.3km short of **Turbigo** (29.5km), is at the end of the blissfully low-horse-power *pista* (track) and the national park. Regular roads advance the ramble. Wander inland for a pinch at Turbigo (detour through its centre for its 13th-century Castello Visconteo) and then ease back into the familiar canal-side course. At **Bernate Ticino** (40km), the 15th-century Palazzo Visconti and a Renaissance castle-convent should be admired. Around 3km further,

ITALIAN ALPS & LAKES DISTRICT

NAVIGLI MILANESI - MILAN

the Ponte Vecchio canal crossing (with a bike shop and the park headquarters, ☎ 02 972 10 205, on the corner) is at the western edge of Magenta, site of memorials to an important and very bloody 1859 battle in the Italian struggle for unification. The path continues along the eastern bank of the canal, glides past sumptuous villas, exits the parkland and crosses the bridge over the Naviglio Grande.

The last 20km run the length of the Naviglio Grande through Parco Agricolo Milano Sud. Stop in **Gaggiano** (61.4km) at the bridge across the canal to glimpse its 15th-century Villa Marino and municipal *palazzo* (palace). In **Trezzano** (64.4km), take in the 10th- to 12th-century Chiesa

di San Ambrogio and 17th-century bridge. Within the Milan city limits, 13th-century Chiesa di San Cristoforo borders right on the canal. These few sights don't complicate directions along this arrow-straight corridor into southern urban Milan.

Day 2: Milan Circuit via Pavia
5½–9½ hours, 102.4km

Like most terrain in the region, this route is flat, hitting the banks of three different *navigli* (canals) – the Grande, Bereguardo (43.5km) and Pavese – and the monument-rich city of Pavia.

The morning ride is to Abbiategrasso along yesterday's Naviglio Grande, but this time from Milan and not Sesto Calende

Day 2: Navigli Milanesi

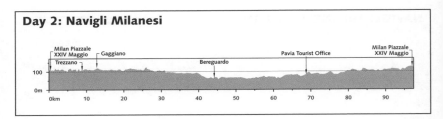

(see map p141 for Milan section). For those averse to the already-seen, westbound local trains from Milan's Stazione Porta Genova, 600m west of Piazzale XXIV Maggio, make the trip in 25 minutes. **Abbiategrasso** has a 12th-century Castello Visconteo and the 15th-century Chiesa Santa Maria Nuova.

Abbiategrasso is just west of the Naviglio Bereguardo along which the route then runs. This waterway is a narrow canal winding through the area's extensive agricultural meadows, much of which was once under the direction of Cistercian monks residing in the 11th-century **Abbazia di Morimondo**, just west of the canal (around 26km). The trail along the canal disappears and the route detours through local villages as far as **Bereguardo**, site of an impressive 13th-century Castello Visconteo.

In Bereguardo head west across to the far bank of the Ticino across a cool *ponte di barche* (boat bridge). The **Bosco Grande** (woods) after Zerbolo is a rare and protected natural riparian forest.

Pavia (see the Lungo Po Argine ride p108) is the turn-around point and a good place for lunch.

The Naviglio Pavese now runs without interruption (and sometimes with gravel embankments) all the way to Milan's Piazzale XXIV Maggio. Along the way, don't dismiss the side trip (76.7km) to the **Certosa di Pavia**, a fabulous 14th- to 15th-century Carthusian monastery (church, cloister and palace) and one of the most notable Italian buildings produced during the Renaissance. Also note the impressive system of locks south of Binasco.

Day 3: Milan to Lecco
4–7½ hours, 77.7km

Like the previous rides, this route is very flat. It follows the same geological sequence as Day 1, only in reverse: from downtown Milan (see map p141 for Milan section),

a canal (the Naviglio Martesana) escapes the urban jungle to the shores of a river (the Adda) that cuts through a green swath of park (Parco dell'Adda Nord) to a city (Lecco) on a great lake (the Lago di Como).

The **Naviglio Martesana** starts just north of Milan's main train station. It's a splendid waterside terrace bounded by family parks and playgrounds, and passing through placid communities riddled with majestic 17th- and 18th-century villas and farmhouses. The bit between Cernusco and Casano d'Adda is particularly rich in architecture. Mind the direction of the canal. At three points – just after Crescenzago, just before Gorgonzola (after which the cheese is named) and before Inzago – you'll need to take a short detour away from the canal.

At **Casano d'Adda** (26km), the road along the canal turns north with the canal. A side trip to the centre of **Casano** runs by the 11th-century Castello Borromeo and a number of lavish villas. Back on the main route, a signed bike path swings back to the west from **Groppello**, but your route continues north, sometimes over gravel, along the wooded bluffs along the canal.

Pavement returns when a hydroelectric facility appears. The arresting, frescoed, 15th-century **Palazzo Melzi d'Eril** at **Vapro d'Adda** is atop the rock face to the left. The gravel path continues along the water.

The nearby church is Trezzo sull'Adda's 17th-century **Santuario della Maternità di Maria**. The Naviglio della Martesana ends here and the course along the west bank of the true Adda River begins. At the time of writing, this riverside route was blocked a short distance north. A ramp up the cliff face sufficed for a fortuitous skip into central Trezzo sull'Adda right by its ancient castle. The road just beyond the castle returns to water level and proceeds along the river.

NAVIGLI MILANESI – DAY 3

CUES		GPS COORDINATES
start	Milan Piazza Duca d'Aosta, Stazione	
		45°27'27"N 9°10'52"E
0km	NW on Via Galvani	
0.4	↱ Via Melchiorre Gioia bike path	
2.3	Naviglio della Martesana bike path	
15.6	Metro Cassina de' Pecchi	45°31'10"N 9°21'55"E
19.2	↙ follow canal bike path	
19.8	Gorgonzola	45°31'50"N 9°24'21"E
21.5	▲↱ cross highway	
	▲↙ (5m) right of barrier to bike path	
23.3	Inzago	45°32'14"N 9°28'45"E
26.5	↰ follow canal bike path	
	(●● ↱ Cassano d'Adda 1km ↻)	
28.2	↑ Groppello, NOT across bridge	45°32'38"N 9°31'26"E
31.2	▲ 3.5km gravel bike path	
35.3	★↑ Vaprio d'Adda, NOT across bridge	
		45°34'34"N 9°31'56"E
35.5	↙▲ 4km gravel bike path	
38.5	▲ cross canal (at Santuario)	
39.5	↖ go up ramp (to castle)	
40	★ Trezzo sull'Adda	45°36'25"N 9°31'17"E
	↱ Via Visconti back to river	
40.4	▲ 6.6km good gravel bike path	
48.8	★ Bertini power station	
49.3	▲ 0.7km gravel bike path	
51.6	★ Paderno d'Adda bridge	
52.8	▲ 1.2km gravel bike path	
55.3	★ Imbersago ferry crossing	45°42'27"N 9°2723"E
55.4	▲ 3.2km gravel bike path	
59.8	Brivio	45°44'22"N 9°26'51"E
60	↑ follow river, ignore dead-end signs	
61.5	▲ 4km dirt single track	
67.2	↱▲ unmarked road, 1.3km gravel path	
68.5	Olginate	45°48'04"N 9°24'54"E
69.2	↰ Via Barozzi (last before bridge)	
68.9	↱ unsigned (main) road	
	↱ (50m) cross brdge `to Calolziocorte'	
70.6	↰ `to Lecco'	
73	↰ Via della Spiaggia `to spaggia'	
74.7	↙ unmarked nonoverpass road	
75.2	↙ Via Figini `to Lecco'	
75.7	↰ Corso Carlo Alberto `to Sondrio'	
77.2	↰ Via Costituzione `to Valtellina'	
77.5	↱ follow curve onto Largo Isonzo	
77.7	↱ Via Saura (after Larius Rest.)	
	(50m) Lecco tourist office	45°51'10"N 9°23'24"E

For 6.6km, a gravel path parallels the rapid waters. A paved road briefly takes over at the **Bettini power station**, designed by the American inventor Thomas Alva Edison and built in 1896 as the first plant

for the long-distance transport of electricity. Shortly thereafter, a new canal appears, the Naviglio di Paderno, and plunges into a beautiful thickly wooded area of winding, sometimes-gravel paths and overgrown canal locks.

The comfortable riverside pace returns once the high 1889 bridge at Paderno wheels into view. The barriers to the Imbersago ferry landing may require two people to lift the bike over. The structure and operating system of the ferry are based on drawings by Leonardo da Vinci, who spent many years studying the waters of the Adda south of Lecco.

Brivio, the next town after a lovely wooded pedal, is the end of the effortless bike paths. Continuing straight along the river's edge, 4km of tough single-track mix with small residential-area trails to avoid the main road and then link with a fine bike path to **Olginate** on its namesake lake.

The bridge here provides the first access to the east bank of the Adda, where you can take a fun spin along **Lake Garlate** to Lecco, the southernmost city on the eastern leg of Lago di Como.

EASTERN LAKES

Duration 3 days
Distance 203.4km
Difficulty moderate
Start Bergamo
Finish Mantua (Mantova)
Summary You'll find clear contrasts here with the charming and understated Lago d'Iseo and Lago di Endine offering a counterpoint to the brash and beautiful Lago di Garda.

Lago di Garda is the largest and most frequented of the Italian Lakes. Its tiny neighbours, Lago di Endine and d'Iseo, although diminutive in surface area are no less grand in appeal. This ride swims through fabulous rolling hills from the former Venetian outpost of Bergamo through these eastern water sensations and down the Fiume Mincio to its terminus, Mantua, on the edge of the Po flood plain.

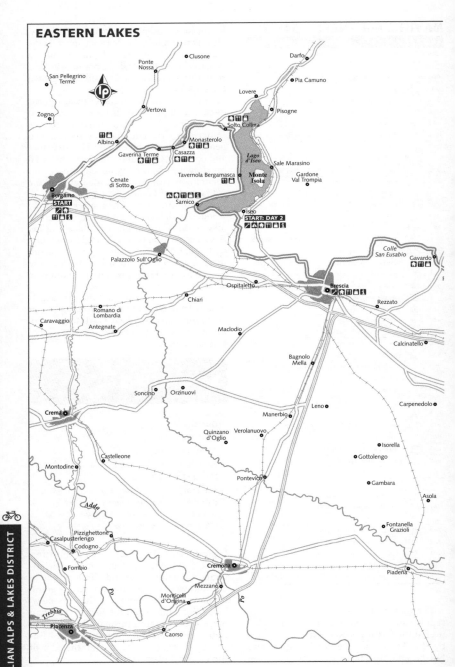

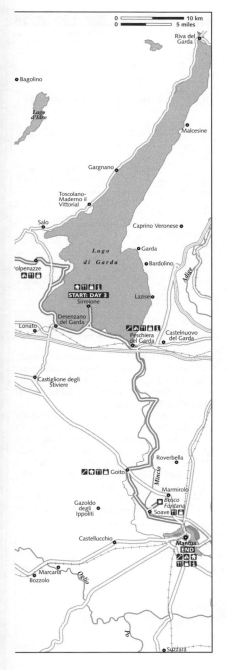

PLANNING
When to Cycle
Like the more central lakes, the eastern basins enjoy a mild climate. Cycling is most enjoyable from spring to autumn, although August can be a very crowded month (especially on Lago di Garda). The afternoon southerly breezes are felt here too.

Maps
Touring Club Italiano's 1:200,000 *Lombardia* map includes the full length of this ride. Regione Lombardia also distributes a 1:50,000 map of *Lago d'Iseo e dintorni* for a close-up of the smaller lakes, and Comunità del Garda makes a simple map of Lago di Garda.

Information Sources
The active FIAB affiliate in Bergamo is **Associazione Rilancio Bicicletta** (☎ 03 536 00 53; www.aribi.it). Along the way on Day 3, you pass **Olympic Bike Centre** (☎ 04 564 01 837; Via Bella Italia 31; right at the turn off to Peschiera). This huge bike shop rents mountain, road and city bikes.

GETTING TO/FROM THE RIDE
Bergamo (start)
BUS
The bus station in Bergamo, across from the train station on Piazzale Marconi, is served by SAB with regular lines to/from the lakes and surrounding mountains. Other companies run to/from nearby big cities (Milan, Brescia, Cremona, Como and Piacenza).

TRAIN
Three rail lines stop in Bergamo: a direct service from Milan (50 minutes); a thrice-daily local from Cremona (1¾ hours) via Treviglio; and the busy route between Brescia (1 hour) and Lecco (35 minutes).

BICYCLE
To cycle to Lago di Como, Lecco is 35km northwest by way of SS639 and SS342.

Mantua (finish)
See p117.

EASTERN LAKES – DAY 1

CUES		GPS COORDINATES
start	Bergamo tourist office	45°41'26"N 9°40'35"E
0	SE on Viale Giovanni XXIII	
	18km easy, gradual climb	
0.5	Via Camozzi to 'Valle Seriana'	
2.2	Via Corridoni	
5	bike shop, Norris Speedy Sport	
6.3	Alzano, to 'Villa di Serio' SP69	45°43'56"N 9°43'45"E
7.1	Via Dalzano to 'Villa di Serio'	
7.2	Viale Piave to 'Villa di Serio'	
7.5	(cross bridge)to 'Villa di Serio'	
7.6	to 'Clusone'	
	take bike path just beyond Roundabout, direction 'Clusone'	
	1.4 packed dirt path	
8.4	to 'Nebro'	
9	Merge with road	
14.2	to 'Abazzia'	
18.7	Abbazia	45°44'56"N 9°50'15"E
	6km tough climb	
24.7	Colle Gallo (763m, Madonna dei Ciclisti)	
	6km twisty descent	
29.9	Gaverina Terme	45°44'51"N 9°54'18"E
32.4	SS42 to 'Lovere'	
33.8	Casazza	45°44'23"N 9°54'24"E
34.2	to 'Monasterolo'	
35.4	to 'Monasterolo'	

CUES CONTINUED		GPS COORDINATES
36.2	Monasterolo, to 'Cassa Della Gente'	45°45'51"N 9°56'00"E
36.7	to 'Endine'	
42.6	SS42 to 'Lovere'	
43.8	to 'Riva di Solto'	
44.6	1.5 km steep climb	
46.7	Solto Collina (430m)	45°46'59"N 10°00'59"E
	4.2km steep descent	
50.5	to 'Sarnico'	
51	Riva di Solto	45°46'30"N 10°02'22"E
51.1	SS469 to 'Sarnico'	
54.2	1.2 km tunnel	
58	Tavernola Bergamasca	45°42'37"N 10°02'53"E
63.8	Predore	45°40'50"N 10°01'10"E
68	(unsigned road) counter flow, where Via Predore becomes Corso Europa	
68.6	merge with road	
68.7	Via V Veneto on red bike path	
69	Sarnico, to 'Iseo'	45°40'04"N 9°57'29"E
69.5	cross bridge to 'Iseo'	
70.8	Teckno Bike Shop	
69.8	Via Mazzini to 'Iseo'	
72.9	Clusane	45°39'47"N 10°00'00"E
76	to 'Iseo'	
78	to 'Iseo'	
79.1	at fountain, follow road along water	
79.5	Iseo tourist office	45°39'39"N 10°02'51"E

THE RIDE
Day 1: Bergamo to Iseo
4½–9 hours, 79.5km

Today's a valley-and-lake kind of day with two intermediate passes. From Bergamo the route eases into the shallow lower Valle Seriana and cranks 430m up the Valle del Lujo to the Colle Gallo and then drops to the little lake gems of **Lago di Endine** and **d'Iseo** for roars along their shores.

After the turn east to **Casazza**, the route begins to climb more steeply. **Colle Gallo** (763m) is a gruelling 6km up beyond the top of an immediately visible ridge. Take a break in **Abbazia** for the important, intact, 12th-century **Benedictine monastery**. Make the obligatory pilgrimage stop at the pass-top **Santuario del Colle Gallo** and its **Madonne dei ciclisti**.

The 7km plummet to the Val Cavallina and the shores of **Lago di Endine** takes only a few minutes and tears through the spa town of **Gaverina Terme**. Slip to the far side of the lake on the quieter road through **Monasterolo** (36.2km) for its view and castle with 13th-century origins.

Monolithic Monte Agolo on Lago d'Iseo is an overwhelming spectacle for anyone

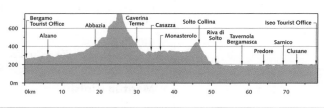

Day 1: Eastern Lakes

EASTERN LAKES – DAY 2

CUES CONTINUED		GPS COORDINATES
start	Iseo tourist office	45°39'39"N 10°02'51"E
0km	SW along water	
0.3	2nd exit, Viale Reppublica/Via XX Settembre	
	{0.5 alt route: Franciacorta	
0.6	Iseo FNME train station	
	{!take train to Brescia}	
0.6	Brescia train station	45°31'56"N 10°12'46"E
	Viale Stazione	
0.8	(2nd exit) Corso Martiri d. Liberta	
1.8	Piazza della Loggia	
{	alt route rejoins}	
1.9	Via Gasparo da Salo	
2.6	Via San Faustino bike path	
2.7	Via Battisti	
2.9	Via Apollonio `to Lago di Garda'	
3.3	Via Galileo Galilei	
3.9	Via San Rocchino	
4.1	9.8km gradual climb `to Ospedale'	
4.5	Via Schivardi	
4.9	to 'Val Trompia'	
6.6	at T intersection	
7.7	unsigned busy street	
12.8	Nave, 10.2km moderate climb	
		45°35'10"N 10°17'19"E

CUES CONTINUED		GPS COORDINATES
22.1	Colle San Eusabio (574m)	
	3.3km descent `to Gavardo'	
30.9	(1st exit) `to Gavardo'	
31.8	unsigned main road (cross river)	
31.9	Gavardo	45°35'04"N 10°26'33"E
32.	Via Fossa/Viale Antonio Ferretti	
32.4	Largo Giacobinelli to 'Muscoline'	
32.6	(2nd exit) to 'Muscoline' (straight thru 2 more)	
33.6	3km moderate climb `to Muscoline'	
36.1	Muscoline, `to Lago di Garda'	
		45°33'45"N 10°27'41"E
38.3	to 'Manerba'	
40.6	4km steep descent to 'Manerba'	
42.1	Via S. Antonio to 'Manerba'	
45	2nd exit to 'Manerba' NOT Soiano	
	{45.5 Manerba di Garda 3km }	
	Via M. d. Liberta to 'Moniga'	
47	Via S. Martino to 'Moniga'	
49.6	Moniga del Garda	45°31'44"N 10°32'18"E
50.5	SS572 to 'Desenzano'	
	{53.2 Padenghe sul Garda 1km }	
58.2	to 'Centro'	
58.5	to 'Sirmione'	
65.4	at stop signed T intersection, to info icon	
67.6	Sirmione tourist office	45°29'30"N 10°36'30"E

heading down from the top of the pass at **Solto Collina** (430m, 46.7km). It dominates the view until the sweet and discreet lakeshore road bends through **Tavernola Bergamasca** and then to the west. Once-fortified medieval **Sarnico** (69km) squats at the narrow end of the lake, from which it is only 10km to the basin's namesake city of **Iseo**.

Day 2: Iseo to Sirmione
4–7 hours, 67.6km

Today's route goes from lake to lake. After a quick morning train through **Franciacorta** or a long alternative route through it to **Brescia**, roads climb one pass to the vineyarded and olive-groved rolling hills of Valtenesi on the western shores of Lago di Garda. A short trip around the southern end culminates in Sirmione, a town at the tip of a narrow isthmus.

Your first morning responsibility: get to Brescia the quick way. The **Ferrovia Nord Milano Esercizio** (www.ferrovienord.it) station is at the end of Via XX Settembre in Iseo. More than 15 trains come through daily, covering the distance to Brescia in 20 minutes (€3).

Brescia is replete with attractions. Its historic centre is dominated by Colle Cidneo and its castle and 13th-century Torre Mirabella, also host to two museums.

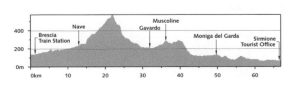

Day 2: Eastern Lakes

Nave · Muscoline · Gavardo · Brescia Train Station · Moniga del Garda · Sirmione Tourist Office

At the foot of the castle are the Roman ruins of **Capitolium** (a temple) and a Roman theatre. The city museum is housed in Monasterio di Santa Giulia. Heading west, on Brescia's central square, Piazza Paolo VI, the 11th-century **Romanesque Duomo Vecchio** is the headliner, although the Renaissance **Duomo Nuovo** dwarfs it. To the northwest is Piazza Loggia, with its 16th-century loggia and Torre dell'Orologio. Modern, fascist-styled Piazza della Vittoria is a perfect example of the period's monumentalism.

From Brescia's Piazza della Loggia, **Colle San Eusebio** (22.1km) is 425m up the Garza Valley. Beyond it are the varied terrain and quiet back roads of the world-famous Lago di Garda area of **Valtenesi**. Ruins of walls, castles and villas pepper the cultivated slopes of this region loved by Goethe, Byron, Lawrence, Ibsen, Rilke, Gide, Pound and many other accomplished writers. The route takes in the villages of **Polpenazze**, with its medieval castle and 16th-century parish church.

From **Moniga**, the main road is the only road around the bottom of the lake. It passes through the major hub of **Desenzano del Garda** before tripping north up a tapered cape to Sirmione. **Desenzano** has ruins of a 4th-century Roman villa (with excellent mosaics), a 14th- to 15th-century castle and the 16th-century Chiesa di Santa Maria Maddalena.

ALTERNATIVE ROUTE: FRANCIACORTA
2–3½ hours, 35.6km

Franciacorta, the Tuscany of the north, is a quality wine region of rolling hills. The name Franciacorta comes from *corti franche* (literally 'short taxes'), a hint of the area's tax-free status dating back to the Venetian Republic, when privileged religious orders tilled the land. The religious centres they left behind, as well as later villas and castles, dot the landscape.

The alternate route swings through Provaglio d'Iseo (Romanesque Monasterio di S. Pietro, Riserva Naturale Torbiere), Bornato, Paderno Franciacorta (14th-century castle), Rodengo-Saiano (15th-century Abbazia di San Nicola), Gussago (10th-century Pieve di Santa Maria) and Cellatica on the way to Brescia.

For more local ride information (there are many signed bike paths), contact the Brescia FIAB affiliate, **Amici della Bici** (☎ 03 037 56 023; www.youthpoint.it/amicidellabic).

Day 3: Sirmione to Mantua
4–6 hours, 55.3km

With the exception of the first 11km running along the southern fringe of Lago di Garda, today's route is entirely within **Parco Regionale del Mincio**, a strip of green bordering the southern arm of the river to Mantua. The road takes in a few low hills when skirting the edge of the western morainic *colline* (hills), but is essentially level.

On the road south of Sirmione, the first and last lakeside community is **Peschiera del Garda** (9.5km), straddling the mouth of the Fiume Mincio. Impressive ramparts dating back to the years of Venetian and Austrian domination girdle Peschiera.

In Peschiera, you hit the best part of the day: the **Ciclopedonale Mantua–Peschiera bike path**, running the full distance between the cities. Only very small sections of it are unpaved, and it's a tranquil riverside ramble flanked by greenery with the occasional castle in the distance.

The divine riverside **Borghetto** (24.4km) visible off to the right should be given a quick tour. Many a local will tell you about its beauty. Up the hill, **Valeggio** is topped by the **Castello Scaligeno** and a typical medieval centre. A short distance to the north, the area's crowning attraction is the 100-acre **Parco Giardino Sigurtà** installed on the grounds of the 17th-century **Villa**

Day 3: Eastern Lakes

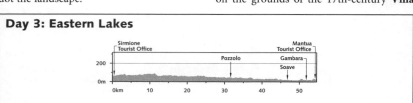

EASTERN LAKES – DAY 3

CUES		GPS COORDINATES
start	Sirmione tourist office	45°29'30"N 10°36'30"E
0km	↰	S along water
3.2	↰	to 'Verona'
		{9.5 ●● ↰ to 'Peschiera' 2km rt
12	↰	to Localita 'Casa Otello', before hotel
12.2	↰	onto 'Ciclo pedonale'
17.3	↰	cross bridge
22.9	↰	on path not road
24	⚠	.4 km gravel
24.4	↑	following bike path signs
		{ ●● ↰ to 'Borghetto'
31.6	↱	Pozzolo, to 'Volta' following bike path
		45°18'05"N 10°42'59"E
38	↱	on bike path, to 'Mantua'
46.6	↱	Soave, across bridge 45°11'25"N 10°43'58"E
46.7	↱	on bike path on other side of canal
49.8	↙	on bike path
	↱	(20m) at T intersection
49.9	↰	first left following bike path signs
50.1	↱	at T intersection after wooden bridge
51.7	↘	to continue on bike path across street
51.9	↱	bike path sign to 'Foresta della Carpaneta'
		Gambara 45°10'44"N 10°46'58"E
52.9	↱	Precorso Ciclopedonale
		(easy to miss – right after path joins traffic)
53.9	↰	under overpass to where path continues
54.2	↰🕭	U turn onto street
54.3	↱	Via Trento/Giovanni Arrivabene
55	↱	Via Domenico Fernelli
55.3		Mantua tourist office 45°09'30"N 10°47'47"E

Maffei and once the headquarters of Napoleon III.

From there, a fine spin through open countryside laced with canals ends in the little town of **Goito** (site of a medieval tower) before the final pedal into Mantua. An interesting side trip can be made from **Soave** (46.6km) to the protected deciduous **Bosco Fontana**, complete with a 15th-century castle.

MOUNTAIN BIKE RIDES

AOSTA

Many trails in the valley are suitable for mountain biking and there are some particularly interesting nature trails in the **Parco Nazionale del Gran Paradiso**. The tourist office gives advice on mountain-biking itineraries and mountain accommodation.

BORMIO

Mountain bikers will find rental material and supplies at **Bormio Ski 7 Bike** (☎ 03 429 01 698; www.bormioskibike.it; Via Morbegno 5). The tourist office has a good amount of information about mountain biking in the area.

Also located in the area is **Alta Rezia** (www.altarezia.eu), a company that organizes bike tours and runs a mountain biking school. Their website offers a lot of fat-tyre information in the area.

IVREA

For a unique way to experience Parco Nazionale del Gran Paradiso, tackle the six-day ascent of 4061m **Gran Paradiso** – first part on bike, second part on foot. Ask at tourist information about **Me Na Vòta** or contact **ATL del Canavese e Valli di Lanzo** (☎ 01 256 18 131; www.granparadiso.it; Corso Vercelli 1).

TIRANO

The tourist office in Tirano gives out free mountain biking and trekking maps and is a good source of information in general.

VALLE DI SUSA AND ITS ALPINE TOWNS

Devoted mountain bikers should ask for the *Montagne doc Due ruote tra i monti* pamphlet. For all information about rentals, trails, events and guides in Bardonecchia check out www.bardonecchiabike.com.

TOWNS & FACILITIES

AOSTA

☎ 01 / pop 34,100

Aosta, the 'Rome of the Alps', is the capital and only major city of the Valle d'Aosta, sitting at its centre on the Fiume Dora Baltea. Opportunities for hiking and other outdoor activities (rock climbing, mountain biking, hang-gliding/paragliding, mountaineering etc) attract tourists in droves to this incredibly postcard-picturesque old town nestled into a mountain valley.

Information

The **APT office** (☎ 01 652 36 627; www .regione.vda.it/turismo, www.aostavalley .com; Piazza Chanoux 8) has loads of information on the entire region, including detailed road maps that are very handy.

Banks are also found on this large central square.

Supplies & Equipment

A very good bike shop, **Cicli Lucchini** (☎ 01 652 62 306; www.ciclilucchini.com; Corso Battaglione Aosta 49–51), with a knowledgeable staff, is 300m west of the old town walls. Mountain bikes can be rented from **Gal Sport** (☎ 01 652 36 134; www .paginegialle.it/galsportsas; Strada Paravera 6) at the base of the *funivia* (cable car).

Sleeping & Eating

Accommodation is sometimes difficult to find. In a pinch, there are cheap and pleasant lodgings in the very near hinterland – check with the APT office.

There are many camp sites in the valley and on the ride route. Check out www .camping.it for more listings.

Milleluci (☎ 01 652 35 278; www .campingmilleluci.com; Loc Porossan Roppoz 15; per person/tent €8–10/€15) is about 1km to the east of Aosta. If you're a camper and your riding partner likes their bed turned down, this is the perfect appeaser.

Hotel Turin (☎ 01 654 45 93; www .hotelturin.it; Via Torino 14; s €34–60, d €58–84) is a modern, boxy affair. Some rooms have mountain views. It's a quick spin to the train station, there's a basement where you can store your bike, and the breakfast (extra charge) will surely sustain you.

Hotel Roma (☎ 01 654 08 21; hroma@ libero.it; Via Torino 7; s €36–54, d €60–76) is a reasonably priced option just outside the old Roman walls, but it does not come with the most cyclist-friendly staff. Breakfast costs extra.

The penny-conscious will find the Mercato Coperto and supermarkets east of the walls at Piazza Cavalieri Vittorio Veneto, and good speciality food shops in Via Sant'Anselmo. Open-air cafés spring up on Piazza Chanoux's terraces in summer.

Ad Forum (☎ 01 654 00 11; Via Mons de Sales 11; mains €12–19; Tue–Sun) is a garden restaurant built on part of the remains of the Roman forum. They serve gargantuan portions of creative and traditional dishes, and the attached *enoteca* (wine bar) has an excellent line-up of wines. **Trattoria degli Artisti** (☎ 01 654 09 60; Via Maillet 5–7; mains €7.50–18) has fabulous Valdostan regional cuisine – like salami, polenta and puff pastries filled with Valdostan fondue.

AVIGLIANA
☎ 01 / pop 11,100

The Susa Valley traces one arm of the Via Francigena, a web of paths between Turin and France hiked for centuries by merchants, mercenaries and pilgrims. Avigliana, at the eastern end of the trail below Sacra di San Michele, was a focal point of valley life. Its many monuments bear witness to a lasting presence.

Information

The **tourist information office** (☎ 01 193 28 650; www.comune.avigliana.to.it; Piazza del Popolo 2a) is centrally located.

Banks are nearby on the square.

Supplies & Equipment

The nearest bike store, **Cicli Giai** (☎ 011 939 93 73; info.cicligiai@libero.it; Via Turin 48), is in Sant'Ambrogio.

Sleeping & Eating

Check out the tourist office website (www .comune.avigliana.to.it) for more listings. About 500m from the lake is **Avigliana Lacs** (☎ 01 193 69 142; campingslacs@libero.it; Via Gaveno 23; per person/site €7/8–12), is a good camping option.

Albergo Miralago (☎ 01 193 69 123; Via Giaveno 3; rooms without bathroom from €42) also has a restaurant with basic pasta dishes and pizzas.

Albergo Vittoria (☎ 01 193 67 367; Corso Torino 90; s/d €45/55) and its restaurant are north of town on the main through road.

One-third of Avigliana's restaurants are on Corso Laghi. **Pizzeria del Pasché** (Corso Laghi 231) always draws a crowd. For a view that will distract you from your primo-quality meal, try **Ristorante Hermitage** (Strada Sacra San Michele 12).

BERGAMO
☎ 03 / pop 113,000

Virtually two cities, Bergamo consists of an enclosed hilltop *città alta* (upper town) surrounded by a 16th-century circle of walls, beyond which is the *città bassa* (lower town), the sprawling modern counterpart to this magnificent former outpost of the Venetian empire. Bergamo has a strong sense of local identity, and this lively town off the tourist track offers much for your discovery.

Information

Città alta **tourist office** (☎ 03 524 22 26; Via Gombito 13) has upper town information only. Città bassa **tourist office** (☎ 03 521 02 04; www.comune.bergamo.it; Piazzale Marconi) has province-wide information, including the lowdown on alpine activities.

Banks are easily found in the lower city in Viale Roma and Viale Papa Giovanni.

Supplies & Equipment

There is a moto/bike shop, **Effendi & Merelli** (☎ 03 524 79 70; Via Corridoni 9a), on the way out of town. **Cicli Bonfanti** (☎ 03 522 50 82; Via GB Moroni 180) is centrally located.

Sleeping & Eating
CITTÀ BASSA (LOWER TOWN)

Nuovo Ostello di Bergamo (☎ 03 536 17 24; www.ostellodibergamo.it; Via Galileo Ferraris 1; dm/s/d €16.50/27/40) is Bergamo's state-of-the-art HI hostel 4km north of the train station.

Hotel San Giorgio (☎ 03 521 20 43; www.sangiorgioalbergo.it; Via San Giorgio 10; s/d €33/53, s/d with bathroom €53/70) is a basic two-star place, around 400m southwest of the train station. It's one of the cheapest options in town, offering clean, simple rooms. Right in the centre of the lower city,

Al Vecchio Tagliere (☎ 03 534 47 25; www.alvechiotagliere.it; Via S Alessandro 13; s/d €40/60) is a heck of a deal for a bed and breakfast, with two large and elegantly decorated rooms and a deservedly popular restaurant. There's a nice internal place to lock bikes.

CITTÀ ALTA (UPPER TOWN)

Il Gourmet (☎ 03 543 73 004; Via San Vigilio 1; set menus €35–40), run by two wine buffs, is a gourmet's haven hidden away in San Vigilio, a few minutes' stroll beyond the upper town's western walls. Its shady terrace and artful Bergamasco and Mediterranean cuisine make it worth seeking out for a meal, but there are also 10 charming boutique rooms (s/d €66/98). Breakfast costs an extra €10.

BORMIO
☎ 01 / pop 4100

Bormio, a pretty little ski resort with a well-preserved medieval centre, occupies a key position on a high plain met by three valleys and criss-crossed by routes over the surrounding Alps. In the 12th century, the commercial Imperial German Road and Ombraglio Highway passed through. Many people come to Bormio today for its nine thermal-mineral springs.

Information

Bormio's **APT office** (☎ 03 429 03 300; www.bormio.it, www.valtline.com; Via Roma 131b) is near the southwest entrance to town and provides a wealth of maps and information. For information about Stelvio National Park, check with the **Consorzio** (☎ 04 729 10 100; www.stelviopark.it; Via Roma 26).

Banks are right around the corner on Via Roma.

Supplies & Equipment

Bobo Moto (☎ /fax 03 429 05 064; Via Milano 53), about 500m from the centre, is a good shop for repair, parts and rental. Mountain bikers will also find rental material and supplies at **Bormio Ski and Bike** (☎ 03 429 01 698; www.bormioskibike.it; Via Morbegno 5).

Sleeping & Eating

About 5km south on the main road (SS38) is **Cima Piazzi** (☎ 03 429 50 298; Via Nazionale 29, Tola Valdisotto; per person/site €7/5.50).

Ask at tourist information about B&Bs around town – hotel rates increase dramatically during peak seasons. In general, pay half-board to economise and because hotel-restaurant food quality is good. Many

ITALIAN ALPS & LAKES DISTRICT

hotels don't even post *meublé* (room only) rates. **Meublé Cima Bianca** (☎ 03 429 01 757; www.ciambianca.it; Via Credaro 5; s €50–70, d €60–80 is a lederhosen kind of place that welcomes cyclists, has a good breakfast, and is just two minutes from the centre of town.

Larice Bianco (☎ 03 429 04 693; www.laricebianco.it; Via Funivie 10; from €67 per night) is about as bike-friendly as they get with rental, bike cleaning services, GPS equipment for hire, maps and trail/road advice available, and a wellness centre with Turkish baths.

Albergo **Dante Meublé** (☎ /fax 03 429 01 329; meubledante@bormio.it; Via Trieste 2; room €90) has sunny rooms in the centre.

Hotel Adda (☎ 03 429 04 627; Via Milano 70; s/d €27/42), 1km west of town on the main road, is one of the cheapest and most pleasant hotels around.

ISEO
☎ 03 / pop 8400

After its heyday as an important command post and commercial centre at the outer reaches of the Venetian empire, Iseo slumbered for years as little more than a fishing town. Today, it's a peaceful holiday resort with antique shops set where fish stalls used to be.

Information
The **IAT office** (☎ 03 098 02 09; Lungolago Marconi 2) overlooks the lake.

Banks can be found next door on Porto Rosa.

Sleeping & Eating
There are 15 camping grounds within easy reach of downtown Iseo. The closest are just east of town, like **Punta d'Oro** (☎ / fax 03 098 00 84; www.puntadoro.com; Via Antonioli 51/53; per person/site €4.70–7.30/€13.30–18.90).

Iseo has three affordable lodges, all with wallet-friendly restaurants. **Albergo Rosa** (☎ 03 098 00 53; Via Roma 47) and **Albergo Arianna** (☎ 03 098 22 082; Via Roma 78; s/d €40/51) are a few streets back from the shore. Right next to the tourist office is **Albergo Milano** (☎ 03 098 04 49; www.hotelmilano.info; Lungolago Marconi 4; s €32–38, d €42–44) which has good-value

rooms looking right over the water. There are more similarly priced hotels in Clusane, 5km west of Iseo.

Self-caterers will find a variety of markets in the old town around Piazza Garibaldi.

IVREA
☎ 01 / pop 23,500

Ivrea is the largest city of Piedmont's Canavese region. A few kilometres from the beginning of the Valle d'Aosta, the view looks out to the wide Po River plain. Although it was established as Eporedia by the Romans, Ivrea is famous for its King Arduino, the early-11th century first King of Italy. He and his legions built the many castles throughout the area.

Information
Ivrea's main **Azienda Turistica Locale** (☎ 01 256 18 131; www.canavese-vallilanzo.it; Corso Vercelli 1) is 1.3km east of the centre. The **central branch** (☎ 01 256 27 603) is on Piazza Ottinetti.

Banks can be found on Via Palestro and its Corso Massimo d'Azeglio extension, and across the river in Corso Nigra.

Supplies & Equipment
Two bike shops, **Cicli Fiore** (☎ 01 256 41 695) and **BiciSport** (☎ 01 254 03 48) are within sight of each other at Corso Nigra 53 and 46, respectively. Local FIAB affiliate, **Amici della Bici – Legambiente** (☎ 01 254 42 02; curzionelli@tiscalinet.it) is in the Centro Gandhi at Via Arduino 75.

Sleeping & Eating
About 2km northeast of town towards the eponymous lake is the campground **Lago San Michele** (☎ 01 256 16 195; Via Lago San Michele 13; sites per person/tent €5/10). There are two hostels in town:

Ostello Canoa Club (☎ 01 254 01 86; www.parks.it/ost/ivrea; Via Dora Baltea 1; per person €15) and **Ostello Salesiano Eporediese** (☎ 01 256 27 268; www.salesiani-icp.net/ivrea/ostello; Via San Giovanni Bosco 58; per person €33 with breakfast).

Albergo Luca (☎ 01 254 87 06; Corso Garibaldi 58; s/d €37/57) is on a quiet courtyard off the main loop road.

Restaurants are mostly attached to hotels, although there are several stand-alone places in Via Arduino and Via Palestro and their Corso Vercelli extension to the east. Try the vaulted **La Mugnaia** (☎ 01 254 05 30; Via Arduino 53; closed Mon), in a side *vicolo* (alleyway), for regional fare. The **Enoteca Ferrando** (Corso Re Umberto 1) is a hip and popular place. Also popular is **Hotel Ristorante Aquila Nigra** (☎ 01 256 41 416; Corso Nigra 56), which spills over with people and serves traditional food and piping hot pizza from its old-fashioned oven.

LECCO
☎ 03 / pop 45,500

Lecco has a long and interesting history. Towered over by the Grigna mountain range and Monte Resegone, but open to Lago di Como's outlet to the Adda River, Lecco is both protected and accessible. This dramatic and strategic location has attracted countless peoples – area digs have uncovered the presence of Bronze-Age folk, Romans and Byzantines, among others. Today, Lecco, a picturesque shore side town on Lake Como, manages to stay low-key without attracting hordes of *turisti*. It's a fave lake town for sure.

Information
The **Lecco APT office** (☎ 03 413 69 390; www.turismo.provincia.lecco.it; Via Sauro 6) is one block back from the lake and is open daily. Banks are on the square, Piazza Garibaldi, just behind it.

Equipment & Supplies
The closest bike shop is **Gilardi** (☎ 03 412 72 523; Via Turbada 15), which is a bit far flung from the city centre. Travel in land from Torrente Bione, and it's off Via Tonio da Belledo.

Sleeping & Eating
Campers should head 4km to the south at Chiuso's *lido* (beach) on Lake Garlate to find **Rivabella** (☎ 03 414 21 143; www .rivabellalecco.3000.it; Via alla Spiaggia 35, Località Chiuso; per site/person €7.50/5.80).

Let the tourist office help you find rooms for rent and B&Bs.

In Lecco's centre is **Hotel Moderno** (☎ 03 412 86 519; Piazza Diaz 5; s/d €65/80), a pricey but good place that's bike-friendly.

Hotel/Ristorante Bellavista (☎ 03 415 81 335; Via Parè 87; r from €60) occupies an idyllic spot 4km southwest across the lake looking at Lecco and serves a hearty breakfast. Follow Day 2's directions to the tunnel entrance and veer right; the hotel is at the far end of the road.

Self-caterers can shop at the supermarkets on Viale Turati – this is also a good area for trattorias. Another restaurant row is to the east in Carlo Alberto and Via Pescatori. Downtown, a local favourite for pizza and pasta is **Taverna ai Poggi** (☎ 03 414 97 126; Via ai Poggi 14).

MANTUA
See the Po River Basin p117.

MILAN
☎ 02 / pop 1,256,000

Milan (Milano) is synonymous with style. Smart and slick at work or play, the Milanese run their busy metropolis with efficiency and aplomb. It's Italy's economic engine room, the powerhouse of world design and a leading fashion centre. That's why it's a kick in the pants to arrive sweaty and road-worn with a bike. Ha! It's also a city for city-lovers and an efficient orientation centre for anyone recently arrived or soon to depart.

Information
The main **IAT/APT office** (☎ 02 725 24 301; www.milanoinfotourist.com; Piazza del Duomo 9a; open daily) also has a **branch office** (☎ 02 725 24 360) at Stazione Centrale. All sell a comprehensive visitor's guide to Milan.

ATMs dispense cash all over town, particularly on important shopping strips and in heavily touristed areas. **Etnoland Shop** (☎ 02 720 99 239; Via Giardino 2; per 15min €1.20) is a central place to log on. **Lavanderia** (Via Tadino 4) is a self-service laundromat – just the place to take your sweat-soaked lycra.

Supplies & Equipment
One of the most central bike shops is **Rossignoli** (☎ 02 80 49 60; www.rossignoli .it; Via Garibaldi 71). Near the central station (and start of Day 2 of the Navigli Milanesi ride, see p142) is **AWS** (☎ 02 670 72 145; www.awsbici.com; Via Ponte

ITALIAN ALPS & LAKES DISTRICT

Seveso 33) which also does rentals. In the south, near Piazza XXIV Maggio (and the terminus for the other Navigli Milanesi ride days), try **I Signori del Ciclismo** (☎ 02 894 01 498; www.isignoridelciclismo.it; Via Ferrari 2).

Check with **Ciclobby** (p138) for others.

Sleeping & Eating

Finding a room in Milan (let alone a cheap one) isn't easy, particularly during the fashion weeks, furniture fair and other exhibitions, when rates skyrocket.

Lonely Planet's online booking service (lonelyplanet.com/hotels) reviews standout properties that can be booked online. Check out **Albergabici** (www.albergabici.it) for bike-friendly recommendations.

The area around the Stazione Centrale has some of the city's least expensive accommodation, but many places double quietly (and often not so quietly) as brothels.

Campeggio Città di Milano (☎ 02 482 00 999; www.parcoaquatica.com; Via G Airaghi 61; per person/tent/car €8/6/6, 2-/3-/4-person bungalow from €40/50/62) is a four-star 'camping village' west of the centre with bar, restaurant, laundry, bike rental and aqua park 9km west of the *duomo* just south of SS11 and east of the *tangenziale ovest* (western bypass).

Il postello (☎ 33 317 52 272; http://postello.realityhacking.org; Via A della Pergola 5; dm €10) is a chilled community arts centre in the Isola district that has 28 dorm beds for like-minded travellers. DJs spin electro beats on Wednesday night and reggae is performed on Sunday night. There's no sign – look for the graffiti-covered blue metal gate concealing the doorbell.

La Cordata (☎ 02 583 14 675; www.ostellimilano.it; Via Burigozzo 11; dm/s/d €18/40/70) is in the canal district, just a quick ride to the centre. The rooms are Spartan but spotless – wi-fi and a self-catering kitchen are available.

Hotel Del Sole (☎ 02 295 12 971; www.delsolehotel.com; Via Gaspare Spontini 6; s without/with bathroom €35/50, d without/with bathroom €50–70/65–85) is one of the best options in the not-always-salubrious Stazione Central area, 400m from the station. Rooms are acceptable,

and some have balconies. If you're a light sleeper, ask for a room overlooking the courtyard.

Hotel Ariston (☎ 02 720 00 556; www.brerahotels.com; Largo Carrobbio 2; s incl breakfast €110–200, d incl breakfast €160–290) is Milan's first ecological hotel and it earns a rating of 'awesome' thanks to the purified air in the rooms, herbal tea made with purified water, organic breakfasts, natural fibre–filled mattresses, soaps and shampoos with all-natural ingredients, and a free loaner bicycle at the door to combat emissions.

Self-caterers, you'll find fresh fruit, veggies and fish at the covered market, **Mercato Comunale** (Piazza XXIV Maggio). **Princi: Il Bread & Breakfast** (☎ 02 659 90 13; Via Della Moscova 52; price by weight) sells slices of pizza, focaccia, cakes, bread and fresh pasta.

If you're on a budget, do as the Milanese do and fill up during *aperitivi* (see boxed text p129) – for the cost of a cocktail, glass of wine or beer at the city's bars. And what better place to do it than **Le Biciclette** (☎ 02 581 04 325; www.lebiciclette.com; Via Torti 4). Once a bike warehouse and now one of the best *aperitivi* bars in Milan, it boasts glassed-in bicycle memorabilia.

Flash (☎ 02 583 04 489; Via Bergamini 1; pizzas €7–10, mains €11–22) gets packed to the rafters with locals tucking into its gargantuan pizzas, fresh pasta and risotto – anything with *cinghiale* (wild boar) is a speciality. **Le Vigne** (☎ 02 837 56 17; Ripa di Porta Ticinese 61; mains €14–18) is a Slow Food restaurant renowned for its use of local cheeses, such as zucchini flowers stuffed with artisan herbed ricotta.

Getting There & Away

AIR

Most European and other international flights use **Malpensa airport** (www.malpensa.com), 56km northwest of the city. It's situated a few kilometres east of the Fiume Adda, along which the Navigli Milanesi bike route (p138) runs. The majority of domestic and a handful of European flights use the more convenient **Linate airport** (www.sea-aeroportimilano.it), 7km east of the city centre. For flight information, call ☎ 02 748 52 200 (both Malpensa and Linate airports).

The **Malpensa Express** (☎ 220 222; www.malpensaexpress.it) train links Stazione Nord with Malpensa airport (one-way €11, 40 minutes, every 30 minutes). Autostradale runs buses roughly every 30 minutes between 4.35am and 9.15pm from Piazza Luigi di Savoia, outside Stazione Centrale, to Malpensa (adult/child €5.50/2.75, 50 minutes). A taxi from Malpensa into Milan will cost at least €65 (and much more during peak hour).

TRAIN
You can catch a train from **Stazione Centrale** (Piazza Duca d'Aosta) to all major cities in Italy. Check schedules at its **information office** (☎ 147 88 80 88). Daily trains (intercity train fares are quoted here) run to and from Venice (€24, 3½ hours), Florence (€27, 3½ hours), Genoa (€15.50, 1½ hours), Turin (€20, 1½ hours), Rome (€51, 4½ hours) and Naples (€62, 6½ hours). Ferrovie Nord Milano (FNM) trains from **Stazione Nord** (Stazione Cadorna; www.fnmgroup.it/orario, in Italian; Piazza Luigi Cadorna) connect Milan with Como (€3.50, 1 hour, hourly). Regional services to many towns northwest of Milan are more frequent from **Stazione Porta Garibaldi** (Piazza Sigmund Freud).

BUS
For many national and international destinations, buses (operated by numerous different companies) leave from the **bus station** (☎ 02 637 9 01; Piazza Sigmund Freud) opposite the main entrance to the Stazione Porta Garibaldi.

OULX, SAUZE & BARDONECCHIA
☎ 01 / pop 2700
Though surrounded by the glories of nature, **Oulx** is generally regarded as the main stepping stone to the ski resorts of the Via Lattea.

A gruelling uphill climb away, **Sauze d'Oulx** (1509m) is one of the Via Lattea resorts. It offers excellent skiing and an après-ski that's more British than Italian. In summer, a popular walking trail leads to the hamlet of **Jouvenceaux,** where the wooden houses and frescoed chapel remain largely unchanged.

Information
The **tourist office** (☎ 01 228 31 596; www.montagnedoc.it; Piazza Garambois 2) here is one of the valley's largest, offering tonnes of mountain biking information.

Sauze has a **tourist office** (☎ 01 228 58 009; www.comune.sauzedoulx.to.it; Piazza Assietta 18), and Bardonecchia's **tourist office** (☎ 0122 990 32; www.montagnedoc.it; Viale della Vittoria 4) has heaps of local information.

Supplies & Equipment
In Oulx you'll find the well-supplied and proficient **Orgeas Sport** (☎ 01 228 31 260; Corso Torino 21).

There are a number of shops in Bardonecchia.

Sleeping & Eating
Check with the tourist office about lodging options in Oulx.

In Sauze, there's **B&B Ico's Lodge** (☎ 01 228 59 524; www.bedandbreakfast-sauze.it; Via Villaggio Alpino 14; d/t/q €68/83/88; closed May, Sep–mid-Nov). Set amongst larch trees, this alpine villa is refreshingly free of concrete. It's a fully equipped apartment that can be used by up to four people.

Il Capricorno (☎ 01 228 50 273; Via Case Sparse 21, Localitá Le Clotes; s/d €150/180) does the trick when you want a touch of chalet chic.

Bardonecchia has **Casa Alpina** (☎ 01 229 99 841; Via Giolitti 11; s €25–30, d €45–55), a cosy little pad on the edge of the Borgovecchio. Casa Alpina is, as its name suggests, an alpine home offering basic rooms for the night. The downstairs **restaurant** (menu €16) specialises in Piedmontese cuisine with a French slant – think fondues and polenta with venison.

In Sauze, the bar- and pizzeria-lined main drag is Via Assietta.

In Bartonecchia, try out **Ristorante Biovey** (☎ 01 229 99 215; www.biovey.it; Via Generale Cantore 2; 1st/2nd courses from €7/12; Wed–Mon). A mix of the modern and traditional, the decor at this elegant restaurant-cum-hotel is as eye-catching as the food.

PINEROLO
☎ 01 / pop 33,500
A distant suburb of Turin at the foot of the mountains, Pinerolo is one of the more

important cities of the upper Po. It's a somewhat sprawling affair redeemed by a charming *centro storico* (historic centre).

Information

The **information office** (☎ 01 217 95 589; www.montagnedoc.it; Viale Giolitti 7/9) is a few blocks from the train station. There is a bank across the street, as well as others under the arches of Corso Torino and around the corner in Piazza Barbieri.

Supplies & Equipment

Two bike shops in town are **Hiper Bike** (☎ 01 213 22 196; Piazza Barbieri 18) and **Ciclo Sport Licheri** (☎ 01 217 39 81; Via Monte Grappa 83).

Sleeping & Eating

Accommodation isn't Pinerolo's strong point, but unless there's an Olympic-sized event going on, you're unlikely to have problems bagging a room in this town.

Villa San Maurizio (☎ 01 213 21 415; www.hotelsanmaurizio.eu; Via de Amicis 3; s/d €47/62) is a charming two-star hotel up the hill from the centre. Rooms are comfortable, bright and airy and the staff helpful. Breakfast is an additional charge.

Il Torrione (☎ 01 213 22 616; www .iltorrione.com, in Italian; Via Galoppatoio; s/d €53/106) is the 17th-century family home to the Marquess Doria Lamba. Standing at the centre of its own 20-hectare park, it is a wonderfully picturesque place to stay.

Self-caterers can check out the speciality food stores on Via Trento. For cheap eats, Piazza Verdi has a slew of cafés and restaurants.

Ristorante Mimosa (☎ 01 21 742 00; Via San Giuseppe 15; 1st/2nd courses €4.50/5) is where locals come for a plate of hearty, no-frills pasta and simple well-cooked meat. Absolutely without pretensions, it's a relaxed place. **Pizzeria Via Trieste** (☎ 01 217 38 08; Via Trieste 63/65; pizza from €4.20, 1st/2nd courses from €5/8) has atmosphere ideal for munching on a large, bubbling pizza charred correctly by a wood-fired oven.

PRATO ALLO STELVIO
☎ 04 / pop 3140

Prato allo Stelvio derives its livelihood from drawing outdoor types to its strategic location at the junction between the Val Venosta (upper Adige valley) and the Stelvio Pass road. Sitting at the gateway to the **Parco Nazionale dello Stelvio**, it's a small town with a distinctly Germanic flavour. Hiking trails abound (get a free list from the tourist office) in Parco Nazionale dello Stelvio. Commercial life focuses on highway SS38, which doubles as the Hauptstrasse (main street). Prato's main square (Hauptplatz/Piazza Principale) is east of SS38, just uphill from the visitor centre.

Information

The **visitor centre** (☎ 04 736 16 034; www.prad.suedtirol.com; Hauptstrasse/Via Principale 29) is an efficient, clean Northern European-esque wealth of information.

Banks can be found on Hauptplatz/Piazza Principale.

Supplies & Equipment

Baldi Sport (☎ 04 736 17 071; Reutweg/Via Nuova 19) rents bikes, sells a wide range of cycling gear, and repairs bikes.

Sleeping & Eating

Located near the tourist office, **Camping Sägemühle** (☎ 04 736 16 078; www .camping.saegemuehle.suedtirol.com; Dornweg/Via delle Spine 12; per person/site €8/9.50) has hot showers, a swimming pool and a sauna.

Pension Café Ortler (☎ 04 736 16 031; Hauptstrasse/Strada Principale 57; B&B per person €20) is a small, family-run place above a downtown bar-café.

Garni Wiesenheim (☎ /fax 04 736 16 189; www.garni-wiesenheim.com; Hauptstrasse/Via Principale 4a; per person €24 with breakfast) sits in a pretty field just out of town.

Gasthof Stern (☎ 04 736 16 123; www .gasthof-stern.it; Silbergasse/Via Argentieri 1; per person with breakfast €34–42), self-proclaimed bike hotel, is a cosy, two-star place just a stone's throw from the tourist office.

Hotel Zentral (☎ /fax 04 736 16 008; www.zentral.it; Hauptstrasse/Via Principale 48; B&B per person €36–51) has a sauna, solarium and fitness centre.

Groceries are available at De Spar supermarket in Hauptplatz/Piazza Principale. **Bäckerei/Konditorei Saurer** (Hauptstrasse/Via Principale 37) is a good bakery where you can starch it up. Casual **Pizzeria Stern** at Gasthof Stern serves tasty pizza and pasta. The other hotels in town also have restaurants.

SESTO CALENDE

☎ 03 / pop 9800

At the southern tip of Lago Maggiore – near the head of the Ticino River – affluent Sesto encompasses the nine *comuni* (municipalities) encircling the historic centre of the original village. Evidence traces prehistoric settlement back to the 6th century BC. Now it's a low-key, pleasant lakeside town.

Information

The local **IAT office** (☎ 03 319 23 329; Via Italia 3) is at right on the lake. Banks are lined up in Via Roma.

Supplies & Equipment

Your best bet is the shops in Milan but in Sesto Calende, **Barberi** (☎ 03 319 24 670; www.barberiauto.it; Via Cavour 21–23) deals more with automotive issues but can do bicycle repairs as well.

Sleeping & Eating

About 1km north of town in Santa Anna is the camping ground **La Sfinge** (☎ /fax 03 319 24 531; www.campeggiolasfinge.it; Via per Angera 1).

For information on lodging check out **Pro Sesto Calende** (www.prosestocalende .it).

Albergo La Pagoda (☎ 03 319 13 776; Via Umberto Maddalena; s/d €16/32), a shout from the train station, is rudimentary at best, but it's fine for a cheap sleep.

Hotel/Ristorante del Parco (☎ 03 319 22 577; Via Marconi 42; s/d with bathroom €55/85) is a mid-range option.

Groceries are available in shops and markets on Via Roma and Via IV Novembre. A number of restaurants are on Via Manzoni.

SIRMIONE

☎ 03 / pop 21,240

Catullus, the Roman poet, celebrated Sirmione in his writing, and his name is still invoked in connection with this popular bathing spot. Water buffs can swim at the beaches on the east side of town; ask at the tourist information about renting *pedalos* (paddle boats), kayaks and windsurfing gear.

Be prepared to navigate the hordes around this little lake town.

Information

Sirmione's **IAT** (☎ 03 091 61 14; www .sirmione.com; Viale Marconi 8) is near the bridge to the islet at the tip of the peninsula. Banks are easy to spot along the peninsula.

Supplies & Equipment

The closest bike shops are in Desenzano del Garda. Try **Girelli** (☎ 03 091 19 797; Via Annunciata 10).

Sleeping & Eating

An inordinate number of hotels are crammed into Sirmione, but many of them close from the end of October to March. Four camping grounds lie near the town.

Camping Sirmione (☎ 03 091 90 45; www.camping-sirmione.com; Via Sirmioncino 9, Colombane; per person €6–10, tent €6–10, tent & car €9–16, 2-bed chalet €45–75, 4-bed chalet €65–110) is an attractive, well-kept site at the base of the peninsula (2.5km from the castle).

Hotel Catullo (☎ 03 099 05 811; www. hotelcatullo.it; Piazza Flaminia 7; d €55–70) is one of Sirmione's oldest hotels, dating back to 1888, with a lovely garden and smart, contemporary rooms; lake-view rooms cost just €5 extra.

Hotel Marconi (☎ 03 091 60 07; hmarconi@tiscalinet.it; Via Vittorio Emanuele II 51; s €40–65, d €65–110) ingratiates itself to the cyclist with the incredible morning spread of cakes, tarts and pies, made (by hand) by the family who run this elegant hotel. Rooms are spotless, and their timber sundeck extends over the lake.

SONDRIO

☎ 03 / pop 21.600

Sondrio is situated in the wide vineyard-terraced waist of the Valtellina between the Rhaetian and Orobic Alps. This quaint and welcoming mountain town isn't particularly geared for tourists, but it's a lovely jumping-off point into some spectacular riding.

Information

The **Valtellina tourist board** (www.valtellina .it) has several information points throughout the region, including the main **tourist**

office (☎ 03 425 12 500; infovaltellina
@provincia.so.it; Via Trieste 12) in Sondrio's train station. Banks are located at
Piazzas Campello and Garibaldi and the
connecting Corso Italia.

Supplies & Equipment
Try **Cicli SAS** (☎ 03 422 12 703; Via
Gorizia 10) for bike-related purchases and
repairs.

Sleeping & Eating
Sondrio has a few places to lodge.
Check with the tourist office for B&B
recommendations.

Il Gembro (☎ /fax 03 422 13 081; www
.sondrio-hotel.com/page4.htm; Via Gorizia
14; s/d €26/38), next door to the bicycle
shop, has spotless rooms, but a depressing
restaurant.

Modern-feeling **Hotel Schenatti** (☎ 03
425 12 424; www.hotelschenatti.it; Via
Bernina 7b; s/d €40–60/€70–90) is at the far
western end of the city. For more options,
check in the towns of **Chiuro** and **Ponte
Valtellina** (both 9km east), and **Montagna
Piano** (3km east).

For mealtime do-it-yourselfers, the
speciality shops in Piazzette Rusconi and
Via Beccaria are excellent. Otherwise, use
the supermarkets in Via Parolo or Via
Trieste. **Il Passatore** (Via Trieste 41; closed
Thur) has a welcoming local atmosphere
and good pizzas.

TIRANO
☎ 03 / pop 3000
At the narrowest point of the Valtellina,
Tirano monitors the traffic triangle
formed by Switzerland, the Alta Valtellina
and Milan. Although the area has been
inhabited for millennia, Tirano truly came
into its own in the earliest years of the
16th century after a reported 'miraculous
appearance' of the Madonna. The basilica
built to commemorate this was once
a Catholic buffer against encroaching
northern Protestant reformist ideas. Today
it's the most important religious building
in Valtellina.

Information
The **tourist office** (☎ /fax 03 427 06 066;
www.valtellinaonline.com) shares the train
station building with the railroad on Piazzale

della Stazione. Another **office** (☎ /fax 03
427 06 066) is hidden near the basilica at
Viale Italia 183. The handiest banks are
located on Viale Italia at its eastern end.

Supplies & Equipment
For bike parts and repairs, go to **Spada
Biciclette** (☎ /fax 03 427 05 033; www
.spadabike.com; Via Benefattori 12). Bicycle
rentals are possible at **Cicli'ama'** (☎ 03 427
04 360; Via Trivigno 2).

Sleeping & Eating
Al Giardino (☎ 03 427 01 723; Via
Calcagno 10; r from €25) has clean rooms
above a local café; be prepared for the
occasional rumble caused by infrequently
passing trains.

Casa Mia (☎ 03 427 05 300; www
.geocities.com/eccocasamia; Via Arcari 6;
B&B s/d €36/62) feels like home right in
the old centre.

Albergo Gusmeroli (☎ 03 427 01 338;
Piazza Cavour 5; per person with breakfast
€27–30) is perfectly situated on sunny Piazza Cavour.

All of the pizzerias on Piazza Basilica or
Via Mazzini (near the train station) are good
bets for economical eats. Another pizza shop,
Chaia di Luna (Via Stelvio 36), just southeast
of the old city, attracts many locals.

TURIN
☎ 01 / pop 865,000
A gracious city of wide boulevards, elegant
arcades and grand public buildings, Turin –
the Savoy capital from 1574 and for a
brief period after unification the seat of
Italy's parliament – rests in regal calm
beside a pretty stretch of the Po River. The
hip, young scene is around Turin's regal
squares – particularly café-lined Piazza
San Carlo and southwest of Piazza della
Repubblica, as well as on Via Po between
Piazza Castello and Piazza Vittorio Veneto.
Don't miss the panoramic views from atop
the indescribable architectural wonder, and
symbol of Turin, called **Mole Antonelliana**
(just north of Via Po). Turin's 'black-and-
white magic' is illuminated on quirky
walking tours with **Somewhere** (☎ 01
166 80 580; www.somewhere.it; via Botero
15). The company also runs other tours on
lesser-known aspects of the city, such as
'Underground Turin'.

Information

The main **tourist office** (☎ 01 153 51 81; www.turismotorino.org; Piazza Castello 161) has a smaller **booth** (☎ 01 153 13 27) at Stazione Porta Nuova. For much more about Turin's attractions, in particular the fantastic museums, see Lonely Planet's guide to *Italy*.

Banks are along Via Roma and on Piazza San Carlo.

Supplies & Equipment

Three of the many bike shops in Turin are **Tuttobici** (☎ 01 152 13 236; Via Cottolengo 2), **Risico** (☎ 01 124 82 519; Corso Brescia 44) and   (01 143 46 028;

Sleeping & Eating

Finding a room in Turin can sometimes, but not always, be difficult for people who pedal. At times, the higher the price range, the more willing the proprietor is willing to work with you and your two-wheeler. Check out **Albergabici** (www.albergabici. it) for hotels playing the 'bike-friendly card'.

Villa Rey (☎/fax 01 181 9 0117; Strada Val San Martino Superiore 27; per person/tent/car from €5/4/1.10) is a very basic camping ground east of the Po River that's nothing to write home about, but it's your only chance to pitch within striking distance (3km east) of the city.

Ostello Torino (☎ 01 166 02 939; ostellotorino.it; Via Alby 1; dm/s/tw without bathroom €14.50/20/38) is Turin's HI hostel, 1.8km from the train station. Facilities are good (including online computers/wi-fi) and breakfast is included, but there's an afternoon lock-out.

Hotel Montevecchio (☎ 01 156 20 023; www.hotelmontevecchio.com; Via Montevecchio 13; s €40–85, d €60–100) is in a quiet residential area just 300m from Stazione Porta Nuova. This two-star hotel is very amicable towards cyclists and has a buffet breakfast and guest laundry.

Victoria Hotel (☎ 01 156 11 909; www. hotelvictoria-torino.com; Via Nino Costo 4; s €135–170, d €190–220) is an English country–style hotel on a quiet pedestrian lane. Mod cons include wi-fi. Prices teeter on top end, but it's worth it for the comfort and atmosphere of this memorable inn.

Eataly (☎ 01 119 506 811; www. eatalytorino.it; Via Nizza 230), 3km south of the city centre, houses a staggering array of Slow Food–affiliated eats and beverages in a huge building that was once a vermouth factory. Around 12.30pm to 2.30pm, each segment serves lunch in its own little restaurant. 1872-established **Pastificio Defilippis** (☎ 01 154 21 37; Via Lagrange 39) makes dozens of varieties of pasta; you can buy it here fresh or dried. **Porta Palazzo** (Piazza della Repubblica), Europe's largest open-air food market, has hundreds of food stalls.

Getting There & Away

AIR

Turin airport (TRN; ☎ 01 156 76 361; www. turin-airport.com) is 16km northwest of the city centre in Caselle. **SADEM** (☎ 01 130 00 166; www.sadem.it, in Italian) runs buses to the airport from Stazione Porta Nuova (40 minutes), stopping also at Stazione Porta Susa (30 minutes). Buses depart every 30 minutes between 5.15am and 10.30pm (6.30am & 11.30pm from the airport).

Turin is also linked directly by bus to Milan's international **Malpensa Airport** (☎ 02 748 522 00; www.malpensa.com, in Italian), 100km to the northeast.

TRAIN

There are four train stations in Turin, although the majority of trains terminate at the main station, **Stazione Porta Nuova** (Piazza Carlo Felice). Regular daily trains connect Turin with Milan (€14.57, 1 hour 45 minutes) and Rome (€40.50, 7 hours). Regionally, there are frequent trains for Modane, Aosta, Domodossola, Milan, Genoa, Cuneo and Ventimiglia. Turin's other train stations are **Stazione Porta Susa** (Corso Inghilterra), **Lingotto** (Via Panunzio 1) and **Stazione Dora** (Piazza Baldissera).

BUS

Turin is very well connected with buses serving international, national and regional destinations. Most, though not all, services terminate at the bus station.

International operator **Eurolines** (☎ 05 535 71 10; www.eurolines.it) departs from the bus station for a number of European destinations, including London (€87), Paris (€54) and Barcelona (€100).

DOLOMITES

HIGHLIGHTS

- Eight 2000m passes **Sella**, **Pordoi**, **Gardena**, **Valparola**, **Falzarego**, **Tre Cime**, **Giau** and **Fedaia** (p170)
- Top-rated bike paths **Adige**, **Noce**, **Sarca** and **Rienza Rivers** (p163)
- Highly developed bike infrastructure in **Bolzano** (p177)
- The unique food and luscious wine of **Trentino-Alto Adige**

SPECIAL EVENTS
- Gran Fésta da d'Jstà or Ladin Festival (August/September), Canazei
- Val Gardena Music Festival (July/August)
- Val Gardena Folklore Festival (August)

CYCLING EVENTS
- Maratona dles Dolomites (June), Dolomites
- Dolomites Superbike MTB Race (July), Val Pusteria
- Giro delle Dolomites (July/August), six days throughout Trentino-Alto Adige
- Drop Down International Cup (July), downhill MTB race, Canazei

FOOD & DRINK SPECIALITIES
- *casunziei* (beet ravioli with poppy seeds), Cortina d'Ampezzo
- *sones* (apple fritters), Canazei
- *crafuncins da ula verda* (half moon-shaped spinach ravioli), Val Gardena
- *strangolapreti* (spinach gnocchi), Trentino-Alto Adige

TERRAIN
Two extremes: steep and mountainous, and flat along major river valleys

Telephone Code – 04	www.dolomiti.org/dengl

Unquestionably one of the most dramatic mountain ranges on earth, the Dolomites thrust their jagged spires skyward over an area of 7000 sq km in Italy's northeastern corner. While the Dolomiti Mountain Passes ride in this chapter is extremely strenuous, excellent bike paths along the Adige and Rienza Rivers offer a rare cycling gift: they're flat and dramatically scenic. The well-maintained paths tour you through utterly spectacular mountain, river and wine-country landscapes. This is a stellar ride choice for beginners.

Furthermore, this region is appealing not only for its geography but also for its cultural diversity, food and wine. Three languages (Italian, German and Ladin) are officially recognised in the Dolomites, and local culture is shaped by a pleasing combination of Italian, Germanic and traditional alpine influences. The gastronomic result of this cultural confluence will make you grateful that you worked up such a hunger cycling.

HISTORY

As glaciers receded in the Mesolithic era, hunters entered the Dolomites in pursuit of wild game. 'Living' proof of these early human migrations came to light in 1992 with the discovery of Otzi, a 5300-year-old alpine man perfectly preserved in ice (see the boxed text **The Iceman Cometh** p162). A more permanent farming and herding culture had evolved by the Bronze Age, as evidenced by village sites discovered in Val di Fassa and Val Gardena.

In 15 BC the Dolomites were conquered by the Romans and incorporated into the alpine province of Rhaetia. The Rhaetians' traditional language mixed with vulgar Latin, spurring the evolution of the Ladin language, which is still spoken widely in the Dolomites today. After Rome fell, the usual succession of Lombards and Holy Roman Emperors swept through the area. In 1027, political jurisdiction over the southern Adige Valley and the Brenta Dolomites passed to the prince-bishops of Trento, while further north the bishops of Brixen and the counts of Tyrol grappled for control of Bolzano and the eastern Dolomites.

The 19th century brought brief periods of Napoleonic and Hapsburg rule, followed by WWI, which transformed the Dolomites into a battle zone. Austrians and Italians staked out positions in the high country and endured terrible conditions, as commemorated in numerous museums and cemeteries throughout the region. At war's end in 1918, Italy won control of South Tyrol. Mussolini, in the fascist spirit of nationalism, imposed new Italian names on all towns and geographical features and divided the Dolomites into three separate political regions, attempting to dilute German and Ladin cultural influence. Almost a century later, however, the Dolomites remain proudly tricultural.

ENVIRONMENT

The Dolomites derive their name from 18th-century French geologist Déodat de Dolomieu. While studying specimens gathered in the Adige Valley, Dolomieu discovered that, unlike normal limestone (calcium carbonate), the local rocks contained magnesium as well. This double carbonate of magnesium and limestone, which occurs

---

THE LADIN LANGUAGE

With roots as old as Italian itself, Ladin is a Romance language spoken by roughly 40,000 people in the Dolomites. Ladin's ancestral language was once spoken throughout the Alps; it evolved from the mixing of Vulgar Latin with the traditional mountain language known as Rhaetian. Rhaeto-Romanic languages other than Ladin have survived elsewhere in remote pockets of the Alps, such as southeast Switzerland's Graubunden canton, where the local variant is known as Romansh and has long been recognised as one of Switzerland's four official languages.

Ladin-speaking residents of Val Gardena and Badia, as part of the autonomous province of Bolzano, have had greater success than the others in achieving official recognition for their language, and Ladin is a now a required subject in the schools in both valleys.

---

elsewhere in the world as well, is today known universally as dolomite.

The Dolomites' unique landscape is the result of uneven weathering of two different kinds of rock. Millions of years ago, this part of northeastern Italy was covered by a warm sea criss-crossed with coral reefs and flanked by two large volcanoes. Over the millennia, shells from sea creatures were compacted into dolomite, while volcanic eruptions created vast areas of cooled magma. Both rock types were exposed to the elements when tectonic pressure caused dramatic uplifting of this ancient sea floor. The extremely durable dolomite remained relatively intact, while the much softer volcanic rock eroded easily, resulting in the Dolomites' characteristic pattern of low-lying valleys and prominent spires.

The mountains' undersea origins are evident in the large number of marine fossils discovered in the area. A particularly good collection can be seen at the **Regoles Museum** in Cortina d'Ampezzo.

CLIMATE

The Dolomites' climate is characterised by warm, wet summers and cold, drier winters. Temperatures and rainfall are highest in July and August and lowest in January. In the mountains the best cycling weather

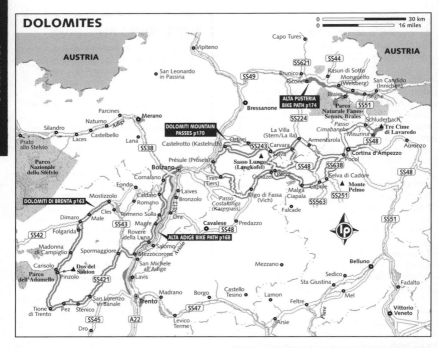

occurs between June and September. Warmer temperatures in the Adige Valley around Bolzano and Trento permit comfortable cycling as early as April and as late as October. Average high temperatures in July and August are 30°C in Bolzano and 22°C in Val Pusteria.

PLANNING
Maps & Books

Touring Club Italia's 1:200,000 *Trentino-Alto Adige* map provides detailed coverage of this entire region.

Both excellent and not-so-excellent maps of *Trentino-Alto Adige* bike paths are available free at tourist bureaus throughout the region.

Dolomites di Brenta Bike (a free booklet available at tourist offices; www.Dolomites brentabike.it) is a top information source for cycling the Dolomiti di Brenta ride.

Place Names

In the eastern Dolomites, place names reflect the region's trilingual heritage. In the northern valleys closest to the Austrian

THE ICEMAN COMETH

It's impossible to resist the magnetic draw of Otzi, the 5300-year-old man found perfectly preserved in ice west of Bolzano in 1992. People flock to the second floor of Bolzano's archaeological museum, waiting reverently in line for a chance to gaze through the tiny opening of Otzi's deep-freeze unit and make contact with their recognisably human Copper Age ancestor. As fascinating as Otzi himself are his clothing and tools, displayed on the same floor in both original and reconstructed versions. Otzi's original leggings, grass cape, soft goatskin underwear, bear-fur hat, and shoes stuffed with hay are remarkable; and his goatskin coat with stripes in alternating colours is downright fashionable.

Otzi's status as a popular cult hero was enhanced in September 2001 when Bolzano's Nuovo Teatro Comunale launched a musical in his honour, *Frozen Fritz*.

border (Val Gardena and Val Badia), road signs can be cumbersomely complex, with Ladin, Italian and German town names all jockeying for position. South of the Trentino-Alto Adige border (Val di Fassa), where German is less commonly spoken, bilingual naming conventions remain in effect, with all localities retaining a traditional Ladin name plus a modern Italian equivalent. The Ampezzo Valley is the most Italianised part of the Dolomites, with signs in Italian only, although even here many people still speak Ladin at home.

In this chapter the Italian place name is always listed first, followed by the German and/or Ladin equivalent in parentheses.

GATEWAY
See Bolzano p177.

DOLOMITI DI BRENTA

Duration 3 days
Distance 173.6km
Difficulty moderate–demanding
Start Mostizzolo
Finish Bolzano
Summary This ride features the kind of bike path that converts people into cyclists: immaculately maintained, utterly safe and crazily gorgeous. Throw a pass in for good measure – now there's a bike ride.

This gem of a ride takes advantage of two of Trentino-Alto Adige's stellar bike paths. You'll wind through thick forests and open valleys with mountains and vineyards of ridiculous beauty flanking both sides. This is not so much a ride for a hammerhead rider, but rather for a cyclist psyched to embrace the extreme splendour of the Dolomiti di Brenta. The route circumnavigates the Dolomites' westernmost peaks, cruising through the lush greenery of the **Val di Sole** and **Val Rendena** on Days 1 and 2, then following the flat and scenic **Strada del Vino** through vineyards on Day 3.

The only challenging climb (1682m, Passo Campo Carlo Magno) comes on Day 1, with a lesser climb to the beautiful mountain lake at Molveno on Day 2.

PLANNING
When to Cycle
June, July and September are good months to ride. The Strada del Vino section on Day 3, due to its lower elevation, is also appealing in spring and autumn and can be combined with the Adige Valley Bike Path (see p168) route to make a loop starting and ending in Bolzano.

Maps
Two useful resources for this ride are Touring Club Italia's *Trentino-Alto Adige* map and the free map of bicycle routes in Trentino-Alto Adige, including those covered on the first two days.

Information Sources
Dolomites di Brenta Bike (a free booklet available at tourist offices; www.Dolomitesbrentabike.it) is a top information source for cycling the Dolomiti di Brenta. Bicycles can be picked up at the open-air **bike rental stall** (☎ 04 719 97 578; Via della Stazione 2; 7.30am–8pm, Easter–Oct) near the train station. **Turismo in Bicicletta** (www.turismoinbicicletta.it) is like a travel agency for cycle tourists. They are based in Bergamo but function in Trentino-Alto Adige as well.

GETTING TO/FROM THE RIDE
Mostizzolo (start)
TRAIN
Mostizzolo train station is best approached from Trento. Several trains daily run from Trento's private **Trento–Malé train line** (☎ 04 612 38 350; www.fertm.it) to

---

MOSTIZZOLO

Ponte Mostizzolo is a bridge spanning the beautiful limestone canyon of the Noce River at the west end of Lago Santa Giustina, and also marks the eastern terminus of the Val di Sole bike path. The Mostizzolo train station, just above the bridge on the northern bank of the river, offers no services of any kind. There is a lonely hotel and restaurant near the station. The ride begins at the station due to the easy train access and the proximity of the Val di Sole bike path.

Mostizzolo (€3, plus €1.75 for bikes, 1¼ hours, regularly). Mostizzolo is a very small station just beyond the large station at Cles.

BICYCLE

It's possible to cycle from Trento to Mostizzolo, although some sections of the route have heavy traffic. From Trento, take the Adige Valley bike path 24km north to Mezzocorona, then follow the Noce River upstream towards Cles and Mostizzolo.

Bolzano (finish)
BUS

Buses run by SAD (www.sad.it) leave from the **bus station** (☎ 84 000 04 71; Via Perathoner) for destinations throughout the province, including Val Gardena (up to 12 daily), Brunico (up to 20 connections daily) and Merano (55 minutes, hourly). SAD buses also head for resorts outside the province, including Cortina d'Ampezzo. Updated timetables are on the SAD website.

TRAIN

Bolzano **train station** (Piazza Stazione) is connected by hourly trains with Merano (40 minutes), Trento (30 minutes) and Verona (2½ hours), with less-frequent connections to Brunico (1½ hours, 6 daily) in the Val Pusteria.

BICYCLE

Cycling from Bolzano to Fiè is very doable. There's a well-maintained bike path that goes from Bolzano, skirting SS12, from which you can turn up ('up' being the operative word) the signposted road to Fiè. The bike path to Merano is of the standard high-quality characteristic of the region.

THE RIDE
Day 1: Mostizzolo to Pinzolo
3–6 hours, 48.1km

The route consists of three roughly equidistant segments: an initial easy stretch along a riverside bike path, a challenging climb and a rousing downhill to end the day.

As you leave the train station at Mostizzolo, the route quickly descends to cross the beautiful gorge at Ponte Mostizzolo, merging with the Val di Sole bike path after

DOLOMITI DI BRENTA – DAY 1

CUES			GPS COORDINATES
Start		Mostizzolo train station	46°23'40"N 11°00'38"E
0km	┌►	SE on SP57 (L out of car park)	
0.2	┌►	to 'Cles'	
0.5	↙	Val di Sole bike path	
5.9	↑	at stop sign, cross SP38	
6.3	┌►	Val di Sole bike path	
7.5	┌►	to 'Male,' bike path	
11.9	┌►	to stay on bike path	
12	┌►	to stay on bike path	
15.2	★	Dimaro train station	
15.4	┌►	to 'Ossana,' bike path	
15.9	↙	after road becomes brick, small bike path sign, SS239	
		Dimaro	46°19'34"N 10°52'24"E
	▲	14.8km steep-moderate climb (1st half harder)	
21.9		Folgarida	46°18'09"N 10°52'01"E
30.7		Passo Campo Carlo Magno	
32.7	↙	to 'Madonna di Campiglio'	
32.8	┌►	at fork, to 'Madonna di Campiglio'	
		(50m) into town	
33.3	↙	Via Pradalago, Madonna di Campiglio	
			46°13'55"N 10°49'38"E
34.1	↙	stop sign at fork, cross stream	
34,2	↘	at fork to road along stream, bike path sign	
35.9	↙	Bike path, to 'Antonio de Mavignola'	
	▲	.4km steep climb	
36.2	┌►	up switchback, not on gravel bike path	
	┌►	(50m) unsigned SS239	
40.6	┌►	Via Corno di Cavento	
40.7	↘	Via Folgorida/bike path	
	▲	2.8km very steep descent	
43.5	┌►	beyond bridge to continue downhill	
44.9	↙	Val Rendena bike path	
46.7	┌►	opp bridge through playground	
46.8	↙	Via dei Pini (unmarked)	
47.7	┌►	SS239	
48	┌►	Via al Sole	
48.1		Pinzolo visitor centre	46°09'22"N 10°46'03"E

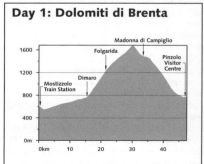

Day 1: Dolomiti di Brenta

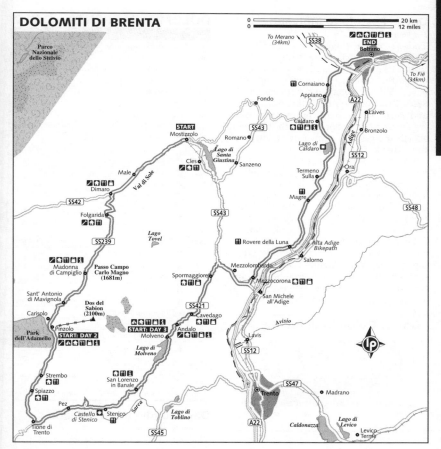

DOLOMITI DI BRENTA

500m. The 15km path meanders languidly through forests, fields and apple orchards, following the roaring Noce River and affording beautiful views of the distant Alps to the west.

At **Dimaro** (15.9km) the route turns south off the bike path and begins the long climb to **Passo Campo Carlo Magno**, named for Charlemagne, who crossed this same pass in the late 1700s during his campaign against the Lombards. **Snoopy Bar** (☎ 04 639 74 135; Via Madonna di Campiglio 78), the internet café on the main drag in Dimaro, makes a mean panini if you want something to sustain you. The ascent from Dimaro is steep at first, then more gradual beyond the town of Folgarida,

where the Dolomiti di Brenta become visible along the eastern horizon.

From the pass, a 2.3km descent leads to the trendy but rather empty-feeling resort town of **Madonna di Campiglio**. The route works its way through the town centre and back streets to avoid a huge tunnel, then rejoins the main highway. The descent spotlights spectacular views of huge rocky crags to the east and the **Adamello glacier** straight ahead. A winding descent through high meadows leads to **Sant' Antonio di Mavignola**, where the bike path resumes, plunging precipitously through a beautiful forest to the Campiglio branch of the Sarca River and then depositing you in Pinzolo.

Day 2: Pinzolo to Molveno
3–6 hours, 50.6km

Today's route lingers a while in the lowlands before climbing gently northeast to the lake at Molveno. The first 11km is delightful, primarily following the well-paved Val Rendena bike path along the Sarca River past sports fields, picnic areas and small towns, with mountains rising regally on all sides. Sometimes the bike path shortly merges with a town street, but don't fret – just keep on trucking.

At 14km, the bike path fizzles out for good, and the route continues downhill on comparatively busy SS239. Beyond Tione di Trento a second short (4km) bike path heads east through cornfields to the miniature town of Pez. Here the route climbs steeply out of the valley on a wonderfully 'untrafficky' tertiary road. Levelling out, the road snakes its way along a mountainside, crossing the steep **Val d'Algone canyon**, passing through a tunnel carved from solid rock and following a deep, wide limestone gorge past a waterfall into Stenico (32.2km).

Day 2: Dolomiti di Brenta

Stenico offers limited services, but the short side trip to imposing **Castello di Stenico** just above town is recommended. Building of the present castle started in the 12th century by the prince-bishops of Trento to guard the important route between Trento and Lombardy. Among its treasures is a wonderful 13th-century fresco of the Virgin Mary tormented by a dragon. Stenico is also noteworthy as the castle depicted in the snowball fight scene in Trento's Torre Aquila frescoes.

The final leg from Stenico to Molveno climbs and dips through pastoral country, ultimately passing through several roughly hewn limestone tunnels and levelling out along the forested shores of Lago di Molveno.

DOLOMITI DI BRENTA – DAY 2

CUES		GPS COORDINATES
start	Pinzolo visitor centre	46°09'22"N 10°46'03"E
0km	W on Via al Sole	
	{!retrace yesterday's route to bike path}	
1.4	↱ Val Rendena bike path	
1.5	cross Sarca River	
	↱ 40m onto bike path	
4.1	↱ following bike path	
6.5	Strembo	46°07'17"N 10°45'08"E
7.5	↱ at T after bridge, following BP	
8.5	Spiazzo	46°06'07"N 10°44'20"E
9.1	↱ bike path downstream	
10.7	↱ cross Sarca River, after bridge onto bike path	
12.9	↱ at T following bike path	
14	↱ SP334, bike path ends	
16.5	↱ to 'Tione'	
16.7	↘ through car park to bike path	
22.9	↘ uphill to 'Pez'	
24.0	Pez	40°03'26"N 10°48'00"E
	↘ main street (unmarked)	
24.1	▲ 1.3km steep climb	
25.3	↱ SP34	
30.1	⚠ 75m tunnel	
31.2	★ Stenico	46°03'07"N 10°51'18"E
31.5	●●↱ Castello di Stenico 1km↺	
32.3	▲ 1.5 moderate climb	
36.7	↱ SS421 to 'Molveno'	
37.4	▲ 3km steep climb	
39.1	San Lorenzo in Banale	46°04'37"N 10°54'29"E
41.3	⚠ Tunnel 700m	
50.3	↙ Via C Battisti 'to Centro'	
50.6	Molveno visitor centre	46°08'32"N 10°57'54"E

Day 3: Molveno to Bolzano
4–6 hours, 72.5km

The spectacular landscapes you pass through today make the ride almost surreal, and certainly a blessing. It's longer than the first two, but less challenging, thanks to long stretches of flat and downhill riding.

After climbing gradually to **Andalo**, the route begins its 13km descent to the **Noce River Valley**. Views are especially nice beyond **Spormaggiore**, where switchbacks drop through a landscape of long, sloping plateaus covered with apple orchards.

At 19.8km, the route crosses busy SS43 to follow an abandoned road labelled SP29. The road is overgrown with bushes and the paving is intermittent, but guardrails remain in place. This traffic-free shortcut drops immediately into the Adige Valley's beautiful vineyard country with a backdrop of limestone cliffs. This section of the route

DOLOMITI DI BRENTA – DAY 3

CUES		GPS COORDINATES
start	Molveno visitor centre	46°08'32"N 10°57'54"E
0km	W through Piazza Marconi	
0.2	SS421, 2km moderate climb	
5.0	Andalo	46°10'01"N 11°00'14"E
9.0	Cavedago	46°11'10"N 11°01'57"E
14.9	Spormaggiore	46°13'08"N 11°02'54"E
19.4	to 'Trento'	
24.0	Mezzocorona	46°12'55"N 11°07'13"E
24.5	Via Romana/SP90 `to Roverè'	
26	to 'Roverè della Luna'	
30.8	Roverè della Luna	46°14'59"N 11°10'17"E
	Via Milano	
32.5	to 'Magrè/Margreid'	
36.4	Strada del Vino to 'Magrè'	
37.7	Magrè	46°17'14"N 11°12'46"E
38	Via Gruntz	
39.7	SP58 to 'Neumarkt/Egna'	
41.8	to 'Kaltern/Caldaro'	
44.1	to 'Klughammer/Campi al Lago'	
45.6	to 'Klughammer/Campi al Lago'	
46.3	Lago di Caldaro nature reserve	
48.2	to 'Klughammer/Campi al Lago'	

CUES CONTINUED		GPS COORDINATES
53.1	onto 'percorso ciclabile caldaro'	
53.9	Strada del Vino (Weinstrasse)	
54.6	bike path to 'Bolzano' (you can follow signs into Caldaro (Kaltern)	46°24'51"N 11°14'46"E
56.2	bike path to 'Bolzano'	
56.9	.6km steep climb	
57.6	hard u-turn, bike path to 'Bolzano'	
	Wineries	
60.6	following bike path (or straight to San Michelle)	
	(30m) bike path to 'Bolzano'	
68.9	bike path to 'Bolzano'	
	(70m) to 'Centro'	
69.2	to 'Centro'	
69.5	bike path to 'Aslago'	
72.9	over yellow bridge	
73.4	bike path to 'Centro'	
73.5	cross Via Garibaldi	
	(20m) when one other side	
	(60m) bike path to 'Centro,' Via Isarco	
74.9	at T intersection after piazza	
75	Piazza Walther (Waltherplatz, Bolzano (Bozen) visitor centre)	46°29'42"N 11°21'15"E

from **Mezzocorona** (24.km) entails some of the most extravagant landscapes. The low traffic combined with the scenery of monstrous mountains bulging at the sides of a valley carpeted by vineyards and apple fields glittering in the sun is something to write home about. Whew!

At 32.5km, the lovely historical centre of **Magrè** (Margreid) warrants a visit, with cobblestone streets and a stone-walled, flower-bedecked canal descending from the cliffs.

A 10km flat stretch through vineyards and apple orchards leads to the south shore of **Lago di Caldaro,** a nature preserve rich in bird life. A birdwatching platform and boardwalk permit easy access. The next several kilometres skirt the lakeshore and then climb through a sea of vineyards to the picturesque wine town of **Caldaro** (Kaltern) at 54.6km. Consider detouring up Caldaro's main street; Goldgasse 1. At 57.6km, instead of U-turning to the left to continue on the bike path, head straight to reach a number of *enoteche* (wine bars) that offer **wine tastings**.

From Caldaro, a handsome bike path follows the old railway bed towards **Cornaiano** (Girlan), gliding through forest with stunning views of terraced orchards dropping off to a small valley. The day's final thrill comes just beyond Cornaiano, where a small farm road plummets from the high vineyards to the Adige Valley floor. From here Bolzano's fine network of bike paths covers most of the remaining distance to the city centre.

Day 3: Dolomiti di Brenta

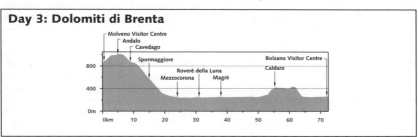

MEZZOCORONA

In the centre of the bike path action is Mezzocorona, a tiny, wine-country town that's under the tourist radar. If you want to base somewhere and capitalise on the easiest biking sections, three bike routes (Dolomiti di Brenta Day 2 reversed, Day 3, and the Trentiono-Alta Adige Bike Path) radiate from the town. Plus Mezzocorona sits on both the Trenitalia and Trento–Malè train lines, so travel back to the town via train is an added planning option.

There's a wonderful, good-value place to stay, **Albergo Caffe Centrale** (☎ 04 616 03 755; www.caloretrentino.com; Piazza San Gottardo 2; s/d €56/96), that has an indoor 'wellness' pool, hot tub and sauna. Appointments with in-house massage therapists can be arranged. The affiliated restaurant next door, **Trattoria Dolcespina** (Piazza San Gottardo 4), will feed you truly scrumptious Trentino-Alto Adige food and show you the best of the region's wine.

ALTA ADIGE BIKE PATH

Duration 3–6 hours
Distance 66.9km
Difficulty easy
Start Bolzano
Finish Trento

Summary If you like to tootle, meander, piddle, casually recreate and dink around while on a bike in miraculous mountain environs, this ride is for you.

The queen of Trentino-Alto Adige's bike paths, this iconic, highly popular route meanders effortlessly downstream from Bolzano to Trento, weaving through vineyards and fruit orchards as it ricochets between the striking limestone cliffs on either side of the Adige Valley.

Cyclists preferring a slightly more challenging loop back to Bolzano can follow the cue sheet for the first half of this ride, then return north via the scenic Strada del Vino route described earlier in this chapter under

Day 3 of the Dolomiti di Brenta ride (p163). To link these two routes, leave the Adige Valley bike path at 34.8km, cross the Adige River and follow signs towards Roverè della Luna. A right turn (1.8km after leaving the bike path) towards Magrè (Margreid) puts you on the Strada del Vino.

PLANNING
When to Cycle
This ride is pleasant anytime between April and October. Fruit blossoms are at their peak in late April and early May.

What to Bring
Picnic benches are more common than towns along this route; a picnic would definitely accentuate the day.

Maps
For maps of the bike paths in and around the area, head to the tourist offices, which have a wide array of materials.

GETTING TO/FROM THE RIDE
Bolzano (start)
See Bolzano p177.

Trento (finish)
BUS
From the intercity **bus station** (Via Andrea Pozzo), local bus company **Trentino-Alto Adige Trasporti** (☎ 04 618 21 000; www .ttspa.it, in Italian) runs buses to and from various destinations, including Madonna di Campiglio, San Martino di Castrozza, Molveno, Canazei and Rovereto.

TRAIN
Trains connect Trento's **main train station** (Piazza Dante) just north of the historical centre opposite the Piazza Dante park. There are direct trains to Venice, as well as to points north and south on the main Bologna–Innsbruck line. One-way fares from Trento include Verona (€4.80, 1 hour), Venice (€8.20, 2½ hours), Bologna (€10.50, 3¼ hours) and Bolzano (€3, 30 minutes). The private **Trento–Malé train line** (☎ 04 612 38 350; www.fertm.it), on the corner of Via Dogana and Via Romagnosi, just north of the FS station, runs daily trains northwest to points in the Val di Non and Val di Sole, including Mostizzolo, the starting point for the Dolomiti di Brenta ride.

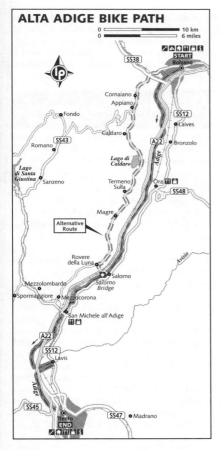

ALTA ADIGE BIKE PATH

0	10 km
0	6 miles

ALTA ADIGE BIKE PATH – DAY 1

CUES			GPS COORDINATES
start		Bolzano (Bozen) visitor centre	46°29'43"N 11°21'15"E
0km	⌐	towards church on main street	
0.1	⌐	to 'pista ciclabile'	
0.4	⌐	to 'pista ciclabile,'	
	⌐ 🚲	(60m) following bike path across Via Garibaldi	
0.6	⌐	bike path to 'Stadio Druso'	
1	⌐	onto bike path after yellow bridge	
3.7	⌐	cross road and continue on bike path	
5	↑	Bike path to 'Trento'	
8.1	⌐	cross bridge to 'Ora'	
12.4	⌐	cross bridge to 'Ora'	
	⌐	(80m) ⌐ bike path to 'Trento'	
12.7	↙	to 'Ora'	
	{ST ↘	to 'Bronzolo (2km RT)}	
18.5	⌐	to 'Ora'	
18.7	⌐	cross street to bike path	
20.2	⌐	at T intersection on bike path	
{ST	⌐	to 'Ora,' 1km RT}	
25.3	↑	to 'Trento'	
{ST	⌐	to 'Neumarkt Egna,' 1km RT}	
34.8	★	Bike café	
	{ ●●⌐	to 'Salorno'	
42	⌐	to 'ciclopedonale' (cross river)	
42.1	⌐	onto bike path	
44	⌐	switchback before S. Michele Train Station	
48	⌐	across bridge, at Nave S. Felice, unsigned	
48.1	⌐	on bike path after bridge	
53.7	⌐	to 'Trento'	
54.2	⌐	to 'Trento' after overpass	
55.3	⌐	following bike path sign	
56.9	↙	onto bike path to 'Trento'	
65.5	◎	3rd exit to 'Centro	
66.1	⌐	Via Giovanni Segantini, to 'Turismo'	
66.4	★	Trento Train Station	
66.8	⌐	to 'Turismo,' Via Torre Vanga	
66.9	⌐	Via Vitorio Alferi	
(50m)	⌐	Trento Tourist Office	46°04'11"N 11°07'18"E

BICYCLE

To get to the Dolomiti Mountain Passes ride (p170), take the Trentino-Alta Adige to Bolzano. From there the Ciclabile lungo l'Isarco can start you off to Fiè allo Sciliar (see p179).

In the tourist office, you can find a brochure that delineates a bike route to Ferrara, a town on the Po Basin and Ciclo-towns ride.

THE RIDE

This ride connects Bolzano and Trento via an impressive, flat riverside bike path used by loads of locals for recreation and commuting.

As you leave Bolzano, you navigate a lattice of bike superhighways, where you'll be able to spot every walk of life on a bicycle. Without self-consciousness, the *bici* is totally an integrated, integral part of the metropolitan culture.

After crossing a bike/pedestrian bridge over the Tálvera (Talfer) River, the route turns downstream towards the Isarco (Eisack) River. The path becomes especially scenic as it straddles the long peninsula between the Isarco and the Adige Rivers near their confluence.

Limestone cliffs loom above vineyards on the left as you enter the Trentino-Alto Adige region. Their drama in contrast to the bike path's tranquillity is a satisfying

BIKE PATH BONUS: BOLZANO TO MERANO TO PRATO ALLO STELVIA

Edge your way north closer to Austria by taking the well-maintained, well-marked bike path to Merano (34km). Visiting Bolzano's more Austrian cousin makes for a lovely, very easy day ride, and you can take the frequently running train back from Merano to Bolzano.

Another option is to take the Val Venosta bike path in Merano to Prato di Stelvio, the beginning of the Alta Rezia ride. This scenic bike path starts to gradually climb into the mountains but the ride from Bolzano to Prato allo Stelvia can certainly be done in a day. There are a couple of small sections of the path that are gravel and sometimes the route takes you on the road for a stint. Detailed bike path maps can be bought at the Merano **tourist office** (☎ 04 732 35 223; www.meraninfo.it; Corso Libertà 35).

If at any point, you want to start saving your legs for the Passo di Stelvio, you can hop onto the uber bike-friendly **Merano–Malles train line** (☎ 04 732 01 500; www.ferrovi-avalvenosta.it), which flanks the Val Venosta bike path. Get off at the Spondigna stop and Prato allo Stelvia is just under 4km away.

mountains. Increasing numbers of joggers, cyclists and picnicking families appear as you near Trento, and soon you are swallowed back into a city again, one with a notable yet not as impressive bike infrastructure.

DOLOMITI MOUNTAIN PASSES

Duration 6 days
Distance 317.9km
Difficulty demanding–very demanding
Start/Finish Fiè allo Sciliar
Summary Up, up and away into the Dolomites' unearthly beauty. Make sure your riding partner is a massage therapist.

The Dolomites reign supreme among all mountain ranges. Castle-shaped rocky outcroppings jut up to incredible heights yet seem as thin as Milan's supermodels. Hulking walls of rock bulge and swirl with patterns of geologic drama. Gigantic mountain slabs heave towards the sky and reign over skirting meadows, forest and precious little towns which are ready to specifically welcome you, the *ciclista*.

This circuit over the Dolomites' highest passes is one of the most breathtaking rides in Italy (both literally and figuratively). Including the two day rides, you'll climb eight 2000m passes (Gardena, Valparola, Falzarego, Tre Cime, Giau, Fedaia, Pordoi and Sella). The toil is handsomely rewarded by incomparable views and a feeling of exhilaration that will stay with you long after the trip.

The Giro d'Italia regularly crosses several of the passes, as evidenced by encouraging messages painted on the pavement. Lest you feel sorry for yourself on the long climbs, remember that Stage 13 of the 2001 Giro required cyclists to climb Passo Pordoi twice in one day, as part of a 224km route that also included Passo Fedaia!

The described route consists of one grandiose four-day loop, with two side-loop options in case you want to cross off all eight passes. If you want to spread out the ride, you can stop at the various *rifugi* (mountain huts) at the tops of the passes – possibly the best seats in the house.

marriage. At 34.8km there's a turn-off over the Salorno bridge that connects to the alternate route back to Bolzano via the Strada del Vino (covered in the Dolomiti di Brenta ride).

At 42.3km the route again crosses the Adige, following the west bank to San Michele all'Adige (42km). A short side trip nearby is recommended to the **Museo degli Usi e Costumi della Gente Trentina** (☎ 04 616 50 314; www.museosanmichele .it; Via Mach 2), one of Italy's largest ethnographic museums. Its fascinating collection includes wonderful scale models of water-driven saws and grain mills, plus farm implements, carts and sleds, butter churns and moulds, looms, ironwork, ceramic stoves, hand-painted furniture, old wedding photos and other relics of rural mountain life.

The remainder of the route zigzags across the emerald valley guarded over by

PLANNING
When to Cycle
This ride is possible between June and September when the mountain passes are free of snow. Late June, early July and early September are the best times for warm weather, without high-season prices and crowds.

What to Bring
Strong, well-adjusted brakes are imperative. Extra water and food are advisable for the many long ascents with limited services. The dirt section on Day 1 requires good tread or a willingness to walk the toughest bits. Make sure you have lights on hand for the tunnels along the route.

GETTING TO/FROM THE RIDE
Fiè allo Sciliar (start/finish)
BUS
There are excellent bus connections between Bolzano and Fiè. SAD (☎ 80 084 60 47; www.sad.it) runs a bus 20 times daily between the two towns (€2.25 one-way plus €1 for bikes, 30 minutes).

BICYCLE
Cycling from Bolzano to Fiè (about 17km) is very doable. The Ciclabile lungo l'Isarco bike path skirting SS12 heads north along SS12 all the way to Vipiteno. You can turn off and up (and we do mean 'up') the signposted road to Fiè. The tourist office offers a brochure about the path.

THE RIDE
Day 1: Fiè allo Sciliar to Selva
3–5 hours, 32.4km
While short in distance, today's ride includes a gruelling climb and an equally precipitous descent, serving as a good tune-up for the greater challenges ahead. You could ride from Bolzano and make this a very full day.

The main route follows a rarely travelled and chunky gravel road through the Alpe di Siusi (Seiser Alm), the largest expanse of high pastureland in the Alps. It is incredibly gorgeous, no doubt, but just be prepared for what is more akin to mountain biking. 'Knobby tyres' are recommended. The alternate route that you might opt for is entirely sealed and involves less climbing, less distance, less adventure and more traffic.

The main road ascends gradually for the first 8.5km through fields at the base of Sciliar. Siusi (Seis) at 7.9km is the last chance for food and water before the big climb. At 8.4km the main route turns steeply uphill, while the alternate route descends straight towards Castelrotto (Kastelruth). The climb's early stages showcase beautiful vistas across green fields to the onion-domed church of San Valentino. A 9km series of switchbacks offers an ever closer and more dramatic look at Sciliar, until the road finally levels off around 17.5km, where is a hotel and restaurant.

For the next several kilometres, the Alpe di Siusi's expansive meadows filled with grazing cattle and backed by the sawtooth spires of Sasso Lungo dominate the view. Smack in the middle of the Alpi lies the remote town of Saltria (Saltner; 22.9km), a good place to refuel on goulash or *canederli* (dumplings). The 6.1km stretch beyond Saltria is a rough gravel road shared with hikers (but no cars). You'll have to open and close several livestock gates along the way.

Almost immediately after rejoining the paved road, a screaming downhill plummets to Santa Cristina (St Christina/S Crestina). Here the alternative route rejoins for the last uphill slog into Selva.

Day 2: Selva to Cortina d'Ampezzo
4–6 hours, 55.4km
Are you ready? Yeah, you are. Today's fantastically gruelling route crosses three major passes en route to the grand valley of Cortina d'Ampezzo.

From Selva the climb to Passo Gardena begins almost immediately. Cyclists have a tendency to appear in large numbers at the junction with the Sella Ring Road (SS243) at 4.8km. Around 6.8km, there is a false summit whose 2km descent allows time to savour the beautiful views of green fields, hay barns and the trapezoidal profile of Sassolungo. The last push up to the pass deposits you at restaurants with terraces serving panoramic views eastward towards Val Badia.

A steady switchbacking descent drops through Colfosco into Corvara, where the route turns downstream, paralleling the Rio Gadera. From La Villa (Stern/La Ila) the next long climb begins gradually, then culminates in 6km of relentless uphill to

DOLOMITI MOUNTAIN PASSES

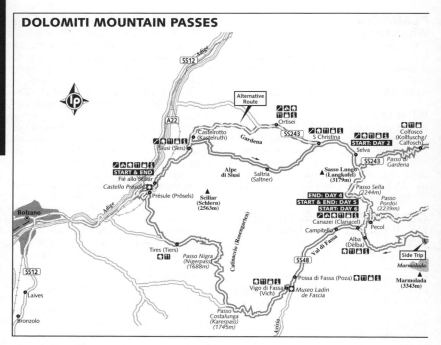

Passo Valparola. At the pass spectacular views unfold to the southwest towards Marmolada, the Dolomites' biggest glacier, and southeast towards the five rugged peaks known as the Cinque Torri. During WWI Italians and Austrians faced off for three years in this desolate landscape, enduring brutal conditions but doing little to change the border relationship between the two countries until war's end. The area's military history is commemorated in the **Museo della Grande Guerra** (37.6km).

From Passo Valparola it's all downhill through spectacular mountain scenery to the third pass of the day (**Passo Falzarego**), and on into Cortina. It's worth stopping at 52.6km for the great viewpoint over Cortina's broad valley backed by sawtooth mountains.

Day 3: Cortina day ride: Tre Cime Loop

4–6 hours, 57km

This classic loop out of Cortina includes the steepest grade (16%) and highest summit (2320m), before climbing to the base of the jagged Tre Cime di Lavaredo.

From Cortina, the initial ascent towards **Passo Tre Croci** traverses open fields, then enters pretty forest with a backdrop of mountain walls in every direction. After **Misurina**, the route turns onto the Superstrada Panoramica toll road. A short but very steep initial climb is followed by a brief downhill and, soon after, another relentless 4.4km slog to the summit. It can be deeply satisfying to whiz past cars and buses waiting to pay the toll.

Exhaust fumes from buses are an unwelcome distraction, but there are fantastic views of the stark, treeless landscape of the high Dolomites, with the tridentate **Tre Cime di Lavaredo** dominating the scene. The climb culminates at **Rifugio Auronzo**, where a lonesome café awaits.

The final downhill/flat 18km through Passo Cimabanche traces an ancient trading route between Venice and Germany.

Day 4: Cortina d'Ampezzo to Canazei

5–7 hours, 62.1km

This is the most challenging day yet, with fabulously gut-wrenching climbs over **Passi**

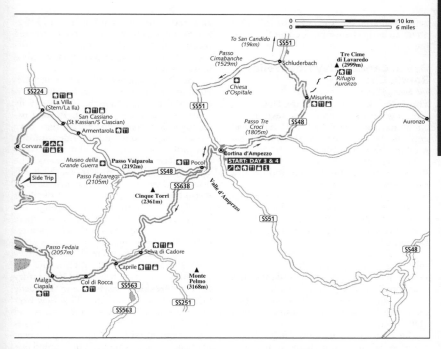

Giau and **Fedaia** (both over 2000m). The heart-stopping descent from Giau leaves little room for relaxation, but the views throughout are sensational, leaving cyclists feeling truly euphoric.

Turn southwest into the stupendous scenery of the quieter Passo Giau road after the little village of **Pocol** (6.8km), your last food stop before the summit. Towards 13km the route emerges onto a vast moorland surrounded by peaks whose noble beauty gives one good reason to pilgrimage long distances just to cycle at their feet. **Passo Giau** (17.6km) comes none too soon.

Giau is arguably the most beautiful pass in the Dolomites, and it's worth stopping at the *rifugio* (mountain hut) to savour the view. The ensuing 9.6km descent is not for the faint of heart, with a sustained pitch of 9.2°. At **Selva di Cadore** (28km), the **Museo Civico della Val Fiorentina** (☎ 04 375 21 068; www.valfiorentina.it; Via IV Novembre 55; open daily in summer) has exhibits on archaeology, history and geology, the most fascinating focusing on the Uomo

di Mondeval, a 6th-century-BC man unearthed locally. Another steep descent with breathtaking southeasterly views towards Monte Pelmo leads to **Caprile** (33.7km), a bustling tourist town.

The climb to Passo Fedaia begins in earnest at 39.5km, immediately past the side-trip turn-off for the spectacular **Serrai di Sottoguda** gorge. The ascent to Fedaia is as steep as the descent from Giau, but the road is straighter, leaving no room for doubt about the challenges ahead. A short but nerve-wracking tunnel in mid-climb doesn't help matters. Make sure to remember lights and to channel all the Italian *ciclisti* who don't think twice about the tunnel. From Passo Fedaia, a delightful lakeside stretch with views of Marmolada glacier leads to the junction (50.3km) where a short side trip provides access to the glacier itself.

On the exhilarating final descent into Canazei, wildflower-choked rivulets descend from high turrets on the right, competing for attention with huge rocky masses rising from the deep valley floor to the left. Just

DOLOMITES

before Canazei, the town of **Alba** (59.5km) offers an early chance for food and accommodation.

Day 5: Canazei day ride: Sella Ronda Circuit
4–6 hours, 62.8km

This is the classic circuit of the Dolomites, crossing four major passes as it circumnavigates the Sella Massif. If you had only one day to cycle in northern Italy, this wouldn't be a bad choice.

The day's profile is fairly straightforward: steeply up and steeply down four times in a row. However, each pass has its own unique personality. The initial climb from Canazei to Passo Pordoi (2239m) is the longest and most obstinate, and the view from **Passo Pordoi** is one of the most dramatic in the Dolomites.

The descent from Pordoi is awe-inspiring, zigzagging through 33 numbered switchbacks into a glowingly verdant valley, occasionally checkerboarded with piles of new-mown hay. From the town of **Arabba** the climb to **Passo Campolongo** is short (3.9km) but steep.

The final climb to **Passo Sella** is another steep one, but with stupendous views throughout. From **Passo Sella**, the views of **Sasso Lungo** and Marmolada are remarkable, making it hard to hop onto your bike and head back down. The final 11km descent to Canazei is worth it just for the remarkable, intestine-like S-curve, which looks like something straight out of Dr Seuss.

Day 6: Canazei to Fiè allo Sciliar
3–6 hours, 49.8km

The return leg to Fiè allo Sciliar involves less climbing than any day on the tour, but the mountain scenery keeps up with the Dolomites standard of being absolutely sensational, and visits to a museum and castle en route provide an interesting cultural dimension.

The ride out of Canazei follows the main road down the Val di Fassa, a long, gradual descent with mountains on either side. Like Val Gardena, Val Badia and Cortina d'Ampezzo, Fassa is a Ladin-speaking valley with strong Ladin cultural influences. The well-organised **Museo Ladin de Fascia** (11.4km) showcases local culture

and traditions on three floors, with interactive touch-screen videos, reconstructed traditional rooms and displays featuring ironwork, farm implements, carnival masks and toys.

The day's toughest hill begins just beyond the museum. Compared to the previous days' ascents, though, it's mercifully short. By the time you reach **Passo Costalunga** (Karerpass, 20.8km) things have already levelled out, and the ride is mostly downhill from here as it skirts the bases of the Catinaccio and Sciliar Massifs. The screaming descent into the lush, barn-dotted valley of St Cipriano just beyond **Passo Nigra** (Nigerpass) is one of the day's highlights, as is the passage through the lovely small town of **Tires** (Tiers), where the onion-domed church signals your re-entry into the German zone.

About 4km before Fiè the route turns onto a small farm road, offering the opportunity to visit the beautiful 13th-century castle at **Presule** (Prösels). From the castle (47.4km) there's a commanding view over the surrounding fields and mountains and the Adige River far below. The route makes a short but mind-bogglingly steep descent to the main road, where you turn uphill one last time to the ride's starting point at Fiè.

ALTA PUSTERIA BIKE PATH

Duration 2½–4 hours
Distance 40km
Difficulty easy–moderate
Start San Candido (Innichen)
Finish Brunico (Bruneck)
Summary If this ride were food, it would be bratwurst: Germanic, juicy, easy going down and wonderfully chased by a beer

The Alta Pusteria bike route is a combination of dedicated bike paths and small farm roads winding through one of northern Italy's most scenic valleys. The region is distinctly South Tyrolean, with onion-domed churches around every corner and Germanic specialities on every menu. While more undulating than the Adige Valley bike path, this route is still manageable for cyclists of any age in reasonable physical condition. The overall trend of the ride is downhill, with a couple of steep climbs and dirt sections thrown in for good measure. The route parallels a train line and there are several bike-rental locations throughout the valley, making it possible to cycle one way (or even just part of the way) and take the train back to your starting point.

PLANNING
When to Cycle
This ride is enjoyable anytime from early June to mid-September, although as usual the period around the Ferragosto holiday (15 August) is best avoided due to crowds and higher prices. Many hotels close down in late September as the weather turns colder, taking a brief break before the ski season.

Maps
Maps showing the route can be found or bought in area tourist offices.

GETTING TO/FROM THE RIDE
San Candido (start)
TRAIN
From Bolzano, take any northbound train to Fortezza (Franzensfeste), then transfer to the slow train to San Candido. (The 2-hour journey costs €9.80.) San Candido's station is a snarl of tracks, serving as the end of the line for both Italian trains (from Fortezza) and Austrian trains (from Lienz). The supplementary bike ticket is €3.50.

BICYCLE
The westbound Alta Pusteria bike path to Brunico described here is only half the story. The same bike path continues 45km east from San Candido to Lienz, Austria. It's a beautiful ride, well maintained and signposted, and mostly downhill. As with the ride to Brunico, it's possible to cycle one way and then return to San Candido by train.

It's also possible to connect the Alta Pusteria ride with the Dolomites ride. Just beyond Dobbiaco Nuova (5km on the Alta Pusteria route), follow signs south towards Lago di Dobbiaco. A 32km mostly unpaved bike path leads from here to Cortina d'Ampezzo, where you can hook up with the Dolomites ride.

Brunico (finish)
TRAIN
Hourly trains run east from Brunico back to San Candido or west to Fortezza, where you can catch a southbound train to Bolzano.

THE RIDE
Throughout the day, the route skirts the southern edge of Val Pusteria, following a mostly paved bike path, which occasionally turns to dirt or merges with small farm roads. Far across the valley, the main road can periodically be seen and heard.

Winding out of downtown San Candido on streets shared with traffic, the route turns to bike path at 1.4km. The first several kilometres run level through green fields dotted with hay barns, with the spiky-topped Dolomites providing a dramatic backdrop along the southern horizon.

After a quick jog through **Dobbiaco**'s train-station car park, the route continues west, closely following a beautiful stream through evergreen forest, then veering briefly but steeply uphill to a picturesque chapel. From here, a long and coasting descent offers sweeping views of gorgeous green farmland and the steeples of **Villabassa** below. At 9.7km, cyclists without fat tyres should beware of the treacherously steep, unpaved crossing under the railroad tracks.

Open fields and deep forests alternate as the route stays left of the river between Villabassa and **Monguelfo**. Halfway between the two towns, a side trip leads to **Lago di Braies** (1494m), a glittering green and turquoise lake backed by craggy, grey mountains.

At 16.9km, just before central Monguelfo, yellow-green signs direct you to a path. The trail descends along the rushing river to the south shore of a manmade lake, then levels out for 3km and traverses a delightfully peaceful forest. Beyond the dam, the route climbs to **Valdaora di Sopra** on busier roads, then re-enters farm country at 23.2km.

The next 5km requires attentive navigation as the route zigzags through cornfields and open pastures, with beautiful cross-valley views to the **Austrian Alps**. The bumpy dirt section beginning at 27.3km will rattle your teeth, but smooth pavement resumes at 28km. After a brief but steep downhill on a road shared with cars, the route resumes

DOLOMITES

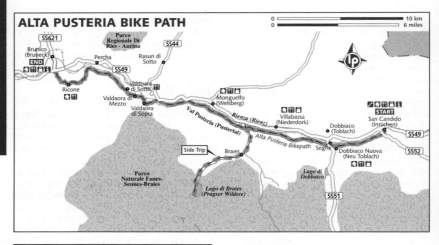

ALTA PUSTERIA BIKE PATH

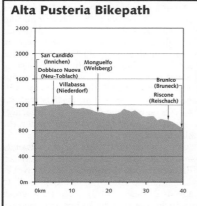

Alta Pusteria Bikepath

an undulating course through pastureland, with barns, woodpiles and cows jingling their bells. At 35km there's a nice view of the crenulated castle tower of **Lamprechtsburg**, just before the long final descent into Brunico.

MOUNTAIN BIKE RIDES

Take one look around and it will be obvious to you that this is one of the most stellar places in Italy to ride the 'knobbies' for a day or two.

DOLOMITES

Mountain biking is great all around Cortina. An excellent guide company in the area that is professional and accommodating is **Tra Cielo Cycling** (www.cielocycling.com).

If you want to venture out solo, mountain bikes can be rented from many places in town. The visitor centre publishes a good free map, *Escursioni in Mountain Bike a Cortina d'Ampezzo*, detailing 15 routes for cyclists of all abilities. **Mountain Bikes Centre** (☎ 04 368 63 861; Corso Italia 294) also publishes its own booklet of mountain bike routes.

Gardena Mountain Adventures (☎ 04 717 94 247; www.gardena-adventures.com; Str Ciampinoi 18) is based in Selva. It rents mountain bikes and also leads adventure tours in the nearby mountains.

Fassa Bike (www.fassabike.com) is a good internet resource for information on mountain bike rides in the Val di Fassa area, where mountain biking is excellent. The Canazei visitor centre distributes a free map, *Escursioni in Mountain Bike*, suggesting 10 itineraries in and around Val di Fassa. In Canazei, **Detomas** (☎ 04 626 02 447; Via Pareda 29/31) and **Northland Bike and Shop** (☎ 04 626 01 656; Strada del Piz 15) both rent mountain bikes. **Fassa Bike Freeride Park** will satisfy the BMX trickster in you.

TRENTINO-ALTO ADIGE

The visitor centres distribute detailed free booklets describing mountain biking routes in Val Rendena. In between Bolzano and Merano, near the bike path, you'll find **KTM Bike Industries** (☎ 04 735 50 355; www.noleggiobici.info; Via Merano, near Valsura Bridge) in Lana. This shop rents everything from city bikes to carbon racing mountain bikes, and you can arrange for them to drop off the rental where you are staying.

TOWNS & FACILITIES

BOLZANO
☎ 04 / pop 100,000

The appealing medieval city of Bolzano (Bozen), the capital of Alto Adige (Südtirol), sits at the gateway to the Alps near the confluence of the Adige (Etsch), Tálvera (Talfer) and Isarco (Eisack) Rivers. This city with its inhabitants chatting in German and Italian has a relaxed feel and some of the best bicycle infrastructure in Italy – yes, Bolzano's intricate, well-marked network of bike paths will amaze you.

Life revolves around Piazza Walther (Waltherplatz), a big square buzzing with sidewalk cafés and graced with a statue of medieval lyric poet Walther von der Vogelweide.

Information
The **visitor centre** (☎ 04 713 07 000; www.bolzano-bozen.it; Piazza Walther 8) is centrally located.

Credito Italiano (Piazza Walther 5) is one of several downtown banks with ATMs.

Supplies & Equipment
One of Bolzano's best bike shops, featuring a huge selection, is **Sportler** (☎ 04 7197 77 19; www.sportler.com; Via Enrico Fermi 14; closed Sun). It also runs a bicycle touring company (www.sportlertours.com) that runs road and mountain bike tours in the region and in Austria.

Sleeping & Eating
Accommodation in Bolzano is on the pricey side.

A few kilometres northwest of the centre is **Camping Moosbauer** (☎ 04 719 18 4 92;

www.moosbauer.com; Meranerstr 101; per person/per tent €8/12.50–15).

Ostello della Gioventù Bolzano (☎ 04 713 00 865; www.jugendherberge.it; Via Renon 23; dm incl breakfast €19.50–21.50, s incl breakfast €22–24) is close to the train station. The three- and four-bed dorms in this new independent hostel are configured for added privacy.

Hotel Feichter (☎ 04 719 78 768; hotel.feichter@dnet.it; Via Grappoli 15; s/d with breakfast €60/100) is an unexceptional but central two-star serving a substantial breakfast.

Hotel Figl (☎ 04 719 78 412; www.figl.net; Piazza del Grano 9; s €80–100, d €100–110) is a well-priced and stylish hotel, centrally located, with chic, contemporary rooms. An 'Italian breakfast' (espresso and brioche) costs €3; a more cyclist-friendly hot and cold buffet costs €11.

You can find most anything in and around Bolzano's famous and bustling fruit, vegetable, cheese and meat **market** (closed Sun) that lines the streets around Piazza delle Erbe. Definitely try the Barolo-soaked *formaggio* (cheese) if you have the chance.

Fischbänke Pic-Nic Bar (☎ 04 719 71 714; Via Dott Streiter 26a; dishes €5–10) has a sign next to the speakers that reads 'This is not McDonald's' – and that says it all. Run by artist/host/*bon vivant* Cobo on the site of the old fish market, the Fischbänke has the market's original white-marble tables, where you can drink a glass of Tyrolean wine and eat some of northern Italy's most beautiful bruschetta. **Hopfen & Co** (☎ 04 713 00 788; Piazza delle Erbe 17) hydroplanes you into the Habsburg era. This venerable 800-year-old inn serves up hearty portions of traditional dishes, including sauerkraut and sausages cooked in beer. **Ristorante al Duomo** (☎ 04 719 71 551; Via Isarco 3) is just off Piazza Walther, located on the bike route. It manages to be intimate and tranquil within the bustling centre as it serves handmade pasta and other scrumptious, well-done dishes.

Getting There & Away
Bolzano airport (Aeroporto di Bolzano; ☎ 04 712 55 255; www.abd-airport.it) is served by flights to Rome, Olbia and Cagliari. Cheap airport transfers are

available through **Locus Coach** (www.locus coach.com).

To reach the airport from downtown Bolzano, follow the Isarco bike path south (see Alta Adige Bike Path ride p168), cross the Isarco River on Ponte Resia, continue straight on Via Volta, turn right on Via Buozzi, turn left on Via Einstein and follow airport signs the rest of the way.

From Bolzano **train station** (Piazza Stazione), one block southeast of the Piazza Walther visitor centre, there are also trains Milan and Venice.

BRUNICO
☎ 04 / pop 14,150

Because of the easy transportation to San Candido and Bolzano, Brunico (Bruneck) is not covered as a destination here. For information on places to stay and eat in Brunico, check with the **visitor centre** (☎ 04 745 55 722; www.bruneck.com; Piazza Municipio 7). just east of the train station

CANAZEI
☎ 04 / pop 1960

Canazei (Cianacei), a summer and winter resort surrounded by stunning mountain scenery, is yet another great base for hiking and mountain biking trips into the surrounding peaks. Here Val di Fassa runs up against the imposing barrier of the Sella group to the north, the steep face of Marmolada to the east and the red-tinged Catinaccio (Rosengarten) to the west. Canazei's centre is small but well-equipped with tourist services.

Information

The **visitor centre** (☎ 04 626 01 113; www .fassa.com; Via Roma 34) provides information about Canazei and the entire Val di Fassa.

There are banks with ATMs along the main drag.

Supplies & Equipment

Detomas (☎ 04 626 02 447; Via Pareda 29/31) is a helpful, well-stocked bike shop with good information about the local area.

Sleeping & Eating

Conveniently located near the river at the east edge of town, **Camping Marmolada**

(☎ 04 626 01 660; campingmarmolada@ virgilio.it; Via Pareda; per person/tent €10/10) has laundry facilities and hot showers.

Garni Stella Alpina (☎ 04 626 01 127; www.stella-alpina.net; Via Antermont 4; d €64–104) is in the heart of the village, but tucked away on a small street lined with impossibly quaint buildings. This immaculate **Ladin B&B** has a muscle-soothing sauna and hot tub.

Hotel Cesa Tyrol (☎ 04 626 01 156; www.hotelcesatyrol.com; Viale Cascata 2; d half-board €94–202) has rooms with views of Canazei's church spire rising above the village. Public areas are modern and elegant, and many rooms have timber balconies.

Hotel Rita (☎ 04 626 01 219; www .hotelrita.com; Streda de Pareda 16; d half-board from €98) sits 20m from the main square at the base of the ski lift. Most importantly, there's an in-house masseuse!

Café Antermont (☎ 04 626 01 040; Piazza Marconi 15; cakes around €3.10) is on the main square and has fresh-baked sponge cake with alpine cream and a shot of espresso, 'righteous'. **El Paél** (☎ 04 626 01 433; Streda Roma 54; set menus €27, mains €14–19.90) is a welcoming typical Trento *osteria* with a traditional Ladin kitchen cooking up specialities of the valley such as nettle dumplings with spinach and Vezzena cheese.

CORTINA D'AMPEZZO
☎ 04 / pop 6090

Cortina has grown dramatically since hosting the 1956 Winter Olympics, and the city you see today comes closer to urban sprawl than anything else in the Dolomites. Even so, the magnificence of the surrounding valley dwarfs the town centre, and Cortina remains more appealing than many other Dolomite resorts where growth has been more recent. Close to Cortina are the **Tre Cime di Lavaredo**, one of the world's most famous climbing locations and a panoramic place to walk. The fact that you can arrive by bus in summer literally at the foot of the Tre Cime means the area swarms with climbers in peak season.

Town life focuses on the long Corso Italia pedestrian zone near the belltower, a pleasant place for a *passeggiata* (stroll) day or night.

Information
The **visitor centre** (☎ 04 36 32 31; www .infoDolomites.it) operates offices at Piazzetta San Francesco 8 and Piazza Roma 1.

There are several banks with ATMs along Corso Italia near the belltower.

Supplies & Equipment
Just north of town, **Cicli Cortina** (☎ 04 368 67 215; Via Majon 148) is one of the town's most excellent bike shops. Proprietor Luigi de Vila offers rentals, clothing, accessories, equipment and great advice on itineraries around Cortina. Another good local shop is **Mountain Bikes Centre** (☎ 04 368 63 861; Corso Italia 294).

Sleeping & Eating
The most convenient of Cortina's four camping grounds, **International Camping Olympia** (☎ /fax 04 36 50 57; www .campingolympiacortina.it; strada Alemagna; per person €4.50–7.50, per tent €7–9) has forested sites near the river, 4km north of town (and just slightly uphill) on the Day 3 route. **Camping Rocchetta** (☎ / fax 04 36 50 63; Via Campo 1; www.camping rocchetta.it; per person/tent €5.50–8.25/€7– 9) is the most cyclist-friendly. It's near the river south of town, on a route that runs steeply downhill from Cortina with very nice (and distracting) valley vistas.

The visitor centre can provide a list of rooms for rent in private homes, generally the cheapest option in high season. Prices listed here are based on a minimum stay of seven nights; contact the hotel to check alternative prices.

Hotel Montana (☎ 04 368 60 498; www .cortina-hotel.com; Corso Italia 94; s/d from €50/77) is right in Cortina's pedestrian-friendly heart. This 1920s hotel has snug, comfortable rooms and is an unbeatable two-star deal.

Oltres B&B (☎ 03 465 203 175; www .oltres.com; Loc Campo di Sotto 70; d €70–120) is a charming little B&B tucked inside a 17th-century house drowsing in a wildflower-filled meadow on Cortina's southeastern outskirts.

La Cooperativa di Cortina (Corso Italia 40) is a big department store with a great supermarket.

Cafés and pizzerias and some stellar gourmet restaurants fill Cortina's centre,

with pavement seating in summer. **Osteria Pane Vino e San Daniele** (☎ 04 368 68 110; Corso Italia 137) is a trendy place for light meals and drinks. At **Croda Caffè** (☎ 04 368 66 589; Corso Italia 163), hungry cyclists can sample the local speciality, *casunziei* (beef ravioli with poppy seeds).

FIÈ ALLO SCILIAR
☎ 04 / pop 3040
Perched in verdant meadows beneath the Sciliar's giant stone hump, Fiè (Vols am Schlern) is a classic South Tyrolean mountain town. Despite its diminutive size, it's a lovely place to spend a night or two, with a medieval main square and an onion-domed church enhancing its stunning setting.

Information
Look for the **visitor centre** (☎ 04 717 25 047; www.seiseralm.it) across from the SAD bus stop, on the corner of Via Bolzano and Via del Paese. Information is available on the Alpe di Siusi, as well as on Fiè.

There are banks near the visitor centre that have ATMs.

Sleeping & Eating
About 3.5km up the hill along the Day 1 route is **Camping Seiser Alm** (☎ 04 717 06 459; www.camping-seiseralm.com; per person/tent €6–8.50/€4.50–11).

The town centre boasts excellent hotels. **Albergo Croce Bianca** (☎ /fax 04 717 25 029; www.albergocrocebianca.info; Piazza della Chiesa 2; per person with breakfast €30–45) is the most affordable.

Hotel Rose-Wenzer (☎ 04 717 25 016; www.hotel-rose-wenzer.it; Piazza della Chiesa 18; rooms half-pension €45–60, full-pension €65–80) is a three-star with a sauna for aching quadriceps and a stunning terrace overlooking the Sciliar Massif.

J Delago Markt am Platz (Piazza della Chiesa 3) sells groceries, cold drinks and sandwiches. Good restaurant meals can be had in all the hotels. Albergo Croce Bianca's prices are among the most economical, while the winner for atmosphere is Hotel Rose-Wenzer, with its great terrace affording a panoramic view.

MOLVENO
☎ 04 / pop 1100
Molveno's setting is dramatic, with the Dolomiti di Brenta's most imposing peaks

soaring dizzyingly above the lake's blue-green waters. There's an array of outdoor recreation opportunities based from here, including rock climbing, windsurfing and boating. The SS421 divides Molveno into two sections: the centre, which sprawls across a hillside above the lake, and the lower town along the lakeshore, where the camping ground, sports facilities and some hotels and restaurants are located.

Information

The **visitor centre** (☎ 04 615 86 924; www .aptDolomitespaganella.com; Piazza Marconi 5) is in the heart of the centre.

There are banks with ATMs close to the visitor centre.

Supplies & Equipment

In Molveno, **For You** (☎ 04 615 86 056; Via Lungolago 11/a) advertises bike services. Or else, Andalo, 5km north along the Day 3 route, has a bike shop, **Danilo Sport** (☎ 04 615 85 907; at Via Piz Galin 10).

Sleeping & Eating

Camping Spiaggia (☎ 04 615 86 978; www .campingmolveno.it; Via Lungolago 25; 2 adults & car €24.50–34), on the shores of Lago di Molveno, has sites that come with free admission to the neighbouring outdoor swimming pool. It's an easy stroll into Molveno's buzzing little village centre.

Hotel Alexander Cima Tosa (☎ 04 615 86 928; www.alexandermolveno.com; Piazza Scuole 7, s €50–66, d €64–92) is in Molveno's village centre. This three-star hotel has spacious, contemporary rooms (most with balconies) and a relaxing sun terrace.

Alp & Wellness Sport Hotel Panorama (☎ 04 615 83 134; www.sportho telpanorama.it; Via Carletti 6, Fai della Paganella; d €88–240) boasts its namesake panoramic views as well as extensive wellness facilities where you can nurture your road-tired body.

Molveno has several centrally located grocery stores, including **Central Market** (Via Paganella 1), across from the visitor centre. There are restaurant choices in the centre and near the lakeshore.

PINZOLO
☎ 04 / pop 3050

Pinzolo is an unpretentious town in the heart of the Val Rendena, much less glitzy than its uphill neighbour Madonna di Campiglio. Traditionally a rural agricultural community, Pinzolo residents now make their living from tourists visiting the nearby **Parco Naturale Adamello-Brenta** and is a fantastic base for myriad outdoor adventures.

Information

The **visitor centre** (☎ 04 655 01 007; www .pinzolo.to; Piazzale Ciclamino 32) at the south end of town has info on hikes in the local mountains (some starting in Pinzolo), in addition to cycling and accommodation information. One of the most popular hikes heads up Val Genova west of town to the **Cascate Nardis** and other waterfalls.

There are banks in the city centre.

Supplies & Equipment

Il Laboratorio Bike (☎ 04 655 03 880; maddmaxx@libero.it; Via Balognini 24) rents skis in the winter and is bike-oriented in the summer. **Makalù Sport** (☎ 04 658 04 512), 5km down the valley at Via Regina Elena 4 in Caderzone, sells, rents and repairs bicycles.

Sleeping & Eating

Camping Parco Adamello (☎ 04 655 01 793; www.campingparcoadamello.it; Carisolo; per person €8–9, tent & car €12–18) is beautifully situated within the Parco Naturale Adamello-Brenta, 1km north of Pinzolo.

Check out **Albergabici** (www.albergabici .it) for the latest on bike-friendly accommodation in Pinzolo.

Hotel Bellavista (☎ 04 655 01 164; www .bellavistanet.com, in Italian; s/d from €47/80, half-board per person per week €273–406) is Pinzolo's 57-room 'beautiful view' hotel – one of the few hotels to open all year. It's a modern place with plain but clean and comfortable rooms.

There's a supermarket just north of the centre. Adjacent to a camping ground in Carisolo is **Ristorante Tipico Magnabò** (☎ 04 655 03 841; www.magnabo.com; Localitá Magnabo), a cosy old wood-and-stone building, specialising in traditional Trentino-Alto Adige cuisine. If you bring a printed-out advertisement from its website, you'll be given a 10% discount. **Ristorante Pizzeria La Botte** (04 655 01 488; Viale Dolomites 12) is lively and makes good pizza the old-fashioned way.

SAN CANDIDO
☎ 04 / pop 3110

Sitting in the upper reaches of the Val Pusteria only 7km from the Austrian border, the Germanic-flavoured town of San Candido (Innichen) has a lovely main square flanked by old churches. People love the town for its pleasant pedestrian zone and relaxed pace of life, and cyclists especially relish it for its location at the midpoint of the heavily used bike path from Lienz, Austria to Brunico.

Information
The **visitor centre** (☎ 04 749 13 149; www.innichen.it; Piazza del Magistrato 1) sells the *Raderlebnis Dolomiten* guide to the area and offers a wealth of other free information.

Near the visitor centre there are banks equipped with ATMs.

Supplies & Equipment
Papin Sport (☎ 04 749 13 450; www.papinsport.com; Via MH Hueber 1) sells everything a cyclist could ever need and also rents bikes at multiple locations throughout Val Pusteria – one-way rentals are permitted.

Sleeping & Eating
Between Dobbiaco and Villabassa, **Camping Olympia** (☎ 04 749 72 147; www.camping-olympia.com; per person/tent €8.50–9.50/€3.50–8.50) is reachable via a right turn off the San Candido–Brunico bike path at 7.3km. **Camping Toblacher** (☎ 04 749 72 294; www.toblachersee.com; per person/tent €6.50–8/€3–8.50) is another option, 8km southwest of San Candido on beautiful Lagi di Dobbiaco.

Near the Drava River and city centre, **Garni Patzleiner** (☎ /fax 04 749 13 211; Via Mantinger 3; www.garnipatzleiner .com; per person €25–32) has flower-filled balconies.

Albergo Orso Grigio (☎ 04 749 13 115; www.orsohotel.it; Via Rainer 2; half-pension s €58–120, d €74–190) is an appealing historic three-star smack in the centre of town.

There are markets in the heart of town. Get your carbohydrates at **Panificio/ Backerei Wachtler** (Benediktinergasse 1 & Via Rainer 9) in the form of delicious baked goods. **Restaurant Wiesthaler** (Via Duca Tassilo 3) is a cosy locals' hangout adjacent to Hotel Weisses Rossl. **Uhrmacher's Weinstube** (☎ 04 749 13 158; Via dei Tintori 1) is a convivial hideaway/*enoteca* serving snacks and 300 different wines until midnight.

SELVA
☎ 04 / pop 1460

Selva (Wolkenstein/Selva Gherdeina) is the highest of Val Gardena's three main towns. Scenically located at the base of two of the Dolomites most famous rock formations, Sassolungo and the Sella Massif. It's an unapologetically touristy resort offering services to skiers in winter and hikers in summer. This area is a walker's paradise with endless possibilities, from the challenging **Alte Vie** of the Gruppo del Sella and the magnificent **Parco Naturale Puez-Odle**, to picturesque strolls for walkers of all abilities in spots such as the Vallunga. Highway SS242, also known as Str Meisules, serves as Selva's main street, and every other building seems to be a hotel or guest house.

Information
Make a stop at Selva's **visitor centre** (☎ 04 717 95 122; www.val-gardena.com; Streda Meisules 213) for information and inspiration.

There's an ATM just outside the visitor centre, and there are others along the main street.

Supplies & Equipment
In the town of Ortisei (St Ulrich/Urtijei), 7.5km downhill, the bike shop **Doi Rodes** (☎ 04 717 86 378; Via Rezia 224) can satisfy your cycling-supply needs. In Selva, **Gardena Mountain Adventures** (☎ 04 717 94 247; www.gardena-adventures.com; Str Ciampinoi 18) rents mountain bikes.

Sleeping & Eating
Selva has no camping grounds, but intrepid souls can push over Passo Gardena to **Camping Colfosco** (☎ /fax 04 718 36 515; www .campingcolfosco.org; Sorega 5, Corvara; per person €5.50–7, site €6–12, 18.5km), east along the Day 2 route.

Thanks to Val Gardena's popularity as a ski destination, Selva has no shortage of accommodation.

Hotel Posta Al Cervo (☎ 04 717 95 174; www.hotelpostaalcervo.com; Via Meisules 116; d half-board €80–100) is a good choice right in Selva's village centre. This friendly and reasonably priced little place has a fine restaurant serving Ladin and Italian cuisine.

For groceries, try **Senoner Market** (Via Puez 3). **Pasticceria Perathoner** (☎ 04 717 73 177; Streda Meisules 175) proudly sells delectable baked goods. Restaurant **Pizzeria Sal Feur** (☎ 04 717 94 276; Via Puez 6) pleases the more upscale palates with its Ladin specialities, wood-fired pizzas and a nice wine list. **Medél** (☎ 04 717 95 235; Streda Meisules 22) also serves tasty local dishes, sometimes accompanied by live music.

TRENTO
☎ 04 / pop 105,000

Trento is a pleasant city on the banks of the Adige. Aesthetically disappointing urban sprawl has greatly expanded its borders, but the historical core remains largely intact – and very lovely. Old palaces with painted facades fan out from central Piazza Duomo.

Information

The **visitor centre** (☎ 04 619 83 880; www .apt.trento.it; Via Manci 2; 9am-7pm daily) has excellent English-language resources and loads of information for the cycle tourist. This office gives out a fat, sleek booklet detailing the bike paths in the region.

Convenient ATMs are located in the train station and across from the visitor centre.

Supplies & Equipment

Trent's best-stocked bike shop is the chain store **Sportler** (☎ 04 619 81 290; www .sportler.com; Via Mantova 12; closed Mon morning & Sun). Those who prefer to support independent shops can check out **Moser Cicli** (☎ 04 612 30 327; www .mosercicli.it; Via Calepina 37; closed Mon morning & Sun).

Sleeping & Eating

One of the closest camping grounds is **Campeggio Moser** (☎ 04 618 70 248; Via Nazionale 64, Località Nave San Felice; open May–Oct), several kilometres north of town between Lavis and San Michele all'Adige.

Ostello della Gioventù Giovane Europa (☎ 04 612 63 484; Via Torre Vanga 9; dm €15–20, s/d €25/40) is the best budget option in town, with a convenient location right near the train station.

Albermonaco (☎ 04 619 83 681; www .albermonaco.it; Via Torre d'Augusto 25; s/ d €60/90) has a soft spot for cyclists. You'll get a 10–15% discount, and the facilities are well-run and maintained.

Hotel Venezia (☎ 04 612 34 114; www .hotelveneziatn.it; Piazza del Duomo 45; s/d €38/55, s/d with bathroom €49/69) is a simple but comfortable two-star hotel split across two buildings in Trento's heart. The price-to-location ratio is first-rate.

Pick up picnic supplies at **Supermercato Trentino-Alto Adige** (Corso III Novembre 4–6).

Osteria Trentina (☎ 04 612 38 841; Via Roma 48; snacks €3–3.50, lunch dishes €5–7) is a great spot to head early evening for a *spritz* (soda and white wine served in a brandy glass with orange slices) along with free happy-hour munchies brought to your table. **Due Giganti** (☎ 04 612 37 515; Via Simonino 14; buffets from €7) is a cheap all-you-can-eat, self-service restaurant where locals flock. **Scringno del Duomo** (☎ 04 612 20 030; Piazza del Duomo 29; upstairs mains €8.50–20, downstairs set menus €50–70) is located in Trento's oldest building, dating back to the 1200s. It actually houses two separate and equally outstanding restaurants serving local specialities; one of them looks into a glassed-in Roman cellar holding more than 1000 different wines.

ADRIATIC COAST

HIGHLIGHTS

- Early Christian mosaics at **Ravenna** (p214) and **Aquileia** (p189)
- Cycling through famous Friulian vineyards of the **Collio** (p187)
- White cliffs and dazzling blue-green waters of the **Conero Riviera** (p198)
- Seldom-visited places and the walled medieval towns of **Umbria** (p197) and **Le Marche** (p200)
- **Ferarra** (p196) and **Ravenna** (p214) – epicentres of bike love

SPECIAL EVENTS
- Barcolana Sailing Regatta (October), Trieste
- Buskers Festival (August), Ferrara
- Corsa dei Ceri (May), Gubbio
- Quintana Medieval Festival (August), Ascoli Piceno

CYCLING EVENTS
- Gran Fondo d'Europa (September), Trieste-Cividale del Friuli
- Transeuganea (May), Euganeian Hills

FOOD & DRINK SPECIALITIES
- *frico* (savoury Friulian cheese-potato cake)
- *cappellacci di zucca* (Ferrarese pumpkin-filled pasta)
- truffles
- miniature Castelluccio lentils
- pork products of Norcia

TERRAIN
Flat along the coast except at Monte Conero (south of Ancona), Monte San Bartolo (north of Pesaro) and the Carso (east of Trieste); hilly to mountainous inland.

| Telephone Codes – 04/05/07 | www.cuorelemarche.com | www.comune.venezia.it |

Ranging from the limestone cliffs along the Slovenian border to the dazzling Conero Riviera south of Ancona, with lagoons, beaches and vast, flat wetlands in between, the Adriatic Coast offers some of Italy's easiest cycling, plus fascinating traces of the region's Byzantine, Lombard and Roman history. It also holds in store the more typical challenging riding through the dramatic landscapes of Le Marche and Umbria. Venturing further inland to the Euganeian Hills near Padua, you'll climb through forests and small hamlets.

CLIMATE

The Adriatic Coast has a Mediterranean climate, with hot, dry summers and moderately cold winters. Spring and autumn are the rainiest seasons, with precipitation increasing inland towards the mountains. Winter brings bone-chilling fog to the Po Delta and Venetian Lagoon, while snow falls at higher elevations.

Average high temperatures for Venice are 28°C in July and August, 18°C in April and October, and 8°C around December and January.

GATEWAY

See Venice (p217).

FRIULI-VENEZIA GIULIA

Italy's northeastern most region, Friuli-Venezia Giulia reflects the influence of its modern Slovene and Austrian neighbours, as well as the Venetians and ancient Romans who once plied its waters. Three languages – Italian, Friulian and Slovene – are widely spoken. The region's cultural diversity is matched by geographic variety, ranging from spare limestone cliffs to lush vineyard-covered hills, from coastal lagoons to the rugged Carnian and Julian Alps.

ACCESS TOWN

See Trieste (p215).

HISTORY

Prehistoric settlement of the Triestine Carso is evidenced by tools, pottery and bones discovered in local caves. Excavations nearby have also revealed hundreds of Bronze Age walled settlements known as *castellieri*.

Ancient Roman influence began in 181 BC with the settlement of Aquileia, followed by the colonisation of Cividale del Friuli (Roman Forum Iulii) and Trieste (Tergeste). All three cities were incorporated into the 10th Roman region, Venetia et Histria.

The region's low alpine passes left it vulnerable to invasion from northern and eastern tribes. Attila the Hun sacked Aquileia in AD 452, and the Lombards founded their first Italian duchy at Cividale del Friuli in AD 568.

The medieval period resulted in ongoing struggles between the patriarchate of Aquileia and the Venetian Republic. In 1420 Venice finally took Friuli, while the eastern provinces of Trieste and Venezia Giulia (now known as Gorizia) fell into Austrian hands.

After a brief period of Napoleonic rule, Austria took control of the entire region in 1815. Friuli joined the Kingdom of Italy in 1866, with Venezia Giulia following in 1918.

ENVIRONMENT

Friuli-Venezia Giulia divides roughly into three geographic zones: the Friulian lowlands, the southeastern karstic highlands (known in Italian as the Carso) and the northern Alps (not covered in this chapter).

The Friulian flatlands, drained by the great Isonzo and Tagliamento Rivers, spread south from the alpine foothills to the sea. As elsewhere along the Adriatic, the land was historically swampy, but large sections, such as the Bonifica della Vittoria near Grado, were gradually reclaimed as farmland to feed a growing population and reduce the risk of malaria. To the west, the Marano and Grado lagoons continue to provide important shorebird habitat.

The Carso is a high, limestone plateau riddled with caves, abysses and sinkholes, spreading eastward into Slovenia from Gorizia in the north and Trieste in the south. Originally called kras by the local Slovenes, its German name karst has since been adopted by geologists to describe similar limestone formations worldwide.

FRIULI RAMBLE

Duration 3 days
Distance 213.5km
Difficulty easy–moderate
Start/Finish Trieste
Summary Dust off the northeastern part of your Italy map. The land of Italy's famous white wine will unroll its easy-pedalling, radiant landscapes for you. They are under visited and a true delight.

By cycling the overlooked, yet spectacular, far-flung reaches of the northeast corner of Italy, you have the unique opportunity to capture an intimate sense of this earthy region. Along the route, Slovenian farmers tend their fields in the strong sun, rows of vines cling to voluptuous hill country, the blaze of sunsets makes the land vibrate with colour, and laid-back locals are happy to stop and chat. Sometimes, there may just be the hum of a tractor in the distance and not another person in sight. This would be the moment to stop, take a drink and lavish being in the heart of Friuli.

As you pedal you'll pass a couple of tourist attractions, like **Aquileia's centre**, with its splendid mosaics and basilica, and the seaside destination of **Grado** with its

medieval centre. Each holds a drawing appeal in its own right. The icing on the cake is the final scenic jaunt down the **Istrian coast**.

This loop showcases southern Friuli-Venezia Giulia's geographic and cultural diversity, and the flat nature of the ride adds an element of tranquillity. In the Friulian hills and plains, adventures await to be uncovered from the fancy-free vantage point and freedom you will enjoy on two wheels.

PLANNING
When to Cycle
This ride is most enjoyable between April and October. August is best avoided, to put it lightly, due to overcrowding in Trieste and on Grado's beaches. In October small, roadside restaurants known as *osmizze* spontaneously pop up in the Triestine Carso, serving simple meals featuring local produce and wine.

What to Bring
Make sure that you have plenty of water-storage capacity. The sun is hot, and sometimes there are significant gaps between towns.

Maps & Booklets
Touring Club Italia's (TCI) 1:200,000 *Veneto Friuli-Venezia Giulia* map covers this ride in its entirety.

The free booklets funded by the **Regione Automoma Fruili Venezia Giulia** (www.turismo.fgv.it) containing *itinerari cicloturistici* (routes for cycle tourists) in Friuli-Venezia Giulia are available at local visitor centres. They describe 21 rides throughout the region, including sections of this route.

MOUNTAIN BIKING: FRIULI-VENEZIA GIULIA

The **Regione Autonoma Friuli Venezia Giulia** (www.turismo.fvg.it) has collaborated with '**Avventura – Bike**' (Associazione Mountain Bike Italia; www.amibike.it) to create a booklet of suggested mountain biking itineraries in the region. You can pick up a copy at visitor centres.

Bikelandia (☎ 43 294 10 44; www.bikelandia.com) is a tour company that will take you riding in the hills and dirt roads of Friuli.

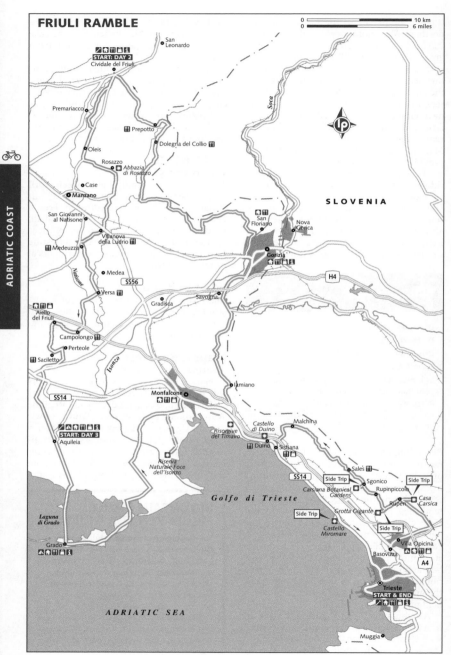

FRIULI RAMBLE

0 ———————————————— 10 km
0 ———————————————— 6 miles

San Leonardo

START: DAY 2
Cividale del Friuli

Premariacco

Prepotto

Oleis

Dolegna del Collio

Rosazzo
Abbazia di Rosazzo

Case
Manzano

San Giovanni al Natisone

Villanova della Ludrio

Medeuzza

Medea

SS56

Versa

Gradisca

Savogna

Aiello del Friuli

Campolongo

Perteole

Saciletto

SS14

START: DAY 3
Aquileia

Riserva Naturale Foce dell'Isonzo

Monfalcone

Iamiano

Castello di Duino

Malchina

Risorgive del Timavo

Duino

Sistiana

Sale's

Side Trip

SS14

Carsiana Botanical Gardens

Sgonico

Rupinpiccolo

Side Trip

Rupen

Casa Carsica

Grotta Gigante

Side Trip

Side Trip

Laguna di Grado

Grado

Golfo di Trieste

Castello Miramare

Villa Opicina

Basovizza

A4

Trieste
START & END

SLOVENIA

Soča

San Floriano

Nova Gorica

Gorizia

H4

Natisone

Isonzo

ADRIATIC SEA

Muggia

FRIULI RAMBLE – DAY 1

CUES			GPS COORDINATES
start		Trieste visitor centre	45°38'59"N 13°46'05"E
0km	⌐►	From visitor centre along Piazza Della Unita	
0.3	↙	Corso Italia (at Piazza Della Borsa)	
0.4	◥⌐	Via Dante Alighieri (turns into Via 30 Ottobre)	
0.9	★	Piazza Oberdan, Tram to Opicina	
0.9		Opicina	45°41'12"N 13°47'14" E
0.9	◥⌐	on SS58 from Tram stop	
1.7	◥⌐	to 'Monrupino'	
5	◥⌐	to 'Rupen'	
6.3		Rupen	45°43'20"N 13°47'38"E
{6.7	●●⌐►	Casa Carsica, 1km ↻}	
6.8	↖	to 'Borgo Grotta Gigante'	
9.3	⌐►	to'Rupinpiccolo'	
		(easy to miss, signed from opposite direction)	
	{●●↑	Grotta Gigante 2km ↻}	
11.3	↖	to 'Carsiana', 'Rupinpiccolo'	45°43'38"N 13°45'48"E
13.8	⌐►	to 'Sales', Sgonico	45°44'12"N 13°44'49"E
	{●●◥⌐	Carsiana Gardens 1.4km ↻}	
16.1		Sales	45°44'53"N 13°43'47"E
16.6	⊙⌐►	to 'Samatorza' (not to Sgonico)	
19.9	◥⌐	to 'Malchina'	
20	◥⌐	to 'Malchina'	
23.8	↖	to 'Visogliano', 'Malchina'	45°47'04"N 13°39'30"E
(50m)	↙	to 'Ceroglie'	
26.7	⌐►	continue downhill at T intersection	
27.1	⌐►⊙	SS14 to 'Venezia', 'Sistiana'	
			45°46'14"N 13°38'20"E

CUES CONTINUED			GPS COORDINATES
31.8	↙	SS55 to 'Gorizia'	
45.2	◥⌐	to 'Savogna'	
47.2	⌐►	to 'Savogna'	
47.6	↙	SP8 to 'Gorizia'	
47.8		Savona	45°54'30"N 13°34'42"
52.5	↖	SS56 to 'Udine', 'Gorizia'	45°56'03"N 13°36'20"E
		{ST VR to go to Gorizia Centro 2km RT}	
53.3	↙	Gradisca/Cervignano exit	
53.5	↙	to 'S. Floriano'	
56.1	◥⌐	to 'S. Floriano'	
57.1	▲	1km steep climb	
61.2	↖	unmarked road downhill, not to 'S. Floriano'	
62	◥⌐	to 'Cormons'	
62.6	⌐►	unsigned T intersection with stop sign	
65.5	◥⌐	at stop sign to 'Cormons'	
66.4	⌐►	to 'Cormons'	
71.1	⌐►	to 'Dolegna'	
71.2		0.9km steepish climb	
71.3	↖	to 'Dolegna'	
74.5	⌐►	SP14 to 'Strada del vino'	
80.5		Dolegna	46°01'52"N 13°28'48"E
80.6	↑	SP21 to 'Mernico'	
83.6	◥⌐	to 'Trattoria da Mario/Farmacia'	
84.2		Prepotto	46°02'48"N 13°28'50"E
84.8	⌐►	'to Cividale'	
92.1	↙	Viale Trieste 'to Centro'	
92.7	↑	Piazza del Duomo	
92.9		Piazza Centrale, Cividale del Friuli visitor centre	
			46°05'36"N 13°25'53"E

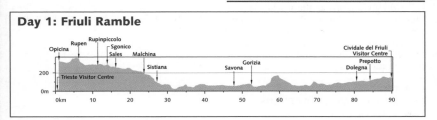

Day 1: Friuli Ramble

THE RIDE
Day 1: Trieste to Cividale del Friuli
5–7 hours, 92.9km

Today the route descends from the stony Carso highlands to the fertile Collio vineyards. This is the tour's longest day, but it's still only moderately challenging. On autumn weekends the hills are abuzz with locals sampling *jota* (bean and sauerkraut soup), Terrano wine, and other regional specialities at the seasonal *osmizze* (roadside eateries).

Trieste's century-old, historic **relic-of-a-tram** tackles the day's steepest climb (supposedly up to 26% grade) and sidesteps city traffic on its way to Villa Opicina. The 25-minute ride costs €1.50, with departures every 20 minutes from Piazza Oberdan. Bikes cost €1 extra and they travel on racks up the front. Be prepared to unload all your baggage to get your bike onto the front rack.

From **Opicina**, traffic becomes extremely light after you turn off SS58 (1.7km). Then the route undulates on peaceful roads through stony hamlets and fields bordered by rocky walls. **Gorizia** (52.5km) makes a nice lunch stop around the midway point.

ADRIATIC COAST

The best trattorias are found in the old-town streets, near the **food market** (Via Verdi 30). You'll want to be fuelled for some of the most beautiful, but hilliest (two short, steep climbs), parts of this generally flat day.

Leaving Gorizia, you'll be on a main road for 1km. After that, farm roads tour you through the famous Colli region's vineyard-covered hills. As the landscape flattens you'll be dabbling in Slovenia (around 60–65km) and wine country that produces Collio, Picolit and Tocai Friulano, amongst other fine wines.

The day's final highlight is the picturesque crossing of the Natisone River gorge on Cividale del Friuli's famous Ponte del Diavolo.

SIDE TRIP: CASA CARSICA
30 minutes, at 6.7km, 1km RT

The **Casa Carsica** (Rupingrande 31; admission free; 11am–12.30pm & 3–5pm Sun only) is a traditional Carso farmhouse on display.

SIDE TRIP: GROTTA GIGANTE
1 hour, at 9.3km, 2km RT

The **Grotta Gigante** (☎ 04 032 73 12; www .grottagigante.it, in Italian; admission €16), is listed by Guinness as the world's largest tourable cave; St. Peter's Basilica in Rome could fit inside. It was inhabited from the ancient times until the Roman era. There are regular 50-minute guided tours given through the grotta.

SIDE TRIP:
CARSIANA BOTANICAL GARDENS
1 hour, at 13.8km, 1.4 RT

This impressive grounds (☎ 04 022 95 73; admission €3; closed Mon) displays 600 plant and tree species native to the Carso.

Day 2:
Cividale del Friuli to Aquileia
3–4 hours, 53.7km

Though the scenery doesn't knock your socks off like the previous day's ride, the short and easy route from Cividale to Aquileia compensates with intriguing sites. You'll have plenty of time to explore both Cividale and Aquileia as well as the Abbazia di Rosazzo en route. The ride is entirely flat except for a short climb early in the day.

FRIULI RAMBLE – DAY 2

CUES			GPS COORDINATES
start		Cividale del Friuli visitor centre	46°05′36″N 13°25′53″E
0km	↱	Corso Mazzini	
.2	↑	Piazza del Duomo	
0.6	↱	Via Manzano (becomes Lazzarda)	
1.2	↑	Cross Via Foraboschi	
1.8	↙	to 'Firmano' at stop sign, Vian Manzano	
6.1	↱	Via Strada di Ipplis	
6.9	↰	Via Strada di Leproso	
9.3	↰	at T intersection stop sign, Via Armentarezza	
9.4	↱	to 'Manzano'	
10.5	↱	to 'Manzano'	
11.4	↰	to 'Rosazzo' Via Rosazzo	
12	↰	'Abbazia di Rosazzo' Via Rosazzo	
14	▲	0.8km steep climb	
{14.8	★	Abbazia di Rosazzo}	
	↑	to 'Corno di Rosazzo'	
17.7	↰	to 'Corno di Rosazzo'	
18.1	↱	Via Dolegnano di Sotto	
19.1	↱	at T intersection, Via Zanon/Via IV Nov/Via Chiopris	
21.4		Villanova del Ludrio (M, R)	45°57′19″N 13°25′16″E
24.5		Medeuzza R	45°56′28″N 13°23′46″E
27.7	↱	SP6 to 'Versa'	
30.1	↱	SS252 to 'Palmanova', Versa	45°54′01″N 13°25′07″E
32.0	↱	to 'Campolongo/Tapogliano'	
32.3	↰	`to 'Campolongo'	
32.6	↱	to 'Campolongo'	
36.0	↱	to 'Aiello del Friuli,' SP120, Campolongo (R)	
			45°51′55″N 13°23′40″E
38.8	↰	to 'Ruda/Perteole', Aiello	45°52′21″N 13°21′51″E
39	↱	Via Petrarca	
42.8	↰	at T intersection, SP30, Saciletto	
			45°50′45″N 13°21′49″E
44.0	↱	Via Garibaldi to 'Grado'	
45.4	↱	to 'Grado'	
45.6	↰	SP54 to 'Aquileia/Grado'	
50.2	↘	SS352 to 'Aquileia/Grado'	
53.7		Aquileia visitor centre on left	45°46′15″N 13°22′02″E

Leaving Cividale, small rural roads parallel the Fiume Natisone through farm country for about 8km. After a brief congested stretch, the route climbs through pretty hills peppered with vineyards, cypresses and poplars to the 11th-century **Abbazia di Rosazzo** (13.6km; open 9am–noon & 3–6pm daily). The well-preserved abbey commands a beautiful view of the valley below and makes a peaceful rest stop.

Descending into the vast Friulian flatlands, the route passes historical villas marked with plaques, while meandering

Day 2: Friuli Ramble

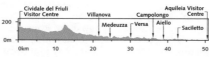

Day 3: Friuli Ramble

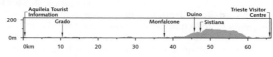

ADRIATIC COAST

through a series of small rural communities. Note that the road changes name several times between 19.1km and 27.7km, but continues straight as it passes through tiny **Villanova del Ludrio** and **Medeuzza**.

Aquileia's distinctive belltower comes into view soon after you join the tree-lined main highway at 49.2km. The ride's last 1km passes old Roman ruins, then ends at the tourist office right off SS352, before the turn into the main square and the basilica. The distance and ease of the route leave room for you to take your time checking out the crypts, mosaics and **basilica of Aquileia**.

Day 3: Aquileia to Trieste
4–7 hours, 67.9km

Highlights of this flat final day include Grado's beaches and appealing medieval historic centre, plus the scenic home-stretch down the Istrian Coast.

From Aquileia, a lovely canopy of syca-more trees leads to a causeway over open water, where billboards proclaim your official entry into **Grado** (Mitteleuropa's Beach). Hype aside, Grado does have some nice beaches. The beautifully preserved historic centre, hidden like a pearl within the ungainly oyster shell of the surrounding modern development, is filled with atmospheric cobblestone streets and lanes leading to a cluster of early Christian churches.

The route leaves Grado via the main Grado–Monfalcone highway, where intermittent bike paths parallel the roadway, offering broad lagoon vistas. A turn-off at 19.9km follows peaceful back roads through

FRIULI RAMBLE – DAY 3

CUES			GPS COORDINATES
start		Aquileia Tourist Information	45°46′15″N 13°22′02″E
0km	↰	Via Giulia Agusta/SS352	
10.4	★	Grado	45°40′43″N 13°23′44″E
	◎↰	to 'Centro'	
10.8	↘	Via Scaramuzza/Riva lataper	
11	★	Bike path flanks SS352 intermittently	
12.6	↑	to 'Trieste'	
19.2	★	Bike path become gravel, return to road	
19.9	↱	Via Grado to 'Fossalon'	
23.5	↰	Via Isonzato	
27	↱	SP19	
30.5	↱	Via del Brancolo `to Marina Giulia'	
{33	●●↱	Riserva Foce dell'Isonzo 3km ↺}	
36.9	↰	cross bridge, to 'Monfalcone'	
36.5	↙	Via Boschetti	
37.7	↙	Via dei Cipressi, Monfalcone	45°48′19″N 13°32′00″E
38.4	↘	Viale Cosulich	
39.4	↱	SS14/Via Boito to 'Trieste'	
39		Cicli Granzon bike shop	
{43.5	★	Risorgive del Timavo}	
45.2	↙	to 'Duino'	
45.7	↰	at T intersection, Duino	45°46′23″N 13°36′15″E
	★	Castello di Duino	
47.2		Sistiana	45°46′09″N 13°38′20″E
48.7	↙	Strada Costiera Miromare/Trieste	
		{59.8 ●●↱ Castello di Miromare 1km ↺}	
66.8	↰	into Piazza dell'\ Unita	
66.9	↰	Trieste visitor centre	45°38′58″N 13°46′06″E

farmland reclaimed from the swamps. You might have the roads all to yourself.

After crossing the Fiume Isonzo on the main highway, the route detours onto another sleepy back road (30.5km) for 5km, following a canal and permitting access to the **Riserva Naturale Foce dell'Isonzo**, a protected wetland bird habitat at the river's mouth.

The return to 'civilisation' at Monfalcone can be a bit jarring if you're riding during a trafficky time of day. There is a bike shop, **Cicli Granzon**, at 39km. At 43.5km is the mouth of the Timavo (a river immortalised in Virgil's *Aeneid*), which flows underground for 35km before emerging here.

At 45.7km, you pass **Castello di Duino** (☎ 04 020 81 20; www.castellodiduino .it; adult/student/child 6–16/child under 6yr €7/4.50/3/free; 9.30am–5.30pm daily Mar–Sep, 9.30am–5.30pm Wed–Mon Oct, 9.30am–4pm Sat & Sun Nov–Feb), a privately owned 14th- and 15th-century bastion filled with all sorts of artwork and curios and surrounded by a verdant garden. The Prague poet Rainer Maria Rilke was a guest here in 1911 and 1912.

The beautiful **Strada Costiera** hugs the Adriatic's edge from 48.7km all the way into Trieste, offering gorgeous views of white cliffs, the sparkling sea and the dramatic **Castello di Miromare** (side trip at 69.8km). As you approach Trieste, traffic gets heavier.

PO DELTA & VENETIAN LAGOON

This section of the Adriatic Coast is overwhelmingly flat and watery, and laced with canals, lakes, rivers and lagoons. Originally valued for its proximity to the sea and as a refuge easily defended from invaders, these lands gave rise to some of Italy's greatest cultural centres, including **Ravenna, Padua, Ferrara** and, of course, **Venice**.

HISTORY

Greek and Etruscan presence in the Po Delta has been documented at Spina (near present-day Comacchio) and Adria (southwest of Chioggia). Rome's many settlements in the region included the important naval port of Classis, established

near modern-day Ravenna by Augustus Caesar.

In AD 402, the emperor Honorius, fearing an onslaught of northern invaders, moved the Roman Empire's western capital to Ravenna, ushering in a golden age for the city as it became first the capital of the Ostrogoths under Theodoric (late 5th Century) and then the Byzantines under Justinian (mid-6th century).

Ravenna's power slowly faded as it came under repeated siege by Lombards and Franks. Meanwhile, the nascent republic of Venice distinguished itself as the only northeastern Italian community capable of staving off the invaders. Protected on their lagoon islands, the Venetians became rulers of the Adriatic and much of the Mediterranean, increasingly declaring their independence from Byzantium and building a land empire in mainland Italy.

The entire region was incorporated into the new Kingdom of Italy in the 1860s.

ENVIRONMENT

The Po, Italy's longest river, drains the country's vastest expanse of flat land, the Pianura Padana. Much of the region was historically marshy and unfit for human settlement, but over the centuries huge tracts were reclaimed for urban and agricultural development. The most substantial remaining wetlands can be found in the Po Delta near the Adriatic Coast. Here, in its eastern reaches, the Po splits into seven distinct channels: the Volano, Goro, Gnocca (Donzella), Tolle, Venezia, Maistra and Levante. In between are islands and large bodies of water known as valli, which provide bird habitat. The Po remains heavily polluted, but with the establishment of **Parco del Delta del Po**, efforts are underway to protect the local environment.

Near the coast a few significant stretches of pinewoods remain, as well as the **Bosco della Mesola**, a forest dating to Etruscan times, which shelters a small herd of native deer.

West of Padua, the rugged **Colli Euganei** (Euganeian Hills) provide an unexpected counterpoint to the region's flatness. Their cone-shaped peaks are remnants of ancient volcanoes.

COLLI EUGANEIAN

Duration 5–7 hours
Distance 78.8
Difficulty moderate–demanding
Start/Finish Padua
Summary If you feel like the cities are making you want to head for the hills, this is a refreshing day jaunt for you.

This loop showcases the lovely vineyards, appealing small towns and rugged to-pography of the Euganeian Hills west of Padua.

PLANNING
When to Cycle
This ride is especially nice in spring and early autumn.

COLLI EUGANEIAN

CUES			GPS COORDINATES
start		Padua (Padova) train station	45°25'01"N 11°52'50"E
0km	⌐	from train station, under overpass, Via G Ermitano	
0.3	↑	Viale Codalunga	
0.8	↖	Via Petrarca/Via Dante	
1.3	⌐	Corso Milano	
1.7	⌐¬	Riviera San Benedetto	
2.1	⌐	Via San Plosdocimo	
2.5	⌐¬	Via Milazzo	
2.8	↗	Via Sorio/Via dei Colli	
10.7	◎ ↖	to 'Montecchia'	
12.8	⌐	⌗ Via Euganea	
		{13.5 ●● ⌐¬ Praglia Abbey 1.6km ↻}	
		{ ●● ⌐¬ Abano Terme 5.km one-way }	
18.2	▲	3.2km moderate climb	
21.4	⌐¬	P43 to 'Castelnuovo', Teolo	45°20'55"N 11°40'20"E
24.1	▲	3km moderate climb	
		Castelnuovo	45°19'48"N 11°41'16"E
	↘	at fork	
24.4	▲	2.3km moderate climb	
26.8	⌐	to 'Faedo/Este', Via Roccolo	
27.4	⌐	to 'Roccolo'	
	▲	1.8km steep climb	
29.2	↘	at fork at top of climb	
32.1		Faedo (follow signs to Fontana Fredda)	45°17'44"N 11°41'24"E
32.4	⌐¬	Via Giarin	
	▲	2.1km steep climb	

Maps
TCI's 1:200,000 *Veneto Friuli-Venezia Giulia* map shows the entire route.

GETTING TO/FROM THE RIDE
Padua (start/finish)
TRAIN
The train station is just north of down-town. Padua is on the main north–south line from Venice to Bologna and also on the main east–west line from Venice to Milan. One-way fares from Padua include Milan (€12.10, 3 hours, regularly) and Venice (€2.70, 30 minutes; every 30–40 minutes).

THE RIDE
It's a wonderful thing to leave a hectic city like Padua on a bicycle and soon be in lus-cious hill country full of vineyards and for-ests. After an easy but traffic-heavy initial cruise through the flatlands southwest of Padua, the route becomes relentlessly hilly,

CUES CONTINUED			GPS COORDINATES
34.7	⌐¬	Via Roverello	
	↗	(20m) NOT on Via Dea Santa, AFTER it34.8	
	↗	(50m) follow red arrows on pavement	
	▲	0.4km moderate unpaved descent	
35.3	↗	follow red arrows	
37.2	↗ ★	Via Monta Piccola, Arqua Petrarca	45°16'12"N 11°43'00"E
38.9	↗	to 'Monselice/Este'	
39.7	⌐¬	SP6 to 'Monselice'	
42.1	⌐¬ ★	to 'Galzignano', 'Monselice'	45°14'34"N 11°44'42"E
45.3	↖	to 'Galzignano' at fork	
	⌐	(80m) SP25dir to 'Galzignano'	
49.1	★	Valsanzibio	45°17'35"N 11°43'44"E
51.0	⌐¬	to 'Galzignano Terme'	
51.5	⌐	to 'Torreglia', 'Galzignano Terme'	5°18'30"N 11°43'42"E
55.2	⌐¬ ◎	SP43 to 'Teolo', 'Torreglia'	45°20'08"N 11°43'56"E
56.3	↗	to 'Teolo' (sign hard to see)	
56.5	⌐¬	to 'Luvigliano'	
60.5	⌐	Euganea Treponte `to Padova'	
65.4	⌐¬	Via Montecchio	
67.4	⌐	at stop sign	
	◎ ⌐	(20m) Via Scapacchio	
73.6	↖	to 'Citta'	
73.9	↗	to 'Centro'	
75.9	↖	to 'Centro'	
76.8	⌐	Corso Milano, to 'Centro'	
77.9	⌐¬	Corso Girabaldi	
78.8		Padua (Padova) train station	45°25'01"N 11°52'50"E

ADRIATIC COAST

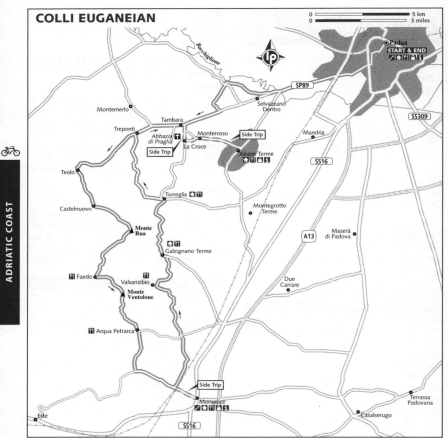

COLLI EUGANEIAN

0 ————— 5 km
0 ————— 3 miles

Bacchiglione

Padua
START & END

SP89

SS309

Montemerlo

Tambara

Selvazzano
Dentro

Treponti

Monterosso

Abbazia
di Praglia

Side Trip

La Croce

Mandria

Side Trip

Abano Terme

SS16

Teolo

Torreglia

Montegrotto
Terme

Castelnuovo

Masarà
di Padova

Monte
Rua

Galzignano Terme

A13

Faedo

Valsanzibio

Monte
Ventolone

Due
Carrare

Arqua Petrarca

Side Trip

Terrassa
Padovana

Este

Monselice

Casalserugo

SS16

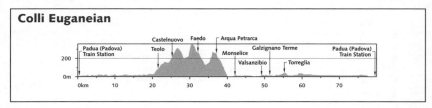

Colli Euganeian

	Castelnuovo	Faedo	Arqua Petrarca			
Padua (Padova) Train Station	Teolo		Monselice	Galzignano Terme		Padua (Padova) Train Station
				Valsanzibio	Torreglia	

200

0m

0km   10   20   30   40   50   60   70

climbing through landscapes thick with trees, carpeted with carefully manicured fields of vines and dotted with the lovely small towns of the **Colli Euganei** (Eugeneian Hills).

It's a bit hairy navigating out of Padua, but starting around 4.5km a bike path appears intermittently. Beyond the city limits, the Via dei Colli (which changes

names a hundred times) zooms through the flats for roughly 15km before climbing towards Teolo. You'll pass two bike shops in the first 15km.

From **Teolo** (21.4km), picturesquely perched at the gateway to the hills, a densely packed series of climbs and descents leads through the heart of the Colli Euganei.

Most gruelling is the 11% grade leading to **Valico del Roccolo**, but the views of the surrounding countryside are spectacular. The 5km stretch from **Faedo** to **Arqua Petrarca** is also alluring as it snakes up through a narrow, vineyard-filled valley, briefly turning to dirt at the summit, then plunges downhill, eventually clattering onto the cobblestones of Arqua Petrarca (37.2km). The lovey-dovey poet Petrarch spent his last five years in this beautifully preserved medieval town; visits to his house and tomb are possible.

Beyond Arqua the route descends to **Monselice** (42.1km), home to a splendid 11th-century **castle** (www.castello dimonselice.it) and several historic villas. At **Valsanzibio** (49.1km), Villa Barbarigo with its 16th-century gardens, fountains and labyrinth makes another worthwhile stop. The remainder of the route rolls along the eastern edge of the hills, continuing its course through vineyards and small towns, eventually rejoining the Teolo–Padua highway at **Treponti** (60.5km).

SIDE TRIP: PRAGLIA ABBEY & ABANO TERME
1–2 hours, at 13.4km, 1.6km RT to monastery
30 minutes – 1 hour, 5.1km one-way monastery to Abono Terme

The **Praglia Abbey** encapsulates lovely 15th-century cloisters and a centre for the restoration of old books. Continue south of the monastery, via La Croce and Monterosso, on back roads to get to Abano Terme. Note that there are also several other turn-offs closer to Padua en route that lead to Abano Terme.

The **Colli Euganei** area is famous for its hot springs or *terme*. The water passes underground from the low mountains of the Pre-Alps north of Padua, where it is heated to more than 85°C, collecting mineral salts in the process. This therapeutic water bubbles up in the Colli Euganei area, and **Abano Terme** is a main spa centre. So if you want to stop in and soak at the end of your ride, you have that lovely option. The gaggle of hotels offers spa services. For a list of hotels, go to the comune's website (www.abanoterme.net/hotel.html). For more information contact the tourist offices of **Abano Terme** (☎ 04 986 69 055; Via Pietro d'Abano 18).

PO DELTA & CICLO TOWNS

Duration 4 days
Distance 242.7km
Difficulty easy
Start Ravenna
Finish Venice
Summary This is the best way for bike aficionados to approach Venice, one of Italy's must-see cities.

This pancake-flat ride over the Po Delta and surrounding wetlands passes through the fantastically bike-lovin' cities of Ravenna and Ferrara, as well as Venice – tourist-infested or not, one of the most beautiful cities in the world. Five ferry crossings add to the ride's appeal, culminating in an island-hopping journey across the Venetian lagoon.

PLANNING
When to Cycle
Spring and autumn are the best seasons for this ride.

What to Bring
Carry extra water and food, as services are few and far between. Insect repellent is a must, for reasons that will become obvious as you cycle through the wetlands.

Maps & Booklets
TCI's 1:200,000 maps of Emilia Romagna and Veneto Friuli-Venezia Giulia are useful resources for most of this ride.

The Day 3 Destra Po bike path section is covered by the free map/brochure *Destra Po*. The map *Cycling in Ferrara* is also very useful for getting into and out of Ferrara. Both are available from Ferrara's visitor centre.

Tourist bureaus in this region provide a wealth of other cycling information. Of particular note are these four: *In bici lungo il Po*, with routes along the river; the free map/brochure *10 itinerari in bicicletta in provincia di Ferrara*, describing additional rides near Ferrara; the booklet *Cycling in Romagna*, which features rides in the Ravenna–Rimini area; and the map/brochure *The Park by Bike*, suggesting cycle itineraries in the Po Delta.

ADRIATIC COAST

ADRIATIC COAST

Information Sources
Ferrara has a very informative website (www.ferrarainbici.it) about everything bike-related in Ferrara.

GETTING TO/FROM THE RIDE
Ravenna (start)
TRAIN
The train station is just east of the centre. Ravenna is on a secondary train line with limited direct service. Most long-distance trips require a change of train in Bologna, Ferrara or Rimini. Trains connect with Bologna (€4.90, 1½ hours, hourly), Ferrara (€4.40, 1¼ hours, 17 daily), Faenza (€2.60, 40 minutes, hourly), Rimini (€3, 1 hour, hourly) and the coast, including Ancona and Venice.

BICYCLE
From Ravenna, it's possible to link up with the **Deep In Le Marche** (see p200) ride at either Urbino or Pesaro via back roads.

If you want to split off the route in Ferarra, there's a bike route to Trent (Trentino) to access the Dolomites rides.

Venice (finish)
See Venice (p217).

THE RIDE
Day 1: Ravenna to Comacchio
4–6 hours, 62.2km
Today's route makes a great S-curve through the wetlands south of Comacchio, with two ferry crossings along the way.

A quick zigzag through Ravenna's cycle-friendly streets leads to the day's first bike path (1.5km). The route to the coast, following bike paths and small roads, is often mobbed with other cyclists. A northward turn on the coastal highway passes scraggly pine forest, beaches and pizzerias en route to the Marina di Ravenna ferry landing.

The port is rather grubby, but the ferry crossing is great, with little black-and-white boats bobbing in the water and hordes of bike-toting locals sharing the three-minute trip. Tickets are less than €2 and can be bought from a dockside machine or on board.

From **Porto Corsini**, navigate north to Casalborsetti on roads interspersed with bike paths. At 19.7km, the smell of salt and fish fills the air as the route crosses a picturesque canal bordered by fishing shacks and docks strung with cables and nets. Turning inland, another canal leads to **Sant'Alberto,** the last chance for food and provisions before Comacchio.

Leaving Sant'Alberto, the road narrows, crosses a dike and finishes completely at the edge of the pretty tree-lined **Reno River**. Here a cable-drawn ferry crosses to the opposite bank, charging cyclists €0.50 for the one-minute ride.

On the north bank, a narrow dike-top road threads the needle between the broad and languid Reno and the vast **Valli di Comacchio lagoon** spreading away to the northern horizon. The insects can be nasty, but there's no traffic, and the wide-open vistas, with huge brick farmhouses looming like ships, are dazzling.

Turning north, another long stretch follows on a narrow strip of land between canal and lagoon, with fishermen lining the banks in early morning. The home stretch into **Comacchio** is through flat agricultural land.

Day 2: Comacchio to Ferrara
4–6 hours, 61.7km
Today starts out through flatlands rich in bird life, then follows the Po into Ferrara.

Herons and pheasants are among the birds thronging the sleepy agricultural back roads leading to Ostellato. Keep your eyes peeled for the turn at 8.2km, and beware that around 22km the pavement gets chucky.

From Ostellato, tiny Strada Pioppa crosses a busy highway (26.3km) and winds through fruit orchards into Migliarino (29.8km), the day's best lunch spot. Walk your bike through Migliarino's main piazza, then turn briefly against the flow of traffic, continuing straight onto Largo Zerbini towards the tiny bike/pedestrian bridge over the Po.

The remainder of the route follows the languid **Po di Volano**, which was one of the Po's biggest branches during Ferrara's medieval heyday but has been reduced to a fraction of its former size. The river ducks in and out of view as you wind along dike-tops past fields, orchards and old brick farmhouses. Stay close to the Po, continuing straight onto a smaller road at 35.8km (the main road veers right here), then hugging the river's edge to cross under a bridge at 38.1km.

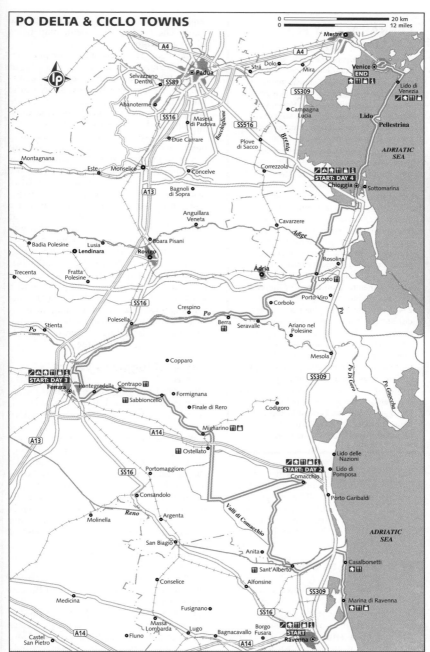

PO DELTA & CICLO TOWNS

ADRIATIC COAST

FERRARA, CITY FOR CYCLISTS

Ferrara might just be the 'cyclin-est' city in Italy. Indeed, studies have awarded it that status and surveys have shown that the Ferrarese ride their bikes as much as residents of cycle-crazed countries like Holland and Denmark. Furthermore, nearly 90% of Ferrara's people own bikes and more do their shopping by bike than by car.

In recognition of these facts, Ferrara has established itself as the first Italian member of the international Cities for Cyclists network, developing an impressive infrastructure in support of cycling. Signs at all city entrances proclaim Ferrara to be a *città per biciclette*. Automobile traffic is limited or banned on many downtown streets, and there's an extensive and expanding network of well-signposted bike paths, including a wonderful circuit of the city's medieval walls. The city government maintains an **Office of Bicycles for Sustainable Mobility** (☎ 05 327 64 224; www.comune.fe.it; Via Kennedy 6) and distributes official bikes to the mayor and all city council people. It also publishes a free bike map (you can download one from their website, too) and runs a Bicicard program offering shopping discounts and free museum admissions to visitors willing to trade their cars for bikes. Dozens of hotels and garages provide free bikes for their clients' use. **Ferarra in Bici** (www.ferrarainbici.it), a FIAB affiliate, has a helpful website with more information.

The river crossing at 43.4km leads to a series of small towns along the south bank. A second crossing at 52.5km signals the beginning of the home-stretch. Ferrara's excellent system of bike paths starts in **Pontegradella** (57.4km), paralleling the main road from here to the town walls.

Day 3: Ferrara to Chioggia
6–8 hours, 96.9km
Today's route reaches Venice's doorstep via a combination of bike paths and small country roads. Food stops are few and far between; consider bringing a picnic.

After a brief stint atop Ferrara's old town wall, the route twists through farmland north of town, following brown bike signs. The *Cycling in Ferrara* map helps with navigation.

The wonderful **Destra Po bike path** begins at 3.7km, reaching the river's edge at 9.7km. It's closed to cars except on the outskirts of towns; even in those spots traffic is next to nil. The path straddles a riverside dike, offering nice views of fields, vineyards, orchards and vast stands of poplars.

From 25.1km to 57.2km, the route follows quiet back roads, bike paths and dike-top streets offering views of the distant Dolomites to the left and the mighty Po on the right. Brief industrial and urban stretches near Loreo give way to tranquil back roads and **crumbling Venetian mansions**. After crossing the wide, slow-flowing Adige at 78km, the route follows canals through farmland to the outskirts of **Chioggia**.

The final few kilometres are a rude awakening, with a slew of roundabouts (88.5km) and a 50m stretch of gravel (91.9km), which leads to a steep, dirt path that passes under a railway (91.7km). The bike path (91.7km) starts again soon after, paralleling the main road and dumping you at the ferry landing. Chioggia's calmer historic centre is a welcome relief at the end of the line.

Day 4: Chioggia to Venice
2–3 hours, 21.9km
This island-hopping odyssey across the lagoon involves as much time on boats as on your bike, but it's an unforgettable way to reach Venice.

An €8.50 ticket covers the first two ferry crossings, from the ferry landing in Chioggia to Pellestrina and Lido, plus the bike charge. Signs warn that bikes may board only at the captain's discretion, but there's usually enough space (five bikes are officially allowed). Boats leave Chioggia roughly hourly for the 20-minute crossing to Pellestrina. There are pleasant views of the lagoon en route.

From the Pellestrina ferry dock, take the island's only road north, passing small residential areas and wispy vegetation on the left, with the massive 18th-century **Murazzi sea wall** on your right.

From Santa Maria del Mare at Pellestrina's northern tip, a larger car ferry makes the 10-minute crossing to Alberoni on Lido. Lido-bound ferries wait for passengers con-

PIAZZA SAN MARCO

Few public spaces in the world can match the allure of **Piazza San Marco**, what Napoleon called 'the finest drawing room in Europe'. It opens to the Grand Canal on one side, surrounded by *loggias* (covered areas on the side of buildings) on three others, and enclosing Venice's two grandest architectural monuments.

At the square's northeastern corner, the **Basilica di San Marco** is a Byzantine masterpiece of mosaics, domes and undulating marble pavement, showcasing the Venetians' twin gifts for artistry and plunder. Next door, the lovely white-and-pink **Palazzo Ducale** was for centuries the residence of Venice's *doges* (chief magistrate) and seat of the republic's government.

necting by bus from the Chioggia–Pellestrina boat – fast cyclists can usually outpace the bus, reaching the boat in plenty of time.

Hugging Lido's western shore for 8km, the route passes through the smaller communities of Alberoni and Malamocco, then circumnavigates Lido's town centre with a short run north along the island's main beach and past the famous casino.

Cyclists wishing to lock their bikes for a spell in Lido de Venezia can take a *vaporetto* (small passenger ferry) from the ACTV ferry dock (18.3km) into Venice. Alternatively, head north another 1.4km (briefly going against traffic) to the Tronchetto car ferry. ACTV boats make the 25-minute crossing every 50 minutes or so.

From Tronchetto, signs lead the remaining 2km to Piazzale Roma, where you can catch a bus to the airport or walk your bike to the train station (15 minutes, one big bridge).

UMBRIA & LE MARCHE

The patchwork fields, picturesque hill towns and undulating topography of Umbria and Le Marche are classically Italian. Umbria is Italy's lone landlocked region, while neighbouring Le Marche boasts some of the Adriatic's most scenic coastline. Each has a long and fascinating history.

HISTORY

Ancient Rome's indelible mark on this region is seen in temples, theatres, gates, bridges, roads and civic layouts, in places such as Gubbio, Assisi and Ascoli Piceno. In 220 BC Caius Flaminius opened the Via Flaminia, which passed through eastern Umbria and the northern Marche, connecting Rome to the Adriatic Coast. The Furlo Gorge tunnel stands as one of the road's enduring engineering achievements.

Umbria in particular has figured prominently in Christian religious history. **St Benedict** and **St Francis** were born in Norcia and Assisi, respectively. The 11th-century Camaldolese St Romuald also walked these hills, establishing nearly 100 monasteries, including the beautifully preserved **Fonte Avellana**.

The early Middle Ages saw a flowering of courtly and artistic life in the Umbrian and Marchigian hills. The **Dukes of Montefeltro** in Urbino were particularly influential patrons of the arts.

Two of the region's most famous sons are Raffaello, from Urbino, and composer Rossini, from Pesaro.

ENVIRONMENT

Coastal Le Marche is generally flat, with notable exceptions at Monte Conero south of Ancona and Monte San Bartolo north of Pesaro. Inland from the coast, hills rise rapidly towards the Appenine Mountains. The highest summits are in **Parco Nazionale dei Monti Sibillini**.

The region's underlying geology is rich in limestone. The **Frasassi Caves** near Fabriano rank among Italy's largest, and rivers have cut dramatic gorges, such as the Gola del Furlo, at several places in the local hills. Exposed rocky outcrops throughout the region provide fascinating opportunities for geologists. In 1978 a team from the University of California at Berkeley (USA), studying rock layers in the hills east of Gubbio, discovered unusually high concentrations of iridium, which contributed valuable evidence to their theory that a great meteorite caused the extinction of the dinosaurs.

The **Piano Grande** east of Norcia is one of Italy's most unusual landforms, a treeless plateau ringed by mountains and carpeted in spring with poppies, buttercups, lilies, daisies and wild tulips. The surrounding Sibillini

ADRIATIC COAST

Mountains are home to alpine flowers such as edelweiss, and also shelter rare fauna such as the Appenine wolf and golden eagle.

CONERO RIVIERA

Duration 3–6 hours
Distance 54.6km
Difficulty moderate
Start/Finish Ancona
Summary Sparkling coastline, wine country and back country roads will entice a cyclist off the beach for a day.

This moderately hilly ride focuses on one of the Adriatic's most picturesque shorelines, the Conero Riviera south of Ancona. This is a convenient ride to fit in if you have a day to kill before tackling the Deep in Le Marche ride (p200).

CONERO RIVIERA

CUES			GPS COORDINATES
start		Ancona train station	43°36'27"N 13°29'59"E
0km	↰	going E on Via Marconi	
0.3	◎↑	Via de Gasperi/Martiri Resistenza	
1.6	↰◎	Piazzale Liberta to 'Centro'	
1.7	▲	500m tunnel (Galleria Risorgimento)	
2.3	↱	Via Isonzo/Via del Conero, to 'Porto Novo'	
	▲	2.5km moderate-steep climb	
		{12.2 ●● ↰ Portonovo 4.4km ↺}	
12.6	▲	2km moderate climb	
		{13 ●● ↱ Poggio}	
14.7	↱	to 'Camerano'	
15.1	▲	0.5km extremely steep descent	
17.3	▲	0.4km killer ascent	
17.7	↰	Via Massignano, Camerano	43°31'54"N 13°33'31"E
18.5	↙	to 'Agriturismo Il Corbezzolo'	
19.0	↱	to 'Agriturismo Il Corbezzolo'	
21.7	▲	0.2km unpaved section	
21.9	↙	at the 'Coppo' cicloturismo post	
23.1	↑	cross busy road	
25.0	↰	to 'Svarchi'	
	↱	(50m) to 'Valcastagno'	
26.1	↰	to 'Ancona'	
26.2	↰	to 'Numana/Sirolo'	
27.2	↑	not to 'Marcelli'	
28.1	↙◎	to 'Marcelli'	
28.7	↰	to 'Spiaggia'	
29.2	◎↰	Via Modena	
29.5	↘	along beachfront, Via Litoranea, Marcelli	
			43°29'25"N 13°37'47"E

PLANNING
When to Cycle
This ride is possible year-round but is best in spring and autumn, and from Monday to Friday, when traffic is lighter.

Maps
TCI's 1:200,000 *Umbria e Marche* map covers the entire region in detail.

Information Sources
Regione Le Marche (www.le-marche.com), the official tourist-office website has useful information on Ancona and its accommodation and sights.

GETTING TO/FROM THE RIDE
Ancona (start/finish)
TRAIN
The train station is west of downtown. Ancona sits at the junction of two major train lines, one running along the Adriatic Coast and the other heading southwest to Rome. One-way fares from Ancona include Rome (€13.80–23, 4 hours), Bologna (€10.50–24, 2¾ hours), Pesaro (€3.25–6.50, 45 minutes), Ravenna (€7.55, 2¾ hours), Florence (€25.50–34, 3–4 hours) and Milan (€30.50–37, 5½ hours). You'll have to pack your bike (see p297) for non-regional trains. Regional trains' supplementary bike ticket is €3.50.

CUES CONTINUED		GPS COORDINATES
31	▲ 1.5km moderate-steep climb	
31.5	Numana	43°29'09"N 13°37'09"E
31.8	↙ to 'Spiaggia/Conchiglia Verde'	
	{32.5 ●● ↱ Sirolo beaches 1.6km ↺}	
32.6	↑ through Arco Gotico, Sirolo	
		43°29'32"N 13°36'53"E
32.8	↰ Via Verdi	
32.9	↘ Via Puccini	
33	hard ↱ Via Cilea	
33.6	↱ to 'Ancona'	
33.7	◎↰ Via Cave	
	{35.2 ●● ↱ Monte Conero 6km ↺}	
51.4	↘ Road becomes Via Isonzo	
52	↙ Via Piave	
52.5	↱ Via Giannelli	
52.7	↰ Via Frediani	
52.9	↘ around Piazza Cavour	
	↱ (70m) Corso Garibaldi	
53.5	↙ Piazza della Repubblica	
	↰ (60m) Via 29 Settembre	
54.2	↙ Via Marconi	
54.6	Ancona train station	43°36'27"N 13°29'59"E

BICYCLE

Ancona sits near the junction of the 1000km Via Adriatica and the 500km Conero–Argentario bike route proposed by FIAB.

These routes connect Ancona with Venice in the north, Santa Maria di Leuin 'in' the south. Visit www.bicitalia.org for details.

THE RIDE

This undulating route initially parallels the Adriatic, then follows smaller back roads inland through the Rosso Conero wine country, concluding with a swing back up the beautiful Conero coast.

From Ancona's train station, the route climbs steadily out of the city. At 12.2km there are spectacular views of the coast, with the option of a long downhill side trip to the beaches and fort at **Portonovo**. Some locals say this stretch of coast is one of the prettiest. The fort, built by Napoleon in 1808, now houses a fancy restaurant with windows overlooking the Adriatic.

Descending precipitously inland at 15.1km, the route commands a bird's-eye view of the Rosso Conero wine country. Red wine from this region has become increasingly popular, winning awards both domestically and internationally. The stretch between 17.7km and 26.1km is narrow and bumpy, but probably one of the most inspiring and gorgeous sections

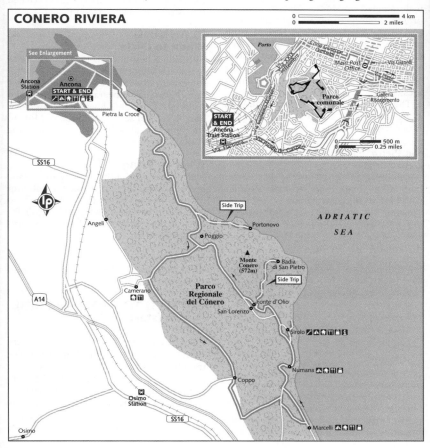

CONERO RIVIERA

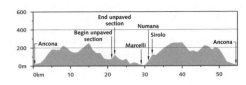

Conero Riviera

as it threads its way through golden hills and vineyards.

Busier roads lead back to the Adriatic Coast. At **Marcelli** (29.5km) the route curves north to follow a flat beach popular with families. Straight ahead, the coastline is dominated by Monte Conero's hulking profile. A steep climb leads to the medieval coastal town of Sirolo at 32.6km. With its stunning cliff-backed beaches (steep downhill side trip at 32.5km) and picturesque town square, **Sirolo** is the perfect spot to cool your heels and take a lunch break.

The return route climbs through forests along the western edge of Monte Conero. A side trip at 35.2km provides access to the mountain's eastern slopes and the **Badia di San Pietro**, perched high above the blue-green Adriatic.

Rejoining the coast at the Portonovo turn-off, the main route retraces its earlier path back to the train station.

This ride follows sleepy back roads through the hills and mountains of Le Marche and eastern Umbria. Highlights include the coastal scenery north of Pesaro; the

DEEP IN LE MARCHE

Duration 6 days
Distance 428.3km
Difficulty moderate–demanding
Start Pesaro
Finish Ascoli Piceno

Summary From the Sibbillini Mountains to the desert-like Piano Grande, you'll cycle hard and delve deeply into some of the lesser-known reaches of Italy.

beautiful hill towns of Urbino, Gubbio and Assisi; the secluded monastery of Fonte Avellana; the dramatic limestone gorge of the Furlo; the rugged grandeur of the mystery-shrouded Monti Sibillini; the stark lunar landscape of the Piano Grande and the appealing but relatively rarely visited towns of Norcia and Ascoli Piceno.

PLANNING
When to Cycle
This ride is best in May, June and September, when temperatures are warm enough to permit passage over the Sibillini Mountains but not as unbearably hot as July and August in the route's lower-lying stretches. May is festival season in Gubbio. Mid- to late June is peak wildflower season on the Piano Grande.

What to Bring
Make sure your bike is in good shape before attempting to cross the Sibillini Mountains on Days 4 to 6. There are no bike shops between Assisi and Ascoli Piceno. Bring extra food and water, as services are limited.

Maps
TCI's 1:200,000 *Umbria e Marche* map covers the entire region in detail.

GETTING TO/FROM THE RIDE
Pesaro (start)
TRAIN
The train station is southwest of the city centre. Pesaro is on the Bologna–Lecce train line and you can reach Rome (€16.10 to €26.15, 4 hours, 9 daily) by changing trains at Falconara Marittima, just before Ancona. There are hourly services to Ancona (€3.25, 45 minutes), Rimini (€2.60–€6, 20–40 minutes), Ravenna (€5.80, 1¾

hours) and Bologna (€7.70–€15, 2 hours). Add a €3.50 fee for a supplementary bike ticket.

BICYCLE
Pesaro is a stop on the 1000km Via Adriatica between Venice and Santa Maria di Leuca, part of a national network of bike routes proposed by FIAB. For more information, check out www.bicitalia.org.

Ascoli Piceno (finish)
TRAIN
The train station is 1km east of the centre, connected by a short spur line to Benedetto del Tronto on the Adriatic Coast. There are three direct daily trains to Ancona (€4.20, 1¼ hour). Several other daily trains make the 30-minute trip to Benedetto del Tronto, allowing connections to points north and south along the coast. Add a €3.50 fee for a supplementary bike ticket.

BICYCLE
Ascoli Piceno is a stop on FIAB's 400km Via Salaria bike route between Rome and San Benedetto del Tronto. Point being, continuing by bike is very possible.

THE RIDE
Day 1: Pesaro to Urbino
4–6 hours, 76.3km

After a brief but scenic meander along the Adriatic, today's ride turns inland through a series of attractive hill towns culminating in the Renaissance gem of Urbino.

Gently climbing from the beach at Pesaro into the coastal hills of **Monte San Bartolo Parco Naturale**, the **Strada Panoramica Adriatica** offers sweeping views both inland and out to sea. Pesaro's modern apartment blocks are soon replaced by farmland framed by pine and olive trees, with occasional glimpses of increasingly sheer drop-offs to the Adriatic. Traffic is relatively light, with bikes sometimes outnumbering cars.

Fiorenzuola di Focara at 15.3km is a picturesque coastal village worthy of a visit. Cobblestone streets lead up through the town gate to a grassy spot with benches overlooking the sea. It's tempting to linger for lunch.

DEEP IN LE MARCHE – DAY 1

CUES		GPS COORDINATES
start	Pesaro tourist office	43°54'47"N 12°55'03"E
0km	go N on Viale Trieste	
1.1	↰ Viale Napoli	
1.8	◎ Continue straight to strada panoramica	
1.9	▲ 3.5km moderate climb	
15.3	Fiorenzuola di Focara	43°57'03"N 12°49'20"E
18.1	↰ Strada di Vincolungo	
	⚠ 1km very steep descent	
19.7	↱ SS16	
20.0	↰ SP47/Strada Ferrata 'to Gradara'	
	{22.1 ●● ↱ Gradara 1km ↺}	
22.3	↰◎ 'to Tavullia'	
	▲ 2.7km moderate climb	
25.0	↱ Strada Pirano 'to S. Giovanni'	
28.7	↰ 'to Urbino'	
29.8	↱ Strada del Piano 'to Saludecio'	
33.5	▲ 1.4 K steep climb	
34.9	↱ SP 38, Tavulia	43°53'53"N 12°45'25"E
36.5	↙ to Urbino	
37.7	↙ to Mondiano	
43.4	◎↑ to Montegridolfo	
44.6	◎↰ to Mondiano	
46.0	↘▲ 'to Mondaino, 4.5km climb	
50.5	↘ Mondaino before city gate, to Rio Salsa (5.7km descent)	43°51'30"N 12°40'12"E
56.2	↱ to Urbino'	
62.9	↙ 'to Urbino'	
	↘ 50m	
64.3	▲ 10.4km gradual climb	
74.7	↙ 'to Centro'	
75.7	↱ Via Bramante (through town gate)	
76.0	↰ Via Raffaelo	
76.3	Urbino tourist office	43°43'30"N 12°38'10"E

At 18.1km an exhilaratingly steep and narrow descent through forest and fields leads inland toward the dramatic medieval hilltop fortress of **Gradara**. The heavily restored town and castle can be visited on a short side trip at 22.1km.

The undulating route continues past the pretty hilltop towns of **Saludecio** and **Mondaino** (50.5km). The latter has a 13th-century fortress and an interesting **museum of palaeontology** (☎ 05 419 81 674 for both). Beyond Mondaino, a long run along the ridgeline offers superb views south towards Urbino and north towards San Marino. On a hillside to the right, the palace façade at **Montefiore Conca** is visible as a striking rectangular silhouette.

ADRIATIC COAST

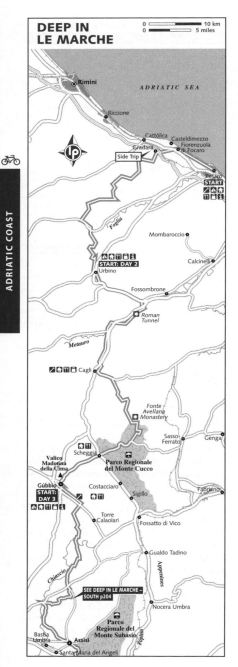

The final 20km includes a long descent followed by a gradual climb through green fields into Urbino.

Day 2: Urbino to Gubbio
5–8 hours, 81.2km

Today's ride takes you through the rugged heart of the **Appenines**.

Zigzagging down to the Metauro Valley, the route offers nice parting vistas of Urbino, then joins (at 15.1km) the ancient Via Flaminia, established as a link between Rome and Rimini by Roman general Caius Flaminius in 220 BC. The most noteworthy Roman remnant is the ancient tunnel at 19.8km, bored out of solid rock by Flaminius' crew, then widened into its current form by Vespasian in AD 76.

Just beyond the tunnel (20km) is the exquisite **Gola del Furlo** gorge, where the Fiume Candigliano's jade-green waters flow beneath towering limestone cliffs shaded at the base by leafy forests. Mussolini was very fond of this area, coming here frequently to dine. A monumental profile of Il Duce was carved into Monte Pietralata west of the gorge, but it was later damaged by partisans.

A rather gritty urban section follows, as the route emerges from the gorge into mountain-fringed flatlands parallelling the national highway. The area around **Acqualagna** (26.6km) accounts for two-thirds of Italian truffle production and hosts the **National Truffle Fair** in October/November.

From **Cagli** (35.7km), the route climbs through increasingly remote country along the flanks of imposing **Monte Catria** (1701m). A narrow, steep descent leads to 11th-century Fonte Avellana (53.3km), which the poet Dante once visited and later mentioned in the 21st canto of his *Paradise*. First glimpsed from above against a stunning mountain backdrop, the monastery seems lost in time. A short visit is recommended – the building's austere stone rooms are beautiful and evocative, especially the well-preserved medieval Scriptorium.

The undulating route continues into Umbria, traversing forest and open grazing country and following another limestone chasm. From the final summit, **Valico Madonna della Cima** (75.8km), a delightful

Day 2: Deep in Le Marche

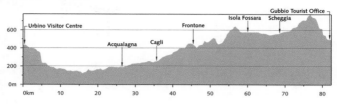

DEEP IN LE MARCHE – DAY 2

CUES		GPS COORDINATES
Start	Urbino visitor centre	43°43'30"N 12°38'10"E
0km	go SW on Via Saffi/ Pucinotti	
0.4	↰	cobblestone street along town wall
0.6	↘	SS73 bis
1.0		SS73bis 'to Roma/Perugia'
11.8	↰	SS73 bis, Via Nazionale, to Calmazzo (pass under railroad tracks)
15.1 hard	↱	'to Passo del Furlo'
17.2	↙	'to Furlo'
{19.8	★	ancient Roman tunnel}
{20.0	★	Gola del Furlo}
26.6	Acqualagna	43°36'49"N 12°40'18"E
28.4	↙	'to Smirra'
28.4	↰	(50m) Via Flaminia (unmarked)
35.7	↰	SS424 'to Frontone', Cagli 43°32'45"N 12°39'00"E
37.8		SP42 'to Frontone
45.5	↑	SP42\Via Fabriano, Frontone 43°30'49"N 12°44'16"E
50.1	↱	'to Fonte Avellana
	⚠	1.4km steep bumpy descent
53.3	↰	to Isola Fossara,SP 226
	▲	1.4 km moderate climb
	●●↺	Fonte Avellana monastery} 6km
56.0	4km descent	
60.0	↙	SS360, Isola Fossara 43°25'56"N 12°44'15"E
68.6	Scheggia	43°24'10"N 12°40'05"E
68.9	↱	SS3 'to Gubbio'
69.2	↘	SS298 'to Gubbio'
72.0	▲	3.8km gradual-moderate climb
75.8	Valico Madonna della Cima	
	⚠	4.2km steep winding descent
80.0	↱	follow town wall
80.5	↰◎	'to Centro'
81.0	↰	<SL> to centro
81.2	Gubbio tourist office (Via della Republica) 43°21'07"N 12°34'42"E	

winding descent reaches Gubbio via the rocky **Gola del Bottaccione**, famous as the site where, in the late 1970s, scientists hatched the meteorite theory of dinosaur extinction.

Day 3: Gubbio to Assisi
3–5 hours, 48.5km

This is the shortest day of the trip, allowing time for sightseeing or relaxing before tomorrow's long haul to Norcia.

After paralleling the main highway along the valley floor for 5.6km, the route climbs south into rolling hills, affording nice views back to the Appenines. A long descent to a small river valley is followed by an equally long climb onto a high plateau between tiny **Colpalombo** and **Carbonesca**.

From the junction at **Casacastalda**, the route plunges downhill on busy SS318 to **Valfabbrica**, then turns onto the challenging but gorgeous 12km **Strada Francescana della Pace**. This steep and narrow tertiary road traces part of the pilgrimage route travelled by the young St Francis between Assisi and Gubbio. Watch carefully for the turn-off, just below Valfabbrica at a point where the main road curves right – signs are only posted for travellers coming from the opposite direction.

The Strada Francescana climbs relentlessly for more than 2km at an angle (16% arena) that tests both patience and stamina, but the views of vineyards and open hills are magnificent and there's virtually no traffic. If you want to avoid this climb opt for the alternative road, sticking to main secondary roads (33.9km). A short side trip at 38.9km leads to the medieval church site of **Pieve San Nicolo**.

The **Basilica of St Francis** comes in-toview just before the 40km mark. At 44.6km, in the middle of a precipitous descent, a particularly dramatic view of the church and the town unfolds, with beautiful olive groves in the foreground.

The route's final kilometres climb steeply through the medieval walls to Assisi's central piazza.

ADRIATIC COAST

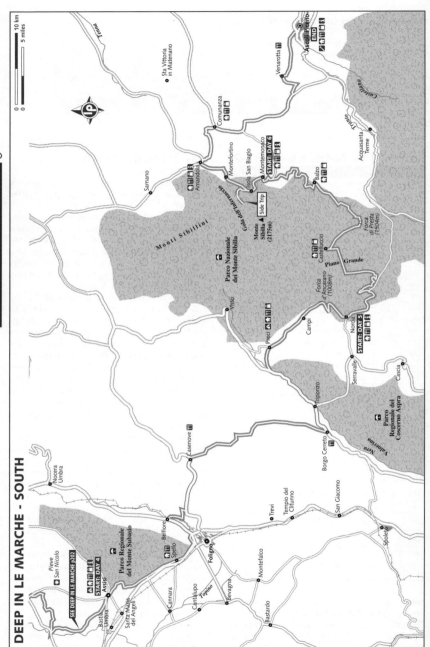

DEEP IN LE MARCHE - SOUTH

Day 3: Deep in Le Marche

DEEP IN LE MARCHE – DAY 3

CUES			GPS COORDINATES
start		Gubbio visitor centre	43°21'07"N 12°34'42"E
0km		S (downhill) on Via della republica	
0.2	↘	to Ancona	
2.1	↑⊙	unmarked	
5.6	⌐	Sp 240, `to Casacastalda'	
5.7	⌐	SP240, Padule	43°19'27"N 12°36'52"E
9.8	▲	1.8km steep climb	
15.5	▲	6.3km moderate climb	
17.0		Colpalombo	43°14'58"N 12°36'45"E
20.0		Carbonesca	43°13'39"N 12°37'28"E
23.2		Descent of 8km	
24.6	⌐	SS318, Casacastalda	43°11'17"N 12°38'49"E
33.2		Valfabbrica	43°09'31"N 12°36'09"E
33.9	↰	Strada Francescana `to Assisi'	
	■■↑	staying on main road 22.5km	
35.2	▲	2.6km extremely steep and difficult climb!	
		{38.9 ●●⌐ Pieve San Nicolo 0.4km (↻)}	
41.9	▲	3.3km very steep descent	
45.4	↰	SS147 `to Foligno'	
47.4	↘	Viale Marconi	
47.7		Porta San Francesco (town gate)	
47.8	↘	Via Fontebella	
48.2	↘	Via Eugenio Brizi/Via Giotto	
48.3	↙	Via Portica	
48.5	↰	Piazza del Comune	
48.5		(10m) Assisi visitor centre	43°04'13"N 12°37'03"E

Day 4: Assisi to Norcia
6–9 hours, 99.9km
This long and challenging day crosses a remote corner of eastern Umbria.

After a winding descent from Assisi, an uninspiring secondary road parallels the *autostrada* for several kilometres. Possible diversions include a visit to historic **Spello** (13.1km), or watching for the Roman ruins poking out of weeds on the left. After a brief stint on busy SS3, traffic decreases and the scenery improves. A steep short-cut beyond tiny **Belfiore** climbs to national highway SS77.

DEEP IN LE MARCHE – DAY 4

CUES			GPS COORDINATES
start		Assisi visitor centre	43°04'13"N 12°37'03"E
0km		go SE through Piazza del Comune	
0.1	↘	Via San Gabriele dell'Addolorata	
0.6	↙	`to Foligno'	
1.5	↘⊙	SS147 `to Foligno'	
7.2	↰	`to Spello'	
13.1	★	Spello	42°59'13"N 12°40'22"E
16.6	↘	Via Clareno/Via Hoffmann	
18.5	↰	SS3	
22.6	⌐	SP449 `to Scanzano/Vescia'	
25.8	↰	Viale Innamorati	
26.2		Belfiore	42°59'00"N 12°45'10"E
27.3	↙	`to Macerata'	
	▲	2.8km steep climb	
30.1	↰	SS77	
37.1	⌐	to Casenove	
37.5		Casenove	42°58'36"N 12°50'38"E
38.2	⌐	SS319 `to Norcia'	
46.0	▲	4km moderate climb	
49.8		Valico del Soglio	
		10km gradual descent	
65.0	↰	SS209, Borgo Cerreto	42°48'52"N 12°54'53"E
		{67.2 ■■⌐ alt route: SS396 17.7km}	
68.4		Triponzo	42°49'40"N 12°56'14"E
76.3	⌐	SP476 `to Norcia/Preci'	
81.2		Preci	42°52'52"N 13°02'18"E
87.0		Campi	42°51'07"N 13°05'41"E
88.8	▲	3.6km steep climb	
92.4		6.6 descent	
93.0		Forca d'Ancarano	
99.1	⌐	SP476 `to Casa del Parco'	
99.6	↰	Corso Sertorio	
		{alt route rejoins (turn right)}	
99.9		Piazza San Benedetto, Norcia	42°47'40"N 13°05'42"E

A moderate climb over a small pass leads to the beautiful **Valnerina** (Nera River Valley). The junction at **Borgo Cerreto** (65km) is one of few food stops. Shortly beyond this point the road splits.

Preci (on the right at 81.2km) is an attractive hill town famous historically for its surgeons, one of whom performed cataract surgery on Queen Elizabeth of England in 1588. The valley beyond town, backed by the Sibillini Mountains, is gorgeous, with a picturesque church at **Campi** (87km or so). The final big push up to **Forca d'Ancarano** (1008m) yields spectacular views down into Norcia's great valley.

Day 5: Norcia to Montemonaco
5–6 hours, 64km

Climbing 17.4km into the mountains above Norcia, the route crosses the other worldly landscape of the Piano Grande, then rides a long series of ups and downs along the Sibillini's eastern slopes. Today is definitely a highlight.

The steady climb from Norcia offers great views of the valley's patchwork quilt of fields. Traffic is light, and skies are often filled with paragliders. Near the summit the landscape becomes starker and more windswept, with shaggy horses roaming about. The first view down onto the **Piano Grande** (20.2km), a vast sheep-grazing plateau ringed by barren peaks, is guaranteed to leave a lasting impression. This enormous, treeless bowl is ablaze with wildflowers in late spring, painted in more-subtle shades of yellow and ochre in summer and autumn.

Sitting on a knoll at the far end of the valley, the lonesome town of **Castelluccio** looks more a Tibetan monastery site than a central Italian hill town. Accessible as a side trip at 27.6km, Castelluccio is famous throughout Italy for its unique, small lentils. The **Festa della Fiorita** is held here every June in conjunction with the annual explosion of wildflowers.

Continuing through sheep country, the route climbs again to the desolate **Forca di Presta** (1540m), then drops steeply down the mountains' eastern flank, providing great close-up views of hulking **Monte Vettore** (2476m), the Sibillini's highest peak.

Another short climb and long descent leads to **Balzo**, an attractive hill community and the only chance for services before Montemonaco. The undulating profile continues, culminating in a long final ascent.

DEEP IN LE MARCHE – DAY 5

CUES		GPS COORDINATES
start		Piazza San Benedetto, Norcia 42°47'34"N 13°05'34"E
0km		Go S on Via Zara 'to Castelluccio'
0.1	⌐	'to Ascoli Piceno'
0.2	⬑	'to Ascoli Piceno'
0.5	⌐	'to Ascoli Piceno/Castelluccio'
2.8	⬑	SP477 'to Castelluccio'
	▲	17.4km moderate-steep climb
7.5	⬑	'to Castelluccio'
18.3	⬑	'to Castelluccio'
20.2		Piano Grande
	⚠	3.3km steep descent
27.6	⌐	'to Ascoli Piceno'
	{ ●●⬑ Castelluccio 4km (↻)}
29.0		4.8km moderate-steep climb
33.8		Forca di Presta
	⚠	6km steep descent
39.8	⬑	'to Montegallo'
	▲	1.6km moderate climb
41.4		Valico Galluccio, 5km steep descent!
47.0		Balzo 42°50'27"N 13°19'51"E
47.5	⬎	to Montemonaco
51.0	▲	3.3km moderate climb
54.3	⬎	at Pescolle summit 'to Montemonaco'
		Descent 3.9km
58.2		SP83 'to Montemonaco'
60.0	▲	4km moderate-steep climb
63.9	⬑	'to Pro Loco'
64.0		Montemonaco visitor centre 42°53'57"N 13°19'43"E

Day 6: Montemonaco to Ascoli Piceno
4–6 hours, 59.6km

The final day is a breeze, with an early, long descent and only a couple of moderate climbs the rest of the way into Ascoli Piceno. The first section is gorgeous – the rest of the ride is functional for getting you to a train station and a visit-worthy town.

The first 12km, on a quiet road hugging the mountains' edge, is a pure delight. At 3.9km the tiny town of **Isola San Biagio** marks the beginning of a bumpy but exhilarating descent. Traffic is next to nil, and the close-up views of the Sibillini are magnificent. At 7.5km, as the paved main road hairpins right, a signposted dirt road continues straight for the side trip to **Gola dell'Infernaccio**, a narrow rocky chasm cut by the raging Fiume Tenna, accessible via a hiking trail at the end of the road.

At 11.7km, with lovely **Montefortino** perched overhead, the route veers away from the mountains and joins increasingly

DEEP IN LE MARCHE – DAY 6

CUES		GPS COORDINATES
start	Montemonaco visitor centre	42°53′57″N 13°19′43″E
0km	go downhill towards main road	
0.1	to Isola San Biagio	
0.6	`to Isola	
3.9	Isola San Biagio	42°54′32″N 13°18′29″E
4.6	6.1km very steep bumpy descent	
	{7.5 ●● Gola dell'Infernaccio 10km ↺}	
11.1	unmarked	
11.7	`to Amandola'	
16.5	SS78 `to Ascoli Piceno', Amandola	
		42°58′35″N 13°21′03″E
20.1	1.2 moderate climb	
24.8	SS78, Comunanza	42°57′27″N 13°24′50″E
29.1	4km moderate climb	
44.8	Via Ponte Pugliese, Roccafluvione	
		42°51′34″N 13°28′37″E
	easily missable turn	
45.1	`to Venarotta'	
	2km moderate climb	
49.3	SP93 `to Ascoli', Venarotta	42°52′54″N 13°29′34″E
57.9	`to Roma'	
58.1 Hard	Via Bengasi `to Centro'	
58.7	Via Berardo Tucci	
58.8	Rione Borgo Solesta (to bridge)	
58.9	Via Elisabetta Trebbiani	
59.2	Via Cairoli	
59.3	Via del Trivio	
59.5	Corso Giuseppe Mazzini	
59.5	(50m) Piazza del Popolo	
59.6	Ascoli Piceno visitor centre	42°51′12″N 13°34′39″E

busy roads – which can be jarring in contrast with the kind of riding you may be used to. The larger town of **Amandola** marks the junction with national highway SS78, which follows a sinuous course through big open fields offering lovely views back to the Sibillini.

At **Comunanza** (the last major town before Ascoli), SS78 veers right, eventually crossing a small pass, then winding downhill through forest. A detour onto smaller roads (keep your eyes open – it's easy to miss) at 44.8km necessitates another short climb but avoids the heavy traffic characterising other approaches to Ascoli. The grand entry into the city is via a **1st-century Roman bridge**, with Ascoli's numerous medieval towers forming a picturesque backdrop.

TOWNS & FACILITIES

ANCONA
☎ 07 / pop 101,000
Founded by Syracusan Greeks in the 4th century BC, with a harbour substantially developed by Roman Emperor Trajan in AD 115, Ancona remains the mid-Adriatic's largest port, nowadays best known among tourists for its passenger ferry service to Croatia, Greece and Turkey. The city centre, heavily bombed in WWII, is relatively uninspiring.

Information
Ancona's visitor centre (☎ 07 135 89 903; www.comune.ancona.it/turismo; Via Thaon de Revel 4), east of town, provides information for the city and the entire Marche region.

Banca delle Marche (Via Marconi 217) is just across from the station.

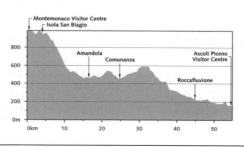

Day 6: Deep in Le Marche

Supplies & Equipment

Bike Maniacs (☎ 07 121 81 600; Via Flaminia 224; closed Sun & Mon morning) is an excellent bike shop north of town along the main highway.

Sleeping & Eating

Camping Internazionale (☎ 07 193 30 884; www.campinginternazionale.com; Via San Michele 10; per person €5–10, per site €9–16) is at the midpoint of the Conero Riviera ride in Sirolo. This gorgeous campground just below town has 230 sites overlooking the beach.

Ostello della Gioventù (☎ /fax 07 14 22 57; Via Lamaticci 7; dm €16) is Ancona's HI-youth hostel. It's divided into a floor for males and a floor for females, each with spotless four- to six-person bedrooms and separate bathrooms.

Residence Vanvitelli (☎ 07 120 60 23, 33 889 74 705; www.residencevanvitelli.it; Piazza Saffi; studio/one-/two-room apt per night €60/75/90, per week €350/450/550) is tucked away in a tiny piazza no more than a 10-minute walk from most of Ancona's sights. It's comfortable, quiet and modern.

Hotel Fortuna (☎ 07 14 26 63; www.hotelfortuna.it; Piazza Rosselli 15; s/d incl breakfast from €56/72) takes the prize in the train station area. The breakfast buffet is enormous by Italian standards.

Mercato delle Erbe (Corso Giuseppe Mazzini 130) is a picnickers' dream-come-true. Dozens of booths line this green-metal-and-glass-enclosed bazaar where you can buy freshly baked pastries and bread, locally produced cheese and meat, and everything else you need for a picnic. **Osteria del Pozzo** (☎ 07 120 73 996; Via Bonda 2; meals €23) has black-ink squid risotto that alone merits a trip. Most locals go for the seafood fixed price dish, €16 worth of the freshest fish of the day. **La Moretta 1897** (☎ 07 120 23 17; Piazza del Plebiscito 52; meals €28) has been run by the same family since that very year: 1897. It features not just Marchigiani cuisine, but dishes specifically native to Ancona. **Cremeria Rosa** (☎ 07 120 34 08; Corso Mazzini 61) serves sundaes as big as your head, with as many spoons as you need.

AQUILEIA

☎ 04 / pop 3330

At first glance you'd never guess that Aquileia once ranked among the Roman Empire's largest and richest cities and served as its busiest Adriatic port. Aquileia was also a major ecclesiastical power, instrumental in the early diffusion of Christianity into central Europe, later ruling Friuli as a powerful patriarchate for several centuries. Nowadays the Adriatic has receded, leaving the Roman port high and dry, but the ruins, mosaics and churches left behind give fascinating glimpses of the town's illustrious past. **Aquileia's basilica** (☎ 04 319 10 67; Piazza Capitolo), founded soon after Constantine's conversion to Christianity in the early 4th century, features a stunning floor mosaic, the largest of its kind in Western Europe.

Information

The **visitor centre** (☎ 04 319 19 491; Piazza Capitolo 4) is across from the basilica, with a another larger centre right off SS352, on the left as you enter the town from the north. Go to www.aquileia.it for more information on the town. ATMs can be found in the centres.

Supplies & Equipment

Motostile Nadalin (☎ 04 319 15 72; via Beligna 1a) can provide basic parts and repairs (or sell you a motorcycle if you get desperate).

Sleeping & Eating

Campers should head north of town, near the old Roman port, to **Camping Aquileia** (☎ /fax 04 319 19 583; www.camping aquileia.it; Via Gemina 10; per person €5–7, per site €8–21; 15 May–15 Sep).

Several places here rent rooms, request a list at the visitor centre, or look for signs on Via Gemina and SS352.

Ostello Domus Augusta (☎ /fax 04 319 10 24; www.ostelloaquileia.it; Via Roma 25; per person €13) is Aquileia's gleaming hostel with a cute garden.

Hotel Restaurant Patriarchi (☎ 04 319 19 595; www.hotelpatriarchi.it; Via Giulia Augusta 12; s/d €58/96) has rooms that are mostly spacious; some have views of the basilica. The restaurant wine cellar is well stocked and the chef is a dab hand at preparing fish dishes.

ADRIATIC COAST

De Spar (Via Giulia Augusta 17) sells groceries. On the way out of town, going south on SS352, you'll find several restaurants that have some righteous provisions.

ASCOLI PICENO
☎ 07 / pop 51,400

While less of a tourist draw than many Italian cities its size, Ascoli Piceno is an appealing place abounding in history and fine architecture. The central Piazza del Popolo, paved in travertine, is one of Italy's prettiest squares. Ascoli's Roman origins can be seen in its straight and perpendicular street layout, the 1st-century Ponte Solesta and the ruins of a Roman gate and amphitheatre. Ascoli, the region's capital, is the largest city in the southern Marche.

Information
Ascoli's visitor centre (☎ 07 362 98 204; iat.ascolipiceno@regione.marche.it; Piazza Arringo 7) has info on sites and lodging. The **City of Ascoli Piceno** (www.comune .ascoli-piceno.it) has information on events and festivals.

Banca Nazionale del Lavoro is located on Viale Indipendeza 63.

Supplies & Equipment
Cicli Falgiani (☎ 07 363 41 866; Via Amalfi 1/3) is a good bike shop southeast of the centre.

Sleeping & Eating
For a town with not many hotels, Ascoli has a good range of accommodation. Tourist offices have lists of other accommodation options, including rooms and apartments, *agriturismi* (farm stay accommodation) and B&B options in outlying districts.

Ostello dei Longobardi (☎ 07 362 61 862, fax 07 362 59 191; Via dei Soderini 26; dm €16, in winter €18) is an 11th-century stone-palace-turned-youth hostel. Don't expect much from the plumbing.

Teamwork runs the show at **B&B Rainbow** (☎ 07 362 51 176, 32 080 82 705; Via Salvadori 2; s €25–30, d €45–50, incl breakfast): he teaches theatre and mime, she teaches yoga and dance, and together the English-speaking couple runs a B&B that's as warm and inviting as it is casual.

Tigre (☎ 07 633 41 000; Viale Indipendenza), the most central of Ascoli's

supermarkets, has a deli and a good wine selection. **Gallo D'Oro** (☎ 07 362 53 520; Corso Vittorio Emanuele 54; meals €26) is a bit outside the tourist area, which may be part of the reason it's so popular with long-time Ascoli residents. This fine establishment has been serving up local fare for decades. **Caffè Meletti** (☎ 07 362 59 626; Piazza delle Popolo) was once a popular spot for the likes of writers Ernest Hemingway and Jean-Paul Sartre. In the shade of the ancient portico you can sip coffee or the area's famous *anisette* as you gaze onto the perfect Italian piazza.

ASSISI
☎ 07 / pop 25,300

Depending on when you visit and how long you stay, the City of St Francis may strike you either as a beautifully preserved medieval town or an oppressive tourist trap — with kitschy Franciscan souvenirs on sale in every other doorway. Either way, it's also a major site of religious pilgrimage, with the faithful flocking in from around the world to worship at the shrine made famous by Assisi's native son.

The massive **Basilica of St Francis** is the reason most people, pilgrims and tourists alike, come to visit, but the town is an appealing destination in its own right, a maze of stone streets, alleyways, gates and arches enclosed by an intact medieval wall. After the tour buses pull out, it's a delightful place for an evening stroll.

Information
The **visitor centre** (☎ 07 581 25 34; info@ iat.assisi.pg.it; Piazza del Comune 22) also has a branch office outside Porta Nuova during high season. There are ATMs near the visitor centre.

Supplies & Equipment
For bike parts and repairs, go downhill 5km to **Angelucci Cicli** (☎ 07 580 42 550; www .angeluccicicli.it; Via Risorgimento 54/a) in Santa Maria degli Angeli.

Sleeping & Eating
Camping/Hotel Fontemaggio (☎ 07 581 23 17; www.fontemaggio.it; Via Eremo delle Carceri 8; per person/tent/car €6/5/3, dm/s/d €20/35/52, four- to six-person bungalow with kitchen €32–110) offers guests the choice of

bungalows, camp sites and hotel rooms. On the way to Eremo delle Carceri, it's a beautiful walk into town, but the restaurant might just keep you for the evening.

We usually suggest staying away from hotel restaurants – most of Assisi's better restaurants though (even the more inexpensive ones) are part of hotels. **Grotta Antica** (☎ 07 581 34 67; Vicolo Buscatti 6; meals €16) has lovely pesto dishes and the wine prices here can't be beaten anywhere in Assisi. **Buca di San Francesco** (☎ 07 581 22 04; Via Brizi 1; meals €29) prepares traditional Umbrian dishes and specialities of the house in a elegant medieval setting. You can choose from the extensive wine list with the help of one of Assisi's only sommeliers.

CHIOGGIA
☎ 04 / pop 51,800

During the Venetian Republic's heyday, Chioggia was Venice's proud sister city. Parallels between the two are harder to find nowadays. Modern Chioggia has more vehicle traffic than canals, and it's dominated by an industrial port zone with nothing to offer the tourist. Even so, if you haven't seen Venice yet, the historic centre of Chioggia gives you a watered-down but tantalising idea of what's in store. The town's northern tip retains hints of its Venetian history, with decaying waterfront *palazzi* (palaces or mansions), and sculpted lions adorning the 16th-century Porta Garibaldi arch and 12th-century Vigo Column at either end of the pedestrianised Corso del Popolo.

Information

The **visitor centre** (☎ 04 140 10 68; www .chioggiatourism.it) is in Sottomarina at Lungomare Adriatico 101.

Banks abound along Corso del Popolo.

Supplies & Equipment

Cicli e Moto Albanese Sergio (☎ 04 140 12 55; Corso del Popolo 970) is a bike/motorcycle shop.

Sleeping & Eating

One of several Sottomarina camping grounds around **Chioggia is Camping Adriatico** (☎ 04 149 29 07; www.campingadriatico .com; Lungomare Adriatico 82; per person €5–7, per site €8–10.50) with private beach, pool, supermarket and restaurant.

Pensione Clodia (☎ 04 140 08 13; www .sottomarina.net/clodia; Calle Forno Filippini 876; with shared bathroom €30–50, d €45–70), just south of Corso del Popolo, is one of the cheapest places in Chioggia proper.

Albergo Caldin's (☎ 04 140 35 82; becaldin@tin.it; Piazzale Peretolo 30; r from €65) is a basic, one-star place overlooking Canale Pero at the western edge of the pedestrian zone.

SISA (Corso del Popolo) is a large supermarket. Corso di Popolo has a number eateries to check as well. **Ristorante al Buon Pesce** (Stradale Ponte Caneva 625; closed Wed) is one of many places specialising in Chioggia-style seafood.

CIVIDALE DEL FRIULI
☎ 04 / pop 11,400

Straddling the Natisone gorge and surrounded by some of Friuli's finest vineyards, Cividale is a pleasant town with a fascinating history. Founded by Julius Caesar in 50 BC as the *municipium* (a self-governing town whose residents did not necessarily qualify for Roman citizenship) of Forum Iulii (from which the modern name Friuli derives), it became the first of 35 Lombard duchies in Italy when King Alboin invaded in AD 568, then served as seat of the Patriarchate of Aquileia from 1077 to 1238. Cividale's multilayered history is evident in its medieval and Renaissance architecture and in the Roman and Lombard remnants preserved in its museums and monuments.

Information

The **visitor centre** (☎ 04 327 10 460; www.cividale.net; Corso Paolino d'Aquileia 10) is just in the main plaza, Piazza Paolo Diacono.

You'll find ATMs in the centre.

Supplies & Equipment

Bicisport di Giovanni Mattana (☎ 04 327 33 542; bicisport@libero.it; via Udine cap 33043) is an excellent, friendly bike shop at the northwest corner of town.

Sleeping & Eating

The tourist office has an extensive list of B&Bs and *agriturismi*. Other than those, the best deal in town is

Locanda al Pomo d'Oro (☎/fax 04 327 31 489; Piazza S Giovanni 20; s/d €50/80), a restored 11th-century inn. It's friendly, family-run and central, with an excellent restaurant.

Hotel Roma (☎ 04 327 31 871; Piazza Picco; s/d €55/80), one of the only other in-town options, is much less inspiring.

Locanda al Castello (☎ 04 327 33 242; www.alcastello.net; Via del Castello 20; s/d €80/130), a 19th-century castle originally built as a Jesuit monastery, sits on a hilltop overlooking vineyards 1km north of town. It features an attached restaurant and a pleasant terrace.

Chow down on *cialcions* (a somewhat sweet dumpling typical of the area) at **Al Monastero** (☎ 04 327 00 808; Via Ristori 9; meals €25–30). In fitting with its old-town location, it is decorated with original frescoes and antique furniture.**Locanda al Pomo d'Oro** (closed Wed) also has great local cuisine. For good company and a lovely environment to try the remarkable wines of the area, check out the wine bar **Gustobase** (☎ 04 327 31 383; www .gustobase.com; Piazza Paolo Diacon 24), which has seating right on Piazza Paolo Diacono.

COMACCHIO
☎ 05 / pop 20,300

Surrounded by low-lying wetlands 5km inland from the Adriatic, Comacchio is better known as an eel-fishing port than a tourist destination. Optimistic local promoters have long dubbed it a miniature Venice because of its small network of canals and unusual 17th-century bridge, but until recently there wasn't much else to see. Two new museums enhance the town's cultural appeal and visitors burned out on the tourist treadmill may even find charm in Comacchio's sleepy unselfconsciousness.

Information
The helpful **tourist office** (☎ 05 333 14 154; www.comune.comacchio.fe.it; Corso Mazzini 4) has loads of information about the area's opportunities for hiking, cycling, birdwatching, horse riding and boat excursions.

You'll find banks with ATMs on Via Zappata and Piazzetta Folegatti.

Supplies & Equipment
Nordi Cicli e Moto (☎ 05 333 11 529; Via Muratori 4), is a small bike shop offering rentals in the heart of town.

Sleeping & Eating
There are nine camping grounds along the beaches east of Comacchio. **Spiaggia e Mare** (☎ 05 333 27 431; Via Strada Provincia Ferrara-Mare 4; per person/site €7/15) is the closest, in Porto Garibaldi.

Lodging options in Comacchio itself are limited. **Albergo Ristorante Tre Ponti** (☎/fax 05 333 12 766; Via Marconi 3; s €25, d €50–70) is the cheapest, but then you get what you pay for at this rather dismal place.

Locanda La Comacina (☎ 05 333 11 547; Via E. Fogli 21; www.lacomacina.it; s/d €50/90) is a nice three-star hotel with the option of half-board. Several B&Bs have appeared recently, one of the cheapest being **La Corte die Ducati** (☎ 05 338 11 56; Via Mazzini 22; www.lacortedei ducati.it; s/d €50/80).

Self-caterers will find markets in the centre. There is no shortage of restaurants along the canals, most offering fish-based menus and eel specialities. One of the best is **Trattoria della Pescheria** (☎ 05 338 15 97; Via E Fogli 93; meals €28, tourist menu €16), where the helpings are huge, the fish is fresh and the chips are a delight.

FERRARA
☎ 05 / pop 131,000

Traces of the past are evident everywhere in the agreeable city of Ferrara. Urban life still revolves around the **Castello Estense**, the moated former dwelling of the Este dukes who ruled this region between the 13th and 16th centuries. The city's medieval core and surrounding walls are largely intact, and Renaissance palaces abound.

Ferrara may well also be the cycle-friendliest city in Italy.

Information
The **visitor centre** (☎ 05 322 09 370; www .ferrarainfo.com; Viale Cavour) is in the heart of town, on the ground floor of the Castello Estense.

There are numerous banks with ATMs along Corso Martiri della Libertà in the centre.

Supplies & Equipment

The *Cycling in Ferrara* map available from the visitor centre lists dozens of bike shops. One of the most convenient is **Barlati** (☎ 05 322 06 863; Via Adelardi 1), near the cathedral.

Sleeping & Eating

Campeggio Comunale Estense (☎ 05 327 52 396; campeggio.estense@freeinternet.it; Via Gramicia 76; per person/tent €5/7) is along the Day 3 route and is the only camp site in Ferrara. Look for it just outside the city walls.

Ostello Estense (☎ 05 322 01 158; ostelloestense@coopcamelot; Corso Biagio Rossetti 24; dm €18) offers the cheapest beds in town. It's clean with no frills.

Locanda Borgonuovo (☎ 05 322 11 100; www.borgonuovo.com; Via Cairoli 29; s/d €55/95) is a gem of a B&B. Breakfast is delicious, and there's a delightfully patio. They have free bike hire for guests. Reservations are essential.

Self-caterers can fill up at the **covered market** (Via Vegri; closed Sun). **Il Ciclone** (☎ 05 322 10 262; 1st fl, Via Vignatagliata 11; pizzas from €4, meals €25) serves a tempting selection of pastas, pizzas, meats and fish. **Trattoria il Mandolino** (☎ 05 327 60 080; Via Carlo Mayr 83; meals €27) has old-fashioned (mandolin-centric) décor to match its traditional Ferrarese, so expect plenty of meat, cheese and salami.

GUBBIO

☎ 07 / pop 31,600

Founded by the ancient Umbrians and known to the Romans as Iguvium, the lovely stone town of Gubbio cascades down a green hillside above the fertile plain of the Saonda and Assino Rivers. The town's most prominent landmark is the amazingly tall face of the medieval Palazzo dei Consoli, rising abruptly from the square below and dwarfing all other buildings in town. With so many bumpy stone streets, Gubbio is not a comfortable place to cycle, but it's a delightful walking town and a fun place to window-shop for ceramics. At sunrise or sunset, Gubbio is a dazzling study in red and grey, its stone and brick buildings exuding a warm glow.

Information

The **tourist office** (☎ 07 592 20 693; www .gubbio-altochiascio.umbria2000.it; Via Repubblica 2) and banks with ATMs are in the centre.

Supplies & Equipment

In town, **Centro Servizi S Spirito** (Via della Repubblica 11) can help you out with the basics.

Sleeping & Eating

The tourist office has an extremely thorough list of all accommodation options within the area.

Città di Gubbio & Villa Ortoguidone (☎ 07 592 72 037; www.gubbiocamping .com; Loc Ortoguidone 49; per person €6–9, tent €7–9, car €3, 2-/4-person apt €30–100), in addition to its full-service, four-star camp site, also has stunning apartments in an old stone manor house. July and August visits require a one-week stay.

From the SS298, follow the signs for 3km to 'Agriclub Villa Ortoguidone'. **Maestro Pie Filippini** (☎ 07 592 73 768; Corso Garibaldi 100; per person €20) is religious accommodation that's more institutional than spiritual. The price and location can't be beaten, as long as you make reservations in advance and can work with the terms: a two-night minimum and a 10.30pm curfew.

At **Residenza di Via Piccardi** (☎ 07 592 76 108; e.biagiotto@tiscali.it; Via Piccardi 12; s/d/apt incl breakfast €30/55/60), you can share a romantic breakfast in the garden or cook dinner in the mini-apartment's kitchenette.

There's is an outdoor **fruit and vegetable market** (Piazza 40 Martiri; closed Sun).

Ristorante La Fornace di Mastro Giorgio (☎ 07 592 21 836; Via Mastro Giorgio 2; meals €40) is a favourite place for a special occasion (not just for the 500-item wine list, either). The seasonal menu includes modern takes on traditional dishes. **Ristorante Fabiani** (☎ 07 592 74 639; Piazza Quaranta Martiri 26; meals €27) has a fabulous patio and garden. The selection here is vast, with a rotating €15 tourist menu.

MONTEMONACO

☎ 07 / pop 690

Tiny Montemonaco enjoys a picture-postcard view over the majestic eastern **Sibillini.**

The Sibillini's countless mystical associations can best be appreciated by hiking up to the legendary sites nearby, such as Lago di Pilato, a lake sometimes turned red by algae where Pontius Pilate reputedly met his fate, and Grotta della Sibilla, the subterranean domain of the prophetess for whom the mountains were named.

Information

Montemonaco's **Pro Loco office** (☎ 07 368 56 411; www.montemonaco.com; Piazza Risorgimento 2) offers general information about the town. The nearby **Casa del Parco** (☎ /fax 07 368 56 462; info.montemoanco@sibillini.net; Via Roma) has plenty of information about Parco Nazionale dei Monti Sibillini.

There are banks in the centre.

Sleeping & Eating

Basic, two-star establishments along Montemonaco's main street include **Ristorante Albergo Carlini** (☎ /fax 07 368 56 127; Via Roma 16/18; r from €50) and **Albergo Sibilla** (☎ 07 368 56 144; Via Roma 52; r from €45).

At Piazza Roma, Alimentari Grilli sells groceries and there are some eateries. There are restaurants at the listed hotels, most specialising in the truffle dishes for which the region is famous.

NORCIA

☎ 07 / pop 4900

Enclosed within 13th-century walls, the remote town of Norcia sits alone in a vast valley ringed by mountains. Already a Roman city in the 3rd century BC (a fact commemorated by the 'Nursia Vetusta' inscription in one of the town gates), it gained fame in AD 480 as the birthplace of St Benedict and in the Middle Ages as a centre for witches and necromancers.

Today Norcia is a popular Italian tourist destination, thanks to its many culinary specialities (pork, mushrooms and truffles prominent among them) and its proximity to the Sibillini mountains, which hold many opportunities for outdoor adventure.

Information

The Casa del Parco **visitor centre** (☎ /fax 07 438 17 090), one block west of Piazza San Benedetto at Via Solferino 22, offers information about Parco Nazionale dei Monti Sibillini and Norcia itself.

There are a couple of banks north of the main square.

Sleeping & Eating

Around 20km north of Norcia, just outside Preci on the Day 4 route is **Centro Agrituristico Il Collaccio** (☎ 07 439 39 005; www.ilcollaccio.com; per person €5.50–8.50, per site €5.50–8.50), an *agriturismo* with lovely camp sites in addition to its hotel. They also rent mountain bikes (half-day €8).

Ostello Norcia (☎ 34 930 02 091; www.montepatino.com; Via Ufente 1/b; dm incl breakfast €15) has 52 tidy rooms holding to 10 beds each, but the hostel often fills up with school or tour groups, so call ahead. They can help you arrange outdoor excursions.

Hotel Grotta Azzura (☎ 07 438 16 513; www.bianconi.com; Via Alfieri 12; s €37–88, d €44–125) has suits of armour in the reception and can be a fabulous deal during the week and in low season. Its Ristorante Granaro del Monte has been open daily for 150 years running. It is a tad touristy, but the food is still excellent and comes in great piles of *porcini* mushrooms, sausages and prosciutto, truffles and *cinghiale* (wild boar).

PADUA

☎ 04 / pop 204,900

Padua (Paddova) is most famous as the site of Giotto's beautiful **Scrovegni Chapel** frescoes, and has also become popular among tourists as a more affordable and less crowded place to overnight while visiting Venice. Its delightful medieval centre and numerous churches and monuments deserve a visit on their own merits.

Information

Padua's main **visitor centre** (☎ 04 987 52 077; www.turismopadova.it) is conveniently located inside the train station.

There's an ATM at the station, with plenty of other banks throughout the city.

Supplies & Equipment

Two of Padua's best bike shops are **Morbiato Cicli** (☎ 04 970 64 63; Via Pontevigodarzare 101–105) and **Cicli Morello** (☎ 04 987 15 650; Via Sorio 54).

Sleeping & Eating

Koko Nor Association (www.bbkokonor
.it) can help you to find B&B-style accommodation in family homes as well as furnished apartments (it has 12 places on the
books) for around €60–80 for two people. If
you have trouble with the website, try www
.bbtibetanhouse.it. The tourist office has a
list of about 30 B&Bs.

Camping Sporting Centre (☎ 04 979 34
00; www.sportingcenter.it; Via Roma 123,
Montegrotto Terme; per person €6.30–
7.30, per site €8.50–12) is the only camping ground in the province of Padua. It's
about 15km away from the city centre and
it boasts a swimming pool and access to
thermal spa facilities.

Padua's best low-budget option is **AIG
Ostello Città di Padova** (☎ 04 987 52 219;
www.ostellopadova@ctgveneto.it; Via A Al-
eardi 30; dm €16), just south of downtown.
A stay there includes breakfast.

Albergo Sant'Antonio (☎ 04 987 51
393; Via San Fermo 118; s/d €60/80), a
nearby, tattered two-star, has some rooms
with bridge and canal views. Check the
stuffiness factor before deciding to stay.

Padua's daily produce market, **Piazza
delle Erbe**, is one of Italy's finest. A sea of
fresh fruit and vegetables fills the central
area, while surrounding stalls sell everything from ice cream to horsemeat.

Caffè Pedrocchi (☎ 04 987 81 231;
www.caffepedrocchi.it; Via VIII Febbraio
15) has been a coffee place for scholars and
artists since 1831. **Osteria Dal Capo** (☎ 04
966 31 05; Via degli Obizzi 2; meals €30), a
wine bar serving quality traditional Veneto
cooking, comes recommended by many
throughout the town. Go to **Enoteca Angelo
Rasi** (☎ 04 987 19 797; www.an gelorasi
.it; Riviera Paleocapa 7; meals €50) for
ombrete e cicheti (little glasses of wine and
snacks), or treat yourself to a full meal. Each
dish, which might include a meat tartare
with several sauces, can be accompanied by
wines suggested by the house.

PESARO
☎ 07 / pop 92,000

Featuring a long expanse of beach and the remains of a medieval centre, Pesaro is a handy
transport junction and the jumping-off point
for one of the Adriatic's prettiest cycling
routes, the **Strada Panoramica Adriatica.**

Information

The **tourist office** (☎ 07 21 6 93 41; www
.comune.pesaro.ps.it; Piazzale della Libertà
11) offers a free *Handy Guide,* in English.
Pesaro Urbino Tourism (www.turismo
.pesarourbino.it) has excellent information
in English, with maps, hotels and sights.

Banks can be found on Piazza del Popolo
and in the historic centre.

Supplies & Equipment

Biciland (☎ 07 214 56 365; Via Carrara 7),
near Via Giolitti in the Calcinari district, is
a large shop selling bikes, parts, accessories
and clothing.

Sleeping & Eating

For a room, contact the **Associazione Pe-
sarese di Albergatori** (☎ 07 216 79 59;
www.apahotel.it in Italian, English, French
& German; Viale Marconi 57) or ask at the
tourist office.

Marinella (☎ 07 215 57 95; www.camping
marinella.it; SS Adriatica at 244km, Loc
Fossosejore; per person/tent/car from
€5/5/3, bungalows d/tr €60/70) has seaside
tent sites, a casual restaurant and other
camping amenities.

Most hotels are square, concrete buildings from the 1960s, uninspiring but close
to or right on the beach.

Oasi San Nicola (☎ 07 215 08 49; www
.oasisannicola.it; Via San Nicola 8; per
person €60–80) is a nice, more expensive,
alternative found a little bit inland in a
converted 13th-century hilltop monastery
surrounded by pine trees.

At **C'Era Una Volta** (☎ 07 213 09 11;
Via Cattaneo 26; pizzas from €3.50) the
raucous atmosphere is almost as fun as
the pizzas, which come topped with peas,
artichokes, *speck,* pancetta or even *patate
fritti* (chips). No glass of wine costs more
than €2.80, and an enormous array of pasta
dishes can be had for under €7.50.

RAVENNA
☎ 05 / pop 134,600

For mosaic lovers, Ravenna is nirvana.
Nowhere else in Italy are so many early
Christian mosaics so readily accessible –
eight local churches and monuments have
been designated Unesco World Heritage
sites. Unlike their more austere late-
Byzantine successors, Ravenna's mosaics

shimmer with brilliant shades of green and blue, their religious subject matter enhanced with portraits of earthly beauty in the form of flowers, fruit, birds and animals.

Aside from its mosaics, Ravenna has a pleasant, prosperous and traffic-free centre where cycling is a popular way of getting around.

Information
There's a **tourist office** (☎ 05 443 54 04; www.turismo.ravenna.it; Via Salara 8) in town and many banks along Via Diaz, plus an ATM at the train station.

Supplies & Equipment
There are three good local bike shops: **Casa del Ciclo** (☎ 05 444 07 495; Via S Mama 148–152; closed Thurs afternoon & Sun), **Cicli Il Pedale** (☎ 05 444 02 274; Via Fiume Montone Abbandonato 293) and **Pezzi di Bici** (☎ 05 444 62 441; Via Maggiore 199).

Sleeping & Eating
Ravenna hotels are generally bland and expensive. **Camping Piomboni** (☎ 05 445 30 230; www.camping piomboni.it; Viale della Pace 421, Marina di Ravenna; per person/tent €7.40/11.50; Easter–mid-Sep) sits within a pine forest 8km from town and near the beach at Lido di Ravenna.

Ostello Dante (☎ 05 444 21 164; www .hostelravenna.com; Via Nicolodi 12; dm/s/d €14/20/36), Ravenna's vibrant HI youth hostel, is right off the bike path on Day 1, 1km east of the train station.

Hotel Ravenna (☎ 05 442 12 204; hotelravenna@ravennablu.it; Via Maroncelli 12; s/d €45/65, s/d with bathroom €55/90) is a stone's throw from the train station. Rooms are bland but comfortable.

Self-caterers and sandwich-fillers should load up at the city's **covered market** (Piazza Andrea Costa). **Naif** (☎ 05 444 22 315; Via Candiano 34; pizzas from €3.80, meals €22) is the pizzeria locals choose for take-away; they also have an extensive menu for eating-in. **Babaleus** (☎ 05 442 16 464; Vicolo Gabbiani 7; pizzas from €4, meals €23) is a popular place in the historic centre that's good for both pizza and pastas.

TRIESTE
☎ 04 / pop 211,200

Trieste is like no other place in Italy, strongly influenced culturally by its Slavic neighbours, while architecturally retaining a faded grandeur from its former life as Austria-Hungary's principal Mediterranean port. The modern-day city is a bit gritty, with its waterfront marred by a busy main road, but there are still plenty of pleasant and intriguing places to discover. The bones of old Roman Tergeste poke out from San Giusto Hill, while the lower-lying Borgo Teresiano is filled with monumental squares and neoclassical buildings.

Information
The **visitor centre** (☎ 04 034 78 312; www.turismo.fvg.it) is in the Piazza dell'Unitá d'Italia. Other informative websites include www.triestetourism.it and www.triestecultura.it. ATMs are available throughout the city.

Supplies & Equipment
Casa del Ciclo di Capponi Pierpaolo (☎ 04 063 80 09; Via Valdirivo 21) is an excellent, bike shop with a helpful staff. It leads tours in the surrounding area and is closed on Sunday and Monday. Or try **Cicli Fleur** (☎ 04 066 04 68; Via Fontane 19).

Sleeping & Eating
Attractively situated high in the hills above Trieste, across from the Obelisco tram stop, is **Campeggio Obelisco** (☎ 04 021 16 55; www.campeggiobelisco.it; per person/site €5/4).

Around 7km north of town on the Day 3 route is **Ostello Tergeste** (☎ /fax 04 022 41 02; www.ostellotregeste.it; Viale Miromare 331; dm €14). It's the best deal around. Its dreary dorm rooms are redeemed by an airy, trellised terrace offering lovely castle and ocean views. There's an 11.30pm curfew

Nuovo Albergo Centro (☎ 04 034 78 790; www.hotelcentrotrieste.it; Via Roma 13; s/d without bathroom €37/54, s/d with bathroom €52/72) is right in the heart of Trieste. This small, family-run hotel is great value for money, offering spick and span, if smallish, rooms.

For self-caterers, there's a good **produce market** (Piazza Ponterosso), alongside the Canal Grande.

To the glory of ravenous cyclists, buffets are a Triestine institution, serving up cheap and authentic local food. Expect lots of boiled bacon, sausages and beer. A classic is *cotto caldo con kren* (a boiled slab of ham served with horseradish). **Buffet Da Siora Rosa** (☎ 04 030 14 60; Piazza Hortis 3; meals €20–25) was opened before WWII. The family-run Siora Rosa is still one of the best and most traditional of Trieste's buffets. **Circus** (☎ 04 063 34 99; Via San Lazzaro 9b; meal €10–15) has an appealing slogan: 'Drinkjokecommunitypeoplefoodmusicjoyfriendlysnack'. The restaurant/bar's decor is a cross between circus big top and old-time cinema. It's known for huge bowls of salad (€5) and a selection of nicely priced *primi* (first courses) and mains.

Getting There & Away
Friuli-Venezia Giulia airport (TRS; ☎ 04 817 73 224; www.aeroporto.fvg.it; Via Aquileia 46), aka Ronchi dei Legionari or **Trieste Airport**, is 33km northwest of Trieste, near Monfalcone.

The train station is just north of downtown. Trieste is the easternmost stop in the Italian train system. Trains run to Venice (€8.20–13.50, 2 hours, hourly), where connections can be made to other Italian destinations and to Rome (€58.10, 6½–7½ hours; most require a change at Mestre). There's also frequent service on the smaller line to Gorizia (€3.55, 50 minutes, hourly) and Udine (€6.60, 1½ hours, hourly).

National and international services operate from the **bus station** (☎ 04 042 50 20; Via Fabio Severo 24). Runs include Udine (€5.10, 1¼ hours, at least hourly) and destinations in Slovenia and Croatia.

Trieste sits at the crossroads between two international bike routes sponsored by the European Cyclists' Federation (ECF; www.ecf.com). The Mediterranean route runs east-west from Cádiz (Spain) to Athens (Greece), while the Baltic to Adriatic route runs north-south from Gdansk (Poland) to Pula (Croatia). For more info contact ECF or its Italian affiliate Federazione Italiana Amici della Bicicletta (FIAB; www.fiab-onlus.it).

URBINO
☎ 07 / pop 15,300
Generally considered one of the prime tourist destinations in Le Marche, Urbino is a classic Italian hill town. With the lovely turrets of its Palazzo Ducale rising from verdant slopes below, it is an aesthetically pleasing blend of architecture and setting, developed to its full splendour by the Dukes of Montefeltro five centuries ago but still thriving as a university and tourist centre.

Information
The **tourist office** (☎ 07 22 26 13, fax 07 22 24 41; www.comune.urbino.ps.it Via Puccinotti 3) provides 10 minutes of free internet access. Banks can be found on Via Vittorio Veneto, the main street running between Piazza della Republica and the Palazzo Ducale. **Assessorato Cultura e Turismo** (www.urbino culturaturismo.it, in Italian) is provided for tourists by the city of Urbino and Unesco. It contains listings for all accommodation (including B&Bs and *agriturismi*) and popular historic, cultural and artistic sights, albeit in Italian.

Supplies & Equipment
Urbino does not have a bike shop. However, there's an excellent one, **Basili Sport** (☎ 07 217 90 077; Via Flaminia) in Cagli along Day 2's route.

Sleeping & Eating
Pleasantly situated 2km east of town is **Campeggio Pineta** (☎ 07 22 47 10; campeggiopinetaurbino@email.it; Via Ca' Mignone 5, San Donato; per person/tent €7/12; Easter–Sep). This camp site is located amid a luscious surrounding of trees. Hot showers, a bar and a market await campers.

San Giovanni (☎ 07 22 28 72, fax 07 223 29 055; Via Barocci 13; s/d €26/40, s/d with bathroom €38/58) is fitting for a university town with its good-value, dormitory-style rooms. Despite the slightly musty smell, the beds are comfy enough and the shared bathrooms are clean.

Albergo Italia (☎ 07 22 27 01; www.albitalia.it; Corso Garibaldi 32; s €45–65, d €65–115, all incl breakfast) is set behind the Palazzo Ducale and could not be better positioned. This modern building is pleasingly quiet for tired cyclists, and business-hotel amenities are available.

There are markets in the centre and on the main square for self-caterers.

Osteria L'Angolo Divino (☎ 07 223 27 559; Via Sant'Andrea 14; meals €32) is a subterranean *enoteca* (wine bar) whose arched brick alcoves overflow with wine bottles that are available for tastings. Pasta is their speciality. The unassumingly simple **Il Coppiere** (☎ 07 223 22 326; Via Santa Margherita 1; meals €23) specialises in typical local dishes at fantastic prices. **Caffè Basili** (☎ 07 22 24 48; Piazza della Repubblica), known to Urbino students and professionals as 'Bar Centrale', is the best of the piazza cafés. Its outdoor tables are a great choice for late-after-noon *aperitivi*.

VENICE

☎ 04 / pop 271,100

Maligned by some as an artificial museum city ruined by tourism, Venice (Venezia) remains for others one of the worlds most magical and romantic places. For cyclists, Venice is not immediately welcoming — indeed, bikes are a useless encumbrance among its bridges, canals and narrow alleyways, and they are prohibited on the *vaporetti* running along the Grand Canal between Piazzale Roma, Santa Lucia train station and Piazza San Marco. Despite these limitations, Venice is an international gateway, a convenient rail hub and an indispensable part of any northern Italian itinerary. Park your bike for a few days and enjoy.

Six *sestieri* (neighbourhoods) constitute the main nucleus of the island city. South and west of the Grand Canal are Sestieri Santa Croce, San Polo and Dorsoduro; north and east are Sestieri Cannaregio, San Marco and Castello. Street addresses commonly include the name of the appropriate *sestiere*. Santa Lucia train station is in Sestiere Cannaregio, while Sestiere San Marco to the east is Venice's tourist hub.

South of the city, the island of Lido is open to traffic, and bikes are a familiar sight on its roads. Cyclists arriving from the airport or riding the Ravenna to Venice route may wish to stash their bikes here for a few days while visiting Venice. Alternatively you can lock your bike at one of the train stations.

It's impossible to do this city justice in a few paragraphs. For more comprehensive coverage, see Lonely Planet's *Italy* guide.

Information

The **APT visitor centre** (☎ 04 152 98 711; www.turismovenezia.it) has offices at the train station, the airport, Piazzale Roma, Piazza San Marco 71f, and Gran Viale Santa Maria Elisabetta 6a in Lido.

There's a ATM in the train station, plus numerous banks and change offices around San Marco and throughout the city. Internet and laundry services can be found respectively at **Planet Internet** (☎ 04 152 44 188; Rio Terà San Leonardo, Cannaregio 1519; per hr €8) and **Laundry** (www.laundry .it; Calle Chioverette, Santa Croce 665b; 8kg wash €4, 12kg dry €4).

Supplies & Equipment

A good bike shop in Mestre (just north of Venice) is **Bicimania** (☎ 04 198 92 60; Via Torre Belfredo 124). Another excellent shop, **Scavezzon** (☎ 04 157 03 092; www .scavezzon.com; Via della Vittorian 141) is 24km west of Venice.

Sleeping & Eating

Booking accommodation ahead is always advisable in Venice.

A booming sector is the B&B business. A good number of B&Bs in Venice are listed at www.guestinitaly.com. The city's **APT tourist board** (www.turismovenezia.it) has some 200 B&Bs and 250 *affittacamere* (rooms for rent) on the books.

For camping, try **Marina di Venezia** (☎ 04 153 02 511; www.marinadivenezia .it; Via Montello 6, Punta Sabbioni; per person/tent €8.25/20.05) on the Litorale del Cavallino. This place has a private beach, shops, cinema, playground and bungalows. You can get the *vaporetto* from Punta Sabbioni to Fondamente Nuove (Cannaregio).

Ostello Venezia (☎ 04 152 38 211; venezia@ostellionline .it; Fondamenta della Croce 86, Giudecca; dm incl breakfast €20), the lone HI hostel in Venice, is located in a peaceful spot on Giudecca. Catch *vaporetto* 41, 42 or 82 to Zitelle from the train station or Piazzale Roma.

Locanda Casa Petrarca (☎ 04 152 00 430; www.casapetrarca.com; Calle delle Schiavine 4386; s/d €70/112, s/d with bathroom €95/135) is a family-run place high up in an ancient apartment building with six simple but sparkling rooms.

Hotel Galleria (☎ 04 152 32 489; www .hotelgalleria.it; Campo della Carità 878a; s/d without bathroom €80/120, d €165) is the only one-star hotel right on the Grand

ADRIATIC COAST

Canal near the Ponte dell'Accademia. Some rooms are canal-side.

Hotel Dalla Mora (☎ 04 171 07 03; www.hoteldallamora.it; Salizada San Pantalon, Santa Croce 42a; s/d €65/95) sits on a small canal just off Salizada San Pantalon. The hotel has clean, airy rooms, some with lovely canal views, and there is a terrace.

Venice is about the most expensive city in Italy for eating out, so you may find yourself resorting to *panini* or *tramezzini* (sandwich triangles) that cost around €2.

Search out little trattorias and *osterie* tucked along side lanes and canals away from the main tourist centres. A Venetian *osteria* is a cross between a bar and a trattoria, where you can usually sample *cicheti* (bar snacks), washed down with an *ombra* (small glass of wine). Some *osterie* also serve full sit-down meals.

Better areas to look include the backstreets of Cannaregio, San Polo and Castello. A sprinkling of good places can be found in Dorsoduro and the Giudecca.

Some stand-out places include: **Ristorante Oniga** (☎ 04 152 24 410; www .oniga.it; Campo San Barnaba 2852; meals €35), offering imaginative pasta firsts and a balance of fish and meat mains. You can dine on the square. **Osteria La Zucca** (☎ 04 152 41 570; Calle del Tentor, Santa Croce 1762; meals €30) is an excellent option for frustrated vegetarians. The menu is a Mediterranean mix and even the vegetable side orders are inspired and plentiful. Meat-eaters are also well catered to. **Ai Tre Scaini** (☎ 04 152 24 790; Calle Michelangelo 53c, Giudecca; meals €25) is 'the' popular local eatery. It's a no-nonsense place for seafood and other goodies in the Giudecca neighbourhood.

Getting There & Away

Marco Polo Airport, 12km northeast of Venice, is served by numerous domestic and international airlines.

The **Alilaguna** (☎ 04 152 35 775; www .alilaguna.com) airport fast-ferry costs €12 to/from Venice or Lido and €6 to/from Murano. Bikes are accepted as free luggage at the captain's discretion. You can pick it up at the Zattere, at Fondamente Nuove or near Piazza San Marco.

The *arancia* (orange) line runs from the Guglie stop via Madonna dell'Orto and Murano to the airport. A faster direct service (the gold line) from San Marco (stopping only at nearby San Zaccaria) costs €25 and runs eight times a day.

The standard water-taxi rate for the ride between Piazzetta di San Marco and Marco Polo airport is €45. To/from Lido costs €55. Keep an eye out for night and baggage surcharges. A group of up to four people could expect to pay around €90 for the ride to San Marco from the airport.

ATVO (☎ 041 38 36 72; www.atvo .it) buses run to the airport from Piazzale Roma (€3, 20 minutes, 27–30 daily). If your plans don't include Venice, Mestre is the closest place to catch a train headed somewhere else. ATVO's Fly Bus service regularly connects Marco Polo airport with Mestre's train.

Venice has two train stations. At the island city's western edge, **Venezia Santa Lucia** provides arriving tourists with immediate picture-postcard gratification, its broad steps descending directly to the Grand Canal. On the mainland north of the city is **Venezia Mestre**, which is a transfer point.

Stazione di Santa Lucia is linked by train to Padua (€2.70–€10, 30–40 minutes, 3 or 4 each hour), Verona (€6.10–€14, 1¼–2¼ hours, 2 each hour). Regular trains race further a field to Milan (€24, 2¾–3 hours), Bologna (€8.20–€21, 1 hour 20 minutes–2 hours 10 minutes), Florence (€15.90–€30, 3–4 hours) and many other cities. Cyclists wishing to stash their bikes can utilise the left luggage facility.

For cycling instructions for getting from Lido to Venice's Santa Lucia train station, see Day 4 (see p196) of the Ravenna to Venice ride. Cyclists whose religion doesn't permit other forms of transportation can pedal the congested and uninspiring few kilometres from Marco Polo airport to Mestre. At the airport exit, turn left on SS14 (Via Triestina). After 5km, veer left (south) at the junction with Via Martiri della Libertà, then turn right towards downtown Mestre on Viale San Marco and follow signs for the station.

THE SOUTH & SICILY

HIGHLIGHTS

- The diverse landscapes and minimal crowds of the **Gargano peninsula** (p231)
- **Puglia's** intriguing peasant architecture of *trulli* (conical stone houses) and *sassi* (cave dwellings) (see boxed text p225)
- The unspoilt forests and mountainous beauty of **Calabria's La Sila** region

SPECIAL EVENTS

- Musicale di Ravello & Wagner Festiva (July), Ravello
- Feast of Santa Maria della Bruna celebrants march through town carrying a statue of the Madonna in a cart (2 July), Matera
- Festival of Peschici's three patron saints, highlighted by a colourful procession through the Medieval quarter (early July), Peschici

CYCLING EVENTS

- Trofeo dell'Etna 200km road race around Mt Etna (March), Sicily
- Trofeo Pantalica 170km road race (March), near Syracuse, Sicily
- Giro della Provincia di Reggio Calabria 190km road race (March), northern Calabria

FOOD & DRINK SPECIALITIES

- *limoncello* (a bright-yellow, lemon liqueur with a hidden kick)

TERRAIN

The mainland's southern half is dominated by the mountainous Apennine range. The only significant plains are the Tavoliere di Puglia and the Pianura Campana around Mt Vesuvius.

Sicily is dominated by the massive Mt Etna to the east and the high ridges of the Peloritani, Nebrodi and Madonie Mountains to the north.

Telephone Codes – 08/09	www.discovertuscany.com/

THE SOUTH & SICILY

Every part of Italy's south offers a distinctly different cycling experience, each in its own way a rich and rewarding insight into a world far removed from the affluent tourist meccas of the north. Preconceptions of the *Mezzogiorno* (literally 'midday' and the name for the south of Italy) are often misguided and are usually fuelled by visions of a hostile, barren landscape and uncivilised backwaters where poverty and vicious Mafiaesque corruption have created a people insular and shuttered. The reality couldn't be more different. Areas of intense natural beauty, dotted with humble villages where the people are warm and generous of spirit, contrast with sophisticated and cultivated cities steeped in history. Some parts – such as the ritzy Amalfi Coast – are famous the world over, but for the most part the rides in this chapter endeavour to uncover hidden treasures that lie along the back roads, waiting to be discovered by the open eyes of relaxed cyclists.

CLIMATE

Sicily and the south have a mild Mediterranean climate, meaning hot, dry summers and short, mild winters with light rainfall. Spring and autumn are almost a toned-down extension of summer, so short is the winter. There can also be quite sharp differences in weather, caused both by the height of the larger mountains and the distance fron the sea. The finest weather is usually found around the coast, with summer temperatures in the mid-thirties and winter averages between 10 to 13°C. The hot sirocco wind blows during the six hottest months of the year, bringing Saharan sand to Sicily's southern and western coasts. The Tyrrhenian coast is usually shielded from the worst effects of the sirocco by the mountainous interior.

Inland, summer days are extremely dry and hot, with little or no respite until sundown – at altitude it can even get quite cold at night. During the short winters (December to February), the weather can be bitterly cold, especially after dark. Substantial snowfalls are common in mountain areas above 1500m. Calabria's La Sila region and the higher reaches of Sicily's Madonie and Nebrodi mountains are often snowbound in January. The upper reaches of Mt Etna can experience snow at almost any time of year.

CAMPANIA

Presided over by Naples, the only true metropolis in the Mezzogiorno, Campania is alive with myth and legend. Stories tell how sirens (sea nymphs) lured sailors to their deaths off Sorrento – how islands in the Gulf of Naples were the domain of mermaids – and how Lago d'Averno (Lake Avernus), in the Campi Flegrei, was believed in ancient times to be the entrance to the underworld.

In the shadow of Mt Vesuvius (Vesuvio; 1277m), southeast of Naples, lie the ruins of Pompeii and Herculaneum, Roman cities buried by the volcano, and the Greek temples of Paestum, among the best preserved in the world. Many writers have waxed lyrical about the natural beauty of the Amalfi Coast and the islands out in the Gulf of Naples, particularly Capri.

AMALFI COAST

Duration 2 days
Distance 81.5km
Difficulty moderate
Start Sorrento
Finish Salerno

Summary Join the sophisticated lovers of the Mediterranean coast as they stand in awe of this bit of coastline that no poet could have conjured. Thanks to your bike, your experience trumps that of any of the sports-car drivers zipping past.

Simply said, this is a sexy ride. The towns are sexy, the scenery is sexy and you feel sexy (barring lycra). This route is perfect for those of you who want to ride through jaw-dropping landscape by day and then sip Bellinis at upscale, ocean-view cafés by night as the sea breeze flutters your clothes against well-toned muscles. There's little to 'discover' on the Amalfi Coast – rather, the best plan of action is to embrace the well-established tourist infrastructure.

This route calls for tolerance of hordes of tourists. People flood the towns and traffic fills the roads. However, the species of tourist here, though decidedly posh, is notably relaxed and sophisticated (especially in appearance). If this doesn't fit your bill, there are a handful of other sparkling but more low-key coastal rides to enjoy in Italy.

Following the route, you'll be as close as safely possible to the cliff's edge, without having to sprout wings. Whether they're biking or driving, there is a sense that everyone is in awe. You know that the guy on that scooter going by is feeling something akin to your bicycle-borne ecstasy as he rushes along the road: a tar ribbon clinging impossibly to cliffs hundreds of metres above azure waters. Nonetheless, you savour the priceless perspective that pedalling is the ultimate way to experience this amazing road.

PLANNING
When to Cycle

Anytime from March to early July is prime. Though heat will be a factor in the warmer

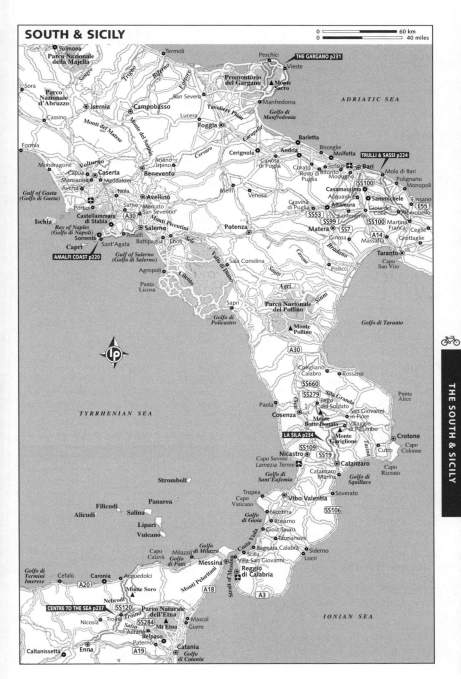

SOUTH & SICILY

0 ——————— 60 km
0 ——————— 40 miles

Sulmona
**Parco Nazionale
della Majella**
Termoli
Peschici
THE GARGANO p231
Vieste

Sora
**Parco
Nazionale
d'Abruzzo**
Isernia
**Promontorio
del Gargano**
▲**Monte
Sacro**

Cassino
Campobasso
San Severo
Manfredonia
ADRIATIC SEA

Formia
Monti del Matese
Lucera
Foggia
*Golfo di
Manfredonia*

Mondragone
Volturno
Caserta
Monti del Sannio
Tavoliere Plain
Barletta
Bisceglie
Molfetta
TRULLI & SASSI p224

Marcianise
Capua
Maddaloni
Nola
Benevento
Ariano
Irpino
Cervaro
Cerignola
Canosa
di Puglia
Andria
Corato
Ruvo di
Puglia
Terlizzi
Bitonto
Modugno
Mola di Bari
Bari
SS100
Polignano
Monopoli

Aversa
Avellino
Mercato
San Severino
Melfi
Venosa
Gravina
di Puglia
Casamassima
Acquaviva
Altamura
Santeramo
Sammichele
SS100
Cassano
Alberobello
E55

Ischia
Portici
Castellammare
di Stabia
Sarno
Monti Picentini
Salerno
Potenza
SS53
SS99
A14
Martina
Franca
Grottaglie
Ceglie

**Bay of Naples
(Golfo di Napoli)**
Sorrento
Capri
Sant'Agata
Amalfi
Battipaglia
Eboli
Sala Consilina
Matera
SS7
Massafra
Taranto
Capo
San Vito

AMALFI COAST p220
*Gulf of Salerno
(Golfo di Salerno)*
Agropoli
Sele
Valle di Diano
Sinno
Pisticci

*Gulf of Gaeta
(Golfo di Gaeta)*

Punta
Licosa
Cilento
**Parco Nazionale
del Pollino**
Golfo di Taranto

*Golfo di
Policastro*
Sapri
Agri
▲**Monte
Pollino**

A30

Congliano
Calabro
Rossano
Punta
Alice

TYRRHENIAN SEA
SS660
SS279
Sila Grande
Lago
del Soldato
San Giovanni
in Fiore
Paola
Cosenza
Monte
Botte Donato ▲
Villaggio
di Palumbo
Crotone
Capo
Colonne

LA SILA p234
Monte
Gariglione ▲
Cutro
Capo
Rizzuto

Nicastro
Lamezia Terme
Capo Suvero
SS109
SS19
Catanzaro
Catanzaro
Marina
*Golfo di
Squillace*

Stromboli
*Golfo di
Sant'Eufemia*

Tropea
Capo
Vaticano
Vibo Valentia
Soverato
SS106

Panarea
Filicudi
Salina
Alicudi
Nicotera
Rosarno
*Golfo
di Gioia*
Gioia Tauro

Lipari
Vulcano
Taurianova
Palmi
Costa Viola
Bagnara Calabra
Siderno
Locri

Capo
Calavà
Milazzo
*Golfo
di Milazzo*
*Golfo
di Patti*
Messina
Scilla
Villa San Giovanni
**Reggio
di Calabria**

*Golfo di
Termini
Imerese*
Cefalù
Caronia
Acquedolci
A20
▲**Monte Soro**
Nebrodi
Monti Peloritani
A18
Strait of Messina

CENTRE TO THE SEA p237
SS120
Troina
**Parco Naturale
dell'Etna**
A3

Nicosia
Troina
SS284
▲Mt Etna
Mascal
Giarre

Caltanissetta
Enna
A19
Salso
Adrano
Belpaso
Paterno
Catania
*Golfo
di Catania*
IONIAN SEA

THE SOUTH & SICILY

months, the rides are short and there are regular rest opportunities and facilities along the route. Weekends equate to major traffic congestion and potentially unpleasant riding conditions; avoid them. Anything you can do to avoid crowds – leaving early, visiting mid-week, travelling in the off-season – is highly recommended.

Maps

The Touring Club Italiano's (TCI) 1:200,000 *Campania & Basilicata* map covers the route.

GETTING THERE & AWAY
Sorrento (start)
BOAT

Alilauro's (☎ 16 660 02 02; www.alilauro .it Via F Caracciolo 11) fleet of *aliscafi* (hydrofoils) make the trip from Molo Beverello in Naples to Sorrento (€11.50/2 per person/ bike, every 2 hours).

BUS

Curreri (☎ 08 180 15 420; www.currerivi aggi.it) has a direct bus service to Sorrento from Naples' *Capodichino* airport (€10, 6 per day, 1 hour).

TRAIN

Regular trains on the **Circumvesuviana** line (☎ 08 177 22 444) make the trip to Sorrento (€3, every 20 to 40 minutes, 1 hour). There's no luggage space for roll-on bikes, and permission to board with one will depend upon who you ask. It's worth a try – if you pack it in a bike bag there should be no problem at all.

BICYCLE

Arriving at or departing the route area on your bicycle is possible, but it's not recommended. It's not worth it due to ever-present traffic and pollution, both in high levels.

Salerno (finish)
BUS

SITA (☎ 08 940 51 45) has buses for Naples (every 25 minutes, about 1 hour), leaving from outside **Bar Cioffi** (where you buy your ticket) at Corso Garibaldi 134. Buonotourist runs a weekday express service to Rome's Fiumicino airport, departing from Piazza della Concordia (also

stopping at EUR–Fermi Metropolitana in Rome). **Simet** (☎ 09 835 20 315) has two buses daily to Cosenza (4 hours) and one daily each to Rome (3 hours) and Naples (1 hour).

TRAIN

Salerno is also a major train stop linking Rome, Naples and Reggio di Calabria and is served by all types of trains. It also has good train links with both inland towns and the Adriatic Coast. There's a direct train to Cosenza (€11.21 plus €3.50 per bike, 3½ hours, 7 per day).

THE RIDE
Day 1: Sorrento to Positano
2–4 hours, 34.8km

The route to Positano gives you exposed views of Sorrento, the sea and islands jagging the horizon. During other ride sections the route winds down shade-dappled, forested roads. There will be just enough climbing today that you'll feel satisfied after 34.8km of riding. At the same time, the leniency of the route allows for tootling at a vacationer's pace.

The biggest ascent of the day, 4.4km, starts 9km into the route. Near the top of that climb is **Mira Capri** (12.9km) a pizzeria, restaurant and bar that has outdoor tables perfectly positioned for a fantastic view of the sea and city. It's a great place for a revitalizing cappuccino.

AMALFI COAST – DAY 1

CUES			GPS COORDINATES
0km	⬏	out of Sorrento tourist office	40°37'42"N 14°22'29"E
	⬏	Piazza S Antonio	
0.2	⬈	Corso Italia to Massa Lubrense	
6.4		Massa Lubrense	40°36'39"N 14°20'42"E
9	▲	4.4 km moderate to hard climb	
11.9		Termini	40°35'27"N 14°20'24"E
12.9	★	Mira Capri Restaurant/ Bar	
13.1	↑	to Sant'Agata on cobbled road	
14.8	⬑	to Sant'Agata, Costiera Amalficana	
15.2	⬋	to Sant'Agata	
17.6		Sant'Agata	40°36'22"N 14°22'28"E
17.8	⬈	to Positano, Sorrento	
18	⬈	to 'Amalfi, Positano'	
18.6	⬋	to 'Positano'	
24.8	⬈	to 'Positano, Amalfi'	
32.7	⬈	to ' Positano, centro'	
34.8		Positano, Piazza dei Mulini	40°37'40"N 14°29'06"E

AMALFI COAST

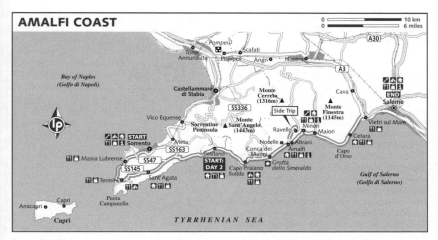

0 — 10 km
0 — 6 miles

Day 1: Amalfi Coast

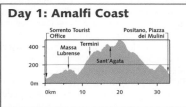

The route then heads east, with the imposing grey cliffs and rugged mountains towering above the distant Amalfi Coast, and it rejoins the SS145 just beyond Sant'Agata (17.6km). After swooping down in a blinding rush of twists and switchbacks, the road leads you to the SS163 (24.8km), the Amalfi Coast road proper. The final run into Positano is truly exhilarating, as the narrow road teeters on almost-sheer cliffs hundreds of metres above the sea – a perilous frolic indeed, were it not for the secure retaining wall and unobtrusive mesh barrier. The dramatic landscape provokes a sense of unearthliness.

Close to Positano, fruit and vegetable stands flank the road and sell *granita* (fresh lemon slush). The final bit on the road into town is narrow and it acts as a pedestrian, cyclist, car and scooter thoroughfare. Ride defensively.

Day 2: Positano to Salerno
2½–5 hours, 46.7km

Today continues merrily along the Amalfi Coast, albeit closer to sea level than before.

AMALFI COAST – DAY 2

CUES			GPS COORDINATES
0km		Positano, Piazza dei Mulini	
			40°37'40"N 14°29'06"E
	↱	uphill from Piazza Mulini	
0.5	↱	to Salerno	
5.2		Praiano	40°36'43"N 14°31'25"E
10.8	★	Grotto dello Smeraldo	
15.6	◉↰	to 'Salerno' uphill	
		Amalfi	40°38'01"N 14°36'08"E
16.3		Atrani	40°38'09"N 14°36'33"E
[17	●●↰	Ravello side trip	
19.4		Minori	40°39'04"N 14°37'32"E
20.5		Maiori	40°38'54"N 14°38'25"E
21.6	▲	2.5km moderate-hard climb	
30.7		Cetara	40°38'52"N 14°42'02"E
36		Vietri su Mare	40°40'22"N 14°43'41"E
	↘	to 'Salerno'	
40	↱	to 'Salerno,' following cobbled road	
	↱	(50meters) to 'Salerno'	
40.3	↑	to 'centro'	
40.5	↘	at fork to 'Salerno'	
42.1	↗	to 'Centro'	
	↗	(40m) to 'centro'	
44.7	◉↑	to 'centro'	
44.8	↰	to 'centro'	
46.6	↰	to 'stazione'	
46.7		Salerno train station & tourist office	
			40°40'31"N 14°46'21"E

It's a short day with rolling elevation (excluding the optional side trip to Ravello at 17.2km), allowing time for lazy beach and coffee stops and the odd walk. You can visit the Grotte dello Smeraldo (Cave of the Emerald) at 10.8km, a spectacular limestone cave accessed by boat via a lift at road level.

Amalfi (15.6km), Atrani, Minori and Maiori form an almost continuous stretch of built-up, yet somehow picturesque, coastal resort towns. **Amalfi** is by far the best known, being one of Italy's most popular seaside holiday destinations. It was a major naval superpower in the 11th century, and its navigation tables, the **Tavole Amalfitana**, formed the world's first maritime code.

The low-key fishing village of **Cetara** (30.7km) is a nice change from the flashier coastal towns. From here to Salerno traffic increases incrementally, especially in the late afternoon. After passing through **Vietri sul Mare** (36km), where many workshops and showrooms display the town's renowned ceramics, the road drops down to the Salerno port area, and an easy ride along the busy esplanade leads to day's end. Coming into town, you'll think you've gone the wrong way – and maybe you have because it's rather confusing – but the route loops north along a busy road before dumping you onto the esplanade. If you don't want to deal with Salerno traffic, a great alternative is to hop onto a bus going into the city from Vietri sul Mare.

Day 2: Amalfi Coast

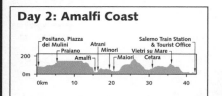

SIDE TRIP: RAVELLO
1½ hours, at 17km, 10.6km RT

For those craving their daily climbing fix, the 5.3km climb through lush ravines on the side trip to Ravello will reward with spectacular views down to Amalfi, Maiori, Minori and the coast beyond. The *duomo* (cathedral) in Piazza Vescovado dates from the 11th century. It houses an impressive marble pulpit and a free museum in the crypt. Other highlights include the 13th-century Villa Rufolo and its gardens and terrace. The villa has housed several popes and was later home to the German composer, Wagner. **Villa Cimbrone** also boasts

beautiful gardens, and the city's three vineyards can all be visited; ask for more information at the tourist office.

PUGLIA

The 'spur' and 'heel' of Italy's boot, Puglia is bordered by two seas, the Adriatic to the east and the Ionian to the south. Its strategic position as the peninsula's maritime gateway to the east made it a major thoroughfare and a target for colonisers and invaders.

The ancient Greeks founded Magna Graecia, a string of settlements along the Ionian coast. Brindisi marks the end of the Roman Via Appia (see p39), which was completed around 190 BC and ran all the way to Rome. The Norman legacy is seen in magnificent Romanesque churches across the region. Foggia and its province were favoured by the great Swabian king, Frederick II, several of whose castles remain. Spanish colonisers have also left their architectural mark, particularly in the province of Lecce.

Puglia's predominant flatness makes it ideal cycling territory. In any case, pedal power offers a passage into many out-of-the-way parts of the province and can open otherwise closed doors into the world of the innately friendly southern Italians. Another indirect advantage is that cycling creates an appetite, and perhaps nowhere in Italy is the produce as fresh and the food as good as it is in Puglia.

TRULLI & SASSI

Duration 3 days
Distance 237.5km
Difficulty easy–moderate
Start/Finish Bari
Summary Flat riding on rural back roads past surreal architectural anomalies in stark, inspiring landscapes just got better: the food of Puglia makes your eyes roll back.

This is one of southern Italy's few easy rides, starting and finishing in Puglia's capital, Bari, and traversing the region's

THE SOUTH & SICILY

broad inland plains known as the Murge. It's mostly flat, but the landscape manages to inspire rather than bore. It touches down in Basilicata, visiting Matera's once infamous *sassi*, then discovers the landscapes dotted with intriguing *trulli*. These quaint, conical-roofed stone houses dot the richly cultivated countryside of the Murge (between Noci and Locorotondo), a region with a justly deserved reputation as the 'garden of Italy'.

PLANNING
When to Cycle

Summer heat can be oppressive in Puglia, especially out on the open plains of the Murge. Ideal riding times are March to July and September to November. If riding in the warmer months, plan to make an early departure to allow for siesta time during the hottest part of the day.

Maps

TCI's 1:200,000 *Puglia* map is fine, covering all but one or two of the minor roads (which aren't shown on any other available maps of the area either).

GETTING THERE & AWAY
Bari (start/finish)
AIR

Bari's **Palese airport** (BRI; ☎ 08 058 35 200; www.seap-puglia.it) is located 10km west of the city centre. It is serviced by a host of international, domestic and budget airlines. To get to the airport, take a train or the **Cotrap** bus (€4.15). Taxis wait outside the airport and the trip into town costs around €20, but you might have to search a bit to find one willing to shuttle a bike box.

BOAT

Bari's **port** (www.porto.bari.it) is the principal port in the Adriatic. Ferries run to

---

TRULLI

Trulli are circular or cube-shaped, stone houses, conical-roofed and whitewashed, and built entirely without mortar. Their roofs are tiled with concentric rows of *chiancarelle* (evenly-shaped slate pieces) and topped with pinnacles or spheres, which are often painted with astrological or religious symbols. Their origin is obscure, with suggestions of a connection to the Nuraghe of Sardinia, the bories of France and other similar structures in parts of Spain and Turkey.

The mortarless construction reputedly enabled feudal lords to deny the exploited peasants who tilled their lands any civil rights, by conveniently moving them on whenever necessary. Another theory is that the dry construction enabled rapid dismantling and rebuilding of the *trulli*, thereby sidestepping decrees forbidding the construction of towns by feudal lords without express royal permission, and avoiding heavy imposts levelled on urban collectives.

The *trulli* area is in the Itria Valley. It extends from Conversano and Gioia del Colle in the west to Ostuni and Martina Franca in the east. The greatest concentration of *trulli* is in and around Alberobello.

Within the more commercialised quarter of Rione Monti, on the south side of Alberobello, more than 1000 *trulli* cascade down the hillside. To its east, on the other side of Via Indipendenza, is Rione Aia Piccola, with 400 *trulli* still mostly used as family dwellings. In the modern part of town, the 16th-century **Trullo Sovrano** (☎ 08 043 25 482; Piazza Sacramento) has been converted into a small museum.

Greece, Albania, Croatia and Montenegro. Bicycles normally travel free.

THE SOUTH & SICILY

Day 1: Trulli & Sassi

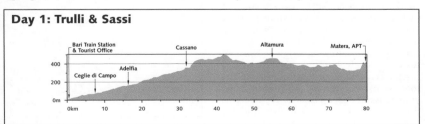

BUS

The **Ferrovie Appulo–Lucane** (☎ 08 057 25 229; www.fal-srl.it, in Italian) services Altamura (€2.60, 1 hour, hourly) and Matera (€4, 1 hour 20 minutes, 10 daily). The south of Puglia is serviced by the **Ferrovie del Sud-Est** (☎ 08 054 62 111; www.fseonline .it, in Italian). Every hour its tiny trains head for some of the most tourist-filled towns in Puglia, like Alberobello (€4, 1 hour 50 minutes) and Martina Franca (€4.60, 2 hours 10 minutes).

TRAIN

Being a transportation hub, Bari has buses to just about anywhere, but riding the train is easier with a loaded bike. The train system out of Bari can be confusing due to the various private and state railway services that operate. Note that Puglia is proudly the only region in Italy without the extra bike charge on its trains!

On Piazza Aldo Moro you'll find the **main train station** (☎ 08 052 44 386; www .trenitalia.com), which is serviced by mainline trains connecting Bari with Milan (1st/ 2nd class €82/61, 8–9½ hours), Rome (€35, 5 hours) and Foggia (€10.40, 1½ hours), where you can connect to Malfredonia and the start of the Gargano ride. Be aware that bikes cannot be taken on *Eurostar* trains unless disassembled and packed (see boxed text p297). There are also trains to towns to the south like Brindisi (€6.80, 1¼ hours) and Lecce (€11.60, 1½–2hours).

THE RIDE
Day 1: Bari to Matera
4½–8 hours, 78km

Today involves an almost imperceptible climb from sea level to 400m. Escaping Bari's urban congestion is relatively quick and pain-free, with traffic thinning out after only a few kilometres. Beyond **Ceglie del Campo** (7.5km) – where you can pick up supplies from the morning produce market – the route heads south through olive groves to Adelfia (15.2km), a small rural town boasting an original Norman tower, a lovely baroque *palazzo* with a clocktower, and a baroque archway to the town's historic centre. Beyond Adelfia, your sense of space becomes expansive as the horizon stretches on forever and the

TRULLI & SASSI – DAY 1

CUES			GPS COORDINATES
Start		Bari tourist office by train station	
			41°07'34"N 16°52'20"E
0km	↰	Head east of station on Via Zuppetta	
0.4	↰	at T unsigned	
	↱	(40m) Hard right at Piazza Luigi de Savoia	
		to underpass	
0.6	↱	at T	
	↰	(60m) Viale Unita d'Italia, to 'Stadio'	
1.8	↱	Via Luigi Sturzo (which becomes Papa Giovanni)	
2.3	↰	Guilio Petroni	
4.9	◎	to 'Carbonara, ospedale'	
5.0	◎	to 'Carbonara, ospedale'	
5.8	↑	Continue straight at intersection	
7.5		Ceglie di Campo	41°03'53"N 16°51'41"E
12.9	↘	to 'Adelfia'	
15.3	↰	to 'Adelfia'	
15.8	↑	to 'centro' at stop sign	

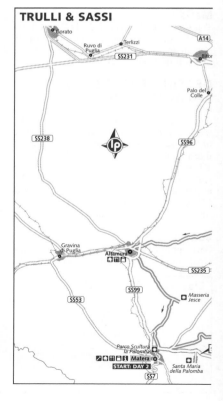

TRULLI & SASSI

CUES CONTINUED			GPS COORDINATES
16.2		Adelfia	41°00'14"N 16°52'05"E
	⌐→	at clocktower	
16.8	⌐→	to 'Birtitto'17	
	↘	to 'Cassona' SP16	
24.5	↑	'to Cassano' (at 'Stop' sign)	
31.2	↑⊙	'to Cassano'	
31.6		Cassano	40°53'30"N 16°46'16"E
	↰	at T intersection	
31.7	⌐→	'to Matera, Santeramo'	
32	↰	'to Matera, Santeramo'	
34.1	⌐→	'to Altamura'	
53.3	↑🏠	uphill	
53.8	⌐→	'to Bari, Matera, Gravina'	
54.2	↰	'to Matera, Gravina'	
54.9		Altamura	40°49'46"N 16°33'15"E
54.9	↘	'Matera, Corato'	
55.1	↰	Viale Martiri (not to 'Matera' to the right)	
55.7	⌐→	Tutte la direzioni, Via Carpintino	
56.5	↑	to Laterza	

CUES CONTINUED			GPS COORDINATES
63.4	↑	to Laterza	
66.1	↰	to Matera SS9	
	●●↑	to side trip to Massuria Jesce up on left 2.6km RT.	
69	↑	to Matera	
72.4	↰	to Matera SS7	
75.5	⌐→	to Matera	
	★	Parco Scultura la Palomba	
	●●↰	to Santuario S Maria della Palomba	
	⌐→	(1.6km) take first right after 20m	
	⌐→	(0.3km) entrance is on the right}	
75.5	↰	to 'Centro'	
	▲	.8km moderate climb	
76.5	↑	at stop sign to Palazzo Lanfrachi	
77.1	↗	merging with main road (Via Nazionale)	
77.5	↑	following information icon	
77.9	⌐→	following info icon on Via Roma	
	⌐→	(10 meters) following info icon	
78	↰	following info icon	
		Matera, APT on left	40°40'02"N 16°36'06"E

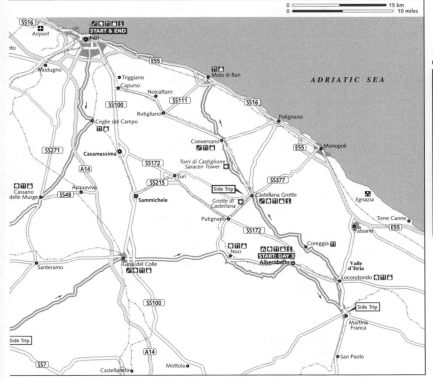

THE SOUTH & SICILY

rock-strewn land is given over to vineyards and fruit orchards.

Cassano delle Murge (30.1km) has a good little bakery, signposted just as you enter the town. Beyond Cassano the minor road is a patchwork of repaired potholes. It's a little rough in places, but pleasant distractions are plentiful in this silent and harshly beautiful landscape of olive groves corralled by rock walls, and vast empty fields stretching away into a distant, hazy horizon.

Altamura (54.9km) is a large rural centre, and negotiating its maze of one-way streets can be confounding. The city's origins date back to Trojan times, but it's the 13th-century **Cattedrale Vergine Assunta** that is of interest. The cathedral is in the old town's main street, Via Federico II di Svevia. Also, don't miss out on Altamura's regionally famous bread (*pane di Altamura*), which will send you straight into carb-loading heaven. Its hard exterior shields soft, thick insides that have an ever-so-slight hint of spice, maybe cinnamon. The route passes right by a few bakeries.

For a few short kilometres, the route traces the original Via Appia Antica (Appian Way), roughly between 60 and 70km, but visions of Roman centurions with clanging shields and sandalled feet quickly dissipate within the roar of traffic that's not particularly heavy, but fast-moving. The route passes **Parco Scultura la Palomba** (75.5km; www.parcoscultTuralapalomba.it), an intriguing display of gigantic, surreal works of art. Barinese Antonio Paradiso is in charge of this project that combines his scientific experience in anthropology and palaeontology with visual art.

The final run up to the day's end at Matera involves one uphill grunt.

SIDE TRIP: MASSERIA JESCE
30 minutes–1hour, at 66.1km, 2.6km RT
This whole region is dotted with *masserias*,

or old Italian farmhouses, that used to be the nuclei of rural farming communities. Many of them have been converted into *agriturismi* (farm stay accommodation). However, **Masseria Jesce**, once a medieval agricultural centre, has definitely not been converted to anything. Rather, it has given time free reign to dilapidate it into a fascinating relic. Believed to have been built between 1400 and 1550, this massive stone structure was intended to be a point of fortification for the community against possible threats brewing in an unsettled countryside.

Though the government intends it to be a historical site for tourists, that project has not manifested and you can wander about this decrepit edifice freely while taking in the stark landscape and imagining what it once must have been like.

SANTUARIO SANTA MARIA DELLA PALOMBA
30 minutes–one hour, at 75.5km, 1.6km RT
Once frequented by vagrants and shepherds who visited the frescoed Madonna Odigitria, this **cave church** (☎ 08 353 30 287; Contrada Pedale della Palomba) dates back to the Byzantine era. Now there is a more recent church structure attached to what used to be just a sanctuary carved out of the cliff, but you can still go and visit the eerie cave portions of this truly provocative structure.

There are hiking trails into the gorge from the courtyard to other minor cave churches if you are up for that additional exercise. After the left turn off the route at 75.5km, follow signs to the church.

Day 2: Matera to Alberobello
4–7 hours, 71.1km
The first half of today's ride heads back across the broad, gently rolling plains of the western Murge. Once you turn off the main

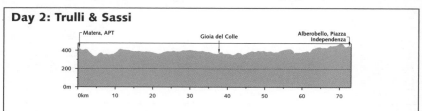

Day 2: Trulli & Sassi

TRULLI & SASSI – DAY 2

CUES			GPS COORDINATES
Start		Matera, APT	40°40'02"N 16°36'06"E
0km		head downhill	
	⌐	(20 meters) on De Viti de Marco	
	⌐	(20 meters) on Via Roma	
0.3	⌐	at T at Stazione Matera	
	⌐ 🚉	(30m) Viale Aldo Moro	
0.5	↗	Via Rosselli	
0.9	⌐ ◎	Via Stigliani, to 'Bari, Taranto'	
2.8	⌐ 🚉	'to Bari, Taranto'	
2.9	⌐	to 'Taranto, Santeramo'	
3.1	⌐	to 'Santeramo'	
6.5	↖	to 'Gioia del Colle'	
17.6	⌐	to 'Gioia del Colle'	
20.7	↑	to 'Gioia del Colle' at stop sign	
36.8	↖	to 'Gioia del Colle' centro	
37.1	⌐	to 'centro' at stop sign	
37.8	↖	to 'Bari'	
		Gioia del Colle	40°47'55"N 16°55'22"E
38.7	◎	First exit to 'Noci'	
39.9	◎ ↖	to 'Noci'	
40.8		at intersection, follow signs to Noci	
40.9	↘	@ fork to 'Noci'	
56.9	⌐	to Motolla	
	↑	if you want to go to Noci centro	
57.2	◎ ↖	to 'Motolla'	
57.6	↑	to 'Motolla'	
58.1	↖	to 'Martina Franca'	
58.4	⌐	to Martina Franca'	
59.6	↑	to Martina Franca'	
60	↘	NOT To Martina Franca, unsigned road	
	★	Vineria Barsento on Left, winery and restaurant	
64.6	↖	at T intersection at stop sign	
65	⌐	at white Trullo	
67	↖	at fork	
70	↑	to Centro at stop sign	
70.3	↘	to centro	
70.7	↙	Via C Battisti	
70.9	⌐	at intersection	
71.1		Alberobello, Piazza Independenza	40°46'57"N 17°14'17"E

road out of Matera, the soft hues of tilled soil and wheat crops mark the long stretch to Gioia del Colle. On warm days the silence may be broken by bizarre, squeaking crickets that do a masterful imitation of derailleur pulleys in dire need of oil. Don't be surprised if you do a time-warp double-take as you pass a mule and cart.

Gioia del Colle (37.8km) is a large rural town with a supermarket, a green-grocer and several bars in the central piazza. From there, it's a straight shot to the turn-off near **Noci**, which leads to possibly the most pleasant part of the day through picturesque trulli territory on other quiet back roads. It's a gentle cruise to day's end at Alberobello.

Day 3: Alberobello to Bari
5–9 hours, 88km

The last day might be the best of all, as the countryside becomes lusher and you wind your way via back roads through *trulli* country. This day is a juicy example of why bicycle touring is one of the best ways to travel. In Alberobello, mobs of tourists flood in to see the *trulli*, and locals present them like appetizers. But roaming the rural countryside, you'll see the *trulli* and realise how they blend with the well-tended orchards and vineyards of the vast landscape. You get a sense of what it might have been like to live in a *trullo* hundreds of years ago.

A short pedal north of **Martina** is **Locorotondo** (17.5km), a completely circular town perched on a hill above the **Valle dei Trulli**. It takes only a minor diversion to access the charming, rambling streets and alleys of the centre, and it's well worth the effort. It also offers a couple of fine restaurants serving delicious home-style food using the freshest local produce.

Leaving Locorotondo, the route continues to roll along quiet roads through undulating farmland marked by a noticeable absence of *trulli*. After the little one-bar

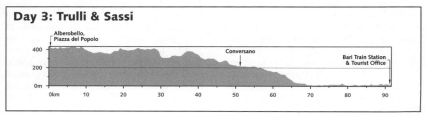

Day 3: Trulli & Sassi

Alberobello, Piazza del Popolo — Conversano — Bari Train Station & Tourist Office

(400 / 200 / 0m; 0km–90km)

TRULLI & SASSI – DAY 3

CUES		GPS COORDINATES
Start		Alberobello, Piazza del Popolo 40°47'06"N 17°14'21"E
0km		Head Downhill on Fausto Arturo Cucci (flanks park on west)
0.1	↰	@ T unsigned 'Largo Martellotta'
0.7	◎↑	to 'Locorotondo'
0.8	↰	to 'Locorotondo'
	↱	to 'Locorotondo'
1.5	↱	to 'Ristorante/Pizzeria di Puglia, Green Park'
2	↰	Strada Aquarulo
9	↰	to "martina Franca" at stop sign
9.5	↘	to 'Martina Franca'
12	↰	to 'Locorotondo' (at 'Stop' sign)
	{ ↱ ●● Martina Franca 4km ↺ }	
12.2	↰	minor road before white trullo, Cupa Rampone Strada
15.7	↑	stay left of train line
16.7	↱	uphill @ T intersection
17.0	↰🚲	'to Fasano'
	●●↑	to Locorotondo centro
17.8	↘	not to Fasano
18.5	↑	'to Contrada San Marco' (right of little church) SP 162
18.6	↰	'to Contrade Catuscio Nunzio' (white sign) SC 190
23.4	↙	no sign at roughly hewn roundabout
24.2	↰	unsigned (green gate on drive-way to the right)
25	↱	at T intersection, at stop sign
25.8	↑	Viale Serenissima (at 'Stop' light)
28.3	↰	'to Castellana Grotte, Putignano'
28.9	↑	'to Putignano' (at 'Stop' sign)
31.6	↱	rock-walled lane, trullo on right
37.4	↘	@ fork
38.9	↰	'to Castellana Grotte'
39.1	↱	'to Monopoli, Polignano a Mare'
	↑	to Castellana Grotte cenrto
	{ ↑ ●● Grotte di Castellana 6.6km ↺ }	
39.4	↰	'to Monopoli, Polignano a Mare'
39.8	↰	'to Brindisi, Monopoli, Polignano a Mare'

CUES CONTINUED		GPS COORDINATES
40.5	↱	'to Monopoli, Brindisi' (at 'Stop' sign)
	↰	(50m) 'to Polignano'
40.7	↰	'to Polignano a Mare'
40.8	↱	'to Polignano' (at 'Stop' sign)
41.7	↰	Via Vecchia, 'to Conversano'
43.1	↑	'to Torre Castiglione'
46.2	↱	'to Conversano'
	{ ●● Saracen tower 1km ↺ }	
48		small road, industrial buildings on right
50.2	↱	at T intersection
50.7	↱	at T intersection
50.8	↰	at T intersection
50.9	↑◎	'to Conversano centro'
51.2		Conversano 40°58'03"N 17°07'02"E
51.5	↱	at T intersection, 'to Bari'
51.8	↑◎	'to Bari, Rutigliano'
52.2	↑	Via Bari (white sign)
53.2	◎	2nd exit, 'to Rutigliano'
53.3	↱	to 'Centro de Vallorizzazione'
57.2	↰	'to Mola'
57.8	↱	'to Mola'
58.5	↱	'to Mola'
63.3	↰	at T intersection
64.4	↱	to 'Cozze' (not to Stadio)
	↑	to centro di Mola di Bari
65.6	↑	at T intersection at waterfront
67.8	↑	to 'Torre de Mare'
69.6	◎↑	to Torre de Mare (don't get on highway)
74.7	↱	Strada Scizze (right before highway entrance)
77.9	↱	.3km of gravel (head under arched overpass)
78.2	↱	Via Abate Eustaso at stop sign
78.4	↰🚲	to 'Bari Lungomare'
86.7	↰🚲	to 'Stazione, Centro' Via Corso Cavour
87.5	↱🚲	Via Prospero Petroni
87.7	↰	Pedestrian/bike thruway, across from Piazza Umberto
88	◎	Bari, Stazione and APT tourist office 41°07'35"N 16°52'20"E

village of **Coreggia** (25.8km), the route heads onto busier roads, skirting **Castellana Grotte** (39.1km) and beginning the long, loping descent to the Adriatic Coast at **Mola di Bari** (64.4km) via **Conversano** (51.2km). Take the short 1km round-trip side trip to the Saracen tower **Torre di Castiglione** (46.2km).

From Mola di Bari, the route is flat and moderately built up, and it hugs the coast for the most part. Traffic density will vary somewhat depending on the time of day and season, but it will increase from what you've been accustomed to over the last couple of days, especially as you get closer

to Bari. On the coastal stretch coming into Bari is a strip where locals buy cheap, fresh seafood and produce.

SIDE TRIP: MARTINA FRANCA
1 hour, at 12km, 4km RT

The short side trip to Martina Franca offers the chance to admire its well-maintained old quarter boasting some fine examples of baroque architecture. Founded in the 10th century by refugees fleeing the Arab invasion of Taranto, Martina Franca flourished from the 14th century, when it was granted tax exemptions (*franchigie*, hence the name Franca) by Philip of Anjou.

SIDE TRIP: GROTTE DI CASTELLANA
2–3hours, At 39.1, 6.6km return

These spectacular **limestone caves** (☎ 08 049 98 211; www.grottedicastellana.it; Piazzale Anelli) form Italy's longest natural, subterranean network. The interlinked galleries, with their breathtaking stalactite and stalagmite formations, were first explored in the 1930s by the speleologist Franco Anelli: today's visitors can follow his route in a guided group. After trudging down 265 steps (or taking the elevator) to a huge cavern known as La Grave, you pass through a series of caves, culminating in the magnificent **Grotta Bianca**.

The caves are only about 2km southwest of the main town and are well signposted. They're open 8.30am–7pm daily, with tours on the hour. Bikes can be left at **Hotel Autostello's** private car park (next to the caves' entrance) at no cost if you purchase lunch at the hotel.

THE GARGANO

Duration 2 days
Distance 166.5km
Difficulty moderate–demanding
Start/Finish Manfredonia
Summary In between bustling enclaves of beachgoers on the coast, you have a spectacular coastal ride. Inland, you'll have diverse landscapes and wildernesses practically to yourself.

This circuit of Puglia's surprisingly unspoilt Gargano Promontory, the 'spur' of the Italian boot, hugs the coast one day and traverses the mountainous interior the next. The ride passes through a rich and amazingly varied landscape of stark limestone terrain, cliffs falling to the sea, ancient forests and beautiful beaches. It's a truly special place, and since public transportation here is not the most convenient, you as the cyclist have the unrivalled opportunity to explore this marvellous territory (while others look at you wistfully through the windows of vehicles).

While parts of the promontory bustle with tourists in summer, it doesn't suffer from overcrowding or gross overdevelopment. The visitors seem to cluster and leave you the beautiful remainder. A midway stopover in the lovely little cliff-top village of Peschici offers seaside lazing and the option to access the superb beech and oak woods of the Foresta Umbra. The terrain is hilly and the two days relatively long and arduous, but opportunities abound for those wishing to linger longer.

You could describe the Gargano as the low-key, second cousin of the Amalfi Coast, where you can experience a dramatic coastline without the dramatic crowds.

ENVIRONMENT
The Gargano Promontory was formed somewhere between 70 and 180 million years ago, and is predominantly composed of dolomite, limestone and sedimentary rock. Traces of human habitation date back to the Neolithic Age.

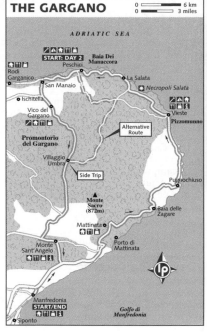

THE GARGANO

THE SOUTH & SICILY

Parco Nazionale del Gargano includes the marine reserves of the Tremite archipelago and covers 120,000 hectares. The park is home to a wide variety of important plant and animal species, such as the 61 species of orchid (the highest concentration in Europe). There are 27,000 hectares of predominantly broad-leaf forest (Italy's largest), where 79 tree species such as the beech, ilex (holm oak), Turkey oak, cerris, ash and elm thrive. Coastal areas are dominated by native pines and Mediterranean maquis.

Significant and endangered native animal and bird species include the *capriolo italico* (Italy's own roe deer), which inhabits the Foresta Umbra, the *gallina prataiola* (a small native bustard) found on the dry fields of the foothills, and the *picchio dorsobianco* (a small white-backed woodpecker). The native wildcat, several other species of woodpecker, peregrine and lanner falcons, buzzards, kestrels, owls (including the rare eagle owl) and sparrow hawks also thrive in the sanctuary of the park.

PLANNING
When to Cycle

While the tourist flocks and high prices of the summer peak in August are best avoided, the beach aspect can be enjoyed during any of the warmer months. The promontory also offers pleasant cycling in spring and autumn, but winters are cold, wet (especially on the northern side) and windy on the coast. If you're riding on the weekend you'll run into more lycra-ed cyclists than vrooming vehicles.

The Gargano is sprinkled with lodging and lots of camp sites (check out www.camping.it), so this route can be extended into any number of enjoyable days. And don't be afraid to explore roads off the route.

Maps

TCI's 1:200,000 *Puglia* map covers the ride.

GETTING TO/FROM THE RIDE
Manfredonia (start/finish)
BUS

Taking a bus means you don't have to change trains, but there are only two daily SITA buses (€12, 1½ hours), leaving from Bari's ATS Viaggi office. Ferrovia del Gargano and SITA also operate regular services between Foggia and Manfredonia (€3.40; 2 hours; frequent).

TRAIN

Trains connect Manfredonia with Foggia (€3 per bike and person; 30 minutes; 5 daily; tickets from Bar Impero, opposite the station), where FS services for many major cities stop, including Bari (€15, 1½ hours).

THE RIDE
Day 1: Manfredonia to Peschici
5–9 hours, 86km

This is a longish day accented by a number of climbs. The first, at 11.9km, is a moderate 3km at 5% not far out of Manfredonia. After skirting **Mattinata** (18.7km) the road is smooth and wide, rising and falling dramatically as it negotiates the rugged coastline, offering sensational panoramas down to the gleaming waters of the Adriatic.

The south coast of the promontory is noticeably drier and the vegetation sparser than on the northern side, so noon heat should be avoided. Rest assured, shady coastal pines bring welcome relief beyond 35km. There are numerous bars, restaurants, hotels and camping villages (many of which are seasonal) dotting the route, so rest stops and accommodation options are never far away.

Vieste (60.3km) is a bright and very popular seaside resort, loaded with tourist facilities and boasting some great beaches. The **IAT tourist office** (☎ 08 847 08 806; Piazza Kennedy) is an excellent source of information on the national park and

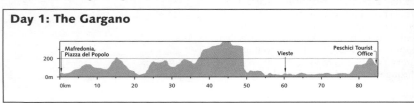

Day 1: The Gargano

Mafredonia, Piazza del Popolo — Vieste — Peschici Tourist Office

200

0m

0km   10   20   30   40   50   60   70   80

THE GARGANO – DAY 1

CUES		GPS COORDINATES
start	Mafredonia, Piazza del Popolo	41°37'46"N 15°55'03"E
0km	north on Corso Manfredi	
0.3	↰ Via Vettor Pisani	
0.4	↱ Via Tribuna	
1.9	↗ to 'Mattinata'	
11.9	↱ 'to Monte S Angelo'	
	▲ 3km moderate climb	
17.9	↱ 'to Vieste'	
18.2	↗ to 'Mattinata'	
18.7	↑ to 'Litoranea, Vieste'	
or	↰ to Mattinata Centro	
22.3	▲ 2.3km moderate climb	
29	↱ to 'Vieste'	
29.9	pensione & camping	
31.5	Villa Scapone	
35.4	▲ 2.3km hard climb	
39.7	▲ 3.6km moderate climb	
49.5	camping village	
60	↱ to 'centro, port'	
60.3	↱ Corso Lorenzo Fazzini	
	★ Vieste	41°53'02"N 16°10'36"E
60.6	↘ Piazza Kennedy, to 'Porto'	
60.9	↑ keep to road above coast	
61.9	↱🅷 Peschici Litoranea	
70.3	★ Necropoli Salata	
78.3	▲ 5.2km moderate-hard climbing	
	(1km break in middle of climb)	
85.9	↱ to info icon Via Petrini	
	Peschici	
86	Peschici Tourist Office on corner of Piazza San Antonio	41°56'50"N 16°00'51"E

places of interest on the promontory. Worth a look in the medieval quarter are the **Chianca Amara** (Bitter Stone), where thousands were beheaded when the Turks sacked Vieste in the 16th century, and the **Museo Malacologico**, exhibiting a collection of seashells from around the world.

On the flat stretch leaving town, the road passes an endless chain of unobtrusive, low-level camping villages. At 70.3km there's a **small Roman ruin** on the left near the church. At 71.8km (100m along the entrance road to Camping Spiaggia Lunga), **Sinergie** (☎ 08 847 06 635; www .agenziasinergie.it) conducts guided tours of the **Necropoli Salata**, underground tombs and burial grounds representing the earliest evidence of Christianity in the region.

There are plenty of secluded bays and little beaches to explore along the final stretch to Peschici, which includes a series of short, steep pinches and one last hefty climb at 78.3km to test weary legs.

Day 2: Peschici to Manfredonia
4½–8 hours, 80.5km

After a short roll along the coast, today's route heads inland and upward, starting with a hard 6km, then levelling out for a further 1km or so to **Vico del Gargano** (18.8km), a major agricultural centre. Encompassing two more moderate yet long climbs, the road maintains the exposed ridgeline, affording superb views down to Peschici and the coast before plunging into the leafy depths of the **Foresta Umbra**. A short side trip (32km) to **Villaggio Umbra** leads to a museum and nature centre, and the leafy surrounds of the picnic areas, kiosk and restaurant nearby make an ideal rest stop.

Back on the promontory's southern side, the vegetation becomes markedly thinner and drier, slowly giving way to more open farmland as the road drops into the steep Valle Carbonara. The forbidding switchback up to **Monte Sant'Angelo** looks worse than it is, and after a steady, but exposed, 5km climb you're in the town (60.7km).

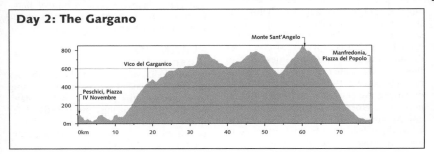

Day 2: The Gargano

THE GARGANO – DAY 2

CUES		GPS COORDINATES
start	Peschici, Piazza IV Novembre	41°56'51"N 16°00'52"E
⌐→	Corso Umbert 1	
0.1	↰ to 'Rodi Garganico,' Corso Garibaldi	
1.5	⌐→ 'to Rodi Garganico'	
2.7	↘ to ' Vico del Gargano'	
3.9	▲ 2.2 moderate climb	
10.3	↰ 'to Vico del Gargano'	
11.8	▲ 5.6km hard climb	
18.8	Vico del Gargano	41°53'46"N 15°57'35"E
	↰⊙ 'to Monte S Angelo'	
32	↙ to 'Monte S Angelo'	
	{●●↘ to 'Vieste' for ST Villaggio Umbra 1km ↻}	
55.1	↰ 'to Monte S Angelo, Manfredonia'	
55.4	▲ 5km moderate to hard climb	
60.7	★ Monte Sant'Angelo	41°42'18"N 15°57'32"E
	⌐→ 'to Manfredonia'	
61.2	⌐→ 'to Manfredonia'	
61.6	↰ 'to Manfredonia,' at stop sign	
63.5	⌐→ 'to Manfredonia'	
73.1	⌐→ 'to Manfredonia'	
77.7	⌐→ 'to Manfredonia nord'	
79	↗ Via Giantommaso Giordani	
79.5	⌐→ Via Torre dell'Astrologo	
	↰ (50m) Via delle Antiche Mura	
80.1	↰ Via Campanile	
80.2	↰ Via Tribuna	
80.3	⌐→ Via Arcivescovado	
80.5	Manfredonia, Piazza del Popolo	
		41°37'44"N 15°55'07"E

The centre is just off the route. For useful tourist information go to the **Pro Loco** (☎ 08 845 65 520; Via Reale Basilica 40) and the **Parco Nazionale del Gargano** head office (☎ 08 845 68 911, www.parcogargano.it; Via Sant'Antonio Abate 121). The town's main attraction is the **Santuario di San Michele**, for centuries the last stop on a gruelling pilgrimage to the place where St Michael the Archangel is said to have appeared before the Bishop of Siponto in AD 490. Opposite the sanctuary is the **Tomba di Rotari**, not a tomb but a 12th-century baptistery. Enter through the facade of the Chiesa di San Pietro. Its intricate rose window is all that remains since a 19th-century earthquake destroyed the church. The town's highest point is a **Norman castle** with Swabian and Aragonese additions. Take time too to enjoy the belvedere, a building situated to give sweeping views of the coast.

With a scintillating switchback descent from 800m to the coast, the last leg to the ride end in Manfredonia is quick and easy.

CALABRIA

Although it may not loom large on the average visitor's list of Italian destinations, Calabria is worth some exploration. The province has its share of ugly holiday villages along parts of the Ionian and Tyrrhenian coasts, but its beaches are among the cleanest in Italy. Lovers of ancient history can explore the sparse reminders of the civilisation of Magna Graecia, but cyclists will love the roads heading inland, where large areas of unspoilt mountains and even the odd picturesque medieval hilltop village await the more adventurous.

LA SILA GRANDE

Duration 2 days
Distance 138.6km
Difficulty moderate
Start Fago del Soldato turn-off
Finish Catanzaro
Summary In the heart of pristine forests and lake country, a cycling adventure awaits you in rural La Sila.

Many people think of Calabria as a dry, forbidding interior surrounded by long stretches of ugly, overdeveloped coastline. As this ride heads into the mountains those preconceptions you carry are soon dispelled; kilometre after kilometre of rich mountain forests, green meadows and placid lakes reveal a region of natural beauty reminiscent of the lower alpine country of northern Europe.

PLANNING
When to Cycle
A high likelihood of snow and road closures on Day 1 negates the possibility of riding in winter months (October to late May), but the altitude brings the benefit of far milder midsummer heat than would be experienced at lower levels. Ideal riding times are from June to September.

Maps
TCI's 1:200,000 *Calabria* map covers the route adequately.

GETTING TO/FROM THE RIDE
Cosenza (start)
FAGO DEL SOLDATO TURN-OFF
In just 30 minutes – and for a mere €1.90 – one of the hourly FC buses will cover the 1100m vertical climb from Cosenza up to the ride start. The bus station is just north-east of Piazza Fera. Catch the Cosenza–Camigliatello Silano bus from *binario* 1 (platform 1) at the main bus station and ask to be dropped off at the *bivio* (turn-off) for **Fago del Soldato**.

BUS
Autolinee Preite (☎ 09 844 13 001) has buses heading daily along the north Tyrrhenian coast, and **Autolinee Romano** (☎ 09 622 17 09) serves Crotone, as well as Rome and Milan.

TRAIN
Stazione Nuova (☎ 09 842 70 59) is about 2km northeast of the centre. Regular trains go to Reggio di Calabria (1st/2nd class €17.40/11.60, 3 hours) and Rome (€50/37, 5½ hours), both usually with a change at Paola, and Naples (€36/25, 3½–4 hours), as well as most destinations around the Calabrian coast.

Catanzaro (finish)
BUS
From Catanzaro, **Ferrovie della Calabria** (☎ 09 618 96 111; www.ferroviedella calabria.it) run three buses daily to Rome (€40, 7 hours) and one daily to Milan (€75, 11½–13 hours) via Perugia, Florence (€60, 10½ hours) and Bologna (€62, 10½–11½ hours), departing from Motel Agip.

TRAIN
From the Catanzaro FS station (about 2km south and downhill from the centre), trains connect with the main Tyrrhenean Coast line at Lamezia Terme for services south to Sicily or north to Naples, Rome, Milan and Turin. The main Adriatic Coast line is accessed from Catanzaro Marina for connections to Bari. There are trains daily to Bari (€27.80–40, 5¼–8 hours, every 2 hours), most involving up to two to three changes.

FC trains leave every 30 to 45 minutes for Catanzaro Marina. Space can be tight. Biking is the easiest way to reach Catanzaro Marina for seaside accommodation options or train connections. It's 13km, mostly downhill. Follow the signs from the centre.

THE RIDE
Day 1: Fago del Soldata turn-off to Villagio Palumbo
4½–8 hours, 75.5km

The route starts out by winding continuously upward on almost deserted (if somewhat rough) roads for 600 vertical metres. The landscape is mostly shady beech woods and the odd meadow dotted with lazily grazing horses. The ride's high point is at the 1920m **Monte Botte Donato** ski station (18km), a good place to stop for a snack and enjoy the incredible view out across **La Sila Grande** to the north and **Lago Arvo** and **La Sila Piccola** to the south.

Descending to the SS108 from the ski station, the flora changes to include oak and pine, and there are short sections of broken bitumen to look out for. Nestled on the banks of picturesque **Lago Arvo, Lorica** (31km) has all the necessary facilities and would make an excellent option for a day or two of rest. After skirting the north side of the lake, the remainder of the day is spent undulating through fertile farmland and rolling easily through oak and pine forest around the smaller **Lago Ampollino**.

Day 2: Villagio Palumbo to Catanzaro
3–5½ hours, 57.9km

This is an easier ride than yesterday's, but there's a 2.6km climb after the hamlet of

Spineto (13.3km) and a 1.9km climb at 39.3km. If you choose the longer route, the day culminates in an almost uninterrupted, 35km downhill roll to Catanzaro. Leaving the main SS179 at 22.6km allows a shorter route, remaining higher for longer (so avoiding climbs), and crossing the dam wall of the picturesque **Lago Passonte** at 25.8km. The alternative route on the SS179 and SS109 through **Villaggio Mancuso** and **Taverna** is 10km longer, and arguably more scenic. It drops more rapidly and necessitates a 300m climb out of Taverna.

The terrain is mostly covered with dense, shady oak and pine until **Sant'Elia** (49.7km), when the mountain vegetation gives way to sparser, drier maquis and the more familiar sight of olive groves on harder-edged, rockier ground. There are a number of hamlets with bars and the odd restaurant dotting the route.

The final run into Catanzaro is short and sweet, but be sure to make the right turn at 54.1km (to Catanzaro centro) to avoid

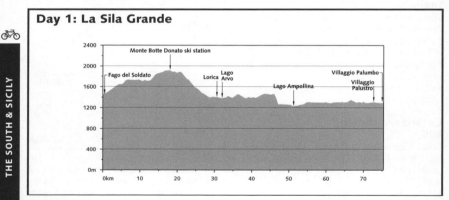

Day 1: La Sila Grande

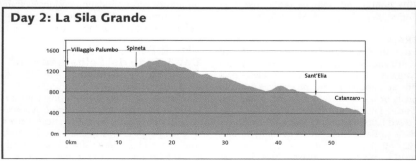

Day 2: La Sila Grande

a series of long, ghastly tunnels with very fast-moving traffic.

SICILY

Strategically located at the heart of the Mediterranean basin, Sicily has been the target of colonisers and settlers from all sides of the sea for more than 6000 years. Each conqueror has undoubtedly contributed to the make-up of modern Sicily, some leaving a rich cultural heritage, others leaving nothing but scars.

Since WWII the Italian government has poured significant resources into the island in an effort to kick-start its moribund economy, but entrenched extortion activity by the region's organised crime groups has hampered their efforts. Italian government figures have indicated that up to 70% of all Sicilian businesses pay some level of protection payments to Mafia groups.

Today, Sicily's infamous cloak of insularity is being cast aside and the Sicilians have begun to open up to the outside world. Yet deep into the island's mountainous interior, away from the bustling cities and trendy beach resorts, change is not so evident, and that shroud of mystery lives on. That's hardly surprising considering that the burden of 6000 years of invasion and occupation weighs heaviest here. Still, many foreign visitors will encounter a type of hospitality here like none other, both warm and generous.

ENVIRONMENT

Sicily's precarious position over two continental plates has resulted in the island being a major centre for volcanic and seismic activity. The eastern half of the island is dominated by the imposing cone of Mt Etna, Europe's largest active volcano, with more than 135 recorded eruptions.

Centuries of exploitation have taken their toll on the island's native flora and fauna. Widespread deforestation that began during Roman times has seen enormous tracts of forest stripped to make way for the large-scale cultivation of grain, particularly in the interior. Vineyards and olive trees were introduced by the Greeks, and citrus groves came with the Arabs. Eucalyptus trees were introduced in the 19th century to combat malarial mosquitoes in the marshlands.

Outside the nature reserves it's unlikely you'll see any creatures other than sheep, while the coastline is home to a regular selection of birds, mostly gulls and cormorants. Even the great schools of tuna, which for centuries were to be found off the western coasts, are fast disappearing into the nets of large Japanese trawlers far offshore.

ROLLING TO THE SEA

Duration 2 days
Distance 138.3km
Difficulty moderate–demanding
Start Enna
Finish Sant'Agata di Militello
Summary At times you might have to wait for goats to be herded off the road. Fortress-like towns almost spill off cliffs and hills into a gigantic valley; you might as well be time travelling. On a bike, you're doing it in style.

Inland Sicily is certainly not noted as a cycle-touring mecca, but anyone with a sense of adventure, a desire to experience the true nature of rural Sicily, and a thirst for out-of-the-way places will reap enormous satisfaction from this strenuous, two-day jaunt from the island's heart to its northern shores. With Etna as a constant backdrop, the ride passes though a rich variety of landscapes and some ancient and impressive mountaintop villages that seem as old as the mountains themselves. As for the riding, the hauls uphill and plunges downhill lull you into a kind of ecstasy that's a cocktail of reverence, exhilaration and resolve.

PLANNING
When to Cycle

Snow is common on the higher parts of the Nebrodi range and midsummer heat can be oppressive. Ideal riding is in April to July and September to October.

Maps

Use TCI's 1:200,000 *Sicily* map.

THE SOUTH & SICILY

GETTING THERE & AWAY
Enna (start)
BUS

SAIS (☎ 095 53 61 68) runs buses from Catania right to the centre of Enna (€10.30, 1½–2 hours, 10 daily) and from Palermo to Enna's bus station (€8.80, 1¾ hours, 6 daily).

TRAIN

Enna's train station is 5km from, and 500 vertical metres below, the town centre, making the train a less attractive option for arriving than the bus. From Catania (€4.75 plus €3.50 per bike; 7 daily) and from Palermo (€7.50; plus €3.50 per bike; 4 daily).

Sant'Agata di Militello (finish)
TRAIN

Regular trains run to Palermo (€7.35) and Messina (€6.65) for connections to Catania, Rome and other mainland cities. The supplementary bike ticket is €3.50.

THE RIDE
Day 1: Enna to Troina
3½–7 hours, 62.8km

The dramatic 12km descent from Enna's lofty heights starts your day better than a cappuccino. You fly through open yet mountainous countryside past cliff-hanging ancient towns. Look behind you and you'll see Enna peering over her precipitous cliff as if she had just stopped herself from plummeting. Then the ride quickly establishes a rhythm of grinding and freewheeling on the rollercoaster of inland Sicily's starkly beautiful and hilly terrain. A couple of tough climbs on the SS121 to **Leonforte** (22.6km) quickly get the legs warmed up and the blood pumping. A detour to the old

centre is recommended. The highlight is the **Granfonte**, an amazing baroque fountain built in 1651 by Nicolò Braciforte and made up of 24 separate jets playing against an ornately sculpted facade. Follow the signposts from the main cathedral.

Nissoria's (27.4km) one-way main street and most facilities can only be accessed from the far end of town, where there's an excellent bakery that also slices cheeses and hams, ready for picnic *panini* (sandwich). From a distance, **Agira** (35.3km) rises up in an almost perfect cone, matching in shape the incredible mass of **Mt Etna**, which totally dominates the eastern horizon. The route bypasses the town, but all food amenities are

Day 1: Rolling to the Sea

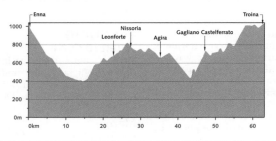

ROLLING TO THE SEA

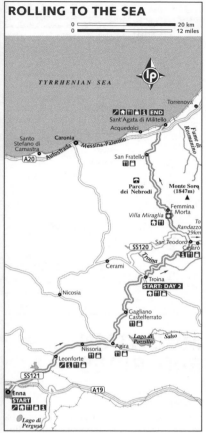

0 — 20 km
0 — 12 miles

TYRRHENIAN SEA

ROLLING TO THE SEA – DAY 1

CUES			GPS COORDINATES
start		Enna, APT tourist office	37°34'00"N 14°16'59"E
0km		uphill on Via Roma	
0.1	↰	Largo Rossi	
	↰	(70m) unnamed street	
0.2	↱	hard right around switch back, Panoramica Casina Bianca, 'to Palermo, Catania'	
1.7	↙	'to Catania, Palermo'	
2.6	↱	'to Leonforte, Pergusa'	
4.4	↑	'to Leonforte, Catania'	
4.6	↑	'to Leonforte, Catania'	
16	↑	'to Leonforte, Catania'	
	▲	2km hard climb	
19.0	▲	1km hard climb	
22.1	↘	to Leonforte	
22.6		one-way road – Leonforte	37°38'38"N 14°24'16"E
23.2	↙	when road forks	
23.8	↑	'to Nicosia, Nissoria, Agira'	
24.8	↑	'to Catania, Nissoria'	
25.0	▲	1km hard climb	
27.4		Nissoria	37°39'12"N 14°27'02"E
28.3	↙	'to Catania'	
29.0	↱	'to Catania, Agira'	
35.3		Agira	37°39'23"N 14°30'42"E
35.4	↘	'to A19 PA-CT, Gagliano c.to, Regalbuto'	
37.1	↙	'to Gagliano'	
39	↰	SP22, 'to Troina, Gagliano c.to'	
43.5	▲	3.7km hard climb	
46	↰	'to Gagliano Castelferrato'	
47	↱	'to Troina, Gagliano centro'	
47.2		Gagliano Castelferrato	37°42'42"N 14°32'15"E
	↘	when road forks	
48.1	↙	on downhill road	
48.8	↘	'to Troina'	
52.0	▲	1.4km hard climb	
55.1	▲	2.9km very hard climb	
61.3	↙	'to Troina, centro'	
61.8	↙	'to centro' at fork	
62.6	↰	Hard left up switch back then left at fork 'to Pro-Loco'	
62.8		Troina, Pro Loco tourist office on the right	37°47'07"N 14°35'46"E

available without entering the centro. After a rapid descent to the valley floor at the Salso, it's another very hard climb to **Gagliano Castelferrato** (47.9km), an amazing array of houses dwarfed by stern, craggy peaks. From here it's all hard work, as the route climbs onto the high, narrow ridge leading to day's end at **Troina**. A glance back to the south after cresting the final ever-steepening 2.9km lung buster affords an inspiring panorama back to the distinctive high plateau of Enna.

Day 2: Troina to Sant'Agata di Militello
4–7 hours, 75.5km
After the succession of tough climbs on Day 1, today presents only one ascent, albeit a

long one. Once beyond the 770m low point at the **Troina River**, the route heads inexorably upwards, reaching 1530m at the top of the Nebrodi range (37km), near **Monte Soro**. Most of the climbing is on moderate gradients.

While exposure to sun and heat can be a factor during the clear days that predominate in late spring and early summer, most of the actual riding time will be spent gazing in awe across the cultivated fields and tilled soil of this starkly beautiful rural

THE SOUTH & SICILY

landscape to the splendour of Mt Etna. The cool, shady forests of the Nebrodi mountains beyond Cesarò bring welcome relief from the heat.

Cesarò (22.4km) is a pretty village with an almost alpine flavour, clinging high on the southern slopes of the Nebrodi mountains. An ideal place to rest, dine or collect lunch supplies, it also hosts a regional office of the **Parco dei Nebrodi** (☎ 09 569 60 08; www.parcodeinebrodi.it), situated on the main approach road at 22.3km. It's an excellent source of maps and information on day and multi-day walks in the park, and it also houses a small museum dedicated to the Nebrodi.

At 37km, buried deep in the leafy oasis of Europe's largest beech forest in the higher reaches of the Parco dei Nebrodi, is **Villa Miraglia** (☎ 09 577 32 133; www .villamiraglia.it; half-/full-board €50/62), a lovely old, stone building originally built as a mountain retreat for an asthmatic count from Taormina, now serving as a small hotel. It's stuffed full of fabulous collectibles: quirky ceramics, colourfully decorated cart panels and old paintings. With good, simple food, it's an alluring retreat well worth considering as an overnight stop or a base for walks in the Nebrodi.

The day ends with an unforgettable, uninterrupted 33km freewheel from the day's high point all the way to sea level, with the mirage-like volcanic forms of the Aeolian Islands a faint blur on the sparkling sea's horizon.

ROLLING TO THE SEA – DAY 2

CUES		GPS COORDINATES
start	Troina, Pro Loco tourist office	37°47'07"N 14°35'46"E
0km	head downhill	
0.2	\<Uturn\> switch back to right at 'Stop' sign	
0.8	⌐↑🏠 'to Catania, Cesarò'	
1.4	↱ 'to Catania, Cesarò '	
2.2	↱ SS120, 'to Cesarò '	
5.7	↑ 'to Cesarò, Randazzo'	
18.5	▲ 3.9km moderate climb	
21.4	↱ 'to S Agata M, Cesarò '	
22.4	Cesarò	37°50'38"N 14°42'55"E
22.6	↱ SP167, 'to S Teodoro'	
27.3	↱ 'to S Fratello, S Agata M'	
33.9	⚠ Caution 3 consecutive 100mt long tunnels. Think about lights.	
	{37.0 ★ Villa Miraglia}	
57.4	San Fratello	38°01'01"N 14°35'57"E
62.7	⌐ S Agata di Militello	
72.3	⌐ SS113, 'to Messina, S Agata di mililtello'	
73.8	↘ 'to S Agata di Militello'	
74.7	⌐ to 'Polizia di Stato'	
	(50m) after turn unsigned bike shop on left	
75.2	↱ 'to centro, Messina'	
75.4	↱ 'to senso unico'	
75.5	↑ Sant'Agata di Militello, Piazza Crispi, Pro Loco tourist office	38°04'08"N 14°38'05"E

MOUNTAIN BIKE RIDES

GARGANO

Check out **Gargano Bike Centre** (☎ 08 847 04 186; www.garganobike.com; Località

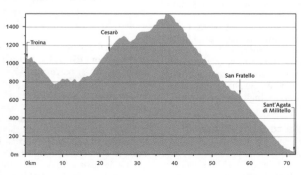

Day 2: Rolling to the Sea

Defensola, Vieste) for tours and information about mountain biking in this mountainous, wild corner of Italy.

MATERA
Trekking and Mountainbike (☎ 08 353 34 549; www.trekkingmountainbike.eu; Via Piave 6 bis) is a company based in Matera that rents mountain bikes and runs guided MTB tours of the surrounding mountains and forests. They also lead hiking trips.

SICILY
See boxed text (p238).

TOWNS & FACILITIES

ALBEROBELLO
☎ 08 / pop 10,900
Alberobello (translated literally as 'beautiful tree') is built on two hills: the eastern hill, made up of 'normal' buildings; and the western one, made up of several thousand fascinating stone structures with *trulli*-style, conical roofs (see the boxed text **Trulli**, p225). Originally founded as a small feudal outpost sometime around the mid-1400s, when heavily exploited peasants tilled the soil (and indirectly cleared the area of rocks), the *trulli* area was declared a national monument in the 1930s and a UNESCO World Heritage site in 1996. Many of these amazing stone structures now only accommodate souvenir shops, boutiques and restaurants.

Information
The **IAT office** (☎ 08 043 25 171) is in the Casa d'Amore, just off Piazza del Popolo, the main square. There is also another tourist office right off the main drag.

Near the centre, there are banks with ATMs on Via Vittime del Fascismo, along Corso Vittorio Emanuele and in Via Trieste e Trento.

Supplies & Equipment
Known as 'the bicycle place across from the post office', this little multi-purpose shop (intersection of Viale Margherita and Via Vitt del Fascismo) will help you out the best they can with the supplies they have.

Sleeping & Eating
Accommodation ranges from camp-sites to the *trulli* themselves. **Camping dei Trulli** (☎ 08 043 23 699; www.campingdeitrulli .it; Via Castellana Grotte; per site €4–6, per person €5–7, d €50) is just out of town. You can hire bikes or *trulli* (per person €20–30) here.

Hotel Didi (☎ 08 043 21 188; Via Piave 22/30; r from €35) is a cute, smaller hotel in the centre that won't break the bank. Some rooms have patios and great views. Bikes are kept in the food-storage room. **Hotel Miniello** (☎ 08 072 11 88; Via Balenzano 14; r from €40) is also fine value.

Pick up self-catering supplies at the little *alimentari* around the centre; big supermarkets are outside of town. **La Cantina** (☎ 08 043 23 473; Via Lippolis 9; meals €20) is a good local restaurant serving fresh seasonal food. Consider it a breath of fresh air in a town full of tourist traps. **Il Trullo d'Oro** (☎ 08 043 21 820; Via Cavallotti 27; meals €35) is a cute, side-street *trulli* restaurant serving generous plates of scrumptious food.

BARI
☎ 08 / pop 316,500
Bari may still be considered the Bronx of southern Italy, but that old reputation is wearing thin these days. Undeniably, things are looking up. Since the civic renaissance of the late 1990s, the old town has transformed from a virtual ghetto to a modestly glamorous *citta vecchia* (old city). Note, however, that even though the infamous *centro storico* (historical centre) is undergoing a gradual rehabilitation, it's a definite no-go at night.

Though Bari is still a far cry from a tourist-friendly city, the drab, concrete-bound exterior hides a prosperous and lively university town with fine restaurants and boisterous Barese who certainly know how to have a good time. Plus, it's a handy starting point for touring the intriguing architecture, land and culture of Puglia.

Information
The **APT headquarters** (☎ 08 052 42 361; www.pugliaturismo.com) is at Piazza Aldo Moro 33a (1st floor). There are plenty of

THE SOUTH & SICILY

banks on Corso Cavour and at the station, most with ATMs.

Supplies & Equipment

Run & Bike (☎ 08 055 76 586; rebrunbike@ libero.it; Via G. Laterza 12/a; closed Sun) is a well-stocked shop in the centre with a knowledgeable owner. Also central is **Mannarini** (☎ 08 055 41 983; www.mannarini .com; Via G Capruzzi, 13; closed Sun), a half-bike/half-motorcycle shop.

Sleeping & Eating

Hotel Adria (☎ 08 052 46 699; www.adria hotelbari.com; Via Zuppetta 10; s €70–80, d €90–110) competes favourably with the larger and more expensive Bari hotels. Bikes go in the basement.

Pensione Fiorini (☎ 08 055 40 788; Via Imbriani 89; s/d €20/40) is probably the best budget accommodation in Murattiano. You'll love its large, bright rooms and the eclectic, retro bric-a-brac the owner displays.

Self-caterers should try the daily **produce market** (Piazza del Ferrarese), or the *alimentari* (deli) that dot the centre.

Pizzeria Enzo e Ciro (☎ 08 055 34 196; Via Cardassi 70; meals €15–20) is the most celebrated pizzeria in town, known for its wafer-thin crusts, cheap beer and boisterous atmosphere. **Osteria delle Travi** (☎ 08 056 17 150; Largo Chiurlia 12; meals €25; Tue–Sat) has great traditional cooking. **La Vineria** (☎ 08 055 83 489; www.lavineria.eu; Via Imbriani 78) is a cool place for serious samplers of vino who want to try local varieties alongside other regional favourites.

CATANZARO
☎ 09 / pop 95,300

Catanzaro replaced Reggio di Calabria as the regional capital in the early 1970s. Set on a rocky peak 13km inland from the Ionian coast, it's generally overlooked by tourists – and it's not difficult to see why. Scarcely anything remains of the old city, and evidence of its Byzantine origins is virtually nonexistent.

The city's seaside 'suburb' of Catanzaro Marina, one of the Ionian Coast's major resorts, is 13km south. Although it's heavily developed, it's less tacky than many other resort towns, and the beaches stretching off in both directions are among the best on this coast. It also has a number of accommodation options.

Information

The **Pro Loco office** (☎ 09 617 41 842; www.proloco-catanzaro.org; Larghetto Educandato 16) is in the centre. There are several banks with ATMs along Corso Mazzinin. **Cicli de Rosa Sabrina** (☎ 09 617 25 956; Via Grecia 141) is a shop that does sales and repairs.

Sleeping & Eating

Catanzaro has few hotels and they are generally expensive.

Albergo Belvedere (☎ /fax 09 617 20 591; Via Italia 33; s/d €38/54) is a pleasant enough budget option.

Grand Hotel (☎ 09 617 01 256; Piazza Matteotti; s/d €90/110) is very central and has bland but comfortable rooms.

There's a big **Conad supermarket** east of Piazza Matteotti, next to the Grand Hotel. Not much has changed since 1892 at **Caffè Imperiale** (☎ 09 617 43 231; Corso Mazzini 159). This belle epoque café on Catanzaro's main thoroughfare is a fab place for coffee or ice cream. Hidden down a narrow side street, **Da Salvatore** (☎ 09 617 24 318; Via Salita del Rosario 28; pizzas from €3, meals €11) is an unpretentious restaurant serving excellent local dishes and pizza. Try the *salsiccia alla Palanca* (sausage with greens), named in honour of a local football hero.

COSENZA
☎ 09 / pop 73,000

Without its wonderful medieval core, Cosenza would be little more than a dismal array of cheek-by-jowl concrete high-rises. The old area, seated at the confluence of the Crati and Busento Rivers, is an unexpected pleasure, with its narrow *vicoletti* (alleys), some no more than steep stairways, winding past elegant (if much decayed) mansions.

Information

The **APT office** (☎ 09 847 32 14; www .aptcosenza.it; Via Galliano 6) is located on the 5th floor of the provincial offices.

There are several banks with ATMs on Corso Mazzini.

Supplies & Equipment

For bike repairs and basic spares try **Barbarossa** (☎ 09 842 11 818; Via Canttaneo 82/b), in the medieval quarter, or **Faraca Sport** (☎ 09 843 92 209; Viale de la Repubblica 373) – the owner, Faraca, was a race champ.

Sleeping & Eating

Cosenza only has a few accommodation options, as it isn't geared towards tourism.

Ostello Re Alarico (☎ 09 847 92 570; www.ostellorealarico.com; Vico II Giuseppe Marini Serra 10; dm/s/d €16/30/50) is a fabulous youth hostel in a beautiful old house. Some rooms have brilliant views over the old city, and there's a fantastic lounge with an open fire and a self-catering kitchen.

Confluenze B&B (☎ 09 847 64 88; www.confluenze.org; Vico IV Santa Lucia 48; s €25–35, d €50–70) is a small, popular B&B in the historic centre. Rooms are cosy and plain with wood ceilings, and there's a community lounge and kitchen.

Self-caterers will find supermarkets, delicatessens and greengrocers on Via Trieste, 50m west of Corso Mazzini at the southern end of town. There's also a daily produce market about 500m uphill from Corso Mazzini, just west of Corso Umberto.

Ristorante Calabria Bella (☎ 09 847 93 531; Piazza del Duomo; meals €25) is one of the best choices in the old town, smack-bang next to the cathedral and busy with locals tucking into Calabrian cuisine, such as *cavatelli con fagioli e cozze* (pasta with beans and mussels), in a series of wood-beamed rooms. **Per…Bacco!!** (☎ 09 847 95 569; Piazza dei Valdesi; meals €25) is a splendid, upmarket but informal restaurant with windows facing onto the square. There's a great choice of wines to accompany the well-executed local dishes.

ENNA

☎ 09 / pop 29,000

Enna sits almost perfectly at Sicily's scorched centre. Perched on a precipitous U-shaped ridge at around 1000m, it offers commanding views across the cultivated valleys and rugged mountains of the island's interior. It's not hard to see why it's nicknamed the *belvedere* (panorama) or *ombelico* (umbilical cord) of Sicily. With several significant archaeological treasures

within easy reach, it makes an excellent base for further exploration.

Information

Staff at the **APT office** (☎ 09 355 28 288; www.apt-enna.com; Via Roma 413) are very helpful and can give you maps and all manner of information on the city and the region. There's also an **AAST office** (☎ 09 355 00 875; Piazza Colaianni 6) next to the Grande Albergo Sicilia for information on Enna itself.

There are several banks with ATMs in the Via Roma precinct.

Sleeping & Eating

For B&B recommendations, contact the tourist office or check out www.bed-and-breakfast-in-italy.com.

There is only one hotel option in Enna, and it's not particularly cheap. However, you do get what you pay for at the **Grande Albergo Sicilia** (☎ 09 355 00 850; www.hotelsiciliaenna.it; Piazza Colaianni 7; s €55–72, d €70–120): a hotel set high in the old centre with comfortable rooms and fabulous views. For self-catering, there is a **market** (Via Mercato Sant'Antonio; open daily) where you can find basics such as delightful fresh fruit, bread and cheese.

Historic **Pizzeria Da Gino** (☎ 09 352 40 67; Viale Marconi 6; pizza €6–8) has outdoor seating, good atmosphere and great views. **Antica Hostaria** (☎ 09 352 25 21; Via Castagna 9; meals €30), Enna's best restaurant, has made it into the Slow Food Movement bible thanks to its pork *ragù* (sauce), an ancient mountain staple. During the summer you should opt for the *orecchiette* (ear-shaped pasta) with broccoli and black olive paste.

MANFREDONIA

☎ 08 / pop 57,700

Manfredonia is a port town founded by the Swabian King Manfred, Frederick II's illegitimate son. Other than providing useful transport links and easy access to some great riding territory on the promontory, it really doesn't merit more than a short stay. At the far end of the main drag, Corso Manfredi, is the town's majestic castle, started by Manfred and completed by Charles of Anjou. Within it, the **Museo Archeologico Nazionale del Gargano** displays local finds.

Information

The **IAT tourist office** (☎ 08 845 81 998; Piazza del Poplolo) is in the same piazza as Banco di Napoli (with ATM).

Supplies & Equipment

For bike spares and repairs, go to **Spano** (☎ 08 845 36 306; www.ciclispano.com; Via di Vittorio 105), found on the main road south towards Siponto.

Sleeping & Eating

There are several camping villages within 5km south of town, but they only open from July to late September.

Hotel Gabbiano (☎ 08 845 42 554; www.albergogab biano.it; Viale Eurostides 20, Siponto; s €65–80, d €75–96) is a clean, modern and friendly hotel nestled in a quiet street 150m from the beach and only 2km from the port. The pizzeria is a lively spot and the outdoor garden café is the perfect place for a morning coffee.

Self-caterers will find supermarkets, bakeries and small grocery stores on Viale di Vittorio.

Il Baraccio (☎ 08 845 83 874; Corso Roma 38; meals €30) is an unpretentious, well-reputed traditional trattoria serving up local specialties such as octopus salad, squid-ink pasta and seafood soup.

MATERA

☎ 08 / pop 57,800

Matera evokes powerful images of a peasant culture, which first began to hew the city's famous cave houses in medieval times or earlier. Now a Unesco World Heritage site, Matera was a troglodyte city of 20,000 until well after WWII – people and animals slept together and, despite an infant mortality rate of more than 50%, a typical family cave sheltered an average of six children. Matera's famous *sassi* (buildings of tufa stone, half constructed, half bored into the rock walls of Matera's twin ravines) were home to the majority of the populace until the local government forcefully relocated them into new residential areas in the late 1950s.

The most striking account of how these people lived is found in Carlo Levi's *Christ Stopped at Eboli*. It took half a century and vast amounts of development money to eradicate malaria and starvation in this region. Today people are returning to live in the *sassi* – but now it's a trend rather than a necessity.

Information

The **APT office** (☎ 08 353 31 983; www .materaturismo.it; Via De Viti De Marco 9) has helpful staff who can give you information about historical tours of the *sassi*.

There are several banks with ATMs in the town centre, including the Banco di Napoli in Piazza Vittorio Veneto.

Supplies & Equipment

There are several bike shops, one good one being **Bici Sport di Caldone** (☎ 08 353 83 612; Via Loperfido FP 8–10). It's well-stocked with most bike spares and has an excellent workshop.

Sleeping & Eating

For camping options near Matera check out www.camping.it.

Good budget accommodation is available at **Sassi Hotel/Hostel** (☎ 08 353 31 009; Via San Giovanni Vecchio 89; dm/s/d €16/60/94) where there are graceful rooms – some in caves, some with balconies. The terrace's view is astounding.

Albergo Roma (☎ /fax 08 353 33 912; Via Roma 62; s/d €42/60) is a clean, budget option near the *sassi* and train station.

Hotel Sant'Angelo (☎ 08 353 14 010; www.hotelsantangelosassi.it; Piazza San Pietro Caveoso; s/d/ste €90/120/160) is a splurge that shows you sleeping in a cave can be a luxury. The rooms are spacious and stylish with a panoramic view of the Idris rock and the wild ravine behind.

For self-caterers, there's a daily **produce market** (off Piazza Vittorio Veneto). **L'Arturo Enogastronomia** (☎ 08 353 30 678; Piazza Sedile 15; panini €2.50) is at the entrance to the *sassi* and has a deli built from recycled materials. It's a great place to crowd around a bottle of wine. **Vecchia Matera** (☎ 08 353 36 910; Via Sette Dolori 62; meals €20–25) serves interesting pizza as well as traditional Lucanian dishes in a cosy, candlelit cave. **La Stalla** (☎ 08 352 40 455; Via Rosaria 73; meals €25) is a family-run *osteria* in a converted stable adorned with rustic artefacts, farming pieces, a feeding trough carved out of the rock and an impressive outdoor terrace.

PESCHICI

☎ 08 / pop 4340

Peschici is a classic medieval coastal village, perched high on a rocky outcrop above a sweeping, sandy bay, with narrow cobbled alleyways and whitewashed houses reminiscent of villages in the Greek islands. It's not hard to see why it's becoming increasingly popular as a summer haven, but the good news is it remains relatively unspoiled.

Information

The closest thing you're going to get to a tourist office is **Agrifolio Tour** (☎ 08 849 62 721; www.agrifogliotour.it; Piazza Sant'Antonio 3). This private travel agency can arrange hotel reservations, cultural tours and trips to the Isole Tremite. See www.peschici.it for more information about the town.

There are two banks with ATMs on Corso Garibaldi.

Supplies & Equipment

Moto e Bici (☎ 08 849 64 905; at Via Montesanto 47) stocks basic spares (tyres, tubes, chains, cassettes etc) for road and mountain bikes. The staff will be happy to order in if required.

Eating & Sleeping

There are numerous camp sites along the coast east and west of town. **Camping Parco degli Ulivi** (☎ 08 849 63 404; www.parco degliulivi.it; per tent/person €4–11/€4–10), downhill from the centre, offers shaded sites in a lovely, ancient olive grove.

Locanda al Castello (☎ 08 849 64 038; Piazza Castello 29; s/d with breakfast €55/70) is a pleasant family establishment situated above the cliffs. It's definitely the pick in the old quarter, due in part to its fine sea views.

La Torretta (☎ 08 849 62 935; www .latorrettapeschici.it; Via Torretta 15; half-board per person €42–80) has views alone that are worth the stay. The rooms at this no-frills are clean and the new *pensione* all face the bay of Peschici.

For self-caterers, **Frutta Verdura de Loretta**, off Piazza San Antonio, has the most luscious produce and even makes its own olive oil. **Ristorante Vecchia Peschici** (☎ 08 849 62 053; Via Roma 31; meals

---

FORESTA UMBRA DAY RIDE

Foresta Umbra offers superb walking and mountain biking, with many well-marked trails and numerous well-maintained picnic areas. Check out **Gargano Bike** (p241) for tours and information about mountain biking in the area. Even though the Day 2 route passes this point (32km), the 28km ride up to Villaggio Umbra in the heart of the forest, via an alternative route, is highly recommended as a day trip. Take the inland road toward Vieste and turn right after 12km. It's a long climb up, which means a long roll all the way back! There's a **small museum and nature centre** (☎ 08 845 60 944; open Jun–Sep), which includes a re-creation of a woodcutters' and charcoal burners' camp. While there, pick up maps of walking trails and feed the roe deer in the adjacent reserve. Nearby, there's a small lake, a **kiosk** (open Apr–Sep) and a **restaurant** (open Jul–Aug).

€20–25) is positioned perfectly for a sunset *aperitvo* (pre-dinner drink) overlooking the Baia di Peschici. This family-run restaurant offers a menu based on fresh seafood and inland meats. **Porta di Basso** (☎ 08 849 15 364; Via Colombo 38; meals €30–40) has fresh seafood and floor-length windows with superb views of the ocean from its cliff -top perch.

POSITANO

☎ 08 / pop 3900

To say that Positano is picturesque doesn't do it justice. Softly-hued, bougainvillea-laced buildings cling to a slope so steep it's hard to believe they don't tumble into the azure waters below. The town is split in two by a cliff that bears the *Torre Trasita* (Trasita Tower). West is the smaller, less crowded Spiaggia del Fornillo beach area and the less expensive side of town; east is Spiaggia Grande, backing up to the town centre. Travelling by bike means a long descent on one-way Viale Pasitea to the centre and a steep climb back out on one-way Via Cristoforo Colombo to rejoin the SS163, which bypasses the town in a huge hairpin high above.

Information

The area below Viale Pasitea is pedestrian-access only, and finding the small **APT tourist office** (☎ 08 987 50 67; www .aziendaturismopositano.it; Via del Saracino 4) at the foot of the Chiesa di Santa Maria Assunta steps means locking bikes or walking them down the narrow, cobbled Via dei Mulini to the seafront at Spiaggia Grande.

Banco di Napoli and Banca dei Paschi di Siena on Via dei Mulini have ATMs.

Sleeping & Eating

Positano has several one-star hotels, which are usually booked well in advance for summer. Ask at the APT office about rooms in private houses. Everything is generally expensive.

Praiano, 5km east of Positano, has the nearest camping, **La Tranquilità** (☎ 08 987 40 84; info@continental_positano.it).

Ostello Brikette (☎ 08 987 58 57; www .brikette.com; Via G Marconi 358; dm €22– 26, d €65–85, apt $155–180) is clean and full of character, and it enjoys a staggering view of the bay.

The lovely **Villa Maria Luisa** (☎ 08 987 50 23; www.pensionemarialuisa.com; Via Fornillo 42; r €65-80) has nothing flashy about it, which only adds to its charm. Quirky, old-fashioned rooms, the sunny communal area and the jovial owner will make this a fun stay.

Pick up all self-catering supplies at reasonable prices at **Bar Internazionale**, where Via Pasitea leaves the SS163. Most restaurants are overpriced for the food they serve. **Da Costantino** (☎ 08 987 57 38; Via Montepertuso; pizzas from €4, meals €20) is a slog up about 300m north of Hostel Brikette. It's worth the work however as it's one of the few authentic places in town, serving honest, down-to-earth Italian grub with some amazing views. **Ristorante Bruno** (☎ 08 987 53 92; Via Cristoforo Colombo 157; meals €28), with its non-existent décor and unspectacular venue, serves superb seafood.

SALERNO

☎ 08 / pop 138,200

In the glamour stakes, Salerno's built-up, urban sprawl comes a very poor second to the photogenic loveliness of the Amalfi Coast. With a legacy of earth tremors, landslides and major damage after the American 5th Army landed in 1943, it's surprising any of Salerno's architectural heritage survives at all. With the exception of a charming, tumbledown medieval quarter and a pleasant seafront promenade, the city today is unexciting, although there have been successful efforts to beautify it. That said, Salerno is an important transport junction, so 'moving on' is well catered for.

Information

The **EPT office** (☎ 08 923 14 32, www .salernocity.com) is near the train station on Piazza Vittorio Veneto, at the eastern end of town, and most intercity buses stop here. They offer maps and are a good source of information.

There are numerous banks with ATMs on Corso Vittorio Emanuele.

Supplies & Equipment

Ugolino Cicli (☎ 08 975 20 64; www .cicliugolino.it; Via Iannuzzi 43–47) has a comprehensive stock-list of cycling supplies. Look for it 3km east of town.

Sleeping & Eating

The HI Ostello Ave **Gratia Plena** (☎ 08 979 02 51; www.ostellodisalerno.it; Via Dei Canali; dm/s/d €14/29/45) has bright rooms and an interesting history: it's housed in a 16th-century convent right in the heart of the centro storico (historic centre).

The more upmarket **Hotel Plaza** (☎ /fax 08 922 44 77; www.plazasalerno.it; Piazza Vittorio Vento 42; s/d €65/100) is comfortable, friendly and close to the train station.

Self-caterers will find supermarkets, fruit and vegetable shops, bakeries and delicatessens in and around the shopping precinct on Corso Vitorio Emanuele. There's also a daily produce market in Piazza Vittorio Veneto.

Ristorante Santa Lucia (☎ 08 922 56 96; Via Roma 182; meals €22) is one of the best eateries on trendy Via Roma, good for delicious seafood and bubbling wood-fired pizzas. **Pinocchio** (☎ 08 922 99 64; Lungomare Trieste 56; meals €24) is a relaxed seafront trattoria reputed for its no-nonsense Italian food and vivacious atmosphere.

SANT'AGATA DI MILITELLO

☎ 09 / pop 12,900

Sant'Agata di Militello is unlikely to win awards in the glamorous Mediterranean seaside resort stakes, but cycling there is the worthwhile, gorgeous part. It has accommodation, good transport options, and a pleasant, seafront dining precinct.

Information

The not so elaborate **tourist office** (☎ 09 417 09 30; www.comune.santagata dimilitello.me.it; Piazza Crispi) operates under irregular hours.

There are several banks with ATMs on Via Medici, the main road through the town centre.

Supplies & Equipment

With a tonne of bikes squished into a tiny space, bike shop **Di Blasi Salvatore** (☎ 09 617 22 781; Via Cernaia s/n; closed Sun) can help you out with your bike needs if such a mood strikes the staff. It's on route on the left 50m after the right turn at 74.7km. At the time of writing, there was no sign for it.

Sleeping & Eating

Hotel Parimar (☎ 09 417 01 888; Via Medici 1; s/d €35/55) is well-priced, if tattered, accommodation. The plus is some rooms have sea-view balconies. For another option, check out B&Bs at the tourist office or www.bed-and-breakfast-in-italy.com.

The huge **SMA supermarket** (Via G Puccini), east of the centre and two streets north of Via Medici, has everything for self-caterers.

There are several good restaurants and pizzerias along the esplanade (Via Cosenz), a short stroll from the centre. Diners at **Ristorante Carletto** (☎ 09 417 03 157; Via Cosenz 151) can choose from a sumptuous array of Sicilian antipasti. The **Break Café** (Via Medici 143/145; internet €3.50/hr) has internet access and a friendly vibe.

SORRENTO

☎ 08 / pop 16,500

According to ancient Greek legend, the Sorrento area was known as the Temple of the Sirens. Sailors of antiquity were powerless to resist the beautiful song of these maidens-cum-monsters, who would lure them and their ships to doom on the reefs. In the high season this unashamed resort town is bursting with holidaymakers, predominantly from Britain and Germany, but there's still enough southern-Italian charm to make a stay here enjoyable – plus it is handy for reaching Capri (15 minutes away).

Information

The **AAST office** (☎ 08 180 74 033; Via Luigi de Maio 35) is within the Circolo dei Forestieri (Foreigners' Club), an office and restaurant complex. There are several banks with ATMs in the centre and up on Via degli Aranci.

Info Sorrento (www.infosorrento.it) has an intensive website with tourist information.

Supplies & Equipment

Emporio Bici (☎ 08 187 70 613; www .emporiobici.com; Via Nizza 58/60) is a well-equipped shop.

Sleeping & Eating

There are a couple of camping grounds just west of town, an easy ride from the centre. **Camping Nube d'Argento** (☎ 08 187 81 344; www.nubedargento.com; Via Capo 21; per person/tent €10/10) is only 200m from the beach and there's a pool on site. It also has bungalows (€50–85).

Pensione Linda (☎ /fax 08 187 82 916; Via degli Aranci 125; s €30–35, d €55–70) offers courteous, friendly service and is excellent value.

Hotel Elios (☎ 08 187 81 812; Via Capo 33; s €35–45, d €60–70) is a modest pension offering no frills (unless you count the views), just impeccable, old-fashioned hospitality and light, airy rooms.

CAPRI

A hop, skip and a jump away from Sorrento is the island of Capri. Visiting this microcosm of Mediterranean appeal with its Roman ruins and rugged seascapes makes for a fine day trip. **Linee Marittime Partenopee** (LMP; ☎ 08 180 71 812; consorziolmp.it; €12.50; 20 minutes; 20 daily) runs hydrofoils daily to/from Capri, as does **Caremar** (☎ 08 180 730 77; www .caremar.it; €8.80; 25 minutes; 4 daily). They depart from the port at Marina Piccola, where you also buy your tickets.

For self-caterers, there are supermarkets within the centre. **Mondo Bio** (☎ 08 180 75 694; Via degli Aranci 146; snacks/pasta €3/6.50), flying the banner for organic, vegetarian food, is a bright shop-restaurant serving a limited range of meatless pastas and tofu-based dishes. **Pizzeria Da Franco** (☎ 08 187 72 066; Corso Italia 265; pizzas €5–7), though more deli than pizzeria, is a hugely popular place that makes the best pizza in town. **Da Emilia** (☎ 08 180 72 720; Via Marina Grande 62; meals €22) is among the cluster of eateries along the Marina Grande seafront. It's the archetypal family-run trattoria serving huge portions of uncomplicated seafood classics.

TROINA
☎ 09 / pop 10,100

On a narrow perch more than 1100m high, Troina is built around a mountaintop fortress dating back to the 6th century. It was later one of the first towns taken by the Normans from the Arabs. Under Norman rule it was the 11th-century base for Count Roger I, who made major changes to the fortifications, and established the convent of San Michele and one of the island's first Christian churches here. There are also archaeological ruins dating back to the ancient Greeks in the area known as Catena, situated below Troina to the southeast.

Information

There's a **Pro Loco** (☎ 09 356 56 981; www .comune.troina.en.it; Via S Silvestro 71–73) and they are very exuberant and helpful when it comes to their tiny town.

Banks with ATMs can be found in Piazza Martiri d'Ungheria, just off Via S Silvestro, and on Via Nazionale, the main approach road west of town.

Sleeping & Eating

There are scant accommodation options.

In town is the new hostel **idria 14** (☎ 09 356 54 589; Via Idria 14; per person €20), which is your best budget option.

About 3km west (turn left at 61.8km on Day 1 and ride 1.3km) is **Eden Hotel** (☎ 09 356 56 676; SS120 bivio diga Ancipa; s/d with bathroom €50/70), a friendly, family-run establishment with excellent rooms, some with balconies and views across to Etna. It also has a very good restaurant/

pizzeria downstairs where you can eat economically.

La Citadelle dell'Oasi (☎ 09 356 53 966; Contrada San Michele; s/d with breakfast €50/75) is a huge and somewhat bizarre multi-storey complex to the east of the town. Choose this one last among Troina's choices.

There are bars and a couple of good delicatessens on or near Via S Silvestro in the centre. There's a Despar supermarket and several bars on the main road circling south of the historic centre. **La Tavernetta** (Via Arcirù 30; pizzas & pasta around €8–10) serves good, basic food.

VILLAGGIO PALUMBO
☎ 09 / pop 2200

Nestled on the southern shores of Lago Ampollino, Villaggio Palumbo is predominantly a winter village serving the small Palumbosila ski resort. In the off-season its position on the lake and the nearby mountains makes it an excellent place to kick back and relax or head up into the trails in the Cotronei forests, and further south, Monte Gariglione and the wilds of Parco Nazionale della Calabria.

Information

The Palumbosila **tourist office** (☎ 34 886 03 354) offers information on walks and supplies a small map of the village. All shopping facilities are in the Centro Commerciale in Piazza Ampollino, about 500m east of the information office. There are a couple of bars, some small markets and a delicatessen.

Sleeping & Eating

The lovely grassy area along the lake shore immediately below the village is open to free camping. Outside the ski season and August, the village's central hotels offer excellent value for the money. The selection includes **Hotel/Ristorante La Baita** (☎ 09 624 93 034; d with breakfast €55–80); **Hotel Lo Sciatore** (☎ /fax 09 624 93 098; carmela. madeo@tin.it; r with breakfast €60–75); and **Hotel Lo Scoiattolo** (☎ /fax 09 624 93 141; www.scoiattolohotel.com; r with breakfast €55–65). All have very good, reasonably-priced restaurants, specialising in *cucina tipica silana* (cuisine of La Sila); try the (mostly vegetarian) antipasto and the porcini mushrooms (in season).

SARDINIA

HIGHLIGHTS

- The coastlines of the **Costa Verde** and **Costa del Sud** with some of the cleanest water and best beaches of the Mediterranean (p255)
- Tasting strong, delicious **Cannanou** and **Carignano** wines in their motherland (p267)
- Superb mountain wilderness areas in the **Barbagia** and **Gennargentu** (p252)

SPECIAL EVENTS

- Bosa Carnival (Saturday before Ash Wednesday), Bosa
- Nostra Signora di Regnos Altos feast (second week in September), Bosa
- La Sagra del Torrone (late March–early April), Tonara
- Festival of Sant'Efisio (1 May), Cagliari

FOOD & DRINK SPECIALITIES

- *bottarga* (dried, pressed tuna roe, served finely grated over piping hot spaghetti)
- *culigiones* (delicious parcels of pasta filled with potato and wild mint)
- *pane carasau/carta musica* (crisp and paper-thin bread, often sprinkled with oil and salt)
- *porcini* (literally 'little pigs'; delectable mushrooms gathered from the forests high in the mountains)
- *seadas* (honey-drenched pastry filled with ricotta, tinged with lemon zest and served hot)
- *torrone di Tonara* (nougat; famed throughout Italy as the best of the best)

TERRAIN

Much of the island is very hilly, with a rugged coastline. A broad, elevated plain in the central-west rises to a range of high, rugged mountains that dominate the centre and drop sharply to the east coast.

| Telephone Code – 07 | www.sardegnaturismo.it/en/ |

The second-largest island in the Mediterranean, Sardinia (Sardegna) has always been considered an isolated land. Its people and culture maintain a separate identity from the mainland, which they call *il continente* (the continent), and even today many Sardinians speak an ancient, Latin-based dialect and proudly maintain traditional customs and costume, especially in the remote interior.

In keeping with its tradition of isolation, Sardinia as a cycling destination offers something quite different from anywhere else in Italy, not the least being its superbly maintained and lightly trafficked roads. You also have its fabulous food, spectacular beaches and archaeological treasures, an isolated, rugged interior of intense natural beauty and people renowned for their graciousness and hospitality. It's hard to find a reason not to head off and start pedalling – all you need is to learn to love hills!

HEADS UP TO THE ADVENTUROUS CYCLIST

Some people are comforted by advanced planning, itineraries and reservations. Other people like to burst into their travel experience, with that carrot of adventure dangling in front of their nose, open to what destiny has scheduled for them...even at the risk of ending up in uncontrollable or unfortunate situations.

If you are in the latter category, Sardinia might just be your cycling kingdom. There are certainly the resources to go the highly-planned route. However, unlike many other places in Italy, you can usually venture off and find a low-traffic (most likely scenic) back road leading from point A to point B.

Sardinia, whose tourist industry is just beginning to blossom, has a wealth of seldom-visited places. You, as the cyclist, have an exceptional opportunity to intimately discover these towns, cultures and landscapes if you choose to let go of a sense of certainty and timetables.

HISTORY

While there are signs of possible human habitation that date back as far as 150,000 years, significant archaeological finds indicate that the Neolithic era holds the first widespread signs of man's presence.

Perhaps the most significant and easily identifiable of Sardinia's earlier inhabitants were the Nuraghic people, whose 7000 *nuraghi* – their conical megalithic stone fortresses – dot the island (see the boxed text **Stone Cone Homes** on p252). These sheep-rearing people lived in separate communities led by warrior-kings, and their culture flourished from around 1800 to 300 BC.

Sardinia's coast was visited by Greeks and Phoenicians, first as traders and then as invaders, and the island was colonised by the Romans. They, in turn, were followed by the Pisans, Genoese, Spanish, Austrians and finally, the Royal House of Savoy, the future kings of a united Italy. In 1948 Sardinia became a semi-autonomous region.

Despite the succession of invaders and colonisers, it is often said that the Sardinians (known as the Sardi) were never really conquered, they simply retreated into the hills. The Romans were prompted to call the island's central-eastern mountains the Barbagia (from the Latin word for barbarian) because of the uncompromising lifestyle of the warrior-shepherds, who never abandoned their Nuraghic customs.

ENVIRONMENT

Sardinia and its close northern neighbour, Corsica, were originally connected to the European continent and share a similar geomorphic ancestry. Major geological upheavals around 300 million years ago created the solid-granite spine that today constitutes more than one-third of the island. But it was the massive volcanic upheaval responsible for the formation of the European Alps that forced both Sardinia and Corsica into their current mid-Mediterranean position.

Once heavily forested, the island has been indelibly marked by centuries of fires, clearing and uncontrolled grazing. In spite of this, there remain some significant tracts of oak, cork oak, chestnut and hazelnut in the higher mountain areas. On the high plateau of the Gennargentu and Sopramonte, mixed scents of wild herbs such as thyme, oregano, sage and rosemary perfume the air. In the sparsely vegetated coastal areas, Mediterranean maquis, juniper, myrtle, rosemary, lentisk and broom dominate.

Wildlife remaining includes the *cinghiale* (wild boar), golden and Bonelli's eagles, peregrine falcon, pink flamingos, herons, the *mouflon* (wild mountain sheep), and Sardinian deer, plus a colony of griffon vultures on the west coast.

CLIMATE

While extremes of temperature in summer and winter can occur, Sardinia's climate in general is relatively mild in comparison to other parts of Italy on a similar latitude. This is due mainly to its position within the Mediterranean, where temperatures are often tempered by sea breezes.

There are three prevailing winds: the northwesterly mistral (which often blows with considerable force), the sirocco from the south, and the levant from the south and southeast.

Altitude plays its part in keeping temperatures to tolerable levels in the warmer months. Average temperatures are 25°C in

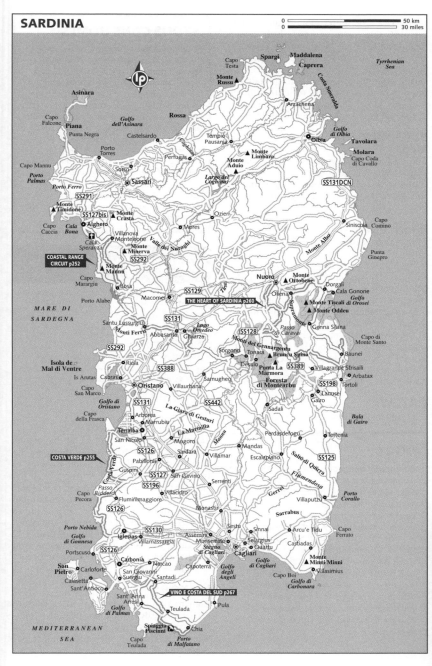

SARDINIA

0 —————————— 50 km
0 —————————— 30 miles

Tyrrhenian Sea

Spargi Maddalena
Capo Testa Caprera

Monte Russu

Costa Smeralda

Arzachena

Asinara

Capo Falcone
Piana
Punta Negra

Golfo dell'Asinara

Rossa

Castelsardo

Tempio Pausania

Golfo di Olbia

Olbia

Tavolara

Monte Limbara

Molara
Capo Coda di Cavallo

Porto Torres

Coghinas

Pertusas

Monte Aduio

Capo Mannu
Porto Palmas
Porto Ferro

Sotso

Sassari

Largu del Coghinas

SS131DCN

SS291

Capo Caccia
Cala Bona

Monte Timidone
SS127bis
Monte Crasta

Ozieri

Mpres

Capo Comino

Siniscola

Alghero
Cala Speranza

Villanova Monteleone

Monte Minerva

Valle dei Nuraghi

SS292

Monte Albo

Punta Ginepro

COASTAL RANGE CIRCUIT p252

Monte Mannu

Nuoro

Monte Ortobene

Dorgali
Cala Gonone

Capo Marargiu

Bosa

Macomei

SS129

Oliena

Monte Tiscali
Golfo di Orosei

MARE DI SARDEGNA

Porto Alabe

THE HEART OF SARDINIA p260

Supramonte

Monte Oddeu

Santu Lussurgiu

Monti Ferru

SS131

Lago Omedeo

Ghilarza

SS128

Sorgono

Tonara

Passo di Caravai

Genna Silana

Capo di Monte Santo

Abbasanta

SS292

Isola de Mal di Ventre

Riola

SS388

Monti del Gennargentu
Desulo
Punta La Marmora

Bruncu Spina

SS389

Villagrande Strisaili

Baunei

Arbatax

Is Arutas
Cabras

Capo San Marco

Samugheo

Villaurbana

Foresta di Montearbu

SS198

Lanusei
Gairo

Tortoli

Oristano

SS131

Capo della Frasca

Golfo di Oristano

SS442

La Giara di Gesturi

Sadali

Bala di Gairo

Arborea
Marrubiu

La Marmilla

Mannu

Perdasdefogu

Tertenia

Terralba

Mogoro
Sardara

Villamar

Mandas

San Nicolo

SS126

Escalaplano

Salto di Quirra

SS125

COSTA VERDE p255

Pabillonis

Costa Verde

Guspini

SS127
San Gavino

Serrenti

Fluminendosa

Villaputzu

Porto Corallo

Passo Bidderdi

SS196

Villacidro

Monastir

Gerrei

Capo Pecora

Fluminimaggiore

SS126

Porto Nebida
Golfo di Gonnesa

SS130

Iglesias

Villamassargia

Assemini
Monserrato

Sestu

Sinnai

Sarrabus

Arcu'e Tidu
Capo Ferrato

Portscuso

SS126

Stagno di Cagliari

Selargius
Quartu

Cagliari

Castiadas

Monte Minni Minni

San Pietro

Carloforte

Carbonia
Narcao

San Giovanni
Suergiu
Santadi

Golfo di Cagliari

Capo Boi

Villasimius

Calasetta

Sant'Anna Arresi

Santadi

Capoterra

Golfo degli Angeli

Golfo di Carbonara

Sant'Antioco

Golfo di Palmas

VINO E COSTA DEL SUD p267

Teulada

Pula

MEDITERRANEAN SEA

Spiaggia Piscinni
Capo Teulada

Chia

Porto di Malfatano

SARDINIA

summer (a little hotter inland) and around 8 to 10C degrees in winter (a little colder inland, naturally decreasing with altitude). July and August are the hottest months and January is the coldest. Rain mainly falls in spring and autumn, and the mountainous interior receives the bulk of it (the higher peaks get snow); the plains and coastal areas in the east and south are significantly drier.

PLANNING
Maps
TCI's (Touring Club Italiano) 1:200,000 map of Sardinia gives good coverage of all routes in this chapter. Another good one is the Istituto Geografico de Agostino's road map of Sardinia.

Information
Ente Sardo Industrie Turistiche (ESIT; ☎ 80 001 31 53, www.esit.net; Via Goffredo Mameli 95) in Cagliari covers all of Sardinia. The excellent website **Sardinia by Bike!** (www.sardiniabybike.cjb.net) offers suggested itineraries and information on organised tours. Another helpful official website (www.sardegnaturismo.it) has links to tourist services, maps and itineraries in each region. **Dolce Vita Bike Tours** (☎ 07 092 09 885; www.dolcevitabiketours.com; Viale Segni 16) provides self-guided tours during which they shuttle your luggage.

GATEWAY
See Cagliari (p271).

DOGS

We encountered more dogs in Sardinia than in the rest of Italy, by far. Be prepared for the cute little free-loping beasts, who are for the most part apathetic – except when they're provoked by weird, rolling things with shiny wheels. In many cases, they are all bark, but you should be prepared for other outcomes. There are many philosophies of dealing with dogs, ranging from yelling, cooing, water-slinging, whistling, or just sprinting with the knowledge that the person you're riding with is slower. Whatever your tactic is, make sure you're prepared to use it.

STONE CONE HOMES

Among the most dominant features of Sardinia's landscape are the 7000 or so *nuraghi* dotted around the island. Dating from 1500 to 400 BC, these truncated, conical structures were made out of huge basalt blocks taken from extinct volcanoes. The towers were used for shelter and for guarding the surrounding territory. The name nuraghe derives from the Sardinian word nurra which means 'heap' or 'mound'. Very little is known about the identity of the Nuraghic people. Judging by their buildings, they were well organised and possessed remarkable engineering skills, although it appears that they left no written word.

COASTAL RANGE CIRCUIT

Duration 2 days
Distance 107.9km
Difficulty moderate
Start/Finish Alghero
Summary Spectacular, traffic-free coastal roads are diamonds in the rough. The other gem is riding through the richly green and rugged coastal range.

Thigh-intensive and outrageously satisfying, this two-day tour from the handsome and upbeat port town of **Alghero on La Riviera de Corallo** (the Coral Riviera) to Bosa's more laid-back shores offers the very best of *il mare* (the sea) and *il monte* (the mountain). You'll savour sensational and enduring panoramas across the entire northern and eastern expanses of the island on Day 1, and the return journey on Day 2 will carry you over one of the finest coastal cycling roads, marked by dramatic beauty and sparse traffic.

HISTORY
Alghero's Nuraghic heritage dates back to before 1000 BC. More recently, its strategic position in the Mediterranean made it a valuable trading port. Originally under Genovese control, it fell in 1354 to the Catalan-

Aragonese who flushed out the Sardinian inhabitants and duly replaced them with Catalonians. The Catalan links are evident in the architecture, and even more so in the local language, which preserves more elements of ancient Catalan than the language spoken today in the Spanish province itself.

PLANNING
When to Cycle
In the warmer months (April to June and September and October), temperatures are ideal for cycling and warm enough for swimming – and the summer hordes are avoided. Wind can be a factor, with the mistral sometimes howling out of the northwest for days at a time. If you ride the coast road (Day 2) on a weekday you'll feel like it's yours alone.

GETTING TO/FROM THE RIDE
Alghero (start/finish)
AIR
The **airport** (☎ 07 993 50 39; www.aero portodialghero.it), about 12km north of town and inland from Fertilia, has domestic flights to major cities throughout Italy. It's easily reached by bike, and regular buses (€.60, 30 minutes) leave from the corner of Via Vittorio Emanuele and Via Cagliari to coincide with flights.

BUS
Intercity buses terminate in and leave from Via Catalogna, by the Giardini Pubblici. You can buy tickets for **ARST** (☎ 07 995 01 79) and **FdS** (☎ 07 995 04 58) at a booth within the gardens.

Many buses (ARST and FdS) run to/from Sassari (€2.32–2.58, 1 hour). ARST also runs buses to Porto Torres (€2.58, 55 minutes, 8 daily) and Bosa (€2.90, 55 minutes, 2 daily).

There are no direct links with Olbia. Instead you have to travel to Sassari, where you can pick up the Turmo Travel link.

To reach the beginning of the Barbagia and Gennargentu ride, you can catch a bus to Mancomer, where you catch a connection to Abbasanta, which is just several kilometres from Ghilarza.

TRAIN
The train station is situated 1.5km north of the old town on Via Don Minzoni. There

are up to 11 trains a day run to/from Sassari (€1.85, 35 minutes) with connections to Cagliari and Oristano.

BICYCLE
The 35km ride to Sassari (for all main transport connections) is a feasible alternative. Leaving from the tourist office, follow Via Vittorio Emanuele directly onto the SS127. Otherwise, you could catch a bus to Bosa and ride to Ghilarza via Santu Lussurgiu (see boxed text p255) for the start of the Barbagia and Gennargentu ride.

THE RIDE
Day 1: Alghero to Bosa
3½–6 hours, 61.6km
This is your classic up-and-over day. Much of the work is accomplished early in gaining the high ridge (around 600m) that is maintained for most of the ride until the drop to the Fiume Temo at Bosa. The roads are excellent and traffic is so light as to go almost unnoticed.

The theme for the day is 'panorama' – the vistas that dominate virtually from the outset are a just reward for a little sweat expended on the climbs. It's not all hard work, though, with the road at times undulating through beautiful open country dotted with cork oak and crisscrossed by low stone walls.

COASTAL RANGE CIRCUIT – DAY 1

CUES			GPS COORDINATES
start		Alghero, AAST tourist office, Piazza Porta Terra	40°33'32"N 8°18'52"E
0km	↑	head up Via Sassari	
0.3	⤵	Via G Carducci	
0.4	⤶	Via Giovanni XXXIII	
1.8	↑🏨	to Bosa, Villanova Monteleone	
3.8	▲	6km moderate climb	
18.1	⤵	not to 'Bosa'	
23.5		Villanova Monteleone	40°30'06"N 8°28'14"E
24.1	⤶	to Bosa, Padria	
25.3	↑	to Montresta, Bosa	
46.1	⤶	at 'T', to Bosa, Montresta	
47.5		Montresta	40°22'28"N 8°30'01"E
61.4	↙	to 'Carabinieri, G di Finanzia,' Via Alberto Lamamora	
61.6	⤶	(40m)	
61.6	⤵	(10m) into Via Azuni	
61.6		Bosa tourist office	40°17'45"N 8°29'52"E

Perched like a natural balcony on the upper slopes of the Colle di Santa Maria is **Villanova Monteleone** (23.5km), a lovely village commanding stunning views over Anglona to the north and Gallura to the east. The centre of town is just off the main route (go straight at 24.1km, instead of turning right as the cue sheet indicates, and follow the 'centro' signs). That's where you'll find a **daily produce market** (open mornings Mon–Sat; follow signs to 'mercato'), a supermarket and a couple of bars.

On the high road beyond Villanova Monteleone, some great coastal views are on offer as the road bobs and weaves through shady woods and across a lacework of pretty, rock-walled meadows. The final 5km climb is far outweighed by the sizzling 10km descent into Bosa.

SIDE TRIP: ALGHERO TO SELLA E MOSCA
3 hours, 16km RT
Prestigious wine producer **Sella e Mosca** is the best-known on the island. From Alghero you can ride to the immaculately maintained property and its **wine cellars** (☎ 07 999 77 00; admission free; tours 5.30pm Mon–Sat, mid-Jun–mid-Oct). Around the low buildings and exquisite gardens spread 600 hectares of vineyards that have been going since 1899. The cellar tour gives you some insights into old and modern production methods. You can visit the *enoteca*

(wine shop; 8.30am–1pm & 3–7.30pm daily) afterwards and sample some of the wares.

From Alghero, Via Don Minzoni hooks up with SP42, (Sella e Mosca is to the side) a little more than 8km down the road. It's not the most spectacular ride, but more a goal-oriented journey.

Day 2: Bosa to Alghero
2½–4½ hours, 46.2km
On a wide and almost empty road with a flawless surface, this gem of a ride weaves and bobs its way along a truly spectacular stretch of rugged, deserted coastline. There's only one significant climb of 6.2km to 350m, but the work involved is

COASTAL RANGE CIRCUIT – DAY 2

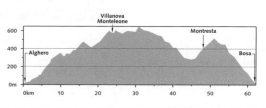

CUES			GPS COORDINATES
Start		Pro Loco tourist office, Bosa	40°17′45″N 8°29′52″E
0km		W on Via Azuni	
0.4	⬑	at 'T'	
0.5	⬏	into Via Alghero	
1.4	⬏	to Alghero (SP49)	
9.1	▲	6.2km moderate climb	
35.4	★	Spaggia la Speranza	40°30′26″N 8°21′24″E
43.7	⬑	Viale Resistenza	
44.7	⬑	Via Fratelli Kennedy	
45.1	⬏	Via XX Settembre	
45.6	⬑🅗	Via Cagliari	
46.2		Alghero tourist office	40°33′32″N 8°18′52″E

Day 1: Coastal Range Circuit

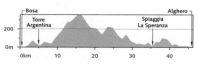

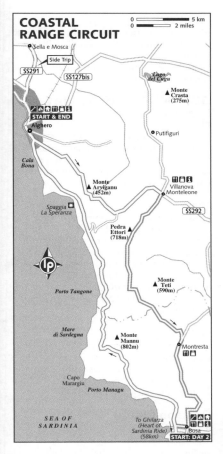

COASTAL RANGE CIRCUIT

CYCLING BOSA TO GHILARZA

You can connect the Coastal Range Circuit (p252) with the Heart of Sardinia (p260) ride by cycling from the Bosa Marina towards Tùras then cutting in towards Magomàdas, where you head south to Cuglieri. From there it's a clear shot east to Ghilarza via Santu Lussurgiu. This ride is absolutely stellar, though after Santu Lussurgiu the landscape flattens and loses some pizzazz. Soon after you leave the bustle of the Marina, the ride becomes traffic-free and the glory of the Sardinian countryside reveals itself. The butt-kicker haul up and over into Santu Lussurgiu is a marvellous submersion into the thickly forested mountainscape. For much of the time on the way to Santu Lussurgiu, a giant cross on top of the neighbouring mountain is in view, adding even more drama to the scenery – scenery that will be shared by just you, the critters and an occasional mushroom hunter.

Other than the path to the beach (5.4km), just south of Torre Argentina, there's no chance to swim until **Spiaggia La Speranza** (35.4km); the long, sandy beach lapped by crystal-clear aquamarine waters looks inviting indeed, and it makes a nice stop before the final run into Alghero.

COSTA VERDE

Duration 3 days
Distance 147.4km
Difficulty moderate
Start Iglesias
Finish Oristano
Summary A smorgasbord of a ride: beaches, ancient hamlets, expansive horizons, engulfment in forest, off-roading and smooth pavement.

more than offset by the commanding views gained in the process. The brilliant white cliffs of **Capo Caccia** (16km) can often be seen on the northern horizon through the Mediterranean haze. A headwind from the northwest is the only thing that could realistically spoil the fun.

In spring, the scent of wildflowers fills the air. Oftentimes, the only signs of life are the jangles of goats' bells from the rugged, high slopes soaring steeply to the right, or a bird of prey winging on thermals high overhead. The area is one of the last habitats of the griffon vulture and it's quite an experience if you are lucky enough to spot one of these huge birds, whose wingspans reach up to 2m.

This route has got you covered. For the beachcomber it has lazy little Mediterranean villages and secluded bays, long unspoilt sandy beaches and stretches of rugged

SARDINIA

coastline, all caressed by an emerald sea. For the culture vulture, it has beautiful medieval towns rich in architectural treasures. For the adventurer, it has mining ghost towns reminiscent of the wild west, open spaces and high, rocky peaks in some of the more isolated and sparsely populated parts of the island. Note that you'll need knobby tyres for a rough section on Day 3.

HISTORY
The rugged and remote mountain region north of Iglesias (known as the Iglesiente) was originally home to the Nuraghic people. It was later colonised by the Phoenicians, but passed successively to the Carthaginians, Romans and Pisans, who all exploited its rich lead, zinc and silver resources. Mining activity began to decline during the centuries of Aragonese control until a boom in the 19th century saw it become Italy's most important mining region. Falls in productivity and demand after WWII led to inevitable mine closures and the eventual death of the industry.

While the area around Oristano lacked the mineral resources of the Iglesiente, it reflects a similar history of Phoenician, Carthaginian and Roman occupation. The Phoenicians established the port town of Tharros, whose later inhabitants moved inland and laid the foundations of Oristano.

ENVIRONMENT
The Iglesiente is an area of major geological significance and provides an incredible keyhole into the past. In the rock strata of the coastal cliffs and the mountains inland, there is clear evidence of the upheavals that created the major massifs of Western Europe more than 500 million years ago. Prized fossil remains from the area, such as the Pre-Cambrian trilobite, are among the oldest known examples of animal life on earth.

PLANNING
When to Cycle
Even though traffic and crowds are never likely to be a real issue, the ride will be best enjoyed on weekdays, preferably in the warmer, off-season months (April–June and September–October). Peak-season crowds aside, July and August are not good months for cycling here because of the heat.

What to Bring
Much of the ride passes through quite isolated countryside, so self-sufficiency is paramount. There are no bike shops. Knobby tyres are recommended for the rough section on Day 3

GETTING THERE & AWAY
Iglesias (start)
BUS
Ferrovie Meridionali Sarde (FMS; ☎ 07 813 28 00, www.ferroviemeridionalisarde.it; Via Crocefisso 92) buses depart the at terminal for Cagliari (€3.50, 1 hour, around 10 per day) and Sassari as well.

TRAIN
From Iglesias, hourly trains also leave and arrive from Cagliari (€5.15 plus €3.50 per bike, 1 hour). There are frequent trains, one about every two to three hours, to Sassari for connections to Alghero, (€8.75 plus €3.50 per bike, 2½–3 hours). Hourly trains leave to Abbassanta/Ghilarza (start of the Gennargentu ride; €2.55 plus extra ticket for bike, 30–40 minutes).

BICYCLE
Iglesias is a relatively easy 55km ride from Cagliari. Head north past the airport and turn left just before Assemini onto the secondary road running parallel to and south of the busy and fast SS130.

Oristano (finish)
BUS
The main intercity bus station is on Via Cagliari. ARST (Azienda Regionale Sarda Trasporti) buses leave for destinations all over the province as well as to Sassari (4 daily) and Cagliari (3 daily).

TRAIN
The main Trenitalia train station is in Piazza Ungheria, east of the town centre. Six or seven trains run between Oristano and Abbasanta and Paulilatino to the northeast.

As many as 20 trains, sometimes involving a change en route, run between Oristano and Cagliari (€4.75, 1–2 hours). Only a handful make the run from Oristano to Sassari (€7.75, 2½ hours, 4 daily). For Olbia there are only two through trains (€9.25, 3 hours); otherwise you have to change at Chilivani.

COSTA VERDE & ORISTANO

0 — 10 km
0 — 5 miles

Is Arutas

San Salvatore

Stagno di Cabras

Cabras

Tirso

Oristano **END**

Simaxis

Torre Grande

San Giovanni di Sinis

Tharros

San Giusta

Villaurbana

Capo San Marco

Stagno di Santa Giusta

Golfo di Oristano

Capo della Frasca

SS131

Arborea

Marrubiu

SS442

Sant'Antonio de Santadi

Marceddi

Terralba

Pistis

Uras

Mogoro

La Marmilla

Torre dei Corsari

San Nicolo

SS126

Terme di Sardara

Sardara

MARE DI SARDEGNA

Monte Arcneutu (785m) ▲

Marina di Arbus

Pabillonis

Santa Maria de is Acquas

Portu Maga

Montevecchio

Guspini

SS197

San Gavino

Costa Verde

Ingurtosu

Arbus

START: DAY 3

Bau

SS126

Passo Bidderdi (492m)

Gennamari

Gonnosfanadiga

SS196

Side Trip

Capo Pecora

Villacidro

Portixeddu

Fluminimaggiore

START: DAY 2

Grotta de su Mannau

Buggerru

Tempio di Antas

To Cagliari (42km)

Cala Domestica

Side Trip

Masua

SS126

Domusnovas

Nebida

START Iglesias

SS130

Golfo di Gonnesa

Funtanamare

Siliqua

Gonnesa

Villamassargia

SS126

Portscuso

To Santadi (Vino e Costa del Sud Ride) (35km)

Portovesme

SARDINIA

BICYCLE

It's a 40km ride from Oristano up to Ghilarza on the Abbassanta Plateau. Follow the SS388 to Fordongianus, then head north to Abbassanta and Ghilarza.

THE RIDE
Day 1: Iglesias to Buggerru
2–4 hours, 34.2km

Day 1 is quite short, leaving plenty of time to enjoy some magnificent stretches of unsullied coastline and marvel at the ruins from mining endeavours of centuries past.

Once off the Iglesias–Sant'Antioco road (8km), any concerns about traffic quickly dissipate as the route heads north on a lovely quiet road, lolling and bobbing its way past pristine white beaches and imposing cliffs. Stop for a swim at **Fontanamare** (11km). Just beyond Nebida (14.5km), the aptly named **Pan di Zucchero** (sugar loaf), an enormous 132m-high mass of pure white limestone, looms above the sea.

COSTA VERDE – DAY 1

CUES			GPS COORDINATES
start		Iglesias tourist office	39°18'35"N 8°32'07"E
0km		W uphill on Via Gramsci-Via Roma	
0.5	⬑	Via Roberto Cattaneo, to Calasetta	
2.9	↑	to Sant'Antioco	
4	↑	to Sant'Antioco (not onto SS162)	
8	⬏	to Nebida	
11	★	Fontanamare	
14.5		Nebida	39°18'50"N 8°26'11"E
17.7		Masua	39°19'53"N 8°26'05"E
		{●● Masua beach 4km ↺}	
	▲	2.6km steep climb	
		{27.3 ●●⬑ Cala Domestica 2.8km ↺}	
33.3	↘	to Carabinieri, downhill	
34.2		Piazza Monumenti ai Caduti, Buggerru	
			39°23'56"N 8°24'00"E

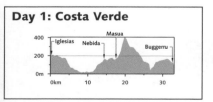

Day 1: Costa Verde

Elevation profile showing Iglesias, Nebida, Masua, Buggerru with heights in metres (0m, 200, 400) along distance (0km, 10, 20, 30).

SIDE TRIP: MASUA'S BEACH
1 hour, at 17.7km, less than 1km RT

Set in a bay below towering grey cliffs, Masua is just off the main route. The side

trip to its small beach offers great views out to Pan di Zucchero, and across the bay to the ancient Porto Flavia, a mining facility carved directly into the cliff face. It involves a 2km descent from 130m, but any urge for a quick dip may be tempered by fears of a 2.6km, lung-busting climb – with an average gradient of 13% – over the pass from Masua.

SIDE TRIP: CALA DOMESTICA
1 hour, at 27.3km, 2.8km RT

Cala Domestica is a stunning, secluded bay lapped by emerald waters – it makes for a very easy and worthwhile side trip. A short tunnel to the right of the beach accesses another pristine cove. Other than a dusty car park, it has no facilities and the beach is only accessible on foot – you must leave your bike.

Day 2: Buggerru to Arbus
2–3½ hours, 31.4km

This is another shortish day on very quiet roads. The route is often flanked by rugged mountains and passes through a variety of terrain from open sandy beaches to high rolling plains dotted with tracts of cork oak. Other than the hard 7.2km climb to the 492m **Passo Bidderdi** there isn't a great deal of hard work involved. **Portixeddu** (5.4km; also written 'Portisceddu') has services and there are a couple of beachfront bar-restaurants, a hotel and a camping ground nearby. An early departure from Buggerru should also leave plenty of time to reach the day's end at Arbus. Unload, and then ride out to Montevecchio.

COSTA VERDE – DAY 2

CUES			GPS COORDINATES
start		Piazza Monumento ai Caduti, Buggerru	
			39°23'56"N 8°24'00"E
0km	↑	uphill on Via Roma	
0.9	↰	to 'Iglesias'	
5.4		Portixeddu	39°26'21"N 8°25'02"E
		{ ●● ↰ Capo Pecora 9km ↺ }	
11.6	↰	to Arbus, Guspini	
12.2	▲	7.2km moderate-hard climb	
18.3	↙	to Arbus, Guspini	
23.4	↑	to Arbus, Guspini	
31.4		Piazza Mercato, Arbus	39°31'36"N 8°36'11"E

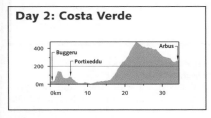

Day 2: Costa Verde

SIDE TRIP: PORTIXEDDU
1–2 hours, at 5.4km, 9km RT

Cycling from Portixeddu to the remote, windswept promontory at Capo Pecora involves a hard climb in both directions to 115m – an easier task if heavy bags are left at one of the obliging restaurants. It's worth the effort for the views alone.

SIDE TRIP: ARBUS TO MONTEVECCHIO
2–3 hours, at 33.2km, 14km RT

The abandoned 150-year-old **Montevecchio mining complex** (☎ 07 097 25 37; www .europroject.it/montevecchio) is an easy and rewarding trip. Head up Via Repubblica to the pass and take the small signposted road to the left. Detailed maps with historical information (in Italian and English) on the entire mining area from Montevecchio to Piscinas are available from the Pro Loco or from Hotel Meridiana.

COSTA VERDE – DAY 3

CUES			GPS COORDINATES
start		Piazza Mercato, Arbus	39°31'36"N 8°36'11"E
0km		retrace last 8km of Day 2	
8.1	⌐	to Ingurtosu, Piscinas	
12.1	★	Ingurtosu mine ruins	
12.8	↰	to Piscinas	
		Ingurtosu	39°31'18"N 8°30'40"E
13.2	⚠	loose dirt 7.2km, steep descent 2km	
19.3	↗	to Gutturu, Flamini	
		{ ●● ↘ Piscinas 3.4km ↺ }	
19.3	⚠	creek crossing, check depth	
20.4		end dirt road	
26.3		Portu Maga	39°34'33"N 8°28'01"E
32.3	↰	no sign (not to Arbus)	
33	⌐	to S Antonio Santadi, Pistis	
47.9		Sant'Antonio di Santadi	39°42'48"N 8°29'10"E
48.4	↰	immediately after inlet; no sign	
49.4	↑	Cross bridge	
52.7	↰	to Arborea, Oristano	
53.5	⌐	to Oristano, Arborea	
57.8	↰	to Oristano	
62.8		Arborea	39°46'12"N 8°34'46"E
72	↑	to Santa Giusta	
74.9	↰	to Santa Giusta	
78.8	⌐	to Pro Loco and EPT	
79	↰	to Pro Loco and EPT; follow one-way	
79.1	⌐	Via Vittorio Emanuele	
79.5	↰	(10m) Oristano, Piazza Eleanora; EPT tour	
			39°54'19"N 8°35'47"E

Day 3: Arbus to Oristano
5–8 hours, 79.5km

Day 3 offers a little off-road adventure, more superb deserted coastline viewed from equally deserted roads, and possibly the longest stretches of uninterrupted flat road in Sardinia.

After retracing the last 8km of Day 2, the route passes through the eerie mining ghost town of **Ingurtosu** (12.1km). This signals the start of the loose-gravel section that descends to Piscinas and the Costa Verde, maintaining the south bank of the

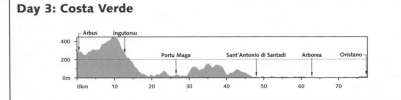

Day 3: Costa Verde

JUSTICE AND EQUALITY FOR ALL

Throughout the island's long history one person stands head and shoulders above the rest: **Eleonora d'Arborea** (1340–1404). Described as Sardinia's Boudicca or Joan of Arc, she was the island's most inspirational ruler, remembered for her wisdom, moderation and enlightened humanity.

She became Giudicessa of Arborea in 1383, when her venal brother, Hugo III, was murdered along with his daughter. Surrounded by enemies within and without (her husband was imprisoned in Aragon), she silenced the rebels and for the next 20 years worked to maintain Arborea's independence in an uncertain world.

Her greatest legacy was the *Carta de Logu*, which she published in 1392. The code was drafted by her father, Mariano, but Eleonora revised and completed it. To the delight of the islanders, it was published in Sardinian, thus forming the cornerstone of a nascent national consciousness. This progressive code, based on Roman law, was far ahead of the social legislation of the period. For the first time the big issues of land use and the right to appeal were codified, and women were granted a whole raft of rights, including the right to refuse marriage and – of perhaps even more significance in a rural society – property rights.

Eleonora remains the most respected historical figure on the island.

rather toxic-looking Rio Naracauli. As the road nears the dunes area there are also a few short sections of soft sand, where walking the bike through may be the most upright option.

Crossing the **Rio Piscinas** should present no drama – it has a firm base, but check the depth if it's running fast and walk the bike through if necessary. Back on the bitumen the road flows for more than 30km through the remote maquis-covered wilderness of the Costa Verde. Every now and then you'll pass the odd coastal hamlet or summer holiday village, some of which have bars or ristoranti open all year. **Portu Maga** (Marina di Arbus; 07 097 72 22; portumaga@tiscali.it) has wonderful *tagliolini con arselle* (handmade pasta with clam sauce). Take your pick of spots to stop and swim.

The left turn (onto the very narrow road that accesses the even narrower causeway) to the tiny fishing village of **Marceddi** is not signposted and is easily missed. It comes immediately after the small bay close to the left verge. The long, straights of the pancake-flat road grid on the Arborea flatlands, a swamp reclamation project initiated by Mussolini in the 1930s, are almost hypnotic after days of up-and-down on *strade nervose* ('nervous' roads). The final section into Oristano from Santa Giusta can be busy, but is easily navigated.

SIDE TRIP: PISCINAS
1 hour, at 19.3km, 3.4km RT

Piscinas has a wide beach and vast protected area of dunes that reach almost 200m in height in places. Other than the restaurant at Le Dune and some snack joints in the summer there is little in the way of services in the area.

HEART OF SARDINIA

Duration 4 days

Distance 293.4km

Difficulty demanding

Start Ghilarza

Finish Nuoro

Summary It doesn't get much more authentic than cycling in the rural mountain range of Sardinia while making your way to Nuoro, where you won't see a tourist. The unreal part is the majesty of the mountains and the glittering coastline you skirt along the way.

This arduous four-day jaunt through Sardinia's central-east region delves into the island's high country, circling the mountains of the Gennargentu, which are dominated by Monte La Marmora (at 1834m, the island's highest peak), and tracing the SS125 through the awesome massifs and gorges of the Parco Nazionale del Golfo.

As you grind up and soar down the dramatic mountainscapes, you'll hear bells tinkling and see fuzzy white dots of sheep on the green hills. You might pass a grandmother picking mushrooms, a farmer with weathered skin checking his crops, or a group of men trying to lasso a horse. In between these scant interludes with humans, there will be gigantic wildness miraculously cut through by the stellar road on which you cycle.

Stopovers in the lazy, coastal towns like Cala Gonone are ideal for recuperation after the hard climbs of Days 2 and 3. The roads are uncluttered and they boast an almost blemish-free surface as they cling to rugged mountainsides, swoop down long, steep valleys, meander through dense green forests, hug the banks of deep lakes and visit picturesque villages. This is some of Sardinia's most remote territory. Some call it the 'real' Sardinia for its lack of major tourist development.

PLANNING
When to Cycle
With some mountain sections of the route at altitudes over 1000m, snow and ice can be a factor. April to June and September and October are ideal, as they're warm enough to allow for beach time and comfortable passage over the mountains.

GETTING TO/FROM THE RIDE
Ghilarza (start)
BUS
Regular ARST buses arrive from Oristano (2 hours).

TRAIN
Abbassanta (only 2km west of Ghilarza) is a major stop on the main north–south line, with almost-hourly trains arriving from Cagliari (€7.60 plus €3.50 per bike, 1½–2 hours) via Oristano (€2.55 plus an extra ticket per bike, 40 minutes). Both towns are close enough for you to catch an early train and head straight off on the ride.

BICYCLE
It's a 40km ride from Oristano up to Ghilarza on the Abbassanta Plateau. Follow the SS388 to Fordongianus, then head north to Abbassanta and Ghilarza. From Bosa, you can bike to Ghilarza via San Lussurgiu.

Nuoro (finish)
TRAIN
Trains run from Nuoro to the interchange station of Macomer (€2.63, 1¼ hours), where you can connect to Cagliari (€10.80, 3½ hours). Bike supplement tickets cost €3.50.

THE RIDE
Day 1: Ghilarza to Tonara
3–6 hours, 50.7km
This is a hard day offering plenty of climbing and great panoramas as the route winds its way up into the verdant forests and high, fertile meadows of the Mandrolisai and the Gennargentu mountains.

The side trip to **Zuri** (4.1km) leads to the beautiful, 13th-century, pink-basalt **church of San Pietro**. The work of Anselmo da Como, it was relocated brick by brick to the new Zuri site before Tirso was flooded in 1922 to form Lake Omodeo. Everything else from the original town went under. Another possible short stop is at **Tadasuni** (5.3km), where you can inspect its small museum of musical instruments.

A pleasant roll around the west bank of the lake then leads to the impressive **Diga Tirso** (Tirso Dam, 16.5km) before the route heads up. Take in the view and catch your breath during the first climb in **Busachi** (20.4km), with its striking old houses of rough-hewn pink and red basalt. A small museum at the top end of town houses a

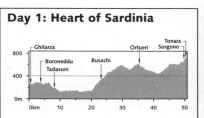

Day 1: Heart of Sardinia

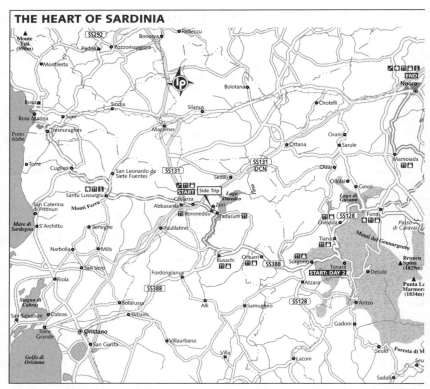

THE HEART OF SARDINIA

permanent display of traditional costumes and intricate designs in hand-woven linen. On that note, looks of mutual fascination between the town's women who still wear traditional dress and cyclists in bright lycra can be expected.

The route eventually crests (32.2km) and rolls through rich meadows, cork-oak woods and a latticework of vineyards. The air becomes noticeably cooler and fresher with the gain in altitude – a welcome relief from the heat in the warmer months. The lovely mountain village of **Sorgono** (47.6km) has all facilities and makes an excellent rest stop before the final ascent through thick old pine and oak forest to Tonara.

Day 2: Tonara to Tortolì/Arbatax
6–10 hours, 103.6km

This is a long day on quiet roads cover-

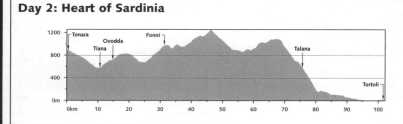

Day 2: Heart of Sardinia

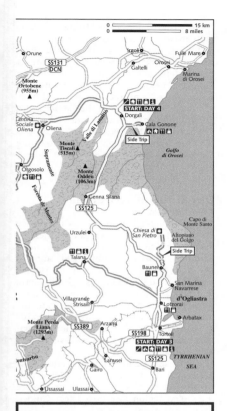

HEART OF SARDINIA – DAY 1

CUES		GPS COORDINATES
start	Ghilarza Municipio, cnr V. Matteotti-V. d Vittoria	40°07'19"N 8°50'19"E
0km	N on Viale Matteotti	
0.8	↑⊙ through traffic island	
3.7	Boroneddu	40°06'48"N 8°52'13"E
	{4.4 ●● ⌐ to 'Zuri' 2.1km↺}	
8	Tadasuni	40°06'39"N 8°53'36"E
8.7	⌐ to Diga Tirso (brown sign)	
19.1	↰ to Busachi	
19.6	↑ to Busachi	
20	10.1km moderate-hard climb	
21.2	⌐ to Busachi (SS388)	
23.1	Busachi	40°01'57"N 8°53'55"E
23.2	↰ to Sorgono	
25.4	↖ to 'Ortueri'	
30.1	↗ to Ortueri	
32.6	1.7km moderate-hard climb	
35.4	Ortueri	40°02'09"N 8°59'13"E
42.5	↗ to 'Sogorno'	
	▲ 3.7km moderate climb	
48	↰ to 'Sogorno' at T intersection	
	▲ hill, 7.1km moderate	
50	Sogorno	40°01'39"N 9°06'14"E
52.1	↗ to 'Tonara'	
58.2	⌐ to 'Tonara'	
50.7	Tonara main piazza	40°01'27"N 9°10'26"E

TONARA TORRONE

Don't leave Tonara without popping into one of the torrone factories to pick up some of the scrumptious **nougat** that has made this town famous; it's also the ultimate pick-me-up when cycling legs seem spent. There are two main commercial producers: **Fabbrica Pili** (Via Vittorio Emanuele 68) and **Pruneddu Torronificio** (Via Ing Porru 5). Tonara takes its torrone heritage very seriously – the town's annual feast day, held in late March–early April, even bears its name – La Sagra del Torrone.

ing myriad terrains, from shady forests and clear mountain lakes to high, rugged, treeless plains and vast coastal bowls. The kilometres spent climbing are more than offset by some long descents, especially the unforgettable drop at day's end.

Descending out of Tonara, the route hugs the west side of the River Tino valley as it meanders and descends through oak and chestnut woods to **Lago di Gusana** (25km), passing through the hamlets of **Tiana** (10.5km) and **Ovodda** (14.7km) along the way – both have small supermarkets and a couple of bars. The pleasant, public rest areas around the lake make an excellent place for a short break before the climbing begins. At an altitude of 1000m, **Fonni** (31.8km) is Sardinia's other high town. Stop for a sit-down lunch or pick up picnic supplies. There are several bars, supermarkets, *alimentari* (deli), *ristoranti (restaurants)* and *pasticcerie* (pastry shop)scattered along the main street. It's also the last place for some time to get water, an essential commodity in hot conditions during the exposed climb up to the 1246m pass of **Arcu Correboi** (47.6km) and beyond. Traffic of any sort is rare on this old high-road (the new road hugs the valley floor and passes through a tunnel hundreds of metres below). It isn't maintained and it's quite rough in places. Plus it's a livestock

SARDINIA

HEART OF SARDINIA – DAY 2

CUES		GPS COORDINATES
start	Tonara main piazza	40°01′27″N 9°10′26″E
0km	retrace last 2.5km Day 1	
2.5	⤴ to Tiana, Fonni	
10.7	Tiana	40°04′07″N 9°08′52″E
14.7	Ovodda	40°05′42″N 9°09′40″E
25.4	⤴ to Fonni, cross bridge	
25.6	⤴ to 'Fonni'	
	▲ 6.1km moderate-hard climb	
31.4	Fonni	40°07′15″N 9°15′10″E
33.1	⤵ to Lanusei	
37	▲ 10.6km moderate climb	
47.6	⚠ herd animals on road next 7km	
57.4	⤴ to Lanusei	
57.4	↑ to Villagrande, Tortoli	
57.6	↑ on road to left, to Villagrande, Tortoli	
61	⤴ to Talana	
61.4	▲ 2.6km moderate climb	
68.5	⤴ to Talana	
	{70.4 ●● ⤴ Bau 'E Tanca Nuraghic ruins 1km ↺}	
75.5	⤵ no sign	
75.8	Talana	40°02′33″N 9°29′51″E
83.6	⤴ to Lotzorai	
98.6	⤴ at 'T'	
99.5	⤴ to Girasole	
103.6	⤴ to Carabinieri, into Corso Umberto	
	⤴ (40m) into Via Mazzini	
103.6	Tortoli tourist office	39°55′27″N 9°39′13″E

OPTION TO GET LOOPY

We know you're out there …cyclists hell-bent on riding looped itineraries. Good thing for you this ride can be tweaked into a loop route. There's a very scenic, hilly road connecting Orguloso to Fonni (see map p262-3) that makes a circuit. This is a good option if you are starting near Tortoli anyway, which is a logical point to start and end. Fonni would be a fine base town, too (there are buses from Nuoro). For B&Bs in Fonni, check out www.sardegnabb.it. So shed your extra weight, leave it at an obliging hotel and go loop it up.

---

party: cows, goats, horses and sheep roam freely, so care should be taken on the long, fast descent.

After meeting the new road in the Calaresu river valley floor, the route heads up onto the southern rim of the vast, open high plains of the northern Gennargentu.

At the eastern edge below **Monte Genziana** (1505m) are the impressive Nuraghic ruins of **Bau 'E Tanca** (70.4km), an easy 500m side trip – look for an unsigned gravel track on the left. The switchback descent into **Talana** (75.8km) hails the beginning of a scintillating 20km freefall – the road literally drops off the edge of the Gennargentu as Sardinia's east coast explodes into view. The scene will take your breath away and the drop is surely the closest thing to riding the face of a 1000m wave. Be sure to keep one eye on the road – the allure of the spectacular panorama is strong indeed.

Day 3: Tortolì to Dorgali
3½–6½ hours, 65.7km

This is an 'up-and-over' day spent entirely on the SS125 (also known as the Orientale Sarda). This section is renowned as one of Sardinia's most panoramic roads and it's not hard to see why. It's a wild, rugged landscape and there isn't a single kilometre that fails to impress with stunning, uninterrupted panoramas unfolding from the moment the road begins to head upwards at Lotzorai (5.2km). While the long ascent to more than 1000m from sea level is hard work, once you're beyond Baunei at 400m (15.4km) the gradient and the effort ease noticeably. From Baunei, consider a very worthwhile stopover or side trip to explore the Golgo region (see boxed text Guided Excursions p265).

Just left of the road at 24km there's a shady pine forest with picnic and barbecue facilities. A path leads to a small pinnacle offering unbeatable 360-degree views – an ideal place for a break. Fill up with water at the signposted *sorgente* (spring).

The only semblance of flat road encountered is a 4km traverse of the northern rim of the vast Gennargentu high plains (31km), an open, rolling meadow bordered by rugged peaks where horses, cows, sheep, goats and enormous wild pigs graze lazily under the watchful eye of their herders. The top of Passo Genna Croce (38.1km) offers a welcome respite from the day's toil. You might want to explore this fascinating region in depth – it's also the base for **Società Gorropu** (see the boxed text Guided Excursions).

From the day's high point of 1017m at **Passo Genna Silana** (43km), it's a su-

Day 3: Heart of Sardinia

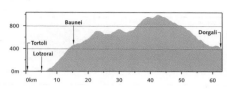

HEART OF SARDINIA – DAY 3

CUES			GPS COORDINATES
start		Tortoli tourist office	39°55'27"N 9°39'13"E
0km		N on Via Mazzini	
		retrace last 5km Day 2	
4	↑	to Lotzorai, Olbia	
5.2		Lotzorai	39°58'15"N 9°39'48"E
7		6.9km hard climb	
15.4		Baunei	40°01'52"N 9°39'50"E
	★↰	left for Golgo excursions	
24	★	panorama and picnic area	
32.8	▲	10.2km moderate climb	
38.1		Sa Domu e S'Orcu	
		{61.7 ●● ↰ Cala Gonone 12km ↻}	
64.7	↰	to Centro	
65.7		Dorgali tourist office	40°17'47"N 9°35'03"E

perb downhill roll all the way to Dorgali. The road clings high to the steep east walls of the spectacular **Gola di Gorropu** (Gorropu Gorge).

Day 4: Dorgali to Nuoro
4–7 hours, 67.7km
The final day follows a fairly circuitous route to Nuoro and continues the trend for experiencing the rugged, natural beauty of the region, highlighted by the spectacular backdrop of the Sopramonte. While the small towns of **Orgosolo** and **Mamoiada** lack major tourist facilities or sights, cycling through them offers the unique possibility to see how locals live in Sardinia's interior. Often regarded as quite guarded and insular, residents are far more likely to warm to travellers arriving under pedal-power.

The route drops quickly out of **Dorgali**, crossing the narrow Lago Cedrino before dropping to the valley floor at the Oliena River with the enormous pale-grey mass of **Monte Sos Nido**s (1349m) looming ever-larger beyond. Traffic between Dorgali and Oliena (21km) is light but fast-moving and

GUIDED EXCURSIONS

FROM BAUNEI INTO THE GOLGO
Cooperativa Goloritzé (☎ 07 826 10 599; www.coopgoloritze.com; Baunei) is a well-organised excursion company, run by young locals, offering guided treks in the magical Golgo area – on foot, on horseback or by donkey. Its base is on the high plain, about 8km from Baunei via a very steep road to the north of the town centre (15.4km, Day 3), indicated by a sign to the church of San Pietro. The co-op is located in a group of low buildings (visible from the road), accessed via a road to the left about 300m before you reach the church. It can also organise pick-ups from Baunei.

FROM SA DOMU E S'ORCU & URZULEI
For inexpensive and efficient guided tours and walks in the Urzulei area call **Società Gorropu** (☎ 07 826 49 282; www.gorropu.com; Via Sa Preda Lada 2, Urzulei), a group of young expert guides based at **Sa Domu E s'Orcu** (38.1km, Day 3). They can help you make the exciting descent into the Gola di Gorropu or explore the area's fascinating underground caves and rivers. This company also organises treks in other parts of the Barbagia and can offer help with renting rooms in private homes in Urzulei – an excellent way to get a feel for the real Sardinia. They offer self-guided options as well.

Coop Ghivine (☎ /fax 07 849 67 21; www.ghivine.com; Via Montebello 5, Dorgali), is a highly professional outfit that organises guided walks, canyoneering, rock climbing and horse trekking in the Sopramonte, Gola di Gorropu, or the Codula di Luna.

SARDINIA

Day 4: Heart of Sardinia

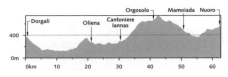

HEART OF SARDINIA – DAY 4

CUES			GPS COORDINATES
start		Dorgali, Pro Loco tourist office	40°17'47"N 9°35'03"E
0km		E on Via La Marmora	
0.1	⌐	Corso Umberto	
0.9	⌐	to Nuoro	
1.2	↖	to Nuoro	
1.8	⌐	to Nuoro	
3.5	⌐	to Nuoro, Oliena	
8	↑	to Oliena	
15.7	▲	5.1km moderate-hard climb	
21		Oliena	40°16'24"N 9°24'16"E
21.5	⌐	to Nuoro	
22	⌐	to Orgosolo	
	▲	8.2km moderate-hard climb	
23.5	⌐	to Orgolsolo	
30.2		Cantoniere Iannas	40°15'14"N 9°20'12"E
35.6	▲	4.3km moderate-hard climb	
40.5	⌐	to Mamoiada	
40.7	⌐	sharp turn	
40.9	⌐	sharp turn, Orgosolo	40°12'19"N 9°21'06"E
41.2	↖	no signs	
41.3	↑	to Mamoiada	
44.6	▲	2.1km hard climb	
50.5	⌐	To Nuoro, Mamoiada	40°12'52"N 9°17'02"E
51	⌐	to 'Stazione di Servizio'	
65.3	↖	to Nuoro	
66.1	↖	follow signs to Centro	
66.6	⌐🏠	at 'T'	
66.7	⌐🏠	sharp turn	
67.1	↑🏠	to Centro	
67.6	↑🏠	to Oliena, Dorgali, Monte Ortobene	
67.7		Nuoro tourist office	40°19'27"N 9°19'50"E

the road lacks a good shoulder. From Oliena onward, the roads are close to empty. In Oliena, however, there is a wonderful stop at the **Cantina Sociale di Oliena** to sip some of the region's noble rot. The turn-off for Orgosolo on the far side of Oliena (22km) is easily missed.

After the meandering 8.2km climb out of Oliena through shady woods, the sudden

> ## CANTINA SOCIALE DI OLIENA
>
> Riding through Oliena (21km), you pass the **Cantina Sociale di Oliena** (☎ 07 842 87 509; www.cantinasocialeoliena. it; Via Nuoro 112), a wine cooperative founded in 1950 to hone the production of Cannonau wine. The vines, originally imported from Spain, have thrived in the dry, sandy soils and beating sunshine of Northern Sardinia. A low-yield crop, the Cannonau has distinct characteristics: deep, garnet-red colour and dry, strong-like-Roman structure. And, *mamma mia*, is it lovely to drink. Try the Nepente di Oliena, named from the homage that poet Gabriele D'Annunzio paid it in 'Elogio del vino di Oliena.'

sight of the Sopramonte's jagged escarpment 700m above as the road crests the pass at **Cantoniere Iannas** (30.2km) is simply breathtaking. The rocky, maquis-speckled terrain of the next valley is like another world, seemingly deserted but for Orgosolo, perched like a lonely eagle's nest high above and reached after a stiff climb from the **Fiume Cedrino** (36.6km).

Orgosolo (40.9km) became famous for its tradition of *banditismo* (banditry), immortalised by the 1963 Italian film *The Bandits of Orgosolo*, but not a locals' favourite subject. Also of interest are the murals decorating the facades of many of Orgosolo's buildings. Dating back to 1973, they originally reflected fairly extreme political views on international issues such as the Vietnam War, South African apartheid, and the Palestinian question. Nowadays they deal mainly with domestic social issues.

The road to Mamoiada remains high, traversing the oak woods and hayfields of the fertile Pratobello plateau, then sweeping through a lush valley of vineyards, crops and orchards – a welcome relief in warmer months from the persistent glare of the sun. Once you're beyond the sleepy mountain hamlet of Mamoiada (50.5km) and onto the superb, swooping 'old' road down to Nuoro (*quella vecchia tortuosa*, 'that twisty old one', as the locals call it with disdain), sighting a car will be rare indeed.

You get sparkling coastline on cliff-hanging roads, luscious wine and challenging picturesque hills. What more is there?

VINO E COSTA DEL SUD

Duration 2 days
Distance 93.6km
Difficulty moderate
Start/Finish Chià
Summary Make it a scintillating day ride, bursting through the coastal, plains and mountain scenery. Or linger on the ride: hang out on the beach, thoughtfully slosh wine in your mouth while noting the undertones and stay the night in little Santadi.

Though this isn't a mileage-intensive route, it has its fair share of hills along the turquoise waters of the Costa del Sud and inland during the second part of Day 2 when you go up and over the small coastal range. The itinerary gives you time to experience the gorgeous wines at Cantina Santadi, creator of the famous Carignano red, while letting you take your time riding through the rolling farmland and coastal range on the second day. Note that the route begins at a crossroads in Chià, known as Baia Chià, because the village is more like an amoeba with floating parts than a cohesive town.

If you aren't interested in wine or carrying panniers, this ride can be done in a day. It's in fact a training route for some local cyclists. If you aren't into tiny beach towns either, it could even be done as a day ride from Cagliari, if you busted your chops to catch the bus to Chià at 6.30am and then make the final bus back around 8pm.

HISTORY

Chià actually stands on what used to be the Phoenician town of Bithia and there are a few scant remains lying about. This part of southwest Sardinia has been prized not just by the Phoenicians but also by the Carthaginians and Romans for its rich mines. Later on the mines also served as Mussolini's bread and butter during the 1936 sanctioning of Italy by the League of Nations.

However, it wasn't only the silver mountains of the interior that caught the colonists' eye – the wild coastline has long played a key role in commerce. Furthermore, the charms of this coast have not been lost on modern developers: the coastline boasts a stretch of luxurious resorts northeast of the start of the route at Chià.

PLANNING
When to Cycle

In the warmer months (April to June and September and October), temperatures are ideal for cycling as it's warm enough for swimming and the summer hordes aren't there. August is an especially crowded month when Italians take their holidays.

What to Bring

Sunscreen and lots of water! Much of the ride is exposed. Be completely self-sufficient as there are no bike shops on route.

GETTING TO/FROM THE RIDE
Chià (start/finish)
BUS

ARST buses to/from Chià run west along the Costa del Sud a couple of times daily in summer, and others serve Cagliari passing through Pula (€2.70, 1½ hours, 8 daily).

BICYCLE

There are a number of ways to cycle from Santadi to Iglesias, the start of the Costa Verde ride. On the main roads, like SS126, it is 42km from Giba. A back-road route will be prettier.

THE RIDE
Day 1: Chià To Santadi
3–6 hours, 53.3km

Get ready to dig in to a truly splendid section of coastline with dazzling capes, craggy outcrops and tranquil turquoise waters. Astonishingly, the traffic is light – unheard of for a coastal road of such a stunning nature. You will work for it, though. The coastal road could be qualified as a bit more than rolling, as the climbs seem to linger on. Conversely, the descents along this wild coastline road inspire a sense of freedom from all confines inherent to the human condition…you know, mostly.

As you make your way inland towards Santadi, the route calms down in respect to scenery and elevation. The town of **Santa Anna Arresi** (35.4km) holds fine potential for lunch. Amazing picnic supplies – onion focaccia, creamy gorgonzola, fruit, sun-dried tomatoes etc – can be found in **Centro Fruta** (**Via Italia**) on the right as you cruise through town. Right before you turn off SS293 to Santadi (50.4km) you'll pass the **Cantina Santadi** (see boxed text p269), only 3km from town. Call ahead in the morning to make arrangements for tasting and to see the winery. If you arrive anywhere between noon and 3pm (the siesta hours),you can

VINO E COSTA DEL SUD – DAY 1

CUES			GPS COORDINATES
start		Baia Chia (Intersection of Viale Chia and Viale Spartivento)	38°53'40"N 8°52'08"E
0km	↰	to 'Teuluda'	
12.8	★	Spiaggia Piscinni	
25.1	↰	to 'Giba,' SS195	
35.4		Sant'Anna Arresi	39°00'11"N 8°38'39"E
41.1	⌐→	Masainas	
43.8	⌐→	to 'Piscinas,' SS293	
		Giba	39°04'18"N 8°38'07"E
50.4	⌐→	to 'Santadi'	
	★	Cantina Santadi	
53	⌐→	to 'Teulada,'	
		Santadi	39°05'38"N 8°42'57"E
	↰	(70m) Via Speranza, to 'Pro Loco'	
53.2	⌐→	Where road hits small piazza, Via Fontane	
	↰	(20m) First left, around piazza	
	↰	(40m) Via Vittorio Veneto	
53.3	★	Santadi Pro Loco (on Left)	39°05'36"N 8°43'01"E

first get settled in the town of Santadi and then make the leisurely pedal back for a tour and tasting.

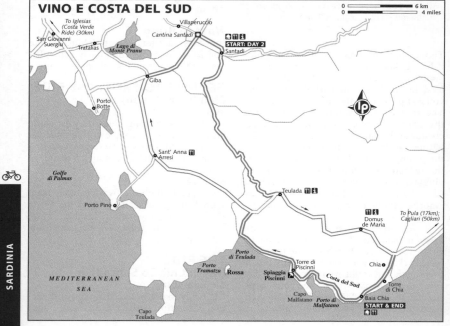

Day 1: Vino e Costa del Sud

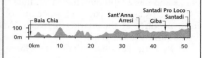

CANTINA SANTADI

The Carignano grape may not be the first to come to mind when you think of great Italian red wines. However, **Cantina Santadi** (☎ 07 819 50 127, Via Cagliari 78; www.cantinadisantadi.it) has quietly created a rich, complex variety that we have seen in a number of wine-savvy restaurants all over Italy. The Carignano wine is not generally well known abroad, but it's a delectable secret to uncover. The Rocca Rubia is a lovely, smooth red that inspires one to linger over a nice meal. They also produce a great dessert wine, Latinia, with notes of honey, caramel and vanilla. Beware that the strong sun of Sardinia makes the wines produced from its soil thusly strong (best to eat something before you go a-tasting). Call ahead to make a reservation to visit; it is open weekdays, mornings and afternoons, with a three-hour, mid-day break.

Day 2: Santadi to Chià
3–5 hours, 40.3km

Don't underestimate this day by the shorter distance. The route is no joke when it comes to climbing and descending. It's not a killer day by any means, but it's significant.

Leaving Santadi, you stroll through fields and farmlands of rural Sardinian countryside speckled with tiny villages. The pavement is smooth and the traffic is oh-so-light. **Teulada** (20.2km), a sweet, upbeat little town, might seem like a logical place to stop for a bite. Just don't eat too much, because you have kilometres of climbing to pass over the top of the utterly gorgeous coastal range, where the landscape again starts its spectacular dramatics. The descent back to the coast and Chià is one you might call someone long-distance just to brag to them about it. You can't go wrong ending

VINO E COSTA DEL SUD – DAY 2

CUES		GPS COORDINATES
Start	Santadi Pro Loco	39°05′36″N 8°43′01″E
0km	Via Vittorio Veneto from Pro Loco	
0.1	Via Mazzini	
	(80m) at stop sign to 'Posta,' Via Fontane	
1.1	to 'Teulada'	
19.5	SS195, to 'Teulada'	
20.2	SS195, Via Cagliari	
	Teulada	38°58′05″N 8°46′20″E
35.5	Domus di Maria	
37.9	to 'Chià'	
40.3	Chià	38°54′25″N 8°53′09″E

the day with a dip in the ocean at one of Chià's beaches.

MOUNTAIN BIKE RIDES

In Sardinia, mountain biking is a new industry, but entrepreneurs are beginning to pick up on the range of opportunities available on this mountain-clad island. There are a number of tour companies in the area that run mountain bike tours, including:

Ichnusa Bike (☎ 07 077 38 424 www .ichnusabike.it) is based in Cagliari and provides rentals and guided tours. The company's values are aligned with FIAB, an active bicycling organisation that strives to create awareness and advancements for cycling in Italy. The proprietor, Marcello, has worked for 10 years as a member of **Cittá Ciclabile** (Cyclable City; www.citta ciclabilecagliari.it), which promotes cycling infrastructure in Cagliari.

Dolce Vita Bike Tours (☎ 07 092 09 885; www.dolcevitabiketours.com; Viale Segni 16) is based in Pula and has high-quality rentals and equipment as well as guided and self-guided tours. An especially nice ride on its docket is one in the Montevecchio area (see p259) that navigates through wilderness and old mining land. You roll through to the gorgeous coastline for a stint before looping back up to Montevecchio.

SARDINIA

TOWNS & FACILITIES

ALGHERO
☎ 07 / pop 38,400

Alghero sits on a small promontory jutting unobtrusively into the idyllic, blue waters of the Mediterranean on Sardinia's north-west coast. Situated in an area of incredible natural beauty, it has understandably become one of this island's most popular tourist resorts. With long, sandy beaches stretching away to the north and plenty of low-key, resort-style accommodation, it's packed with sun-seeking tourists in July and August.

Beyond the beach umbrellas is a town with an attractive historic centre reminiscent of old Spain, part of a rich cultural heritage left by the Catalan-Aragonese.

Information

The **AAST office** (☎ 07 997 90 54; www .comune.alghero.ss.it; Piazza Porta Terra 9) on the west side of the park, has material on the town's history, places of interest and available services.

There are numerous banks with ATMs in town, two of which (Banca Carige and Banco Nazionale di Lavoro) are within a stone's throw of the AAST office.

Supplies & Equipment

For bike repairs and an excellent range of spares for road and mountain bikes, try **Velosport** (☎ 07 997 71 82; Via Vittorio Veneto 90; closed Mon morning). It also hires bikes.

Sleeping & Eating

There's no shortage of accommodation options. Outside August you shouldn't have too much trouble finding a room, but booking ahead is advised.

Camping Calik (☎/fax 07 993 01 11; www.campeggiocalik.it; SS127, Fertilia; per person €9–16), about 6km north of Alghero, has pleasant, shady sites and a pizzeria.

B&B El Buric (☎/fax 07 998 92 019; www.bed-and-breakfast-sardinia.com; Via Enrico Costa 26; d low/high season €55/75)

is simple, neat and summery. It's full of books and has a fabulous shaded veranda.

For self-caterers, you can stock up on fresh produce at the market between Via Sassari and Via Cagliari.

At Pizzeria Paradiso (Via Carlo Alberto 8) a big wedge of pizza won't cost more than €4. **Il Ghiotto** (☎ 07 997 48 20; Piazza Civica 23; meals €10–15) is a crowded deli-cum-wine-bar with an excellent wine list. It's one of the few places where you can try a glass (€8) of the famous Turriga, a renowned Sardinian wine of small production.

ARBUS
☎ 07 / pop 7100

The small town of Arbus has always relied on agriculture and grazing, but the mining boom of the 19th century signalled a new era of prosperity. Production peaked after WWII but a gradual decline in profitability led to total mine closures in the 1970s. Today, Arbus strives to attract tourists, overseeing and promoting not only the areas of natural beauty like the Costa Verde and the wilderness areas of Monte Arcuentu, but also the heritage left by 150 years of mining – what the Sardinians call *arceologia industriale* (industrial archaeology).

Information

Pro Loco (☎ 07 097 54 063; www.arbus.it; Piazza dell'Immacolata) is uphill from the church of San Sebastiano. Their website has many listings for B&Bs and other services.

The main road through town is Via Repubblica, and most services can be found scattered along it.

Sleeping & Eating

Check out the tourist office's website or office for B&B listings.

The only *albergo* is **Hotel Meridiana** (☎ 07 097 58 283; www.wels.it /hotelmeridiana; Via Repubblica 172; B&B €41, half-board €55). Fortunately it is a very good hotel with large, well-appointed rooms, many with balconies and pleasing views.

Pick up supplies from the **ISA supermarket** (Via Repubblica 163–165). **Ristorante Sa Lolla** (☎ 07 097 54 004; Via Libertà 225) is one of Arbus' best eating options, with good pasta and pizzas, and full meals for €25–35.

BOSA

☎ 07 / pop 8000

Bosa is becoming more popular as a tourist destination, but it is yet to show signs of becoming touristy. Sitting in a deep valley at the mouth of the Fiume Temo, its easy pace, fine historic centre and proximity to clean beaches make it a very pleasant little seaside haunt.

Information

The **Pro Loco M Melis tourist office** (☎ 07 853 77 108; www.infobosa.it; Via Azuni 5) is open daily and can provide a town map and useful information. Within the main town centre, **Banco di Sardegna** (Piazza IV Novembre) and **Credito Italiano** (Corso Vittorio Emanuele) have ATMs.

Sleeping & Eating

There are several hotels in Bosa Marina, a somewhat ordinary, modern resort town at the mouth of the Temo about 2.5km south of the centre, but Bosa has the best options. All prices rise considerably in late July and August.

Ostello della Gioventù (☎ 07 853 75 009; www.valevacanze.com Via Sardegna 1, Bosa Marina; dm €16–20) and **Hotel Perry Clan** (☎ 07 853 73 074; Via Alghero 3, Bosa; s/d with bathroom €25/45) are budget places close to the centre of town, with functional rooms. Hotel Perry's restaurant serves good food. **Hotel Sa Pischedda** (☎ 07 853 73 065; Via Roma 8; €70/78; meals €25–30) is a gem of a hotel. Its restaurant is recognised by the Slow Food Movement; it has an excellent wine list and won't leave you disappointed.

In the centre, self-caterers will find appeasing *alimentari*.

BUGGERRU

☎ 07 / pop 1200

Set within the natural walls of a steep valley, Buggerru (buh-jeh-ruh) is a quiet, Mediterranean delight. This little seaside town's origins date back to around 1860, when it was established to serve a thriving zinc- and lead-mining industry. In the early 20th century, the population swelled to more than 12,000. A gradual decline in mining activity from around 1940 shrunk it to around 1300 permanent inhabitants.

The main preoccupation these days is trying to attract the valuable tourist dollar, and there's little evidence of crass development. The atmosphere is relaxed and welcoming.

Information

All shops and services, including a bank with an ATM, are on Via Roma, the main drag running straight down the hill from the coast road to the port. There's little in the way of tourist infrastructure. The **Pro Loco** (☎ 07 815 40 23; www.sardegna turismo.it; Via Roma 17) only opens in high summer; outside of that, try the folks at the **Palazzo Municipio** (town hall; Via Roma 53), which is open most of the year. The staff are happy to offer information on places of interest or to help find a bed in a private home.

Any of the bars or supermarkets in town can also help in finding a cheap bed. Expect to pay around €25–50 per night. There are known to be places to free-camp on the road south of town, or you can head 10km up the road to **Camping Ortus de Mari** (☎/fax 07 815 49 64; camp sites per adult/tent €7.75/10.33), a little way northeast of the beach, about 1km from the Capo Pecora turn-off.

CAGLIARI

☎ 07 / pop 164,200

The capital of the island as well as its transportation hub, Cagliari is an attractive city that's noted for its interesting Roman and medieval sections, its beautiful beach, Poetto, and its wide marshes populated by diverse birds. As with the rest of the island, the city passed through the hands of various conquerors, including the Pisans, the Spanish and the Piemontese House of Savoy, before joining unified Italy. Cagliari was savagely bombed during WWII, suffering significant destruction and loss of life.

Information

If you arrive by boat, you'll find yourself at the port area of Cagliari. At the northwestern end of Via Roma is Piazza Matteotti and the **AAST office** (☎ 07 066 92 55, aast.ca@tiscalinet.it), along with the ARST intercity bus station and the train station. There's also a **tourist information booth** (☎ 07 066 83 52) at the ferry terminal and one at the airport.

There are several major banks (all with ATMs) on Largo Carlo Felice, which runs uphill from Piazza Matteotti.

Supplies & Equipment

The bike shop **Runner** (☎ 07 066 92 18; www.runnernet.it; Corso Vittorio Emanuele 296) has a good workshop and a wide range of spares for road and mountain bikes. Another good place is **Probike** (☎ 07 092 080 77; www.probikepula.it; Corso Vittorio Emanuele 118), in Pula.

Sleeping & Eating

Around 11km from Cagliari is **Camping Pini e Mare** (☎ 07 080 31 03; www.pinie mare.com; Via Leonardo da Vinci, Quartu Sant'Elena; per person €9–18).

Hotel Aurora (☎ 07 065 86 25; www .hotelcagliariaurora.it, in Italian; Salita Santa Chiara 19; s/d €30/45, with bathroom €45/60) has a shabby exterior, but inside it's bright and breezy with city views.

Hotel Clamamosca (☎ 07 037 16 28; www.hotelcalamosca.it; Viale Calamosca 50; s/d €54/84) is a big, boxy beach hotel with sunny rooms, a terrace and a good location.

For picnic supplies, head for Via Sardegna, where there are several good *alimentari* (deli), some greengrocers and a *forno* (bakery). You can make up your own gourmet deli lunch at one of the *salumerie* (delicatessens) in the marina quarter.

Corso Vittorio Emanuele is lined with a plethora of good restaurants and bars. Pop into **Disizos** (Via Napoli 72) for handmade pastas and delicious *seadas* (see boxed text p249). **Isola del Gelato** (☎ 07 065 98 24; Piazza Yenne 35) has sensational gelati, including soy-based varieties.

Getting There & Away

AIR

This island province is well-serviced with busy air and sea routes. Cagliari's **Elmas airport** (www.sogaer.it) is just off the SS130, 8km northwest of the city, and is easily reached by bike. ARST buses leave regularly from Piazza Matteotti to coincide with flights.

BOAT

The cheapest and easiest, though slowest, way to arrive with a bike is by ferry. Ferries arrive at the port just off Via Roma. **Moby Lines** (☎ 19 930 30 40; www.mobylines.it) runs ferries from Olbia to Civitavecchia, Genoa, Corsica and Livorno. **Sardinia Ferries** (☎ 07 894 67 80; www.corsicaferries .com) runs from Golfo Aranci to Corsica. **Tirrenia** (☎ 19 912 31 99; www.tirrenia .it) has connections to Civitavecchia, Fiumicino (Rome), Palermo, Trapani, Naples and Genoa, as well as Tunisia (via Trapani) from Olbia, Cagliari and Arbatax.

BUS

The main bus station is on Piazza Matteotti. Local and intercity **ARST** (Azienda Regionale Sarda Trasporti; ☎ 80 086 50 42; www.arst.sardegna.it) buses use the station. There are services to nearby Pula (€2, 1 hour, hourly) and Villasimius (€2.90, 1½ hours, 10 daily Mon-Fri, 4 daily Sat–Sun) as well as to Oristano (€5.85, 1 hour 35 minutes, 4 daily) and Nuoro (€9.50, 3½ hours, 4 daily). Curiously, the ticket counters are in the attached McDonald's.

FMS (☎ 80 004 45 53; www.ferrovie meridionalisarde.it, in Italian) runs services to Iglesias (€3.45, 1–1½ hours, 6 daily), Carbonia (€4.45, 1½ hours, 6 daily), Portovesme (€4.90, 2 hours, 3 daily) and the Sulcis area. Buses depart from Piazza Matteotti. Buy tickets in the café inside the station.

TRAIN

The main **Trenitalia** (www.ferroviedel lostato.it) station is on Piazza Matteotti. Trains serve Iglesias (€2.75, 55 minutes, 8 daily) and Carbonia (€3.50, 1 hour, 6 daily from Mon–Sat, 2 on Sun) in the southwest, while the main line proceeds north to Sassari (€12.10, 4¼ hours, 5 daily) and Porto Torres via Oristano (€4.75, 1–2 hours, hourly).

The **FdS** (Ferrovie della Sardegna; ☎ 07 050 02 46; www.ferroviesardegna.it, in Italian) station for trains north to Dolianova, Mandas and Isili is on Piazza Repubblica. In summer (19 June–11 September), the scenic trenino verde (www.treninoverde.com) runs between Cagliari and Mandas (€2.65, 2 hours, hourly) and between Mandas and Arbatax (€16.50, 5 hours, 1 daily) on the east coast on Heart of Sardinia ride (see p260). It's a slow ride on a steam locomotive through some wild country. Another similar line runs from Mandas to Sorgono (€12, 2½ hours, 1 daily).

CHIÀ
☎ 07 / pop 1800

Chià sits on bay of silky sand with clear Caribbean-like waters and is adorned with hoary juniper trees and magnificent sand dunes. It's a paradise for wind- and kite-surfers who very often do their thing off its beaches. It's not by any stretch the biggest or flashiest of the Sardinia beach towns, but it's a convenient jumping-off point. There is frequent transport to Chià from Pula and Calgliari, so it's not necessary to stick around if you just want to arrive from Cagliari the morning of the ride.

Information
There is no tourist office in tiny Chià, but check out www.sardegna.com for a list of B&Bs.

Supplies & Equipment
The nearest bike shop is in Pula, **ProBike** (see p272).

Sleeping & Eating
For cheaper options, **Campeggio Torre Chià** (☎ 07 092 30 054; fax 07 092 30 055; www.campeggiotorrechia.it; camp sites per adult/tent €6/8, 4-person villas up to €112) is a few hundred metres back from Spiaggia Su Portu. Note that it's usually full in August.

Your next bet would be the modest **Il Gabbiano** (☎ 07 092 30 160; www.hotel ilgabbiano.net; Località` Is Tramazzeddus; s/d €90/145). For the ultimate splurge, check into the **Le Meridien Chià Laguna** (☎ 07 09 23 91; www.lemeridien.com; Località Chià; half-board per person €220) and ask for sea-view rooms.

There are a handful of places to grab a bite, but self-caterers might want to stock up on supplies before coming.

DORGALI & CALA GONONE
☎ 07 / pop 8200

Whether visitors choose to stay in Dorgali or Cala Gonone will probably be determined by their preference for sea or mountains. Dorgali is dominated totally by the Sopramonte to its south, the vast 500-sq-km high-plain (around 1000m above sea level) and the awesome Gola di Gorropu gorge that cuts deeply into it. Opportunities for excursions on foot abound – guided

walks, from day trips to week-long excursions come highly recommended.

The coastline that extends south from Cala Gonone, the sleepy fishing village turned coastal resort town immediately east of Dorgali, is truly exceptional, even by Sardinian standards. Much of this vast, unspoilt stretch of coast is accessible only on foot or by boat. It's a seemingly endless line of limestone cliffs and crags dotted with caves of every dimension, interrupted only by pristine beaches nestled in secluded bays. It's a 6km ride into or out of Cala Gonone, but there's always the option of catching the bus with your bike.

Information
Dorgali's main street, Via Lamarmora, runs one-way, so the town can only be entered from the lower, western end. The helpful staff at the **Pro Loco** (☎ /fax 07 849 62 43; www.dorgali.it; Via Lamarmora 108) can provide maps and information on accommodation and the vast array of natural and archaeological wonders in the area. There's also a **tourist office** (☎ 07 849 36 96; www .calagonone.com; Viale Bue Marino 1/a) at Cala Gonone open April to October.

Banks with ATMs are on Via Lamarmora.

Supplies & Equipment
For limited bike spares, try **Ditta Pier Paolo Melis** (☎ 0784 9 62 30; Via Lamarmora 74).

Sleeping & Eating
Accommodation and dining choices in Dorgali are a bit slim. Try the tourist office for B&B suggestions.

Hotel S'Adde (☎ 07 849 44 12; www .hotelsadde.it; Via Concordia 38; s/d €60/108) is a good, centrally located hotel with clean rooms, terraces and a decent pizzeria/*ristorante* downstairs.

For self-caterers, there are a number of stores located close to the centre. **Ristorante Colibri** (Via Grasci 14; meals €27–30) offers excellent regional dishes.

Cala Gonone offers far greater choice. Note that free-camping is strictly forbidden in the area. **Camping Cala Gonone** (☎ 07 849 31 65; www.campingcalagonone.it; Via Collodi 1; per person €13–19, 4-bed bungalows €126–206; open June–Oct) is one of Sardinia's best camping grounds, with excellent facilities.

Hotel Costa Dorada (☎ 07 849 33 32; www.hotelcostadorada.it; Lungomare Palmasera; s/d €90/180) is a lovely, low-key hotel situated at the southern end of the *lungomare* (seafront promenade).

There are a couple of small supermarkets in the centre of town. **Ristorante Il Pescatore** (Via Marco Polo; full meals from €25–30), just near the port, specialises in fish and seafood.

GHILARZA
☎ 07 / pop 4600

Ghilarza is a small town of around 4500 people that sits just west of Sardinia's mountainous heart. It's one of three towns (the others being Abbassanta and Norbello) that have grown to the point where they virtually merge; they're perched on a broad, volcanic high-plain that provided the basalt for the construction of many of their striking, stone buildings.

Information

Ghilarza's primary importance in this ride is its proximity to the main rail line at Abbassanta, making it an effective gateway to the fabulous cycling territory of the Gennargentu to the east. With little tourist infrastructure, it has a **Pro Loco** (☎/fax 07 855 23 96; www.sardiniacnos.it/ghilarza; Piazza A Gramsci 3) and a handful of B&Bs. Riders might be keen to saddle up and head into the hills.

The main thoroughfare, Corso Umberto, has a couple of banks (with ATMs) and supermarkets within easy reach.

Supplies & Equipment

Ciclomania (☎ 07 855 27 68; Via Nessi 22) is a good bike shop with spares and repair facilities for road and mountain bikes.

Sleeping & Eating

There are a number of B&Bs. You can check an updated list at www.sardegnaturismo.com.

Ianam B&B (☎ 320 378 04 23; www.ianam.com; via Giovanni XX111, #17; s/d €25/40) is a true gem. Right near the city centre, this tiny and immaculate zen-style B&B will treat you to organic food and good conversation. You can't beat this deal.

Ristorante Al Marchi (Via Concezione 4) is one of the town's best eateries.

IGLESIAS
☎ 07 / pop 28,200

Iglesias' history is inexorably linked to mining. Much of the town's prized architecture dates back to the Pisans, who took control in the 13th century and changed its name from Villa di Chiesa (City of Churches) to Argentaria (City of Silver), in obvious recognition of the rich reserves of silver they discovered in the surrounding hills. When the Aragonese arrived in 1323 they rekindled the ecclesiastical theme and gave the city its current name of Iglesias (Spanish for 'church'). Today it is a bustling, rural centre with strong cultural traditions and it proudly bears the indelible imprint left by centuries of mining. There's nothing brash or flashy about Iglesias and, while it's not high on most tourists' agendas, you might uncover something worthwhile with a bit of fossicking.

Information

The **tourist office** (☎ 07 814 17 95; www.prolocoiglesias.it; Via Roma 10) provides a wealth of information on the city's history and places of interest.

There are several banks with ATMs on and around Piazza Quintino Sella.

Sleeping & Eating

Accommodation options are limited. Check the tourist office for B&B options, or check out **Hotel Artu** (☎ 07 812 24 92; www.hotelartuiglesias.it; Piazza Q Sella 15; s €45–76, d €58–86 with breakfast), the best option. It sits just metres from the *centro storico* (historic centre) and offers a friendly, helpful staff and clean, functional rooms.

For food supplies, visit the **produce market** (Via Gramsci) and the numerous pastry shops, takeaways and grocery shops in the shopping area around Via Martini and Via Azuni in the centro storico. **Bar Capocabana** (Via Gramsci 4) welcomes all for drinks and snacks.

NUORO
☎ 07 / pop 36,700

There isn't a lot of appeal to sticking around in Nuoro, but it is a major transport hub and offers good possibilities for a speedy exit, if desired. The old centre of town is around Piazza delle Grazie, Corso Garibaldi and Via Italia, near the tourist office.

Information

The **EPT office** (☎ 07 843 00 83; www .enteturismo.nuoro.it; Piazza Italia 19) is near several banks with ATMs around Piazza Italia.

Supplies & Equipment

For bike spares (mostly mountain bike), try **Soddu Tonino** (☎ 07 842 00 750; Via della Resistenza 1) about 2km east of the centre.

Sleeping & Eating

There are no real budget accommodation options in Nuoro. From the outside, **Hotel Grillo** (☎ 07 843 86 78; www.grillohotel .it; Via Monsignor Melas 14; s/d with bathroom €55/75) is pretty ugly, but its rooms are pleasant and the place is centrally located.

If you want to make your own meals, pick up fresh produce at the *mercato* on Piazza Goffredo Mameli and other goods at the **UPIM** (Viale del Lavoro) supermarket, near the train station. **Il Rifugio** (☎ 07 842 32 355; Via Antonio Mereu 28–36; set lunch €16, meals €25–30) draws the locals – and you'll love it too, especially if you grab a table in front of the entertaining *pizzaioli* (pizza maker).

ORISTANO

☎ 07 / pop 31,200

Oristano grew to prominence in the 14th century, particularly under the *giudicessa* (queen-judge) Eleonora d'Arborea (see boxed text p260), who opposed the Spanish occupation of the island and drew up a body of laws known as the *Carta de Logu*, a progressive legal code which was eventually enforced throughout the island.

Today, Oristano is the commercial hub of a thriving agricultural industry and an important trading port. Its historic centre, rich in architectural monuments, is a fine showcase of its medieval heritage.

Information

The **EPT office** (☎ 07 833 68 31; www .inforistano.it; Piazza Eleonora d'Arborea 19) has loads of information on the town and the province and will advise on accommodation. There's also a **Pro Loco office** (☎ 07 837 06 21; Via Cuitadella di Menorca 4).

There are several banks with ATMs on and around Piazza Roma.

Supplies & Equipment

Ciclo Sport (☎ 07 837 27 14, Via Busachi 2), in the area east of Via Cagliari, is an excellent place for any spares or repairs.

Sleeping & Eating

Oristano lacks good budget hotel options and the nearest camping grounds are about 7km west. You can pitch a tent at **Camping Torregrande** (☎ /fax 07 832 22 28; www .campeggiotorregrande.com; Località Marina di Torre Grande; per person/tent €6/8).

If you are looking to stay in a private house rather than a hotel, check out **Sardinian Way** (☎ 07 837 51 72; www .sardinianway.it; Via Carmine 14) for listings. Otherwise there is **Eleonora B&B** (☎ 07 837 04 35; www.eleonora-bed-and-breakfast.com; Piazza Eleonora d'Arborea 12; s/d €35/60) situated on the main piazza with three converted en-suite rooms and loads of character.

For food supplies try the Vinci supermarket and covered **produce market** (Via Mazzini 54) between Piazza Roma and Piazza Mariano. **La Grotta** (Via Diego Contini 3–7; pizza €6–8) boasts a wood-burning stove – the sign of a good pizzeria. It's only open in the evenings. **Antica Trattoria del Teatro** (☎ 07 837 16 72; Via Parpaglia 11; meals €28–35) exudes subtle elegance and serves vegetarian options and a hearty minestrone.

SANTADI

☎ 07 / pop 3800

Santadi is a tiny village with its fair share of charm in that rural Sardinian kind of way. Its location is the perfect stopover point after your full day of riding the exquisite Costa del Sud and your careful exploration of Carignano wine at Cantina Santadi (see boxed text p269), only three kilometres away. Plus, this is a fine place to get to know small-town Sardinia. You are unlikely to see many tourists, during any season. Live it up.

Information

Along with your rich cultural experience, comes little tourist infrastructure. Santadi has a tiny **Pro Loco** (☎ 07 819 55 178; www.santadi.it; Via Vittorio Veneto 2), which has a list of B&Bs (it also has lodging information on its website). There are about six B&Bs, but you'll do best with a reservation. There are no hotels. In town there are a number of places to eat and an *alimentari*.

TONARA
☎ 07 / pop 600

At around 950m, Tonara is one of Sardinia's highest towns – therefore snow covers it during the island's colder winters. Perched like a sentinel on the southern slopes of Monte Muggianeddu (1467m), this picturesque town serves as a commercial centre for the surrounding region. It proudly maintains its centuries-old traditions, most notably the hand-manufacture of Sardinia's jangling *campanacci* (herd-animal bells) and the prized Tonara *torrone* (see boxed text p 263), recognised as Italy's very best nougat.

Information
There is no tourist office in Tonara, but the amicable president of the **Pro Loco** association, Mr Gabriele Casula (☎ 07 846 36 47; prolocotonara@tiscali.it), can be contacted for information on services, places of interest, and things to do and see in and around the town.

There is a bank with ATM on Via Sant' Antonio in the town centre.

Sleeping & Eating
For such a small centre, accommodation options are excellent and offer great value.

Ostello della Gioventù Il Castagneto (☎ 07 846 10 005; ilcastagneto@tiscalinet.it; Via Muggianeddu 2; camping per person/bed €10/17), 1km up a steep hill from the centre, offers a lovely panoramic aspect with terrace and evening *ristorante*-pizzeria.

Hotel Belvedere 1 (☎ 07 846 37 56; Via Belvedere 24; s/d €35/60) has great views and clean rooms. It's a friendly, family-run hotel, serving excellent local cuisine in a downstairs restaurant. Brace yourself for a skimpy breakfast, though.

Self-caterers will find everything they need in and around the small centre. **Locanda del Muggianeddu** (☎ /fax 07 846 38 85; Via Monsignor Tore) is an award-winning restaurant serving excellent local cuisine.

TORTOLI/ARBATAX
☎ 07 / pop 10,000

Set about 4km inland of Capo Bellavista, Tortoli is a bustling business town that becomes a bit of a summer haven for the tourists lured by the nearby beaches and a lively holiday scene. About 4km east is Capo Bellavista, with Arbatax (the major central east–coast port for ferries from Civitavecchia and Cagliari) to its immediate north.

Information
The **Pro Loco tourist office** (☎ /fax 07 826 22 824, proloco.tortoli@tiscali.it; Via Mazzini 7) has excellent maps and loads of information in English on the town and area. During the summer it also has an **office** (☎ 07 826 67 690; Via Lungomare 21) in Arbatax. There are several banks with ATMs in and around the main centre of Tortoli.

Sleeping & Eating
Other than camping, there are no good budget options, and all prices rise in midsummer. **Camping Telis** (☎ 07 826 67 140; Località Porto Frailis; per person/site €6–12/€8–11), set in a protected bay, enjoys a very pleasant beach location.

Hotel Victoria (☎ 07 826 23 457; www.hotel-victoria.it; Via Monsignor Virgilio 72; s/d with breakfast €79/118) is a very comfortable, upmarket hotel with an excellent restaurant in a central location.

For self-caterers, try any of the little *alimentari* in the centres or the big **Sisa supermarket** (Lungomare 60) in Arbatax. **Da Lenin** (☎ 07 826 24 422; Via San Gemiliano 19; meals €30) is a restaurant signposted south of the main road connecting Tortolì with Arbatax. It's worth seeking out for the homemade pasta and good seafood served on the terrace.

SARDINIA

Cyclists Directory

ACCOMMODATION

For someone travelling with a bike, accommodation can be trickier to secure. For one, hoteliers at times aren't too keen on the dirty bike and the sweaty bike tourist and, secondly, the hotels have to meet a cyclist's criteria as well. Two standard things to check for in a hotel or B&B are safe bike storage (you can't bring bikes to rooms generally) and breakfast status (is it a buffet or just a croissant?). Laundry service will be a rare bonus. Generally, it's not a problem: they want your business and you want a place to stay, and so it gets worked out. That said, the more people (and bikes) you have in your party the more complicated it becomes.

A new resource, sponsored by FIAB (p29) that is available to cyclists is **Albergabici** (www.albergabici.com), which is basically free advertisement for establishments that are bike-friendly. Check tourist offices in popular cycling areas for bike-friendly hotel listings.

Accommodation in Italy can range from the sublime to the ridiculous with prices to match. Hotels and *pensioni* (guesthouses) make up the bulk of accommodation, covering a rainbow of options from cheap, nasty and ill-lit dosshouses near stations to luxury hotels considered among the best on the planet. Youth hostels and camping grounds are scattered across the country. Other options include charming B&B-style places that continue to proliferate, villa and apartment rentals, and *agriturismo* (farm stays). Some of the latter are working farms, while others are converted farmhouses (often with pools).

In this book a range of prices is quoted from low to high season, and this is intended as a guide only. Half-board equals breakfast and either lunch or dinner; full-board includes breakfast, lunch and dinner.

Prices can fluctuate enormously depending on the season, with Easter, summer (especially August), and the Christmas/New Year period being the typical peak tourist times. Expect to pay top prices in the mountains during the ski season (December-March). There are many variables. Summer is high season on the coast but in the parched cities it can equate to low season. In August especially many city hotels charge as little as half price. It is always worth considering booking ahead in high season (although in the urban centres you can usually find something if you trust it to luck).

Here's a rough guideline: a budget double room can cost up to €80, a midrange one from €80 to €200, and top-end anything from there to thousands of euros for a suite in one of the country's premier establishments. Price depends greatly on where you're looking. A bottom-end budget choice in Venice or Milan will set you back the price of a decent mid-range option in, say, Campania.

Some hotels barely alter their prices throughout the year. This is especially true of the lower-end places, although in low season there is no harm in trying to bargain for a discount. You may find hoteliers especially receptive if you intend to stay for several days.

For more on costs, see p279.

Agriturismo & B&Bs

Holidays on working farms, or *agriturismi*, are increasingly popular, both with travellers and property owners looking for extra revenue. Accommodation can range from simple, rustic affairs to luxury locations where little farming is done and the swimming pool sparkles. Agriturismo business booms in Tuscany and Umbria, but it's also steadily gaining ground in other regions. Local tourist offices can usually supply lists of operators. For detailed information on *agriturismo* facilities throughout Italy check out **Agriturist** (www.agriturist.com) and **Agriturismo.com** (www.agriturismo. com). Other sites include **Network Agriturismo Italia 2005** (www.agriturismo-italia2005.com), which in spite of its name is updated annually, **Agriturismo-Italia. Net** (www.agriturismo-italia.net), **Agriturismoitalia.com** (www.agriturismoitalia.com) and **Agriturismo Vero** (www.agriturismovero.com).

B&B options include everything from restored farmhouses, city palazzi and seaside bungalows to rooms in family houses. Tariffs per person cover a wide range from around €25 to €75. For more information contact **Bed & Breakfast Italia** (☎ 06 687 86 18; www.bbitalia.it; Corso Vittorio Emanuele II 282, Rome, 00186).

Camping

Camping is growing in popularity in Italy. Many camping grounds in Italy are major complexes with swimming pools, restaurants and supermarkets. They are graded according to a star system. Charges often vary according to the season, rising to a peak in July and August. Such high-season prices range from €2 to €20 per adult, free to €12 for children under 12 and from €5 to €25 for a site. In the major cities, grounds are often a good bit from the historic centres. Many camping grounds offer the alternative of bungalows or even simple, self-contained flats.

Independent camping is not permitted in protected areas but, out of the main tourist season, independent campers who choose spots that aren't visible from the road and who don't light fires shouldn't have too much trouble. Get permission from the landowner if you want to camp on private property.

Lists of camping grounds are available from local tourist offices or can be looked up on various sites. The most inclusive is www.camping.it is the best, but you can also try www.campeggi.com and www.italcamping.it. The Touring Club Italiano (TCI) publishes the annual *Campeggi in Italia* (Camping in Italy), listing all camping grounds, and the Istituto Geografico de Agostini publishes *Guida ai Campeggi in Europa* (Guide to Camping in Europe), sold together with *Guida ai Campeggi in Italia*. Both are available in major bookshops.

Other sites worth looking up are www.canvasholidays.com, www.eurocamp.co.uk, www.keycamp.co.uk and www.select-site.com (on this site it's possible to make individual site bookings).

Convents & Monasteries

Some convents and monasteries let out cells or rooms as a modest revenue-making exercise and happily take in tourists, while others are single-sex and only take in pilgrims or people who are on a spiritual retreat. Convents and monasteries generally impose a fairly early curfew. Charges hover around €35/70/100 for a single/double/triple.

As a starting point, take a look at the website of the **Chiesa di Santa Susana** (www.santasusanna.org/comingtorome/convents.html), an American Catholic church in Rome. On this site, it has searched out convent and monastery accommodation options around the country. Getting a spot generally requires contacting the individual institution – there are no central booking agencies for convents and monasteries (yet!).

Another site worth a look is www.initaly.com/agri/convents.htm. You pay US$6 to access the online newsletter with addresses. At www.realrome.com/accommconvents.html you will find a list of Roman convents that generally take in young, single women. **Dolce Vita Travel** (www.dolcevita.com/travel) lists a 'top 10' of convents and monasteries in Italy. A useful if aging publication is Eileen Barish's *The Guide to Lodging in Italy's Monasteries*. Another is *Guida ai Monasteri d'Italia,* by Gian Maria Grasselli and Pietro Tarallo. It details hundreds of monasteries, including many that provide lodging.

Hostels

Ostelli per la Gioventù (youth hostels) are run by the **Associazione Italiana Alberghi per la Gioventù** (AIG; ☎ 06 487 11 52; www .ostellionline.org; Via Cavour 44, Rome), affiliated with **Hostelling International** (HI; www.hihostels.com). A valid HI card is required in all associated youth hostels in Italy. You can get this in your home country or direct at many hostels.

Pick up a booklet on Italian hostels, with details of prices, locations and so on, from the national head office of AIG. Nightly rates vary from around €14 to €20, which usually includes a buffet breakfast. You can often get lunch or dinner for €9.50.

Accommodation is in segregated dormitories and it can be basic, although many hostels offer doubles and/or family rooms (usually at a higher price per person). Hostels will sometimes have a lock-out period between about 9am to 1.30pm. Check-in is usually not before 1pm, and in many hostels there is a curfew from around 11pm. It is usually necessary to pay before 9am on the day of departure.

A small but growing contingent of independent hostels offers alternatives to HI hostels. Many are barely distinguishable from budget hotels. One of many hostel websites is www.hostelworld.com.

Hotels & Pensioni

There is often little difference between a *pensioni* and an *albergo* (hotel). However, a *pensioni* will generally be of one- to three-star quality and traditionally it has been a family-run operation, while an albergo can be awarded up to five stars. *Locande* (inns) long fell into much the same category as *pensioni,* but the term has become a trendy one in some parts, thus it reveals little about the quality of a place. *Affittacamere* are rooms for rent in private houses; they are generally simple affairs.

Quality can vary enormously and the official star system gives only limited clues. One-star hotels/*pensioni* tend to be basic and usually do not offer private bathrooms. Two-star places are similar but rooms will generally have a private bathroom. At three-star joints you can usually assume reasonable standards. Four- and five-star hotels offer facilities such as room service, laundry and dry-cleaning.

Prices are highest in major tourist destinations. They also tend to be higher in northern Italy. A *camera singola* (single room) costs from €25. A *camera doppia* (twin beds) or *camera matrimoniale* (double room with a double bed) will cost from around €40.

Tourist offices usually have booklets with local accommodation listings. Many hotels are also signing up with (steadily proliferating) online accommodation-booking services. You could start your search here:

Alberghi in Italia (www.alberghi-in-italia.it)
All Hotels in Italy (www.hotelsitalyonline.com)
Hotels web.it (www.hotelsweb.it)
In Italia (www.initalia.it)
Italy Hotels Discount (www.italy-hotels-discount.com)
Travel to Italy (www.travel-to-italy .com)

Rental Accommodation

Finding rental accommodation in the major cities can be difficult and time-consuming; rental agencies (local and foreign) can assist, for a fee. Rental rates are higher for short-term leases.

If you're looking for an apartment or studio to rent for a short stay (such as a week or two) the easiest option is to check out the websites of agencies dealing in this kind of thing, starting with the following:

Guest in Italy (www.guestinitaly.com) An online agency, with apartments (mostly for two to four people) ranging from about €115 to €385 a night.
Holiday Lettings (www.holidaylettings .co.uk) Has hundreds of apartments all over the country.
Interhome (www.interhome.co.uk) Here you book apartments for blocks of a week, starting at around UK£400 for two people in Rome.

Villa Rentals

Long the preserve of the Tuscan sun, the villa-rental scene in Italy has taken off in recent years, with agencies offering villa accommodation, often in splendid rural locations not far from enchanting medieval towns or Mediterranean beaches, up and down the country.

For villas in the time-honoured and most popular central regions, particularly Tuscany and Umbria, check out the following:

Cuendet (www.cuendet.com) One of the old hands in this business; operates from the heart of Siena province in Tuscany.

Invitation to Tuscany (www.invitation totuscany.com) A wide range of properties across Tuscany.

Italian Retreats (www.italianretreats .com) Properties from Tuscany to Campa nia, with a sprinkling in Venice.

Simpson (www.simpson-travel.com) Concentrates on Tuscany, Umbria and Sicily.

Summer's Leases (www.summerleases. com) Properties in Tuscany and Umbria.

Some agencies concentrate their energies on the south (especially Campania and Puglia) and the islands of Sicily and Sardinia:

Costa Smeralda Holidays (www.costas .meralda-holidays.com) Concentrates on Sardinia's northeast.

Long Travel (www.long-travel.co.uk) From Lazio and Abruzzo south, including Sardinia and Sicily.

Operators offering villas and other short-term-let properties across the country:

Carefree Italy (www.carefree-italy.com) Apartments and villas.

Cottages & Castles (www.cottagesand castles.com.au) An Australian-based specialist in villa-style accommodation in Italy.

Parker Villas (www.parkervillas.co.uk) Has properties all over Italy.

Veronica Tomasso Cotgrove (www.vt citaly.com) This London-based company also acts in the sale of property in Tuscany and Umbria.

BUSINESS HOURS

Generally markets open from 9am to 1pm and 3.30pm to 7.30pm (or 4pm to 8pm) Monday to Saturday. Many close on Saturday afternoon and some close on a Monday morning or afternoon, and sometimes again on a Wednesday or Thursday afternoon. In major towns most department stores and supermarkets have continuous opening hours from 10am to 7.30pm Monday to Saturday. Some even open from 9am to 1pm on Sunday.

Banks tend to open from 8.30am to 1.30pm and 3.30pm to 4.30pm Monday to Friday. They close at weekends but ex-change offices usually remain open in the larger cities and in major tourist areas.

Bike shops are usually open during the week in the morning and then in the afternoon after the siesta hours. Saturdays tend to be a half-day, with morning hours. On Sunday most shops are closed, but occasionally shops pick a different rest day.

Farmacie (pharmacies) are generally open 9am to 12.30pm and 3.30pm to 7.30pm. Most shut on Saturday afternoon, Sunday, and holidays, but a handful remain open on a rotation basis for emergency purposes. Closed pharmacies display a list of the nearest ones open.

Many bars and cafés open from about 8am to 8pm. Others then go on into the night serving a nocturnal crowd - while still others - dedicated more exclusively to nocturnal diversion, don't get started until the early evening (even if they officially open in the morning). Few bars remain open anywhere beyond 1am or 2am. Clubs (disco-teche) might open around 10pm (or earlier if they have eateries on the premises), but things don't get seriously shaking until after midnight.

Restaurants open noon to 3pm and 7.30pm to around 11pm or midnight (sometimes even later in summer and in the south), although the kitchen often shuts an hour earlier than final closing time. Most restaurants and bars close at least one day a week.

The opening hours of museums, galleries and archaeological sites vary enormously, although at the more important sites there is a trend towards continuous opening from around 9.30am to 7pm. Many close on Monday. Some of the major national museums and galleries remain open until 10pm in summer.

CHILDREN

Adventure Dad: Rescuing Families from the Couch One Expedition at a Time by Joe Kurmaskie is an inspirational book that might inspire you to get the kids into the saddle. Also, try *Bicycling with Children* by Trudy Bell.

See Lonely Planet's *Travel with Children* as well as the websites www.travelwithyourkids .com and www.familytravelnetwork.com.

BICYCLE TOURING WITH CHILDREN

Children can travel by bicycle from the time they can support their head and a helmet, at around eight months.

Disadvantages, especially over long distances, can include exposure to weather, the tendency of a sleeping child to loll, and the loss of luggage capacity at the rear. With a capacity of up to 50kg (versus around 18kg for a child seat), trailers can accommodate two bigger children and luggage. They give better, though not always total, protection from sun and rain and let children sleep comfortably.

From the age of about four, children can move on to a 'trailer-bike' (effectively a child's bike, minus a front wheel, which hitches to an adult's bike) or to a tandem (initially as 'stoker', as the back seat is called, with 'kiddy cranks', crank extenders). This lets them assist with the pedalling effort. The tandem can be a long-term solution, keeping you and your child together and letting you compensate if the child tires.

Be careful of children rushing into touring on a solo bike before they can sustain the effort and concentration required. Keep their energy and interest up. When you stop, a child travelling in a seat or trailer will be ready for action, so always reserve some energy for parenting. This means more stops, including at places like playgrounds. Before setting off on a major journey, try some day trips to check your set-up and introduce your child to cycling.

The very fit and adventurous may not need to compromise to ride with children; others will still find it worthwhile. As with other activities, children bring a new perspective and pleasure to cycle touring. Far more often than not, they love it.

Alethea Morison

CLIMATE

Situated in the temperate zone and jutting deep into the Mediterranean, Italy is regarded by many tourists as a land of sunny, mild weather. However, due to the north–south orientation of the peninsula and the fact that it is largely mountainous, the country's climate is variable and some areas get quite cold. See p24 for more information on when to go.

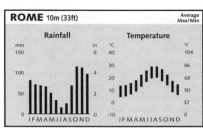

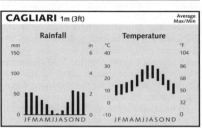

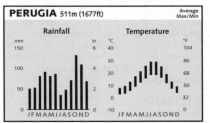

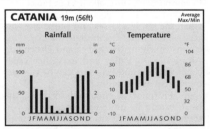

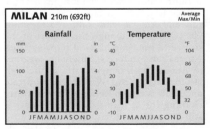

In the Alps, temperatures are lower and winters can be long and severe. Generally the weather is warm from July to September, although rainfall can be high in September. While the first snowfall is usually in November, light snow sometimes falls in mid-September and heavy falls can occur in early October. Freak snowfalls in June are not unknown at high altitudes. Mind you, with climate change, many ski resorts can remain distressingly snow-free until early January.

The Alps shield northern Lombardy and the Lakes area, including Milan, from the extremes of the northern European winter, and Liguria enjoys a mild, Mediterranean climate similar to that in southern Italy because it is protected by the Alps and Apennine range.

Winters are severe and summers torrid in the Po valley. Venice can be hot and humid in summer and, although it's not too cold in winter it can be unpleasant during rain or when the sea level rises and acque alte (literally 'high waters') inundate the city. This is most likely in November and December. Along the Po Valley and in Venice especially, January and February can be surprisingly crisp and stunning.

As Florence is encircled by hills, the weather can be quite extreme, but as you travel towards the tip of the boot, temperatures and weather conditions become milder. Rome, for instance, has an average July and August temperature in the mid-20s (Celsius), although the impact of the *sirocco* (a hot, humid wind blowing from Africa) can produce stiflingly hot weather in August, with temperatures in the high 30s for days on end. Winters are moderate and snow is rare in Rome, although winter clothing (or at least a heavy overcoat) is still a requirement.

The south of Italy and the islands of Sicily and Sardinia have a Mediterranean climate. Summers are long, hot and dry, and winter temperatures tend to be relatively moderate, with daytime averages not too far below 10°C. These regions are also affected by the humid *sirocco* in summer.

CUSTOMS

Duty-free sales within the EU no longer exist (but goods are sold tax-free in European airports). Visitors coming into Italy from non-EU countries can import the following items duty-free: 1L of spirits (or 2L wine), 50g perfume, 250mL eau de toilette, 200 cigarettes, and other goods up to a total of €175. Anything over these limits must be declared on arrival and the appropriate duty paid. On leaving the EU, non-EU citizens can reclaim any Value Added Tax (VAT) on expensive purchases (see p287).

DANGERS & ANNOYANCES

Long queues are the norm in banks, post offices, train stations and government offices.

Pollution

Noise and air pollution, caused mainly by heavy traffic, are problems in the major cities. A headache after a day of sightseeing in Rome or Milan is likely to be caused by breathing in carbon monoxide and lead, rather than simple tiredness. Some cyclists wear protective filter masks. Dirty air is just one of those things that a cyclist must deal with when riding in the great cities.

Italy's beaches can be polluted by industrial waste, sewage, and oil spills from the Mediterranean's considerable sea traffic. The best and cleanest beaches are on Sardinia, Sicily, less-populated southern areas of the mainland and Elba.

Smoking

Since early 2005 smoking in all closed public spaces (from bars to elevators, offices to trains) has been banned – and believe it or not, the ban is being enforced.

Theft

For your bike, use a U-lock made after 2006. If your wheels are worth anything, bring a cable to lock them to the U-lock. This manner of security is also necessary if you are going to be riding and sightseeing in a big city or otherwise sketchy area, of if you will be locking your bike at night or leaving it unsupervised for an extended amount of time. Make sure that you lock your bike to something not easily cut through or dismantled. Also, double check that you actually U-locked your bike to the right thing (it happens).

Pickpockets and bag-snatchers operate in most cities, especially Naples and Rome.

Especially in those cities, watch for groups of dishevelled-looking women and children asking for money. Their favourite haunts are train stations, tourist sites, and shopping areas.

In case of theft or loss, always report the incident at a police station within 24 hours and ask for a statement – otherwise your travel-insurance company won't pay out.

Traffic
See Safety on the Bike (p332).

DISCOUNT CARDS
At museums and galleries, never hesitate to enquire after discounts for students, young people, children, families, or the elderly.

Senior Cards
Senior citizens are often entitled to public transport discounts, but usually only for monthly passes (not daily or weekly tickets); the minimum qualifying age is 65 years.

Seniors (over 60) travelling by rail can get a 15% reduction on all fares by purchasing the annual Cartaviaggio Relax card (€30). The card is available at train stations.

Student & Youth Cards
Free admission to some galleries and sites is available to under-18s. Discounts (usually half the normal fee) are available for some sights to EU citizens aged 18–25. An **International Student Identity Card** (ISIC; www.isic.org) is no longer sufficient at many tourist sites, as prices are usually based on age. A passport, driver's licence, or **Euro<26** (www.euro26.org) card is preferable.

Nonetheless, an ISIC card may still prove useful for cheap transport, theatre and cinema discounts, and occasional discounts in some hotels and restaurants (check the lists on the ISIC website); similar cards are available to teachers (International Teacher Identity Card, or ITIC). For non-student travellers under 25, the International Youth Travel Card (IYTC) offers the same benefits.

Student cards are issued by student unions, hostelling organisations, and some youth travel agencies. In Italy, the **Centro Turistico Studentesco e Giovanile** (CTS; www.cts.it) youth travel agency can issue ISIC, ITIC and Euro<26 cards.

EMBASSIES & CONSULATES
For foreign embassies and consulates in Italy not listed here, look under 'Ambasciate' or 'Consolati' in the telephone directory. In addition to the following, some countries run honorary consulates in other cities.

Australia Rome (☎ 06 85 27 21; emergencies 800 877 790; www.italy.embassy .gov.au; Via Antonio Bosio 5, 00161); Milan (☎ 02 777 04 217; www.austrade.it; Via Borgogna 2, 20122)

Austria Rome (☎ 06 844 01 41; www .bmaa.gv.at; Via Pergolesi 3, 00198)

Canada Rome (☎ 06 44 59 81; www .dfait-maeci.gc.ca/canadaeuropa/italy; Via Zara 30, 00198)

France Rome (☎ 06 68 60 11; www .france-italia.it; Piazza Farnese 67, 00186); Milan (☎ 02 655 91 41; Via della Moscova 12, 20121); Naples (☎ 081 598 07 11; Via Francesco Crispi 86, 80121); Venice (☎ 041 522 43 19; Palazzo Morosini, Castello 6140, 30123)

Germany Rome (☎ 06 49 21 31; www .rom.diplo.de; Via San Martino della Battaglia 4, 00185); Milan (☎ 02 623 11 01; www .mailand.diplo.de; Via Solferino 40, 20121); Naples (☎ 081 248 85 11; www.neapel.diplo. de; Via Francesco Crispi 69, 80121)

Ireland Rome (☎ 06 697 91 21; www .ambasciata-irlanda.it; Piazza Campitelli 3, 00186)

Japan Rome (Map p000; ☎ 06 48 79 91; www.it.emb-japan.go.jp; Via Quintino Sella 60, 00187); Milan (☎ 02 624 11 41; Via privata Cesare Mangili 2/4, 20121)

Netherlands Rome (☎ 06 322 86 002; www.olanda.it; Via Michele Mercati 8, 00197); Milan (☎ 02 485 58 41; Via San Vittore 45, 20123); Naples (☎ 081 551 30 03; Via Agostino Depretis 114, 80133); Palermo (☎ 091 58 15 21; Via Enrico Amari 8, 90139)

New Zealand Rome (☎ 06 441 71 71; www .nzembassy.com; Via Zara 28, 00198); Milan (☎ 02 499 02 01; Via Guido d'Arezzo 6, 20145)

Switzerland Rome (☎ 06 80 95 71; www .eda.admin.ch/roma; Via Barnarba Oriani 61, 00197); Milan (☎ 02 777 91 61; www.eda.admin.ch/milano; Via Palestro 2, 20121); Naples (☎ 081 410 70 46; www.eda .admin.ch/napoli; Via dei Mille 16, 80121)

UK Rome (☎ 06 422 00 001; www .britishembassy.gov.uk; Via XX Settembre

80a, 00187); Florence (☎ 055 28 41 33; Lungarno Corsini 2, 50123); Milan (☎ 02 72 30 01; Via San Paolo 7, 20121); Naples (☎ 081 423 89 11; Via dei Mille 40, 80121)

USA Rome (☎ 06 4 67 41; www.usis .it; Via Vittorio Veneto 119a, 00187); Florence (☎ 055 26 69 51; Lungarno Amerigo Vespucci 38, 50123); Milan (☎ 02 29 03 51; Via Principe Amedeo 2/10, 20121); Naples (☎ 081 583 81 11; Piazza della Repubblica, 80122).

FOOD & DRINK

Eating in Italy is a diverse and decadent highlight for visitors to the expensive cities such as Milan and Venice and the considerably cheaper towns across the south. Indeed, a restaurant rated as mid-range in one place might be considered cheap as chips in Milan. It is best to check the menu, usually posted by the entrance, for prices. Most eating establishments have a cover charge (called *coperto;* usually around €1–2) and a *servizio* (service charge) of 10–15%.

A *tavola calda* (literally 'hot table') normally offers cheap, prepared food and can include self-service pasta, roast meats and *pizza al taglio* (pre-cut pizza).

A *trattoria* is traditionally a cheaper and often family-run version of a *ristorante* (restaurant) with less-aloof service and simpler dishes. An *osteria* is likely to be either a wine bar offering a small selection of dishes with a verbal menu, or a small *trattoria.* You can sometimes get food to accompany your tipples in an *enoteca* (wine bar).

Bars are popular hangouts, serving mostly coffee, soft drinks and alcohol. They often sell *brioche* (breakfast pastry), *cornetti* (croissants), *panini* (bread rolls with simple fillings), and *spuntini* (snacks) to have with your drink.

Vegetarians and vegans, see boxed text.

ON THE RIDE

Unless you are very tied to your energy bar of choice, leave them behind. There's usually at least one bar in even the smallest of towns that has freshly made pastries or some other treat. Many times they have *spremute*, freshly squeezed orange juice, which is a healthful choice. Otherwise, a

---

SPECIAL DIETS: VEGAN, VEGETARIAN, GLUTEN FREE

You'll find vegetarian and vegan restaurants in larger cities, such as Rome and Milan. Most eateries have delectable vegetable starters and side dishes, so vegetarians will do just fine. Vegans can have a tough time, but they'll definitely find enough food. Italians have wonderful vegetable and salad dishes, and bread and pasta are usually vegan; a good lunch on the ride can consist of a sandwich of common deli items such as sundried tomatoes, pine nuts and marinated eggplant. Many Italians seem to think all cheese is vegetarian, so if you can't be sure that the cheese in question does not contain rennet or other non-milk animal substances you should order your dish '*senza formaggio*' (without cheese). Of course, you'll order it thusly if you are vegan. Boutique health food stores are found in cities and some large towns.

Gluten-free foods will be hard to come by in the land of bread and pasta, but nearly all menus offer salad and vegetable sides and many fantastically prepared meat dishes. Rice dishes are more popular up north, but finding them will still be hard.

---

market of any size will have a deli section laden with fresh cheese, bread of the day, sundried tomatoes soaked in olive oil, and fresh meats, and you can fill in the rest in the produce section. Note that markets close during the lunch hours, so you'll have to think ahead. Pocket knives and hand wipes are very useful items to carry.

Of course, going out to lunch along the way is a lovely way to savour Italian culture. It is customary to drink at lunch; if you have hills or traffic ahead, beware of overindulging in wine.

WATER

Drinking water is safe and actually pretty good in Italy, even in light of the fact that the culture is obsessed with bottled water. If you fill from the sink, people may look at you as if you are a barbarian. They might say, 'No, no, no, that water is bad', when they actually mean not that it's not potable but that to them your manner of getting your drinking water is uncivilised.

Along most routes, especially as you get farther north, there will be public springs and fountains, sometimes in a town, sometimes in the middle of nowhere. This water is the freshest and tastiest around.

On remote routes, you know how much water you will need. Add one bottle to the amount you think you'll need, and you'll be set.

See Health & Safety (p323).

HOLIDAYS

Most Italians take their annual holiday in August. This means that many businesses and shops close for at least a part of that month. The *Settimana Santa* (Easter Week) is another busy holiday period for Italians.

Individual towns have public holidays to celebrate the feasts of their patron saints (see individual chapter Highlight boxes). National public holidays include the following:

New Year's Day (Capodanno or Anno Nuovo) 1 January
Epiphany (Epifania or Befana) 6 January
Easter Monday (Pasquetta or Lunedì dell'Angelo) March/April
Liberation Day (Giorno della Liberazione) 25 April – marks the Allied Victory in Italy, and the end of the German presence and Mussolini, in 1945
Labour Day (Festa del Lavoro) 1 May
Republic Day (Festa della Repubblica) 2 June
Feast of the Assumption (Assunzione or Ferragosto) 15 August
All Saints' Day (Ognissanti) 1 November
Feast of the Immaculate Conception (Immaculata Concezione) 8 December
Christmas Day (Natale) 25 December
Boxing Day (Festa di Santo Stefano) 26 December

INSURANCE

A travel-insurance policy to cover theft, loss and medical problems is a good idea. It may also cover you for cancellation or delays to your travel arrangements. Paying for your ticket with a credit card can often provide limited travel accident insurance, and you may be able to reclaim the payment if the operator doesn't deliver. Ask your credit-card company what it will cover.

For information on health insurance, see p323.

INTERNET ACCESS

Most travellers make constant use of internet cafés which are present, if not always abundant, in all cities and most main towns. However, sometimes you'll be surprised by the lack of access in a larger town and the ready availability in a one-horse town. Prices hover around the €5–8 mark per hour.

WOMEN RIDING SOLA

'Da sola? Da sola? Da sola? You're travelling alone?' This is what a solo female bike tourist in Italy might be incredulously asked multiple times daily. In general, Italy is not a dangerous country for women to travel in. The same goes for cycling, but if you do embark on a solo journey consider bringing pepper spray. One must always be prepared for any situation. The author rode her bike around for three months and only encountered one half-way sketchy situation. The verdict: Go for it. Especially in the more populated areas.

Of course, Italian men have that flirting-and-flattering thing going on. Viable reponses: laugh and redirect, walk away, mention your *marito* (husband) or *fidanzato* (boyfriend), ignore, or flirt back if he's a strapping young buck. Always be polite unless you feel unsafe or invaded upon, in which case you should approach the nearest police officer.

Throw a fit if someone touches you in a crowded place. A loud *'Che schifo!'* ('How disgusting!') will usually do the trick. Report more serious incidents to the police, who are then required to press charges.

Follow common sense and standard protocol, avoiding late-nights on dark streets and solo hitchhiking. Maybe we should say something about modest dress, but you're going be wearing lycra all day. Moot point.

Here are some recommended rides for jittery, first-time-solo female cyclists. The criteria we used are the safety of the location, the available services there, and ease of navigability. The top three are:

• Dolomiti di Brenta (p163)
• Val d'Aosta (p48)
• Chianti Classic (p48)

LEGAL MATTERS

For many Italians, finding ways to get around the law is a way of life. This is partly because bureaucracy has long been seen by most (with some justification) as a suffocating clamp on just about all areas of human activity.

The average tourist will only have a brush with the law if victimised by a bag-snatcher or pickpocket.

Alcohol & Drugs

Italy's drug laws were toughened in 2006, and now possession of any controlled substances, including cannabis (marijuana), can get you into hot water. Those caught in possession of five grams of cannabis can be considered traffickers and prosecuted as such. The same applies to tiny amounts of other drugs. Those caught with amounts below this threshold can be subject to minor penalties. The centre-left coalition government that came to power in April 2006 has vowed to repeal these tough laws.

The legal limit for blood-alcohol level is 0.05%, and random breath tests do occur.

Police

If you run into trouble in Italy, you may deal with the *polizia statale* (state police) or the *carabinieri* (military police).

The *carabinieri,* who are directed by the Ministry of Defence, are more concerned with civil obedience. They deal with general crime, public order and drug enforcement (often overlapping with the *polizia*).

One of the big differences between the police and carabinieri is the latter's reach – even many villages have a *carabinieri* post.

Your Rights

Italy still has antiterrorism laws on its books that could make your life difficult if you are detained. You should be given verbal and written notice of the charges laid against you within 24 hours by arresting officers. You have no right to a phone call upon arrest. The prosecutor must apply to a magistrate for you to be held in preventive custody awaiting trial (depending on the seriousness of the offence) within 48 hours of arrest. You have the right not to respond to questions without the presence of a lawyer. For serious crimes, it is possible to be held without trial in preventive custody for up to two years.

MAPS

City Maps

Tourist office maps are generally adequate. More detailed maps are available in Italy at good bookshops, such as Feltrinelli. De Agostini, Touring Club Italiano (TCI) and Michelin all publish detailed city maps.

Cycling Maps

The best map for cycling in Italy is a Touring Club Italiano (TCI, www.touring club.it) 1:200,000 *Grande Carta Stradale d'Italia*. There are 15 overlapping regional foldouts (€7 each) roughly corresponding to Italy's division into 20 major regions. The attention to details like secondary and tertiary lanes, elevation markings, measured distances, and arrows showing every hill's direction and severity of incline are invaluable. Parks and scenic roads are also clearly represented. For a small scale, Kompass publishes maps of various parts of Italy of 1:50,000 and several in other scales (including one at 1:7500 of Capri). Again, many times the tourist offices will have free, detailed maps of the region – and don't forget to ask about bike specific maps. Tourist offices tend to give out gorgeous, free cycling guides and maps.

MONEY

The euro is Italy's currency. The seven euro notes come in denominations of €500, €200, €100, €50, €20, €10 and €5. The eight euro coins are in denominations of €2 and €1, and 50, 20, 10, five, two and one cents.

For the latest exchange rates, check out www.xe.com. For some hints on costs in Italy, turn to p27.

Cash

There is little advantage in bringing foreign cash into Italy. True, exchange commissions are often lower than those for travellers cheques, but the danger of losing the lot far outweighs such gains.

Credit & Debit Cards

Credit and debit cards can be used in an ATM (*bancomat*) displaying the appropriate sign. ATMs are pervasive, even in smaller towns. Visa and MasterCard are among the most widely recognised, but others like Cirrus and Maestro are also well covered. Only some banks give cash advances over the counter, so you're better off using ATMs. Cards are also good for payment in most hotels, restaurants, shops, supermarkets and tollbooths.

Most banks now build a fee of around 2.75% into every foreign transaction, and ATM withdrawals can attract a further fee, usually around 1.5%.

It is not uncommon for ATMs in Italy to reject foreign cards. Try a few more ATMs displaying your card's logo before assuming the problem lies with your card.

If your card is lost, stolen or swallowed by an ATM, you can telephone toll-free to have an immediate stop put on its use:

Amex (☎ 800 914 912)
Diners Club (☎ 800 864 064)
MasterCard (☎ 800 870 866)
Visa (☎ 800 819 014)

Moneychangers

You can change money in banks, at the post office, or in a *cambio* (exchange office). Post offices and most banks are reliable and tend to offer the best rates. Commission fluctuates and depends on whether you are changing cash or cheques. Generally post-office commissions are lowest and the exchange rate is reasonable. The main advantage of exchange offices is the longer hours they keep – just watch out for high commissions and inferior rates.

Taxes & Refunds

A value-added tax of around 20%, known as IVA (Imposta di Valore Aggiunto), is slapped onto just about everything in Italy. If you are a non-EU resident and spend more than €155 on a purchase, you can claim a refund when you leave. The refund only applies to purchases from affiliated retail outlets that display a 'tax-free for tourists' (or similar) sign. You have to complete a form at the point of sale, then get it stamped by Italian customs as you leave. At major airports you can then get an immediate cash refund; otherwise it will be refunded to your credit card. For information, pick up a pamphlet on the scheme from participating stores.

Tipping

You are not expected to tip on top of restaurant service charges but you can leave a little extra if you feel the service warrants it. If there is no service charge, the customer should consider leaving a 10% tip, but this is not obligatory. In bars, Italians often leave small change as a tip, maybe only €0.10. Tipping taxi drivers is not common practice, but you are expected to tip the porter at top-end hotels.

Travellers Cheques

Traditionally a safe way to carry money (and not a bad idea as back-up), travellers cheques have been outmoded by plastic. Various readers have reported having trouble changing travellers cheques in Italy, and it seems most banks apply hefty commissions, even on cheques denominated in euros.

Visa, Travelex and Amex are widely accepted brands. Get most of your cheques in fairly large denominations to save on per-cheque commission charges. Amex exchange offices do not charge commission to exchange travellers cheques.

It's vital to keep your initial receipt, along with a record of your cheque numbers and the ones you have used, separate from the cheques. Take along your passport as identification when you go to cash travellers cheques.

Phone numbers to report lost or stolen cheques:

Amex (☎ 800 914 912)
MasterCard (☎ 800 870 866)
Travelex (☎ 800 872 050)
Visa (☎ 800 874 155)

POST

Poste Italiane (☎ 8031 60; www.poste.it), Italy's postal system, is not as reliable as it could be, although it has improved much over the years. The most efficient mail service is posta *prioritaria* (priority mail).

Francobolli (stamps) are available at post offices and authorised tobacconists (look for the official *Tabacchi* sign: a big 'T', usually white on black). Since letters often need to be weighed, what you get at the tobacconist for international airmail might be an approximation of the proper rate.

TELEPHONE
Domestic Calls

As elsewhere in Europe, Italians choose from a host of choices for phone plans and rates, making it difficult to make generalisations about costs. A local call from a public phone costs €0.10 every minute and 10 seconds. For a long-distance call within Italy you pay €0.10 when the call is answered and then €0.10 every 57 seconds. Calling from a private phone is cheaper.

Telephone area codes all begin with 0 and consist of up to four digits. The area code is followed by a number of anything from four to eight digits. The area code is an integral part of the telephone number and it must always be dialled, even when you're calling from next door. Mobile phone numbers begin with a three-digit prefix such as 330. Toll-free (free-phone) numbers are known as *numeri verdi* and usually start with 800. National call rate numbers start with 848, 899, 166 or 199. Some six-digit national rate numbers are also in use (such as those for Alitalia and rail and postal information).

For national directory inquiries, telephone ☎ 12.

International Calls

Direct international calls can easily be made from public telephones by using a phonecard. Dial ☎ 00 to get out of Italy, then dial the relevant country and area codes, followed by the telephone number.

A three-minute call to a landline in most European countries and across North America will cost about €0.90. Australasia would cost €2.90. Calling mobile phones is generally more expensive. You are better off using your country's direct-dialling services paid for at home-country rates (such as AT&T in the USA and Telstra in Australia); get their access numbers before you leave home. Alternatively, try making calls from cheap-rate call centres or using international calling cards, which are often on sale at newspaper stands.

To make a reverse-charges (collect) international call from a public telephone, dial ☎ 170. All phone operators speak English. In Italy the number for international directory inquiries is ☎ 4176.

To call Italy from abroad, call the international-access number (usually 00), Italy's country code (☎ 39), and then the area code of the location you want, including the leading 0.

Mobile Phones

Italy uses GSM 900/1800, which is compatible with the rest of Europe and Australia but not with North American GSM 1900 or the totally different Japanese system (though some GSM 1900/900 phones do work here). If you have a GSM phone, check with your service provider about using it in Italy and beware of calls being routed internationally (very expensive for a 'local' call).

Italy has one of the highest levels of mobile phone penetration in Europe, and you can get a temporary or prepaid account from several companies if you already own a GSM phone or a dual- or tri-band cellular phone. You will usually need your passport to open an account. Always check with your mobile-service provider in your home country to ascertain whether your handset allows use of another SIM card. If yours does, it can cost as little as €10 to activate a local, prepaid SIM card (sometimes with €10 worth of calls on the card).

Of the four main mobile phone companies, TIM (Telecom Italia Mobile) and Vodafone have the densest networks of outlets across the country.

Pays & Phonecards

Partly privatised, Telecom Italia is the largest telecommunications organisation in Italy, and its orange public payphones are liberally scattered about the country. The most common accept only *carte/schede telefoniche* (phonecards), although you'll still find some that take cards and coins. A few card phones accept credit cards.

Telecom payphones can be found in the streets and train stations and some stores as well as at Telecom offices, post offices, tobacconists and newsstands. You must break off the top left-hand corner of the card before you can use it. Phonecards have an expiry date. This is usually 31 December or 30 June depending on when you purchase the card.

Other companies, such as Infostrada and BT Italia, also operate a handful of public payphones, for which cards are usually available at newsstands.

You will find cut-price call centres in all of the main cities. Rates can be considerably lower than from Telecom payphones for international calls. You simply place your call from a private booth inside the centre and pay for it when you've finished.

TIME

Italy is one hour ahead of GMT. Daylight-savings time, when clocks are moved forward one hour, starts on the last Sunday in March. Clocks are put back an hour on the last Sunday in October. Italy operates on a 24-hour clock. See the World Time Zones Map on p356.

TOILETS

Bars present a really good option for on-the-road pit stops. Of course, you will need to buy a bottle of water or a *dulce* (a pastry or sweet), but generally private establishments in Italy keep their bathrooms clean.

What Mother Nature provides will be your only option on some of the more remote rides. If you're a woman travelling solo and you don't want to leave your bike unattended, hang your tush off a pasture wall the side of the road, and people will think you're just sitting taking a break.

TOURIST INFORMATION

Although the various kinds of tourist offices have different names, they offer roughly the same services.

Throughout this book, offices are referred to as tourist offices rather than by their more elaborate titles. The **Azienda Autonoma di Soggiorno e Turismo** (AAST) is the local tourist office in many towns and cities of the south. AASTs have town-specific information. The **Azienda di Promozione Turistica** (APT) is the provincial (ie main) tourist office, which should have information on the town and the surrounding province. **Informazione e Assistenza ai Turisti** (IAT) has local tourist office branches in towns and cities, mostly in the northern half of Italy. Pro Loco is the local office in small towns and villages and it is similar to the AAST office. Most tourist offices will respond to written and telephone requests for information.

Tourist offices are generally open from 8.30am to 12.30pm or 1pm, and 3pm to 7pm Monday to Friday. Hours are usually extended in summer, when some offices also open on Saturday or Sunday.

Information booths at most major train stations tend to keep similar hours, but in some cases they operate only in summer. Staff can usually provide a city map, a list of hotels, and information on the major sights.

English, and sometimes French or German, is spoken at tourist offices in larger towns and major tourist areas. German is spoken in Alto Adige and French in much of the Valle d'Aosta.

Regional Tourist Authorities

As a rule, the regional tourist authorities are more concerned with planning and marketing than offering a public information service, with work done at a provincial and local level. In the case that you need to look for the tourism or turismo link within the regional site, the website of the Italian **National Tourist Office** (www.enit.it) provides details of all provincial and local tourist offices across the country.

Tourist Offices Abroad

Information on Italy is available from the **Italian National Tourist Office** (ENIT; ☎ 06 4 97 11; www.enit.it; Via Marghera 2, Rome, 00185) and in the following countries:

Australia (☎ 02-9262 1666; italia@ italiantourism.com.au; Level 4, 46 Market St, Sydney, NSW 2000)

Austria (☎ 01-505 16 39; delegation .wien@enit.at; Kärntnerring 4, Vienna, A-1010)

Canada (☎ 416-925 4882; www.italian tourism.com; Suite 907, South Tower, 175 Bloor St East, Toronto, M4W 3R8)

France (☎ 01 42 66 03 96; www .enitfrance.com in French; 23 rue de la Paix, Paris, 75002)

Germany Berlin (☎ 030-247 8398; www .enit.de, in German; Kontorhaus Mitte, Frie-drichstrasse 187, 10117); Frankfurt (☎ 069-259 126; Kaiserstrasse 65, 60329); Munich (☎ 089-531 317; Lenbachplatz 2, 80333)

Japan (☎ 03-3478 2051; www.enit.jp; 2-7-14 Minamiaoyama, Minato-ku, Tokyo, 107-0062)

Netherlands (☎ 020-616 82 46; enitams@wirehub.nl; Stadhouderskade 2, 1054 ES Amsterdam)

Switzerland (☎ 043 466 40 40; info@enit .ch; Uraniastrasse 32, Zurich, 8001)

UK (☎ 020-7408 1254; italy@italian touristboard.co.uk; 1 Princes St, London W1B 2AY)

USA Chicago (☎ 312-644 0996; www .italiantourism.com; 500 North Michigan Ave, Suite 2240, IL 60611); Los Angeles (☎ 310-820 1898; 12400 Wilshire Blvd,

Suite 550, CA 90025); New York (☎ 212-245 4822; 630 Fifth Ave, Suite 1565, NY 10111).

VISAS

Italy signed the Schengen Convention, an agreement whereby 13 EU member countries (excluding the UK, Ireland and the new members that have entered the union since 2004) plus Iceland and Norway agreed to abolish checks at common borders. Legal residents of one Schengen Convention country do not require a visa for another. Citizens of the remaining 14 EU countries and Switzerland are also exempt. Nationals of some other countries, including Australia, Brazil, Canada, Israel, Japan, New Zealand and the USA, do not require visas for tourist visits of up to 90 days.

All non-EU nationals (except those from Iceland, Norway and Switzerland) entering Italy for any reason other than tourism (such as study or work) should contact an Italian consulate, as they may need a specific visa. They should also have their passport stamped on entry as, without a stamp, they could encounter problems when trying to obtain a residence permit (*permesso di soggiorno*).

The standard tourist visa is valid for up to 90 days. A Schengen visa issued by one Schengen country is generally valid for travel in other Schengen countries. However, individual Schengen countries may impose additional restrictions on certain nationalities. It is worth checking visa regulations with the consulate of each country you plan to visit.

You must apply for a Schengen visa in your country of residence. You can apply for only two Schengen visas in any 12-month period and they are not renewable inside Italy. If you are going to visit more than one Schengen country, you should apply for the visa at a consulate of your main destination country or the first country you intend to visit.

For more information on the wonderful world of Schengen visas, check out www.eurovisa.info/SchengenCountries.htm.

EU citizens do not require any permits to live or work in Italy, but may be asked to report to a local police station after three months have elapsed. After five years' continuous residence, they may apply for a document granting permanent residence.

Copies

All-important documents (passport data page and visa page, credit cards, travel insurance policy, tickets, driver's licence etc) should be photocopied before you leave home. Leave a copy with someone at home and keep one with you, separate from the originals.

Permesso di Soggiorno

Non-EU citizens planning to stay at the same address for more than one week are supposed to report to the police station to receive a *permesso di soggiorno* (a permit to remain in the country). Tourists staying in hotels are not required to do this.

A *permesso di soggiorno* only really becomes a necessity if you plan to study, work (legally) or live in Italy. Obtaining one is never a pleasant experience; it involves long queues and the frustration of arriving at the counter only to find you don't have the necessary documents.

The exact requirements, like specific documents and *marche da bollo* (official stamps), can change. In general, you will need a valid passport (if possible containing a stamp with your date of entry into Italy), a special visa issued in your own country if you are planning to study (for non-EU citizens), four passport photos and proof of your ability to support yourself financially. You can apply at the *ufficio stranieri* (foreigners' bureau) of the police station closest to where you're staying.

EU citizens do not require a *permesso di soggiorno*.

Study Visas

Non-EU citizens who want to study at a university or language school in Italy must have a study visa. These can be obtained from your nearest Italian embassy or consulate. You will normally require confirmation of your enrolment, proof of payment of fees and adequate funds to support yourself. The visa covers only the period of the enrolment. This type of visa is renewable within Italy but, again, only with confirmation of ongoing enrolment and proof that you are able to support yourself (bank statements are preferred).

Transport

CONTENTS

GETTING THERE & AWAY

ENTERING THE COUNTRY

Entering Italy is relatively simple. Land crossings from neighbouring EU countries don't require a passport check.

Airport security is much more stringent than in the past. You will need to arrive earlier at the airport than you may have previously – allowing around two hours or more is advisable for international flights. Many airlines allow you to check in online, even if you have baggage, which can save time.

Check what the current policy is regarding restrictions on hand luggage, electronic items, and liquids before you travel, as this is subject to change. Most airlines now specify that only one piece of hand luggage is permitted per person, plus one briefcase or laptop. At the time of going to press, liquids, gels, foams and foodstuffs were allowed in hand baggage in limited quantities by most airlines – usually in amounts not over 100mL (if you have over this amount you can usually buy transparent bottles at the airport in which to decant them). If you carry baby milk you may have to taste it in front of security staff. To save hassle, pack liquids in your luggage and only keep absolute essentials

THINGS CHANGE...
The information in this chapter is particularly vulnerable to change. Check directly with the airline or a travel agent to make sure you understand how a fare (and a ticket you may buy) works and be aware of the security requirements for international travel. Shop carefully. The details given in this chapter should be regarded as pointers and are not a substitute for your own careful, up-to-date research.

(such as baby milk or medicines) your hand luggage.

Passport

Citizens of the EU-member states can travel to Italy with their national identity cards. People from countries that do not issue ID cards, such as the UK or USA, must carry a valid passport. All non-EU nationals must have a full, valid passport. If applying for a visa, check that the expiry date of your passport is at least some months off. See p290 for more information about obtaining a visa and permits for longer stays.

AIR

High seasons in the air are June to September, Christmas and Easter. Shoulder season will often run from mid-September to the end of October and again in April. Low season is generally November to March.

Airports & Airlines

Italy's main intercontinental gateway is the **Leonardo da Vinci Airport** (Fiumicino; ☎ 06 6 59 51; www.adr.it) in Rome, but many low-cost carriers land at Rome's **Ciampino Airport** (☎ 06 6 59 51; www .adr.it) – see p294 for more details. Regular intercontinental flights also serve Milan's **Malpensa Airport** (☎ 02 748 52 200; www .sea-aeroportimilano.it), 50km from the city. Plenty of flights from other European cities also fly to regional capitals (see p294 for more details).

Many European and international airlines compete with the country's national carrier, Alitalia. Listed here are some of the more frequent carriers, with Italian contact telephone numbers unless otherwise stated:

Aer Lingus (airline code EI; ☎ 02434 5 83 26; www.aerlingus.com) To/from Dublin.

Air Canada (airline code AC; ☎ 06 650 11 462, 1-888-247-2262; www.aircanada.com)

Air France (airline code AF; ☎ 848 88 44 66; www.airfrance.com)

Air Malta (airline code KM; ☎ 800 662 22 111; www.airmalta.com)

Air One (airline code AP; ☎ 199 20 70 80, 06 488 80 069; www.flyairone.it)

Alitalia (airline code AZ; ☎ 06 22 22; www.alitalia.it)

American Airlines (airline code AA; ☎ 06 6605 3169, 1-800-433-7300; www.aa.com)

Blue Panorama (airline code BV; ☎ 899 10 33 53; www.blue-panorama.com)

Blu Express (airline code BV; ☎ 06 602 14 577; www.blu-express.com)

BMI (airline code BD; ☎ 199 40 00 44; www.flybmi.com) To/from London Heathrow.

British Airways (airline code BA; ☎ 199 71 22 66; www.britishairways.com)

Delta Air Lines (airline code DL; ☎ 848 78 03 76; www.delta.com)

EasyJet (airline code U2; ☎ 848 88 77 66; www.easyjet.com)

Emirates Airlines (airline code EK; ☎ 06 452 06 060; www.emirates.com)

Eurofly (airline code GJ; ☎ 199 50 99 60; www.eurofly.it) To/from Moscow and New York.

KLM (airline code KL; ☎ 199 41 41 99; www.klm.com)

Lufthansa (airline code LH; ☎ 199 40 00 44; www.lufthansa.com)

Meridiana (airline code IG; ☎ 89 28 98 39, in Europe +39-0789 52 682, in the UK 0845 35 55 588; www.meridiana.it)

Qantas (airline code QF; ☎ 848 35 00 10; www.qantas.com.au)

Ryanair (airline code FR; ☎ 899 67 89 10; www.ryanair.com)

Singapore Airlines (airline code SQ; ☎ 02 777 29 21; www.singaporeair.com)

TAP Portugal (airline code TP; ☎ 351 707 205 700, in Portugal; www.flytap.com)

Thai Airways International (airline code TG; ☎ 064 478 13 304; www.thaiair.com)

BAGGAGE RESTRICTIONS

Airlines impose tight restrictions on carry-on baggage. No sharp implements of any kind are allowed onto the plane, so pack items such as pocket knives, camping cutlery and first-aid kits into your checked luggage.

If you're carrying a camping stove you should remember that airlines also ban liquid fuels and gas cartridges from all baggage, both check-through and carry-on. Empty all fuel bottles and buy what you need at your destination.

TUIfly (airline code X3; ☎ 199 19 26 92; www.tuifly.com) To/from several German cities.

United Airlines (airline code UA; ☎ in the US 1-800-538-2929, in Italy 02 69 63 37 07; www.united.com)

Virgin Express (airline code TV; ☎ 899 800 903; www.virgin-express.com).

Tickets

World aviation has never been so competitive, and the internet is fast becoming the easiest way to find and book reasonably priced seats.

Full-time students and those under 26 have access to discounted fares. You have to show either a document proving your date of birth or a valid International Student Identity Card (ISIC) when buying your ticket. Other cheap deals are the discounted tickets released to travel agents and specialist discount agencies. Most major cities carry newspapers with Sunday travel sections containing ads for these agencies, often known as brokers, consolidators or bucket shops. Also check the websites directly for deals on low-cost carriers, such as Ryanair, Easyjet and Virgin Express. Note that some have started charging extra for hold luggage.

Many of the major travel websites can offer competitive fares, such as:

Booking Buddy (www.bookingbuddy.com)

Cheap Flights (www.cheapflights.com)

Deckchair (www.deckchair.com)

Discount-Tickets.com (www.discount-tickets.com)

CYCLE-FRIENDLY AIRLINES

There aren't too many airlines that will carry a bike free of charge these days – at least according to the official policy. Most airlines regard the bike as part of your checked luggage. With European, Asian and Australian carriers, the usual luggage allowance is 20kg – which doesn't leave much room for your gear – and being over the limit can mean hefty excess baggage charges.

US and Canada-based carriers work on a slightly different system: you are generally allowed two pieces of luggage, each of which must be 32kg or less. Excess-baggage fees are charged for additional pieces, rather than for excess weight. On some airlines a bike may be one of your two pieces; others charge a set fee for carrying a bike, which may then be carried in addition to your two other pieces.

When we looked into the policies of different carriers, we found that not only does the story sometimes change depending on whom you talk to and how familiar they are with the policy, but the official line is not necessarily adhered to at the check-in counter. If your flight is not too crowded, the check-in staff are often lenient with the excess charges, particularly for sporting equipment.

The times when you are most likely to incur excess baggage charges are on full flights – and, of course, if you inconvenience the check-in staff. If you suspect you may be over the limit, increase your chances of avoiding charges by checking in early, being well organised and being friendly and polite: a smile and a thank you can go a long way!

Ebookers.com (www.ebookers.com)
Expedia (www.expedia.com)
Kayak (www.kayak.com)
Last minute (www.lastminute.com)
Orbitz (www.orbitz.com)
Priceline (www.priceline.com)
Travelocity (www.travelocity.com)

Africa

From South Africa many major airlines fly to Italy, most notably: British Airways from Cape Town and Johannesburg through the UK; Air France with connections throughout Europe; and Lufthansa from Cape Town, Durban and Johannesburg connecting through Germany. Ethiopian Airlines flies from Johannesburg to Rome. Emirates Airlines flies between Dubai and Rome. In South Africa try **Flight Centre** (☎ 0860 400 727; www.flightcentre.co.za) or **STA Travel** (☎ 0861 781 781; www.statravel .co.za).

Asia

Bangkok, Singapore and Hong Kong are the best places to find discount tickets. **Cathay Pacific** (www.cathaypacific.com) flies nonstop from Hong Kong to Rome. **STA Travel** (www.statravel.com) has offices in Hong Kong, Japan, Singapore, Taiwan and Thailand. In Hong Kong many travellers use the **Hong Kong Student Travel Bureau** (☎ 2730 3269; www.hkst .com, in Chinese).

Singapore Air flies to Rome three to seven times per week with one or two stops en route. Thai Airways runs regular flights direct from Bangkok to Rome, as well as to Milan Malpensa. Both airlines also have connecting flights with Australia and New Zealand.

Similarly, discounted fares can be picked up from Qantas, which usually transits in Kuala Lumpur, Bangkok or Singapore.

Australia

Flights from Australia to Europe generally go via Southeast Asian capitals. Qantas and Alitalia have occasional direct flights or more-regular trips that make one stop. Also try Malaysia Airlines and the **Star Alliance** carriers (www.staralliance.com), such as Thai Airways, Singapore Airlines or Austrian Air. Flights from Perth are generally a few hundred dollars cheaper.

STA Travel (☎ 134 782; www.statravel .com.au) and **Flight Centre** (☎ 133 133; www.flightcentre.com.au) both have dozens of offices throughout Australia and are renowned for offering cheap deals.

Canada

Alitalia flies direct to Milan from Toronto, with connections to Rome. Air Transat flies nonstop from Montreal to Rome in summer.

Air Canada flies daily from Toronto to Rome, direct and via Montreal and Frankfurt. British Airways, Air France, KLM and Lufthansa all fly to Italy via their respective home countries. Canada's main student-travel organisation is **Travel Cuts** (☎ 1 866 246 9762; www.travelcuts.com), with offices in all major cities.

Continental Europe

All national European carriers offer services to Italy. The three largest, Air France, Lufthansa and KLM, have offices in all major European cities. Italy's national carrier, Alitalia, has a huge range of offers on all European destinations. TAP Portugal serves Portugal.

The cheapest way to fly is via a low-cost airline:

Air Berlin (www.airberlin.com) Flies from Berlin.

Air One (www.flyairone.it) Flies from Munich, Frankfurt, Hamburg and London.

Clickair (www.clickair.com) Flies from Valencia.

Easyjet (www.easyjet.com) Flies from Paris, Berlin, Lyon, Geneva and Basel.

Iberia (www.iberia.com) Flies from Madrid.

Meridiana (www.meridiana.it) Flies from Barcelona and Madrid.

Ryanair (www.ryanair.com) Flies from Brussels, Dublin, Barcelona, Madrid, Stockholm and various other cities.

SAS (www.scandinavian.net) Flies from Copenhagen and Stockholm.

Sky Europe (www.skyeurope.com) Flies from Prague, Bratislava and Budapest.

SN Brussels Airlines (www.flysn.com) Flies from Brussels.

Spanair (www.spanair.com) Flies from Barcelona.

Virgin Express (www.virgin-express.com) Flies from Brussels.

Vueling (www.vueling.com) Flies from Madrid.

New Zealand

Singapore Airlines flies from Auckland through Singapore to Rome's Fiumicino – sometimes with more than one stop. **Air New Zealand** flies via London. **Flight Centre** (☎ 0800 24 35 44; www.flightcentre.co.nz) and STA Travel (☎ 0800 47 44 00; www.statravel.co.nz) have offices in Auckland, as well as in various other cities.

UK & Ireland

The cheapest way to fly to Italy from the UK and Ireland is the no-frills way. **EasyJet** (www.easyjet.com) flies to Milan, Rome, Pisa, Rimini, Venice, Naples and Palermo. The main competitor is Irish **Ryanair** (www.ryanair.com) – its tickets are usually cheaper and it flies to more destinations, including Brindisi, Bari, Milan, Parma, Pisa, Rome, Turin, Genoa, Venice, Rimini and Palermo. Some of these routes are seasonal. **BMI Baby** (www.bmibaby.com) flies to Naples from London and Birmingham (April to October). British Midland also offers some excellent deals; prices vary wildly according to season and depend on how far in advance you book. Italian Air One (www.flyairone.it) also operates flights between London City Airport and Bari, Brindisi, Palermo, Rome, Turin and Venice.

The two national airlines linking the UK and Italy are British Airways and Alitalia, both operating regular flights to Rome, Milan, Venice, Florence, Naples, Palermo, Turin and Pisa.

STA Travel (☎ 0870 160 0599; www.statravel.co.uk) and **Trailfinders** (☎ 020 7292 18 88; www.trailfinders.com), both with offices throughout the UK, sell discounted and student tickets.

Most British travel agents are registered with the Association of British Travel Agents (ABTA). If you have paid for your flight through an ABTA-registered agent who then goes bust, ABTA will guarantee a refund or some alternative.

USA

Delta Airlines and Alitalia have nonstop daily flights from New York's JFK airport to Rome Fiumicino and Milan Malpensa, while Continental flies nonstop to both from Newark. American Airlines flies from Chicago and JFK to Rome.

Discount travel agencies in the USA are known as consolidators. San Francisco is the ticket-consolidator capital of America, although some good deals can be found in other big cities.

STA Travel (☎ 800 781 40 40; www.statravel.com) has offices in Boston, Chicago, Los Angeles, New York, Philadelphia, San Francisco and many more locations. Fares vary wildly depending on season, availability and luck. **Discover Italy** (☎ 1 866 878 74 77; www.discoveritaly.com)

offers booking services for flights, hotels and villas.

LAND

There are plenty of options for entering Italy by train, bus or private vehicle. Bus is the cheapest option, but services are less frequent, less comfortable and significantly longer than the train. Check whether you require a visa to pass through any countries on your way.

Border Crossings

The main points of entry to Italy are the Mont Blanc Tunnel from France at Chamonix, which connects with the A5 for Turin and Milan; the Grand St Bernard tunnel from Switzerland, which also connects with the A5; the Gotthard tunnel from Switzerland (which will have a new parallel railway tunnel, Gotthard Base Tunnel, possibly by 2015, and which will cut travel time from Zurich to Milan by one hour); the new Swiss Lötschberg Base Tunnel (opened in 2007) which connects with the century-old Simplon tunnel into Italy; and the Brenner Pass from Austria, which connects with the A22 to Bologna. All are open year-round. Mountain passes are often closed in winter and sometimes even in autumn and spring, making the tunnels a more reliable option. Make sure you have snow chains if driving in winter.

Regular trains on two lines connect Italy with the main cities in Austria and on into Germany, France or Eastern Europe. Those crossing the frontier at the Brenner Pass go to Innsbruck, Stuttgart and Munich. Those crossing at Tarvisio in the east proceed to Vienna, Salzburg and Prague. Trains from Milan head for Switzerland and on into France and the Netherlands. The main international train line to Slovenia crosses near Trieste. For information on visas see p290.

Bus

Eurolines (www.eurolines.com) is a consortium of European coach companies that operates across Europe with offices in all major European cities. Italy-bound buses head to Milan, Rome, Florence, Siena or Venice and all come equipped with on-board toilet facilities. You can contact them

in your own country or in Italy, and their multilingual website gives comprehensive details of prices, passes and travel agencies where you can book tickets.

Car & Motorcycle

When driving in Europe, always carry proof of ownership of a private vehicle. Third-party motor insurance is also a minimum requirement. Ask your insurer for a European Accident Statement (EAS) form, which can simplify matters in the event of an accident. A European breakdown-assistance policy is also a good investment. In Italy, assistance can be obtained through the **Automobile Club Italiano** (ACI; ☎ 803 116, for 24-hour information 02 661 65 116; www.aci.it in Italian).

Train

If you have the time, a train can be a glorious, nostalgic and relaxing way to travel to Italy, with comfortable couchettes, civilised dining cars and arrival directly in the centre of your destination city.

CONTINENTAL EUROPE

The *Thomas Cook European Timetable* has a complete listing of train schedules. The timetable, which is updated monthly, is available from Thomas Cook offices worldwide for around €15. It is always advisable, and sometimes compulsory, to book seats on international trains to/from Italy. Some of the main international services include transport for private cars. Consider taking long journeys overnight, as the €20 or so extra for a sleeper costs substantially less than Italian hotels.

UK

The passenger-train **Eurostar** (☎ 0870 518 61 86; www.eurostar.com) travels between London and Paris, and London and Brussels. Alternatively you can get a train ticket that includes crossing the Channel by ferry, SeaCat or hovercraft.

For the latest fare information on journeys to Italy, including Eurostar fares, contact the **Rail Europe Travel Centre** (☎ 0870 84 88 48; www.raileurope.co.uk). A Trenitalia Pass can be bought in advance in the UK from **Rail Pass Direct** (☎ 0870 084 1413; www.railpassdirect.co.uk) or **Rail Choice** (www.railchoice.com).

SEA

Dozens of ferry companies connect Italy with virtually every other Mediterranean country. The helpful website **TraghettiOnline** (www.traghettionline.com, in Italian) covers all the ferry companies in the Mediterranean; you can also book online. Tickets are most expensive in summer, and many routes are only operated in summer. Prices for vehicles usually vary according to their size.

Ferry companies and their destinations:

Adriatica (☎ 199 12 31 99; www.adriatica.it) Brindisi to Durrës (Durazzo) in Albania.

Agoudimos Lines (☎ 0831 52 14 08; www.agoudimos.it; Via Giannelli 23) Brindisi to Igoumenitsa, via Corfu.

Blue Star Ferries (☎ 080 52 11 416; www.bluestarferries.com) Brindisi and Ancona to Patras and Igoumenitsa.

Endeavor Lines/Hellenic Mediterranean Lines (☎ 0831 52 85 31; www.ferries.gr; Corso Garibaldi 8) Brindisi to Corfu, Igoumenitsa and Patras, and to Cephalonia – whence you can get a ferry to Zante (Schinari).

Grandi Navi Veloci (☎ 010 209 45 91; www1.gnv.it) Genoa to Barcelona.

Grimaldi Ferries (☎ 081 49 64 44; www.grimaldi-ferries.com) Plies the Mediterranean between Civitavecchia, Livorno, Salerno and Palermo to Tunisia and Barcelona (the Spain routes are part of the Eurail pass system).

Jadrolinija (in Croatia ☎ 0385 51 666 111; www.jadrolinija.hr) From Ancona to destinations along the Croatian coast, including Split and Zadar and from Bari to Dubrovnik.

Marmara Lines (☎ 0831 56 86 33; www.marmaralines.com; Corso Garibaldi 19) Brindisi to Cesme (Turkey).

Minoan Lines (in Greece ☎ 030 2810 399800; www.minoan.gr) Venice, Brindisi and Ancona to Igoumenitsa, Corfu or Patras.

Montenegro Lines (☎ 080 578 98 27; www.morfimare.it) Reservations via Morfimare Travel Agency; Bari to Bar (Montenegro), Cephalonia, Igoumenitsa and Patrasso.

Skenderbeg Lines (☎ 0831 52 54 48; www.skenderbeglines.com; Corso Garibaldi 88) Brindisi to Vlore (Valona; in Albania).

SNAV (☎ 0831 52 54 92; www.snav.it) Brindisi to Corfu and on to Paxos.

Superfast (☎ 080 528 28 28; www.superfast.com) Bari to Igoumenitsa and Patras (Greece), and Corfu. Accepts Eurail, Eurodomino and Inter-Rail passes (port taxes and a high-season supplement payable).

Tirrenia Navigazione (☎ 081 0171998; www.tirrenia.it) Connects all major Italian ports, including on Sicily and Sardinia.

Ventouris Ferries (☎ 080 521 76 99/521 27 56 (Greece/Albania line); www.ventouris.gr) Bari to Igoumenitsa, Corfu and Durrës (Albania).

Virtu Ferries (☎ 095 53 57 11; www.virtuferries.com) Malta to Catania.

GETTING AROUND

You can reach almost any destination in Italy by train, bus or ferry, and services are efficient and cheap; for longer distances there are plenty of domestic air services. With a bicycle in the equation, you can access the far-flung corners of Italy.

AIR

Internal flights in Italy are increasingly competitive, with an increase in low-cost traffic. Some domestic airlines in Italy:

Air Alps (airline code A6; ☎ 045 288 61 40; www.airalps.it)

Air Dolomiti (airline code EN; ☎ 045 288 61 40; www.airdolomiti.it)

Air One (airline code AP; ☎ 199 20 70 80, 06 488 80 069; www.flyairone.it)

Alitalia (airline code AZ; ☎ 06 22 22; www.alitalia.it)

Alpi Eagles (airline code E8; ☎ 899 50 00 58; www.alpieagles.com)

Blu Express (airline code BV; ☎ 06 602 14 577; www.blu-express.com)

Club Air (airline code 6P; ☎ 045 861 77 15; www.club air.it)

Meridiana (airline code IG; ☎ 89 29 28, in Europe +39-0789 52 682, in the UK 0845 355 5588; www.meridiana.it)

MyAir (airline code 81; ☎ 899 50 00 60; www.myair.com)

Volare Web (airline code VA; ☎ 070 460 33 97; www.buy.volareweb.com)

Wind Jet (airline code IV; ☎ 899 65 65 05; www.volawindjet.it).

PACKING YOUR BIKE FOR AIR TRAVEL

We've all heard the horror stories about smashed/lost luggage when flying, but a more real threat to cycle tourists is arriving in a country for a two-week tour only to find the checked bicycle spread out in pieces around the baggage carousel.

How do you avoid this? Err on the side of caution (consider it an extra insurance policy) and box your bike. Otherwise, trust airline baggage handlers if you want (we're told some people actually do) and give it to them unboxed. If you do it this way, turn the handlebars 90°, remove the pedals, and deflate your tyres (partially, not all the way). But is it worth the risk? We recommend that you only do it on your homeward flight, when you can get your favourite bike shop to fix any damage at your leisure.

Some airlines sell bike boxes, but most bike shops give them away free.

HOW TO PACK YOUR BIKE

1. Loosen the stem bolt and turn the handlebars 90°.

2. Remove the wheels, seatpost and saddle (don't forget to mark its height before removing it), and pedals.

3. Undo the rear derailleur bolt and tape it to the inside of the chainstay. There's no need to undo the derailleur cable. Some people also like to remove the chain, and while it can make things easier it isn't necessary.

4. Cut up some spare cardboard and tape it to the underside of the chainwheel, to prevent the teeth from penetrating the floor of the box and being damaged. If you forget this and several teeth are damaged, chances are you'll still be able to ride on them – a professional mechanic with a European road-racing team was notorious for refusing to replace chainrings damaged by riders dragging their bike bags across airport floors.

5. Deflate the tyres of your bike; otherwise the increased pressure during flight could cause them to burst. Remove the quick-release skewers from the wheels and wrap a rag (or two) around the cluster so it won't get damaged (or damage anything).

6. Place the frame in the box, so it rests on the crankset and forks. You might want to place another couple of layers of cardboard underneath the forks. Sometimes the box will be too short to allow your front pannier racks to remain on your bike; if so, remove them. The rear ones should be fine.

7. Place the wheels beside the frame, on the side towards which the handlebars have been turned. You might want to separate the wheels from the frame using a large piece of cardboard.

8. Now add the saddle and seatpost, your helmet, tools, and any other bits and pieces into the vacant areas. Wrap the skewers, chain etc in newspaper to prevent their doing damage to your bike, and then add cardboard or newspaper packing to any areas where metal is resting on metal.

9. Tape the box up extremely well, not covering carrying holes, and write your name, address, and the word 'FRAGILE' on several sides. Ask the airlines to put 'fragile' stickers on your box as well.

10. Strap your panniers together and take them with you as carry-on luggage.

BIKE BAGS & BOXES

If you bring your own bike box, and you're arriving and departing from the same location, sometimes you can talk hotel staff into storing your box for you if you make reservations in their establishment on your way back through town.

TRANSPORT

Lots of domestic flights use the secondary airports, such as in Rome (Ciampino), Pisa, Milan (Linate), Naples, Palermo, Catania, Venice, Florence, Bologna and Cagliari, and other, smaller airports throughout the country. But many internal flights also use the larger airports such as Rome Fiumcino. Domestic flights can be booked online (for low-cost airlines, this is the only way), or you can contact any travel agency (listed throughout this guide).

Alitalia and Lufthanza offer regular domestic flights, with a range of discounts for young people, families, seniors and weekend travellers, as well as advance-purchase deals. A one-way fare is generally half the cost of the return fare. Spanair, the Spanish low-cost airline, also offers some internal flights.

Airport taxes are factored into the price of your ticket.

BOAT

Navi (large ferries) service Sicily and Sardinia, and *traghetti* (smaller ferries) and *aliscafi* (hydrofoils) service the smaller islands. The main embarkation points for Sardinia are Genoa, Livorno, Civitavecchia and Naples; for Sicily the main points are Naples and Villa San Giovanni in Calabria. The main points of arrival in Sardinia are Cagliari, Arbatax, Olbia and Porto Torres; in Sicily they are Palermo and Messina. Usually there will be an extra fee for bicycles on ferries, ranging from €2-10.

For a comprehensive guide to all ferry services into and out of Italy, check out **TraghettiOnline** (www.traghettionline.com, in Italian). The website lists every route and includes links to ferry companies, where you can buy tickets or search for deals.

Tirrenia Navigazioni (☎ 0810 171 998; www.tirrenia.it) services nearly all Italian ports. Other companies include Grandi Navi Veloci, Superfast, Ventouris, and Montenegro Lines.

See the Getting There & Away sections of individual chapters.

BUS

Travelling on buses with a bike in tow is not as convenient as travelling on trains, but it's still relatively easy. There will be an extra fee (€1-4) for the bike and you'll have to store it in the undercarriage. In this case, keeping your panniers on will actually be better because they prop up your bike, protecting the derailleur and drive chain against turbulence and luggage traffic. It's always good to take a seat where it's easy to see luggage loading/unloading at stops, so you can watch your bike. If the bus is loaded down with luggage and people, the bus driver might be ornery about taking you on board; they might be ornery anyway and make up a rule that prevents you from boarding. We were told to be polite and ingratiating. Your second line of defence is to claim injury.

Bus services within Italy are provided by numerous companies and vary from local routes meandering between villages to fast and reliable intercity connections. As a rule, buses are not always cheaper than the train, but they can be invaluable for getting to smaller towns.

It is usually possible to get bus time-tables from local tourist offices. In larger cities most of the intercity bus companies have ticket offices or operate through agencies. In some villages and even good-sized towns, tickets are sold in bars or on the bus. Note that buses almost always leave on time.

CAR

We must also mention car travel, a major form of transport in Italy. Italians love their cars. The extensive public transportation systems should get you to where you need to go, sometimes more quickly, more easily and most definitely more cheaply than by car. Some downfalls include these three facts: *benzina* (petrol) and *autostrada* (highway) tolls are quite expensive, crazy Italian-style driving can be stressful, and parking your car in Italian cities and many towns is a nightmare.

That said, driving in the chaos, even we admit, can be exhilarating. **Avis** (☎ 199 10 01 33; www.avis.com) has a nice option of renting in one location and dropping off the vehicle in another (a one-way rental) for a fee. Two people and two bikes with panniers can be stuffed into an economy-sized car if they pack well.

For information on Road Rules see p232.

HITCHING

Hitching is extremely uncommon in Italy. Hitchhikers could get stranded for hours, and women would be extremely unwise to hitch.

LOCAL TRANSPORT

All the major cities have good transport systems, with bus and underground-train networks usually integrated. However, in Venice your only options are *vaporetti* (small passenger ferries) or your feet.

Bus & Underground Trains

You must buy bus tickets before you board the bus and validate them once on board. If you get caught with an unvalidated ticket you will be fined on the spot (up to €50 in most cities).

There are *metropolitane* (underground systems) in Rome, Milan and Naples, as well as the new automated **MetroTorino** (www.metrotorino.it) in Turin, which is partially up and running. Again, you must buy tickets and validate them before getting onto the train, with fines of up to €50 if you don't. You can get a map of the network from tourist offices in the relevant city.

Every city or town of any size has an efficient *urbano* (city) and *extraurbano* (intercity) system of buses that reach even the most remote of villages. Call ahead if you want to travel on a Sunday, though, as many services come to a virtual halt.

Tickets can be bought at *tabacchi* (tobacconists) or newsstands or from ticket booths or dispensing machines at bus stations and in underground stations. They usually cost around €1. Most large cities offer good-value 24-hour or daily tourist tickets.

Taxi

You can usually find taxi ranks at train and bus stations, or you can telephone for radio taxis. Most cyclists will use taxis to get themselves and a huge bike box from the airport/train station to the hotel. Sometimes it's hard to find taxis that will haul bike boxes. If travelling with a group, expect to take several taxis. Usually you pay an extra fee for the bikes: sometimes they take you for a ride in more ways than one.

It's best to go to a designated taxi stand, as it's illegal for them to stop in the street if hailed. If you phone a taxi, bear in mind the meter starts running from when you have called rather than when it picks you up.

With a minimum charge of €2.33–4.91, depending on the time of day or night, plus €0.78 per km, most short city journeys end up costing between €10 and €15. In Rome, once you go outside the ring road, it costs €1.29 per km. No more than four or five people are allowed in one taxi.

TRAIN

See the boxed text (p300) about travelling on Italian trains with a bike. Trains in Italy are good value – they're relatively cheap compared to those in other European countries – and the better categories of train are fast and comfortable.

Trenitalia (☎ 800 89 20 21; www.trenitalia.com, in Italian) is the partially privatised, state train system that runs most services. Other private Italian train lines are noted throughout this book.

There are several types of trains. Some stop at all stations, such as *regionale* or *interregionale* trains, while faster trains, such as the Intercity (IC) or the fast Eurostar Italia (ES), stop only at major cities. It is cheaper to buy all local train tickets in Italy.

Almost every train station in Italy has either a guarded left-luggage office or self-service lockers. The guarded offices are usually open 24 hours or from 6am to midnight. They charge around €3 per for each piece of luggage.

Classes & Costs

There are 1st and 2nd classes on most Italian trains; a 1st-class ticket costs just under double the price of a 2nd-class ticket.

To travel on Intercity and Eurostar trains you are required to pay a supplement (€3–16) determined by the distance you are travelling. On the Eurostar, the cost of the ticket includes the supplement and booking fee. If you are simply heading over a town or two, make sure you check whether your 40-minute journey requires a supplement. You might arrive 10 minutes earlier but pay €5 more for the privilege. Check up-to-date prices of routes on the Trenitalia website.

On overnight trips within Italy it can be worth paying extra for a *cuccetta* (a sleeping berth in a six- or four-bed compartment)which can cost just €20 more but save you the cost of a hotel.

TRANSPORT

TRAIN TRAVEL WITH BICYCLES

Some of you out there might be intimidated by the thought of taking your bike on the train. Others might be naïve about the challenge. Don't be daunted and don't be fooled. If you have patience tempered with determination and a sense of humour, travelling by train in Italy turns out to be a fantastic way of getting around. We love you, Trenitalia!

There are some essential tips that will set you up for success. Here's our advice in chronological order:

Check train times by either visiting the station or going online to www.ferroviadellostato.it. Calling is usually fruitless. Sometimes the times posted on bulletin boards are outdated, so look at electronically posted times or ask a Trenitalia employee (they wear uniforms).

Regional versus intercity/intercountry trains are designated bike areas on regional trains. However, bikes are 'not allowed' on fast, intercity trains. Though it's a huge pain in the bum, you CAN get away with taking fast trains with your bike. A large part of this restriction comes from the fact that the Italians don't want you to get things dirty with your bike (of course). To travel on fast trains, get industrial sized rubbish bags (black ones are best), take your bike apart, put the wheels in one bag and the frame in the other (using two trash bags taped together to cover the frame). Next, you must somehow manage to get yourself, the pieces of your bike, and your panniers on the train in the 35 seconds it stops for you.

Try buying the rubbish bags from a supermarket; otherwise, you can usually wheel and deal (no pun intended) with a bar employee, who might just give them to you. Once you're on the train, there are usually nice, large places for luggage in each car (on InterCity trains it's more of a squeeze). Mind your free-hanging derailleur: keep it out of reach of other luggage and use a bungee cord to stabilise it.

This whole process is more difficult if you don't have a 'partner in crime', but is still possible. Accept that the train employee might be having a bad day and might choose not to let you on anyway. You can try to deny that your bike is a bike and say that it's just luggage ('*No e una bici, e la mia valigia*'). Problems are less likely to happen if you are female and even less likely if you can cry on cue! Try to take apart your bike out of sight of the train you will be boarding, if possible. A very polite and clueless attitude lubricates this whole situation.

Supplement bike tickets: Beyond your normal fare, you have to pay a fee for your bike which is usually €3.50 and is valid on any train for 24 hours. If your own fare is less than €3.50, you can just buy an extra ticket for your bike at the same price. Just remember that you might want to buy a supplement bike ticket instead if you are taking another train in 24 hours. (There are a couple of other small regional train companies, like in the Lombardy and the Trentino areas that will have slight variations on these fees.)

Bike tickets can be purchased at the ticket windows, but usually not from self-service kiosks (though it's possible from newer kiosks at the larger stations). To buy a supplement bike ticket from a compatible self-service kiosk you must enter in all your travel information and purchase the supplement. Then you have to do the whole process again to buy the regular ticket. This annoys the impatient people behind you, but it's what you have to do.

If you know that you will need multiple supplement bike tickets, we recommend you buy numerous ones from a ticket window and validate them at the stations as needed. There are

Reservations

Reservations on trains are not essential but advisable, as without one you may not be able to find a seat on certain trains. Bookings can be made when you buy your ticket, usually costing an extra €3. Reservations are obligatory for many of the Eurostar trains.

You can make train ticket bookings at most travel agencies, in many cases on the internet, or you can simply buy your ticket on arrival at the train station (allow plenty of time for this). There are special booking offices for Eurostar trains at some train stations.

usually lines for the ticket and you can waste a lot of time or miss a train while waiting. Many times bike supplements aren't checked. If they are and you don't have one, you can be given a hefty fine (the author was given an €18 fine once) or be kicked off the train if the employee is in uber-butthead mode. They won't care that you weren't able to purchase a supplement because the station of departure only had a dated, self-service kiosk. If you get caught, your best bet is to play dumb while speaking in crummy Italian, apologise, and say next time you will get one. Puglia is the only region that proudly does not require supplement bike tickets.

Give yourself a nice chunk of time before the train departs, especially if you don't have a bike supplement. Even at the self-service kiosks lines go incredibly slowly. If you know where you will be going next by train, you can preemptively buy a ticket and validate it when needed; in that case you only need to arrive about 10 minutes early. For those who don't fly by the seat of your pants, you can also buy your tickets online.
Don't forget to validate your ticket at the little yellow machines.

　　Various other obstacles can deter your progression to catching your train. You are not allowed to cross tracks to get to different *binarios* (stations). There are usually stairs to underground passageways, and it's a pain to take them with a fully loaded bike. Usually (sometimes not) there are ramps across the tracks; look at the far ends of the station. Sometimes the train station employees get fussy and insist that they escort you across. Sometimes stalled trains block your ramp and force you down and up stairs. The biggest stations have lifts, which are great, or else have all *binarios* on one navigable level.

Catching the train. Lots of regional trains, but not all, have bicycle-designated cars that are usually, but not always, marked with a bicycle icon. You never know if the bicycle car is at front or back of the train, which is a pain because you have 20 seconds to board before the train departs again. One strategy is to wait, ready to run, in the middle. If you see the bicycle icon in the front, start sprinting to the front. If you don't see it, start sprinting to the back. It might not be there at all, but it usually is. Don't miss your train trying to find the bike car. If worse comes to worse, board wherever and bungee your bike in a boarding compartment in between cars. If the train guy hassles you, you can move your bike, but they most likely won't. Sometimes on older trains the bike car is a holding cell where you have to lift your bike really high to load it. This is nearly impossible to do with the combination of a loaded bike and time restraints. Just go for a compartment in between cars in this case.

Once you're on the train, the single most important object to make your life easier is a bungee cord. You can sit unperturbed without fretting about your bike crashing over if you use the bungee. There are ridiculous 'bike racks' on some of the trains that stabilise your bike via ground racks that balance the bike upright using the spokes. This is crappy and bad for the spokes, even more so with a loaded bike. Creative bungeeing is encouraged. If you can't see your bike from your seat, lock it to something or the back wheel to the frame, and keep valuables with you. But never be far away. You may even want to stay with your bike in the bike car. Be totally prepared to disembark at the stop previous to yours. It's usually unannounced, so find out the station order from the departure bulletin board or ask a lovely Trenitalia attendant. You only have a second to get yourself and your loaded bike off the train.

Good luck and have fun.

Train Passes

Trenitalia offers its own passes for people travelling within Italy. These include the Cartaviaggio Smart, which is free and means you can then buy Ticket Sconto Smart, which has a 10% discount (25% discount for international tickets) for people aged from 12 to 26 years of age. If you get the Cartaviaggio Relax (free) and are over 60, you can buy Ticket Sconto Relax for €30 (free for the over-75s), with discounts of 15% on 1st- and 2nd-class tickets and 20% on couchettes. Children between four and 12 years are entitled to a 50% discount;

TRAIN PASSES & FARES

CATEGORY	4 DAYS	6 DAYS	8 DAYS	10 DAYS
1ST CLASS	€217	€261	€305	€349
2ND CLASS	€174	€210	€246	€282
YOUTH	€145	€175	€205	€235 (2ND CLASS)
GROUPS	€149	€179	€209	€239 (2ND CLASS)

those under four travel free. (For information on train passes, see p302.)

The Trenitalia Pass allows for four to 10 days of travel within any two-month period. Only available to non-residents, passes may be bought from all major train stations or through a travel agent in your home country. Prices for different passes are detailed in the table over.

TRANSPORT

YOUR
BICYCLE

Fundamental to any cycle tour you plan is the bicycle you choose to ride. In this chapter we look at choosing a bicycle and accessories, setting it up to best accommodate your needs and learning basic maintenance procedures. In short, everything you need to gear up and get going.

CHOOSING & SETTING UP A BICYCLE

The ideal bike for cycle touring is (strangely enough) a touring bike. These bikes look similar to road bikes but generally have relaxed frame geometry for comfort and predictable steering; fittings (eyelets and brazed-on bosses) to mount panniers and mudguards; wider rims and tyres; strong wheels (at least 36 spokes) to carry the extra load; and gearing capable of riding up a wall (triple chainrings and a wide-range freewheel to match). If you want to buy a touring bike, most tend to be custom-built these days, but Cannondale (www.cannondale.com) and Trek (www.trekbikes.com) both offer a range of models.

Of course you can tour on any bike you choose, but few will match the advantages of the workhorse touring bike.

Mountain bikes are a slight compromise by comparison, but are very popular for touring. A mountain bike already has the gearing needed for touring and offers a more upright, comfortable position on the bike. And with a change of tyres (to those with semi-slick tread) you'll be able to reduce the rolling resistance and travel at higher speeds with less effort.

Hybrid, or cross, bikes are similar to mountain bikes (and therefore offer similar advantages and disadvantages), although they typically already come equipped with semi-slick tyres.

Racing bikes are less appropriate: their tighter frame geometry is less comfortable on rough roads and long rides. It is also difficult to fit wider tyres, mudguards, racks and panniers to a road bike. Perhaps more significantly, most racing bikes have a distinct lack of low gears.

Tyres – Unless you know you'll be on good, sealed roads the whole time, it's probably safest to choose a tyre with some tread. If you have 700c or 27-inch wheels, opt for a tyre that's 28–35mm wide. If touring on a mountain bike, the first thing to do is get rid of the knobby tyres – too much rolling resistance. Instead, fit 1–1½ inch semi-slick tyres or, if riding unpaved roads or off-road occasionally, a combination pattern tyre (slick centre and knobs on the outside).

To protect your tubes, consider buying tyres reinforced with Kevlar, a tightly woven synthetic fibre very resistant to sharp objects. Although more expensive, Kevlar-belted tyres are worth it. An added benefit is that they are usually light and 'foldable' (they can literally be folded flat), which makes them very simple to pack for long-haulers wishing to carry a spare.

Pedals – Cycling efficiency is vastly improved by using toe clips, and even more so with clipless pedals and cleated shoes. Mountain-bike or touring shoes are best – the cleats are sufficiently recessed to allow comfortable walking. However, you should avoid shoes with excessive flexibility as they reduce pedalling efficiency and can create hotspots on the balls of the feet.

FOLD & GO BIKES

Another option is a folding bike. Manufacturers include: Brompton (www.bromptonbike.com), Bike Friday (www.bikefriday.com), Birdy (www.birdybike.com), Slingshot (www.slingshotbikes.com) and Moulton (www.alexmoulton.co.uk). All make high-quality touring bikes that fold up to allow hassle-free train, plane or bus transfers. The Moulton, Birdie, Brompton and Slingshot come with suspension and the Bike Friday's case doubles as a trailer for your luggage when touring.

TOURING BIKE

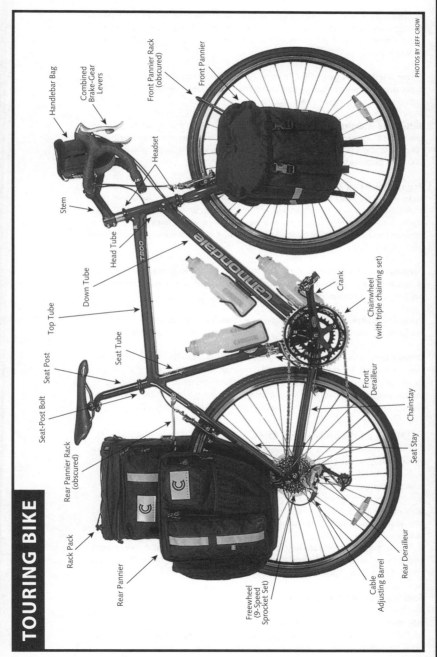

PHOTOS BY JEFF CROW

- Handlebar Bag
- Combined Brake-Gear Levers
- Front Pannier Rack (obscured)
- Front Pannier
- Headset
- Stem
- Head Tube
- Down Tube
- Top Tube
- Seat Tube
- Seat Post
- Seat-Post Bolt
- Rear Pannier Rack (obscured)
- Rack Pack
- Rear Pannier
- Freewheel (9-Speed Sprocket Set)
- Cable Adjusting Barrel
- Rear Derailleur
- Seat Stay
- Chainstay
- Front Derailleur
- Chainwheel (with triple chainring set)
- Crank

YOUR BICYCLE

Mudguards – Adding mudguards to your bike will reduce the amount of muddy water and grit that sprays you when it rains or the roads are wet. Plastic clip-on models are slightly less effective but not as expensive, and they can be less hassle.

Water Bottles & Cages – Fit at least two bottle cages to your bike – in isolated areas you may need to carry more water than this. Water 'backpacks', such as a Camelbak, make it easy to keep your fluids up.

Reflectors & Lights – If riding at night, add reflectors and lights so you can see, and others can see you. Modern LED technology has revolutionised light efficiency, and a small headlight can also double as a torch (flashlight). Flashing LED tail-lights are cheap, compact and highly effective.

Pannier Racks – It's worth buying good pannier racks. The best are aluminium racks made by Blackburn. They're also the most expensive, but come with a lifetime guarantee. Front racks come in low-mounting and mountain bike styles. Low-mounting racks carry the weight lower, which improves the handling of the bike, but if you're touring off-road it is a better idea to carry your gear a bit higher.

Panniers – Panniers range from cheap-and-nasty to expensive top-quality waterproof bags. Get panniers that fit securely to your rack and watch that the pockets don't swing into your spokes.

Cycle Computer – Directions for rides in this book rely upon accurate distance readings, so you'll need a reliable cycle computer, preferably GPS enabled.

Other Accessories – A good pump is essential. Make sure it fits your valve type (see boxed text 'Valve Types'). Some clip on to your bicycle frame, while others fit 'inside' the frame. The stroke volume and high-pressure capability of mini-pumps vary considerably, so shop around. Also carry a lock. Although heavy, U- or D-locks are the most secure; cable locks can be more versatile.

RIDING POSITION SET UP

Cycling is meant to be a pleasurable pursuit, but that isn't likely if the bike you're riding isn't the correct size for you and isn't set up for your needs.

In this section we assume your bike shop did a good job of providing you with the correct size bike (if you're borrowing a bike get a bike shop to check it is the correct size for you) and concentrate on setting you up in your ideal position and showing you how to tweak the comfort factor. If you are concerned that your bike frame is too big or small for your needs get a second opinion from another bike shop.

The following techniques for determining correct fit are based on averages and may not work for your body type. If you are an unusual size or shape get your bike shop to create your riding position.

Saddle Height & Position

Saddles are essential to riding position and comfort. If a saddle is poorly adjusted it can be a royal pain in the derriere – and legs, arms and back. In addition to saddle height, it is also possible to alter a saddle's tilt and its fore/aft position – each affects your riding position differently.

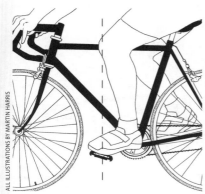

Saddle Tilt – Saddles are designed to be level to the ground, taking most of the weight off your arms and back. However, since triathletes started dropping the nose of their saddles in the mid-1980s many other cyclists have followed suit without knowing why. For some body types, a slight tilt of the nose might be necessary. Be aware, however, that forward tilt will place extra strain on your arms and back. If it is tilted too far forward, chances are your saddle is too high.

Fore/Aft Position – The default setting for fore/aft saddle position will allow you to run a plumb bob from the centre of your forward pedal axle to the protrusion of your knee (that bit of bone just under your knee cap).

Fore/Aft Position: To check it, sit on your bike with the pedals in the three and nine o'clock positions. Check the alignment with a plumb bob (a weight on the end of a piece of string).

Saddle Height – The simplest method of roughly determining the correct saddle height is the straight leg method. Sit on your bike wearing your cycling shoes. Line one crank up with the seat-tube and place your heel on the pedal. Adjust the saddle height until your leg is almost straight, but not straining. When you've fixed the height of your saddle pedal the cranks backwards (do it next to a wall so you can balance yourself). If you are rocking from side to side, lower the saddle slightly. Otherwise keep raising the saddle (slightly) until on the verge of rocking.

The most accurate way of determining saddle height is the Hodges Method. Developed by US cycling coach Mark Hodges after studying the position of dozens of racing cyclists, the method is also applicable to touring cyclists.

Hodges Method

Standing barefoot with your back against a wall and your feet 15cm apart, get a friend to measure from the greater trochanter (the bump of your hip) to the floor passing over your knee and ankle joints. Measure each leg (in mm) three times and average the figure. Multiply the average figure by 0.96.

Now add the thickness of your shoe sole and your cleats (if they aren't recessed). This total is the distance you need from the centre of your pedal axle to the top of your saddle. It is the optimum position for your body to pedal efficiently and should not be exceeded; however, people with small feet for their size should lower the saddle height slightly. The inverse applies for people with disproportionately large feet.

If you need to raise your saddle significantly do it over a few weeks so your muscles can adapt gradually. (Never raise your saddle above the maximum extension line marked on your seat post.)

Handlebars & Brake Levers

Racing cyclists lower their handlebars to cheat the wind and get a better aerodynamic position. While this might be tempting on windy days it doesn't make for comfortable touring. Ideally, the bars should be no higher than the saddle (even on mountain bikes) and certainly no lower than 75mm below it.

YOUR BICYCLE

Pedals

For comfort and the best transference of power, the ball of your foot should be aligned over the centre of the pedal axle (see right).

If using clipless pedals consider the amount of lateral movement available. Our feet have a natural angle that they prefer when we walk, run or cycle. If they are unable to achieve this position the knee joint's alignment will be affected and serious injury may result. Most clipless pedal systems now have some rotational freedom (called 'float') built in to allow for this, but it is still important to adjust the cleats to each foot's natural angle.

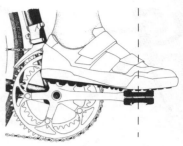

Pedal Alignment: The ball of your foot should be over the centre of the pedal axle for comfort and the best transfer of power.

COMFORT CONSIDERATIONS

Now that you have your optimum position on the bike, there are several components that you can adjust to increase the comfort factor.

Handlebars come in a variety of types and sizes. People with small hands may find shallow drop bars more comfortable. Handlebars also come in a variety of widths, so if they're too wide or narrow, change them.

With mountain bike handlebars you really only have one hand position, but 'riser' bars tend to have a more comfortable angle for touring than 'flat' bars; adding a pair of bar-ends increases hand position options. On drop bars the ends should be parallel to the ground. If they're pointed up it probably means you need a longer stem; pointed down probably means you need a shorter stem.

On mountain bikes the **brake levers** should be rotated downwards to around 45 degrees from horizontal, which ensures your wrist is straight – it's the position your hand naturally sits in. For drop bars the bottom of the lever should end on the same line as the end section.

Getting the right **saddle** for you is one of the key considerations for enjoyable cycling. Everybody's sit bones are shaped and spaced differently, meaning a saddle that suits your best friend might be agony for you. A good bike shop will allow you to keep changing a new (undamaged) saddle until you get one that's perfect. Women's saddles tend to have a shorter nose and a wider seat, and men's are long and narrow.

Brake Levers: Adjust your drop bars so the end section is parallel to the ground and the brake lever ends on this same line.

If you feel too stretched out or cramped when riding, chances are you need a different length **stem** – the problem isn't solved by moving your saddle forward/aft. Get a bike shop to assess this for you. Height-adjustable stems (with a pivot) are also a versatile option, but the correct length is still required.

RECORD YOUR POSITION

When you've created your ideal position, mark each part's position (scratch a line with a sharp tool like a scribe or use tape) and record it, so you can recreate it if hiring a bike or when reassembling your bike after travel. The inside back cover of this book has a place to record all this vital data.

YOUR BICYCLE

MAINTAINING YOUR BICYCLE

If you're new to cycling or haven't previously maintained your bike, this section is for you. It won't teach you how to be a top-notch mechanic, but it will help you maintain your bike in good working order and show you how to fix the most common touring problems.

If you go mountain biking it is crucial you carry spares and a tool kit and know how to maintain your bike, because if anything goes wrong it's likely you'll be miles from anywhere when trouble strikes.

If you want to know more about maintaining your bike there are dozens of books available (*Richard's 21st Century Bicycle Book*, by Richard Ballantine, is a classic; if you want to know absolutely everything get *Barnett's Manual: The Ultimate Technical Bicycle Repair Manual* or *Sutherland's Handbook for Bicycle Mechanics*) or inquire at your bike shop about courses in your area.

PREDEPARTURE & DAILY INSPECTIONS

Before going on tour get your bike serviced by a bike shop or do it yourself. On tour, check over your bike every day or so (see the boxed text 'Predeparture & Post-Ride Checks').

SPARES & TOOL KIT

Touring cyclists need to be self-sufficient and should carry some spares and, at least, a basic tool kit. How many spares/tools you will need depends on the country you are touring in – in countries where bike shops aren't common and the towns are further spread out you may want to add to the following.

Multi-tools (see right) are very handy and a great way to save space and weight, and there are dozens of different ones on the market. Before you buy a multi-tool though, check each of the tools is usable – a chain breaker, for example, needs to have a good handle for leverage otherwise it is useless.

Adjustable spanners are often handy, but the trade-off is that they can easily burr bolts if not used correctly – be careful when using them.

THE BARE MINIMUM:
o pump – ensure it has the correct valve fitting for your tyres (look for one that adapts to both types)
o water bottles (2)
o spare tubes (2)
o tyre levers (2)
o chain lube and a rag
o puncture repair kit (check the glue is OK)
o Allen keys to fit your bike
o small Phillips screwdriver
o small flat screwdriver
o spare brake pads
o spare screws and bolts (for pannier racks, seat post etc) and chain links (2)

FOR THOSE WHO KNOW WHAT THEY'RE DOING:
o spoke key
o spare spokes and nipples (8); can be taped to the lower rear forks
o tools to remove cassette/freewheel
o chain breaker
o pliers with side-cutters
o spare chain links; Shimano HyperGlide chains require new rivets once broken, but quick-release chain links such as the SRAM Powerlink and Wipperman Connex are an excellent alternative
o spare rear brake and rear gear cables

ALWAYS HANDY TO TAKE ALONG:
o roll of electrical/gaffer tape
o nylon cable ties (10) – various lengths/sizes
o hand cleaner (store it in a film canister)

FIXING A FLAT

Flats happen. And if you're a believer in Murphy's Law then the likely scenario is that you'll suffer a flat just as you're rushing to the next town to catch a train or beat the setting sun.

Don't worry – this isn't a big drama. If you're prepared and know what you're doing you can be up and on your way in five minutes flat.

Being prepared means carrying a spare tube, a pump and at least two tyre levers. If you're not carrying a spare tube, of course, you can stop and fix the puncture then and there, but it's unlikely you'll catch that train and you could end up doing all this in the dark. There will be days when you have the time to fix a puncture on the side of the road, but not always. If it's a wet day, be aware that patches may not glue satisfactorily. Carry at least two spare tubes; ones with holes can be patched at day's end.

1 Note which cog the chain sits on, for reference when refitting. Take the wheel off the bike. Remove the valve cap and locknut (see 'Valve Types') on Presta valves. Deflate the tyre completely, if it isn't already.

2 Make sure the tyre and tube are loose on the rim – moisture and tube-pressure often fuse the tyre and rim.

3 Work the tyre bead as far into the central well of the rim as possible to create maximum play where the tyre is being lifted over the rim (removal and fitment). If the tyre is really loose you should be able to remove it by hand. Otherwise you'll need to lift one side of the tyre over the rim with tyre levers. Pushing the tyre away

from the lever as you insert it should ensure you don't pinch the tube and puncture it again.

4 When you have one side of the tyre off, you'll be able to remove the tube. It's imperative before inserting the replacement tube that you carefully inspect the tyre (inside and out) for what caused the puncture; it's often easier to remove the tyre completely. Remove anything embedded in the tyre. Also check that the rim tape covers all spoke nipples and that none protrude through it.

VALVE TYPES

The two most common valve types are Presta (sometimes called French) and Schraeder (American or 'car'). To inflate a Presta valve, first unscrew the round nut at the top (and do it up again after you're done); depress it to deflate. The valve may need to be depressed before pumping as they can stick closed with time. To deflate Schraeder valves depress the pin (inside the top). Ensure your pump is set up for the valve type on your bike.

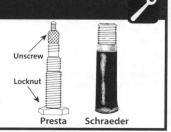

Unscrew

Locknut

Presta   Schraeder

5 Time to put the new tube in. Start by partially pumping up the tube (this helps prevent it twisting or being pinched) and insert the valve in the rim-hole. Tuck the rest of the tube in under the tyre, making sure you don't twist it. Make sure the valve is straight – most Presta valves come with a locknut to help achieve this.

6 Work the tyre back onto the rim with your fingers (refer to Step 3). If this isn't possible, and again, according to Murphy's Law, it frequently isn't, you might need to release a little air and even use your tyre levers for the last 20cm to 30cm. If you need to use the levers, make sure you don't pinch the new tube, otherwise it's back to Step 1. All you need to do now is pump up the tyre and put the wheel back on the bike. Don't forget to fix the puncture that night.

YOUR BICYCLE

FIXING THE PUNCTURE

To fix the puncture you'll need a repair kit, which usually comes with glue, patches, sandpaper and, sometimes, chalk. (Always check the glue in your puncture repair kit hasn't dried up before heading off on tour.) The only other thing you'll need is clean hands.

1. The first step is to find the puncture. Inflate the tube and hold it up to your ear. If you can hear the puncture, mark it with the chalk; otherwise immerse it in water and watch for air bubbles. Once you find the puncture, mark it, cover it with your finger and continue looking – just in case there are more.

2. Dry the tube and lightly roughen the area around the hole with the sandpaper. Sand an area larger than the patch.

3. Follow the instructions for the glue you have. Generally you spread an even layer of glue over the area of the tube to be patched and allow it to dry until it is tacky.

4. Patches also come with their own instructions – some will be just a piece of rubber and others will come lined with foil (remove the foil on the underside but don't touch the exposed area). Press the patch firmly onto the area over the hole and hold it for 2–3 minutes. If you want, remove the excess glue from around the patch or dust it with chalk or simply let it dry.

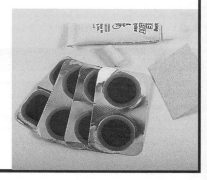

5. Leave the glue to set for 10–20 minutes. Inflate the tube and check the patch has worked.

CHAINS

Chains are dirty, greasy and all too often the most neglected piece of equipment on a bike. There are about 120 or so links in a chain and each has a simple but precise arrangement of bushes, bearings and plates. Over time all chains stretch, but if dirt gets between the bushes and bearings this 'ageing' will happen prematurely and will likely damage the teeth of your chainrings, sprockets and derailleur guide pulleys.

To prevent this, chains should be cleaned and lubed frequently (see your bike shop for the best products to use).

No matter how well you look after a chain it should be replaced regularly – wear depends on the quality of the chain and riding conditions, but about every 5000–8000km on average. Seek the advice of a bike shop to ensure you are buying the correct type for your drivetrain (the moving parts that combine to drive the bicycle: chain, freewheel, derailleurs, chainwheel and bottom bracket).

If you do enough cycling you'll need to replace a chain (or fix a broken chain), so here's how to use that funky-looking tool, the chain breaker. Of course, if you use a quick-release chain link you can avoid all of the following steps (see 'Chain Options' boxed text).

1 Remove the chain from the chainrings – it'll make the whole process easier. Place the chain in the chain breaker (on the outer slots; it braces the link plates as the rivet is driven out) and line the pin of the chain breaker up with the rivet.

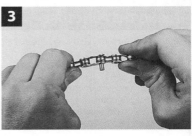

2 Wind the handle until the rivet is clear of the inner link but still held by the outer link plate.

3 Flex the chain to 'break' it. If it won't, you'll need to push the rivet out some more, but not completely – if you push it all the way out, you'll have to remove two links and replace them with two spare links. If you're removing links, you'll need to remove a male and female link (ie, two links).

4 Rejoining the chain is the reverse. If you turn the chain around when putting it on you will still have the rivet facing you. Otherwise it will be facing away

---

CHAIN OPTIONS

Check your chain; if you have a Shimano HyperGlide chain you'll need a special HyperGlide chain rivet to rejoin the chain. This will be supplied with your new chain, but carry a spare.

A really cool alternative is to fit a two-piece joining link, such as Sachs Powerlink or Wipperman Connex Speed Connector – available for all 8-, 9- and 10-speed chains. You'll still need a chain breaker to fix a broken chain or take out excess links.

5

from you and you'll need to change to the other side of the bike and work through the spokes.

Join the chain up by hand and place it in the breaker. Now drive the rivet in firmly, making sure it is properly lined up with the hole of the outer link plate. Stop when the rivet is almost in place.

5 Move the chain to the spreaders (inner slots) of the chain breaker. Finish by winding the rivet into position carefully (check that the head of the rivet is raised the same distance above the link plate as the rivets beside it). If you've managed to get it in perfectly and the link isn't 'stiff', well done!

Otherwise, move the chain to the spreaders on the chain breaker and gently work the chain laterally until the link is no longer stiff.

If this doesn't work (and with some chain breakers it won't), take the chain out of the tool and place a screwdriver or Allen key between the outer plates of the stiff link and carefully lever the plates both ways. If you're too forceful you'll really break the chain, but if you're subtle it will free the link up and you'll be on your way.

PREDEPARTURE & POST-RIDE CHECKS

Each day before you get on your bike and each evening after you've stopped riding, give your bike a quick once-over. Following these checks will ensure you're properly maintaining your bike and will help identify any problems before they become disasters. Go to the nearest bike shop if you don't know how to fix any problem.

PREDEPARTURE CHECKLIST
o **brakes** – are they stopping you? If not, adjust them.
o **chain** – if it was squeaking yesterday, it needs lube.
o **panniers** – are they all secured and fastened?
o **cycle computer** – reset your trip distance at the start.
o **gears** – are they changing properly? If not, adjust them.
o **tyres** – check your tyre pressure is correct (see the tyre's side wall for the maximum psi); inflate, if necessary.

POST-RIDE CHECKLIST
o **pannier racks** – check all bolts/screws are tightened; do a visual check of each rack (the welds, in particular) looking for small cracks.
o **headset** – when stationary, apply the front brake and rock the bike gently; if there is any movement or noise, chances are the headset is loose.
o **wheels** – visually check the tyres for sidewall cuts/wear and any embedded objects; check the wheels are still true and no spokes are broken.
o **wrench test** – pull on the saddle (if it moves, tighten the seat-post bolt or the seat-clamp bolt, underneath); pull laterally on a crank (if it moves, check the bottom bracket).

YOUR BICYCLE

YOUR BICYCLE

BRAKES

Adjusting the brakes of your bike is not complicated and even though your bike shop will use several tools to do the job, all you really need is a pair of pliers, a spanner or Allen key, and (sometimes) a friend.

Check three things before you start: the wheels are true (not buckled), the braking surface of the rims is smooth (no dirt, dents or rough patches) and the cables are not frayed. With disc brakes the wheel should spin freely without any noticeable drag.

Begin by checking that the pads strike the rim correctly: flush on the braking surface of the rim (see right and opposite) and parallel to the ground.

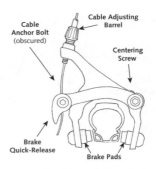

Dual-Pivot Calliper Brakes

Calliper Brakes

It's likely that you'll be able to make any minor adjustments to calliper brakes by winding the cable adjusting barrel out. If it doesn't allow enough movement you'll need to adjust the cable anchor bolt:

1 Undo the cable anchor bolt – not completely, just so the cable is free to move – and turn the cable adjusting barrel all the way in.

2 Get your friend to hold the callipers in the desired position, about 2–3mm away from the rim. Using a pair of pliers, pull the cable through until it is taut.

3 Before you tighten the cable anchor bolt again, check to see if the brake lever is in its normal position (not slack as if somebody was applying it) – sometimes they jam open. Also, ensure the brake quick-release (use it when you're removing your wheel or in an emergency to open the callipers if your wheel is badly buckled) is closed.

4 Tighten the cable anchor bolt again. Make any fine-tuning to the brakes by winding the cable adjusting barrel out.

🔧 BRAKE CABLES

If your brakes are particularly hard to apply, you may need to replace the cables. Moisture can cause the cable and housing (outer casing) to bond or stick. If this happens it's often possible to prolong the life of a cable by removing it from the housing and applying a coating of grease (or chain lube) to it.

If you do need to replace the cable, take your bike to a bike shop and get the staff to fit and/or supply the new cable. Cables come in two sizes – rear (long) and front (short) – various thicknesses and with different types of nipples.

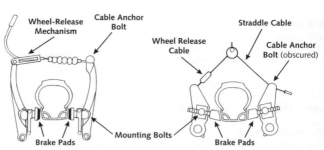

Cantilever Brakes (new style)   Cantilever Brakes (old style)

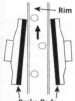

When Braking

Cantilever Brake Toe-In: This is how the brake pads should strike the rim (from above) with correct toe-in.

Cantilever Brakes

These days most touring bikes have cantilever rather than calliper brakes. The newest generation of cantilever brakes (V-brakes) are more powerful and better suited to stopping bikes with heavy loads.

On cantilever brakes ensure the leading edge of the brake pad hits the rim first (see left). This is called toe-in; it makes the brakes more efficient and prevents squealing. To adjust the toe-in on cantilever brakes, loosen the brake pad's mounting bolt (using a 10mm spanner and 5mm Allen key). Wiggle the brake pad into position and tighten the bolt again.

If you only need to make a minor adjustment to the distance of the pads from the rim, chances are you will be able to do it by winding the cable adjusting barrel out (located near the brake lever on mountain bikes and hybrids). If this won't do you'll need to adjust the cable anchor bolt:

1 Undo the cable anchor bolt (not completely, just so the cable is free to move) and turn the cable adjusting barrel all the way in. Depending on the style of your brakes, you may need a 10mm spanner (older bikes) or a 5mm Allen key.

2 Hold the cantilevers in the desired position (get assistance from a friend if you need to), positioning the brake pads 2–3mm away from the rim. Using a pair of pliers, pull the cable through until it is taut.

3 Before you tighten the cable anchor bolt again, check to see if the brake lever is in its normal position (not slack as if somebody was applying it) – sometimes they jam open.

4 Tighten the cable anchor bolt again. Make any fine-tuning to the brakes by winding the cable adjusting barrel out.

Disc Brakes

Disc brakes have traditionally only been used on mountain bikes, but they are starting to make an appearance in the touring bike market these days. The higher-end models offer the advantage of strong, fade-free stopping power in wet and dry conditions, plus none of the rim wear associated with all calliper and cantilever brakes. Once correctly adjusted to eliminate dragging, they are relatively trouble-free, and they are well worth considering when looking at a new bike purchase or upgrade.

Due to the many different brands and adjustment systems available for disc brakes, unless you are very familiar with your particular model, we recommend taking your bike to a reliable repairer for any maintenance or adjustment.

GEARS

If the gears on your bike start playing up – the chain falls off the chainrings, it shifts slowly or not at all – it's bound to cause frustration and could damage your bike. All it takes to prevent this is a couple of simple adjustments: the first, setting the limits of travel for both derailleurs, will keep the chain on your drivetrain, and the second will ensure smooth, quick shifts from your rear derailleur. Each will take just a couple of minutes and the only tool you need is a small Phillips or flat screwdriver.

Front Derailleur

If you can't get the chain to shift onto one chainring or the chain comes off when you're shifting, you need to make some minor adjustments to the limit screws on the front derailleur. Two screws control the limits of the front derailleur's left and right movement, which governs how far the chain can shift.

When you shift gears the chain is physically pushed sideways by the plates (outer and inner) of the derailleur cage. The screws are usually side by side (see photo No 1) on the top of the front derailleur. The left-hand screw (as you sit on the bike) adjusts the inside limit and the one on the right adjusts the outside limit.

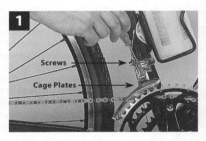

After you make each of the following adjustments, pedal the drivetrain with your hand and change gears to ensure you've set the limit correctly. If you're satisfied, test it under strain by going for a short ride.

Front Derailleur: Before making any adjustments, remove any build up of grit from the screws (especially underneath) by wiping them with a rag and applying a quick spray (or drop) of chain lube.

Outer Limits – Change the gears to position the chain on the largest chainring and the smallest rear sprocket. Set the outer cage plate as close to the chain as you can without it touching. Adjust the right-hand limit screw to achieve this.
Inner Limits – Position the chain on the smallest chainring and the largest rear sprocket. For chainwheels with three chainrings, position the inner cage plate between 1–2mm from the chain. If you have a chainwheel with two chainrings, position the inner cage plate as close to the chain as you can without it touching.

Rear Derailleur

If the limit screws aren't set correctly on the rear derailleur the consequences can be dire. If the chain slips off the largest sprocket it can jam between the sprocket and the spokes and could then snap the chain, break or damage spokes or even break the frame.

The limit screws are located at the back of the derailleur (see photo No 2). The top screw (marked 'H' on the derailleur) sets the derailleur's limit of travel on the smallest sprocket's (the highest gear) side of the freewheel. The bottom screw ('L') adjusts the derailleur's travel towards the largest sprocket (lowest gear).

Outer Limits – Position the chain on the smallest sprocket and largest chainring (see photo No 3). The derailleur's top guide pulley (the one closest to the sprockets) should be in line with the smallest sprocket; adjust the top screw ('H') to ensure it is.
Inner Limits – Position the chain on the largest rear sprocket and the smallest chainring (see photo No 4). This time the guide pulley needs to be lined up with the largest sprocket; do this by adjusting the bottom screw ('L'). Make sure the chain can't move any further towards the wheel than the largest sprocket.

Guide
Pulleys

Cable Adjusting Barrel

If your gears are bouncing up and down your freewheel in a constant click and chatter, you need to adjust the tension of the cable to the rear derailleur. This can be achieved in a variety of ways, depending on your gear system.

The main cable adjusting barrel is on your rear derailleur (see photo No 5). Secondary cable adjusting barrels can also be found near the gear levers (newer Shimano combined brake-gear STI levers) or on the downtube of your frame (older Shimano STI levers and Campagnolo Ergopower gear systems) of some bikes. Intended for racing cyclists, they allow for fine tuning of the gears'

operation while on the move.

Raise the rear wheel off the ground – have a friend hold it up by the saddle, hang it from a tree or turn the bike upside down – so you can pedal the drivetrain with your hand.

To reset your derailleur, shift gears to position the chain on the second smallest sprocket and middle chainring (see photo No 6). As you turn the crank with your hand, tighten the cable by winding the rear derailleur's cable adjusting barrel anti-clockwise. Just before the chain starts to make a noise as if to shift onto the third sprocket, stop winding.

Now pedal the drivetrain and change the gears up and down the freewheel. If things still aren't right you may find that you need to tweak the cable tension slightly: turn the cable adjusting barrel anti-clockwise if shifts to larger sprockets are slow, and clockwise if shifts to smaller sprockets hesitate.

If you've made all these adjustments and gear changes are still not smooth over the entire range, it is highly likely that there is fine grit contaminating the cable housing or a minute crimp in the inner cable. Even very slight friction in the cabling can cause shifting problems, and the easiest solution is to completely replace the inner cable and outer housing. There are devices available that seal out dirt (especially useful for bikes with cables running down the rear frame stay, which allow water to run directly into the cable outer) and aid in reducing friction at the sharp bend into the rear derailleur; a good combo is the Avid Rollamajig and the SRAM Nightcrawler.

YOUR BICYCLE

REPLACING A SPOKE

Even the best purpose-made touring wheels occasionally break spokes. When this happens the wheel, which relies on the even pull of each spoke, is likely to become buckled. When it is not buckled, it is considered true.

If you've forgotten to pack spokes or you grabbed the wrong size, you can still get yourself out of a pickle if you have a spoke key. Wheels are very flexible and you can get it roughly true – enough to take you to the next bike shop – even if two or three spokes are broken.

If you break a spoke on the front wheel it is a relatively simple thing to replace the spoke and retrue the wheel. The same applies if a broken spoke is on the nondrive side (opposite side to the rear derailleur) of the rear wheel. The complication comes when you break a spoke on the drive side of the rear wheel (the most common case). In order to replace it you need to remove the cassette, a relatively simple job in itself but one that requires a few more tools and the know-how.

If you don't have that know-how fear not, because it is possible to retrue the wheel without replacing that spoke and without damaging the wheel – see 'Truing a Wheel' (below).

1 Remove the wheel from the bike. It's probably a good idea to remove the tyre and tube as well (though not essential), just to make sure the nipple is seated properly in the rim and not likely to cause a puncture.

2 Remove the broken spoke but leave the nipple in the rim (if it's not damaged; otherwise replace it). Now you need to thread the new spoke. Start by threading it through the vacant hole on the hub flange. Next lace the new spoke through the other spokes. Spokes are offset on the rim; every second one is on the same side and, generally, every fourth is laced through the other spokes the same way.

Spoke Key

3 With the spoke key, tighten the nipple until the spoke is about as taut as the other spokes on this side of the rim. Spoke nipples have four flat sides – to adjust them you'll need the correct size spoke key. Spoke keys come in two types: those made to fit one spoke gauge or several. If you have the latter, trial each size on a nipple until you find the perfect fit.

Truing a Wheel

Truing a wheel is an art form and, like all art forms, it is not something mastered overnight. If you can, practise with an old wheel before leaving home. If that's not possible – and you're on the side of the road as you read this – following these guidelines will get you back in the saddle until you can get to the next bike shop.

1 Start by turning the bike upside-down, so the wheels can turn freely. Check the tension of all the spokes on the wheel: do this by squeezing each pair of spokes on each side. Tighten those spokes that seem loose and loosen those that seem too tight. Note, though, the spokes on the drive side of the rear wheel (on the same side as the freewheel) are deliberately tighter than the non-drive side.

2 Rotate the wheel a couple of times to get an idea of the job at hand. If the wheel won't rotate, let the brakes off (see 'Brakes').

3 Using the chalk from your puncture repair kit, mark all the 'bumps'. Keep the chalk in the same position (brace the chalk against the pannier rack or bike's frame) and let the bumps in the wheel 'hit' the chalk.

4 In order to get the bumps out you'll need a constant point of reference – to gauge if the bumps are being removed. Often, if it is not a severe buckle, you can use a brake pad. Position the brake pad about 2–3mm from the rim (on the side with the biggest buckle).

5 With your spoke key, loosen those spokes on the same side as the bump within the longest chalked area, and tighten those on the opposite side of the rim. The spokes at the start and the finish of the chalked area should only be tightened/loosened by a quarter-turn; apply a half-turn to those in between.

6 Rotate the wheel again; if you're doing it correctly the buckle should not be as great. Continue this process of tightening and loosening spokes until the bump is as near to gone as you can get it – as the bump is removed turn the nipples less (one-eighth of a turn on the ends and a quarter-turn in between). Experienced exponents can remove buckles entirely, but if you can get it almost out (1mm here or there) you've done well.

7 If the wheel has more than one bump, move onto the second-longest chalk mark next. As each bump is removed you might find it affects the previous bump slightly. In this case, remove the previous chalk mark and repeat Steps 4–6. Continue to do this until all the buckles are removed.

Don't forget to readjust the brakes.

If you've trued the wheel without replacing the broken spokes, have them replaced at the next bike shop.

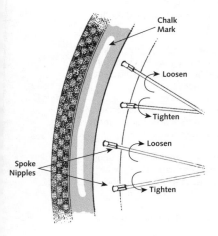

YOUR BICYCLE

LOADING YOUR BICYCLE

If you've ever been to Asia and seen a bike loaded with boxes piled 2m high or carrying four, five or six people, plus a chicken or two, you'll realise that there are more ways to carry your gear than would otherwise seem. More realistic options for you come from a combination of front and rear panniers, a handlebar bag or trailer.

'Credit-card tourists', who are intent on travelling lighter, further and faster and who are happy to stay in hotels or hostels, can get by with a handlebar bag and/or rear panniers (see top right). The downside to this configuration is poor bike-handling; the steering feels particularly 'airy'. It's possible to adopt the 'lighter, further, faster' principle and still camp, but it means frugal packing.

If you want to be more self-sufficient or you're carrying 20kg or more, you'll probably find it easier (and your bike will handle better) with front and rear panniers. The tried-and-tested configuration that works best for a touring bike is to use four panniers: two low-mounting front panniers with two high-mounting rear panniers (see bottom right). The only other thing you might want to add is a small handlebar bag for this book, snacks, sunblock, money, camera etc.

Pannier configurations: the four-pannier system is the best way of carrying your gear and having a bike that handles well; packing light saves weight but the compromise can be poor bike handling.

This combination, with a few light but bulky items on the rear rack (eg, tent, sleeping mat etc), allows you to carry a large load and still have predictable and manageable bike-handling.

If you're riding a mountain bike and riding off-road you'll probably want high-mounting front panniers to give you more clearance.

PACKING YOUR GEAR

It's frequently said that, in packing for a cycle tour, you should lay out everything you need to take and then leave half of it behind. The skill is in knowing which half to leave behind. Almost as much skill is needed in organising the gear in your panniers. Here are some tried and tested tips.

Compartmentalise Pack similar items into nylon drawstring bags (stuff sacks), to make them easier to find again (eg, underwear in one, cycling clothes in another, and even dinner food separated from breakfast food). Using different coloured stuff sacks makes choosing the right one easier.

Waterproof Even if your panniers are completely waterproof, and especially if they're not, it pays to put everything inside heavy-duty plastic bags. Check bags for holes during the trip; replace them or patch the holes with tape.

Reduce Flood Damage If your panniers are not waterproof and they pool water, you can reduce problems by putting things that are unaffected by water, say a pair of thongs, at the bottom of the bag. This keeps the other stuff above 'flood level'. Try using seam sealant on the bags' seams beforehand, too.

Load Consistently Put things in the same place each time you pack to avoid having to unpack every bag just to find one item.

Balance the Load Distribute weight evenly – generally around 60% in the rear and 40% in the front panniers – and keep it as low as possible by using low-mounting front panniers and packing heavy items first. Side-to-side balancing is just as critical.

Group Gear Pack things used at the same time in the same pannier. Night/camp things like your mat, sleeping bag and pyjamas, which you don't need during the day, could all be in the bag most difficult to access – likely to be on the same side as the side of the road you are riding on, since you will probably lean that side of the bike against a tree, pole or roadside barrier.

Put all clothing in one pannier, if possible, sorted into separate bags of cycling clothes, 'civilian' clothes, underwear, wet weather gear and dirty clothes. Keep a windproof jacket handy on top for descents.

In the Front Food and eating utensils are convenient to have in a front pannier along with a camping stove. Toiletry items, towel, first-aid kit, reading material, torch and sundry items can go in the other front bag.

In the Pockets or Bar Bag Easily accessible pockets on panniers or on your cycling shirt are useful for items likely to be needed frequently or urgently during the day, such as snacks, tool kit, sun hat or sunscreen. A handlebar bag is good for these items if your panniers don't have pockets, but remember that weight on the handlebars upsets a bike's handling.

Keep Space Spare Remember to leave some spare space for food and, if using a camping stove, for the fuel canister. Be mindful when packing foods that are squashable or sensitive to heat and protect or insulate them – unless you're working on a gourmet pasta sauce recipe that includes socks.

YOUR BICYCLE

ANOTHER OPTION – TRAILERS

Luggage trailers are gaining in popularity and some innovative designs are now on the market. By spreading the load onto more wheels they relieve the bike and can improve rolling resistance. Their extra capacity is a boon for travelling on a tandem or with a young family. They can be combined with racks and panniers, but the hitch (point it connects with the bike) of some trailers may interfere with your panniers, so check first.

PHOTO BY PETER HINES

Two-wheeled trailers are free standing and can take very heavy loads, including babies and toddlers. Often brightly coloured, they give a strong signal to car drivers who tend to give you a wide berth. However, their relatively wide track can catch a lot of wind and makes them ungainly on rough, narrow roads or trails. Single-wheeled trailers such as the BOB Yak share the load with the bike's rear wheel.

They track well and can be used on very rough trails and may be the easiest option for full-suspension bikes. The load capacity of these units is somewhere between that of a bike with a rear rack only and a fully loaded (four panniers plus rack-top luggage) touring bike.

Prevent 'Internal Bleeding' Act on the premise that anything that can spill will, and transfer it to a reliable container, preferably within a watertight bag. Take care, too, in packing hard or sharp objects (tools, utensils or anything with hooks) that could rub or puncture other items, including the panniers. Knives or tools with folding working parts are desirable.

Fragile Goods Valuables and delicate equipment such as cameras are best carried in a handlebar bag, which can be easily removed when you stop. Alternatively, carry these items in a 'bum bag', which will accompany you automatically.

Rack Top Strap your tent lengthways on top of the rear rack with elastic cord looped diagonally across from front to rear and back again, and maybe across to anchor the rear end. Be sure the cord is well tensioned and secure – deny its kamikaze impulses to plunge into the back wheel, jamming the freewheel mechanism, or worse.

WHAT TO LOOK FOR IN PANNIERS

Panniers remain the popular choice for touring luggage. They offer flexibility, in that one, two or four can be used depending on the load to be carried and they allow luggage to be arranged for easy access.

Many people initially buy just a rear rack and panniers, and it is wise to buy the best quality you can afford at this stage. These bags will accompany you on all of your tours as well as for day-to-day shopping and commuting trips for years to come. The attachment system should be secure, but simple to operate. That big bump you hit at 50km/h can launch a poorly designed pannier and your precious luggage.

The stiffness of the pannier backing is another concern – if it can flex far enough to reach the spokes of the wheel the result can be catastrophic. Good rack design can also help avoid this. The fabric of the panniers should be strong and abrasion- and water-resistant. You can now buy roll-top panniers, made from laminated fabrics, that are completely waterproof. Bear in mind that these bags are only waterproof until they develop even the smallest hole, so be prepared to check them and apply patches occasionally. Canvas bags shed water well, but should be used in conjunction with a liner bag to keep things dry. Cordura is a heavy nylon fabric with excellent abrasion resistance. The fabric itself is initially waterproof, but water tends to find the seams, so using a liner bag is a good idea once again.

Pockets and compartments can help to organise your load, but the multitude of seams increase the challenge of keeping the contents dry in the wet. A couple of exterior pockets are great for sunscreen, snacks and loose change that you need throughout the day. Carrying front panniers as well as rear ones allows more opportunities to divide and organise gear. When fitting rear panniers check for heel strike. Long feet, long cranks and short chainstays will all make it harder to get the bags and your body to fit.

Health & Safety

Keeping healthy on your travels depends on your predeparture preparations, your daily health care and diet while on the road, and how you handle any medical problem that develops. Few touring cyclists experience anything more than a bit of soreness, fatigue and chafing, although other problems are possible. The sections that follow aren't intended to alarm, but they are worth a skim read before you go.

BEFORE YOU GO

HEALTH INSURANCE

Buy a policy that generously covers you for medical expenses, theft or loss of luggage and tickets, and for cancellation of and delays in your travel arrangements. Check your policy doesn't exclude cycling or mountain biking as a dangerous activity.

Buy travel insurance as early as possible to ensure you'll be compensated for any unforseen accidents or delays. If items are lost or stolen get a police report immediately – otherwise your insurer might not pay up.

If you're an EU citizen (or from Switzerland, Norway or Iceland), a European Health Insurance Card (EHIC) covers you for most medical care in public hospitals free of charge, but not for emergency repatriation home or non-emergencies. The card is available from health-centres and (in the UK) from post offices. Citizens from other countries should find out if there is a reciprocal arrangement for free medical care between their country and Italy (Australia, for instance, has such an agreement; carry your Medicare card). If you do need health insurance, make sure you get a policy that covers you for the worst possible scenario, such as an accident requiring an emergency flight home.

Find out in advance if your insurance plan will make payments directly to providers or reimburse you later for overseas health expenditures.

IMMUNISATIONS

No jabs are required to travel to Italy. The World Health Organization (WHO), however, recommends that all travellers should be covered for diphtheria, tetanus, the measles, mumps, rubella and polio, as well as hepatitis B.

FIRST AID

It's a good idea at any time to know the appropriate responses in the event of a major accident or illness, and it's especially important if you are intending to ride off-road in a remote area. Consider learning basic first aid through a recognised course before you go, and carrying a first-aid manual and small medical kit.

Although detailed first-aid instruction is outside the scope of this guidebook, some basic points are listed in the section on Traumatic Injuries (see p331) in this chapter. Undoubtedly the best advice is to avoid an accident in the first place. The Safety on the Bide section on p332 contains tips for safe on-road and off-road riding, as well as information on how to summon help should a major accident or illness occur.

FIRST-AID KIT

A possible kit could include:

First-Aid Supplies

o bandages & safety pins
o butterfly closure strips
o elastic support bandage for knees, ankles etc
o gauze swabs
o latex gloves (several pairs)
o nonadhesive dressings
o scissors (small pair)
o sterile alcohol wipes
o sticking plasters (Band Aids)
o irrigating syringes & needles – for removing gravel from road-rash wounds
o thermometer (note that mercury thermometers are prohibited by airlines)
o tweezers
o blister kit
o body systems isolation CPR mask (travel size)

Medications

o antidiarrhoea, antinausea drugs and oral rehydration salts
o antifungal cream or powder – for fungal skin infections and thrush (p328)
o antihistamines – for allergies, eg, hay fever; to ease the itch from insect bites or stings; and to prevent motion sickness
o antiseptic powder or solution (such as povidone-iodine) and antiseptic wipes for cuts and grazes
o calamine lotion, sting relief spray or aloe vera – to ease irritation from sunburn and insect bites or stings
o cold and flu tablets, throat lozenges and nasal decongestant
o laxatives
o nappy rash cream
o painkillers (eg, aspirin or paracetamol/cetaminophen in the USA) – for pain and fever
o general antibiotic
o for women: yeast infection and UTI treatments (p328)

Miscellaneous

o insect repellent, sunscreen, lip balm and eye drops
o water purification tablets or iodine

PHYSICAL FITNESS

Most of the rides in this book are designed for someone with a moderate degree of cycling fitness. As a general rule, however, the fitter you are, the more you'll enjoy riding. It pays to spend time preparing yourself physically before you set out, rather than let a sore backside and aching muscles draw your attention from some of the world's finest cycle touring countryside.

Depending on your existing level of fitness, you should start training a couple of months before your trip. Try to ride at least three times a week, starting with easy rides (even 5km to work, if you're not already cycling regularly) and gradually building up to longer distances. Once you have a good base of regular riding behind you, include hills in your training and familiarise yourself with the gearing on your bike. Before you go you should have done at least one 60km to 70km ride with loaded panniers.

As you train, you'll discover how to adjust your bike to increase your comfort – as well as any mechanical problems.

STAYING HEALTHY

The best way to have a lousy holiday (especially if you're relying on self-propulsion) is to become ill. Heed the following simple advice and the only thing you're likely to suffer from is that rewarding tiredness at the end of a full day.

Reduce the chances of contracting an illness by washing your hands frequently, particularly after working on your bike and before handling or eating food.

HYDRATION

You may not notice how much water you're losing as you ride, because it evaporates in the breeze. However, don't underestimate the amount of fluid you need to replace – particularly in warmer weather. The magic figure is supposedly 1L per hour, though many cyclists have trouble consuming this much – remembering to drink enough can be harder than it sounds. Sipping little and often is the key; try to drink a mouthful every 10 minutes or so and don't wait until you get thirsty. Water 'backpacks' can be great for fluid

GETTING FIT FOR TOURING

Ideally, a training program should be tailored to your objectives, specific needs, fitness level and health. However, if you have no idea how to prepare for your cycling holiday these guidelines will help you get the fitness you need to enjoy it more. Things to think about include:

Foundation You will need general kilometres in your legs before you start to expose them to any intensive cycling. Always start out with easy rides – even a few kilometres to the shops – and give yourself plenty of time to build towards your objective.

Tailoring Once you have the general condition to start preparing for your trip, work out how to tailor your training rides to the type of tour you are planning. Someone preparing for a three-week ride will require a different approach to someone building fitness for a one-day or weekend ride. Some aspects to think about are the ride length (distance and days), terrain, climate and weight to be carried in panniers. If your trip involves carrying 20kg in panniers, incorporate this weight into some training rides, especially some of the longer ones. If you are going to be touring in mountainous areas, choose a hilly training route.

Recovery You usually adapt to a training program during recovery time, so it's important to do the right things between rides. Recovery can take many forms, but the simple ones are best. These include getting quality sleep, eating an adequate diet to refuel the system, doing recovery rides between hard days (using low gears to avoid pushing yourself), stretching and enjoying a relaxing bath. Other forms include recovery massage and hot soaks. Yoga is an excellent way to wholly recover.

If you have no cycling background the program below will help you get fit for your cycling holiday. If you are doing an easy ride (each ride in this book is rated; see Table of Rides (p18-9), aim to at least complete Week 4; for moderate rides, complete Week 6; and complete the entire programme if you are doing a hard ride. Experienced cycle tourists could start at Week 3, while those who regularly ride up to four days a week could start at Week 5.

Don't treat this as a punishing training schedule: try cycling to work or to the shops, join a local touring club or get a group of friends together to turn weekend rides into social events.

	MONDAY	TUESDAY	WEDNESDAY	THURSDAY	FRIDAY	SATURDAY	SUNDAY
WEEK 1	10KM*	–	10KM*	–	10KM*	–	10KM*
WEEK 2	–	15KM*	–	15KM*	–	20KM*	–
WEEK 3	20KM*	–	20KM*	25KM*	–	25KM*	20KM†
WEEK 4	–	30KM*	–	35KM*	30KM†	30KM*	–
WEEK 5	30KM*	–	40KM†	–	35KM*	–	40KM†
WEEK 6	30KM*	–	40KM†	–	–	60KM*	40KM†
WEEK 7	30KM*	–	40KM†	–	30KM†	70KM*	30KM*
WEEK 8	–	60KM*	30KM†	–	40KM†	–	90KM*

*steady pace (allows you to carry out a conversation without losing your breath) on flat or undulating terrain

† solid pace (allows you to talk in short sentences only) on undulating roads with some longer hills

The training program shown here is only a guide. Ultimately it is important to listen to your body and slow down if the ride is getting too hard. Take recovery days and cut back distances when you feel this way. Don't panic if you don't complete every ride, every week; the most important thing is to ride regularly and gradually increase the length of your rides as you get fitter.

For those with no exercise background, be sure to see your doctor and get a clearance to begin exercising at these rates. This is especially important for those over 35 years of age with no exercise history and those with a cardiac or respiratory condition of any nature.

Kevin Tabotta

HEALTH & SAFETY

regulation since virtually no physical or mental effort is required to drink. Keep drinking before and after the day's ride to replenish fluid.

Use the colour of your urine as a rough guide to whether you are drinking enough. Small amounts of dark urine suggest you need to increase your fluid intake. Passing reasonable quantities of light yellow urine indicates that you've got the balance about right. Some other obvious signs of dehydration include headache and fatigue. For more information on the effects of dehydration, see Dehydration & Heat Exhaustion (p328).

Water
The simplest way of purifying water is to boil it thoroughly. Vigorous boiling for five minutes should do the job.

Simple filtering will not remove all dangerous organisms, so if you can't boil water treat it chemically. Chlorine tablets will kill many pathogens, but not giardia. Iodine is very effective in purifying water and is available in tablet and liquid form, but follow the directions carefully and remember that too much iodine can be harmful. Flavoured powder will disguise the taste of treated water and is a good thing to carry if you are spending time away from town water supplies.

Sports Drinks
Commercial sports drinks such as Gatorade and PowerAde are an excellent way to satisfy your hydration needs, electrolyte replacement and energy demands in one. On endurance rides especially, it can be difficult to keep eating solid fuels day in, day out, but sports drinks can supplement these energy demands and allow you to vary your solid fuel intake a little for variety. The bonus is that those all-important body salts lost through perspiration get re-stocked. It's important to remember to drink plenty of water as well.

If using a powdered sports drink, don't mix it too strong (follow the instructions) in order to maximise the hydration benefits.

NUTRITION
One of the great things about bike touring is that it requires lots of energy, which means you can eat more of Italy's fabulous food. Depending on your activity levels, it's not hard to put away huge servings of food and be hungry a few hours after.

Because you're putting such demands on your body, it's important to eat well – not just lots. As usual, you should eat a balanced diet from a wide variety of foods.

It's usually helpful if the main part of your diet is carbohydrates rather than proteins or fats. While some protein (for tissue maintenance and repair) and fat (for vitamins, long-term energy and warmth) is essential, carbohydrates provide the most efficient fuel. They are easily digested into simple sugars, which are then used in energy production. Foods like pasta, rice, bread, fruits and vegetables are all high in carbohydrates.

Eating simple carbohydrates (sugars, such as lollies or sweets) gives you almost immediate energy – great for when you need a top-up (see boxed text 'Avoiding the Bonk' p327); however, because they are quickly metabolised, you may get a sugar 'high' then a 'low'. For cycling it is far better to base your diet around complex carbohydrates, which take longer to process and provide 'slow-release' energy over a longer period. (But don't miss the opportunity to indulge guiltlessly in pastries…).

For breakfast, Italians grab a *cornetto* (croissant) and a cappuccino and go. This will not do you any good. Many hotels have buffets (which you will embarrass yourself at) and if they don't, make sure you supplement with some hardy carbohydrates like whole grain bread or oatmeal. In the evening, it's hard not to eat a carbohydrate intensive meal in Italy, which is perfect for recovery.

If you can get hold of a copy, the out-of-print, *Cycle Food: A Guide to Satisfying Your Inner Tube* by Lauren Hefferon, is a handy reference for nutrition and health advice with practical recipes.

AVOIDING CYCLING AILMENTS
Saddle Sores & Blisters
While you're more likely to get a sore bum if you're out of condition, riding long distances does take its toll on your behind. To minimise the impact, always wear clean, preferably padded bike shorts (also known as 'knicks' or 'the costume'). Ill-fitted shorts can chafe, as can underwear (see Clothing under What to Bring on p25). It's suggestible to shower soon after stoping and put

AVOIDING THE BONK

The bonk, in a cycling context, is not a pleasant experience; it's that light-headed, can't-put-power-to-the-pedals, weak feeling that engulfs you (usually quite quickly) when your body runs out of fuel.

If you experience it the best move is to stop and refuel immediately. It can be quite serious and risky to your health if it's not addressed as soon as symptoms occur. It won't take long before you are ready to get going again. However, after bonking, you won't generally recover all your robustness, and you'll be more tired the next day so try to avoid it.

The best way to do this is to maintain your fuel intake while riding. Cycling for hours burns considerable body energy, and replacing it is something that needs to be tailored to each individual's tastes. (see Food & Drink p284)

The touring cyclist needs to target foods that have a high carbohydrate source. Foods that contain some fat are okay as well. Good on-bike, Italian-style cycling foods include:

o bananas (in particular) and other fruits

o croissants: (the Italian sports bar) with fat, simple sugars, and complex carbohydrates

o *panini*

o foccacia.

During lunch stops (or for breakfast) you can try including potato-based dishes, pasta, and/or bread.

It's important not to get uptight about the food you eat. As a rule of thumb, base all your meals around carbohydrates of some sort, but don't be afraid to also indulge in local culinary delights.

on clean, preferably nonsynthetic, clothes. Emollient creams especially for the cyclist's crotch help guard against chafing. Apply liberally before riding. For information on correctly adjusting your bike seat, see the Your Bicycle chapter (p303).

If you do suffer from chafing, wash and dry the area and carefully apply a barrier (moisturising) cream.

Wearing gloves and correctly fitted shoes will reduce the likelihood of blisters on your hands and feet. If you know you're suscep-tible to blisters in a particular spot, cover the area with medical adhesive tape before riding.

Knee Pain

Knee pain is common among cyclists who pedal in too high a gear. While it may seem faster to turn the pedals slowly in a high gear, it's actually more efficient (and better for your knees) to 'spin' the pedals – that is, use a low enough gear so you can pedal quickly with little resistance. For touring, the ideal cadence (the number of pedal strokes per minute) ranges from 70 to 90. Try to maintain this cadence even when you're climbing.

It's a good idea to stretch before and after riding, and to go easy when you first start each day. This reduces your chances of injury and helps your muscles to work more efficiently.

You can also get sore knees if your saddle is too low, or if your shoe cleats (for use with clipless pedals) are incorrectly positioned. Both are discussed in greater detail in the Your Bicycle chapter (p303).

Numbness & Backache

Pain in the hands, neck and shoulders is a common complaint, particularly on longer riding days. It's generally caused by leaning too much on your hands. Apart from discomfort, you can temporarily damage the nerves and experience numbness or mild paralysis of the hands. Prevent it by wearing padded gloves, cycling with less weight on your hands and changing your hand position frequently (if you have flat handlebars, fit bar ends to provide more hand positions).

When seated, your weight should be fairly evenly distributed through your hands and seat. If you're carrying too much weight on your hands there are two ways of adjusting your bike to rectify this: either by raising the height of your handlebars or, if you are stretched out too much, fitting a smaller stem (talk to your local bike shop). For more guidance on adjusting your bicycle for greater comfort, see the Your Bicycle chapter (p303).

Fungal Infections

Warm, sweaty bodies are ideal environments for fungal growth, and physical activity,

HEALTH & SAFETY

combined with inadequate washing of your body and/or clothes, can lead to fungal infections. The most common are athlete's foot (tinea) between the toes or fingers, and infections on the scalp, in the groin or on the body (ringworm). You can get ringworm (which is a fungal infection, not a worm) from infected animals or other people.

To prevent fungal infections, wash frequently and dry yourself carefully. Change out of sweaty bike clothes as soon as possible.

If you do get an infection, wash the infected area at least daily with a disinfectant or medicated soap and water, and rinse and dry well. Apply an antifungal cream or powder like tolnaftate. Expose the infected area to air or sunlight as much as possible, avoid artificial fibres and wash all towels and underwear in hot water, change them often and let them dry in the sun.

Staying Warm

Staying warm when cycling is as important as keeping up your water and food intake. Particularly in wet or sweaty clothing, your body cools down quickly after you stop working. Muscle strains occur more easily when your body is chilled and hypothermia can result from prolonged exposure (for prevention and treatment, see Hypothermia p329). Staying rugged up will help prevent colds and the flu.

You can get caught suddenly in bad weather at any time of year, especially in the mountains. No matter when you go, always be prepared with warm clothing and a waterproof layer. Protect yourself from the wind on long downhill stretches – even stuffing a few sheets of newspaper under your shirt in a pinch cuts the chill considerably.

Female Specific Issues

Bike shorts are a ripe environment for yeast infections, and especially so if you happen to be taking antibiotics. Make sure that you are putting on fresh shorts every day. Sink washing and night drying is essential. Off the saddle opt for looser aerated clothes and make sure you have a yeast infection specific antifungal in your first-aid kit.

Urinary tract infections are not as big an issue, but when you're on the road, you don't want to get caught without a nice round of Ciprophlaxin and an over-the-counter UTI pain medication. Preventive measures include eating yogurt, staying hydrated, and urinating after sexual contact.

On that same note, if you and your partner are on a bike honeymoon of sorts, know that sex can increase the likelihood of either one of these issues. However, if you are aware of this and take care, you shouldn't have a problem, which is good because cycling vacations are the most romantic.

MEDICAL PROBLEMS & TREATMENT

ENVIRONMENTAL HAZARDS

Sun

Sun exposure can suck the much-needed liquids from your body faster than you think, and sunburns can be really painful. Both prospects are no fun. Here are some tips to prevent overexposure:

o Wear a white long-sleeved shirt and a peaked helmet cover. A 'legionnaire's flap' for your helmet is geeky but protects the back of your neck and ears.

o Choose a water-resistant, high protection (30+ or higher) 'sports' sunscreen. During the strongest hours, reapply as you sweat it off. Protect your neck, ears, hands, and feet.

o Wear good quality sunglasses.

o Sit in the shade during rest breaks.

Mild sunburn can be relieved with a cool cloth or aloe vera.

Heat

Treat heat with respect. In a hot climate, don't set yourself a demanding touring schedule as soon as you arrive; take things lightly until you acclimatise.

DEHYDRATION & HEAT EXHAUSTION

Dehydration is a potentially dangerous and easily preventable condition caused by excessive fluid loss. Sweating and inadequate fluid intake are common causes of dehydration in cyclists, but others include diarrhoea, vomiting and high fever – see Diarrhoea (below) for details on appropriate treatment in these circumstances.

HEALTH & SAFETY

The first symptoms are weakness, thirst and passing small amounts of very concentrated urine. This may progress to drowsiness, dizziness or fainting when standing up and, finally, coma.

It's easy to forget how much fluid you are losing via perspiration while you are cycling, particularly if a strong breeze is drying your skin quickly. Make sure you drink sufficient liquids (see Hydration p324). You should refrain from drinking too many caffeinated drinks such as coffee, tea and some soft drinks (which act as a diuretic, causing your body to lose water through urination) throughout the day; don't use them as a water replacement.

Dehydration and salt deficiency can cause heat exhaustion. Salt deficiency is characterised by fatigue, lethargy, headaches, giddiness and muscle cramps; salt tablets may help, but adding extra salt to your food is probably sufficient.

If one of your party suffers from heat exhaustion, lie them down in a shady spot and encourage them to drink slowly but frequently. If possible, seek medical advice.

HEATSTROKE
This serious and occasionally fatal condition can occur if the body's heat-regulating mechanism breaks down and the body temperature rises to dangerous levels. Continuous periods of exposure to high temperatures and insufficient fluids can leave you vulnerable to heatstroke.

The symptoms are feeling unwell, not sweating very much (or at all) and a high body temperature (39°C-41°C or 102°F-106°F). Where sweating has ceased, the skin becomes flushed and red. Severe, throbbing headaches and lack of coordination will also occur, and the sufferer may be confused or aggressive. Eventually the victim will become delirious or convulse.

Hospitalisation is essential, but in the interim get the casualty out of the sun, remove their clothing, cover them with a wet sheet or towel and then fan continuously. Give them plenty of fluids (cool water), if conscious.

Cold
HYPOTHERMIA
Hypothermia occurs when the body loses heat faster than it can produce it and the core temperature of the body falls. It is surprisingly easy to progress from very cold to dangerously cold due to a combination of wind, wet clothing, fatigue and hunger, even if the air temperature stays above freezing.

Symptoms of hypothermia are exhaustion, numb skin (particularly toes and fingers), shivering, slurred speech, irrational or violent behaviour, lethargy, stumbling, dizzy spells, muscle cramps and powerful bursts of energy. Irrationality may take the form of sufferers claiming they are warm and trying to take off their clothes.

To prevent hypothermia, dress in layers (see Clothing under What to Bring on p25). A strong, waterproof outer layer is essential. Protect yourself against wind, particularly for long descents. Eat plenty of high-energy food when it's cold; it's important to keep drinking too – even though you may not feel like it.

To treat mild hypothermia, get the person out of the wind and/or rain, remove wet clothing and replace it with dry, warm clothing. Give them hot liquids – not alcohol – and some high-calorie, easily digestible food. Do not rub victims: instead, allow them to slowly warm themselves. This should be enough to treat the early stages of hypothermia; however, medical treatment should still be sought, urgently if the hypothermia is severe. Early recognition and treatment of mild hypothermia is the only way to prevent severe hypothermia, a critical condition.

Hay Fever
If you suffer from hay fever, bring your usual treatment.

INFECTIOUS DISEASES
Diarrhoea
Simple things like a change of water, food or climate can cause a mild bout of diarrhoea, but a few rushed toilet trips with no other symptoms are not indicative of a major problem. More serious diarrhoea is caused by infectious agents transmitted by faecal contamination of food or water, by using contaminated utensils or directly from one person's hand to another. Paying particular attention to personal hygiene, drinking purified water and taking care of what you eat are important measures to take to avoid getting diarrhoea while touring.

Dehydration is the main danger with any diarrhoea, particularly in children or the elderly, as it can occur quickly. Under all circumstances, the most important thing is to replace fluids (at least equal to the volume being lost). Urine is the best guide to this – if you have small amounts of dark-coloured urine, you need to drink more. Weak black tea with a little sugar, soda water, or soft drinks allowed to go flat and diluted 50% with clean water are all good. With severe diarrhoea it's better to use a rehydrating solution to replace lost minerals and salts. Commercially available oral rehydration salts should be added to boiled or bottled water. In an emergency, make a solution of six teaspoons of sugar and a half-teaspoon of salt in a litre of boiled or bottled water. Keep drinking small amounts often. Stick to a bland diet as you recover.

Gut-paralysing drugs such as diphenoxylate or loperamide can be used to bring relief from the symptoms, although they do not actually cure the problem. Only use these drugs if you do not have access to toilets, that is, if you must travel. These drugs are not recommended for children under 12 years of age, or if you have a high fever or are severely dehydrated.

Seek medical advice if you pass blood or mucus, are feverish or suffer persistent or severe diarrhoea.

Another cause of persistent diarrhoea in travellers is giardiasis.

Giardiasis

This intestinal disorder is contracted by drinking water contaminated with the giardia parasite. The symptoms are stomach cramps, nausea, a bloated stomach, watery and foul-smelling diarrhoea, and frequent gas. Giardiasis can appear several weeks after you have been exposed to the parasite. The symptoms may disappear for a few days and then return; this can go on for several weeks. Seek medical advice if you think you have giardiasis but, where this is not possible, tinidazole or metronidazole are the recommended drugs. Treatment is a 2g single dose of tinidazole or 250mg of metronidazole three times daily for five to 10 days.

Rabies

Rabies is a fatal viral infection. It is contracted by a bite from an infected animal, which could be a dog, pig, cat, fox or bat: their salvia is infectious. Once symptoms have appeared, death is inevitable, but the onset of symptoms can be prevented by a course of injections with the rabies vaccine, which you will need irrespective of whether or not you have been immunised.

Tetanus

This disease is caused by a germ that lives in soil and in the faeces of horses and other animals. It enters the body via breaks in the skin. The first symptom may be discomfort in swallowing, or stiffening of the jaw and neck; this is followed by painful convulsions of the jaw and whole body. The disease can be fatal. It can be prevented by vaccination.

BITES & STINGS
Dogs

You're bound to encounter barking dogs while riding in Italy, and some are likely to be untethered. As rabies exists in Italy (see Infectious Diseases p329), all dogs should be regarded as dangerous, and preventative action taken to avoid them. Ride through their territory quickly and try shouting at them. A squirt from the water bottle or tap with the bike pump may provide added deterrent if the animal won't take the hint – though use the pump as a last resort, especially if the owner is in sight.

Bees & Wasps

These are usually painful rather than dangerous. However, anyone allergic to these can suffer severe breathing difficulties and will need medical care.

Calamine lotion or a commercial sting relief spray will ease discomfort, and ice packs will reduce the pain and swelling. Antihistamines can also help.

Mosquitoes & Sandflies

Mosquitoes appear after dusk. The Milan area seems to be especially inundated. Avoid bites by covering bare skin and using an insect repellent. Mosquitoes may be attracted by perfume, aftershave or certain colours. They can bite you through thin fabrics or on any small part of your skin not covered by repellent.

Leishmaniasis is a group of parasitic diseases transmitted by sandflies and found in coastal parts of Italy. Cutaneous leishmaniasis affects the skin tissue and causes ulceration and disfigurement; visceral leishmaniasis affects the internal organs. Avoiding sandfly bites by covering up and using repellent is the best precaution against this disease.

The most effective insect repellent is called DEET, an ingredient in many commercially available repellents. Look for a repellent with at least a 28% concentration of DEET. Note that DEET breaks down plastic, rubber, contact lenses and synthetic fabrics, so be careful what you touch after using it. It poses no danger to natural fibres.

Jellyfish

Italian beaches are occasionally inundated with jellyfish. Their stings are painful but not dangerous. Dousing in vinegar will deactivate any stingers that have not fired. Calamine lotion, antihistamines and analgesics may reduce the reaction and relieve pain.

Snakes

Italy's only dangerous snake, the viper, is found throughout the country except on Sardinia. To minimise the possibilities of being bitten, always wear boots, socks and long trousers when walking through undergrowth If bitten, wrap the bitten limb tightly, as you would for a sprained ankle, and immobilise it with a splint. Keep the victim still and seek medical assistance; it will help if you can describe the offending reptile. Tourniquets and sucking out the poison are now totally discredited.

TRAUMATIC INJURIES

Although we give guidance on basic first-aid procedures here remember that, unless you're an experienced first aider and confident in what you're doing, it's possible to do more harm than good. Always seek medical help if it is available, but if you are far from any help, follow these guidelines.

Cuts & Other Wounds

Here's what to do if you suffer a fall while riding and end up with road-rash (grazing) and a few minor cuts. If you're riding in a hot, humid climate or intend continuing on your way, there's likely to be a high risk of infection, so the wound needs to be cleaned and dressed. Carry a few antiseptic wipes in your first-aid kit to use as an immediate measure, especially if no clean water is available. Small wounds can be cleaned with an antiseptic wipe (only wipe across the wound once with each). Deep or dirty wounds need to be cleaned thoroughly:

o Clean your hands before you start.
o Wear gloves if you are cleaning somebody else's wound.
o Use plenty of water – squirt it forcefully on the wound from a water bottle (three bottles if you can spare).
o Use bottled or boiled water (allowed to cool) or an antiseptic solution like povidone-iodine.
o Embedded dirt and other particles can be removed with tweezers or flushed out using a syringe to squirt water (you can get more pressure if you use a needle as well) – this is especially effective for removing gravel.
o Dry wounds heal best, so avoid using antiseptic creams that keep the wound moist; instead apply antiseptic powder or spray.
o Dry the wound with clean gauze before applying a dressing – alternatively, any clean material will do as long as it's not fluffy (avoid cotton wool), because it will stick.

Any break in the skin makes you vulnerable to tetanus infection – if you didn't have a tetanus injection before you left, get one now.

A dressing will protect the wound from dirt, dust and flies. Alternatively, if the wound is small and you are confident you can keep it clean, leave it uncovered. Change the dressing regularly (once a day to start with), especially if the wound is oozing, and watch for signs of infection.

If you have any swelling around the wound, raising the affected limb can help the swelling settle and the wound to heal.

It's best to seek medical advice for any wound that fails to heal after a week or so.

HEALTH & SAFETY

Major Accident

Crashing or being hit by an inattentive driver in a motor vehicle is always possible when cycling. When a major accident does occur what you do is determined to some extent by the circumstances you are in and how readily available medical care is. However, remember that emergency services may be different from what you're used to at home. As anywhere, if you are outside a major town they may be much slower at responding to a call, so you need to be prepared to do at least an initial assessment and to ensure that the casualty comes to no further harm. First of all, check for danger to yourself. If the casualty is on the road ensure oncoming traffic is stopped or diverted around you. A basic plan of action is:

o Keep calm and think through what you need to do and when.
o Get medical help urgently; send someone to phone (local emergency number)
o Carefully look over the casualty in the position in which you found them (unless this is hazardous for some reason, eg, on a cliff edge).
o Call out to the victim to see if there is any response.
o Put on latex gloves.
o Check for pulse (at the wrist or on the side of the neck), breathing and major blood loss.
o If necessary (ie, no breathing or no pulse), and you know how, start resuscitation. If you aren't familiar with the person you'll want to have a body systems barrier.
o Check the casualty for injuries, moving them as little as possible; ask them where they have pain if they are conscious.
o Don't move the casualty if a spinal injury is possible.
o Take immediate steps to control any obvious bleeding by applying direct pressure to the wound.
o Make the casualty as comfortable as possible and reassure them.
o Keep the casualty warm by insulating them from cold or wet ground (use whatever you have to hand, such as a sleeping bag). If they are in the hot sun, make sure they are in shade.

BLEEDING WOUNDS

Most cuts will stop bleeding on their own, but if a blood vessel of any size has been cut it may continue bleeding for some time. Wounds to the head, hands and at joint creases tend to be particularly bloody.

To stop bleeding from a wound:

o Wear gloves if you are dealing with a wound on another person.

o Lie the person down if possible.

o Raise the injured limb above the level of the casualty's heart.

o Use your fingers or the palm of your hand to apply direct pressure to the wound, preferably over a sterile dressing or clean pad.

o Apply steady pressure for at least five minutes before looking to see if the bleeding has stopped.

o Put a sterile dressing over the original pad (don't move this) and bandage it in place.

o Check the bandage regularly in case bleeding restarts.

Never use a tourniquet to stop bleeding as this may cause gangrene – the only situation in which this may be appropriate is if the limb has been amputated.

SAFETY ON THE BIKE

ROAD RULES

General rules are:
o Ride on the right side of the road.
o Ride in single file, and always keep to the extreme right, unless you are turning left or passing.
o Obey all traffic lights and road signs, and use hand signals to indicate turns. Avoid sudden movements.
o Never ride the wrong way down a one-way street.
o Always yield to pedestrians.
o Do not ride on footpaths unless there is road construction or cobblestones, in which case you must ride slowly and give priority to pedestrians.
o Keep a suitable distance from parked cars.

For a list of commonly seen road signs, see the Language chapter (p335).

Road Use

Cyclists may use all roads except *autostrade* (autoroutes), *strade statali* (state roads) when posted signs specifically prohibit two-wheel motorless vehicles, and roads paralleled by a compulsory bike path. A round blue sign with a white bicycle symbol indicates a *pista ciclabile* (bicycle path). You are obliged to use it, especially if it is signed with the word *obligatorio* (compulsory). The end of a *pista ciclabile* is indicated by the same sign, with a red line through it.

Priority to the Right

The most confusing – and dangerous – traffic law in Italy is the notorious 'priority to the right' rule, under which any car entering an intersection (including a T-junction) from a public road on your right has right-of-way no matter how small the road.

Rotatorie/rotonde (roundabouts)

As a cyclist, use extreme caution. Road decorum calls for you to enter the roundabout and move left to allow enough room for cars to exit (if you are not taking the first exit). However, many Italian cyclists remain in the centre of the outside lane (to discourage drivers' overly aggressive manoeuvring). When you approach your exit, indicate with a right hand turn signal to let cars know you are exiting. Make certain that the driver of the car behind you or to your right has seen you.

Rider Safety

Although helmets are not compulsory in Italy, we strongly recommend you wear one whenever in the saddle. Make sure it fits properly: It should sit squarely on your head with the front low on your brow to protect your forehead. It should be snug, but not tight, once it has been fastened, and there should be no slack in the straps. If it has been in a crash, replace it.

Whether it is day or night, it is always a good idea to wear brightly coloured clothing, and at night garments with reflective strips. Do not hesitate to use your bell or voice to make your presence felt.

Road Conditions

Some Italian roads look like they haven't been retouched since chariots were in vogue. This is especially true in out-of-way rural reaches, where some of the least-run roads have deteriorated to or been left with gravel surfaces. The routes in this book try to keep you off these roads.

Cobblestones are the other major road nuisance. Some major city (Rome's for example) streets are paved with them.

Some steep mountain lanes and most Italian cities include areas paved with rough square stones separated by ruts wide and deep enough to catch, trip and mangle a cyclist's wheels. This is particularly true in Naples. Steer carefully and pedal slowly (especially on steep curvy downhills) when you encounter this.

Italian Driving Habits

Italian drivers (and not just the men) are famous for their aggressive behind-the-wheel shenanigans. Their reputation for unrestrained recklessness is not entirely undeserved. However, before levelling the standard accusations at them, it is important to understand a little Italian driving culture, because they – more than many other cultures – are used to cyclists and, most of the time, respect them.

Why do Italian drivers steer so close? Actually, they don't think they do. They are accustomed to the tight corners of narrow Italian streets and roads. They are not swerving menacingly at you; rather, they are nimbly and ably guiding their vehicles into spaces through which they confidently know they will fit. If you handle your bike with the same self-assurance and dexterity – following your line, making no sudden moves – you will have no trouble. That said, there is no real excuse for the Italian engine-revving love of overtaking at high-speeds on the blind curves of winding mountain roads.

Why do Italian drivers keep cutting you off? They don't think they are. They see what they consider to be a space between (in front of or alongside) you and a vehicle or turn and so accelerate into it. It doesn't help that Italian law actually permits cars to overtake bicycles near an intersection. However, once again, if you pedal with deliberate and clear motions and look around you at intersections, you should run no risks.

Why do Italian drivers ignore traffic rules? Actually, although the problem used to be rampant, there are fewer and fewer law evaders today; especially in cities where automotive congestion is a serious problem and traffic laws are more and more strictly enforced.

RIDING OFF-ROAD

Always tell someone where you are going and when you intend to be back – and make sure they know that you're back! Trail etiquette requires mountain bikes to yield to hikers and equestrians. But it's more important just to use common courtesy while on the trail. Bike paths are often shared with pedestrians; ring your bell or give a holler before passing on the left.

Bring warm clothing, matches and enough food and water in case of emergency repairs. Carry a map and take note of the surroundings as you ride. If you get really lost, stay calm and stop. Try to work out where you are or how to retrace your route. If you can't, or it's getting dark, find a nearby open area, put on warm clothes and find or make a shelter. Light a fire to help searchers.

EMERGENCY NUMBERS

If you need an ambulance anywhere in Italy, call ☎ 118. For emergency treatment, head straight to the *pronto soccorso* (casualty) section of a public hospital, where you can also get emergency dental treatment.

For the police, dial ☎ 112/113. For fire, dial ☎ 115.

HEALTH & SAFETY

Language

If you've managed to gain more than the most fundamental grasp of the language you will need to be aware that many older Italians still expect to be addressed by the third person polite, that is, *lei* instead of *tu*. Also, it is not considered polite to use the greeting *ciao* when addressing strangers, unless they use it first; it's better to say *buongiorno* (or *buona sera*, as the case may be) and *arrivederci* (or the more polite form, *arrivederla*). We have used the polite address for most of the phrases in this guide. Use of the informal address is indicated by (inf). Italian also has both masculine and feminine forms (in the singular they often end in 'o' and 'a' respectively). Where both forms are given in this guide, they are separated by a slash, the masculine form first. If you'd like a more comprehensive guide to the language, pick up a copy of Lonely Planet's *Italian Phrasebook*.

PRONUNCIATION

With a little practice, Italian pronunciation is quite easy. Just follow the guides included with each phrase in our language guide and you'll be well on the way to mastering your spoken lingo.

Word stress generally falls on the second-last syllable, as in spa-*ghet*-ti, but when a word has a written accent, the stress falls on that syllable, as in cit-*tà* (city). Stress is shown in our pronunciation guide by italics.

ACCOMMODATION

I'm looking for a ...	Cerco ...	*cher*·ko ...
guesthouse	una pensione	oo·na pen·*syo*·ne
hotel	un albergo	oon al·*ber*·go
youth hostel	un ostello per la gioventù	oon os·*te*·lo per la jo·ven·*too*
room in a private house	una camera in una casa privata	oo·na *ka*·me·ra in oo·na *ka*·sa pree·*va*·ta

What is the address?
Qual'è l'indirizzo? kwa·*le* leen·dee·*ree*·tso
Could you write the address, please?
Può scrivere l'indirizzo, per favore? pwo *skree*·ve·re leen·dee·*ree*·tso per fa·*vo*·re

EMERGENCIES

Help!		
Aiuto!		a·*yoo*·to
There's been an accident!		
C'è stato un incidente!		che *sta*·to oon een·chee·*den*·te
I'm lost.		
Mi sono perso/a.		mee *so*·no *per*·so/a
Go away!		
Lasciami in pace!		la·*sha*·mi een *pa*·che
Vai via! (inf)		va·ee *vee*·a
Call ...!		
Chiami ...!		kee·*ya*·mee ...
a doctor		
un dottore/medico		oon do·*to*·re/*me*·dee·ko
the police		
la polizia		la po·lee·*tsee*·ya

Do you have any rooms available?
Avete camere libere? a·*ve*·te *ka*·me·re *lee*·be·re
Are bikes a problem at the hotel?
È un problema portare le bici all'albergo? e oon prob·*le*·ma por·*ta*·re le *bee*·chee al· al·*ber*·go
Do you have a safe place to store bikes?
Avete un posto sicuro lasciare bici? a·*ve*·te oon *pos*·to·see *koo*·ro la·*sha*·re *bee*·chee

I'd like (a) ...		
Vorrei una camera ...		vo·*ray* oo·na *ka*·me·ra ...
single room		
singola		*seen*·go·la
double room		
matrimoniale		ma·tree·mo·*nya*·le
room with two beds		
doppia		*do*·pya

How much is it per night/per person?
Quanto costa per la notte/per persona? *kwan*·to *ko*·sta per la *no*·te/per per·*so*·na

CONVERSATION & ESSENTIALS

Hello.	Buongiorno.	b w o n · *j o r* · n o
	Ciao. (inf)	chow
Goodbye.	Arrivederci.	a·ree·ve·*der*·chee
	Ciao. (inf)	chow
Yes.	Sì.	see
No.	No.	no

Please.	*Per favore/*	per fa·*vo*·re/
	Per piacere.	per pya·*che*·re
Thank you.	*Grazie.*	*gra*·tsye
That's fine/	*Prego.*	p r e · g o
You're welcome.		
Excuse me.	*Mi scusi.*	mee *skoo*·zee
I'm sorry.	*Mi scusi/*	mee *skoo*·zee/
	Mi perdoni.	mee per·*do*·nee

What's your name?
Come si chiama?   *ko*·me see *kya*·ma
Come ti chiami? (inf)   *ko*·me tee *kya*·mee
My name is ...
Mi chiamo ...   mee *kya*·mo ...
Where are you from?
Da dove viene?   da *do*·ve *vye*·ne
Di dove sei? (inf)   dee *do*·ve *se*·ee
I'm from ...
Vengo da ...   *ven*·go da ...

Bike Banter
Where have you ridden from?
Da dove hai   da *do*·ve ai pe·da·*la*·to
pedalato? (inf)
Where are you riding to (today)?
Dove pedali (oggi)? (inf) *do*·ve pe·*da*·li (*o*·jee)
I'm going from ... to ...
Vado da ... a ...   *va*·do da ... a ...
Would you like to ride together?
Vuoi pedalare   vwoy pe·da·*la*·re in·*sye*·me
insieme? (inf)

FOOD & DRINK
breakfast
(prima) colazione   (*pree*·ma) ko·la·*tsyo*·ne
lunch
pranzo   *pran*·tso
dinner
cena   *che*·na
restaurant
ristorante   ree·sto·*ran*·te
grocery shop
alimentari   a·lee·men·*ta*·re

I'd like the set menu.
Vorrei il menù turistico. vo·*ray* eel me·*noo* too·*ree*·stee·ko
That was delicious!
Era squisito!   e·ra skwee·*zee*·to
Please bring the bill.
Mi porta il conto, per mee *por*·ta eel *kon*·to per
favore?   fa·*vo*·re

HEALTH
I'm ill.   *Mi sento male.*   mee *sen*·to *ma*·le
It hurts here.   *Mi fa male qui.*   mee fa *ma*·le kwee

antiseptic	*antisettico*	an·tee·*se*·tee·ko
condoms	*preservativi*	pre·zer·va·*tee*·vee
contraceptive	*contraccetivo*	kon·tra·che·*tee*·vo
diarrhoea	*diarrea*	dee·a·*re*·a
sunblock cream	*crema solare*	*kre*·ma so·*la*·re
tampons	*tamponi*	tam·*po*·nee

I'm ...	*Sono ...*	*so*·no ...
asthmatic	*asmatico/a*	az·*ma*·tee·ko/a
diabetic	*diabetico/a*	dee·a·*be*·tee·ko/a
epileptic	*epilettico/a*	e·pee·*le*·tee·ko/a

I'm allergic ...
Sono allergico/a ...   *so*·no a·*ler*·jee·ko/a ...
to antibiotics
agli antibiotici   a·lyee *an*·tee·bee·*o*·tee·chee
to penicillin
alla penicillina   a·la *pe*·nee·see·*lee*·na
to peanuts
alle arachidi   a·le a·ra·*kee*·dee

LANGUAGE DIFFICULTIES
Do you speak English?
Parla inglese?   *par*·la een·*gle*·ze
Does anyone here speak English?
C'è qualcuno che   che kwal·*koo*·no ke
parla inglese?   *par*·la een·*gle*·ze
What is this called in Italian?
Come si chiama questo *ko*·me see *kya*·ma *kwe*·sto
in italiano?   een ee·ta·*lya*·no
I (don't) understand.
(Non) Capisco.   non ka·*pee*·sko

NUMBERS
0	*zero*	*dze*·ro
1	*uno*	*oo*·no
2	*due*	*doo*·e
3	*tre*	tre
4	*quattro*	*kwa*·tro
5	*cinque*	*cheen*·kwe
6	*sei*	say
7	*sette*	*se*·te
8	*otto*	*o*·to
9	*nove*	*no*·ve
10	*dieci*	*dye*·chee
11	*undici*	*oon*·dee·chee
12	*dodici*	*do*·dee·chee
13	*tredici*	*tre*·dee·chee
14	*quattordici*	kwa·*tor*·dee·chee
15	*quindici*	*kween*·dee·chee
16	*sedici*	*se*·dee·chee
17	*diciassette*	dee·cha·*se*·te
18	*diciotto*	dee·*cho*·to
19	*diciannove*	dee·cha·*no*·ve
20	*venti*	*ven*·tee

21	*ventuno*	ven·*too*·no
22	*ventidue*	ven·tee·*doo*·e
30	*trenta*	*tren*·ta
40	*quaranta*	kwa·*ran*·ta
50	*cinquanta*	cheen·*kwan*·ta
60	*sessanta*	se·*san*·ta
70	*settanta*	se·*tan*·ta
80	*ottanta*	o·*tan*·ta
90	*novanta*	no·*van*·ta
100	*cento*	*chen*·to
1000	*mille*	mee·*le*
2000	*due mila*	*doo*·e mee·la

SHOPPING & SERVICES

I'm looking for ...
Cerco ... cher·ko ...

a bank
un banco oon *ban*·ko

a bike shop
un negozio di bici oon ne·*go*·tsyo dee *bee*·chee

a chemist/pharmacy
una farmacia oo·na far·ma·*chee*·ya

a laundry/laundrette
una lavanderia oo·na la·van·de·*ree*·ya

the market
il mercato (civico) eel mer·*ka*·to (*chee*·vee·ko)

the post office
la posta la *po*·sta

a public toilet
un gabinetto oon ga·bee·*ne*·to

a supermarket
un supermercato oon soo·per·mer·*ka*·to

the tourist information office
l'ufficio di turismo loo·*fee*·cho dee too·*reez*·mo

At the Bike Shop

Where can I find a bike repair shop?
Dove posso trovare un riparatore di bici?
do·ve *pos*·so tro·*va*·re oon ree·pa·ra·*to*·re dee *bee*·chee

I'd like to buy ...
Vorrei comprare ... vo·*lyo* kom·*pra*·re ...

arm warmers
manicotti ma·nee·*ko*·tee

an elastic (ocky) strap
un elastico per attaccare oon ee·*las*·tee·ko per
at·ta·*ka*·re
  i bagagli ee ba·*gal*·yee

glasses
occhiali o·*kya*·lee

gloves
guanti *gwan*·tee

a helmet
un casco oon *kas*·ko

knicks
pantaloncini pan·ta·lon·*chee*·nee

a jersey
una maglia oo·na *mal*·ya

leg warmers
gambali gam·*ba*·lee

tights
calzamaglia kal·za·*mal*·ya

a tube
una camera a aria oo·na *ka*·me·ra a *a*·ree·a

How much is it?
Quanto costa? *kwan*·to *ko*·sta

May I look at it?
Posso dare un'occhiata? *po*·so *da*·re oo·no·*kya*·ta

Do you accept credit cards?
Accettate carte di a·che·*ta*·te *kar*·te dee
credito? *kre*·dee·to

I'd like to hire ...
Vorrei noleggiare ... vo·*ray* no·le·*ja*·re ...

a (road) bike
una bici (di strada) oo·na *bee*·chee (dee *stra*·da)

a mountain bike
una 'mountain bike' oo·na mountain bike

a child's seat
un sediolino per oon se·dyo·*lee*·no per
bambini bam·*bee*·nee

a ... trailer
un carrello ... oon ka·*re*·lo
  child's
  porta bambini *por*·ta bam·*bee*·nee
  luggage
  porta bagagli *por*·ta ba·*gal*·yee

Could you ...?
Potresti ...? po·*tres*·ti ...

adjust the gears
regolare il cambio re·go·*la*·re eel *kam*·byo

adjust the saddle
regolare la sella re·go·*la*·re la *sel*·la

inflate the tyres
gonfiare le gomme gon·*fya*·re le *gom*·me

true the wheel
centrare il cerchione chen·*tra*·re eel cher·*kyo*·ne

tighten the ...
serrare il/la ... se·*ra*·re eel/la ...

I have a puncture.
Ho una foratura. o oo·na fo·ra·*too*·ra

I have a broken spoke.
È rotto un raggio. e *ro*·to oon *ra*·jo

TIME & DATES

What time is it?	*Che ore sono?*	ke o·re *so*·no
It's (8 o'clock).	*Sono (le otto).*	*so*·no (le o·to)
in the morning	*di mattina*	dee ma·*tee*·na

in the afternoon	di pomeriggio	dee po·me·*ree*·jo
in the evening	di sera	dee *se*·ra
When?	*Quando?*	*kwan*·do
today	*oggi*	*o*·jee
tomorrow	*domani*	do·*ma*·nee
Monday	*lunedì*	loo·ne·*dee*
Tuesday	*martedì*	mar·te·*dee*
Wednesday	*mercoledì*	mer·ko·le·*dee*
Thursday	*giovedì*	jo·ve·*dee*
Friday	*venerdì*	ve·ner·*dee*
Saturday	*sabato*	*sa*·ba·to
Sunday	*domenica*	do·*me*·nee·ka
January	*gennaio*	je·*na*·yo
February	*febbraio*	fe·*bra*·yo
March	*marzo*	*mar*·tso
April	*aprile*	a·*pree*·le
May	*maggio*	*ma*·jo
June	*giugno*	*joo*·nyo
July	*luglio*	*loo*·lyo
August	*agosto*	a·*gos*·to
September	*settembre*	se·*tem*·bre
October	*ottobre*	o·*to*·bre
November	*novembre*	no·*vem*·bre
December	*dicembre*	dee·*chem*·bre

TRANSPORT

What time does the ... leave/arrive?	*A che ora parte/ arriva ...?*	a ke *o*·ra *par*·te/ a·*ree*·va ...
boat	*la nave*	la *na*·ve
(city) bus	*l'autobus*	*low*·to·boos
(intercity) bus	*il pullman*	eel *pool*·man
train	*il treno*	eel *tre*·no
I'd like a ...	*Vorrei un*	vo·*ray* oon
ticket to (...)	*biglietto ... (a ...)*	bee·*lye*·to ... (a ...)
one way	*di solo andata*	dee *so*·lo an·*da*·ta
return	*di andata e ritorno*	dee an·*da*·ta e ree·*toor*·no

the first	*il primo*	eel *pree*·mo
the last	*l'ultimo*	*lool*·tee·mo
platform (two)	*binario (due)*	bee·*na*·ryo (*doo*·e)
ticket office	*biglietteria*	bee·lye·te·*ree*·a
timetable	*orario*	o·*ra*·ryo
train station	*stazione*	sta·*tsyo*·ne

I'd like to hire a car.
Vorrei noleggiare una vo·ray no·le·*ja*·re oo·na
macchina ma·*kee*·na
Where's a service station?
Dov'è una stazione do·ve oo·na sta·*tsyo*·ne
di servizio? dee ser·*vee*·tsyo

Please fill it up.
Il pieno, per favore. eel *pye*·no per fa·*vo*·re
I'd like (30) litres.
Vorrei (trenta) litri. vo·*ray* (*tren*·ta) *lee*·tree

| **diesel** | *gasolio/diesel* | ga·*zo*·lyo/*dee*·zel |
| **petrol/gasoline** | *benzina* | ben·*dzee*·na |

Transport with a Bike
Does the (bus/hydrofoil/train) carry bikes?
(L'autobus/l'aliscafo/il treno) trasporta le bici?
(lau·to·boos/la·lee·*ska*·fo/eel *tre*·no) tra·*spor*·ta le *bee*·chee
The bike must be in a bag.
La bici dev'essere in una sacca.
la *bee*·chee de·*ve*·se·re een oon *sa*·ko
When is the next train allowing non-bagged bikes?
Quando è il prossimo treno che permette bici non smontate?
kwan·do e eel *pro*·see·mo *tre*·no ke per·*me*·te *bee*·chee non smon·*ta*·ta
Where on the train does the bike go?
Dove nel treno dovrei mettere la bici?
do·ve nel *tre*·no dov·*ray* *me*·te·re la *bee*·chee
Where is the luggage car?
Dov'è il bagagliaio?
do·ve eel ba·gal·*ya*·yo

Directions & Road Conditions
Where is ...?
Dov'è ...? *do*·ve ...
Which road do I take for ...?
Quale strada devo *kwa*·le *stra*·da *de*·vo
prendere per ...? *pren*·de·re per ...
Can you show me on the map?
Potrebbe mostrarmi po·*treb*·be mos·*trar*·mee
sulla carta? soo·la *kar*·ta
Go straight ahead.
Si va sempre diritto. see va *sem*·pre dee·*ree*·to
Vai sempre diritto (inf). va·ee *sem*·pre dee·*ree*·to
Turn left.
Gira a sinistra. *jee*·ra a see·*nees*·tra
Turn right.
Gira a destra. *jee*·ra a *des*·tra
at the traffic lights
al semaforo al se·*ma*·fo·ro
at the next corner
al prossimo angolo al *pro*·see·mo *an*·go·lo
at the next crossroad
al prossimo incrocio al *pro*·see·mo een·*kro*·cho
Is it near/far?
È vicino/lontano? e vee·*chee*·no/lon·*ta*·no
How many kilometres to ...?
Quanti kilometri per ...? *kwan*·tee kee·*lo*·me·tree per ...
Is it hilly?
È collinoso? e ko·lee·*no*·so

<table>
<tr><th colspan="2">ROAD SIGNS</th></tr>
<tr><td>**Attenzione/ Pericolo!**</td><td>Danger!</td></tr>
<tr><td>**Dare Precedenza**
(a Destra)</td><td>Give Way (to Right)</td></tr>
<tr><td>**Deviazione**</td><td>Detour</td></tr>
<tr><td>**Divieto di Accesso**</td><td>No Entry</td></tr>
<tr><td>**Lavori in Corso**</td><td>Roadworks</td></tr>
<tr><td>**(...) Obligatorio**</td><td>(...) Compulsory</td></tr>
<tr><td>**Passo/Valico Chiuso**</td><td>(Road Over) Pass Closed</td></tr>
<tr><td>**Senso Unico**</td><td>One Way</td></tr>
<tr><td>**Strada Accidentata**</td><td>Rough Road</td></tr>
<tr><td>**Strada Chiusa**</td><td>Road Closed</td></tr>
<tr><td>**Strada Scivolosa**</td><td>Slippery Surface</td></tr>
<tr><td>**Strada Sterrata**</td><td>Gravel Road</td></tr>
<tr><td>**Strade Ghiacciate**</td><td>Icy Roads</td></tr>
<tr><td>**Tutte le Direzioni**</td><td>All Directions</td></tr>
</table>

Is it steep?
È ripida?   e *ree*·pee·da

There are lots of hills.
Ci sono tante salite.   chee *so*·no *tan*·te sa·*lee*·te

The road climbs/descends.
La strada sale/scende.   la *stra*·da *sa*·le/*shen*·de

Is there a lot of traffic?
È molto trafficato?   e *mol*·to tra·fee·*ka*·to

Is this road OK for bikes?
Va bene per bici, questa   va *be*·ne per *bee*·chee kwe·sta
strada?   *stra*·da

via ...
per mezzo di .../   per *met*·so dee .../
attraverso ...   a·tra·*ver*·so

behind
dietro   *dye*·tro

in front of
davanti   da·*van*·tee

to stop off at ...
fare una tappa a ...   fa·re oo·na *tap*·pa

north/south/east/west
nord/sud/est/ovest   nord/sood/est/*o*·vest

bitumen road
strada asfaltata   stra·da as·fal·*ta*·ta

gravel/unpaved road
strada bianca/sterrata   stra·da *byan*·ka/ste *ra*·ta

shoulder (of road)
spalla   *spal*·la

in good condition
in buona condizione   een *bwo*·na kon·dee·*tsyo*·ne

potholes
buche   *boo*·ke

headwind
vento contro   *ven*·to *kon*·tro

tailwind
vento a favore   *ven*·to a fa·*vo*·re

GLOSSARY OF THE BICYCLE

The masculine/feminine Italian articles *un/una*, (a) or *il/la* (the) are included to help you identify each noun's gender.

Allen key/wrench
una chiave (a brugola/   oo·na *kya*·ve (a *broo*·go·la/
esagonale)   e·sa·go·*na*·le)

Allen-head bolt
un bullone (a brugola/   oon bu·*lo*·ne (a *broo*·go·la/
esagonale)   e·sa·go·*na*·le)

axle (of wheel)
il perno (asse)   eel *per*·no (*as*·se)

bar ends
corne ('horns')   *kor*·ne

a battery/some batteries
una batteria/   oo·na ba·te·*ree*·ya/
delle batterie   de·le ba·te·*ree*·ye

bearings (ball)
i cuscinetti (a sfere)   ee koo·shee·*ne*·tee (a *sfe*·ra)

bike carrier (for car)
un portabici   oon *por*·ta·*bee*·chee

bolt
un bullone   oon bu·*lo*·ne

bottom bracket
il movimento centrale   eel mo·vee·*men*·to chen·*tra*·lay

brake/s
il freno/i freni   eel *fre*·no/ee *fre*·nee

brake pad
un pattino del freno   oon pa·*tee*·no del *fre*·no

cable
un cavo   oon *ka*·vo

cable housing/outer
la guaina (di cavo)   la gwa·*ee*·na (dee *ka*·vo)

caliper (of disc brake)
una pinza   oo·na *pin*·za

carry rack
un portapacchi   oon *por*·ta·*pa*·kee

cassette
il pacco pignoni a   eel *pa*·ko pee·*nyo*·nee a
cassetta   ka·*se*·ta

chain
una catena   oo·na ka·*te*·na

chainring
una corona   oo·na ko·*ro*·na

cleat
una placchetta/piastrina   oo·na pla·*ke*·ta/pya·*stree*·na

clipless pedals
pedali a sgancio rapido   pe·*da*·lee az·*gan*·cho

cog/sprocket
un pignone   oon pee·*nyo*·ne

crankset
la guarnitura   la *gwar*·nee·too·ra

cyclocomputer
un computerino   oon kom·pyoo·te·*ree*·no

derailleur (general)
il deragliatore   eel de·ra·lya·*to*·re

disc brake
un freno a disco   oon *fre*·no a *dees*·ko

a flat; flat (adjective)
una foratura; sgonfiato   oo·na fo·ra·*too*·ra; zgon·*fya*·to

fork
la forcella   la for·*che*·la

frame
il telaio   eel te·*la*·yo

freewheel
la ruota libera   la ru·*wo*·ta *lee*·be·ra

front
anteriore   an·te·*ryo*·re

glue (for patch)
il mastice   eel *mas*·tee·che

grease
il grasso (lubrificante)   eel *gra*·so (loo·bree·fee·*kan*·to)

grip
una manopola   oo·na ma·*nee*·po·la

handlebar tape
il nastro manubrio   eel *nas*·tro ma·*noo*·bree·o

handlebars
il manubrio   eel ma·*noo*·bree·o

headset
una serie sterzo   oo·na *se*·ree·e *ster*·tso

hub
un mozzo

lever (brake, gearchange etc)
una leva   oo·na *le*·va

link (of chain)
una maglia (della catena)   oo·na *mal*·ya (de·la ka·*te*·na)

light bulb
una lampadina   oo·na lam·pa·*dee*·na

lube/lubricant
il lubrificante   eel loo·bree·fee·*kan*·te

mountain bike
una mountain bike   oo·na *moun*·tain baik

mudguard
un parafango   oon pa·ra·*fang*·go

pannier
una borsa   oo·na *bor*·sa

patch (for tube)
una pezza/toppa   oo·na pe·tsa/*top*·pa

pedal
un pedale   oon pe·*da*·le

pin (for chain)
un perno   oon *per*·no

pressure (eg tyre)
la pressione   la pre·*syo*·ne

pump/mini-pump
una pompa/pompetta   oo·na *pom*·pa/pom·*pet*·ta

puncture
una foratura   oo·na fo·ra·*too*·ra

quick-release (for wheel)
uno sgancio rapido (di ruota)   oon *zgan*·cho ra·pee·do (dee roo·*o*·ta)

rear
posteriore   pos·te·*ryo*·re

rim
una cerchione   oo·na cher·*kyo*·ne

saddle
la sella   la *sel*·la

(a) screw
una vite   oo·na *vee*·te

seat bag
una borsetta   oo·na bor·*se*·ta

seatpost
un cannotto reggisella   oon ka·*no*·to re·jee·*se*·la

shifters
i comandi del cambio   ee ko·*man*·dee del *kam*·byo

shifting system
il cambio   eel *kam*·byo

shoes
scarpe   *skar*·pe

skewer
un bloccaggio   oon blo·*ka*·jo

spanner/wrench
una chiave (fissa)   oo·na *kya*·ve (*fee*·sa)

spoke
un raggio   oon *ra*·jo

spoke nipple/s
un nipplo/dei nippoli   oon *nee*·plo/day *nee*·po·lee

spoke spanner/wrench
un tiraraggi   oon tee·ra·*ra*·jee

sprocket
un pignone   oon pee·*nyo*·ne

steering/head stem
l'attacco/la pipa   la·*tak*·ko/la *pee*·pa

suspension fork
una forcella ammortizzata   oo·na for·*che*·la a·mor·tee·*tsa*·ta

tooth/teeth (of sprocket)
un dente/i denti   oon *den*·te/ee *den*·tee

to true (a wheel)
centrare   chen·*tra*·re

tyre
un copertone   oon ko·per·*to*·ne

tube
una camera a aria   oo·na *ka*·me·ra a *a*·ree·a

bidon/bottle cage
un portaborraccia   oon *por*·ta·bo·*ra*·cha

valve
una valvola   oo·na *val*·vo·la

wheel
una ruota   oo·na roo·*wo*·ta

Glossary

A

AAST – Azienda Autonoma di Soggiorno e Turismo; local tourist office
abbazia – abbey
aereo – aeroplane
affittacamere – rooms for rent
agriturismo – tourist accommodation on farms
AIG – Associazione Italiana Alberghi per la Gioventù; Italian Youth Hostel Association
albergo – hotel (up to five stars)
alimentari – grocery shop, delicatessen
aliscafo – hydrofoil
alto – high
ambasciata – embassy
ambulanza – ambulance
anfiteatro – amphitheatre
antipasto – starter, appetiser
appartamento – apartment, flat
APT – Azienda di Promozione Turistica; regional tourist office
AST – Azienda Soggiorno e Turismo; local tourist office
autostazione – bus station or terminal
autostop – hitchhiking
autostrada – motorway, freeway

B

bagno – bathroom, toilet
bancomat – ATM
belvedere – panoramic viewpoint
benzina – petrol
benzina senza piombo – unleaded petrol
bicicletta – bicycle
biglietto – ticket
biglietto chilometrico – kilometric card (train pass)
binario – (train) platform
borghetto – burg

C

cambio – money exchange
camera – room
campeggio – camp site
campo – field
cantine – wine cellars
cappella – chapel
carabinieri – police with military and civil duties
Carnevale – carnival period between Epiphany and Lent

carta – menu
carta telefonica – phonecard; see also scheda telefonica
casa – house
castello – castle, citadel
cattedrale – cathedral
cava – quarry (as in the pumice quarries at Campobianco)
centro – centre
centro storico – historic centre
chiesa – church
ciclopedonale – bike path
cin cin – cheers (a drinking toast)
città – town, city
colazione – breakfast
colline – hills
comune – equivalent to a municipality or county; town or city council; historically, a (self-governing town or city)
consolato – consulate
convalida – ticket stamping machine
coperto – cover charge in restaurants
corso – main street, avenue
CTS – Centro Turistico Studentesco e Giovanile; Centre for Student & Youth Tourists

D

deposito bagagli – left luggage
digestivo – after-dinner liqueur
diretto – direct; slow train
distributore di benzina – petrol pump
dolce – sweet, dessert
duomo – cathedral

E

elenco degli alberghi – list of hotels
ENIT – Ente Nazionale Italiano per il Turismo; Italian Tourist Board
enoteca – wine bar
espresso – express mail; express train; short black coffee

F

farmacia (di turno) – pharmacy (open late)
fermo posta – poste restante
Ferragosto – Feast of the Assumption, 15 August
ferrovia – rail system
festa – festival
fiume – river

focaccia – flat bread
fontana – fountain
forno – bakery
fortezza – fortress
francobollo – postage stamp
FS – Ferrovie dello Stato; State Railway
funivia – cable car

G

gabinetto – toilet, WC
gasolio – diesel
gelateria – ice-cream parlour
gelato – ice cream
gola – gorge
golfo – gulf
granita – drink of crushed ice flavoured with lemon, strawberry, coffee and so on
grappa – grape liqueur
grotta – cave
guardia di finanza – fiscal police
guardia medica – emergency doctor service

I

IC – Intercity; fast train
imbarcadero – embarkation point
interregionale – long-distance train that stops frequently
isola – island

L

lago – lake
lavanderia – laundrette
lavasecco – dry-cleaning
lido – beach
locale – slow local train
locanda – inn, small hotel
lungolago – lakeshore drive
lungomare – esplanade, seafront road, promenade

M

mare – sea
menù del giorno – menu of the day
mercato – market
mezza pensione – half-board
Mezzogiorno – literally, midday; name for the south of Italy
monte – mountain
motorino – moped
meublé – room only
municipio – town hall, municipal offices
museo – museum

N

Natale – Christmas
nave – large ferry, ship
navigli – canals
necropoli – (ancient) cemetery, burial site

O

Ognissanti – All Saints' Day, 1 November
ospedale – hospital
ostello per la gioventù – youth hostel
osteria – snack bar, cheap restaurant

P

palazzo – palace or mansion; large building of any type, including an apartment block
palio – contest
panetteria – bakery
panino – bread roll with filling
paninoteca – sandwich bar
Pasqua – Easter
passeggiata – traditional evening stroll
pasta – cake; pasta; pastry or dough
pasticceria – shop selling cakes, pastries and biscuits
pensione – small hotel, often with board
pensione completa – full board
pianta della città – city map
piazza – square
piazzale – (large) open square
pinacoteca – art gallery
pinoli – pine nuts
polizia – police
ponte – bridge
porta – gate, door
portico – portico; covered walkway, usually attached to the outside of buildings
porto – port
posta – post office
posta aerea – airmail
pranzo – lunch
primo – first, starter (meal)
Pro Loco – local tourist office

Q

questura – police station

R

rapido – fast train
regionale – slow local train
rifugio – mountain hut
riserva naturale – nature reserve
rocca – fortress, rock

ronda – roundabout
rosso – red
ruderi – ruins

S

sagra – festival (generally dedicated to one food item or theme)
sala – room
salumeria – delicatessen
santuario – sanctuary
scalinata – staircase, steps
servizio – service charge in restaurants
spiaggia (libera) – (public) beach
stazione – station
stadio comunale – municipal stadium
stazione di servizio – petrol or service station
stazione marittima – ferry terminal
strada – street, road
strada provinciale – main road; sometimes just a country lane
strada statale – main road; often multi-lane and toll free
superstrada – motorway; highway with divided lanes
supplemento – supplement, payable on a fast train

T

tabaccheria – tobacconist's shop
tavola calda – literally, 'hot table'; pre-prepared meat, pasta and vegetable selection, often self-service
teatro – theatre
tempio – temple
terme – thermal baths
torre – tower
torrente – stream
torrone – type of nougat
traghetto – ferry, boat
trattoria – cheap restaurant
treno – train

U

ufficio postale – post office
uffizi – offices

V

vacanza – holiday, vacation
via – street, road
viale – avenue
vicolo – alley, alleyway
vigili urbani – traffic police; local police
villa – town house or country house; also the park surrounding the house

Behind the Scenes

THIS BOOK

This guidebook was commissioned in Lonely Planet's Melbourne office, and produced by the following:

Publisher Chris Rennie
Associate Publisher Ben Handicott
Commissioning Editor Bridget Blair, Janine Eberle
Coordinating Cartographer Anita Banh
Managing Cartographer David Connolly
Cover Designer Mary Nelson Parker
Cover Layout Designer Indra Kilfoyle
Project Manager Jane Atkin
Thanks to Lucy Birchley, Rebecca Dandens, Laura Jane, Clara Monitto, Darren O'Connell, Paul Piaia, Julie Sheridan, Simon Tillema
Production [recapture]

OUR READERS

Many thanks to the travellers who used the last edition and wrote to us with helpful hints, useful advice and interesting anecdotes: Rigmor Bjorgo, Dawn Murphy, Gord Smith

ACKNOWLEDGMENTS

Internal photographs by Lonely Planet Images; Ellee Thalheimer p2 (#2, #4), p4 (#1, #2), p5 (#2), p6 (#1), p7 (#2), p9 (#2, #3), p10 (#2, #3), p11 (#1, #2); Bruce Bi p3 (#3); Kevin Levesque p3 (#1); Wayne Walton p5 (#1); Hannah Levy p6 (#2); Witold Skrypczak p7 (#1); Stephen Saks p8 (#2); Russell Mountford p8 (#1); Rocco Fasano p12.

All images are the copyright of the photographers unless otherwise indicated. Many of the images in this guide are available licensing from Lonely Planet Images: www.lonelyplanetimages.com.

SEND US YOUR FEEDBACK

We love to hear from travellers – your comments keep us on our toes and help make our books bettter. Our well-travelled team reads every word on what you loved or loathed about this book. Although we cannot reply individually to postal submissions, we always guarantee that your feedback goes straight to the appropriate authors, in time for the next edition. Each person who sends us information is thanked in the next edition – and the most useful submissions are rewarded with a free book.

To send us your updates – and find out about Lonely Planet events, newsletters and travel news – visit our award-winning website: **lonelyplanet.com/feedback**.

THE LONELY PLANET STORY

Fresh from an epic journey across Europe, Asia and Australia in 1972, Tony and Maureen Wheeler sat at their kitchen table stapling together notes. The first Lonely Planet guidebook, *Across Asia on the Cheap*, was born.

Travellers snapped up the guides. Inspired by their success, the Wheelers began publishing books to Southeast Asia, India and beyond. Demand was prodigious, and the Wheelers expanded the business rapidly to keep up. Over the years, Lonely Planet extended its coverage to every country and into the virtual world via lonelyplanet.com and the Thorn Tree message board.

As Lonely Planet became a globally loved brand, Tony and Maureen received several offers for the company. But it wasn't until 2007 that they found a partner whom they trusted to remain true to the company's principles of travelling widely, treading lightly and giving sustainably. In October of that year, BBC Worldwide acquired a 75% share in the company, pledging to uphold Lonely Planet's commitment to independent travel, trustworthy advice and editorial independence.

Today, Lonely Planet has offices in Melbourne, London and Oakland, with over 500 staff members and 300 authors. Tony and Maureen are still actively involved with Lonely Planet. They're travelling more often than ever, and they're devoting their spare time to charitable projects. And the company is still driven by the philosophy of *Across Asia on the Cheap*: 'All you've got to do is decide to go and the hardest part is over. So go!'

Index

000 Map pages
000 Photograph pages

INDEX

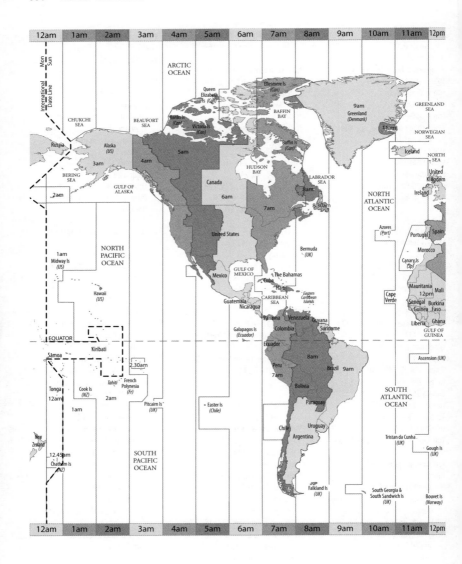

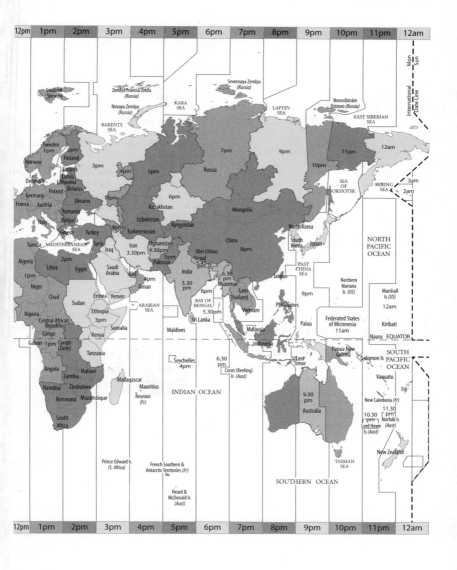

LONELY PLANET OFFICES

Australia
Head Office
Locked Bag 1, Footscray, Victoria 3011
☎ 03 8379 8000, fax 03 8379 8111
talk2us@lonelyplanet.com.au

USA
150 Linden St, Oakland, CA 94607
☎ 510 250 6400, toll free 800 275 8555
fax 510 893 8572
info@lonelyplanet.com

UK
2nd fl, 186 City Rd,
London EC1V 2NT
☎ 020 7106 2100, fax 020 7106 2101
go@lonelyplanet.co.uk

Although the authors and Lonely Planet have taken all reasonable care in preparing this book, we make no warranty about the accuracy or completeness of its content and, to the maximum extent permitted, disclaim all liability arising from its use.

PUBLISHED BY LONELY PLANET PUBLICATIONS PTY LTD

ABN 36 005 607 983

Cover photograph: Italy, Tuscany, Mount Amiata and church near Pienze, David Noton/Getty Images. Many of the images in this guide are available for licensing from Lonely Planet Images: www.lonely planetimages.com.

Printed through Colorcraft Ltd, Hong Kong
Printed in China.

Mixed Sources
Product group from well-managed forests and other controlled sources
www.fsc.org Cert no. SGS-COC-005002
© 1996 Forest Stewardship Council
FSC